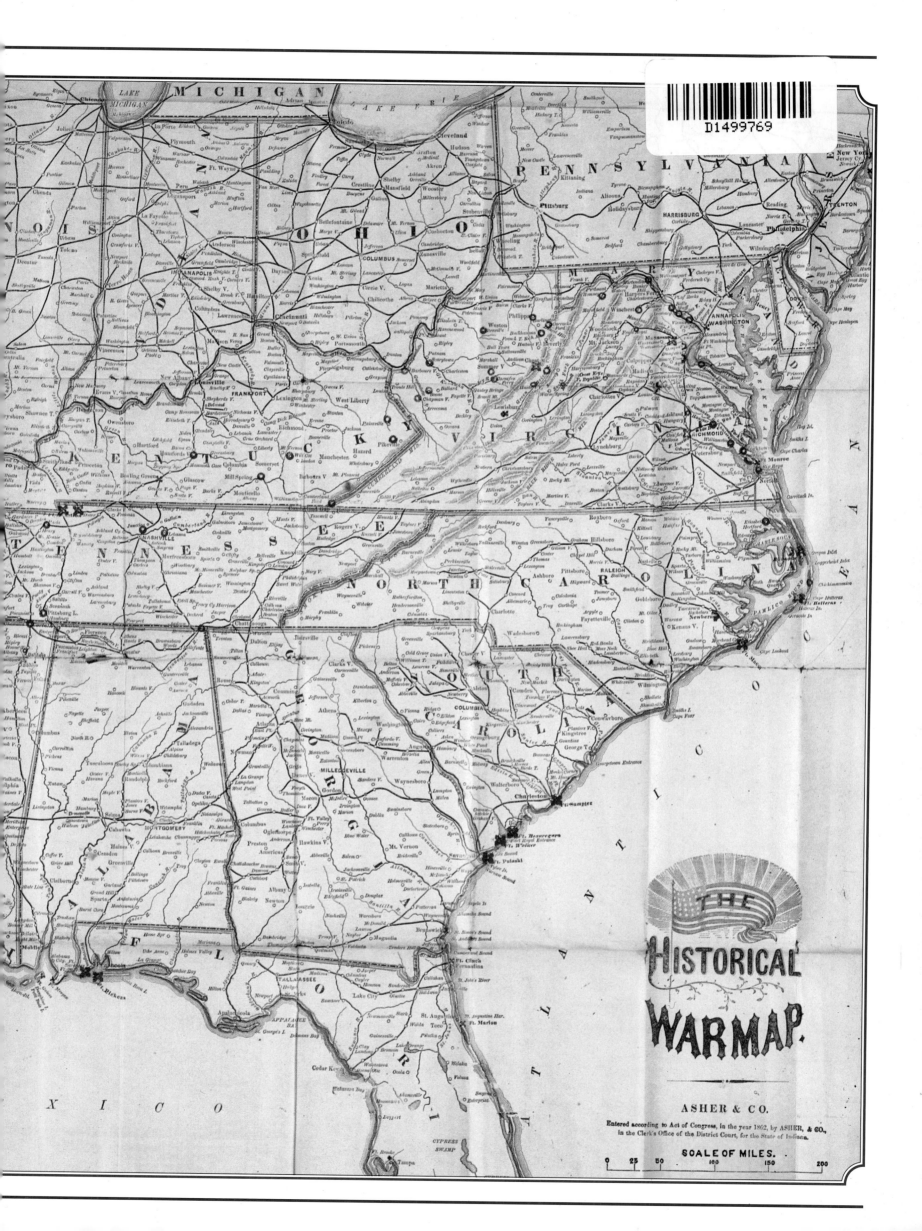

THE

HISTORICAL

WAR MAP.

ASHER & CO.

Entered according to Act of Congress, in the year 1862, by ASHER, & CO.,
in the Clerk's Office of the District Court, for the State of Indiana.

SCALE OF MILES.

0   25   50   100   150   200

NAVAL BATTLES
OF THE CIVIL WAR

NAVAL BATTLES
OF THE CIVIL WAR

CHESTER G. HEARN

THUNDER BAY
P·R·E·S·S

CREDITS
Project Manager: Ray Bonds
Designed by Mitchell Strange
Color reproduction by G Canale
Printed in Italy

CONTENTS

CHAPTER ONE

THE OUTBREAK OF WAR

The seeds for the American Civil War were not sown in the eleven states of the South. They were planted on September 17, 1787, by the original thirteen states when the makers of the Constitution of the United States failed to solve the slave issue. For 73 years the problem incubated and sprouted and, as each year passed, Congress cultivated the question with compromise and fertilized it with an exchange of invectives. Preston Brooks, pro-slavery senator from South Carolina, struck the first physical blow on May 26, 1856, when he attacked Massachusetts Senator Charles Sumner, an abolitionist, on the floor of the Senate and beat him unconscious with a cane. South Carolina struck the next blow on December 20, 1860, when she seceded from the Union. During the next six months, 10 more southern states joined South Carolina and established an independent government, the Confederate States of America.

The economy of these southern states depended upon the export of cotton for revenue and the import of goods to sustain their standard of living. They operated few manufacturing enterprises and lived mainly off the land. To support an economy based on imports and exports, the new Confederacy needed a navy to keep her ports open, but on the day southern delegates formed their government, they had no armed vessels, only a few small revenue cutters confiscated from the United States Treasury Department.

For the North to be able to blockade southern ports and interdict the trade upon which the South depended also required ships – hundreds of them – because the Confederacy occupied more than 3,500 miles of coastal waters. For decades, the Congress of the United States had allowed its Navy to deteriorate, half of its 90-odd vessels still being of the sailing type. Few of these vessels were engaged in active service and none of them was capable of performing missions of war. The difference, however, was that the Union had all the ships and the Confederacy had none.

One of the most remarkable features of the Civil War is how the North and the South used their resources to build their navies. By the end of the war, both sides had produced unique vessels unlike anything the world had ever seen. In doing so, they rendered obsolete the navies of the world.

In 1861, on the eve of the outbreak of hostilities between the North and the South, the United States Navy's fleet consisted of a mere 90 ships. Of that number only 42 vessels were in active service, and most of those were biding their time off foreign stations. Another 27 vessels were available but not in commission, a matter that irked hundreds of officers who lived on half pay while waiting to be called to active duty. Some 29 vessels, listed as unserviceable, languished in navy yards and included

At 4:30 a.m., April 13, 1861, General Pierre G. T. Beauregard opened fire on Fort Sumter and and initiated the first action of the Civil War. Major Robert Anderson, USA, surrendered the following day.

nine ships of the line and three frigates. For this pathetic state of readiness, Secretary of the Navy Isaac Toucey could be blamed. Toucey, a Southern sympathizer, wanted it this way.

Prior to Toucey's appointment as Secretary of the Navy, Congress acknowledged the shabby condition of the nation's navy and appropriated funds for building six sloops of war, each powered by two steam engines to drive a screw propeller, and augmented by a full set of sloop-rigged sails set on three masts. Toucey was in no hurry to see the vessels launched, so that if the South should secede, not all of them would be ready for service.

It never occurred to the old salts sitting on the Naval Appropriations Board to build ironclads. They still believed in sail, partly because a sailing ship was less expensive to operate and partly because they did not know enough about marine steam engines to draw up specifications. Such short-sightedness bothered them not at all, despite the knowledge that both American and

Left: At the beginning of the Civil War, the U.S. Navy had only five screw steamers rated as first-class wooden sloops. The 3,000-ton U.S.S. *Pensacola*, pictured off Alexandria, Virginia, represented one of them.

Below: The U.S.S. *Winona* was one of the many commercial vessels purchased by the Union and converted into one of the Navy's 90-day gunboats. Lightly armed, she did good service under Admiral Farragut on the Mississippi.

English shipbuilders had been putting iron-hulled steamers to sea for two decades.

In 1859 Stanislas Dupuy de Lôme built *Gloire*, a 253-foot conventional wooden steamer, but he attached 4 $\frac{1}{2}$ inch plates of iron to the beams and made her an armor-clad. Napoleon III of France liked the design so much that he ordered 20 more. In the same year the British Admiralty began work on *Warrior* and *Black Prince*, 9,210-ton genuine ironclads which, unlike *Gloire*, had frames as well as hulls made of iron. At the outbreak of the Civil War in America, Britain's Admiralty had 10 ironclads built or under construction, some clad with more than six inches of iron.

Yet this enormous buildup of armored warships in Europe seemed to go unnoticed by the Naval Appropriations Board in Washington, despite the fact that wooden-hulled men-of-war were becoming obsolete as far back as 1824, when General Henri J. Paixhans introduced the shell gun. Unlike cannon balls, which would bounce off the enemy or become embedded in a

Right: Commissioned in May, 1860, the 4,582-ton U.S.S. *Niagara* followed the older frigate design fitted with a steam-driven screw. She carried twelve 11-inch Dahlgren smoothbores in broadside and an 80-pounder in pivot.

Below: Before being raised from the river and converted to an ironclad by the Confederacy, the five-year-old 3,200-ton U.S.S. *Merrimac* had been rigged as a wooden frigate and was powered by a steam-driven propeller.

timber, shells could penetrate like a ball but explode and create massive internal damage. During the Crimean War, the Russian fleet at Sinope, using Paixhans shells, completely obliterated a squadron of Turkish warships and transports. America had observers in the Crimea, but they seemed to have learned nothing from the lesson.

Owners of commercial shipyards could see what the unresourceful fogies in the United States Navy refused to see. These were the men who perfected the design of the majestic clipper ships that "walked the water." To keep pace, their technology in steam-powered vessels had expanded right along with the advancements in naval

Left: Hampton Roads, Virginia, served as a supply center for the Army and Navy. Ammunition schooners loaded at Philadelphia and Brooklyn held their cargoes in the Roads until orders arrived designating a destination.

Below: The Washington Navy Yard continued to operate during the war, acting mainly as a repair center for shallow-draft vessels and a reception center for the constant traffic in steamers carrying dispatches.

engineering in Europe. Donald McKay, who owned one of America's foremost ship-yards, called upon the navy to build a fleet of armored vessels, writing, "It would be easy for us to build in one year, a fleet of 500 to 600 men-of-war ships, from a gunboat to the largest class of iron-cased frigates." He knew the futility of trying to convince the navy that when using steam, ships no longer needed sail. In battle, tumbling masts, spars, tackle blocks, and rigging on a steamer created a hazard, but, knowing this argu-ment would be shoved aside by the navy, McKay kept it to himself and instead suggested that battle frigates be cut down a deck or two and cased in iron to protect the gun decks.

But ships cost money, and neither Secretary Toucey nor President James Buchanan demonstrated the least interest in expanding appropriations beyond the six

Whoever controlled Hampton Roads controlled Chesapeake Bay and the Potomac River. The James River flowed directly through Richmond, the Confederate capital. Without Hampton Roads, Virginia had no direct access to the Atlantic Ocean. Neither side could afford to lose t. One of the fiercest naval battles fought during the war occurred on its waters, the duel between the *Monitor* and the *Virginia*.

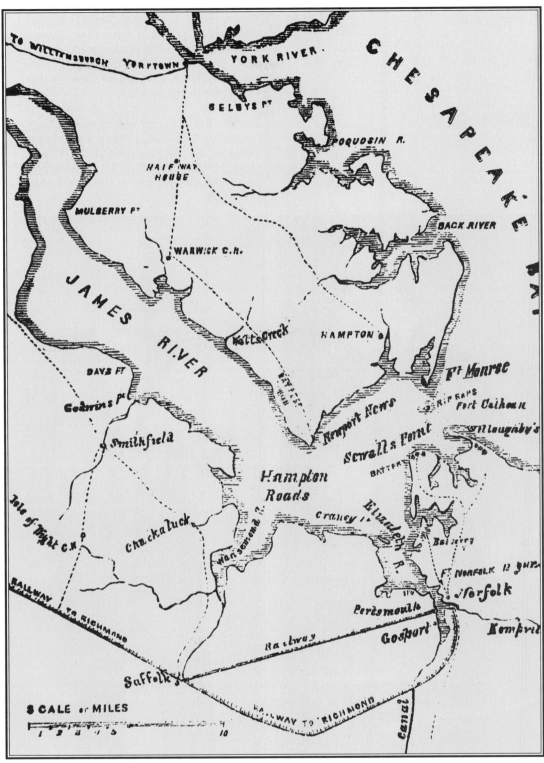

sloop-rigged steamers authorized by the 33rd Congress under President Franklin Pierce in 1854. Of the six to be built, the U.S.S. *Merrimac* (sometimes spelled *Merrimack*) would be the first completed.

Between the date of Abraham Lincoln's election to the presidency on November 6, 1860, and his inauguration on March 4, 1861, incumbent James Buchanan watched indolently as seven Southern states seceded from the Union. He neither had a plan, nor did he seem to want one. He did nothing when the Louisiana militia occupied Fort Jackson and Fort St. Philip on the lower Mississippi. Nor did he take action when Alabamans took possession of Fort Morgan at the entrance of Mobile Bay, or when Floridians appropriated the Pensacola Navy Yard. Union Major Robert Anderson created a bigger problem for Buchanan when he transferred his garrison from Fort Moultrie to the more defensible Fort Sumter. Anderson's move interrupted the plans of

South Carolinians to take possession of all forts in Charleston's harbor and rid themselves of Yankees. Buchanan now had to either evacuate Fort Sumter or maintain it. Neither alternative appealed to him, so he began counting the remaining days of his presidency, anxious to shift his problems to the "rail-splitter" from Illinois.

Lincoln faced an especially touchy problem. Virginia, North Carolina, Tennessee, and Arkansas had not seceded, nor had other so-called "Border States" such as Delaware, Maryland, Kentucky, and Missouri. Of them all, Virginia acted as the linchpin. Her boundaries touched North Carolina, Tennessee, Kentucky, Maryland, and, but for the Potomac River, Washington, D.C. She also controlled the mouth of the James River, which passed through Richmond and swallowed up the Elizabeth and Nansemond rivers, passing through Hampton Roads and into Chesapeake Bay before mingling its waters with the Atlantic.

Below left: Union Secretary of the Navy Gideon Welles ran a tight ship. He watched the Union pocketbook, made wise decisions, and in four years brought the Navy from a third rate force to the strongest in the world.

Below: Assistant Secretary of the Navy Gustavus Vasa Fox, having served many years in the Navy, augmented Welles's strategic planning with boundless energy, judicious advice, and at times a touch of mischief.

Hampton Roads formed one of the finest natural harbors in America, protected at the entrance by Fort Monroe. Whoever controlled Hampton Roads controlled Chesapeake Bay, and whoever controlled the Bay also controlled the Potomac River, up which lay the national capital and the Washington Navy Yard.

But the greatest prize lay inside Hampton Roads – the Gosport Navy Yard at Portsmouth on the Elizabeth River, and the vast naval shops and ordnance facilities across the river at Norfolk. For repair at Gosport lay some of the Union's finest vessels, chief among them the U.S.S. *Cumberland*, one of the nation's newer sailing ships, and the U.S.S. *Merrimac*, a wooden screw steamer with a frigate rig whose cranky engines needed an overhaul. Buchanan had hamstrung Lincoln with a puzzling dilemma. If he sent Federal troops to protect the navy yard, it might offend Virginia and push her to the other side. But the situation was equally as bad in Charleston Harbor. If he attempted to relieve Fort Sumter, it could bring about an engagement with South Carolina that could sweep the entire South into the secession movement. What to do became a choice of alternatives, neither of them good.

For his cabinet Lincoln had chosen men of strong opinions, men who often disagreed with him but more often disagreed among themselves. Secretary of State William B. Seward and Secretary of the Treasury Salmon P. Chase each believed that they were better suited to run the government than their boss – the elected president – and on matters of policy, they seldom agreed with each other. Secretary of War Simon Cameron came into the office because of a deal cut by Lincoln's backers

that the president knew nothing about until after the election. To the surprise of many, one of the most balanced thinkers among the cabinet proved to be Secretary of the Navy Gideon Welles, who Lincoln affectionately dubbed "Father Neptune."

Welles, at age 58, was best known as a Hartford newspaper editor, a Democrat turned Republican, and a postmaster. During his career he had held minor political offices, including a brief appointment as head of the Naval Bureau of Provisions and Clothing during the Mexican War. Although untrained in naval matters,

Welles had a reputation for sound administrative ability, honesty, and competency. One historian wrote, "By temperament, Welles was a combination of stubborn righteousness and hard-bitten practicality, mixed with devotion to duty and a penchant for thrift." His photographs portraying a man of size were deceptive. He was short and slender with an oversized face that he covered with a flowing white beard to hide a cleft chin. He wore spectacles, except when being photographed, because they gave him an elderly appearance. He offset small cosmetic quirks

Above: The Confederacy wasted too many precious resources building floating batteries, such as this one at Charleston, because each structure sapped away iron plating and cannon needed for their ironclad rams.

Above: Naval recruiting offices received a flood of volunteers having no interest in plodding through mud, rain and snow, sweltering in trenches, marching with 50-pound packs, and eating hardtack filled with grubs.

Above left: Edmund Ruffin for many years had been an outspoken "fire-eater" in favor of secession, and when General Beauregard looked for a man anxious to fire upon Fort Sumter, he found a willing volunteer in Ruffin.

Left: For five months, Maj. Robert Anderson held the only bastion in Charleston harbor still under Union control. On April 14, 1861, after a 34-hour bombardment, he yielded to Confederate demands and surrendered.

by his mental and physical energy and by his devotion to the president.

Lincoln recognized Welles's deficiency in naval matters and provided him with a capable assistant, Gustavus Vasa Fox, a small package of inexhaustible energy who had spent 20 years in the navy before resigning to become an agent for Bay State Mills. At first, Welles was not happy to have Fox thrust upon him, but the two men complemented each other, and with a rebellion about to ensnare the nation in civil war the two men needed each other.

Hopes of keeping Virginia in the Union began to dwindle at 3:20 a.m. on April 12, 1861, when two Confederate captains rowed out to Fort Sumter and demanded its surrender. Major Anderson expected reinforcements, which were standing off the harbor, and refused to capitulate. At daybreak the first of many Confederate shells arced its way toward the bastion and exploded on the brickwork. Anderson mustered his garrison on the parade ground, warned the men to take no unnecessary risks, and ordered them to the guns. For the next 34 hours a lopsided duel

Above: President Jefferson Davis, a military man and a brilliant individual, tried to run the Confederate war machine through Richmond and became the victim of his own despotic military policies.

Below: Prize money attracted thousands of recruits to the Navy while the Army struggled to fill its ranks by offering bonuses. Among the perks provided by the Navy was grog money, an inducement unmatched by the Army.

ensued while Fox, rocking at sea in company with a supply ship and two gunboats, nervously paced the deck while waiting for an outcome. His wait ended on the afternoon of April 13. Anderson capitulated, the firing stopped, and surrender arrangements were made for the following day. Confederate General Pierre G. T. Beauregard took possession of the fort, loaded Anderson's garrison on a steamer, and transported the men to the Union vessels anchored off the harbor.

When word reached Washington, it tipped over the proverbial domino that sent the nation tumbling toward its ultimate mess. Lincoln called for 75,000 volunteers to drive the seceded states back into the Union. Incensed by Lincoln's action, Virginia seceded on April 17, followed with less haste by Arkansas, North Carolina, and Tennessee. Confederate President Jefferson Davis moved the government from Montgomery, Alabama, to Richmond, Virginia, and immediately accelerated preparations for war. Among the first of many prizes coveted by the Confederacy was the Gosport Navy Yard and the naval

stores at Norfolk. The Confederacy had no navy, only a few small steamers and revenue cutters bought from shipowners or confiscated from the Union. The Confederacy's Secretary of the Navy, Stephen R. Mallory, could barely wait to get his hands on the Gosport Yard and Norfolk's store of ordnance.

Unlike Welles, Mallory had better than average credentials for managing the affairs of the Confederate navy. As a senator from Key West, Florida, he became the powerful chairman of the Naval Affairs Committee in 1855 and used his influence to press for a larger and stronger Union navy. When Florida seceded, Mallory went south and, being a close colleague of President Davis, became the natural choice as Secretary of the Navy. For the next four years, creating a navy without ships, money, or facilities became his life's work. To Mallory's credit, he would be the Confederacy's only Secretary of the Navy while Jefferson Davis went through five Secretaries of War trying to find someone who thought exactly as he did. Mallory would not always be in good standing with his peers, the public, his

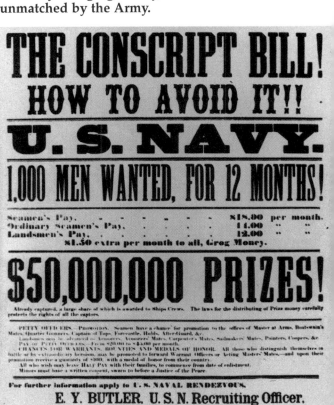

Left: Secretary of the Navy Stephen R. Mallory had a strong vision of how to create a Confederate navy and, if the congress could have supplied him with sufficient funds, his program might have reached his expectations.

Below: Observation balloons played a role in the Civil War. In November, 1861, this one ascended from the "flattop" U.S.S. *George Washington* over the Potomac River near Budd's Ferry below Mount Vernon.

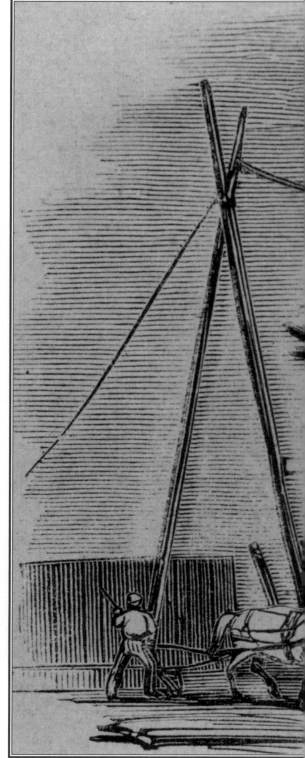

officers, or with the Confederate congress, but Davis could not find a better man in the South to build a navy for the Confederacy.

With the nation dividing, two strategies emerged. In the North, Lincoln conferred daily with General-in-Chief Winfield Scott, the aged hero of the Mexican war. Scott, though ailing and infirm, devised the Anaconda Plan, advocating a blockade of Southern seaports combined with a strong thrust down the Mississippi Valley to split the South apart. He believed that by forcibly securing the Mississippi River from Cairo, Illinois, to the Gulf, in conjunction with an effective blockade, the Confederacy would be sealed off from outside help. Scott's notion that the South could be squeezed like a boa constrictor "to military death" had its flaws, but Lincoln adopted the plan, proclaimed a blockade of Southern ports, and put Welles to work on building a navy to achieve it.

Jefferson Davis nursed a strategy that never had much hope from the beginning. He believed that if the South withheld shipments of cotton to Great Britain and France, the resulting unemployment in both countries would compel European governments to recognize the Confederacy. To resupply the mills with raw cotton, both countries would, he believed, declare war on the Union, knock down the blockade, and force the Lincoln administration to sue for peace. For this strategy to work, Davis knew that the South must prolong the war until raw cotton stores in Europe had been consumed by the mills. In the meantime, the Confederacy must demonstrate their determination by maintaining independence on the battlefield.

To show any resolve afloat, the Confederacy needed ships, and the fastest way to obtain worthy vessels was to steal them from the North. Sitting in a berth at

Norfolk were several fine Union warships, among them the powerful new *Merrimac* and the majestic *Cumberland*. Welles desperately wanted to move Merrimac to a place of safety, but her machinery lay dismantled, and Commodore Charles S. McCauley, the yard's commander, showed too little energy. On April 11, the day before Confederate batteries opened on Fort Sumter, Welles sent his chief engineer, Benjamin Isherwood, to Norfolk to get *Merrimac* back together again.

Four days later, Isherwood had *Merrimac's* machinery reinstalled and running, but McCauley, who had been drinking heavily, would not release the vessel. Days passed quickly, and, following Virginia's secession on April 17, Welles, fearing the yard would be attacked, persuaded General Scott to send a regiment of infantry to Norfolk. He also made arrangements for Commander John A.

Above: Many of Welles's "90-day" gunboats were commercial steamers purchased and converted for warfare. Some were built from scratch, like the U.S.S. *Senaca*, launched from J. Simonson's yard on August 7, 1861.

Above: Hiram Paulding evacuated the Norfolk Navy Yard on April 20, 1861, leaving the U.S.S. *Merrimac* to be raised by the enemy. Welles assigned him to the ironclad board, where he decided upon John Ericsson's *Monitor* design.

Left: Chief Engineer Benjamin Isherwood, seated center, sits with his staff of the Bureau of Steam Engineering. He directed the design and construction of all machinery connected with the new steam Navy.

Right: John A. B. Dahlgren, chief of the Bureau of Ordnance, designed the powerful class of smoothbore cannon known as "Dahlgrens," which packed a wallop at close range but were not as accurate as rifled cannon.

Below: In an action at Hatteras Inlet on August 27-29, 1861, seven Union warships and two transports, led by Flag Officer Silas Stringham, subdued Forts Hatteras and Clark in the war's first amphibious operation.

Dahlgren, an ordnance expert, to take a vessel loaded with explosives to Gosport and destroy, if necessary, any vessel or supplies that could be used by the Confederacy. Welles failed to notify McCauley that relief was on the way. Hearing rumors that a force of Virginia militia were on the road to Norfolk, McCauley panicked and scuttled all the ships in the navy yard. Three hours later, the

first of Welles's relief ships arrived.

Captain Hiram Paulding, the commander of the relief force, now decided that the navy yard should be destroyed, even though he had brought enough men to defend it. Details hurriedly burned the shops, set fire to the remaining vessels, and lit a match to the ordnance stores, which for hours boomed and thundered across the waters. Three hours later, after performing a thoroughly sloppy piece of destruction, Paulding pulled away from the Gosport Navy Yard, towing but three of the vessels which had been berthed there. A few hours later, Major General William B. Taliaferro's command entered the naval facilities

without a fight. He found one thousand cannon in usable condition, tons of unharmed supplies, machinery and equipment untouched, the graving dock undamaged and, resting on the bottom of the river, her machinery and hull saved from the fire by her sinking, the U.S.S. Merrimac.

Two days later, the good news reached Richmond. The press took the words right out of Mallory's mouth, declaring that with the capture of Gosport and Norfolk, "We have material enough to build a navy of iron-plated ships." Since the early 1850s Mallory had been an advocate of ironclad vessels. Now he would have his chance to build them.

CHAPTER TWO

A MONSTER
SHEATHED IN IRON

The naval battles of the Civil War became as much a battle of ingenuity as a battle of might. In the early stages of the naval enterprise, the South anticipated Union strategy and developed countermeasures to regain and protect its ports and inland waterways. Using their vast resources of timber, the Confederates framed vessels with rough-hewn hardwoods and covered them over with plates cut from railroad tees or rolled iron. Having no facilities for building engines, they removed them from riverboats, made small modifications, and installed them in iron-sheathed monoliths that could crawl through the water under steam. Their first ironclad happened to be a Union vessel raised from the waters of the Elizabeth River in Virginia. With a casemate shaped like the roof of a barn, it became the model for all the others.

In addition to "Yankee ingenuity," the Union enjoyed all the resources the South lacked – factories, shipyards, foundries, skilled mechanics, and an unlimited supply of men and money. Secretary of the Navy Gideon Welles maximized the use of his resources, but during the first year of the war his old ships of the line at Hampton Roads, Virginia, received a shock that sent terror up the Potomac River and to the very doors of the White House. Some of the Old Navy men who joined the Confederacy took their "Yankee ingenuity" with them when they went south and gave the Union Navy its first of dose of Confederate determination.

On June 3, 1861, Secretary Mallory arrived in Richmond to develop plans for mobilizing a navy. He did not wait to become settled before meeting with Lieutenant John M. Brooke that same evening to discuss ironclads. At first, he had embraced the notion of buying such vessels in Europe, but Brooke felt they could be built in the South. So on June 7, Brooke went to work preparing cost estimates and drawing up a rough plan for the Confederacy's ironclad navy.

Brooke's concept of an ironclad looked nothing at all like the French *Gloire* or the British *Warrior*. Instead, he proposed a practical design – a shallow-draft vessel, sharply pointed at the bow for ramming but rounded astern, and with a deck to lay slightly above the water line. In the center of the craft would sit an iron-armored casemate sloped at an angle like the roof of a barn and touching the very outside edges of the deck. Ports cut in the casement would provide openings for running out a battery

of guns in broadside, and ports forward and aft would carry pivot guns that could swivel to fire through ports on either beam or straight ahead. Machinery and boilers would be installed below the water, leaving the deck and the casemate as the only portion of the vessel exposed to enemy fire. Brooke expected the angular arrangement of the casemate to deflect any projectile striking it but, to make certain, he proposed to layer it with several inches of iron backed with two feet of lumber, with a lesser amount provided for the deck.

The concept of an ironclad went back at least eighty years to the floating batteries of Europe, but Brooke expected his design to move about with good speed and maneuverability. Mallory liked Brooke's approach because the vessels could be built quickly, cheaply, and without a great deal of sophisticated equipment.

Until recently John L. Porter, a fifty-eight-year-old native of Portsmouth, Virginia, had been the naval constructor at the Norfolk

On the U.S.S. *Monitor*, the Union's first ironclad, there was no place to be comfortable except on deck or underneath the canopy atop the turret, which contained the vessel's two 11-inch Dahlgren smoothbores.

yard. Since 1846 he had been urging the United States Navy to build an ironclad much like Brooke's design. Mallory included the Confederacy's chief engineer, William P. Williamson, in the project and set both men to work with Brooke on refining the design. When finished, Williamson predicted that such a vessel could not be built in less than a year.

In the meantime, a local rigging company raised the *Merrimac* and under Porter's supervision moved her into dry dock. Porter examined the vessel, returned to Richmond, and said, "I can adapt this model to the *Merrimac* and utilize [the] machinery in her." The whole work would cost about $173,000. Mallory approved the project and dispatched Porter to Gosport to develop the drawings. Porter worked assiduously for two weeks and on July 11 delivered the plans to Mallory. Three days later the secretary issued orders to Captain French Forrest, commandant at the Gosport Navy yard, to start work on the ship's conversion.

The steam-driven, screw-propellered

Above: Captain French Forrest was sent to the Gosport Navy Yard to raise the U.S.S. *Merrimac* and convert her into an ironclad. He did so with much trouble, and always resented having not been placed in command of her.

Right: Catesby ap Roger Jones participated in cladding and preparing the battery for the *Merrimac*, and when the vessel was later commissioned as the C.S.S. *Virginia*, he became her second in command.

Merrimac displaced 3,200 tons and had a history of trouble. Commissioned on February 25, 1856, and sent on a cruise to the West Indies, she returned one year later for repairs. Her last cruise took her to the Pacific, returning to Gosport in early 1860 for an extensive overhaul of her engines. There she sat until April 20, 1861, when old drunken McCauley panicked and attempted to scuttle her. As one historian noted, "Her only travel since [1860] had been to the bottom of the Elizabeth River and back up again."

Forrest took one look at the hulk's charred timbers and twisted fittings and called the project hopeless. The decking had been destroyed by fire, and once the machinery hit the atmosphere, every article made of iron began to rust.

With Hampton Roads snugly in control of the enemy, Mallory had visions of using *Merrimac* to clear out the Yankees and open the waterway to blockade runners delivering arms and supplies to the Army of Northern Virginia. To accelerate work on the vessel, he sent the three men who had studied her most – Porter to oversee construction, Brooke to arrange for her armor and weaponry, and Williamson to refurbish the engine and machinery. From the very beginning the trio never got along well together, and areas of overlapping responsibility only made matters worse. Brooke and Porter disliked each other, and Williamson competed with both men, demanding credit for many of their ideas. As a consequence, feuding among the three project managers affected the attitudes of the workmen and grumbling became pervasive.

Porter's turbulent and undistinguished career as a constructor in the United States Navy followed him into the Confederacy and, in a dour sort of way, he set about to vindicate himself. With fifteen hundred workers at hand, he soon had the vessel cut down to within three feet of the water line. He began laying a new gun deck weeks before the Confederate Congress allocated money to buy so much as a rivet. In August, he erected the backing for *Merrimac*'s casemate, and this gave him an opportunity to criticize Brooke for not having her armor available. Both men caused delays. They argued over plating, and after several tons of one-inch plates had been made, Brooke decided that two-inch plates would be better. The Tredegar Iron Works, who supplied the iron, could not punch two-inch plates and lost weeks re-tooling.

To resolve the issue, Mallory ordered tests made on the plating by using the heavy guns of a nearby Confederate battery. For the trial, Brooke chose Lieutenant Catesby Rogers Jones, a forty-year-old navy veteran who specialized in ordnance. Jones replicated a 12-foot section of *Merrimac*'s casemate and on backing two feet thick mounted three layers of one-inch plate. He set the target at a 37 degree angle and, at a distance of 327 yards, fired a solid ball from an 8-inch columbiad charged with 10 pounds of powder. Shots shattered the plates and penetrated the backing. Using two two-inch plates and a 9-inch columbiad,

Above: Two old commanders of the C.S.S. *Virginia*, Admiral Franklin Buchanan (left) and Commodore Josiah Tattnall (right). Buchanan fought her and Tattnall blew her up, leaving the two skippers with opposite legacies.

the outer plate shattered, but the inner plate only cracked, and no damage occurred to the backing. So on October 12 Jones submitted his report, and until February, 1862, the Tredegar Iron Works consumed the bulk of its capacity – 24 hours a day, 7 days a week – on plates for *Merrimac*. "We are now pressed almost beyond our endurance," gasped one of the owners as two-inch plates rolled slowly out of the mill.

As the time for launching drew near, skeptics doubted whether the ironclad would float. Jones, soon to become her executive officer, would not stand on her deck when on February 17, 1862, she was launched. Only four marine privates and a corporal occupied her bow as water rushed into the dry dock and set her afloat exactly as Porter had predicted. Though commissioned C.S.S. *Virginia*, the name Merrimac would

Left: When Cornelius S. Bushnell visited John Ericsson to discuss the matter of building an ironclad, he entered a room cluttered with designs and documents illuminated by the inventor's highly reflective lamp.

Below: John Ericsson had an ingenious mind, abundance of confidence in himself, and very little patience with those who disagreed with him. Only through the desperation of war could he have sold the *Monitor* concept to Welles.

never leave her, not even to the men who soon became her crew.

Far from being finished, she still swarmed with workers, and but for the ports, she looked much like a barge stacked with a pile of rusty iron plates. From bow to stern she measured just under 263 feet. A casemate 178 feet long sat dead center, sloping at a 36 degree angle to three feet below the water line. On each side of the casemate Porter had cut four ports, behind which Brooke had mounted two 6.4-inch rifled cannon and six smoothbores. Cut at the ends were three ports for 7-inch pivot rifles. Over each port was fitted a heavy iron shutter, which could be opened, a gun run out and fired, and quickly closed. On the ship's bow, Porter installed a 1,500-pound cast-iron ram, configured like a beak. When bolted to the bow, a flange cracked. Because Porter never approved of the beak, he did nothing to repair or replace it.

No one could deny that *Virginia* represented a formidable floating fortress, but on the day of her launching, she leaked badly and never got much better. Jones admitted never being on a vessel so damp and unhealthy and, to substantiate his claim, one third of the crew were perpetually on the sick list.

Porter, after complaining almost daily about Brooke's design changes, now faced his own predicament. He miscalculated the ship's weight, and when she slid into the water, her fore and after decks did not submerge as planned, leaving her beams vulnerable to a well-placed shot. Porter brought the mistake to Brooke's attention but would not admit making it. Porter, in his calculations, had failed to subtract the weight of the ship's masts, spars, and the upper deck, but he blamed the problem on Brooke's changes in the armor. Mallory cared little about casting blame. He simply

wanted the problem solved and the Yankees driven from Hampton Roads. So Porter set men to work stowing hundreds of tons of pig iron in empty spaces on the vessel.

Jones wanted to command *Virginia*, but seniority operated in the Confederacy as it did in the U. S. Navy. Mallory waited almost until the last minute to disappoint him. On February 24 he named sixty-two-year-old Captain Franklin Buchanan commander of the James River Squadron and presented him with *Virginia* as his flagship. The appointment contained a small amount of irony. After forty years of service, Buchanan, a Marylander, had resigned from the Union navy at a time when he felt certain his state would secede. When Maryland remained loyal, Buchanan asked Welles to reinstate him. The secretary had already dismissed him from the navy and would not take him back. Buchanan then offered his services to Mallory, who despite the captain's tangled

loyalties put him in command of the most important vessel in the Confederacy. In addition to bringing forty years of service in the old navy to the Confederacy, Buchanan also brought a lot of hostility toward Welles. Mallory hoped to capitalize on Buchanan's enmity toward his former boss and routinely urged him to get underway and smash up the Union blockaders in Hampton Roads.

Mobilizing *Merrimac* could not be kept secret. Civilians with passes shuffled back and forth between Norfolk and Fort Monroe for the ostensible purpose of changing residence. The Union tug *Dragon* picked them up off Norfolk and conveyed them to Fort Monroe. Major General John Wool, commanding the fort, soon learned that *Merrimac* had been raised and that work was underway to refit her as an ironclad. Through spies and disaffected Southerners, Wool maintained a close watch on *Merrimac*'s progress and kept Washington regularly informed.

In May, 1861, when *Merrimac* emerged from the bottom of the Elizabeth River, Welles had no armored vessels, nor had he given much thought to building one. Soon rumors trickled into Washington of other ironclads in the works, so he asked Congress for $1.5 million dollars to finance the development of three prototype ironclads. Funds finally came in August. Now he needed to find a way to spend them, so he advertised, asking designers to submit their ideas to a three man board composed of Commodore Joseph Smith, Commodore Hiram Paulding, and Captain Charles H. Davis. The two aging commodores represented the core within the navy who knew little about steam and nothing at all about ironclads.

Above: Ericsson built the *Monitor* at Green Point, Long Island. The vessel is being brought through the door of the shiphouse, where she will be lowered into drydock to receive her plating, machinery, and cannon.

Left: The ironclad *Galena* did not reach Hampton Roads until after the battle between *Monitor* and *Virginia*, but in the days that followed, she received a shot through her smokestack while patrolling Hampton Roads.

Of 17 proposals, the board winnowed them to two, one from Cornelius S. Bushnell and the other from the Philadelphia firm of Merrick and Sons. As the war progressed, Bushnell would eventually build the ironclad *Galena*, and Merrick and Sons would build *New Ironsides*, but the board had questions about the stability of the proposed vessels and wanted those questions answered before issuing contracts. Bushnell knew that great profits could be made, so he sought advice from John Ericsson, an irascible Swede whose genius as an engineer and inventor was surpassed only by his ego.

Instead of giving due consideration to Bushnell's problems, Ericsson dug through some old papers and located a roll of musty drawings that would render obsolete the navies of the world. He called his creation an "iron-clad steam-battery" whose chief feature was a cylindrical revolving turret housing one gun. The novel vessel came in three pieces – a lower hull section of wood, 132 feet long and 34 feet wide; and iron-plated upper hull section 172 feet long, 41 feet wide, and tapered to points at both ends; and an iron-plated turret that sat upon a revolving screw. If rammed, the plated overhang of the upper hull protected the lower portion from being penetrated, making the vessel nearly ram-proof.

Below deck, the machinery lay fully protected inside the armored upper hull. Because of heat generated by the furnaces, Ericsson provided a ventilation system using blowers to pull in outside air to exhaust the fouled air. Instead of the traditional two-cylindered steam power plant, he saved space by using a single cylinder driven by two pistons. The propeller shaft extended through the rear of the lower hull into a cavity to carry a four-bladed propeller, and behind it the ship's rudder, all neatly protected from enemy fire or ramming.

The idea of a rotating turret had been around for nearly a century, but not in the package envisioned by Ericsson. His final design provided for a turret encased with eight layers of one-inch plates and with space enough for two 12-inch Dahlgren smoothbore cannon (he eventually settled

for 11-inch guns). Both guns fired through two ports cut side-by-side in the turret and, when the shutters opened, the effect was like staring into the mouth of a giant double-barreled shotgun. The turret sat atop a polished brass ring, its weight forming a watertight seal. A small steam engine below deck powered the revolving turret, but controls for its rotation were placed on the gundeck.

Bushnell recognized the superiority of Ericsson's design and rushed off to present it to Welles. Relations between the navy and Ericsson had never been good, mainly because the Swede thought of the Naval Appropriations Board as technological nitwits and minced no words telling them so. Welles, however, saw merit in Ericsson's design and urged Bushnell to bring the engineer to Washington. Under normal circumstances, Ericsson would not leave his New York home to visit anybody, much less the navy. To coax the Swede into Washington, Bushnell lied, telling him that the board had accepted his design and only wished to talk to him about the details. Bushnell knew that once he got Ericsson to Washington, the Swede could be a very compelling salesman. Bushnell also set the stage by seeing Lincoln and Assistant Secretary of the Navy Fox, who both voiced interest in the design.

So, by deception and clever planning, Bushnell brought Ericsson before the so-called "Examining Board." Because the Swede believed the design had been accepted, he extolled its virtues, and instead of lambasting the board as ignoramuses, he answered their questions with knowledge and eloquence. At 3:00 p.m. on the afternoon of September 15, Welles brought Ericsson into his office and told him a contract for $275,000 would be sent to him in New York. Ericsson was delighted. But, down in Virginia, workmen were busy attaching the first iron plates to the resurrected creature in the Elizabeth River.

Days after Welles promised Ericsson a contract, senior naval officers began to complain. They predicted that Ericsson's craft would be a dismal failure and disgrace the board for making a stupid decision.

information given to him by the men who worked on her. From Abbot, Welles learned of *Virginia*'s size and configuration, the number of ports cut in her casemate, her ram, and with somewhat less accuracy, her weaknesses. Then began an almost daily blur of new reports and suggestions emanating from sources ranging from Edwin M. Stanton, the new Secretary of War, Major General George B. McClellan, the general of the army, officers in command of vessels at Hampton Roads, and deserters from the Confederate camp.

On February 20 Welles named forty-two-year-old Lieutenant John L. Worden, a native New Yorker, commander of the "Ericsson." The lieutenant had been in the navy for 27 years and had already been captured once while attempting to return by train to the North after delivering secret orders to the Union force at Pensacola Bay. When exchanged seven months later, thoughtless Confederates sent him home through Norfolk. When in January Worden recovered from his captivity, Welles sent him to the Continental Iron Works on Long Island to test the vessel Ericsson now called the *Monitor*, and the name stuck. Much to Welles's dismay, as he had hoped to destroy *Virginia* while she lay helpless in dry dock, Worden reported the 776-ton *Monitor* unfinished.

Welles held up payments to Ericsson but at the same time urged Worden to get the vessel under steam. Having no crew, Worden plucked men from two old receiving ships. He named a twenty-one-year-old Marylander, Lieutenant Samuel Dana Greene, as his executive officer, and filled out his crew with 57 men and 10 officers, many of whom envisioned light duty and the security of being protected by the vessel's heavy armor.

No one had thought to requisition guns, so Worden went to the Brooklyn Navy Yard and removed two 11-inch Dahlgrens from the U.S.S. *Dacotah*. Cast in 1859, the guns were comparatively new. They were fired by yanking a lanyard which ignited a friction primer placed in the breech vent. The vent led to a 15-pound powder charge which propelled a 166-pound solid iron ball. One 11-inch ball weighed almost as much as the combined weight thrown by a broadside from the navy's old frigates.

Commissioned a fourth-rate ship on February 25, 1862, *Monitor* became the Union's first ironclad, and not a moment too soon. In a single package, Ericsson had incorporated all the features of the battle cruisers yet to come – a revolving turret,

Welles had boxed himself in a corner, but he kept his word and three weeks later sent Ericsson the contract. The Swede must have chuckled when he signed it. Welles had bent to the wishes of critics and stipulated that the ironclad be fitted with masts and spars to make six knots under sail as well as the promised eight knots under steam. The navy's naysayers could evidently not grasp the significance of the rotating turret guns, which might, when in battle, accidentally shoot down the ship's superfluous masts and spars. Some of Welles's other conditions might have rankled a conventional shipbuilder, but there was nothing conventional about Ericsson. He had already raised money and begun the work. He signed the contract, ignored the absurd conditions, and with help from Bushnell proceeded to build the ship he had designed. During the same period, contracts also went out for what would become Bushnell's *Galena* and Merrick and Son's *New Ironsides*.

October 4, 1861 – the day the navy signed

the contract for "Ericsson's folly" – also stood out as the day Commodore Louis N. Goldsborough, commanding the North Atlantic Blockading Squadron at Hampton Roads, sent Welles a dispatch to warn that Confederates were planning to attack his fleet with the reconstructed *Merrimac*. Welles had been looking for a way to test Ericsson's boat, and now he had one. Neither Lieutenant Jones, fretting daily over the problems of preparing the C.S.S. *Virginia* for war, or John Ericsson, running from one subcontractor to another for parts, knew they were in a race with each other – a race that would culminate in one of the greatest and far-reaching coincidences in naval history.

Not until early January, 1862, did Welles get a true picture of what was taking place on the Elizabeth River. For several months Master's Mate William A. Abbot had been a prisoner at Norfolk. When exchanged, he came to Washington and described in detail *Virginia*'s strengths and weaknesses using

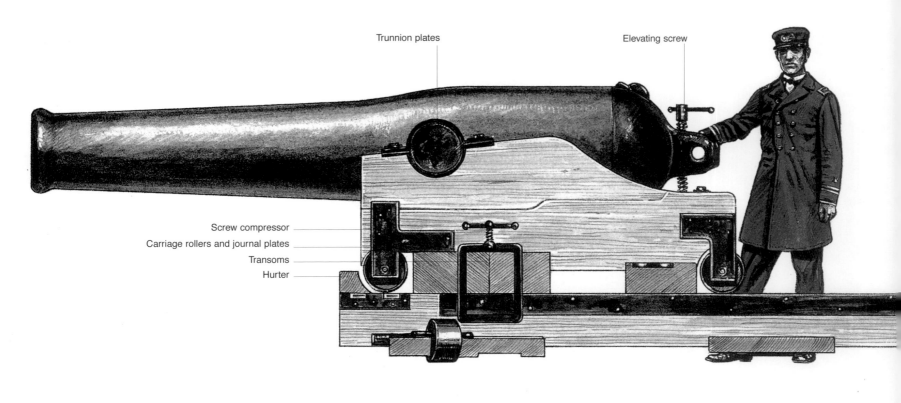

Trunnion plates

Elevating screw

Screw compressor

Carriage rollers and journal plates

Transoms

Hurter

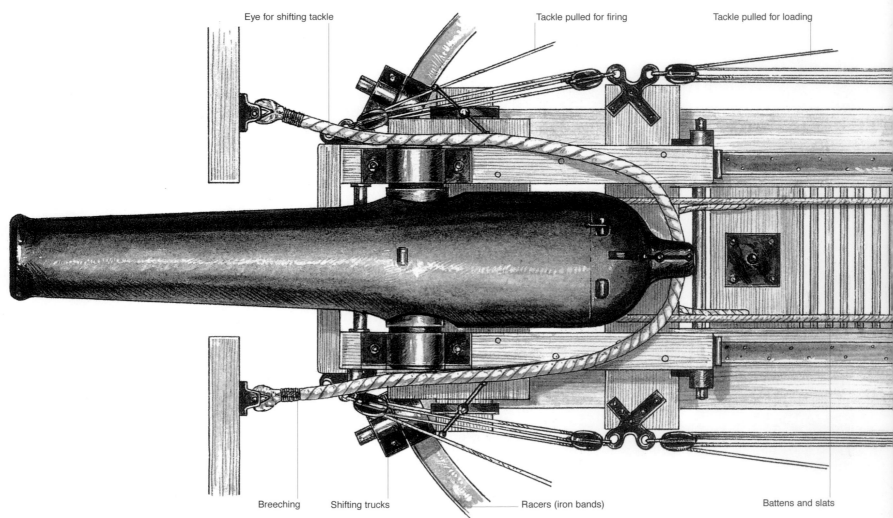

Eye for shifting tackle

Tackle pulled for firing

Tackle pulled for loading

Breeching

Shifting trucks

Racers (iron bands)

Battens and slats

large-bore shell guns, a low freeboard, light draft, good speed and maneuverability, and the use of steam power for multiple purposes such as ventilation and turret rotation. In a single prototype, Ericsson had meshed together revolutionary technology that would otherwise have taken years to combine. But, as a prototype, *Monitor* had its defects, and only with time would the navy awake to the marvel of Ericsson's creation.

On February 27, while *Monitor* took on 80 tons of coal and fired her boilers,

Buchanan began loading 18,000 pounds of powder on *Virginia*. Since February 17 he had been busy planning the attack on Hampton Roads, and every day's delay added to his mounting impatience. *Patrick Henry*, *Raleigh*, *Beaufort*, and *Jamestown*, small gunboats of the James River Squadron, patrolled the mouth of the Elizabeth River, waiting for Buchanan's orders to attack. He intended to keep them out of the line of fire, using them as utility vessels. He would let *Virginia* do the fighting.

Buchanan planned a two-pronged attack. While he smashed the Union squadron at Hampton Roads, Brigadier General John Bankhead Magruder would moved a force by land and capture Newport News. At the last minute Magruder reneged, blaming late winter rains for creating a sea of mud through which his artillery could not be moved. So Buchanan planned to go it alone.

Standing off Hampton Roads were some of the finest vessels in the Union navy. Should *Virginia* make an appearance,

Weighing 16,000lb, the 11-inch Dahlgren smoothbore gun was most likely to be found on the U.S. Navy's seagoing sloops and cruisers. It could hurl a 130-pound shell almost a mile. Here, the gun is shown in the favored pivot arrangement, with iron-shod wheels moving along overlapping irons bands (racers) fixed to the deck planking, allowing movement over a full 360 degrees. The gun crew used rope and tackle to pull the gun out for firing and back for loading. Rate of fire could be rapid (two minutes per shot) or sustained (three minutes per shot). Some ships had pivot guns fore and aft, and maybe one or two amidships as well.

Below: On July 9, 1862, officers pose before the turret of *Monitor*. On December 30, 1861, several would die when the vessel foundered of Cape Hatteras and took four officers and 12 men to the bottom.

Rails　Compressor battens　Transom　Hurter

Rail plates　Preventer breeching

Training trucks　Eye for training tackle

as every sailor expected, Commodore Goldsborough had assembled quite an imposing squadron to meet the challenge. The 1,869-ton screw frigate *Congress*, though 20 years old, boasted 50 guns – 10 8-inch smoothbores and 40 32-pounders. A single broadside could hurl nearly a half-ton of metal at the enemy. Commander William Smith liked his vessel but not her guns. None was rifled, which reduced their range and accuracy. An enemy vessel armed with rifled guns could stand out of range and

pummel his ship while every shot from *Congress*'s smoothbores fell short.

The sloop of war screw steamer *Cumberland* mounted 24 guns, all 9-inch and 10-inch smoothbores with a single exception, one 70-pounder rifle. During March, the executive officer, Lieutenant George Morris, commanded the ship while her regular captain, William Radford, was absent on court-martial duty.

The six-year-old *Minnesota*, the newest of the trio, was also a sister ship of the *Merrimac*. Armed with 47 guns, she could throw more metal than *Congress* but suffered the same deficiency in rifled guns. She had already seen a small amount of fighting in 1861, during the lopsided affair at Hatteras Inlet, North Carolina. Before Goldsborough departed in December to lead the attack on Roanoke Island, North Carolina, he used *Minnesota* as his flagship, though she was actually commanded by Captain Gershom J. Van Brunt.

At Hampton Roads, Captain John Marston commanded the screw frigate *Roanoke*, another sister ship of *Cumberland* and a vessel that shared the latter's main deficiency – chronic engine trouble. He could do little with her but complain about the ship's crippled condition, which he did

with regularity. But he had more to worry about than *Roanoke*. When Goldsborough departed, he left Marston in charge of the squadron. Thirteen other naval vessels lay in the Roads, and in battle, none of them had the firepower to look after themselves.

If *Virginia* attacked, Marston planned to meet her in the channel that flowed by Sewell's Point. Over a seven mile stretch of water beginning at Newport News and ending at Fort Monroe he placed in line *Cumberland*, *Congress*, *Minnesota*, *Roanoke*, and the old sailing frigate *St. Lawrence*, spacing them as he saw fit. Each vessel posted sentinels around the clock, while 2,000 sailors and 188 guns waited day after day for *Virginia*'s debut. On March 8, the wait ended.

For more than a week Buchanan had been delayed by shortages in munitions, poor weather, mechanical problems, and timorous pilots. Now, on the morning of March 8, came a sudden outbreak of fair weather. With the vessel's casemate heavily greased to carom away enemy projectiles, *Virginia* cast off and steamed down the Elizabeth River to keep her appointment with destiny.

Those on board did not expect Buchanan to fight that day. To them he had said

nothing. Those on shore watched her go, some predicting failure. Others followed in boats, clogging the artery with everything from an "army tug-boat to the oysterman's skiff." One observer hollered, "Go on with your old metallic coffin! She will never amount to anything else!" But all watched eagerly, lining both sides of the banks as the ironclad pressed downstream at six knots. Lieutenant John Taylor Wood, one of *Virginia*'s officers who thought Buchanan intended to take the vessel on a trial run,

also believed one was needed because "She steered so badly that, with her great length, it took from thirty to forty minutes to turn… She was as unmanageable as a water-logged vessel." To help with steering the ironclad, Buchanan hitched a towline to the steamer *Beaufort*.

As *Virginia* approached the mouth of the river at Craney Island, Buchanan could see, seven miles off, slightly to port and beyond Sewell's Point, the anchored *Congress* and *Cumberland*. His men were just finishing a

noon meal when he stepped down to the gun deck and called them together. Pointing to the Union vessels ahead he said, "Sailors, in a few minutes you will have the long-expected opportunity to show your devotion to the country and our cause." His was a short pep talk, followed by the order – "Beat to quarters."

For more than an hour, lookouts in the tops of *Roanoke* and *Minnesota* nervously watched the trail of black smoke coming down the Elizabeth River. But this time it

Left: The C.S.S. *Patrick Henry* is typical of the type of steamer seized by the Confederate government and converted into a gunboat. Captain Buchanan used the vessel as part of his James River Squadron in Hampton Roads.

Below: Lt. William H. Parker, commanding C.S.S. *Beaufort*, opened the fight on March 8, 1862, which led the first day's battle during which the C.S.S. *Virginia* destroyed the U.S.S. *Cumberland* and the U.S.S. *Congress*.

just kept coming. At 1:08 p.m. a Union lookout vessel, standing off Sewell's Point, signaled the approach of the Confederate squadron. A few minutes later *Virginia*, glistening a greasy brown in the sunlight, came in sight. When she reached Sewell's Point, all the smaller Union vessels headed down the main channel to Fort Monroe. *Congress* and *Cumberland*, laying off Newport News, still doubted that the long dreaded day of battle had finally come. Lieutenant Joseph B. Smith, commanding

Congress in place of her captain, waited 20 minutes before running out the guns and ordering the decks cleared for action. Lieutenant George N. Morris, executive officer in charge of *Cumberland* moved no faster. He let the men finish their noonday meal before beating to quarters. Sailors on both vessels then moved quickly, spreading sand on the gundecks to soak up blood and gore that would be spilled in battle. Others double-charged the guns with powder, packing in shot and shell.

Morris wanted confirmation and signaled Acting Master Henry Reaney of the tugboat *Zouave* to slip down to the mouth of the Nansemond River to see what was coming. "It did not take us long to find out," Reaney recalled, "for we had not gone over two miles when we saw what to all appearances looked like the roof of a very big barn belching forth smoke as from a chimney of fire." Reaney had a rifled 30-pounder Parrott mounted in the bow and fired the first shot of the day. He got off four more before *Cumberland* recalled the tug by signaling for assistance.

Shore batteries at Newport News, followed by broadsides from *Cumberland* and *Congress*, opened on *Virginia*, but Buchanan ignored the shots and slowly pressed forward. He noticed, however, that without waiting for orders Lieutenant William H. Parker, commanding the canal boat *Beaufort*, fired on *Congress* with his rifled 32-pounder. The battle having been started by a tugboat on one side and a converted canal boat on the other, Buchanan signaled his squadron to take their positions and engage the enemy.

Slogging up the James River's north channel to Newport News, Buchanan planned to attack *Cumberland* and *Congress*,

and then work his way down Hampton Roads taking *Minnesota* and anything else the Union could throw in his way. He came within easy range of *Cumberland* before ordering Lieutenant Charles C. Simms to fire the rifled 7-incher mounted in the bow. The shell screeched up the river, struck *Cumberland*'s starboard-quarter, sent huge splinters flying, and wounded a group of marines standing nearby.

Cumberland's forward gun crew quickly replied but missed the mark. As they reloaded to try again, Simms fired another round from *Virginia*'s rifled Brooke. The shell burst in the midst of *Cumberland*'s gun crew, killing every man but the powder boy and the gun captain, the latter having both arms severed at the shoulder. Lieutenant

Selfridge, in charge of *Cumberland*'s forward guns, wrote, "The groans of these men, as they were carried below, was something new [to us]."

Cumberland then opened fore and aft as fast as the guns could be fired. The shots seemed to have no effect upon *Virginia*. Selfridge noticed that too many of them missed, and those that struck the ironclad either bounded off the casemate or broke to pieces on impact. His own deck was awash with blood. As men fell, he had the dead pitched to port and the wounded carried below to the surgeon.

Buchanan took a position between *Cumberland* and *Congress*, where his broadside and pivot guns could engage both vessels at the same time. *Congress* had

been firing for some time, her shots rattling against the plated casemate without effect. Lieutenant John R. Eggleston looked out one of *Virginia*'s ports, waiting for the ironclad to turn enough to bear on *Congress*. He had loaded two guns with hot shot and held steady, ready to fire. Slowly the big Union frigate came into view, centered perfectly through the starboard gunports. Eggleston yanked the lanyards. One hot shot ripped through *Congress* and settled in a port cabin, starting a blaze that could not be put out. The second shot started a fire near the frigate's magazine and threatened to touch it off.

But Buchanan had his eye on *Cumberland*, the uppermost vessel in the Union chain. Closer and closer he came. As the ironclad's

Left: Cmdr. William Radford commanded the U.S. squadron at Hampton Roads during the attack on the *Virginia*, and when *Monitor* arrived he expressed disgust that so small a craft would be sent to fight the Rebel ironclad.

Right: Capt. Gershom J. Van Brunt commanded the U.S.S. *Minnesota* in Hampton Roads, which grounded during the battle with *Virginia*. He vowed to fight her to the end but was saved by the timely appearance of the *Monitor*.

broadsides concentrated on *Congress*, Buchanan focused all his attention on *Cumberland*. A pilot on the Union vessel looked down on the slowly approaching monster sheathed in iron and spied her beak. "It was impossible for us to get out of her way," he declared.

Buchanan stood where he had been since the opening of the action, fully exposed but miraculously unharmed in an open hatch on the top deck. The constant racket of shot and shell striking the casemate seemed not to bother him in the least. Some asserted that he called out to *Cumberland* to surrender, and that Lieutenant Morris replied, "Never!" but the likelihood of being heard over the roar of guns and the confusion of battle casts the claim into question.

As the ironclad approached *Cumberland*'s beam, Buchanan dropped into the pilothouse and ordered Chief Engineer H. Ashton Ramsay to reverse *Virginia*'s engines the moment she struck the enemy, and to not wait for orders to do so. In the meantime Buchanan changed his mind. Moments before the iron prow made contact, he signaled Ramsay to stop engines and throw them into reverse. A few seconds later, men on *Virginia* experienced a slight jar, much like a vessel going aground. Those on the gundeck did not know the cause until Lieutenant Robert Minor came running by, waving his hat and hollering, "We've sunk the *Cumberland*!"

The ironclad's beak crushed through a barrier of timbers put there by *Cumberland*'s crew to fend off floating enemy mines. It bit deep into the sloop's forward starboard quarter, ripping open like a cleaver a seven foot hole below the water line. At the moment of impact, Simms fired another shell into the very bowels of the rammed vessel. With uncontainable force, water flooded *Cumberland*'s hold. But down in *Virginia*'s engine room, Ramsay frantically struggled without success to extract the ironclad's beak. The sinking *Cumberland*, listing badly where rammed, now threatened to grip *Virginia* in place and pull her to the bottom. In the engine room, Ramsay could feel the ironclad tilt as her bow dipped lower. The whole vessel shook from the laboring of the engines, but she could not break loose.

Good luck more than anything else saved the ironclad from disaster. The force of the tidal current began to slowly swing the trapped ironclad until her starboard side came nearly parallel with *Cumberland*'s. A wave then rolled the sloop just enough to raise her bow. When she came down from the swell, she snapped off the embedded beak, and *Virginia* broke free.

Though their ship was sinking, gun crews on *Cumberland* continued to throw shot and shell at *Virginia*, leaving dimples here and there on the ironclad's casemate. Buchanan stood off and let his gunners finish the work, but they left their ports open, thinking *Cumberland* was done. One Yankee gun found its mark. A shell hit Midshipman H. H. Marmaduke's forward port broadside gun and exploded, slicing a foot off its muzzle, killing one man, and wounding or stunning the others. A few minutes later a shell struck a loaded hot-shot gun aft. It broke off most of the muzzle, set the charge off, and sent the hot shot into the sinking *Cumberland*. Later, Buchanan discovered that he could no longer use either gun because firing them set the wooden backing around the port on fire.

At 3:35 p.m. Morris knew he could no longer keep *Cumberland* afloat and ordered the ship abandoned. A number of cutters put out from Newport News to save the crew and take off the wounded, but most of the men jumped in the water to swim for shore. With a great bubbling hiss, the ship went to the bottom, but the tips of her masts with colors flying continued to mark her resting place in the days to come.

During the fight with *Cumberland*, Buchanan's gunners never let up on *Congress*, firing whenever they could get the right angle. But to face the ironclad downriver, Buchanan had to run up the James to make the slow, wide turn where water was the deepest. The temporary departure of *Virginia* gave men on *Congress* something to cheer about until they realized she was only turning around.

Ranging now behind Buchanan were his three gunboats, Patrick Henry, *Teaser*, and *Jamestown*, and all four vessels steamed in formation toward *Congress*. Batteries at Newport News fired at the squadron as it approached. One shot clipped *Patrick Henry*'s boiler and forced her to retire. During the battle *Beaufort* and *Raleigh* had remained below, trading shots with *Congress*, but the latter had pulled out of range after a shell from the frigate disabled her only gun.

Men on *Congress* took hope when they spotted *Roanoke*, *Minnesota*, and *St. Lawrence* steaming to their support. *Roanoke*, her engines in disrepair, ran upon a bar known as the Middle Ground about three miles west of Sewell's Point. *Minnesota* got a little further down the channel before grounding on the same bar. The 52-gun frigate *St. Lawrence* had just come into Hampton Roads to relieve *Congress* and her commander, Captain H. Y. Purviance, did not know until 2:30 p.m. what was happening. Yet she, too, grounded not far from *Minnesota*. All three vessels opened on *Virginia* with what guns they could bring to bear, but their

Right: Rammed by the *Virginia*, the men of the U.S.S. *Cumberland* remain at their stations to fight their guns, though the gun decks are in shambles, dead and wounded lay everywhere, and the vessel is slowly sinking.

smoothbores could not reach the ironclad. They had the added annoyance of being under fire from Confederate batteries on Sewell's Point and from sharpshooters who waded into the water with rifles.

With fires still burning on *Congress*, Lieutenant Joseph Smith ordered sails set and signaled the tugboat *Zouave* to abandon *Cumberland* and come to his aid. With help from a light breeze and a tow from *Zouave*, Smith hoped to beach the frigate off Newport News in water too shallow for the deep-draft *Virginia* to follow. He did not know that the ironclad had lost her beak.

By the time *Virginia* completed her turn and came within range, *Congress* was underway and heading for shore. But by 4:00 p.m. the ironclad had returned, taking a position 200 yards off *Congress*'s stern. Buchanan opened with a broadside that raked the frigate, tearing up the deck and sending enormous splinters flying. Union blood flowed across the deck, trickled over the side, and spattered the deck of *Zouave*. A shot decapitated Lieutenant Smith, and the command devolved on Lieutenant Austin Pendergrast. By 4:20 p.m., *Congress* could no longer fight. Fires ravaged the ship, her

stern was smashed, and her guns could no longer be served. Buchanan's three consorts, *Beaufort*, *Jamestown*, and *Patrick Henry*, then came up and added their firepower to that of the ironclad's.

Pendergrast succeeded in grounding the vessel off Newport News but not out of harm's way. He ordered the wounded topside, intending to put them on boats for shore, but the smoke from fires raging inside the vessel, combined with a constant shelling from the enemy, made evacuation impossible. At 4:45 p.m., after commanding *Congress* for 25 minutes, Pendergrast ran up the white flag and surrendered. *Zouave* cut her lines and backed into the current. She steamed toward *Minnesota* to give aid, but a Rebel shell snipped off her rudder post and left her without steerage.

Upon seeing a white flag hoisted on *Congress*, Buchanan stepped out on deck and signaled for Lieutenant Parker. He told him to take *Beaufort* and *Raleigh* alongside *Congress* and accept her surrender. Intend-ing to take the officers off as prisoners and set the crew free, Parker placed *Beaufort* off one beam of the stricken vessel and *Raleigh* off the other. In the midst of the surrender ceremony,

shore batteries opened on both Confederate gunboats, killing two officers on *Raleigh* and killing or wounding every man on the hurricane deck of *Beaufort*. A bullet grazed Parker, two passed through his clothing, and another tore away part of his cap.

Brigadier General Joseph K. F. Mansfield, commanding Newport News, knew he had no business firing on an enemy taking possession of a surrendered vessel, but a shell from *Virginia* had destroyed his headquarters. When reminded by a junior officer of military protocol, Mansfield replied, "I know the d___d ship has surrendered, but we haven't."

Mansfield's fire, coming from the guns of the 20th Indiana Infantry, not only riddled *Beaufort*'s crew but killed and wounded men coming off *Congress*. Pendergrast asked permission to go back on board to help with the wounded, and Parker agreed, but when Pendergrast did not return, Parker assumed the lieutenant had been injured. Moments later, men on *Congress* began shooting at the boarding party. Parker had seen enough. He blew the whistle to withdraw, and both vessels beat a hasty retreat back to the ironclad.

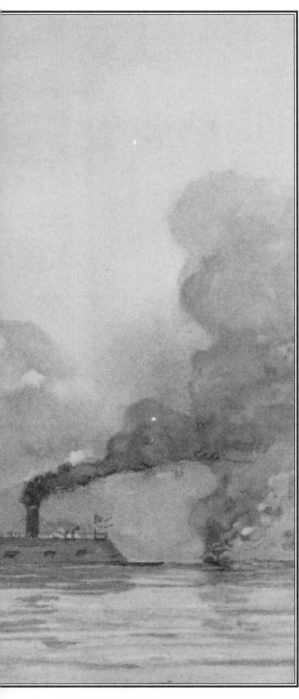

Left: As the rammed U.S.S. *Cumberland*, with her flag still flying, begins to sink, *Virginia* stands off, her crew watching as men from the burning Union vessel topple into the water before flames touch her magazine. Although several of the crew were rescued as she sank, it was later determined that *Cumberland* suffered almost 150 casualties, including wounded.

Buchanan fumed at Parker for not fulfilling his mission, so he sent Lieutenant Minor in the ironclad's boat. Minor came within 250 yards of the frigate when sharpshooters opened from shore. With two men wounded, and being hit himself, Minor signaled for help, passed a line to the tug *Teaser*, and returned to *Virginia*.

Furious, Buchanan snorted, "Destroy the __ __ ship!" Once again *Virginia* took position close astern of the frigate. With broadsides and hot shot, she tore *Congress* to pieces, setting her on fire from end to end. Buchanan could not contain his anger and, seeking his own form of revenge, called for his rifle. Out on deck he went, firing wildly at the sharpshooters along shore. They soon spotted him, and every Union musket turned upon him. A ball struck Buchanan in his left thigh and disabled him. Men carried him below and put him in the cabin with Lieutenant Minor.

Lieutenant Jones took command of the ironclad and, finding *Congress* hopelessly ablaze, steamed across North Channel to destroy the grounded *Minnesota*. *Roanoke* and *St. Lawrence* had freed themselves and moved back toward Fort Monroe, leaving their tugboats behind to assist *Minnesota*. *Jamestown* and *Patrick Henry* had already been peppering the frigate when *Virginia* approached, but Jones did not want to run the risk of grounding. The only way he could get in comfortable range was to navigate around the Middle Ground and come around by way of the South Channel. By then it would be dark, and the ironclad's pilots warned Jones to take her to Sewell's Point before nightfall. Jones fired a few parting shots, content that tomorrow would be another great day for the Confederate Navy.

At 8:00 p.m. hundreds of Virginians converged on Sewell's Point to meet and greet the men of the victorious ironclad. With only two dead and eight wounded, *Virginia* had come through the fires of hell without any injury to the ironclad. At the time, nobody knew how many men had died on *Congress* and *Cumberland*, but the guns of the ironclad had been devastating. Days later, Lieutenant Morris counted *Congress*'s missing. Of 376 men known to be on board when the fight began, he could account for only 255, including his wounded, which meant 121 seamen had gone down with the ship. *Cumberland*'s loss approached 150, including her wounded. *Minnesota* had lost a dozen men and, if Buchanan had his way, there would be plenty more in the morning.

Off in the distance the glow of the burning *Congress* cast a reddish hue against a cloud created by the smoke. "A pretty good day's work," said Lieutenant Eggleston to Jones. "Yes," replied Jones, "but it is not over." All understood that tomorrow they must return to destroy *Minnesota*, *Roanoke*, and *St. Lawrence*. They did not expect to encounter much trouble. Neither the ailing Buchanan nor his executive officer could have predicted the surprise awaiting them in the morning.

Below: When Capt. Hiram Paulding evacuated the facilities at Norfolk, he left behind more than a thousand guns, most of which the Confederates were able to salvage and deploy against the Union in ships and forts.

CHAPTER THREE

DUEL OF THE IRONCLADS

Battles won or lost are often determined by a series of coincidences, and this is probably more true at sea than anywhere else. Probably no fight between two vessels ever resulted from more coincidences than the engagement between the U.S.S. *Monitor* and the C.S.S. *Virginia*.
During every phase of the construction and mobilization of both vessels, the combination of time, trouble, and weather all seemed to be guided toward a fateful date in March 1862. From the summer of 1861 to the night of March 8, 1862, any small alteration in the day-to-day, or even hour-to-hour, arrangements in preparing these vessels for service could have produced an entirely different outcome and might have changed the sequence of the war. Battles fought in June on the Virginia Peninsula between the Army of the Potomac and the Army of Northern Virginia would probably have been fought somewhere else. Coincidences continued right through the morning of the most famous naval battle of the Civil War, but no coincidence hurt the Confederacy more than the March 8 wounding of Buchanan, who would never give an inch in battle, and the survival of the Monitor when she escaped certain death in heavy seas by an almost magical change in weather conditions.
But the day of the battle between the first ironclads would produce its own coincidences and leave both vessels to face their own deferred destinies until a later time.

On March 3, five days before *Virginia* steamed into Hampton Roads and destroyed two of the Union's finest warships, *Monitor* prepared for another trial run. Being hard to steer, she collided with a New York gas works on the river bank. The commandant at the Brooklyn Naval Yard wanted to detain her long enough to modify the rudder, but Ericsson would have none of it. He claimed the work would take weeks and made the adjustments himself. His was an act of providence, as would be other acts soon to follow.

On a bone-chilling day of rain mixed with sleet, *Monitor* pulled into the East River for her final test. Inspectors huddled behind a canvas awning, noting that the vessel steered well but made only seven knots – not the nine promised by Ericsson. The inspecting officers wanted to get her to sea and on March 4 decreed her ready. Now all Lt. John L. Worden, the vessel's commander, needed was to wait for the storm to pass.

March 6 promised to be a pleasant afternoon, so at 4:00 p.m. *Monitor* shoved off

from the Brooklyn yard and stood down the East River for Sandy Hook. Nobody knew her destination but Welles, Worden, and the skippers of *Sachem*, *Currituck*, and *Seth Low*, the tugs that towed her.

Because mechanics never stopped work until the very hour of her departure, the crew had not tested the guns or worked the turret enough to feel comfortable with so new and novel an arrangement. Ericsson had made the vessel as comfortable as possible by installing blowers to circulate heat and outside air. After a light supper, those not on watch crawled into their hammocks. Tomorrow would be a full day of exercises. *Seth Low*, with a hawser tied to the ironclad, plowed through a calm sea while moonbeams danced about in the vessel's wake. *Monitor*'s engines pulsated softly and rhythmically, calming jangled nerves. Men smoked cigars and wrote letters home. All was quiet.

Early in the morning, men awoke to a different scene. A strong westerly kicked up the sea, sending waves streaming over the

Union vessels carried howitzers, mainly because they were not fixed guns and could be moved about. The 12-pounder on the deck of a monitor became a handy utility weapon when firing from the deck.

Below: Every vessel carried its own forge and blacksmiths. Something always needed repair on *Monitor*, and the crew on her deck were busily engaged making rivets for refastening plates loosened during the battle.

deck. The wind steadily increased, building enormous waves. *Monitor*'s turret had been jacked up before leaving the navy yard and a thick hemp rope inserted between the brass ring and the bottom of the turret to act as a seal against leaks. It failed miserably. As waves broke over the deck, seawater poured through the seal, down the gun deck, and onto the berth deck, driving men from their hammocks. Worden discovered water coming through hatches, deck lights, and every other seam and opening to the outer deck. By noon the waves increased to a height that crashed over the turret, swept across the smokestacks, and dumped a column of water down the funnels and into the fire-bed. Water streamed through the intakes, wetting the drive belts that turned the blowers. Belts slipped and finally snapped. Without the blowers working, poisonous gas from the coal furnaces threatened to asphyxiate the crew. Executive Officer Lieutenant Greene went below to check on the pumps and found they could not be operated for lack of steam, so he set up hand pumps and formed a bucket brigade.

To escape the fumes, men crowded onto the gun deck. Some climbed outside to sit atop the turret, huddling under a piece of canvas. Greene attempted to signal *Sachem* and *Currituck*, but neither vessel responded. He finally got the attention of *Seth Low* and ordered her to change course to the west where *Monitor* could get to the leeward and into calmer water. Five hours later the weather improved enough for Greene to evacuate the gases, restart the ventilation system, fire the boilers, and get the steam pumps working. But the weather did not improve much, and shortly after midnight another storm struck. Once again *Monitor* wallowed in tons of seawater that streamed into the vessel through the blower intakes. Greene, having seen little sleep since leaving New York, spoke for the crew when he said, "We then commenced to think the *Monitor* would never see daylight," but at 3:00 a.m. the storm began to ease. Five hours later, about the time when Buchanan decided to take *Virginia* into Hampton Roads on her first day's mission of destruction, the weather turned warm and balmy like a day in May.

Steaming along at six knots, *Monitor* passed Cape Charles at noon and two hours later entered Chesapeake Bay. At three o'clock the vessel passed Cape Henry and an hour later Worden and his officers

thought they heard heavy firing coming from the vicinity of Fort Monroe. They gathered on the top of the turret, peering westward, where a thick column of smoke curled skyward and spread into a vast dark cloud. When 10 miles from Hampton Roads, Acting Assistant Paymaster William F. Keeler claimed to see white puffs of smoke from shells bursting in air. To do so would have required very good eyes.

Worden hailed a passing pilot boat and brought on board a pilot to guide the ship to Fort Monroe. The pilot knew only that *Virginia* had come into the Roads and attacked the Union squadron. The closer *Monitor* came to Old Point Comfort, the better the crew could see a frigate burning farther up the Roads. Nobody thought of

dinner. They geared themselves to enter a fight, but darkness fell and the firing stopped.

South of Hampton Roads the Confederates occupied Sewell's Point, Craney Island at the mouth of the Elizabeth River, and Pig Point off the mouth of the Nansemond River. Over time the Rebels had placed batteries along shore from Norfolk to

Right: The 3,274-ton U.S.S. *Wabash* made frequent stops at Hampton Roads, where her sister ship, the U.S.S. *Minnesota*, lay at anchor waiting for the dreaded *Virginia* to come into the Roads and do battle.

Below: Paymaster William F. Keeler (standing center), Master E. V. Gager (left) 2nd Asst. Engr. A. B. Campbell (front), and Lt. William Flye (right), all of *Monitor*, joined an assembly of officers gathered for a group photograph weeks after the battle.

Sewell's Point. On the west side of the Elizabeth River, more batteries had been planted on Craney Island and along Craney Flats. When Buchanan attacked the Union squadron, he fully intended to sweep the Union force out of Hampton Roads, capture Newport News and Fort Monroe, and return the lower section of the upper peninsula to Virginia. Though disabled, he fully expected Lieutenant Jones to finish the work on March 9. From his perspective, the Union had no force in Hampton Roads that could defeat the C.S.S. *Virginia*.

Since the beginning of the war, the huge North Atlantic Blockading Squadron had controlled Hampton Roads and Newport News. When Goldsborough took command of the squadron in September, he constantly

warned Welles of the coming of *Virginia*. He urged the government to build a fleet of 30 armored warships, but nobody listened. When he departed in December to lead the attack on Roanoke Island, he transferred command of the squadron at Hampton Roads to Captain John Marston. Goldsborough did not expect to get an ironclad, but Marston did. Days before *Monitor* sailed from Brooklyn, Welles notified Marston not to let the experimental vessel go under fire "except for some pressing emergency." Then on March 6 he wired Paulding at the Brooklyn Navy Yard to divert *Monitor* to Washington if *Virginia* attempted to come up the Potomac. The message providently arrived too late. *Monitor* had sailed. Unaware of his change in orders, Worden steamed toward his appointment with the old *Merrimac*.

At 9:00 p.m. *Monitor* entered Hampton Roads and came to anchor near *Roanoke*. Worden went aboard with Chief Engineer Alban C. Stimers to speak with Marston, who glumly warned that *Virginia* would be back in the morning to finish off *Minnesota*. He then explained new instructions from Welles, ordering the ironclad to Washington. Worden argued that the "pressing emergency" was not at Washington but in Hampton

Roads, and if *Monitor* could put an end to *Virginia*, Welles would not need her in Washington. Conversely, if *Monitor* could not defeat *Virginia* here, she would not be able to defeat her at Washington, so why not do battle now and save the Union squadron? So both men agreed to ignore Welles's order and deploy *Monitor* in the morning to defend *Minnesota*.

Lieutenant Greene took a cutter down to *Minnesota* to advise Captain Van Brunt to look for *Monitor* shortly and not fire upon her. The captain hoped to float the frigate off the Middle Ground with the incoming tide at 2:00 a.m., but he had not lightened the vessel enough to accomplish his purpose. Nor could he afford to offload shot and powder that may be needed for the expected fight at daylight.

Monitor came alongside at 1:00 a.m. and dropped anchor. Her crew had just bedded down when fires on *Congress* touched off the frigate's magazine. The explosion rattled the timbers of every vessel for miles around. "It went straight to the marrow of our bones," wrote Greene. Men scrambled topside to witness the sight, all vowing vengeance in the morning.

The explosion also brought *Minnesota*'s men to the deck. They gaped at the

diminutive ironclad tied alongside the frigate's beam and were not at all cheered by the sight of the "little black 'Pill Box' on a 'shingle.'" The creature fell far short of matching the average seaman's conception of a formidable fighting ship, and their grumbling intensified when they learned she carried only two guns.

Not an hour passed between midnight and dawn that a lookout posted in the tops did not imagine seeing *Virginia* crawling down the river to attack the grounded frigate. Nobody any longer tried to sleep. Some of the men on *Monitor* had been on their feet for more than two days with barely a nap. Those who tried to sleep were shaken awake at 2:00 a.m. when Van Brunt, thinking he gotten *Minnesota* afloat, asked Worden to move *Monitor* out of the way. An hour later he discovered the ship was still stuck and would remain that way at least until the next tide.

Because the telegraph to Washington malfunctioned on March 8, Welles did not learn of the Hampton Roads disaster until the following morning. Lincoln then called a cabinet meeting to discuss defensive measures. Secretary of War Stanton paced about in a state of panic. Every so often he strolled to the window and peered outside

Above: Carpenters serving on board were expected to look after the ship and make alterations as needed, using drawings and a variety of tools, such as the adjustable square and the adze for shaving timber.

Above left: An officer's desk might contain a cap button and the ship name plate (right), a signal book (bottom), parallel dividers (left), a general order book (left center), and a pen and ink well (not shown).

Left: Officers of *Monitor*, Robinson W. Hands, Louis N. Stodder, Albert B. Campbell, and William Flye, standing left to right, watch from the deck as workmen repair damage to the revolving turret.

as if he expected to see *Virginia* creeping up Pennsylvania Avenue to beseige the White House.

All but Lincoln turned on Welles. They demanded to know what the navy intended to do to stop the Confederate ironclad. Welles replied that *Monitor* would be there, but such assurance did not satisfy Stanton. He wanted to know her size and strength and how many guns she carried. Welles answered as best he could, but when he admitted that she only carried two Dahlgrens, Stanton flew into a rage that verged on convulsions. The two men never liked each other, and the trouble at Hampton Roads gave Stanton a marvelous opportunity to expectorate his gall. Welles did not feel composed, but he looked composed, and this only made Stanton madder. Several army and navy officers attended the conference, and Lincoln calmly asked them to prepare a plan of defense for the city.

Later they met again. Stanton wanted to sink fully loaded canal barges in the lower Potomac to prevent *Virginia* from coming up the river. Welles said the idea made no sense because the shallowness of the river would stop the ironclad long before she reached Washington. Lincoln told Stanton to go ahead with his plan if he thought it would work but to not sink the barges unless it became necessary.

Weeks later Lincoln and Stanton went downriver in company with other officials. As they passed hundreds of barges stretched along shore, the president pointed to them and said, "That is Stanton's navy." But on the morning of March 9, 1862, the only person willing to gamble that such drastic action would not be needed was Gideon Welles. He placed his confidence not on *Monitor* but on the shoals of the Potomac. From the odd-shaped prototype others called "Ericsson's folly," he hoped for the best and confined his doubts to himself.

As dawn streaked the eastern horizon, aboard *Virginia* Lieutenant Jones peered across the Roads from Sewell's Point and spied *Minnesota* still fast to the Middle Ground. It would be another good day for the Confederacy and an opportunity to finish the work started by Buchanan, who had been taken ashore with the other wounded. At 6:30 Jones weighed anchor and steamed into Hampton Roads, followed by *Patrick Henry, Jamestown,* and *Teaser.* A light mist still clung to the river, but the morning sun began to burn it off. He heard the report of a signal gun at Fort Monroe and knew his movement had been detected.

On entering Hampton Roads, Jones observed a queer object anchored beside *Minnesota.* It looked like a small floating ironclad battery. Lieutenant Eggleston glanced out a port and described her as "the strangest looking craft we had ever seen before." Others believed that *Minnesota's* crew were escaping on a raft that looked like a shingle fitted with "a large cheese box" for shelter. The joking continued, but every man in the small Confederate squadron admitted

being completely surprised by the presence of the odd craft standing by the frigate. Whatever she was, Lieutenant John Taylor Wood affirmed that, "She could not possibly have made her appearance at a more inopportune time."

As the morning sun evaporated the mist overhanging the river, Union infantry manning batteries along the north shore got their first look at *Monitor*. They were as baffled as the Confederates and equally unimpressed. Seamen who had escaped from the burning *Congress* believed the little ironclad would be quickly swallowed-up by the Rebel leviathan. "We do not have much faith in the *Monitor*," said a survivor from *Congress*, but it became apparent to all observers that, without help, *Minnesota* would be knocked to pieces and set ablaze by mid-morning.

Men on *Monitor* were still eating breakfast when they felt the vessel move. They hurried topside as the ironclad slithered by the majestic frigate. To some, it

appeared that *Minnesota* had given up all hope of salvation. Men were leaving the ship and taking boats to shore. Others on deck were pitching cannon into the river. Worden hailed Van Brunt, asking the latter's intentions. Van Brunt replied that he was lightening his ship in an effort to float her. Worden knew better. Removing men and jettisoning a few cannon would not lighten the ship. Van Brunt had given up because he expected Worden's two-gun *Monitor* to be blown to bits by the monster ironclad steaming across the Roads.

Worden called the men to quarters and took his position in the pilothouse with helmsman Peter Truscott and the pilot. Greene took command of the turret with Chief Engineer Stimers on one gun and Acting Master Louis N. Stodder on the other. Paymaster Keeler, with nothing more to do than watch, sat with others atop the turret. A shot from *Virginia*, the first of the day, whizzed overhead and smashed into *Minnesota*. Worden climbed up through the

Above: A Union officer poses before the cladded iron turret of a monitor. Heavy 3-inch diameter rivets hold four inches of armor against a framework of 12 inches of oak. Thickness varied as the war continued.

Above left: The C.S.S. *Teaser*, a gunboat in the James River Squadron, carried two 32-pounders. The gun is mounted on a recoil slide with rope stops. A jackscrew is used to raise and lower the barrel for different ranges.

hatch and hollered, "Gentlemen, that is the *Merrimac*, you had better go below," and they all tumbled back into the turret.

As *Monitor* slowly closed on *Virginia*, gunners inside the turret slid 175-pound projectiles into the barrels of their 11-inch Dahlgrens. They worked in near darkness, the only light coming through gratings in the top of the turret and a few dim lanterns inside. With the shutters closed, they could see nothing outside and silently waited for orders from the pilothouse. They heard sporadic firing – what sounded like two or three shots from *Virginia* and perhaps a broadside from *Minnesota*. As they steeled for battle, the speaking tube from the pilothouse to the turret stopped working, so Greene sent Keeler forward to get instruc-tions. Worden replied, "Tell Lieutenant Greene to not fire until I give the word, to be cool & deliberate, to take sure aim & not waste a shot."

Worden planted *Monitor* squarely between *Minnesota* and *Virginia*, and when coming in range, he ordered the engines stopped and sent Keeler back to the turret with orders to commence firing. Stodder actuated the steam engine that turned the turret and rotated it until the guns bore on the enemy. Greene ordered the shutters opened, ran out the guns, and pulled the lanyards. Smoke billowed into turret, making it difficult for Greene to see whether the shots took effect. From the pilothouse Quartermaster Truscott had a better view, declaring, "You can see surprise on a ship just the same as you can see it in a human being and there was surprise all over the *Merrimac*."

Jones quickly recovered from his surprise. The first projectiles from *Monitor* had no more effect on *Virginia*'s shield than did a broadside from the 9-inch Dahlgrens on *Minnesota*. He ordered the pilots to take him within a half mile of the frigate and to ignore the bothersome *Monitor*. But shallow water lay in his path, as did *Monitor*, and Jones never got closer to *Minnesota* than a mile, still close enough to wreak havoc on the frigate with his rifled cannon. It also bothered Jones that *Monitor* could outmaneuver him, and after the two

ironclads closed to within 100 yards, he decided to fight her first before attending to *Minnesota*.

Closer together they came, circling like a David and a Goliath at 50 yards. Worden soon discovered *Virginia*'s inability to turn and tried to keep *Monitor* in a position where Jones could not bring his powerful broadsides to bear. Lieutenant Eggleston voiced frustration at not being able to put a shot through *Monitor*'s small ports. He had never seen such a thing as a rotating turret, one that could move to firing position, slide open both ports, fire, and rapidly rotate away before he could reply. Neither vessel appeared to be injuring the other, but Eggleston could hear and feel the heavy impact of *Monitor*'s shots slamming into the ironclad's angular shield. He complained to Jones that he could not bring his guns to bear because *Monitor* moved about too quickly and presented too small a target.

Neither Worden nor Greene knew whether *Monitor* would be able to withstand the fire of *Virginia*'s rifled guns. After the first few shots dented the turret and caromed off, the early uneasiness passed. When Chief Engineer Stimers explained that the cladding on the turret had been designed to bend but not to break, the powder-begrimed faces of the gun crews wore a new look of confidence. With fears allayed, they stripped to the waist and vigorously set about the task of whipping the enemy, boasting that they soon would finish her off.

The men of *Monitor*, however, did have a problem. The ports opened only long enough to run out the guns, fire, and close. Neither Greene nor his gun crew could see whether the shots did any harm, though they felt confident of hitting something. After each shot, Greene sent Keeler to the pilothouse to get a report from Worden, who acted as observer. Worden could see the 11-inch projectiles bound off the ironclad's casemate but said nothing to discourage the gunners from keeping up a steady fire.

Because of close quarters on the gun deck, swabbers had to run the handle of the

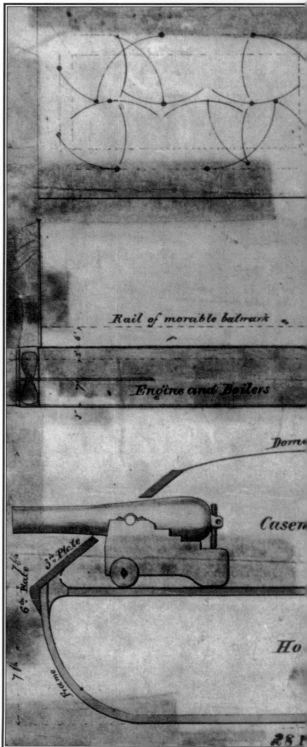

Left: On March 9, 1862, neither *Monitor* nor *Virginia* could gain an advantage over the other. Each attempted to ram the other, and when *Monitor* tried, the helmsman sheered off slightly at the last minute.

Below: Ironclads such as the *Monitor* were not unique to the outer waters. Many similar but shallower draft vessels were built by James Eads in St. Louis for duty on the Mississippi River and its tributaries.

device through a small hole in the turret, push the swab into the mouth of the cannon, and then run it back and forth until the barrel had been cleaned of sparks and powder residue. The awkwardness of the process took time, so Greene decided to speed it up by leaving the ports open. This put *Monitor* at some risk from a lucky shot, but the ports were small enough for Greene to take the chance. He may have escaped misfortune when Stimers reported that he could rotate the turret but no longer stop it precisely on the mark for firing the guns. So Greene decided to let the turret revolve in perpetuity and fire the guns on the fly. This accelerated *Monitor*'s rate of fire, enabling both guns to send off a round every seven to eight minutes, though with some reduction in accuracy.

Worden continued to send orders from the pilothouse to the gun deck, but Keeler, being unaccustomed to naval terminology, often miscarried the instructions. It made

little difference because *Monitor*'s shots, though they cracked a few plates, bounded harmlessly away.

On *Virginia*, Jones was beginning to experience a number of bothersome problems, however. Ramming *Cumberland* had snapped off the ironclad's beak and started a leak that required steam to operate the pumps. With the added weight of water in her hold, she could barely steer, and some of the crew feared she would suddenly sink. It took 15 minutes to bring her about by a few degrees just to fire a broadside. The engines threatened to give out because her smokestack had been so badly riddled that air could not be drafted down to feed her fires. To make matters worse, the day had not gone as they planned. They could not out-maneuver the pestiferous *Monitor*, damage her, or get free of her.

Jones noticed that Union projectiles, though not penetrating the iron casemate, had weakened it in spots. If *Monitor*

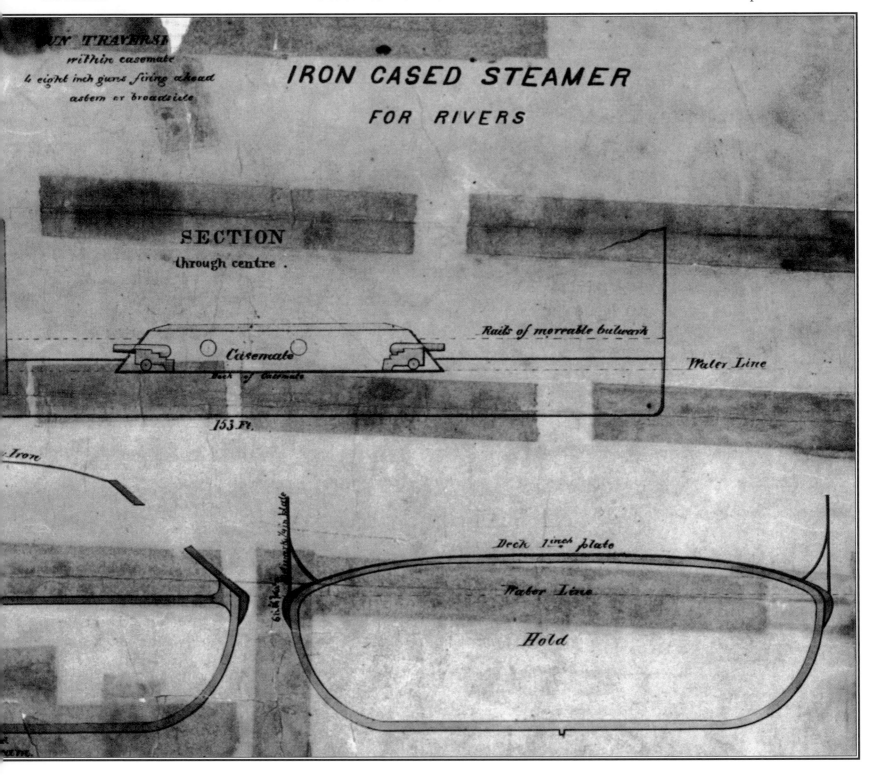

Left: Before the Confederates went to work on the *Merrimac*, she looked much like the U.S.S. *Minnesota*. They saved only part of her hull and built her back up with an iron casemate, an iron deck, and a new battery.

Below: *Monitor* maneuvered constantly to keep *Virginia* away from *Minnesota*. They circled each other, each intent on destroying the other, but whenever *Virginia* had the chance she would lob a shell at *Minnesota*.

concentrated its fire on the same section of *Virginia*'s shield, repeated shots would eventually break through the wooden backing, and once a shell got inside the casemate, the damage would be horrendous. He also worried that a projectile fired at his water line would strike just below the overhanging eaves, hull the vessel, and send her to the bottom. She had used almost all her coal, and had it not been for the water in her bilge, her hull would have risen above the water line. Jones did not know that Greene could no longer control *Monitor*'s turret or take aim at any particular spot of weakness on *Virginia*.

After two hours of fighting and drawing no closer to *Minnesota* than a mile, *Virginia*'s pilots lost track of their position and ran aground. Drawing half the water of *Virginia*, *Monitor* worked in close and began hammering the ironclad fore and aft. The situation enabled Worden to place *Monitor* close enough to *Virginia* to maximize the effect of his shots while denying Jones the opportunity to fire back. Though Greene's firing continued to be helter-skelter, a few shots nearly went through the ports while others cracked plates and began to crush through the wooden backing.

Jones knew *Virginia* would be finished if Ramsay could not work her off the shoal. Her engines had always been cranky, but the situation now became desperate. Ramsay tied down the boilers' steam safety valves and heaved oil, turpentine, and other fast-burning combustibles into the furnaces. Needles on steam gages crept beyond the danger point and continued to climb. The vessel shuddered as the propeller stirred the mud. Boilers threatened to explode, pistons hammered, heat rose to unendurable levels in the engine room, and while men on the gun deck solemnly waited, *Monitor* continued to throw projectiles against the ironclad's casemate at eight minute intervals.

Ramsay reached the point of being unable to do more when he felt the vessel move a bit. He gave the engines all they could bear, and then some, and she slowly backed off the shoal. Men on the gun deck gave a loud cheer and hurried back to their weapons – all but Eggleston. Jones walked by and asked, "Why are you not firing, sir?" Eggleston replied, "It is quite a waste of ammunition…. Our powder is precious, sir, and I find I can do the *Monitor* as much damage by snapping my finger at her every five minutes." Jones shrugged and walked on, saying, "Never mind, we are getting ready to ram her."

Jones did not know *Virginia* had lost her beak and by ramming he would endanger the ship's wooden bow. Had Worden also known this, he would have made every effort to let it happen. Instead, he saw her coming at full speed and anticipated her intentions. He sent a message to Greene to give her both guns, and then he put the helm hard away to avoid the blow. Moments before contact, Jones changed his mind. Fearing the prow – one he no longer had – would become embedded in *Monitor* and take both vessels to the bottom, he told Ramsay to back the engines. Worden's

turning lessened the effect even more. *Virginia*'s bow struck a glancing blow, knocked some men off their feet, and left on *Monitor*'s beam a small number of wooden splinters where the butt occurred.

Monitor twirled about from the blow, but the only damage reported occurred on *Virginia*. The leak in her bow increased to the point of consternation. But even more worrisome were the two shots fired by Greene that struck the port just above Wood's pivot gun and caved in the casemate. The concussion knocked all the men to the floor, causing them to bleed from the nose and ears. Reflecting on the close call, Wood later admitted that "Another shot at the same place would have penetrated."

By 11:00 a.m. Greene had exhausted the supply of shot and powder on *Virginia*'s gun deck. To get more, the turret had to be rotated over a hatchway leading to a storage area below. Knowing the guns could not be fired during the transfer, Worden pulled the *Monitor* out of the fight and stood off for 30 minutes.

Jones, thinking *Monitor* had been damaged, turned his batteries loose on

Minnesota. Simms opened with the forward pivot gun and sent a shell screeching through four of the frigate's cabins and started a fire. His second shot struck the boiler of the tug *Dragon*, standing alongside, and blew it up. Van Brunt answered with a steady but ineffective fire. In an effort to cut down on the damage to *Minnesota*, Worden hurried back into the fight and again closed to within a few yards of *Virginia*. At times the two vessels touched, firing into each other at point blank range.

Jones soon realized that *Monitor* could not be injured and that something drastic

must be done before a well-placed shot disabled *Virginia*. Aware of *Monitor*'s low freeboard, Lieutenant Wood suggested forming a group of volunteers to board the vessel. He now understood how the turret operated. Volunteers using hammers would drive wedges between the deck and the turret. If the turret could be jammed so that its guns bore on the ship's own pilothouse, the enemy would no longer be able to fire them.

Jones wisely decided not to try it. Worden had plenty of hand grenades ready in the turret and would have given the

Rebels a hot reception. When nothing happened, *Monitor* steamed on by, and Worden set his mind to finding other ways to get at the ironclad.

After nearly three hours of inconclusive fighting, Worden believed he had discovered *Virginia*'s Achilles' heel – her rudder and propeller. He ordered *Monitor* to come about and ram the enemy aft. Once disabled, *Virginia* could surrender or drift, but either way she would no longer be a threat to the Union. Using *Monitor*'s superior speed and maneuverability, Worden lined up on *Virginia*'s stern and steamed ahead at full speed.

Above: A navy boarding axe with its leather case. The belt at left is Model 1962 with iron frame friction buckle by Goodyear. The other belt is old style with simple hook for adjustment.

Above right: Modified schooners were fitted to carry 13-inch mortars that fired 200-pound shells distances up to two miles. They were used to demolish forts and earthworks and always came to anchor before firing.

Right: Every sloop of war carried at least one pivot gun, usually a 100- or 150-pounder rifled Parrott in the bow and often a smaller pivot gun aft. Working such a gun required a larger gun crew than a broadside gun.

The day's battle had already become a series of coincidences, and Worden's ramming run became another. *Monitor*'s steering apparatus malfunctioned, causing the vessel to sheer off moments before impact, missing the enemy by no more than a few feet. Jones admitted that had *Virginia* been struck, her career would have come to an end.

Instead, Jones now had the opportunity to experiment on *Monitor*'s weakness, her pilothouse. As she steamed by, Lieutenant Wood trained his pivot gun on the pilothouse and, at a distance of 20 yards, fired. The shell struck and exploded, sending burnt powder and small pieces of metal through the grate and into Worden's eyes. Paymaster Keeler, who had been standing below the pilothouse waiting for orders, rushed to the commander's side to ask if he was injured. Worden, holding his hands to his face, answered, "My eyes. I am blind."

Keeler looked into Worden's blackened face and observed dozens of tiny wounds that oozed small rivulets of blood. He led Worden down from the pilothouse and sent

for Greene. For a while the guns stood silent while the officers consulted with their commander. Worden put the vessel in Greene's hands and said, "Save the *Minnesota* if you can."

After making Worden comfortable, Greene turned the gun deck over to Stimers and went up to the pilothouse. A quick assessment convinced him that another well-placed shot would kill anyone standing there. A half-hour had passed since the wounding of Worden, and during that time Greene had taken *Monitor* into water too shallow for *Virginia* to follow.

Monitor's withdrawal gave Jones the mistaken impression that he had knocked the Union vessel out of the fight. He now felt unencumbered to finish off *Minnesota*, but the receding tide created concern among the pilots. He could not get closer to the frigate without grounding, the leak in the bow fretted him, and his men were all exhausted. Every officer but one thought the vessel should go back to Norfolk for repairs. The exception, Wood, proposed that the ship be taken down to Fort Monroe to smash up the frigates still anchored there. Jones thought

not, and shortly after noon he ordered Ramsay to take her back to the Elizabeth River.

At almost the same instant, Greene brought *Monitor* about and steamed back to resume the fight. Jones must have seen the ironclad's movement but nonetheless reported, "Had there been any sign of the *Monitor*'s willingness to renew the contest we would have remained to fight her." Greene, seeing *Virginia* steaming toward Sewell's Point, believed that Jones had abandoned the fight. Each commander held the mistaken impression that he had won the day, but the edge goes to Greene.

As *Virginia* withdrew and *Monitor* advanced, both vessels continued to exchange fire, and there should have been little question in Jones's mind that the fight had resumed. Jones's orders were to destroy *Minnesota* while Greene's orders from Worden were to defend her. With Worden wounded and in need of medical aid, and with *Virginia* in apparent retreat, Greene broke off the engagement and returned to *Minnesota*.

Spectators to the fight lined the shores on both sides of Hampton Roads. One Union sailor, watching from the rigging of a frigate, summed up the thoughts of his fellow seamen when he wrote, "To tell the truth, we did not have much faith in the *Monitor*. We all expected to see the *Merrimac* destroy her."

A selection of Confederate naval officers' uniforms and equipment includes: (above left) lieutenant's frock coat and (below left) jacket; other frock coats (below center and above right); Adams revolver and holster; captains' swords and scabbards (above center); sword from C.S.S. *Alabama* (top of group of three, bottom center); Raphael Semmes's field glass (bottom left), revolver and holster (below right), and cap (top right).

Right: As the war progressed, monitor design changed depending upon the service intended for the ship. Double-turreted monitors became more prevalent on rivers such as the James and the Mississippi.

Ensign   Master   Lieutenant   Lieutenant Commander   Commander   Captain   Commodore   Rear Admiral

Ensign

Commander

Master

Captain

Lieutenant

Commodore

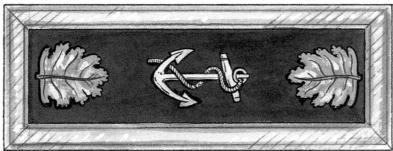

Lieutenant Commander

Rear Admiral

Instead, what he witnessed was "one of the grandest fights between two war vessels that the world has ever seen." From Sewell's Point, Ex-Governor Henry A. Wise of *Virginia* watched the fight with his son and could not believe that *Monitor* survived. "We could not doubt that the *Merrimac* would, either by shot or ramming, make short work of the cheese-box; but as time wore on, we began to realize that the newcomer was a tough customer." When he saw *Virginia* steaming back toward Sewell Point with *Monitor* in chase, he lamented, "dear old Buchanan would never have done it." In Mobile Bay, 29 months later, "dear old Buchanan" would validate Wise's lament.

Though neither ironclad tactically whipped the other, *Monitor* accomplished her purpose while *Virginia* did not. Without the timely appearance of Ericsson's novel warship, *Virginia* would undoubtedly have destroyed *Minnesota* and every other Union vessel that could not escape from Hampton Roads. Over time, she would likely have forced the evacuation of Fort Monroe, opened Hampton Roads to blockade runners, and disrupted the plans of Major General George B. McClellan to invade Virginia's peninsula.

In the weeks to come there would be other duels in Hampton Roads. *Virginia* would come down the Elizabeth River, and

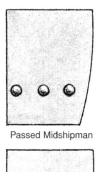

Passed Midshipman

Passed Midshipman

Passed Midshipman

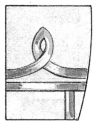

Master

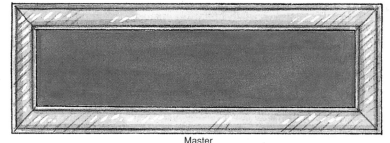

Master

Master

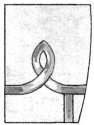

Lieutenant

Lieutenant

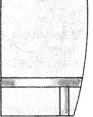

Commander

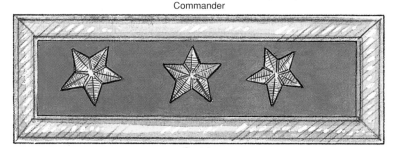

Commander

Commander

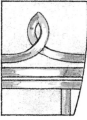

Captain

Captain

Captain

Flag Officer

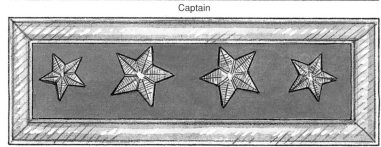

Flag Officer

Flag Officer

Monitor would come up to meet her, but neither seemed particularly anxious to resume the fight left unfinished on the afternoon of March 9. Yet *Virginia's* success vindicated Secretary Mallory, and he promptly obtained funds to build more ironclads to defend the Confederacy's waterways. And in the North, John Ericsson created an entirely new class of ironclad warships having single turrets, double turrets, and even triple turrets, and they would all be called monitors.

In Great Britain, the Admiralty took immense interest in the standoff in Hampton Roads. While its members deliberated on its impact on the Royal Navy,

the London Times succinctly summarized the outcome in one sentence, writing, "Whereas we had available for immediate purposes one hundred and forty-nine first-class war-ships, we have now two, these two being the [ironclads] *Warrior* and her sister *Ironsides*."

Being prototypes, *Virginia* and *Monitor* each had flaws. With all her defects, *Virginia* turned out to be one of the best ironclads built by the South, while for the North, the original *Monitor* became among the worst. Neither vessel lasted to see the end of the war. When in May Confederates abandoned Norfolk, they left *Virginia* without a home. Her new commander, Commodore Josiah

A selection of Confederate naval officers' insignia. As with their army insignia, the Confederates deliberately designed naval insignia that would be different from that of the old Union. Shoulder straps insignia were particularly more in keeping with those of officers of comparable ranks in the army. The most unusual feature was the creation of a regulation ranking of flag officer, traditionally an honorary position. The Confederate Navy also mandated four admirals, although only one was ever appointed, and no insignia for that rank was ever officially prescribed.

Above: Confederates became very proficient at developing "torpedoes" (mines) as an effective weapon. The Union then designed raking attachments to clear the rivers of the devices, such as the one mounted on the U.S.S. *Saugus*.

Below: On December 26, 1862, when *Monitor* foundered of Cape Hateras, she was under tow by the U.S.S. *Rhode Island*, whose crew rescued all the men from the sinking ship apart from four officers and twelve seamen.

Bottom left: The early river ironclads designed by the Union looked much like their Confederate counterparts, but most were lightly clad with iron and propelled by paddlewheels mounted on the sides aft.

Tattnall, could not get the vessel up the James River, so he took her back to Craney Island and blew her up.

Monitor suffered a more dismal fate. Though having never been a seaworthy craft, the Navy Department ordered her to Beaufort, North Carolina, for duty off Charleston. Like her maiden voyage to Hampton Roads, the voyage started in good weather and ended in a storm. All her sailing defects manifested themselves once more, but this time she filled with sea water and on December 31, 1862, sank in 220 feet of water, 15 miles south of Cape Hatteras.

Thus ended the brief careers of the first ironclads, making obsolete the majestic wooden-hulled navies of the world.

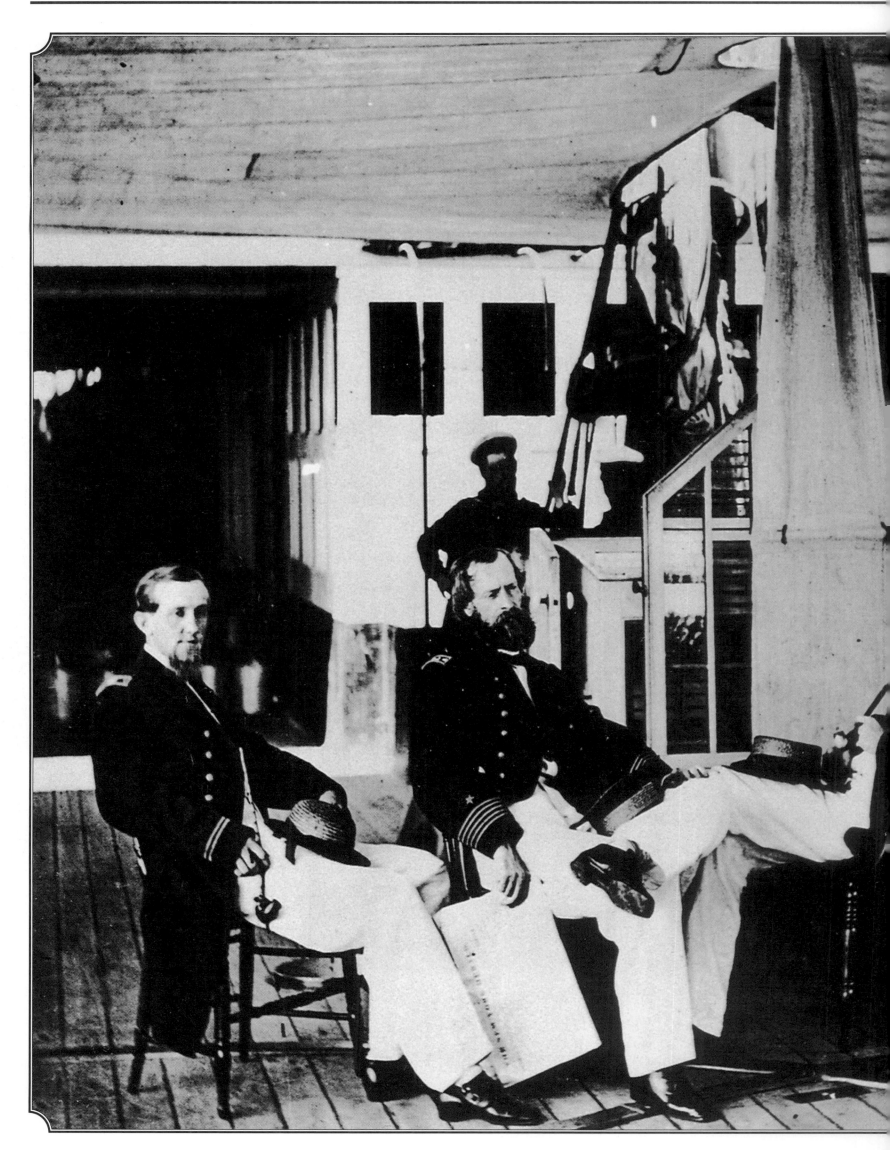

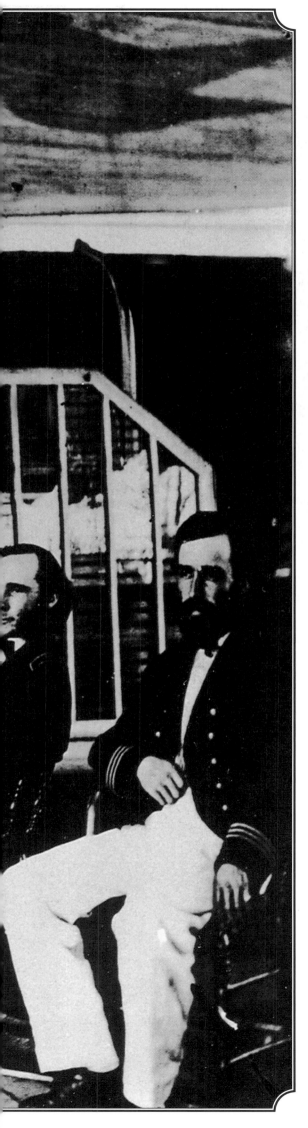

CHAPTER FOUR

RUNNING THE GAUNTLET

A few years before the Civil War, Congress appropriated enough money for the Navy to build five wooden first-class sloops-of-war powered by steam and driven by propeller. They were heavy vessels approaching 3,000 tons and armed with more than 20 guns, mostly 9-inch Dahlgren smoothbores. The ships were designed for service on the oceans and equipped with both sail the steam, but during the winter of 1862 Secretary Welles turned four of them over to Flag Officer David Glasgow Farragut for deployment in the Mississippi River. Under normal circumstances, vessels of this size had no business fighting battles in a river.

About a hundred miles north of the mouth of the Mississippi lay New Orleans, the greatest and wealthiest city of the Confederacy. Her location far upriver gave the Confederate government a measure of comfort because any vessel ascending the mighty watershed would have to pass through the batteries at Fort Jackson and Fort St. Philip, two of the strongest bastionsin the entire country. Most authorities North and Southdid not believe wooden vessels could do this. Wellesthought otherwise, and so did Farragut, provided that the attack came as a surprise.

Like so many hurriedly conceived campaigns, events never materialize according to plan, and a commander more faint-hearted than Farragut would not have been condemned for scrapping the mission. In one of the greatest naval episodes of the Civil War, Farragut, who had not been in a battle since the War of 1812, decided to attempt the impossible.

Secretary of the Navy Stephen R. Mallory used the reconfigured *Merrimac* as the model for all the ironclads subsequently built by the Confederacy, but down in New Orleans, Louisiana, a few enterprising investors created their own version of an impregnable ram. Their motivation had less to do with patriotism and more to do with prize money because on May 27, 1861, Commander Charles H. Poor anchored the 24-gun ship-rigged steamer U.S.S. *Brooklyn* off Pass a l'Outre and sent a dispatch boat up the river to notify Major Johnson K. Duncan at Fort Jackson that the Mississippi was now under Union blockade. Two days later the sidewheel steamer U.S.S. *Powhatan*, commanded by Lieutenant David D. Porter, arrived off Southwest Pass, the other main artery of the Mississippi flowing into the Gulf of Mexico. John A. Stevenson viewed the presence of Union blockaders as an opportunity to cash in on the war. To destroy a warship such as *Brooklyn* would net investors at least $500,000 in prize money. All he needed was the right kind of vessel.

With this in mind, Stevenson opened subscription books at the New Orleans Merchant's change to raise $100,000. He needed the money to purchase the prize packet steamer *Enoch Train*, captured by the steamer C.S.S. *Ivy*, and convert it into an ironclad capable of destroying any vessel posted by the Union navy off the passes. Stevenson discussed his plan with Mallory, who recognized it as a private venture. The secretary voiced his approval and confirmed that letters of marque and reprisal would be issued to enable the vessel to operate as a Confederate privateer.

Stevenson returned to New Orleans, bought *Enoch Train*, and immediately set to work stripping the vessel down to her deck.

Captain Melancton Smith (left center) relaxes with his officers on board the U.S.S. *Mississippi*. To the far right is Lt. George Dewey, who would later command a squadron in the Spanish-American War.

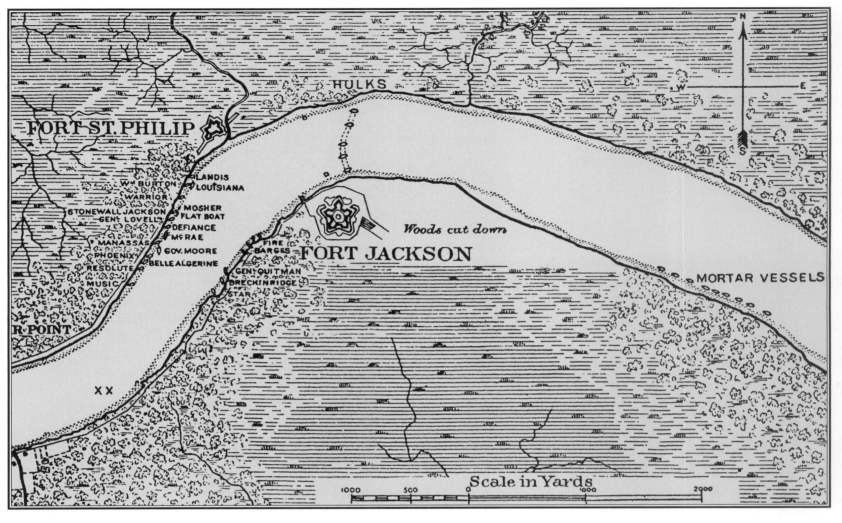

The map includes the following labels: HULKS, FORT ST. PHILIP, W™ BURTON, LANDIS, LOUISIANA, STONEWALL JACKSON, MOSHER, GEN'L LOVELL'S, FLAT BOAT, WARRIOR, DEFIANCE, M°RAE, MANASSAS, GOV. MOORE, PHOENIX, FIRE BARGES, BELLE ALGERINE, RESOLUTE, GEN'L QUITMAN, MUSIC, BRECKINRIDGE, STAR, R. POINT, FORT JACKSON, Woods cut down, MORTAR VESSELS, Scale in Yards, 1000 500 0 1000 2000, N S E W

Two of the strongest forts in the Confederacy lay in the lower Mississippi, 70 miles below New Orleans. Fort Jackson and Fort St. Philip had been built in such a way that the guns of both could enfilade any squadron of warships attempting to pass upriver. Additional defenses in the form of obstructions had been strung across the river below Fort Jackson, where a water battery had been built to fire upon intruders.

He lengthened her from 128 feet to 143 feet, increased her beam from 26 to 33 feet, and deepened her from 12 feet 6 inches to 17 feet. He added 17-inch thick beams 20 feet long to strengthen her bow for ramming, and over this mass of lumber he layered a covering of iron plates to make the exposed portion of the vessel shot-proof.

When finished, the vessel looked like an elongated turtle, shaped to deflect any projectile striking her armor. The only protrusions topside consisted of two retractable smokestacks, a pilothouse aft, and a small hatch. Because Stevenson intended to use the vessel solely as a ram, she carried but one gun, a 32-pounder carronade inside the hatch. When the rebuilt *Enoch Train* took her first trial run, Stevenson discovered what any naval engineer could have told him. He had added so much weight to the vessel that *Enoch Train's* once powerful engines could now barely stem the current.

Nonetheless, the building of the ram now named *Manassas* did not go unnoticed by sailors serving on blockade duty. By late summer the "boat with the iron horn" created enough concern that seamen began to develop an incurable dread known in navy circles as "ram fever."

In the meantime, Union Secretary of the Navy Gideon Welles sent sixty-one-year-old Captain William W. McKean to the Gulf as the new commander of the blockading squadron. Soon after arrival, McKean steamed over to the Mississippi Passes to speak with the senior officer, Captain John Pope. They discussed the difficulty of blockading the delta from the Gulf and concluded that by taking the vessels inside

the river and posting them at Head of Passes, where all the outlets to the Gulf branched, they would then be able to blockade the river at its stem rather than its branches. The strategy made sense, especially since it was McKean's idea, so Pope moved into the Mississippi through Southwest Pass.

Of the four vessels comprising his squadron, the 22-gun sloop-rigged screw steamer *Richmond* served as his flagship. Her draft of 17 feet made crossing the bar difficult, but Pope brought her inside and steamed to an anchorage near Head of Passes. The light-draft sidewheeler *Water Witch*, commanded by Lieutenant Francis Winslow, carried only four light guns, but Pope brought her in to act as scout. The U.S.S. *Vincennes*, a 19-gun sailing sloop skippered by Commander Robert Handy, had no business in a river where she depended a tow but, because she carried a fair amount of firepower, Pope brought her up the river and moored her beside *Richmond*. A schooner, *Frolic*, had been captured as a prize and Pope sent her a few miles above *Richmond* to serve as a sentinel. Aside from that, he made no provision to repel a surprise attack.

On October 5 Lieutenant Joseph Fry took the C.S.S. *Ivy* down to Head of Passes and spotted Pope's squadron. For a while he watched from a distance, then he opened fire on *Richmond* with two rifled 24-pounders. Pope replied with his 9-inch smoothbores, but the shots fell short. Unaccustomed to being under fire, Pope began to worry that while his heavy guns could not reach *Ivy*, the enemy's two popguns could reach him. Pope expressed

Above: The U.S.S. *Richmond*, **the newest ship in Farragut's squadron, had been designed to fight at sea. Vessels such as this struggled in the river, but Farragut made good use of them because they were all he had.**

Right: Commodore George Hollins, C.S.N., was a no-nonsense commander who maximized the use of his small squadron. He did not like his boss, Secretary of the Navy Mallory, and did not always obey orders he thought were wrong.

his jitters to McKean, writing, "We are entirely at the mercy of the enemy. We are liable to be driven from here at any moment, and, situated as we are, our position is untenable. I may be captured at any time by a pitiful little steamer mounting only one [actually three] gun."

Having seen enough, Fry steamed up to Fort Jackson to report the intruders to Commodore George N. Hollins. At the age of sixty-two, Hollins still possessed the combativeness he first displayed when at age fifteen he fought the British during the War of 1812 while serving under Stephen Decatur. Mallory had sent him to New Orleans to build a squadron to defend the river. By the beginning of October Hollins had assembled a half dozen vessels. *McRae*, an 830-ton sloop-rigged steamer carried seven guns. *Ivy* carried three guns, and the tugs *Tuscarora* and *Jackson* each carried two. *Calhoun*, formerly a privateer, carried five, and *Pickens*, a schooner, carried three. With the exception of a 9-inch rifled 132-pounder on *Ivy*, a 9-inch pivot gun on *McRae*, and an

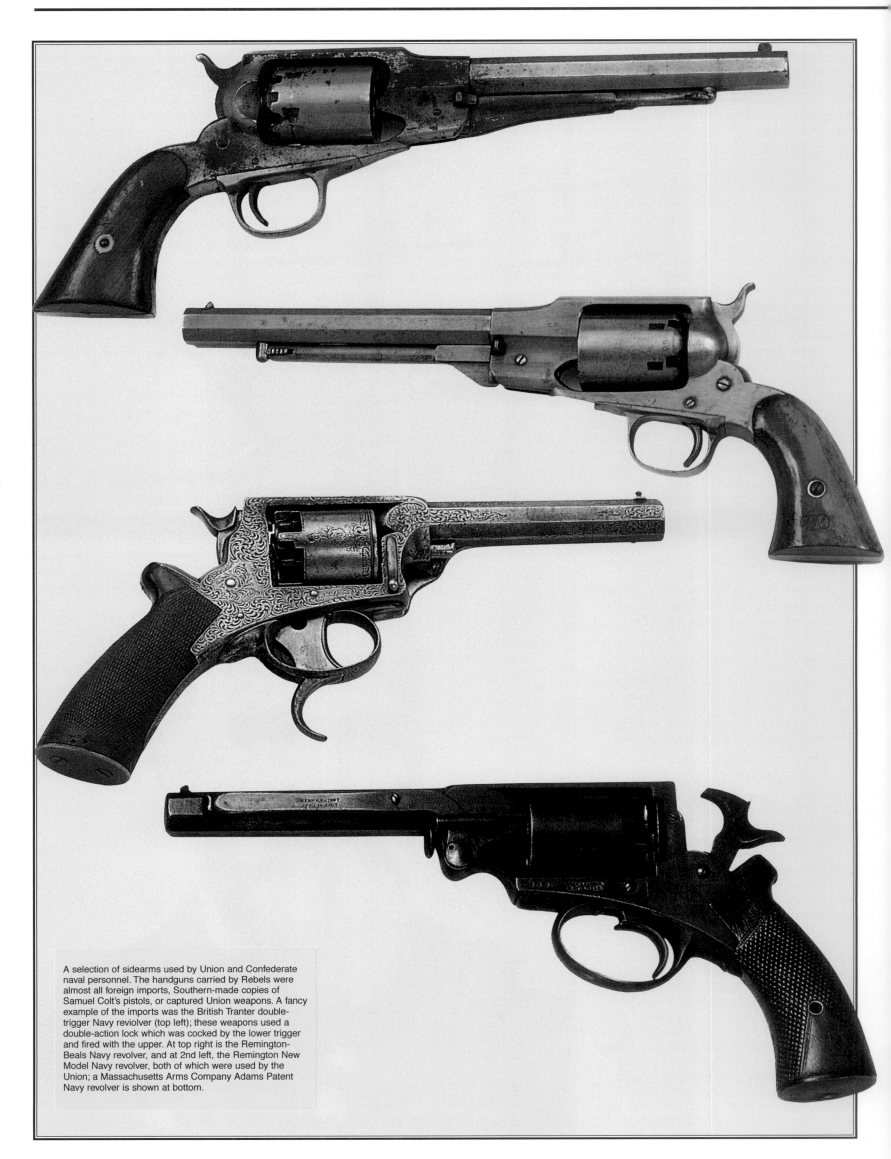

A selection of sidearms used by Union and Confederate naval personnel. The handguns carried by Rebels were almost all foreign imports, Southern-made copies of Samuel Colt's pistols, or captured Union weapons. A fancy example of the imports was the British Tranter double-trigger Navy reivolver (top left); these weapons used a double-action lock which was cocked by the lower trigger and fired with the upper. At top right is the Remington-Beals Navy revolver, and at 2nd left, the Remington New Model Navy revolver, both of which were used by the Union; a Massachusetts Arms Company Adams Patent Navy revolver is shown at bottom.

8-inch columbiad on *Tuscarora*, all the other guns were 32-pounders or smaller. Because Hollins's squadron lacked firepower, local newspapers fell into the habit of calling it the Mosquito Fleet. One broadside from *Richmond* could throw more weight than all the guns of the Mosquito Fleet combined.

With three Union warships already in the river, Hollins felt an urgency to oust them before Pope could be joined by others. His worries were legitimate because a few days later Commander Henry French's U.S.S. *Preble,* another sailing sloop also having no business in the river, came in through Pass a l'Outre. Pope wanted her 10 guns added to his squadron's firepower, but this still did not satisfy him. He now asked for two steamers to move the sloops about.

To attack Pope, Hollins needed more than the Mosquito Fleet, but the only vessel on the lower river that might even the odds was Stevenson's privately-owned *Manassas*. Knowing that Stevenson had taken her down to Fort Jackson, Hollins sent C.S.S. *McRae* and Lieutenant Alexander F. Warley with a boarding party to "politely" seize her. When Stevenson refused to budge, Warley came on board with a revolver. He sent Stevenson and 14 privateersmen ashore, and

without so much as a "thank you" seized the boat and impressed part of her crew.

Hollins waited until the moon set on October 12 to make his attack on the Union vessels. His plan was simple. Warley would lead the attack in *Manassas*, search for the largest enemy vessel, crush its hull, back off, and go down the line ramming each vessel he encountered. After striking the first ship, Warley would send up a rocket, signaling men on *Ivy*, *McRae*, and *Tuscarora* to cut loose three fire rafts tied to each other by a cable. The tugs would then spread the cabled rafts across the river so they would drift down and become entangled with the sailing sloops. Then, with the Union squadron in a state of panic, the Mosquito Fleet would descend and mop up any enemy vessel still in the river.

Manassas presented unknown variables. Having less than a day to run her through tests, Warley found her sluggish to handle in swift water, slow to respond to her helm, and barely able to stem the current. If he drove her into the side of a Union vessel, he could not be certain her engines had enough power to back her out. Fire rafts created another concern. He had visions of becoming caught in the cable and being

roasted with his crew in their own iron pot.

Hollins's attack proceeded quietly through a thin mist draped over dark water. Warley took the lead, peering through a four-inch opening in the forward hatch. Just above Head of Passes he came abeam *Preble* but spotted her too late and passed on by. A short distance below and to starboard he spied *Richmond* with a coaling schooner at work beside her. "Let her out!" he shouted down to the engine room, and firemen tossed prepared buckets of combustibles into the furnaces. Running with the current, the dial in the engine room registered 10 knots.

Pope had given no thought to organizing his squadron to meet an attack, and only by accident did a midshipman on *Preble* notice an odd-looking steamer approaching off the forward port quarter. He rushed into Commander French's cabin shouting, "Captain, here is a steamer right alongside of us." French peered through a port just in time to see "an indescribable object... moving with great velocity toward the bow of the *Richmond*." The officer of the deck had already hoisted a red signal light, and French arrived on deck just as *Preble's* broadside boomed high over the shadowy

The packet of six paper cartridges incorporating bullet and charge were suitable for use with the Colt Navy pistol (top), while next to this is an opened tin of percussion caps. Below this is a pistol bullet mold device. At the bottom is a Whitney Navy revolver (left)

shape below and rattled through trees along the opposite shore.

Pope saw *Preble's* warning light and heard her broadsides, but he seemed to be stupefied by the commotion. Not until *Manassas* appeared off *Richmond's* forward port quarter did Pope grasp the fact that his vessel was about to be rammed. The coaling schooner probably saved *Richmond*. *Manassas* tore her loose before piercing *Richmond* two feet below the waterline, crushing in three planks and leaving a seam of five inches through which water poured.

Warley had no trouble backing *Manassas*

off because the blow had been deflected by the schooner. Thinking he had done serious injury to *Richmond*, he ordered the helmsman to head upstream and get the vessel in position to ram *Preble*, which could not raise her anchor. Ramming *Richmond*, however, had disarranged one of *Manassas's* engines, and she limped along in the current with only one engine. With some hesitation, Warley launched his signal rockets, revealing to officers on *Richmond* the location of the ram.

Pope put the leaking flagship under steam and bore down on the slow-moving

ironclad. As *Manassas* limped by, every vessel in the Union squadron opened on her. One projectile struck her plating, leaving a small dent. Another severed one of her smokestacks, and a third knocked the remaining stack against the vent of the other, causing the engine room to fill with asphyxiating gases.

Pope then spotted the fire rafts, realized that his ship was headed directly into an inferno, and reversed course. He sped downriver, hollering at each ship to "Proceed down the Pass." French could not believe that Pope was abandoning his

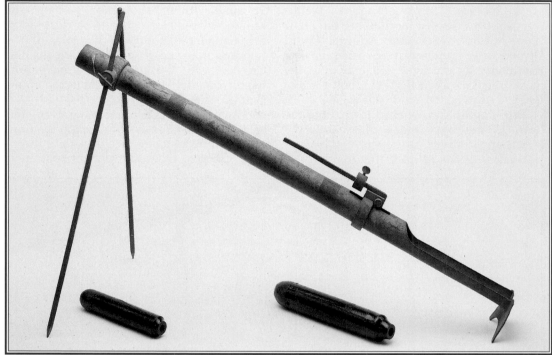

Left: Naval officers enjoyed the opportunity of posing for a photograph because most of their time passed without much for them to do. Newspaper reporters, such as is probably the man standing above the others, also liked to be seen.

Above: The Hale patent rocket launcher in 2.25-inch caliber. The system was invented by British civil engineer William Hale in 1844, and was approved by Union naval ordnance expert Captain (later Admiral) John A. Dahlgren in 1847.

Although inaccurate, Hale rockets were used throughout the war in several calibers. Below the launcher are variants of the projectiles, which were placed in the open breech. Elevation was adjusted at the bipod using the sight on the top. Once in flight the rocket achieved stability in flight by means of a vane inside the exhaust nozzle, which caused the rocket to spin.

Below: U.S. Navy Model 1861 percussion signal pistol, which was made at the U.S. Navy Yard, Washington, D.C.

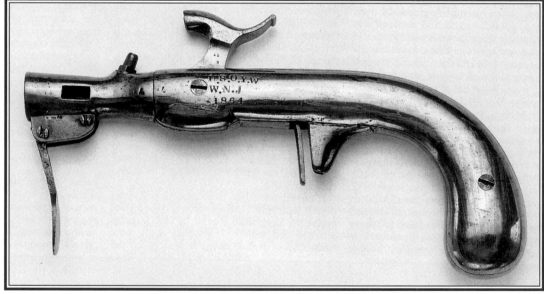

squadron, but when the flaming rafts came within 150 yards of *Preble,* he ordered the anchor cable cut, and with *Vincennes,* set what sails would draw and hurried after the flagship. Because of darkness, Lieutenant Winslow, who had anchored *Water Witch* across from Preble, did not see his companions skedaddle, so he remained upriver and prepared to fight his ship. He carefully avoided the fire rafts and started upriver to meet the enemy. At daylight he observed the Mosquito Fleet coming down to meet him and for the first time realized that the squadron had abandoned him. Not

prepared to fight alone, he sheered off and headed down the river.

Ivy led the chase but encountered *Manassas* lodged on a mudbank along shore. Warley explained that when smoke from the engine room temporarily blinded the pilot, he had to act fast to get *Manassas* out of the way of the fire rafts. With what little power she could muster from one engine, he headed for shore to keep the vessel from drifting down to the enemy. Lieutenant Fry offered Warley a line, but the latter could fight no more and preferred to wait until the engagement ended.

Pope took his squadron out of the river and into the Gulf, and Hollins came down the pass far enough for his rifled cannon to bear on *Vincennes* and *Richmond,* both having grounded during their eagerness to flee the river. For a few hours the two squadrons exchanged fire, neither doing any damage to the other. Hollins had neither the coal nor the ammunition to continue the fight, so he returned to the forts.

The episode in the river produced two diametrically opposite outcomes. When Hollins returned to New Orleans, a cheering crowd of thousands greeted him with a grand parade. In Washington, Welles registered his disgust by dubbing the affair "Pope's Run." Years later, Admiral David Dixon Porter summed it up, writing, "Put this matter in any light you may, it is the most ridiculous affair that ever took place in the American Navy." And so it was.

But "Pope's Run" opened the eyes of the navy to the importance of closing the Mississippi River to every form of resistance. Welles realized that it could not

be done with lightly armed gunboats or sailing sloops. Nor could it be done with commanders like Pope. The prize lay a hundred miles upriver – New Orleans, the Crescent City, the largest, wealthiest, and most cosmopolitan metropolis in the entire Confederacy.

Welles recognized that blockading the river from the Gulf would not stop the flow of munitions and supplies passing through New Orleans. Blockade runners continued

to operate, using Lake Pontchartrain and Berwick Bay, and the source of all contracts and commercial activities on the river still came through New Orleans.

Heavy warships could not invest the city from Lake Pontchartrain because of its shallowness. The Mississippi River provided the only body of water deep enough to carry the Union's first class sloop-rigged screw steamers. But there was a problem. Seventy miles below New Orleans

lay two of the strongest forts on the North American continent, Fort Jackson on the western bank and Fort St. Philip on the opposite bank. The two forts were so positioned that a hostile force coming up the river would come into a crossfire from both forts.

By November the situation for Welles had become even more complicated and was daily growing more so. Five days after Hollins chased Pope out of the river, Major General Mansfield Lovell had taken charge of the district and established headquarters at New Orleans. He immediately began strengthening Forts Jackson and St. Philip and improving the defenses around the city. Welles was not aware at the time that Lovell was also lobbying Confederate Secretary of War Judah P. Benjamin for funds to fit out 14 riverboats with iron prows to be used as lightly armed battering rams. Welles also heard rumors that two more ironclads

Above: Union Navy Secretary Gideon Welles, though conservative by nature, took great risks when he promoted the idea of capturing New Orleans, and he gambled again by picking Farragut to lead it, an untried captain.

Left: When at anchor during the hot days of summer, seamen slung awnings over the deck and hoped for a breeze. The old salt beside the rifled 100-pounder Parrott knew where to stand for an impressive photograph.

similar to the *Merrimac* design were being built at New Orleans, and that *Manassas* was back in service. If he had any real hope of capturing New Orleans, he would have to do it fast.

Welles needed a plan, a captain, and a squadron of powerful ships. Commander David Dixon Porter happened to be in Washington on November 12 and got into the secretary's office by using the coattails of two Republican senators on the Naval Affairs Committee. He had just arrived from Southwest Pass and proposed a novel method for demolishing Forts Jackson and St. Philip. By mounting 13-inch mortars on a squadron of schooners, Porter claimed that he could destroy the forts in 48 hours. Welles had doubts, but if Porter could do half of what he claimed, then it might be feasible for a large squadron of heavy warships to reach New Orleans. Lincoln liked the idea, and, after General McClellan promised to provide 15,000 troops, he told Welles to proceed with the expedition.

Now that Welles had the genesis of a plan, he needed a flag officer. There were dozens of captains on the navy list, and Welles knew that most of them were more than sixty-years-old and made better administrators than fighters. Since he intended to keep his plans secret, but had already taken Porter into his confidence, he showed the commander the captain's list

and asked his opinion. Porter spotted the name of David Glasgow Farragut, his foster brother, 37 lines down the list and recommended him for the job. Welles already had a favorable impression of Farragut, but like many men in the navy, the only real action Farragut had seen was as a thirteen-year-old midshipmen during the War of 1812. Welles shifted about the navy office asking innocent questions about what others thought of Farragut, and after a month of delicate research, decided that he had found the best man. Not everyone agreed with him, but Welles had an innate ability for evaluating people and rarely made a mistake.

Born in Tennessee on July 5, 1801, Farragut was a true Southerner, and the fact that he spent several years of his youth in New Orleans only made him more so. When Farragut's mother died, the father of David Dixon Porter took the youngster into the family, brought him back to Pennsylvania, provided for his education, and raised him as his own. At the age of nine, Farragut entered the navy as a midshipman, and eventually married a woman from Virginia. He and his family lived in Norfolk, giving him every reason to remain a Southerner, but when the rebellion began he repudiated secession and moved to New York.

Members of the Naval Affairs Board questioned the wisdom of Welles's choice of

Left: David D. Porter became an admiral, but in the lower Mississippi he served under Farragut as a commander. Though they were foster brothers, Porter always competed with Farragut to the point of being disruptive.

Below: A view of the main deck of U.S.S. Hartford, looking aft from the forecastle. Built for ocean-going duty, she spent a lot of time during the Civil War in battles on the Mississippi. Probably the most important vessel of the war, she was the flagship of undoubtedly the most notable naval officer, David Glasgow Farragut.

Farragut because the latter still had relatives living in New Orleans. But Welles had made his decision and on January 9, 1862, cut orders giving Farragut command of the West Gulf Blockading Squadron. The command stretched from western Florida to the Rio Grande and incorporated such points of military importance as Pensacola, Mobile Bay, the lower Mississippi, New Orleans, Galveston, and Brownsville.

For the New Orleans expedition, Welles also trusted Farragut with a squadron of 18 powerful warships, many of them having drafts so deep that getting them over the bar and into the river required a Herculean effort. When Farragut learned the depth of the bar at Southwest Pass had risen from 20 to nearly 16 feet, he began to despair of getting his most powerful vessels into the

river. The 44-gun steam frigate *Colorado*, drawing 22 feet aft, never made the effort, leaving Farragut with 17 steamers and Porter's Mortar Flotilla to do the work.

Porter's flotilla represented one of the many novelties of the Civil War. It consisted of seven steamers, 19 mortar schooners, two barks, and a brig. The decks of the sailing vessels had been cut back and reinforced to carry 13-inch mortars. The seven steamers served a dual purpose, acting as towboats and gunboats. Each carried a battery ranging from four to seven guns, some as large as 11-inch Dahlgrens and others as small as 24-pounder howitzers.

Farragut's steamers consisted of all the fighting ships that Welles could spare and still maintain a thin blockade covering more than 3,500 miles of the coastal South. Only

by the slimmest of margins did Farragut get his flagship *Hartford* over the Southwest bar. Because she drew 17 feet aft, he lightened her at Ship Island, Mississippi, before bringing her through the pass. Three sister vessels, *Brooklyn*, *Pensacola*, and *Richmond*, all built along the same lines and all first-class sloop-rigged screw steamers, encountered similar difficulties crossing the bar. Brooklyn scraped across in early March and occupied Head of Passes with three of Farragut's light-draft steamers, *Kennebec*, *Kineo*, and *Winona*. *Richmond*, which had been in the river under Pope and was now under Commander James Alden, tried to enter the river at Pass a l'Outre and lunged into a mound of mud, shaking her masts and upsetting the crew. Alden eventually backed her off but, being a stubborn man, he

Left: Comdr. Porter sailed his mortar schooners from the east coast and towed them up the Mississippi. Men called the 13-inch mortars "chowder pots," but nobody ever used them for making soup.

Below: Farragut would have preferred to fight his wooden ships on the ocean, for which they were built, but he attempted what most thought impossible when he took them to war on the Mississippi.

tried three more times before giving it up. Sailing around to Southwest Pass, he refused help and once again put the ship on a bar. There he remained as the rest of the squadron mirthfully watched.

Porter brought his steamers over to the pass to help *Pensacola, Mississippi,* and *Richmond* over the bar. *Pensacola,* drawing 18 feet, and the old sidewheel steamer *Mississippi,* drawing more than 20 feet, had all been lightened down to their decks at Ship Island, but it still took 14 days to get the two vessels into the river. There were times when it appeared that *Mississippi* might spend the remainder of the war stuck on the bar. Having been careened over on her side, the lower paddlewheel scooped a cavity in the bar, but the suction created by the motion held her fast.

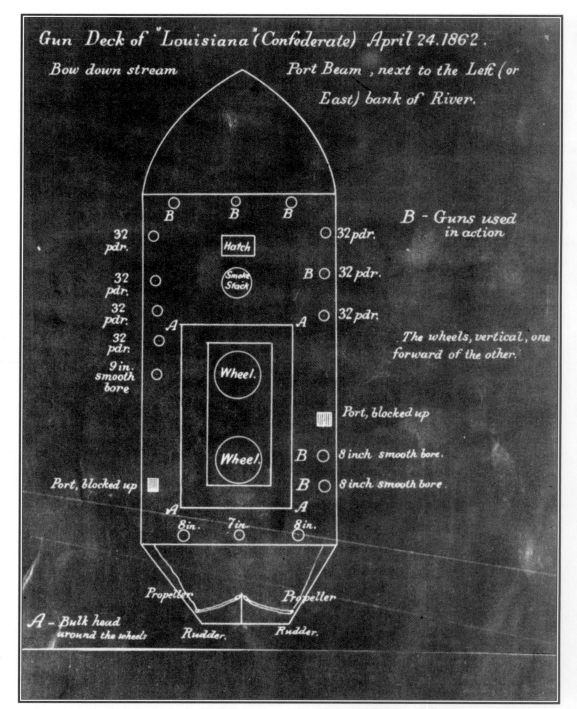

Gun Deck of "Louisiana" (Confederate) April 24. 1862.

Bow down stream

Port Beam, next to the Left (or East) bank of River.

B — Guns used in action

32 pdr.

32 pdr.

32 pdr.

32 pdr.

9 in. smooth bore

Hatch

Smoke Stack

Wheel.

Wheel.

32 pdr.

B 32 pdr.

32 pdr.

The wheels, vertical, one forward of the other.

Port, blocked up

B 8 inch smooth bore.

B 8 inch smooth bore.

Port, blocked up

8 in.   7 in.   8 in.

Propeller   Propeller

A — Bulk head around the wheels

Rudder.   Rudder.

Right and below: The C.S.S. *Louisiana*, had she been built exactly as designed, would have been the most formidable ironclad ram on the Mississippi, but she came down to Fort St. Philip with her guns mismounted and her engines incapable of providing the mobility she needed to maneuver. Had the builders been given another week or two to prepare her for service, Farragut might still have passed the forts, but with far fewer vessels.

Far right: Major General Benjamin F. Butler, sitting in a tent on Ship Island, never got the chance to bumble operations at Forts Jackson and St. Philip because Farragut and Porter spared him the trouble.

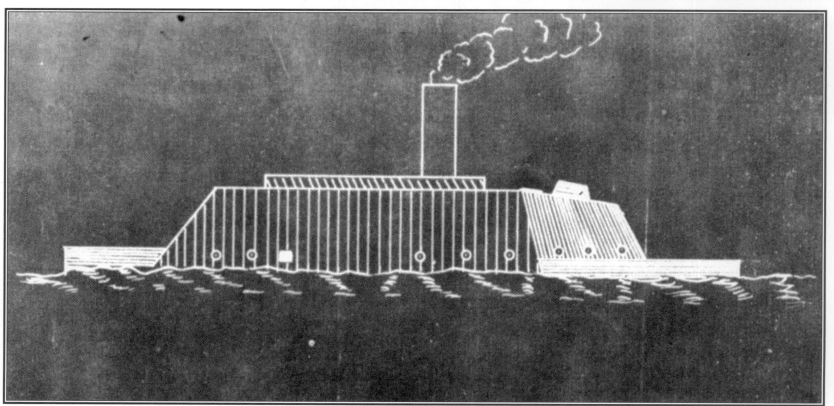

Farragut needed his big vessels. *Brooklyn, Hartford, Mississippi, Pensacola,* and *Richmond* were the backbone of his squadron. Each carried between 22 and 28 guns, most of them being 9-inch Dahlgren shell guns. Not until April 8 did he have all his vessels in the river. By then, news of the March battle between *Monitor* and *Virginia* reached Farragut's squadron and created another outbreak of "ram fever."

Farragut and Porter's Mortar Flotilla had been in the river for a month, and during that time refugees from upriver told of two ironclads being built at New Orleans. To Farragut, the C.S.S. *Louisiana* sounded like an exact replica of *Virginia,* and the C.S.S. *Mississippi,* which was farther from being finished, not much different. He also learned that *Manassas* had come down to the forts and was back in fighting trim. Urgency took on a new meaning. For the expedition to succeed, he must pass the forts, get up to New Orleans, and destroy the ironclads before they could fight.

His original plan had been to sweep into the river suddenly and send Porter's bomb boats ahead to demolish in 48 hours Forts

Jackson and St. Philip, thereby enabling the West Gulf Squadron to pass the forts with minimal damage. Major General Benjamin F. Butler's force of 7,000 men would then land near the forts while the heavy vessels of the squadron moved upriver to invest New Orleans. Problems of getting his ships over the bar destroyed the element of surprise and gave the enemy time to prepare a stiffer defense. What Farragut did not know was that Jefferson Davis had moved most of the regiments formed in Louisiana to other battlefields, and that Mallory had sent the Mosquito Fleet under Hollins upriver to contend with Flag Officer Andrew Hull Foote's Mississippi flotilla in the Tennessee and Cumberland rivers.

Davis and Mallory did not feel that Farragut's entry into the lower river posed a threat to New Orleans. They believed that wooden vessels could not get beyond the defenses of Forts Jackson and St. Philip. If any vessels did, they would either be mopped up by Confederate gunboats or, not having a source for supplies, eventually captured or destroyed. Such thinking made sense far back in Richmond, but neither

Davis nor Mallory paid enough attention to the serious threat confronting the wealthiest and most populous city in the Confederacy.

When General Lovell reached New Orleans in October, 1861, he found the entire area in a deplorable state of unreadiness. With much effort, he arranged for dozens of heavy guns captured at Norfolk to be transferred to the forts protecting New Orleans. Many of the guns went to Forts Jackson and St. Philip to replace old relics mounted on decaying wood. He also had a water battery dug to face downriver so any enemy vessel approaching Fort Jackson would more quickly come under fire.

By the beginning of April 1862, Fort Jackson boasted 74 guns, including three 10-inch columbiads, five 8-inch columbiads, six 42-pounders, and a number of rifled cannon, the bulk of which were mounted either in barbette or casemates. Across the river, Fort St. Philip carried another 52 guns, mainly in the 42- to 24-pounder range. Together, the two forts could bear on about four miles of river. An average steamer running against the 4- to 5-knot current would be under fire for up to 40 minutes and, to make certain that the forts would sink any vessel that tried, Lovell had anchored a barrier chain across the river just below Fort Jackson and supported it with a string of hulks.

Lovell also attempted to compensate for Mallory's ineptitude in sending away the Mosquito Fleet. In January, Commander John K. Mitchell arrived, and with Hollins gone, took over the naval operations at New Orleans. Because Mitchell busied himself expediting work on the two ironclads, Lovell turned his attention to mobilizing the River Defense Fleet with funds provided through Secretary of War Benjamin, the only person in Davis's cabinet who came from Louisiana. Lovell believed that lightly armed riverboats with bows reinforced and sheathed in iron could sink wooden warships by ramming them. As long as the boat faced the enemy, she could not be seriously damaged because the plated battering ram on the bow would deflect the shot.

Benjamin authorized Lovell to build 14 battering rams, but Lovell could only find about a dozen good boats. Each carried a single gun in the bow, usually a 32-pounder, though some carried two. Instead of using naval personnel to command the rams, Lovell recruited riverboatmen, and when he later tried to turn his creation over to the navy, Commander Mitchell did not want them.

Instead, Mitchell confined his squadron to *Manassas, McRae, Jackson,* and two Louisiana gunboats, *General Quitman* and *Governor Moore.* He planned on including the ironclads *Louisiana* and *Mississippi,* but to do so required that they be finished. When it appeared that Farragut actually intended to attack the forts, Mitchell pulled resources from *Mississippi* and concentrated every effort on completing *Louisiana.* Without *Louisiana,* which was designed for 16 guns, his entire squadron would carry only 15 guns, mainly 32-pounders.

John A. Stevenson, who had the

misfortune of building *Manassas* only to have her seized by the Confederate navy, now had the distinction of commanding Lovell's River Defense Fleet. He did not like Mitchell any more than he liked the Confederate navy. So on April 13, 1862, when Farragut made a reconnaissance of Fort Jackson to draw fire and find the range of the fort's guns, the Confederate naval forces represented a hodgepodge of vessels under no one person's command.

Farragut used the reconnaissance for another purpose – to shield the work of men from the Coast Survey who had come with Porter to stake out positions for placing the bomb boats. For five days they labored under shellfire from the forts and sharpshooters hidden in the brush along shore.

On the 15th Porter moved up three schooners to test the range at 3,000 yards. To the sailors of the fleet, Porter's mortars had become "chowder pots" and his 13-man crews "bummers," and those present

watched as the bomb boats opened a slow fire on Fort Jackson. The first 216-pound shell, propelled by a 20-pound powder charge, thumped somewhere inside the fort, and the next one exploded beside the parapet. Content that his mortars had the range and could do the job, Porter withdrew his boats to enable the Coast Survey to finish their work.

Porter divided his squadron into three divisions, each consisting of six to eight boats. On April 18 he placed the first division, under Lieutenant Watson Smith, and the third division, under Lieutenant K. Randolph Breese, along the sheltered west bank. He stretched the second division, under Lieutenant Walter W. Queen, in an exposed position from bank to bank across the river. Once anchored into position, the lead boats lay about 2,850 yards from Fort Jackson and 3,600 yards from Fort St. Philip. Observers tied themselves to the highest mast of each schooner and peered over the treetops as the first big shells arced their way skyward and plummeted into the fort with a thump. A billow of smoke followed each shot, smothering the observer, and once all the bomb boats opened, it became difficult to distinguish one boat's projectile from another. The 48-hour clock now began to run on Porter.

When rifled cannon from the forts got the range of Queen's division, Farragut and Porter sent gunboats ahead to draw the fort's fire. As they came in easy range, shelling from the forts became so intense that Farragut, who needed all of his ships to ascend the river, recalled them. Fort Jackson then re-shifted its guns to Queen's division and caused enough damage to compel Porter to move the boats out of sight and place them closer to the protective screen of cotton-woods along the west bank. After doing so, fewer shots fell into the Fort Jackson.

By late afternoon pillars of smoke could be seen rising from inside Fort Jackson, and

Below: The U.S.S. *Ouachita* was once a lovely steamboat hauling passengers up and down the Mississippi. Many boats like her were cut down and rebuilt, but *Ouachita* remained much as she was, but with a battery of guns.

firing had ceased from the parapets. Porter, thinking he had all but destroyed the fort with mortars, called a halt to the firing at sunset. It was a mistake, compounded by an earlier mistake. All the damaging fire had come from Queen's division. It was closest to Fort Jackson, and the bummers could distinctly see the effects of their firing and make adjustments. Once moved under the screen of trees, most of their shots, like those of the first and third division, fell outside the fort.

Porter's second mistake was not continuing the bombardment through the night. Mortars landing inside Fort Jackson had set the barracks and citadel on fire and threatened to touch-off the magazine. Embrasures had been knocked apart, guns dismounted, and the garrison inside had reached the brink of panic. By not keeping the mortars busy through the night, Porter gave General Duncan an opportunity to quench the fires and restore order. He also lost his opportunity to demolish Fort Jackson because the bummers were never able to equal their first day's marksmanship.

Porter realized the demoralizing effect of a 24-hour bombardment one day too late. For the next five days the chowder pots roared around the clock, but for the most part ineffectually. On April 20 Farragut finally ran out of patience and ordered the barrier below Fort Jackson cut so his

squadron could run the gauntlet.

When news of Porter's bombardment reached New Orleans on April 19, Commander Mitchell assigned two towboats to the C.S.S. *Louisiana* and hurried her down to Fort St. Philip. Still unfinished and without motive power, *Louisiana* represented at best a floating battery, but she looked ugly and impregnable. Her formidable battery consisted of three 9-inch shell guns, four 8-inch shell guns, two 7-inch rifled guns, and seven rifled 32-pounders. How Mitchell intended to use all this firepower had not been determined.

On the following day, the builders of the ironclad C.S.S. *Mississippi* frantically splashed her into the river, but she was still a hulk without engines. Whether she would ever become a factor in the fight to come depended upon how much time Farragut would give the builders to finish her.

When *Louisiana* reached Fort St. Philip, an argument ensued between General Duncan, who commanded the forts, and Commander Mitchell, who commanded the navy. Duncan wanted the ironclad placed where she could use her 16 guns to enfilade Porter's mortar schooners and rake any of Farragut's warships should they round the bend below Fort Jackson. Because the ironclad lacked motive power, Mitchell wanted the vessel snugged safely along shore above Fort St. Philip. Duncan

appealed to Lovell, who came down to the fort to urge Mitchell to comply with the general's wishes. Since the navy controlled the ironclad, Mitchell got his way.

Duncan also believed that the time had come for Mitchell to take command of the Stevenson's River Defense Fleet. Mitchell did not like the idea any better than Stevenson and refused. Mitchell's entire squadron consisted of *Manassas*, four gunboats, a few tugs, and the ironclad. Why he refused to incorporate six armed battering rams into his defensive efforts left Duncan doubly perplexed. The general had no idea how to deploy the rams because Mitchell seemed to have no plan. Dozens of fire rafts had been prepared and tied above the forts, so Duncan put Stevenson in charge of the rafts and told him that if Farragut attacked, to set them ablaze and cut them loose. During all these discussions, Porter's bummers never stopped pounding Fort Jackson with mortar shells.

On April 23, Farragut set the time of attack for 2:00 a.m. He divided his squadron into three divisions, placing Captain Theodorus Bailey in charge of the first division, himself in charge of the second division, and Captain Henry H. Bell in command of the third. He assigned the four-gun *Cayuga* the point position of the first division, followed by *Pensacola, Mississippi, Oneida, Varuna, Katahdin, Kineo,* and

Below left: On the night of April 24, Farragut's squadron breached the obstructions below Fort Jackson and, with very little damage to his ships, paraded through the smoke covering the river and destroyed the Confederate fleet.

Right: *Hartford* was a much faster and more maneuverable a vessel than either of the Confederate ironclad rams, which appeared to be standing in wait, but neither of them ever touched her as she passed.

Flag Officer David G. Farragut faced serious obstacles in passing the forts. To do so, he needed to cut a chain barrier below Fort Jackson and take 17 warships upriver. Cmdr. David D. Porter's mortar schooners and gunboats would remain behind to bombard the forts as Farragut's squadron ran the gauntlet. On the night of April 24, 1862, Farragut organized his squadron into three divisions and pressed ahead.

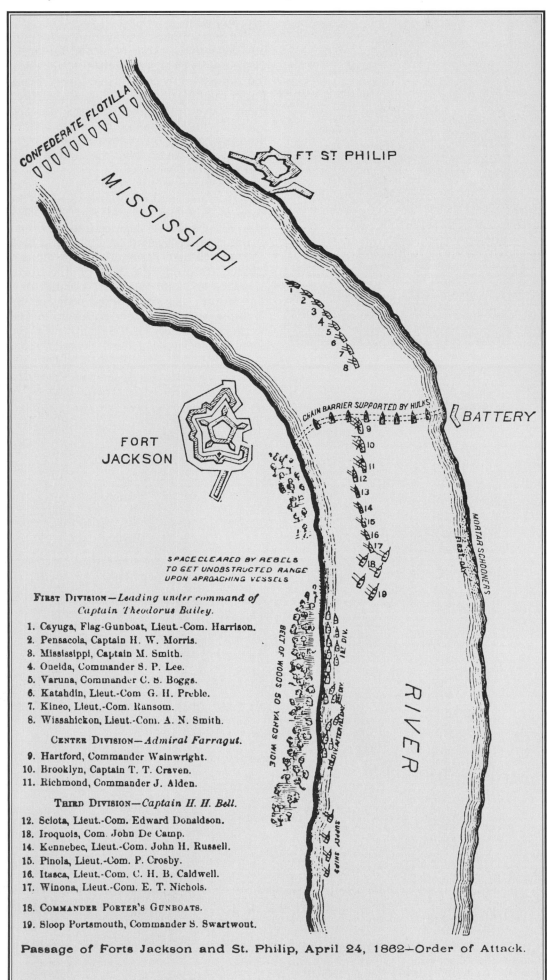

CONFEDERATE FLOTILLA

MISSISSIPPI

FT ST PHILIP

FORT JACKSON

CHAIN BARRIER SUPPORTED BY HULKS

BATTERY

MORTAR SCHOONERS first div.

RIVER

SPACE CLEARED BY REBELS TO GET UNOBSTRUCTED RANGE UPON APROACHING VESSELS

BELT OF WOODS 50 YARDS WIDE

First Division—*Leading under command of Captain Theodorus Bailey.*

1. Cayuga, Flag-Gunboat, Lieut.-Com. Harrison.
2. Pensacola, Captain H. W. Morris.
3. Mississippi, Captain M. Smith.
4. Oneida, Commander S. P. Lee.
5. Varuna, Commander C. S. Boggs.
6. Katahdin, Lieut.-Com G. H. Preble.
7. Kineo, Lieut.-Com. Ransom.
8. Wissahickon, Lieut.-Com. A. N. Smith.

    Center Division—*Admiral Farragut.*

9. Hartford, Commander Wainwright.
10. Brooklyn, Captain T. T. Craven.
11. Richmond, Commander J. Alden.

    Third Division—*Captain H. H. Bell.*

12. Sciota, Lieut.-Com. Edward Donaldson.
13. Iroquois, Com. John De Camp.
14. Kennebec, Lieut.-Com. John H. Russell.
15. Pinola, Lieut.-Com. P. Crosby.
16. Itasca, Lieut.-Com. C. H. B. Caldwell.
17. Winona, Lieut.-Com. E. T. Nichols.

18. Commander Porter's Gunboats.

19. Sloop Portsmouth, Commander S. Swartwout.

Passage of Forts Jackson and St. Philip, April 24, 1862—Order of Attack.

Wissahickon. In the second division, Farragut took the point position with *Hartford,* followed by *Brooklyn* and *Richmond.* Bell would bring up the rear with six gunboats, *Sciota, Iroquois, Kennebec, Pinola, Itasca,* and *Winona.* Porter would open with all his mortars and bring up his gunboats to shell Fort Jackson's water battery, but he would stay below the forts to protect the schooners. Porter did not like the idea of being left behind and grumbled unsuccessfully to his foster brother against being deserted. In the morning, General Butler would send 7,000 men across Black Bay and land them near the quarantine station above Fort St. Philip. With all his plans in place, Farragut went to bed, leaving orders to wake him at midnight.

At 2:00 a.m., April 24, Farragut ordered two red lanterns hoisted on *Hartford's* mizzen, the signal for the squadron to file into formation. The vessels shuffled about in the dark, *Cayuga* quickly taking the point, but *Pensacola,* the second vessel in line, could not haul up her anchor. Referring to the ship's commander, Captain Henry W. Morris, Farragut growled, "Damn that fellow! I don't believe he wants to start," and an hour passed before *Pensacola* fell into position behind *Cayuga.*

Not until 3:30 a.m. did Bailey, in the first

Right: Captain Melancton Smith commanded the old side-wheeler U.S.S. *Mississippi*, which received a severe butt from the C.S.S. *Manassas*. Mad as the devil, he spotted the ram aground and dispatched a detail to burn her.

Below: Admiral Porter's mortar fleet on the Mississippi. The campaign was a great naval success for the Union, with the vessels under Porter's command securing the surrender of the Confederate forts, while Farragut's ships captured New Orleans.

division, get the signal from Farragut to advance. Lieutenant Commander Napoleon B. Harrison, *Cayuga's* skipper, stood on deck with Captain Bailey and led the gunboat through the opening cut in the chain barrier. Six ships were to follow, guiding on *Cayuga* as she hugged the bank and crept toward Fort St. Philip.

For several minutes, everything remained still but the swishing sounds of paddlewheels. The bummers watched as the first vessels of the squadron rounded the lower bend. Porter put his gunboats in motion, anchored them 500 yards below Fort Jackson, and opened with shrapnel on the water battery. Bummers pulled their lanyards, and 20 13-inch mortars arced over the cottonwoods and fell upon Fort Jackson.

At 3:40 came the reply as the water battery roared into action, followed by the guns of Fort Jackson and Fort St. Philip. Mitchell's squadron steamed into the center of the river above Fort St. Philip and took positions to rake Farragut's squadron as it crossed through the fire of the forts. *Manassas* slid into the river, looking for a ship to ram. *Louisiana* lurked near Fort St. Philip's upper water battery, tucked securely and barely visible against the bank. Stevenson's battering rams steamed about

in a state of confusion. Their skippers cut loose a few fire rafts and then bumbled about uncertain of their roles.

As young Lieutenant George Hamilton Perkins, executive officer of *Cayuga*, piloted the ship through the break in the barrier, both forts opened fire. Shells burst around the ship, tearing up masts and rigging. Perkins noticed that the guns of both forts bore on the center of the river, so he steered close to the walls of Fort St. Philip. He looked back in search of *Pensacola* but could not see a single Union vessel. "I thought they all must be sunk by the forts," he recalled. Then, looking ahead, he saw "eleven of the enemy's gunboats coming down on us, and it seemed as if we were 'gone' sure." One gunboat, said Perkins, "made a dash to board us, but a heavy charge from our eleven-inch gun settled [her]." Having dodged one attack, Perkins then spied *Manassas* bearing on *Cayuga's* beam and conned the ship enough to cause the ram to pass astern. "Just then," Perkins declared, "some of our gunboats, which had passed the forts, came up, and then all sorts of things happened."

Pensacola's disappearance occurred when the vessel stopped to engage "in almost a yardarm conflict" with Fort St. Philip. Farragut's orders had been to press on through and stop for nothing but, smothered by smoke from gunpowder, Captain Morris lost all sense of direction. He eventually ordered the vessel to port, found himself running across the river toward Fort Jackson, and ended up in front of Farragut's second division. He could not fire a broadside without fear of hitting Farragut's flagship, *Hartford. Pensacola* began to absorb shell fire from both forts and from a number of gunboats arrayed ahead of him. Lieutenant Francis A. Roe, handling the steerage, sighted an "iron ram dead ahead, coming down upon us." He conned the vessel into position to fire a broadside, and as the ironclad passed, guns barked "from forward aft, clean through the whole battery." He watched *Manassas* go downriver, lost in gunfire from the trailing *Mississippi*.

Captain Melancton Smith, commanding *Mississippi*, followed *Pensacola* into the gauntlet. Because he could not see well at night, Smith turned the piloting of the vessel over to twenty-four-year-old Lieutenant George Dewey. Coming out from under the smoke of *Pensacola's* broadside, Dewey spotted "what appeared to be the back of an enormous turtle, painted lead color."

Having no time to discuss tactics, Dewey sheered into the path of *Manassas*, convinced that the superior tonnage of *Mississippi* would sink the ironclad.

Lieutenant Warley, his ears still ringing from *Pensacola's* broadside, had once served on *Mississippi* and knew she was a sluggish ship. *Manassas* was no better, but she had the advantage of a four-knot current. As Dewey sheered to strike *Manassas*, Warley did the same and nipped *Mississippi* a glancing blow abaft the port paddlewheel, tearing out a section of planking seven feet long, four feet wide, and four inches deep. During the fray, 10 shots from the forts struck *Mississippi*, eight of them going in one side of the vessel and out the other.

Pensacola's hesitation off St. Philip's lower water battery had backed up the first division. Commander S. Phillips Lee of the U.S.S. *Oneida* got caught in the stack-up, steered into the middle of the river and, finding his ship under the guns of Fort Jackson, wheeled to starboard and came under the batteries at Fort St. Philip. Running in close to the fort, he could hear shells screaming overhead. To port, *Manassas* glided by. Ahead, one of Stevenson's rams presented its beam. Lee ran into it with a full head of steam and

sliced through the vessel's starboard quarter. He then lost her in the darkness as she drifted downstream, totally disabled.

Ahead lay a number of gunboats, but Lee could not tell if they belonged to the enemy. He looked to the rear for *Varuna*, which should have been right behind him, but he could not find her. At 5:05 he came abeam *Cayuga* and asked Bailey if anyone had seen *Varuna*. No one had. So Lee started up the river to see if she had gone to Quarantine.

Unlike the ships that had stacked up behind *Pensacola, Varuna*, commanded by Charles S. Boggs had broken formation, swung around the column, plunged through the smoke like a race horse, and suddenly Boggs found his craft alone and among a swarm of Confederate gunboats. *Varuna* carried eight 8-inch Dahlgrens and two rifled 30-pounders, and Boggs loaded them with grape and five-second shells. He had no idea what vessels he attacked, but they were probably part of Stevenson's River Defense Fleet. He struck four with shells, set them on fire, and drove them ashore. Across the river Boggs spotted a gunboat firing at *Oneida* but sheering toward him. A shot had nipped *Varuna's* steam system when passing the forts, and Boggs could not get enough pressure to evade the gunboat slanting toward him.

Captain Beverly Kennon, formerly of the United States Navy, had spotted *Varuna* chewing up the River Defense Fleet and decided to take matters into his own hands. The Louisiana gunboat *Governor Moore* carried only two rifled 32-pounders, one forward and one aft. His vessel had already been riddled by *Cayuga, Pensacola*, and *Oneida*, but he intended to stay in action as long as his guns could be served. He came up behind *Varuna* and opened with his forward 32-pounder. Boggs countered with his stern chaser. Sixteen of 33 men on *Moore's* forecastle had already been killed or wounded, and Kennon was operating the gun himself.

Boggs did not have the steam to helm over and fire his broadsides, and Kennon could not depress his forward gun enough to rake *Varuna*. But when the gun came off its mount, Kennon used the vessel's speed to come off *Varuna's* beam. He fired the gun through *Moore's* deck and raked *Varuna* fore and aft, killing three men and wounding nine. After firing the shot, the smoke cleared and Kennon unexpectedly found himself off *Varuna's* beam. Boggs emptied a broadside into *Governor Moore* that Kennon reported "swept his decks of nearly every living object." But *Moore* still had enough steam to come about and ram *Varuna* on the starboard side, breaking through her ribs. Boggs gave *Moore* another broadside, and with both vessels in sinking condition, they each headed for the shallows. Kennon set *Moore* on fire and blew her up. Boggs got *Varuna* close to shore farther upriver and let her settle on the mud. Because Boggs had sprinted ahead of the first division and gone farther upriver than any other Union vessel, *Varuna* was not found until daylight.

Lieutenant George H. Preble, commanding *Katahdin*, followed *Varuna* through the chain barrier but soon became

Above: After losing most of his crew, Captain Beverly Kennon, commanding *Governor Moore*, ranged up beside the injured *Varuna*, fired a 32-pounder through his own bow, hulled *Varuna*, and forced Boggs to run her to the bank.

Left: Comdr. Charles Boggs pressed *Varuna* through the gauntlet so fast that he found himself in the midst of the Rebel fleet with no support. He sank several vessels before his craft was fully disabled by the C.S.S. *Governor Moore*.

Brig. Gen. Johnson K. Duncan, C.S.A., anticipated the attack on Forts Jackson and St. Philip and attempted to meet it with the guns of both forts, fire rafts, and help from the Confederate navy. Comdr. John K. Mitchell, C.S.N., a reluctant partner in the defense, placed his squadron, including two ironclads, below Fort St. Philip to resist the attack. The ironclad *Louisiana* lay just below St. Philip, but Mitchell used the ram only as a stationary battery.

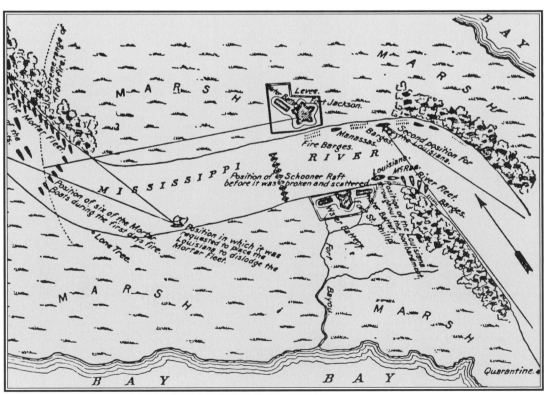

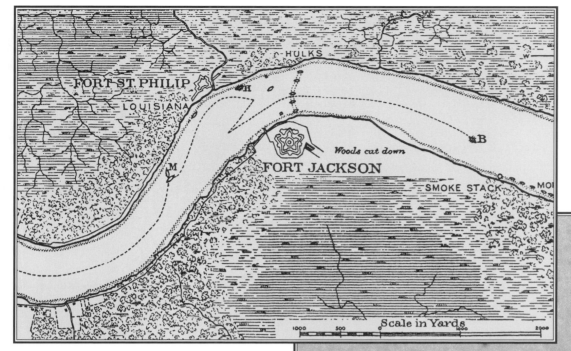

enmeshed in the stack-up created by *Pensacola*. Because so many of the Union vessels had lost their bearings in the smoke, Preble hugged the high walls of Fort St. Philip. Several vessels had already passed above the fort, but Preble was the first to mention *Louisiana*. It came as a surprise to find himself within 50 yards of her. Mitchell had tucked the ironclad alongside the upper water battery where he disguised her as an extension of the battery. *Louisiana's* guns had been poorly mounted, and Mitchell never got off a shot. Preble, however, fired his 11-

The U.S.S. *Brooklyn* (B), commanded by Capt. Thomas T. Craven, got off to a bad start, careened into the chain barrier, collided with U.S.S. *Kineo*, passed up the wrong side of the river, got caught in a strong eddy, sheered across the river, almost struck Fort St. Philip, passed the burning *Hartford*, crossed into the path of the C.S.S. *Manassas* (M), and received a butt almost severe enough to send her to the bottom.

Right: The U.S.S. *Hartford*, Farragut's elegant flagship, had no more business in the river than most of his vessels. Farragut expected to return to the Gulf after capturing New Orleans but spent almost two years in the river.

inch Dahlgren and tore a hole the size of the shell through the iron plating on *Louisiana's* bow. Mitchell claimed the damage had been done by *Hartford,* which came along later, but men on *Hartford* never saw the ironclad though they may have fired on her.

Kineo and *Wissahickon,* the last two vessels in the Union first division, tried to make a fast run past the forts. Lieutenant George M. Ransom, commanding *Kineo,* did not know that the second division had already started through the barrier. *Brooklyn,* which had just sheered to starboard to fire a

broadside at Fort Jackson, collided with *Kineo,* carrying away the latter's bowsprit and head, and wrenched the frame of the vessel. By an amazing stroke of good fortune, *Kineo's* machinery remained aligned and she passed up the river, absorbing 10 shots from the forts that caused far less damage than the collision with *Brooklyn.*

Wissahickon avoided the congestion in the river, and though her commander, Lieutenant Albert N. Smith, worried at times of being run over by the vessels

behind him, he eased over toward Fort Jackson and made his run through smoke draped along the western side of the river.

When Farragut observed *Pensacola* stacking up the first division, he ordered Commander Richard Wainwright to get the second division underway. He knew his decision might add further to the mix-up but, with dawn approaching, he could wait no longer. He planned on using *Hartford, Brooklyn,* and *Richmond* to engage Fort Jackson as the heavy sloops passed upriver. But once through the barrier chain, he could

see nothing. Farragut held his fire because he needed to know what he was shooting at, so he climbed into the port mizzen and stood with his feet on the ratlines and his back against the shrouds. Using a pair of borrowed opera glasses, he got high enough above the smoke to see Porter's mortar shells arcing into Fort Jackson and exploding. From his elevated post, Farragut sent orders down to the steerage to bring the vessel into position to fire a broadside. In the meantime, shells whistled over Farragut's head and began to chip away at the rigging. Urged by his officers to come back to the deck, Farragut made the descent moments before a shell exploded where he had been standing.

Two eddies swept around the forts, one on each side of the river. Every vessel passing the forts got caught in one of the eddies and, when immersed in smoke, the helmsman lost his bearings. Eddies contributed to the confusion because pilots, when coming out of the smoke, found themselves not where they expected to be. The same problem affected the pilots of *Hartford*, *Brooklyn*, and *Richmond*.

Farragut intended to engage Fort Jackson while passing up the river but instead found *Hartford* bearing on Fort St. Philip. The surprise was followed by another when a lookout reported a fire raft dead ahead, pushed by the tugboat *Mosher*. *Hartford's* helmsman overreacted and grounded the vessel just above the fort. With the flagship stuck in the mud, the raft drifted into her and set her port beam on fire. While one crew fought the fire, the starboard gun crew engaged St. Philip's upper water battery. Because of the light caused by the fire raft, nobody on *Hartford* ever reported seeing *Louisiana*, though she must have been there. The signal officer on *Hartford* put an end to the fire raft by dropping three shells into the flames and blew it up. When *Hartford* finally backed off the mud, her port beam smoldered from a severe scorching.

Brooklyn's collision with *Kineo* resulted from Captain Thomas T. Craven's poor sailing. He tried to fire on Fort Jackson before passing through the chain barrier, got off track, swung along the hulks holding the chains, and bungled into Kineo. Backing from the collision, he struck a hulk near the opening, and caught the ship's steam anchor in the chains. After cutting the ship free, Craven steamed along the barrier in the wrong direction, crashed into a raft of logs, and became entangled for the third time. Fire rafts drifted toward the ship, shells from Fort Jackson thudded into the vessel's deck, and flying splinters cut through human flesh.

By the time *Brooklyn* cleared the barrier, she had lost most of the 35 men killed or wounded that morning but, instead of beating up the river, she got turned about in the eddy off Fort St. Philip, swung across the river, and came directly under the guns of Fort Jackson. Craven came hard to starboard, steamed into the current off Fort Jackson, swung back across the river, and found himself scraping bottom 60 yards off Fort St. Philip. Seeing *Hartford* on fire upriver, Craven crept forward to offer assistance, only to spy *Louisiana* lurking in the shadows. A broadside from *Brooklyn* failed to injure the ironclad, but a shot from Mitchell's 9-inch shell gun struck *Brooklyn's* bow a foot above the waterline. Had it exploded, *Brooklyn* would have gone to the bottom.

Craven decided to leave *Louisiana* alone and beat a hasty retreat upriver. Instead, he wandered into the same eddy and once more found his vessel off Fort Jackson. As the ship came about, lookouts spotted the battering ram *Warrior*, commanded by Stevenson, lined up to make a run at Brooklyn's starboard beam. Stevenson changed his mind and gave a quick sheer just as *Brooklyn's* broadside cut loose with all

10 guns. With steam and flames pouring from the injured *Warrior*, Stevenson got her ashore in time to save his men.

When the smoke cleared, the *Brooklyn's* starboard gunners, peering through ports, spotted *Manassas* maneuvering to strike the sloop. Craven shouted to the steerage, "Put your helm hard-a-starboard," but a few moments too late. *Manassas* opened with her carronade, hulling *Brooklyn* five feet above the waterline, and seconds later crashed into ship's chain armor, jarring her fore and aft but doing little damage. Craven, badly jangled by his misadventures, let the Confederate gunboat *McRae* slip by his broadsides and beat upriver to join the squadron.

When *Brooklyn* became entangled in the chain barrier, Commander James Alden conned *Richmond* aside, pressed through the opening, and made a splendid run upriver. Though his vessel sustained 17 hits, all were above the waterline. Only two men lost their lives and four suffered wounds. Compared

with other vessels, *Richmond* got off easy.

Bell's third division, led by Lieutenant Edward Donaldson's *Sciota*, followed in *Richmond's* wake. Donaldson never lost sight of the larger vessel and drew little fire, but *Oneida*, following next, ran into trouble with Lieutenant Thomas B. Huger's C.S.S. *McRae*. A converted packet ship armed with eight guns, *McRae* had already been all over the river exchanging shots with Union vessels passing upstream. Huger had once served on *Oneida* and recognized her immediately. He also knew Lieutenant John De Camp, who commanded her. Huger put two broadsides into *Oneida* before De Camp got off his first shot, an 11-inch shell that exploded in *McRae's* sail room, setting the ship on fire near the shell lockers. Fearing flames would set off the shells, Huger nosed the vessel against the bank to put out the fire. Several Union vessels passed, firing shells and shrapnel into *McRae*. One fragment mortally wounded Huger, and Lieutenant Charles W. Read took command

of the vessel. Read got the fire under control, took the vessel back to Fort St. Philip, and anchored her near *Louisiana*. On *Oneida*, De Camp counted eight men dead, 24 wounded, and several holes in the ship's hull from his brief encounter with *McRae*.

The first yellow wisps of dawn dappled the eastern sky as the last four ships of the third division tried their luck at the gauntlet. *Kennebec*, commanded by Lieutenant John H. Russell, ran into the chain barrier, received a shot at the waterline, and limped back downstream to join Porter's gunboats. *Pinola*, commanded by Lieutenant Pierce Crosby, dodged *Kennebec* at the barrier, slipped through the opening, and dashed up the river. The only Confederate gunboat still operating on the river was *McRae*, and he put two shells into her as he passed upriver. *Itasca* and *Winona* missed the opening and became entangled with each other. Fort Jackson's gunners disabled *Itasca* by smashing her boiler. Her skipper, Lieutenant Charles H. B. Caldwell, conned her back to

Porter's anchorage. *Winona*, commanded by Lieutenant Edward T. Nichols, tried to run by the forts, but daylight and the guns of Fort Jackson drove him back through the barrier and into Porter's command.

At daylight, Captain Smith noticed *Manassas* lying near the east bank, obviously injured and out of commission. He pulled *Mississippi* out of the squadron and with *Kineo* ran her aground. Warley cut the ironclad's delivery pipes and escaped into the swamp with his men. Sailors from *Mississippi* boarded her, set the ship on fire, and towed her back into the river. As she floated by Fort Jackson, gunners mistook the ram for an injured Union vessel and fired upon her as she passed.

Though three gunboats failed to get above the forts, and *Varuna* had been sunk by *Governor Moore*, Farragut was delighted that his five heaviest ships and eight others had made it up to Quarantine with slight damage. He proved that heavily armed forts could be passed by wooden ships, but in

making the effort he had 37 killed and 147 wounded. He had annihilated the small Confederate squadron, leaving only *McRae* and *Louisiana* behind. Because the ironclad played so minor a role in the battle, he suspected that she would not be a threat to Porter.

The river now lay open to New Orleans. Butler landed his troops at Quarantine, and Farragut started upriver to beseige the city. Before Butler's infantry could cross through the swamps to the forts, the men inside Fort Jackson mutinied. After half of them deserted, General Duncan surrendered to Porter. Commander Mitchell, instead of surrendering *Louisiana* to Porter, set her on fire, cast her loose, and sent her down the river. She blew up off Porter's flagship during surrender talks.

On April 25, a few hours before Farragut reached New Orleans, Commander William C. Whittle, the officer in charge of the unfinished C.S.S. *Mississippi*, ordered her set on fire and pushed into the river.

New Orleans never surrendered because General Lovell took his small force and skipped town. After much difficulty with city officials and angry mobs, Farragut finally raised the stars and stripes on federal buildings and waited for Butler to bring up the infantry. On the afternoon of May 1, Butler marched into New Orleans while his band played "Yankee Doodle."

If Gideon Welles ever had doubts about picking the right man for the New Orleans expedition, those doubts vanished the day Farragut passed the forts with his squadron still in fighting trim.

For the Union, Farragut's capture of New Orleans became the greatest feat performed by the Union Navy during the Civil War. There would be other battles, but none of them ever matched the New Orleans expedition. It was not only a national success, but more importantly a diplomatic success, and it sent a message to Great Britain and France not to meddle with America's rebellion.

With Farragut's squadron in the river, Welles set his eyes on opening the Mississippi, but capturing Vicksburg would not be so easy.

Left: As *Hartford* steams beyond Fort St. Philip, she is met by the C.S.S. *Louisiana* on her starboard and *Manassas* off to port, but she passes both ironclads without sustaining any serious damage.

CHAPTER FIVE

MEMPHIS – COLLISION OF THE BATTERING RAMS

Of all the naval engagements during the Civil War, the one least understood occurred off Memphis, Tennessee, in June, 1862. It was the only battle between two fleets where a fort was not involved. What made the fight even more unique were the vessels involved – not conventional warships but battering rams. The use of ships as battering rams went all the way back to the days of the ancient galleys when oarsmen would row their vessel into enemy. The concept was not unique. Both the C.S.S. *Virginia* and the C.S.S. *Manassas* were called rams because they carried a beak on their bows for ramming. Every ironclad built by the Confederacy also carried a reinforced prow for ramming. With the single exception of *Manassas*, Confederate ironclads were built for fighting and well-armed with heavy guns. Confederate battering rams carried two or three small guns, but they mainly relied on speed and the iron casing fastened around their bows. Union battering rams carried no guns. They defied every description of a fighting vessel, were discredited by the Navy, and were commanded by Army officers and river boatmen. They were, by all standards, modified steamboats – sidewheelers and sternwheelers – a curiosity of the Civil War. Their real usefulness during a war that lasted four years came during less than one day. Their commanders, however, were a different breed of men, accomplishing what traditionalists might call the impossible.

During March 1862, at the time when *Monitor* fought *Virginia* and Farragut inched his battle squadron into the lower Mississippi, naval operations above Memphis, Tennessee, took on an entirely different character. After cooperating with Brigadier General Ulysses S. Grant in the capture of Forts Henry and Donelson during February, fifty-five-year-old Flag Officer Andrew Hull Foote moved his Mississippi flotilla back to the river of its name and set his sights on Island No. 10, the next cog in the Confederate defense of the upper river. During the action against Fort Donelson, splinters from a shell had struck Foote near the ankle and put him on crutches. Being as resolute a fighter as Farragut, Foote ignored his surgeon's orders and refused to leave his command.

After losing the forts to a combined Union attack, the remnants of the Confederate Mosquito Fleet moved down to Tiptonville, a town about 30 river miles below Island No. 10 but by land only four miles across the base of a huge horseshoe bend. There it was joined by Captain James E. Montgomery's battering rams, being the other half of the River Defense Fleet organized by General Lovell. At Tiptonville, the Confederate assemblage of vessels united into a single command under Montgomery.

Although in great discomfort, Foote mapped his strategy with Brigadier General John Pope for capturing the island and the enemy fortifications emplaced along the river. His broader plan included a sweep down the river, gobbling up Fort Pillow, Fort Randolph, Memphis, Vicksburg, and any other obstacle that stood between his flotilla and New Orleans, where he hoped to join forces with Farragut. But six weeks passed since the capture of Fort Donelson, giving the Confederates ample time to strengthen their defenses.

> James Eads of St. Louis designed and built most of the Union "City Class" river ironclads, such as the U.S.S. Mound City. The vessels drew about six feet of water and carried up to fourteen guns, plus howitzers.

For several weeks Charles Ellet, Jr., a civil engineer living in Washington, had been making frequent visits to the Navy Department with a scheme to build battering rams. Secretary of the Navy Welles classified Ellet as a pest and, after the first meeting, refused to see him. He had enough problems on his mind and did not want to be bothered by a landsman who knew nothing about naval affairs.

During the Crimean War, Ellet had presented the same plan to Russia, and after that failed he tried with no better success to interest the British Royal Navy. He believed that fast steamers equipped with iron prows could demolish heavy warships, even those with armor, by ramming them at great speed. In 1855 he had made the same proposal to Secretary of the Navy at the time, James C. Dobbin, whose reaction was about the same as Welles's. Ellet did not know then that General Lovell had already adopted the concept for the Confederates

Left: Flag Officer Andrew Hull Foote, U.S.N., distinguished himself during early naval operations at Fort Henry, Fort Donelson, and Island No. 10. Wounded in battle, he was replaced by the less competent Charles H. Davis.

Below: In the first major naval engagement on the Tennessee River, the Union flotilla under Flag Officer Foote, in support of Brig. Gen. Ulysses S. Grant's division, bombarded Fort Henry into submission.

Early operations of the Ram Fleet extended from Cairo, Illinois, to a short section of river below Memphis. The first action took place at Fort Pillow, where the Ram Fleet occupied the earthwork, pressed downriver to capture Fort Randolph, and proceeded from there to Memphis, where the Mississippi flotilla, commanded by Flag Officer Charles H. Davis, joined in the attack on the River Defense Fleet.

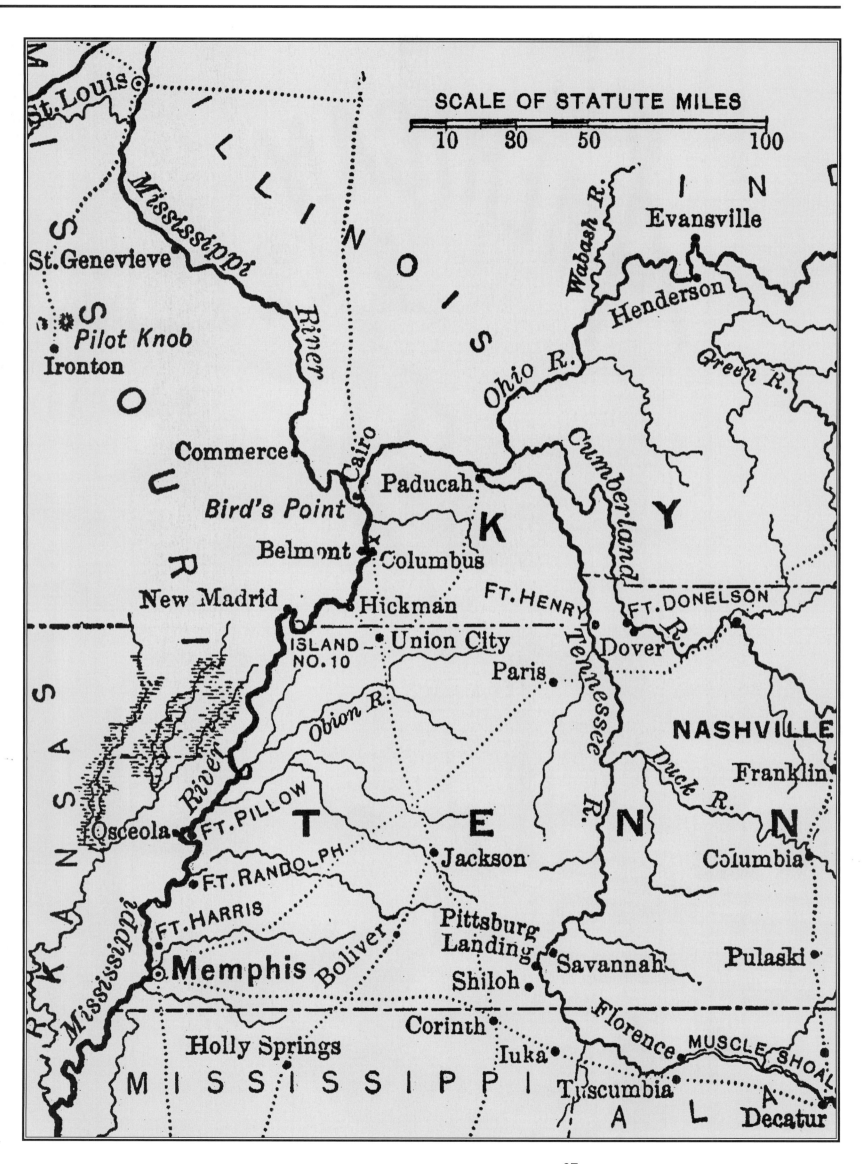

and that a dozen battering rams had been fitted at New Orleans.

After Welles rejected the concept, Ellet took his proposal and a bundle of drawings to the Secretary of War. Stanton showed no interest in battering rams until March 9, the day after the C.S.S. *Virginia* appeared in Hampton Roads, destroyed the U.S.S. *Cumberland* and the U.S.S. *Congress,* and sent shock waves up the Potomac River and into the White House. A few days later Major General Henry W. Halleck reported that the Confederacy had ironclads "like the *Merrimac*" under construction at New Orleans. In the meantime Ellet learned about Lovell's battering rams and warned Stanton that if fitted properly, they would "most likely sweep our flimsy naval craft from the Mississippi waters." Farragut would eventually prove otherwise, but Stanton, thinking Welles too "weak-minded" on the subject, decided to take matters into his own hands.

Stanton had no more business creating his own navy than Welles would have had if he had tried to form a brigade of infantry. The two men did not like each other, but when Stanton agreed to finance Ellet's battering rams, he did so out of patriotism – though he knew that such intrusion into naval affairs would certainly irritate Welles.

On March 27, 1862, Stanton issued orders to Ellet instructing him to "provide steam rams for defense against ironclad vessels on the Western waters." Such an unorthodox arrangement was bound to cause trouble somewhere along the line, especially since Ellet was a civilian who privately hoped to command the rams as an independent squadron responsible only to himself. He had reached a small crisis in his life as a civil engineer and needed money. Though highly motivated to succeed at whatever task he attempted and indefatigable in his pursuits, Ellet was also aware that capturing or destroying Confederate property could lead to a fat bundle of prize money. With this in mind, he assured Stanton that as soon as the boats were ready he intended to go down to Island No. 10, "or any other stronghold of the rebels… and run down before the batteries and drive our rams at full headway into the rebel boats."

Above left: By 1863, the concept of ironclad rams had made so deep an impression on the American public that composer R. S. Frary decided to put words to music, dedicating the satirical work to Secretary Gideon Welles.

Far left: Before Charles Ellet, Jr., could mobilize his battering rams, Flag Officer Foote took his flotilla down to Island No. 10, bombarded the earthwork using mortar boats, and opened the way for the Army.

Left: Alfred W. Ellet, the brother of Charles Ellet, commanded the ram *Monarch* during the Battle of Memphis, and after his brother's death, continued to lead the unit until the end of the war.

Right: Flag Officer Charles Henry Davis, a trained scientist, had never been in a naval battle and was poorly prepared for fighting on the river.

Far right: Charles Ellet, Jr., a civil engineer, conceived a notion that fast, unarmed steamers could sink the Confederate ironclads by ramming.

Below: The clash of rams off Memphis became frantic. *Monarch* **(M) rams** *General Beauregard's* **starboard beam.** *Queen of the West* **(left) staggers from a butt toward the Arkansas shore while others mix in the action.**

Ellet worked at lightning speed. After buying three sternwheelers at Pittsburg – *Lioness, Sampson,* and *Mingo* – he worked down the Ohio River to Cincinnati buying four fast side-wheelers, *Queen of the West, Monarch, Switzerland,* and *Lancaster*. All the boats ranged from 170 to 180 feet in length, 30 to 40 feet in width, with holds ranging from 5 to 8 feet in depth. He then bought two tenders, *T.D. Horner* and *Dick Fulton,* both stern-wheeled towboats not intended for fighting. He did not buy the boats himself. An agent from the Quartermaster's Department followed him from place to place with the equivalent of a limitless checkbook.

Shipyards along the Ohio River bulged with work for the navy, but Ellet managed to shove enough of it aside to convert his steamboats into rams. He removed superfluous weight by cutting down the upperworks, replacing them with heavy bulwarks to protect the boilers. He added three layers of 12- to 16-inch square timber, extending it from stem to stern on the main deck and fastening it to the hull. He tied one heavy beam back to the keelson, using it to absorb the shock of ramming, and reinforced the bows to carry a layer of iron plating. Iron

stays strapped the boilers and machinery into position in such a way that they could not be dislodged by impact. Each vessel received a coat of shiny black paint and a pennant showing the first initial of the vessel's name. Unlike the Confederates' rams, he did not weigh down the bows with excessive plating or the decks with cannon. Instead, he depended upon speed, maneuverability, and surprise. Because he viewed his rams as expendable, he refrained from sharing this information with others, knowing that a crew could not be recruited to serve on a vessel intended to be used as an implement of self-destruction.

Now that the War Department owned nine steamboats, Stanton offered to send "two or three good naval officers" to "take command of your squadron when it is ready." Ellet wanted no intruders disrupting his plans and replied, "I prefer daring and skillful river men… to handle the boats," but he calmed the secretary's concerns by agreeing to apply for naval officers should they be needed. Stanton had not quite grasped the notion that Ellet intended to command the Ram Fleet. Because the matter had never been discussed with the secretary, Ellet now made certain that all his correspondence with the secretary referred to himself as the person in command.

Flag Officer Foote learned that a number of riverboats were being converted along the Ohio River. Thinking they were intended for his flotilla, he sent Lieutenant Wilson McGunnegle upriver to expedite their completion. When Foote learned from McGunnegle that the boats were worthless "brown paper rams" being built for the War Department, he kept his opinions to himself, but Fleet Captain Alexander Pennock grumbled, "I am glad the Navy is not responsible."

Meanwhile, Foote sent a gunboat around Island No. 10 on April 4, General Pope landed four transports of infantry on the eastern shore of the Mississippi three days later, and the combined force trapped 3,500 Confederates with all their equipment. The Union victory at Island No. 10 opened the way to Fort Pillow and gave Stanton an opportunity to reconsider the viability of the Ram Fleet. He chose to keep it rather than have it refused by the Navy, hoping that the boats might still do some good.

Stanton now faced the problem of legitimatizing the Ram Fleet. Ellet hoped to keep his creation a family affair, so he

Above: Union Secretary of War Edwin M. Stanton believed that Ellet's scheme to destroy Confederate ironclads had merit and upstaged the Navy by funding the project.

Left: Secretary of War Stanton placed Col. Charles Ellet's Ram Fleet under the command of Maj. Gen. John C. Frémont, pictured here, but he told the general to not interfere with Ellet's operations.

Below: All of James Eads's "City Class" ironclads, built at St. Louis, followed the same design. Several vessels were similtaneously under construction, and after the first was finished, the others went fast.

suggested that his brother, Captain Alfred W. Ellet, be transferred from the 59th Illinois Infantry as second in command. Because the rams carried no cannon, he also asked that Alfred be permitted to bring with him several lieutenants and a company of infantry to serve as boat guards. The balance of the crews – some 300 men – would be composed of civilian riverboatmen engaged to serve for six months.

By naming his brother as second-in-command, Ellet implied that he intended to be in overall command, and since the secretary had not given much thought on how best to organize the Ram Fleet, he decided to leave Ellet in charge and make him a colonel. Ellet replied that he preferred no rank. He wanted the Ram Fleet to remain under civilian control where he could do with it as he pleased, operating the boats much like a band of privateers collecting prizes under letters of marque. When Stanton insisted that the rams be led by a man of official military rank, Ellet said he

would rather be a general. The secretary could not make anyone a general without the approval of Congress, so Ellet reluctantly became a colonel. He refused to buy a uniform until Alfred arrived and insisted that his brother could not go to war without one.

On April 27 Stanton learned that Farragut had captured New Orleans, and to those in Lincoln's cabinet it appeared that before the summer of 1862 ended the entire Mississippi would be in Union hands. If so, why did Stanton any longer need Ellet's rams? They would make better transports for moving troops. But the secretary, having just made Ellet a colonel and his brother Alfred a lieutenant colonel, decided to retain his personal navy and hope for the best. He attached Ellet to the staff of Major General John C. Frémont but made him subject only to orders from himself. He then told General Halleck that Ellet would be subject to the orders of Flag Officer Foote, but he did not tell this to Foote. On May 9,

Foote, because of his injury, turned the Mississippi flotilla over to Captain Charles Henry Davis and departed, leaving no instructions regarding Ellet's Ram Fleet because he had none to give.

Fifty-five-year-old Charles Henry Davis possessed a brilliant scientific mind which had enabled him to rise in rank more rapidly than others in the Navy. On the matter of intelligence, Davis and Ellet had much in common, but their personalities were exact opposites. Ellet thought swiftly, acted swiftly, and had little patience for indecision. Davis dissected every problem in an effort to grasp a foothold on each detail before drawing a conclusion that led to action. Warfare and logic seldom made a close connection with reality. Unexpected occurrences perplexed Davis and destroyed his mental equilibrium. He thrived on order, and he wanted to command the Mississippi flotilla like an orchestra without an instrument out of tune. Foote had left him with a mission, to coordinate with the Army

Left: The gunboat U.S.S. *St Louis* (later called *Dr. Calb*). When Farragut attacked Forts Jackson and St. Philip, he had no ironclads. All the Eads-built river ironclads were upriver in Foote's squadron and better armed than many of the wooden gunboats in the Gulf Squadron.

Right: One day after Charles H. Davis took command of the Mississippi flotilla, the River Defense Fleet launched a surprise attack below Fort Pillow, damaging two of Davis's ironclads and giving him a permanent scare.

Below: The C.S.S. *General Bragg* of the River Defense Fleeet was a steamboat converted at New Orleans to a battering ram, fitted with iron plating on its bows, and armed with 32-pounder pivot guns fore and aft.

in capturing Fort Pillow, Fort Randolph, and Memphis. After that, Foote hoped to be back with the flotilla. Six weeks later he died, smitten by infection in a wound that would not heal.

Davis suffered his first upset on May 10, the very next day after Foote's departure. Captain Montgomery brought eight gunboat-rams of the River Defense Fleet up from Fort Pillow and attacked seven Union vessels at Plum Point Bend. The boats rammed two of Davis's lightly plated ironclads – *Cincinnati* and *Mound City* – and caused enough damage to force the Union vessels into the shallows to keep from sinking. After 30 minutes of fighting, Montgomery took his rams back to Fort Pillow with only two killed and one wounded. Davis had failed to post a picket boat, and the surprise attack left him shaken and more fearful of Montgomery's rams than their tactical strength warranted. To cover his ineptitude, Davis informed Welles that three enemy vessels had been destroyed and, because Montgomery withdrew, he also claimed victory. Welles had no way of proving otherwise, and Davis's story found its way into the Navy's Official Records.

Davis's next surprise occurred a few days later when Alfred Ellet arrived at Plum Point Bend with six boats from the Ram Fleet. Ellet passed through Davis's squad-ron and anchored where he pleased. Davis had no idea what boats they were or why a lieutenant colonel commanded them. On May 25 Colonel Charles Ellet arrived with the balance of the fleet and, wanting action, sought an interview with Davis. The meeting started cordially and ended badly. Ellet departed in disgust, advising Stanton that Davis refused to "assume any risk at this time." Two days later Ellet returned to *Benton*, Davis's flagship, to propose a joint attack on Montgomery's River Defense Fleet, thereby opening the way to capture Fort Pillow. Davis

promised to reply but never did, so Ellet decided to mount his own attack.

When rumors circulated through the Ram Fleet that Ellet intended to launch what some crew members described as a suicide attack, a pilot on *Monarch* demanded his pay and quit. Ellet released the man but worried that others might follow. He then laid plans to capture an enemy picket boat, but the captain of the converted side-wheeler *Queen of the West* and several members of the crew had seen enough and departed on a barge with their baggage. On June 4 Ellet rallied enough volunteers to set the trap, but the picket boat retreated to Fort Pillow and put Montgomery's River Defense Fleet on alert.

The exercise enabled Ellet to make a reconnaissance of the fort, but the action infuriated Davis. In a combined operation with Colonel Graham N. Fitch's regiments, Davis claimed to have planned a surprise attack. Because he had said nothing about his plans to Ellet, the Ram Fleet's attempt to capture a picket boat put the fort on alert, forcing Davis and Fitch to cancel their attack. Davis summoned Ellet to *Benton* and demanded to know under whose authority the Ram Fleet operated. Ellet produced papers showing that his authority came from the War Department. Davis reacted with bewilderment because neither Welles nor Stanton had said a word to him about Ellet's command. Davis then promised to make Ellet "acquainted with all the details" of his plans and invite his cooperation, but promptly did the opposite.

During the early morning hours of June 5, Ellet spotted Davis's flotilla coming downriver. As the first vessel rounded Craighead Point, he hailed the captain and learned that the squadron intended to bombard Fort Pillow. Ellet put his rams underway, sped down to Fort Pillow, and observed smoke billowing from the abandoned earthwork. Alfred Ellet landed, signaled his brother to come ashore, and planted the Stars and Stripes on the smoldering fort. The colonel held the fort, waiting for Davis to arrive, and sent Alfred downriver in *Monarch* to look in on Fort Randolph. Alfred found Fort Randolph also abandoned and its guns dismounted. He obtained the town's surrender and ran up a second national emblem. Colonel Ellet rejoined his brother at Fort Randolph and sent the following message to Stanton, "I presume there will be no further obstacles unless we encounter one at Memphis." The secretary expressed glee when learning that his private navy had bested Welles's professional sailors.

After securing Fort Randolph, Colonel Ellet started back upriver to communicate with Davis. He found the Union squadron already underway and hailed the flagship *Benton*. Davis snubbed him and continued down the river toward Memphis, anchoring at Wolf's Island, two miles above the city. Ellet gathered the rams together and followed, but darkness intervened and forced him to anchor about 16 river miles above Davis's flotilla.

At 5:00 a.m. on June 6, Ellet heard the deep rumble of firing in the vicinity of Memphis. Taking the lead in *Queen of the West*, he hailed *Monarch*, *Switzerland*, and *Lancaster*, shouting for them to follow. Davis had been looking for the rams, but he had mentioned nothing to Ellet about using them. The colonel had intended to confer with Davis in the morning, but the sound of gunfire induced him to forego the meeting and push straight into the action. As *Queen* rounded the bend above Memphis, Ellet could see through a thin veil of smoke the River Defense Fleet roving in plain sight off the city. From the hurricane deck of *Queen*, he hollered to his brother on *Monarch*, "Round out and follow me! Now is our chance!" Under a full press of steam, the two rams sped downriver. Ellet expected *Switzerland* and *Lancaster* to follow. Had he looked back, he would have noticed they were not there. *Lancaster* had broken her rudder, and *Switzerland* did not press forward because her orders were to follow *Lancaster*.

The River Defense Fleet had arrived off Memphis the previous day. Being short of fuel, Montgomery seized the coal of five commercial steamers moored off the city and scoured the town for more. Having no defenses, Memphis placed its fate in Montgomery's hands and, since he vowed to sink the invaders, they gave him whatever he wanted.

That evening, Montgomery met with Brigadier General M. Jeff Thompson of the Missouri State Guard in the Gayoso House. Earlier in the day, Thompson had received orders from General Beauregard to cooperate with the navy in the defense of the city. During a public gathering, Montgomery promised to "sink the Yankee fleet" in one hour. "I have come here," he boasted, "that

Below: The ram *Switzerland*, depicted without great accuracy by a contemporary artist. She never got into the action off Memphis, but she played a role throughout the career of the Ram Fleet. Later, she would pass the batteries at Vicksburg and serve under Farragut on Red River.

you may see Lincoln's gunboats sent to the bottom by the fleet which you built and manned." Montgomery had not learned of Ellet's rams. Had he done so, it would not have changed a word he said.

Montgomery's rams were fitted and armed identically to the boats that half-heartedly attempted to attack Farragut's squadron when it passed Fort Jackson and St. Philip. Each boat had clad bows, thought to be shot-proof, and Montgomery believed that as long as the rams faced the enemy, the boats could not be seriously injured. This left the beams and stern without protection. General Lovell had created the fleet, later referring to its several riverboat captains as "a breed of men who would never agree on anything once they get underway." While the boats at Fort Jackson carried two guns, Montgomery's rams carried from three to

five guns, 32-pounders and smaller. The flotilla consisted of Montgomery's flagship, *Little Rebel*, and seven other boats: *General Beauregard, General Price, General Bragg, General Jeff Thompson, General Van Dorn, Sumter,* and the sole survivor from Farragut's passage of the forts, *General Lovell*. At this stage of the war, Montgomery commanded the only assemblage of Confederate vessels that could be legit-

imately called a fleet, and after whipping Davis's ironclads at Plum Point Bend he had great confidence in them.

The gunfire heard at dawn by Ellet resulted from two of Davis's ironclads exchanging fire at long range with Montgomery's rams. Davis intended to attack, but before doing so he moved out of range to enable the men to breakfast on coffee, bread, and beef. Montgomery

mistook the movement as a withdrawal and believed that Davis would not engage at close quarters, so he pressed forward with his three best rams – *Little Rebel, General Lovell,* and *General Price* – in the lead. Davis misread Montgomery's intentions, thinking the commodore intended to surrender without a fight. Both men were wrong.

As Montgomery steamed upstream to engage Davis, Colonel Ellet on *Queen* and

Alfred Ellet on *Monarch* came in sight of the Union flotilla. Without pausing to confer with Davis, the Ellets steamed through, running with the current at more than 20 knots. Davis's sailors waved their caps and cheered, probably wondering why their flag officer remained idle while two of Ellet's unarmed vessels rushed to engage the enemy. A large crowd of spectators gathered along the Memphis bank to watch Montgomery smash-up the timid Union flotilla, but from above the thin layer of smoke covering the river they spied two pair of smokestacks proceeding at great speed through Davis's squadron. Tension mounted as they waited for the vessels to come into sight off the city.

Desultory firing from two Union ironclads stopped after the gunners observed Ellet's rams plunging into battle. Out of the smoke they came, bearing directly on Montgomery's three leading rams. *Little Rebel* came head on, but Ellet observed that *General Lovell* and *General Price*, caught completely by surprise, began to back, breaking formation off Beale Street. Both vessels compared in size to *Queen* and *Monarch*, but the captain of *Lovell* made a fatal error when he attempted to turn and run. He underestimated *Queen's* speed and

Below: Ellet's Ram Fleet, moored in a row beginning with *Monarch*, *Queen of the West*, *Lioness*, *Switzerland*, and *Horner*. They carried no guns and depended entirely upon their iron-cladded bows, which the contemporary artist omitted.

exposed his unprotected beam. Ellet waved his hat to his brother, motioning for *Monarch* to attack *General Price*. Then, with a full head of steam aided by a five-mile current, he drove *Queen* into *Lovell's* forward quarter just ahead of the wheelhouse, crushing timbers and all but slicing the vessel in two. The impact jettisoned every loose article on *Queen's* deck onto *Lovell*, jarred loose the latter's smokestacks, and toppled them over *Queen's* bow. Had the rams collided head-on, they would have sent each other to the bottom.

As *Lovell* began to sink, *Queen's* iron bow remained embedded in her victim's beam.

Ellet shoved the machinery into reverse, and the paddlewheels beat the river into a froth, but no amount of backing could free the vessel. Off *Queen's* beam, *General Beauregard* wheeled into position and fired a shell from her forward gun. Seconds later she slammed into *Queen's* wheelhouse, causing a snapping of boards that could be heard on shore. The impact jarred *Queen* loose, but cut her tiller ropes, crushed in her wheel, and left her nearly helpless. The crew had barely gotten back on their feet when *Sumter* ranged off the other beam. Alfred Ellet spotted *Sumter* pressing down on his brother's disabled vessel and wheeled over to cut her down.

Seeing *Monarch* approaching dead ahead, Sumter sheered off and barely got out of the way as *Monarch* steamed by.

Charles Ellet started out of *Queen's* pilothouse to investigate the damage to her wheel, but as he came on deck a pistol shot from *Beauregard* struck him just above the knee. Disabled, he refused to go below and ordered *Queen* onto the shallows along the Arkansas side. While the surgeon bandaged his wound, Ellet remained on deck to follow the engagement of *Monarch*.

Moments after *Queen* struck *Lovell*, *Monarch* crashed into *General Price*, shearing off the enemy's starboard wheel and

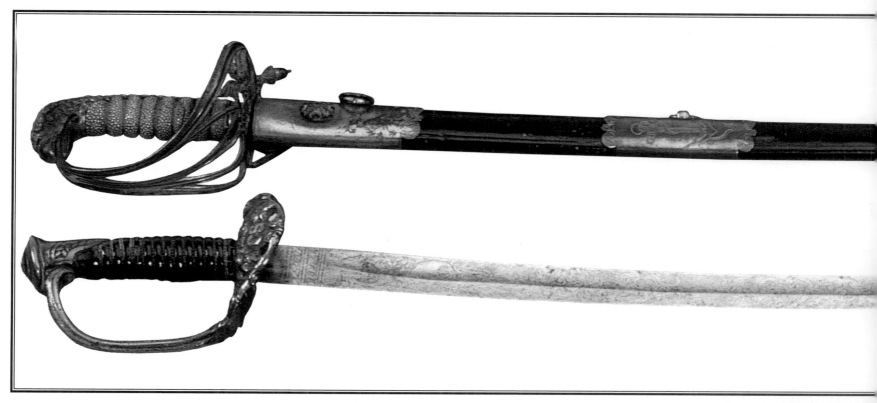

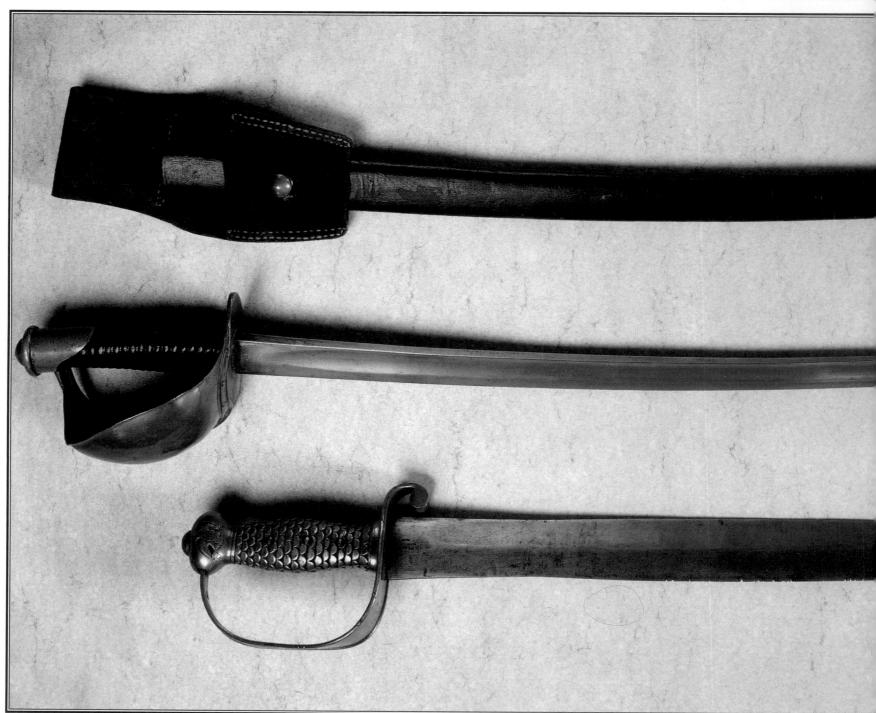

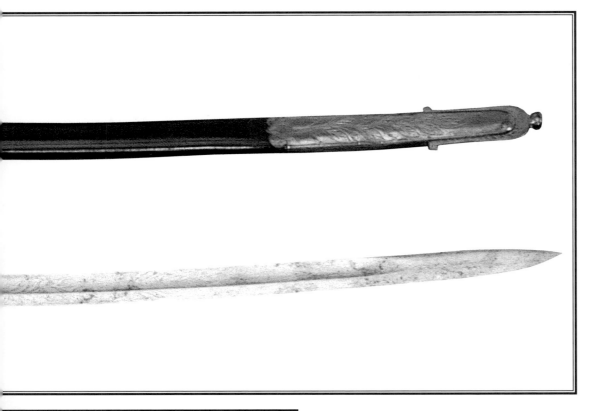

Left: Swords as carried by Confederate naval captains.

Below left: The brothers Ames capitalized on the Civil War by producing swords and bayonets. They each owned foundries and competed viciously against each other for U.S. government contracts. Oakes Ames of Chicopee, Mass., produced the Model 1860 navy cutlass shown at center, with its copper-riveted leather scabbard above it. His brother, Nathan P. Ames of Springfield, Mass., produced the Model 1842 cutlass at bottom. Its fish-scaled brass hiult is reminiscent of the Model 1833 artillery short sword. Naval supply personnel constantly confused one Ames with the other.

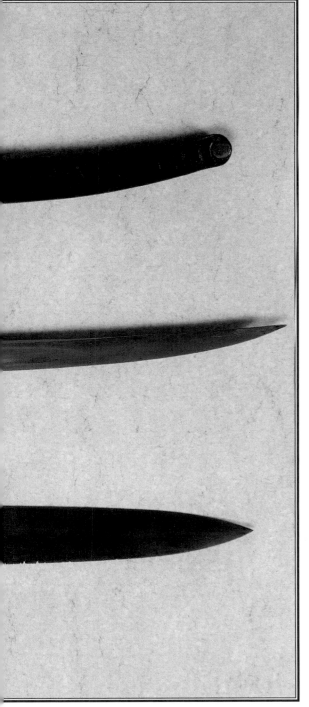

gouging a hole below the waterline. In sinking condition, Price used its port wheel to beat to shore. Being unable to steer, she collided with *Queen*. The butt did no damage, but the jolt gave Ellet another shot of pain. He shouted for the marines to board the vessel and soon found himself in possession of 81 prisoners.

After recovering from the concussion of striking *Price, Monarch* gathered headway and chased after *Beauregard*, which had just disengaged from butting *Queen*. *Beauregard* exposed her beam, and *Monarch* struck her at full speed. With a cracking of timbers that sounded like a barn collapsing, *Beauregard* shuddered from stem to stern. A shot from a Union gunboat narrowly missed *Monarch* and whipped through *Beauregard*, slicing through her boiler and engulfing the ram in steam. Men waving anything white emerged from the vapors and surrendered. Alfred Ellet made no effort to take control of the vessel. He let her drift and went after *Little Rebel*.

Montgomery's flagship had been hit by shellfire from Davis's gunboats and could make little headway. Ellet spotted her limping for the Arkansas shore and set his sights on taking a quick prize. With no guns to stop her from reaching shore, *Monarch* caught up with *Little Rebel* just as she touched the shallows off Hopewell. Ellet butted her hard aground, but Montgomery and most of his crew waded ashore and vanished into the underbrush.

Alfred Ellet observed Davis's squadron coming down the river, so he hurried back to *Beauregard* and took her in tow. When she filled to the boiler deck, he began to remove the prisoners. All about him lay wreckage and floating debris from the River Defense Fleet. A dispatch boat from the colonel came alongside with orders for him to continue the pursuit "as long as there is any hope of overtaking the enemy." Alfred left a number of survivors clinging to the roof of the captain's cabin on *Beauregard* and headed downriver.

During the battle between the battering rams, Davis's gunboats had kept up a steady fire on Montgomery's rams. Because of the constant mixing of vessels, *Monarch* and *Queen* came under friendly fire, but most of the shells fell harmlessly into the water. As the River Defense Fleet began to scatter, one shell struck *General Jeff Thompson* and forced her ashore. The crew escaped, but the vessel blew to pieces when fires reached the magazine. With *Queen* disabled and Alfred Ellet chasing after *General Van Dorn*, Montgomery's two remaining rams, *Sumter* and *General Bragg*, surrendered to Davis. Unable to overtake *Van Dorn*, Alfred Ellet began to worry about his brother's injury and abandoned the chase. As he started upriver for Memphis, he sighted Davis's squadron ranging below the city, scrambling about the river to collect prizes.

What action Davis would have taken were it not for the attack led by the Ellets will never be known. Davis's flotilla consisted of battle-hardened veterans unafraid to fight. The only timorous officer seemed to be Davis, who had already been frightened on May 10 by Montgomery's rams. But soon after the Ellets engaged the enemy, it did not take Davis long to get underway.

Never expecting to be attacked by rams, Montgomery lost all control of his senses when Queen of the West and Monarch emerged from a thin blanket of smoke and minutes later smashed-up two of his largest rams, General Lovell and General Price. After inviting all of Memphis to watch his rams destroy the Union gunboats, he slunk into the woods with his men and never bothered to submit a battle report. General Thompson, who had been a witness to Montgomery's boast, also witnessed the battle. "I saw a large portion of the engagement," he declared, "and am sorry to say that in my opinion many of our boats were handled badly or the plan of battle was very faulty." Most observers would agree that Thompson was probably right on both accounts.

Davis had embellished his official report on Plum Point Bend and Fort Pillow to make himself look audacious in battle, and he did it again at Memphis, giving little credit to Ellet's rams. He praised the Ellets for "conspicuous bravery" but let Welles believe that the entire affair had been a cooperative effort organized by himself when in fact there had been no communication with the Ellets. Observers on Davis's gunboats set the record straight, one writing that Ellet's much maligned "rotten and worthless steamboat rams... left us far behind," sinking two of the enemy boats and throwing the others into such confusion that

by the time Davis got his squadron into the fight, "the rebels started off on a grand skedaddle."

Davis eventually salvaged four of the Confederate rams – *General Price, General Bragg, Little Rebel,* and *Sumter.* He discovered they were much better boats than he had first thought, but he offered none of them to the Ellets. Not until long after the war was the matter of prize money settled, and Davis and his officers got most of it.

When Davis steamed down river to claim prizes, he left behind some unfinished business. A member of *Queen's* crew spotted white flags flying at Memphis and reported

them to Ellet. Unable to go ashore because of his injury, and because his brother had gone downriver, the colonel sent his son, Medical Cadet Charles Rivers Ellet, to accept the city's surrender. Against his mother's wishes, Charlie had joined his father at Plum Point on June 1, the day of his nineteenth birthday. While a nineteen-year-old lad may not have been the ideal envoy to demand the surrender of Memphis, the colonel wanted the name of Ellet connected with the city's capitulation and not the name of Davis. He gave Charlie a revolver and dispatched him on the ram Lioness, together with Lieutenant Warren D. Crandall and

two marines from the 59th Illinois.

The four men landed in a rowboat at the levee and walked to city hall. Charlie Ellet delivered his father's ultimatum to Mayor John Park, a 300-pound chief magistrate who claimed that as a civilian he could make no surrender of a military nature. The colonel had anticipated this argument and had told his son to tear down Confederate flags and hoist the Stars and Stripes over all the federal buildings. Park told the mini-surrender committee that if they attempted to raise the national emblem, a riot would ensue, and he would not be able to protect them because his police department had

vanished. To avoid further trouble, Park suggested the emissaries return to their boat. Charlie Ellet refused, so the mayor reluctantly agreed to lead the four men to the post office. Each marine carried a flag, and during the stroll to the post office a citizen of Memphis crept up behind one of the marines and stole his flag, leaving but one for the hanging.

Men at the post office led Charlie Ellet and Warren Crandall up the stairs to the fourth floor, where a stanchion with slats led to a hatchway on the roof. After posting two guards on a lower level, Ellet and Crandall stepped onto the roof. They looked for a

Above: Closing scene of the clash of battering rams off Memphis. In the aftermath, wreckage of the Confederate River Defense Fleet is scattered all along the river.

flagstaff but found none, so Crandall returned to a lower floor and found a plank about six feet long. He carried it back to the roof and split it down the center. Charlie spliced the two pieces together with bandages, tied on the banner, shoved the makeshift flagstaff into a flue, and draped the flag over the front of the post office. While Ellet and Crandall admired their creation, a prankster locked the hatchway to the roof from the inside. As soon as the Union colors caught the notice of spectators on the street, Memphis citizens began hurling stones at the flag-raisers on the roof, and from the other side of the building, a few shots from small arms fire erupted. Ellet and Crandall hunkered down on the roof while a few badly aimed bullets whizzed about their heads.

Thousands who had watched the battle on the river early that morning now converged on the post office. Park feared that if Ellet's men were injured, Union gunboats would retaliate and bombard the city, so he lumbered down to *Lioness* to find help. Captain Shrodes threatened to fire upon the city "if those men were not released in ten minutes" – a hollow threat because Lioness carried no guns. Shrodes took all the boat's marines ashore and, with Park at his side, led them into the city. Hundreds of civilians surrounded the rescue force as it marched to the post office, but an enormous explosion in a warehouse near the river distracted the crowd, and they

Right: The ram *Lioness*, acting under the orders of Colonel Ellet, conveys his nineteen-year-old son Charlie and three Marines to the levee below Memphis to demand the surrender of the city from Mayor Park.

Below: The Union Navy was always in search of swift, light-draft paddlewheelers like the U.S.S. *General Sherman*, which could be used in tributaries during the shallow water months of summer to carry troops and supplies.

peeled away to investigate. Shrodes placed four men outside the post office while the others went to the fourth floor and opened the hatchway. Ellet and Crandall, once safely back on the street, gathered the men together and marched through town, stopping to remove Confederate flags wherever they found them.

At 3:00 p.m. Colonel Fitch's infantry appeared off Memphis and began landing at the levee. An hour later Davis's squadron returned from below. Colonel Ellet detached a boat to advise Davis that four men from the Ram Fleet had taken possession of the city but would need military assistance to hold it. Davis ignored the message, steamed over to the levee, and sent a note to Mayor Park demanding the surrender of Memphis – a formality already executed by Ellet, but Davis did not want to lose the credit. Park could not understand why the Union force on the river required two surrenders when one would usually sufficed, so he told Davis essentially what he told Charlie Ellet – that as a civilian he could not surrender the city but the Yankees may take it if they wished.

In Washington, Secretary of War Stanton praised Ellet for capturing Memphis, and Secretary of the Navy Welles praised Davis for doing the same. Stanton felt vindicated that his investments in the Ram Fleet produced good dividends, but on June 18 Colonel Ellet died from his wound.

The Ram Fleet had served its purpose, and the time had come to turn the boats over to the navy, but Stanton would not do it. McClellan's Army of the Potomac had invaded Virginia, but it wavered as it stumbled forward to Richmond. Having

Left: After Charles Rivers Ellet went to the roof of the Memphis Post Office to raise the Union colors, a prankster locked the trap door to the roof, and the flag-raisers came under smallarms fire before being freed.

Above: Medical Cadet Charles Rivers Ellet joined his father's Ram Fleet a few days before the battle of Memphis. At the age of nineteen, he became one of the youngest colonels in the Union Army, if not the youngest.

swiped a victory from Welles at Memphis provided Stanton with a measure of smugness he did not deserve. After the death of Charles Ellet, he gave command of the Ram Fleet to Alfred Ellet and made him a brigadier general. Charlie Ellet stayed with the Ram Fleet and became perhaps the youngest colonel in the Union army. There would be other adventures for the Ram Fleet, but never quite like the one at Memphis where two unarmed rams attacked a squadron of eight gunboat-rams and began the destruction of the last Confederate assemblage of vessels dignified as a fleet. It was the only battle ever staged on the American continent by two squadrons of riverboats fitted-out for the sole purpose of battering each other's vessels until they sank.

CHAPTER SIX

THE DEADLY C.S.S. ARKANSAS

After losing the Gosport Navy Yard in 1862, the Confederate Navy had no shipyards, so the Rebels built their ironclads in unconventional places. The typical boat could be framed along the bank of a river by house carpenters, which most of them were. Once the heavy wooden inner structure was finished, the shell could be launched into the river, tied to a wharf, and finished. The most difficult work involved getting the boilers and machinery on board and connecting the drive shafts to the propellers. Cannon usually went on last, two or three guns in each broadside and two pivot guns, one fore and the other aft.

Unlike Union vessels, which carried mostly 9- or 11-inch smoothbores, Confederate ironclads carried 6- or 7-inch rifled cannon, which packed a wallop, had greater range, and better accuracy. Union shell guns were immensely effective at close range against wooden vessels or bricked forts but almost worthless against ironclads. The Confederacy's Secretary of the Navy, Stephen R. Mallory, used good judgement when he decided to build ironclads instead of wooden gunboats, as some advisers had suggested. The weakness in the strategy was his government's inability to provide the finances to build the ironclads swiftly, and the Confederacy's technological inability to produce reliable engines.

One little ironclad, however, could cause a mountain of trouble, and on an early morning in July, 1862, did just that.

On April 26, 1862, news reached Memphis that Farragut had captured New Orleans, and the shock rippled down to the waterfront at nearby Fort Pickering where two Confederate ironclads lay unfinished. The officer in charge panicked and destroyed one of them before Secretary of the Navy Mallory could stop him. Had the government retained the second ironclad at Memphis and bent their efforts to finishing her, the C.S.S. ram *Arkansas* might have been completed in time to defend the city. Her main deck had already been iron-plated to several inches below the water line. Though not yet operative, her two engines and boilers had been installed, and her casemate needed only its armor to become impregnable. Instead, not knowing whether the next naval attack would come from Farragut or Foote, the steamer *Capitol* hawsed onto the unfinished ironclad and towed her downriver. A few miles above Vicksburg, *Capitol* brought *Arkansas* into the Yazoo River and began the trip upstream to Greenwood, Mississippi.

At Greenwood, *Arkansas* lay for a month moored to a dock in the flooded Yazoo with little progress made on finishing her. General Beauregard, commanding the district and feeling pressed by the huge Union army under General Halleck, demanded that a more energetic officer be dispatched to Greenwood. Mallory sent Lieutenant Isaac N. Brown, who arrived on May 29 and replaced Lieutenant Charles H. McBlair. Offended by his removal, McBlair argued with Brown before leaving for Richmond to lodge his complaint with Mallory. Brown experienced some difficulty shedding McBlair, writing, "I came near shooting him and must have done so had he not consented and got out of my way."

Some men who fought for the South came from Border States, and Brown was one of them. A Kentuckian with 28 years in the United States Navy, he had earned a reputation for getting things done. He soon realized why his predecessor accomplished so little. The facilities at Greenwood were deplorable, so he moved the vessel down to Yazoo City where there were repair shops,

The new ironclad U.S.S. *Essex*, commanded by William "Dirty Bill" Porter, is being coaled for action against the formidable C.S.S. *Arkansas* moored at Vicksburg.

sawmills, boat-building equipment, and manpower. He borrowed 200 men from the army and set a detachment to work mounting the guns. Another detachment circulated through Mississippi gathering shot and powder for the guns and supplies for the crew. Work progressed rapidly because two Union squadrons – Farragut's and Davis's – were converging on Vicksburg.

Farragut had no business bringing his heavy sloops-of-war up the Mississippi on the eve of summer, but he did so because Secretary Welles believed that Vicksburg would fall as easily as New Orleans. After the Union Army occupied Memphis, Farragut drove his warships past Vicksburg's batteries and came to anchor on the far side of De Soto Point, a huge horseshoe bend opposite Vicksburg. Porter's bomb boats remained below to shell Vicksburg and to protect transports carrying 3,300 infantry brought up by Brigadier General Thomas Williams to occupy and hold the city. Alfred Ellet found Farragut off Young's Point near the base of the bend and dispatched a boat to notify Captain Charles Davis.

While waiting for Davis's flotilla to arrive, Farragut learned of *Arkansas* and sent the rams *Monarch* and *Lancaster* on a reconnaissance up the Yazoo to investigate. Alfred Ellet and his nephew, Medical Cadet Charlie Ellet, took the two rams 65 miles into the river before they came upon obstructions supported by a four-gun battery at Liverpool. Below the battery lay three gunboats – *Polk, Livingston,* and *General Van Dorn,* the last being the only survivor from Montgomery's River Defense Fleet. Unaware that Ellet's rams carried no cannon, the enemy foolishly set fire to two of their boats, one of which swung abeam *Van Dorn* and set her on fire. Fearing flames would ignite gunpowder carried on the boats, crews cut the lines and set the burning vessels adrift. *Monarch* and *Lancaster* backed around a point just as *Van Dorn* exploded. At Yazoo City, 25 miles above the obstructions, lay the nearly finished *Arkansas,* but the Ellets never saw her.

On the morning of July 1, Davis arrived at Young's Point with the river ironclads *Benton, Carondelet, Cincinnati,* and *Louisville,* followed by four steamers, three tugs, four mortar boats, and two hospital boats. Farragut greeted Davis cordially and, after a brief reunion by two men who knew each other well, Farragut got down to the business of forcing the surrender of Vicksburg. They agreed upon a joint bombardment but, after several days of pounding the enemy's batteries without effect, Farragut wrote General Halleck, urging him to send a force to assault Vicksburg from the rear. Halleck refused to participate, forcing Farragut and Davis to wait in the falling river for further developments. The vessels anchored along shore and, because of a shortage of coal, most of them banked their fires or killed them completely.

The Union's Ram Fleet made periodic excursions up the Yazoo looking for

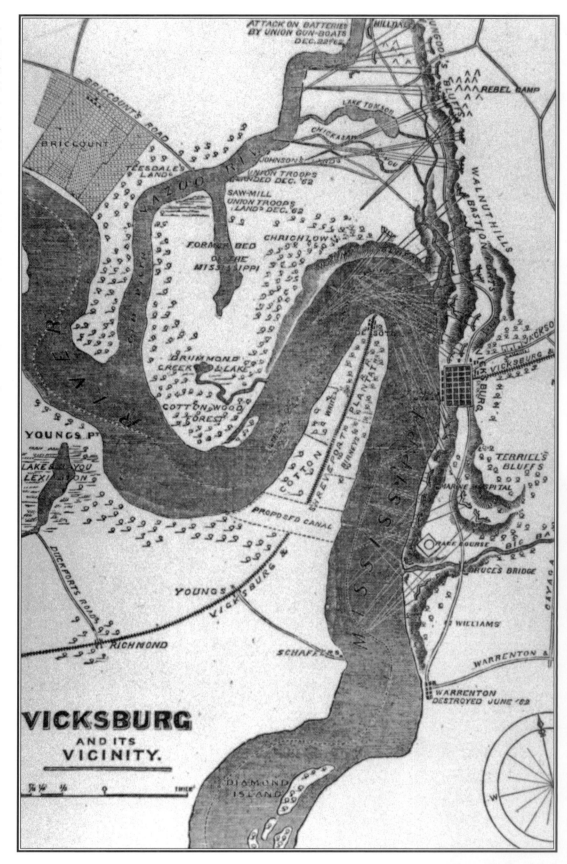

VICKSBURG
AND ITS
VICINITY.

Arkansas, but guerrilla bands operating along the banks with howitzers succeeded in driving the unarmed boats away. From Farragut's perspective, if the unverified ironclad up the Yazoo actually existed, he had better find and destroy her before the enemy cut her loose. Aware that obstructions supported by batteries prevented his vessels from ascending to Yazoo City, he believed that regular patrols should be sent up the river with the combined purpose of removing the obstructions while watching for *Arkansas.* Farragut could not use his deep draft ocean vessels in the shallow Yazoo. So after much arm-twisting, Davis agreed to send Commander Henry Walke's *Carondelet* up

For the next ten months of the war, the focus of the Union will fall upon the capture of Vicksburg. Welles had been in error when he believed the city would fall as readily as New Orleans, the difference being that Vicksburg had become an armed fortress and batteries were being rapidly emplaced at Grand Gulf. Far up the Yazoo another creature of the Confederacy was underway, the C.S.S. ram *Arkansas.*

After the capture of Memphis, Union naval operations moved to the west side of De Soto Point, the peninsula opposite Vicksburg and downriver from the Yazoo. Vicksburg's guns covered a broad range of fire, giving discomfort to any vessel attempting to pass. Farragut's and Davis's squadrons lay along the shore between De Soto Point and the Yazoo River on the morning the C.S.S. *Arkansas* made her appearance.

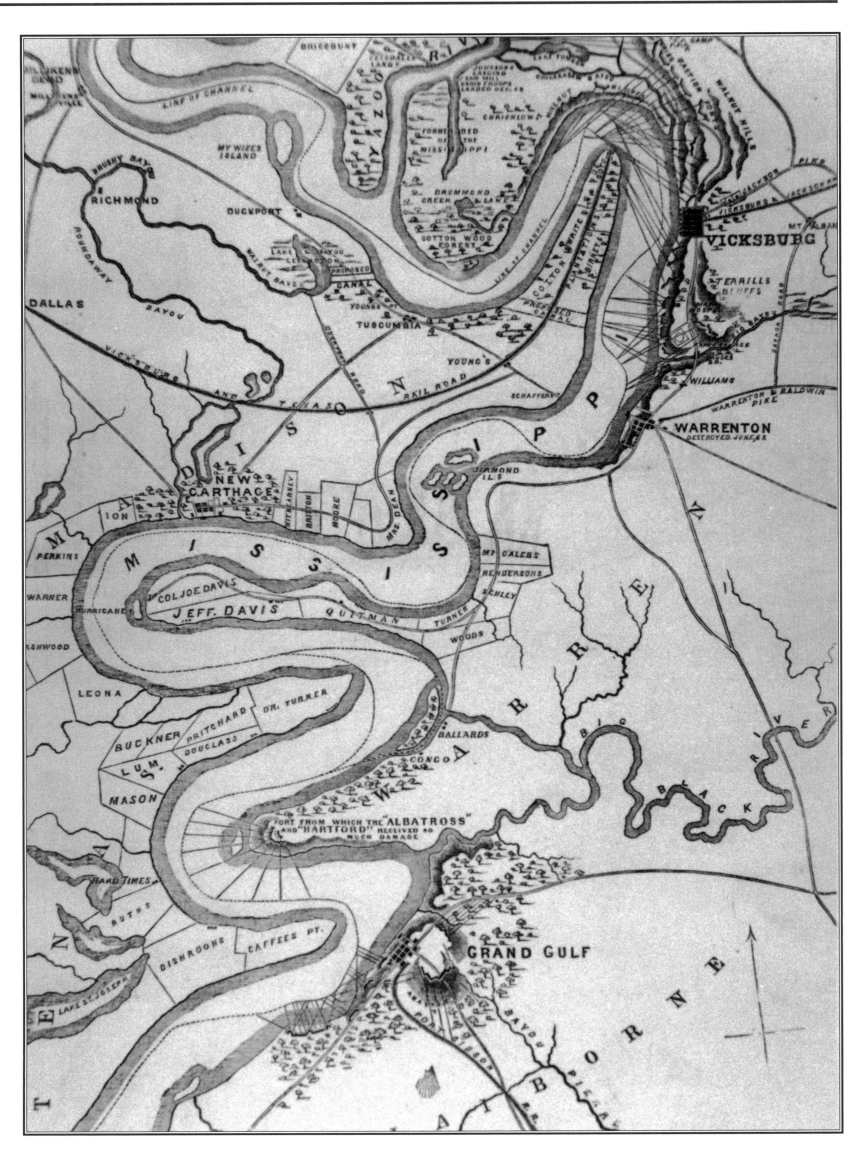

the Yazoo on the morning of July 15 in company with Lieutenant William Gwin's gunboat *Tyler* and Lieutenant James M. Hunter's ram *Queen of the West*.

At 4:15 a.m. *Carondelet*, *Tyler*, and *Queen of the West* steamed into formation and started up the Yazoo. Each vessel had specific orders. Being armed with six 8-inch shell guns and a 32-pounder, and being much faster and more maneuverable than *Carondelet*, *Tyler* swung into the point position. A mile behind, Walke followed with *Carondelet*, a river ironclad armed with eight 32-pounders and three 8-inch shell guns. Hunter followed in the rear with *Queen*, his orders from Ellet being to follow Gwin, and "If the *Tyler* should be attacked by the [*Arkansas*], to dash to her rescue… sinking the enemy's boat by running full speed right head into her." Hunter, an infantry officer from the 63rd Illinois Infantry, had commanded *Queen's* marines during the battle of Memphis. As he rounded into the Yazoo, he assured *Queen's* crew that the early morning exercise was no more than another harmless reconnaissance. Gwin stopped briefly at *Lancaster* to borrow her pilot, Richard Smith, who had been up the Yazoo on past occasions and knew the bars. Then off they went, disappearing in a light morning mist.

For the past six weeks Lieutenant Brown had exerted every effort to finish work on *Arkansas*. Though one of the Confederacy's smaller ironclads, being but 165 feet in length and 35 feet abeam, she carried a draft of $11^1/_2$ feet – a worrisome problem for Brown with the river rapidly dropping. Like *Virginia's* design, her casemate sloped at an angle and carried $4^1/_2$ inches of iron plating. On her gundeck she mounted two 8-inch columbiads forward, two 6-inch guns aft, and a 9-inch, 6-inch, and 32-pounder in each broadside, giving her a battery of 10 guns. Brown filled out the crew with 200 men and on the morning of July 15 took the ironclad down to Old River near the mouth of the Yazoo. A few days before, he had ridden a

Above: There was a striking difference between Farragut's ocean-going vessels and the cladded gunboats operating on the upper Mississippi, such as the U.S.S. *Cairo*, buit. at St. Louis by James Eads.

Right: The officers and men of the U.S.S. *Cincinatti*, moored along shore, spend a casual summer day cooling themselves under canopies while the day's wash dries on a rope fastened to the mizzenmast.

Below right: Ships the size of *Hartford* did no more cruising in the river than necessary. Sunny days provided an opportunity to dry out the sails and the sailor's wash. Farragut kept *Hartford* chain-armored at all times.

horse to a cliff overlooking the Mississippi and with a glass studied the Union vessels idling in the river with their fires down. He knew exactly where to find them.

Through the early morning mist, lookouts on *Arkansas* spotted three steamers crawling up the Yazoo. Knowing what they were, Brown opened on *Tyler* with the 8-inch columbiads and ordered steam. Gwin answered but began backing downstream. *Arkansas'* bow guns belched again, tearing up *Tyler's* deck. Gwin had no business engaging an ironclad with his flimsy gunboat, but he knew the unprepared condition of the fleet below and tried to hold off *Arkansas* until Walke came up in *Carondelet*.

Walke, seeing *Tyler* in desperate trouble, brought *Carondelet* into the fight, enabling Gwin to stand off. Walke and Brown had been messmates in the Navy, but neither was aware of the presence of the other. For nearly an hour the two ironclads exchanged shots, with little damage done to either, but as they slowly closed, Brown decided to ram *Carondelet*. Walke observed *Arkansas'* shift of direction and moved his shallower draft ironclad closer to shore. Brown detected the movement and concluded that

Walke intended to lure him into shallows where *Arkansas* would go aground, so he sheered off, almost touching *Carondelet* as he passed. As *Arkansas* slithered by, the Confederate gun crew depressed their guns and fired a full broadside into *Carondelet's* hull. Moments later, a shot from one of the ram's stern guns swept away *Carondelet's* wheel ropes. Walke had fired 70 rounds and watched every shot bounce off the ironclad's casemate. With his steerage shot away, he drifted against the bank, losing 30 men: four killed, 18 wounded, and eight missing, presumably from drowning.

Brown turned his attention again to *Tyler*, which had been standing off with *Queen of the West*. The best Gwin could do was to stay a few hundred yards ahead of the ironclad by backing and working the 32-pounder mounted in pivot in the bow. At two to three hundred yards, *Arkansas'* two 8-inch forward columbiads ripped into *Tyler's* flimsy decks and tore them to pieces. But two shots from *Tyler's* 32-pounder did more damage than all the rounds fired by *Carondelet*. The first ball struck *Arkansas'* shield and knocked Brown temporarily unconscious. A second shot crashed into the pilothouse, broke a piece off the wheel, and

Above: The Union gunboats *Tyler,* *Lexington,* **and** *Conestoga* **were all riverboats purchased by Capt. John Rodgers, refitted with guns, and transferred by the War Department to the Union squadron on the upper Mississippi.**

Left: Both Davis and Porter used the U.S.S. *Benton,* **in the foreground, as their flagship. She was slightly larger than the "City Class" steamers** *Louisville* **and** *St. Louis* **off her starboard.**

Above right: The U.S.S. *Louisville,* **one of the "City class" ironclads. They all had very much in common. They all looked alike, were 140-feet long, drew about six feet of water, carried 14 guns, and were driven by a center paddlewheel.**

mortally wounded the pilot. During the early morning battle, several shots had struck the ram's smokestack. One severed the breechings between the funnel and the furnaces, causing her steam pressure to drop. By the time *Arkansas* reached the Mississippi, she no longer had the speed to ram and could barely generate three miles an hour. Much of the damage had been done by Gwin's 32-pounder, but the duel with *Arkansas* cost him 13 killed, 34 wounded, and several missing.

When *Arkansas* attacked *Tyler,* Lieutenant Hunter failed to bring *Queen* into the action and dash to Gwin's aid as ordered. Instead, he brought *Queen* about and headed downriver. When Gwin looked for *Queen* and found her nowhere in sight, he believed that Hunter had gone off to warn Farragut and Davis. Hunter, however, lost precious time by dallying out of range. When Farragut and Davis heard faint sounds of firing up the Yazoo, each attributed it to bushwhackers exchanging artillery fire with Davis's two gunboats. As the sound drew nearer, men on some of the vessels took independent action and prepared for a fight. Not until 7:15 a.m., when *Queen of the*

West came beating down the river, did the watch on Farragut's flagship *Hartford* suspect that the action upriver represented something more than a skirmish with guerrillas.

Hunter, however, was slow in getting his message to Farragut, who came on deck in his nightgown and seemed astonished by the unexpected attack. When rounding off *Hartford's* stern, Hunter fouled in her anchor chains, swung alongside, and became entangled with the flagship. Men on deck then spotted *Tyler,* and someone shouted, "There comes the *Tyler* with a prize," but a puff of smoke from the so-called prize, followed by a report from 8-inch columbiads, soon convinced everyone that the strange looking customer firing on *Tyler* was actually a Confederate ironclad.

Men went quickly to quarters, but with fires down, few vessels could get up steam. Both squadrons lay like sitting ducks, Farragut's ships and Davis's gunboats on Mississippi side of the river and a line of transports on the Louisiana side. Nearest to the Yazoo were four unarmed rams commanded by Lieutenant Colonel Alfred Ellet.

Above: On July 17, 1862, the ram C.S.S. Arkansas made an unexpected appearance and caught the Union Navy asleep, hammering each vessel as it passed downriver.

Right: Rear Admiral Porter liked the *Benton* better during the summer than during the winter, complaining that in the cold months the vessel was the draftiest ship he had ever sailed an among the most uncomfortable.

When *Arkansas* rounded into the Mississippi, she steamed slowly down the center of the river, moving barely faster than the flow of the current. Heat from her furnaces escaped through the severed breechings, raising temperatures in the engine room to more than 130 degrees and on the gundeck to 120. Brown no longer had options. He must reach the safety of Vicksburg, 12 miles downriver, and to do so meant fighting the combined squadrons of Farragut and Davis – some 30 vessels – with his wounded ironclad.

Serving as a picket boat, the battering ram *Lancaster* lay at the upper end of the naval squadron. As soon as *Arkansas* hove in sight, Medical Cadet Ellet cut the boat's cable and nosed upriver to give the ironclad "a little of our kind of warfare." His intentions, however heroic, proved to be reckless. *Arkansas'* columbiads sent a ball into *Lancaster's* bulwarks that plowed through eight feet of coal, nipped three feet off the steam drum, scalded the engine crew, and instantly crippled the vessel. A crew member described the horror of watching as "the scalded men jumped overboard, and some of them never came to the surface again." As *Lancaster* drifted downstream, *Arkansas* slowly passed, sending eight more

balls into the wheelhouse. Then, as Brown concentrated his guns on Farragut's ships, fire from the Union squadron passed over the ironclad, striking *Lancaster's* port timbers with three balls and several hundred pounds of canister.

Arkansas passed Ellet's rams, and Brown, though still reeling from his concussion, noticed that all the warships aligned along the left bank still lay at anchor. He ordered the pilot to steer close into them, as it would minimize the risk of being rammed. As soon as he came abreast of *Kineo*, the first gunboat in Farragut's column, both vessels opened fire on each other. Moments later, every Union gun that could be brought to bear fired on *Arkansas*. Some guns could not be depressed enough to do more than nip the very top of the ironclad's casemate. Most shots just bounded away, but not all. One shell from either *Hartford* or *Richmond* penetrated her armor and 20 inches of wood backing before it exploded, killing four men serving the 32-pounder and knocking 10 men to the floor. Another shell burst near a gunport and killed a sponger. A bolt then entered through a port and wiped out the gun crew on the starboard side. A fourth shot passed through the ironclad and gouged another hole in the smokestack, forcing the men on the gundeck to take refuge near the ports to get fresh air.

It took 30 minutes for *Arkansas* to weave through the Union squadron, and she never stopped firing. Oddly enough, she sank no vessels and caused very little damage except to the reputations of Farragut and Davis, whom she caught completely by surprise. Had there been wind to clear away the smoke, *Arkansas* might have done damage to the Union flotilla, but after the first few minutes of firing, thick waves of gun-smoke smothered the river so completely that a vessel could only be

located from the flash of its cannon. Most of Farragut's squadron reported minor damage and few killed, and by the time *Arkansas* worked down to Davis's squadron, many of her guns could no longer be served.

Davis's flagship *Benton*, a river ironclad, was the last warship in line, and her crew had used the time to fire the furnaces and build a head of steam. Rather than pull into the current to engage *Arkansas*, Davis exchanged a broadside and let her pass. Then, with *Arkansas* making no more headway than one mile an hour above the speed of the current, Davis signaled a sister gunboat to follow and initiated a cautious chase. *Benton's* heaviest guns were in the bow; *Arkansas'* weakest guns were aft. Instead of overhauling *Arkansas* in an attempt to drive her ashore, Davis followed at a safe distance. He allowed the wounded ironclad to round De Soto Point and come under the protective batteries at Vicksburg. He said nothing of his timid pursuit to Farragut, who believed that Davis had made a desperate effort to sink the enemy ironclad.

Twenty thousand spectators watched the fight from Vicksburg's heights, among them General John C. Breckinridge and General Van Dorn, who observed the action from the dome of the courthouse. When *Arkansas* appeared, both fleets were in plain view, and though smoke soon blanketed the action, the constant firing of guns assured the spectators that their ironclad was still in the fight. When she rounded the upper bend, townsfolk swarmed down the bluffs to greet her. Van Dorn effused praise, declaring that Brown "immortalized his single vessel, himself, and the heroes under his command by an achievement the most brilliant ever recorded in naval annals."

When *Arkansas* backed into the wharf below the courthouse, hundreds of people

brimming with adulation pressed on board the vessel, only to view war at its ugliest. A powder-blackened crew streaked with sweat and blood met them at the hatchway. As one observer grimly noted, "Blood and brains bespattered everything, whilst arms, legs, and several headless trunks were strewn about. The citizens and soldiers of the town crowded eagerly aboard, but a passing look at the gundeck was sufficient to cause them to retreat hastily from the sickening spectacles within."

Those with strong stomachs stayed on board. They circulated through the vessel, listening to the groans and whimpers of the wounded carried below. A quick look at the gundeck told the story. A gun captain, acting as stretcher-bearer, described the scene, writing "the embrasures, or portholes, were splintered, and some were nearly twice the original size; her broadside walls were shivered, and great slabs of splinters were strewn over the deck of her entire gunroom; her stairways were so bloody and slippery that we had to sift cinders from the ash pan to keep from slipping." The happiest men on board the ironclad were a detachment of army volunteers who had signed-on the vessel for only one week. They grabbed their baggage and disappeared into the city before Brown could stop them, leaving *Arkansas* with less than half a crew.

In his report to Secretary Mallory, Brown reported 10 killed, 15 wounded, and dozens more slightly wounded. "We are much cut up," he added, "our pilot house smashed, and some ugly places through our armor." Brown counted 68 holes in the ram's smokestack. One officer lamented about having to fight using a green crew while the

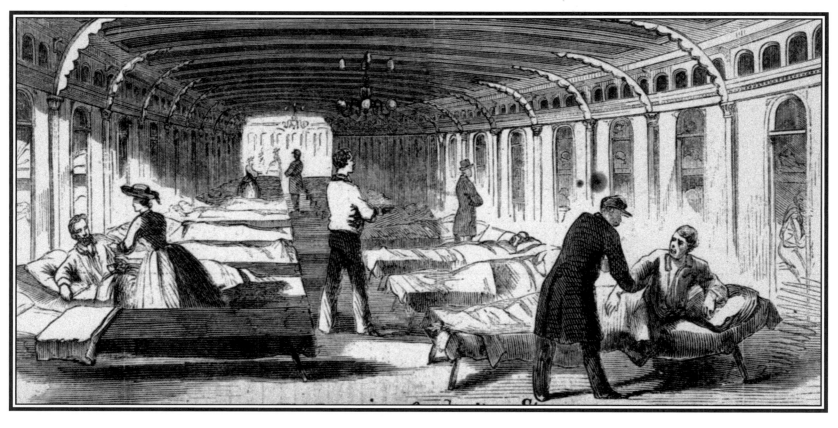

Left: The C.S.S. *Arkansas*, having been started on the banks of the Mississippi below Memphis, was one of the Confederacy's smaller ironclads, but her 64- and 100-pounders packed a powerful punch.

Below: Every flotilla carried at least one hospital ship and, like the U.S.S. *Red Rover*, many were once elegant riverboats. Tied to *Red Rover*'s port bow is an ice barge, a welcome treat for ailing servicemen.

Above: On the typical hospital ship, many of the fancy staterooms had been knocked out to provide open spaces for cots running the entire length of the ship's salon and lower decks, providing easy access to patients.

men who had served on *Virginia* bided their time "in a shore battery [at Drewry's Point] near Richmond."

Neither Farragut nor Davis knew whether *Arkansas* had been damaged. Farragut believed that she behaved like a crippled vessel. He wanted to finish her off, but Davis urged caution. If *Arkansas* cut loose from Vicksburg and steamed downriver, Farragut knew she would smash-up the vessels he had left below the city. *Brooklyn*, *Katahdin*, and *Kennebec* were still there with the boats from Commander William B. Renshaw's mortar flotilla. Renshaw now commanded the remnants of Porter's squadron and, though at the moment he reported to Captain Henry Bell of *Brooklyn*, he became overtly nervous about the safety of his flimsy boats. He speculated that Farragut's squadron had been damaged and, with such fears manifesting his thoughts, he foolishly burned the steamer *Sidney C. Jones* after she accidentally went aground. Farragut understood the vulnerability of the ships he left behind, which made him all the more determined to sink *Arkansas* while she lay at the wharf below Vicksburg.

Farragut assessed the condition of his squadron. *Richmond* carried the sick, but he found her fit for battle. He then wrote Davis, "We were all caught unprepared for him, but we must go down and destroy him. I will get the squadron underway as soon as the steam is up, and run down the line with your ironclad vessels. We must go close to him and smash him in. It will be warm work, but we must do it; he must be destroyed." Farragut had not yet written Welles to express his embarrassment for

Right: Union Navy insignia. Top center is a shoulder board for a mate, with side-by-side boards for pilots. Below center is a Civil War campaign medal, with a pair of 1852 captain's eagles on either side.

Below: The U.S.S. *Tuscumbia*, a riverboat refit as a gunboat, often acted as a tug, hauling two or more mortar boats (see alongside). Tinclads (see No. 10) carried little draft and could operate in four to five feet of water.

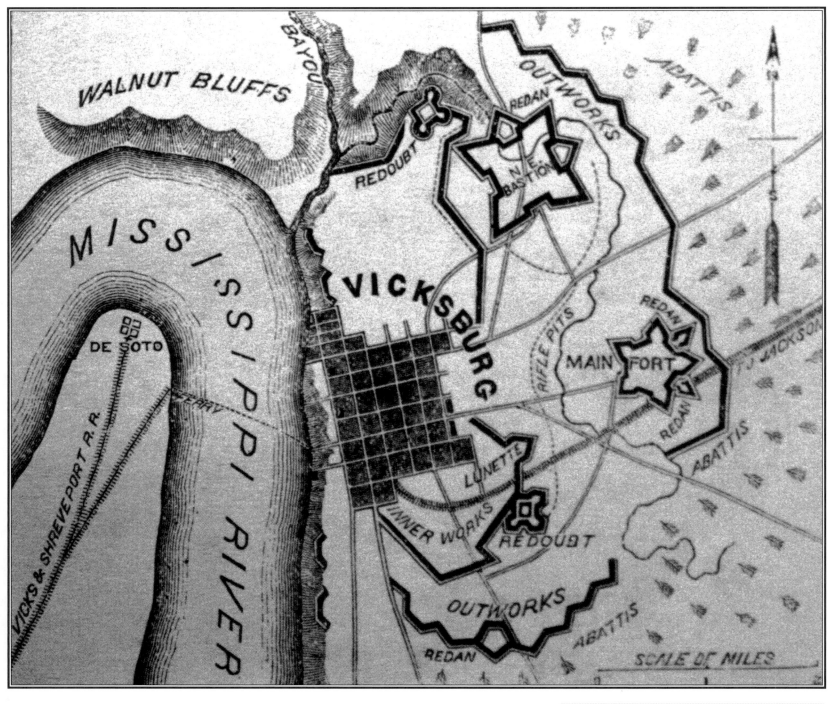

being caught napping, and intended to erase the stain by eliminating the source.

Davis, always deliberately cautious, fought Farragut's impetuosity by refusing to aid an attack if made during daylight. Farragut had no ironclads, Davis did, but the latter refused to risk them. Farragut argued that *Arkansas*, whose form and color resembled a pile of rusty pig iron stacked on a barge, could not be seen at night. Davis compromised and agreed to run his ironclads down to the bend and engage Vicksburg's batteries at 5:00 p.m. Because of delays in the details and a violent mid-afternoon thunderstorm, Farragut did not get his squadron underway until 6:40 p.m. To his commanders, he must have sounded like Lord Nelson when he said, "No one will do wrong who lays his vessel alongside of the enemy or tackles the ram. The ram must be destroyed" – which is precisely what Farragut intended to do with *Hartford*.

Darkness descended as Farragut's squad-ron rounded De Soto Point. He placed his heaviest ships close to shore, keeping the lighter gunboats on the far side of the river. Davis's ironclads – *Benton*,

Louisville, and *Cincinnati* – came around the point and engaged Vicksburg's batteries while *Brooklyn*, *Katahdin*, and *Kennebec* came up from below and with Renshaw's mortars created a cross fire.

The barrage from the combined fleets partially silenced the enemy's batteries, enabling *Hartford* and *Richmond* to drift by Vicksburg within 30 yards of shore. Smoke combined with darkness to cloak *Arkansas* where she lay at the wharf. "Not one of us could see her," declared Commander Alden of *Richmond*. Farragut, after passing below the city, wrote, "I look with all the eyes in my head to no purpose. We could see nothing but the flash of the enemy's guns to fire at." Knowing he would have to report a second failure to Welles, he lamented, "[I] would have given [my]... commission to have [had] a crack at her." One 160-pound stray bolt, however, had pierced *Arkansas* at the water line, killed two men, wounded three in the engine room, and started a severe leak.

Farragut now had no choice but to write Welles the grim news, confessing that, "It is with deep mortification that I announce to

the Department that notwithstanding my prediction to the contrary, the ironclad ram *Arkansas* has at length made her appearance and took us all by surprise."

Davis, however, showed no remorse over the affair, curiously describing it to his wife as "a very exciting and pleasing sight" and condemning Farragut for being too anxious to put vessels in harm's way just to destroy a single enemy ironclad. Davis had little to fear from *Arkansas* returning upriver, while Farragut had every reason to be concerned about the ironclad ram attacking his wooden warships and driving them all back to the gulf.

On July 16, with his full squadron once again below Vicksburg, Farragut pulled his senior officers together and suggested another attack be made on *Arkansas* that

Right: When *Arkansas* attacked the Union fleet, Davis's flotilla lay mainly along the bank, anchored and inactive, and provided easy targets for the enemy ironclad as she wove her way through both sqaudrons.

Below: The Mississippi Squadron made an impressive show wherever it went, and the vessels seldom steamed about the river without the entire fleet being involved. Under Davis, they seldom went on solo missions.

Far right When Welles purchased steamers to augment his navy, he bought a few ferry boats, armed them with four or five guns, and set them to work on the river. They transported troops and supplies, and performed picket duty.

night. Bell favored a daylight effort, but Alden thought the attack should be made by Davis's ironclads, since it was their "specialty." Farragut grumbled that he could not control Davis and "could only trust in his own vessels."

During the day, Farragut spotted *Arkansas'* hiding place and prepared to make the night attack, using the captured battering ram *Sumter* to sink her. He then changed his mind, partly because Davis preferred to destroy the ram by bombarding it with mortars. When that failed, Farragut lost patience. Had he known that Congress, on July 16, had passed an act creating the grade of rear admiral and that he would be the first to receive it, he would not have allowed Davis to temporize.

Davis had recently taken into his squadron a new ironclad, the 6-gun *Essex*, a center-wheeler 159 feet long and 47 feet abeam. Her captain, Commander William "Dirty Bill" Porter, was David D. Porter's brother and, like all the Porters, had the reputation for being both courageous and reckless. Porter wanted promotion, and he felt certain that by destroying *Arkansas* he would get it.

Lieutenant Colonel Ellet wanted both promotion and prize money, so on July 20 he wrote Davis offering to take one of his battering rams and personally attack *Arkansas*, provided that the joint squadrons would agree to draw the fire of the batteries.

Disgusted with Davis's timidity, Farragut walked across the base of the peninsula to consult with his counterpart directly. During the conference, Ellet repeated his offer. Whatever was discussed lit a fire under Davis because he agreed to a plan. At 3:00 a.m., Davis would send down to the bend *Benton, Louisville,* and *Cincinnati* and open on Vicksburg's upper batteries. Porter's *Essex* and Ellet's *Queen of the West* would work along shore and attack *Arkansas*. As soon as the firing started, Farragut would open with Renshaw's mortars and bring up his fleet to engage the city's lower batteries. The battering ram *Sumter* would join *Essex* and *Queen*, and between the three of them, sink *Arkansas* by ramming her and crushing in her beams.

Farragut could not have picked a better time to attack *Arkansas*. The ironclad leaked badly and could not be moved, all but 28 men of Brown's crew were hospitalized, and no replacements were expected until the following day.

Like most operations with Davis, the attack started two hours late. *Essex* rounded De Soto Point and came under fire from the upper water battery. Lagging behind came *Queen of the West*, which by a misunderstanding had been stopped by Davis. Evidence suggests that Davis considered *Queen* a standby vessel and that he neglected to tell Porter to watch for Ellet to join in the attack.

At 5:00 a.m. Brown was ashore, but as soon as Vicksburg's batteries opened, he hurried down to the ram. He had only enough men on board to fight two guns. He soon spotted Porter's ironclad *Essex* sheering toward them and made ready to receive her. Expecting to be rammed, and

Right: Mounting guns was never easy in the field, but a simple tripod with a hoist was usually enough to lift a bronze Parrott, slide a carriage under it, set it on its mount, and hoist it into a vessel.

Below right: Tinclads like *Forest Rose* became some of the handiest vessels in the Mississippi Squadron. They could go almost anywhere while serving as a gunboat, tug, transport, or supply vessel.

Below: On a Union warship, barely a day passed without exercising the gun crew. Eleven-inch Dahlgrens required about ten men and a gun captain to perform the process, and usually a powder monkey to bring up charges.

just before the impact, he let go the bowline and drifted stern on. Porter struck a glancing blow that caromed *Essex* into the bank. Both ironclads exchanged fire while Porter made a desperate effort to back. Several hundred sharpshooters came down from the city with howitzers and began ringing shots off *Essex's* 1-inch plating. For 10 minutes Porter found himself in a hornet's nest. He finally backed away, but instead of rejoining Davis's squadron, he escaped downriver and joined Farragut.

As *Essex* steamed off, Ellet moved into position in midstream and attempted to line-up on *Arkansas'* vulnerable beam. By doing so, *Queen* lost a little headway. Fifty yards from *Arkansas* she struck an eddy, causing the boat to veer at a sharper angle and lose more momentum. Brown slacked off on the hawser and went ahead on the starboard screw, coming about so that the ram could present her prow to *Queen*. *Arkansas* opened with two broadside guns, jarring *Queen* moments before impact. Ellet delivered a hard but glancing blow that sheared several lengths of plating off the ironclad's beam. Had Ellet struck *Arkansas* head on, he would likely have gone with *Queen* to the bottom. Instead, *Queen* bounded off the ironclad's forward quarter and grounded near shore.

The same howitzers that fired on *Essex* now opened on *Queen,* sending dozens of balls into her heavy planking and through the cabins. Brown also opened with his stern guns and sent two shells across *Queen's* deck, neither of which exploded. Though *Queen* sustained a several battering, she suffered no serious injuries.

Ellet backed off the bank and steamed up the river. Much to his disgust, he found *Essex* nowhere in sight, and Davis's gunboats had withdrawn around the point. "I had the undivided attention of all the enemy's batteries and sharpshooters," he grumbled to Stanton, and "the consequences were that the *Queen* was completely riddled with balls and very much damaged." It appeared to Ellet that Davis would do anything to shed the Ram Fleet, and if necessary, one boat at a time.

Porter, rather than Ellet, missed a marvelous opportunity to capture *Arkansas*. Brown had only 34 men on board, six of them being officers. Instead of coming head on, Porter swerved, and at the moment of collision, the guns of both vessels were muzzle to muzzle. Each fired broadsides, but Porter's Dahlgren's drove plates through the forward starboard port, and the second shot passed diagonally through the gundeck, killing eight and wounding six – nearly half of Brown's crew. "Had Porter… thrown fifty men on our upper deck," said Brown, "he might have made fast to us with a hawser, and with little additional loss might have taken the *Arkansas*."

Because Porter abandoned the fight, the remnants of Brown's crew had just enough time to reload and send a broadside into *Queen*. Brown claimed that *Queen* butted *Arkansas* "so gently that we hardly felt the shock." The statement made good fodder for the Rebel press, but Lieutenant George Gift, an officer on board, admitted that *Queen's* prow "made a hole through our side and caused the ship to roll and careened heavily, but we knew in an instant that no serious damage had been done…." Gift's more accurate version had no effect on General Van Dorn, who joyously wired Jefferson Davis, "An attempt made this morning by two ironclad rams to sink the *Arkansas*. The failure so complete that it was almost ridiculous." Had anyone checked the alignment of the ram's engines, they might not have been so comforted. Though unknown at the time, the engines' connecting rods had absorbed the shock, but the hidden damage would not manifest itself for several days to come.

With the river level dropping, Farragut turned his squadron downriver and regrettably left *Arkansas* behind. He continued to watch for her, placing *Essex* and several gunboats at Baton Rouge to intercept the ironclad should she make a run for New Orleans. Davis wanted nothing to do with the ram, but instead of remaining above Vicksburg to secure the upper portion of the river he returned to Memphis. Once again the Confederacy enjoyed free and

Above: The U.S.S. *Choctaw* **presented one of the strangest vessels in the Mississippi Squadron. Though rated as an ironclad, the huge vessel could make only two knots against the current and carried only seven guns.**

Right: During an effort to flank Vicksburg, one of General Butler's pipe dreams had been to dig a canal across the De Soto peninsula and divert the current of the Mississippi enough to allow for the passage of boats.

untroubled use of the river between Memphis and Baton Rouge, reopening to commerce the watersheds of the Yazoo, Arkansas, and Red Rivers.

Brown worked around the clock getting *Arkansas* battle-ready, but during a quick trip to Grenada, Mississippi, he fell ill. While there, he received a telegram from Lieutenant Henry Stevens, the executive officer then in command, who stated that General Van Dorn wanted *Arkansas* taken down to Baton Rouge to cooperate with General Breckinridge's attack on the city. Brown wired back for the ram not to be moved until he returned. When Van Dorn insisted that Stevens not wait for Brown, the lieutenant asked advice of the area navy commander, Captain William F. Lynch, who instructed him to go to Breckinridge's aid. Stevens knew there were problems with the ram's engines, but nobody on site had any experience with a screw vessel or short-stroke engines. Nevertheless, at 2:00 a.m. on August 3, Stevens cut loose, swung into the current, and steamed downriver at eight knots.

Breckinridge planned to attack the Union force at Baton Rouge on the morning of August 5. He expected his brigade to be shelled by the Union gunboats lying off the city, and for this reason he wanted *Arkansas* on hand to drive them off. Stevens made good progress until midnight on the morning of the attack. Twenty-two miles from Baton Rouge the starboard engine broke down, and the engineer said she must be tied up for repairs. Mechanics worked through the night re-aligning the engine and at eight o'clock pushed off.

After covering 14 miles, a connecting rod

broke, and Stevens again tied-up along the bank, this time to forge a sleeve. Men worked through the day, and at times they could hear the distant rumble of Union naval guns bombarding Breckinridge's 3,000 infantry. Union General Thomas Williams, who had spent the spring unsuccessfully digging a canal across the base of the De Soto peninsula, garrisoned the city with a force of the same size. Towards evening, the sound of artillery fire subsided. Stevens sensed an urgency to be there, but the ram could not be moved. In the dim light of kerosene lamps, work in the engine room continued through the night.

Early in the morning, Stevens shoved off once more. After steaming a few miles downriver, the engine room reported more trouble but could not be certain of its cause. Out came the blacksmith's forge for the second time. In the meantime, Breckinridge's infantry killed General Thomas and pushed his force back upon the river. Union gunboats picked up the slack, pounded the advancing Confederates, and forced Breckinridge to retire to the outskirts of the city.

In 1862, Baton Rouge lay at the end of a straight section of river four miles below an upper bend. *Arkansas* had rounded the bend

and gone ashore in sight of Baton Rouge. At 8:00 a.m. on August 6 she was spotted, and four Union gunboats – *Essex*, *Cayuga*, *Katahdin*, and *Sumter* – started up the river to engage her. Stevens conferred with his officers, who unanimously agreed to attack. "We had not steamed any distance," said Master's Mate Wilson, "when the port engine broke. The ship was then headed for shore, and in a few moments the starboard engine suddenly gave way and we drifted toward the enemy in a helpless condition, they opening fire upon us."

In conning her ashore, the helmsman got the ram entangled in a group of submerged cypress stumps, and she lay there with only her stern guns bearing on the enemy. *Essex* stayed out of range, far enough away that neither vessel could do harm to the other. With the ironclad's engines beyond repair, Stevens knew it would only be a matter of time before she would fall into the hands of the enemy. The crew set to work opening the magazines, setting powder trails, scattering shells and cartridges about, and breaking up the machinery. After loading the guns and running them out, the crew shoved her into the current and fled with nothing more than their side arms and the

clothing on their backs.

Arkansas drifted downriver, her guns discharging as the fire touched them off. Porter gave her a wide berth, and for an hour she floated toward Baton Rouge. A few minutes after noon she blew up with a terrific explosion that sent her casemate and plates soaring into the air and the rest of her plunging to the bottom.

The career of the ironclad *Arkansas* lasted but 23 days but included, as one observer wrote, "so much action that there probably never was another vessel that averaged anything like as much fighting per day as did the *Arkansas*."

Among the many ironies of the ram's brief career, none was more distinctive than the cause that led to her destruction. For several days as she lay at Vicksburg, the ram had faced the guns of two squadrons – Farragut's and Davis's – and on two occasions she scared away the ironclad *Essex*. Though William "Dirty Bill" Porter attempted to take credit for destroying her, his lies cost him his career. The vessel that crippled *Arkansas* was Alfred Ellet's unarmed battering ram *Queen of the West*. The butt had disarranged her poorly mounted engines and sealed her fate. Years later a member of *Arkansas'* crew admitted to Charles D. Flaconer, who served on *Queen*, that the butt had sealed the ram's fate by jolting her engines out of alignment. The Ellets had come into the war because they sought prize money, but for the destruction of *Arkansas* they would never receive a cent.

The year of 1862 had been hard on Mallory's ironclad program, but there would be more.

Left: A contemporary depiction of the erroneous report of how Porter's *Essex* destroyed the Rebel ram *Arkansas*, a claim that would cost Porter his career.

Below: What actually happened was that when Alfred Ellet's *Queen of the West* rammed *Arkansas* at her moorage below Vicksburg, she disarranged the ironclad's engines, forcing her crew to abandon the ram and set her afire weeks later above Baton Rouge.

CHAPTER SEVEN

THE $8.23 IRONCLAD

When the Confederacy lacked artillery and wanted to delude the Union into thinking that a particular defensive position contained rows of heavy cannon, they cut logs, hewed them to size, painted them black, and laid them behind a mound of dirt to give the impression of a heavily fortified earthwork. To add to the deception, they sometimes mounted the logs on gun carriages. Lieutenant Charles "Sazez" Read did the same with the C.S.S. *Clarence*, a small sailing vessel armed with one small howitzer and a menacing broadside of harmless wooden guns. The ruse often worked, and the wooden counterfeits became known as "Quaker guns."

During the early months of 1863, Rear Admiral David D. Porter, commanding the Union's Mississippi Squadron above Vicksburg, encountered a rash of unexpected problems having no simple solution. Wily Confederates captured Union gunboats that should not have been captured and turned them against the Union. One partially submerged gunboat, a new ironclad having a battery fore and aft of 9- and 11-inch guns, lay out of Porter's reach below Vicksburg. While Confederate crews worked assiduously to raise the ironclad, Porter needed to find a way to destroy the vessel without risking another gunboat from his weakened squadron. What he devised gave new meaning to the term "Quaker gun."

I n September 1862, Union Secretary of the Navy Welles removed Davis from command of the Mississippi Squadron and replaced him with David Dixon Porter. Having just censured Porter's brother for falsely claiming to have destroyed the C.S.S. *Arkansas*, Welles may have questioned his own judgment in placing another Porter in so important a command. If to no one else, the Secretary at least explained his reasoning in his diary, writing, "He has, however, stirring and positive qualities, is fertile of resources, has great energy, excessive and sometimes not over-scrupulous ambition, is impressed with and boastful of his powers, [and] given to exaggeration of himself – a Porter infirmity… it is a question, with this mixture of good and bad traits, how he will succeed." So Welles straddled his uncertainties by making forty-nine-year-old Davy Porter an acting rear admiral instead of a full rear admiral and sent him to the Mississippi to employ his "fertile resources" on the enemy.

In November, there had been a wordy scuffle between Welles and Secretary of War Stanton during a cabinet meeting over the unification of Ellet's command with Porter. Lincoln gave the Ram Fleet to Welles, who never wanted it. Stanton, who lost the battle, promoted Alfred Ellet to brigadier general and the youthful Charles Rivers Ellet to colonel. Alfred Ellet went to St. Louis to organize the Mississippi Marine Brigade, and Charlie Ellet took command of the Ram Fleet. An acting rear admiral now operated the only flotilla in the Navy commanded by Army officers.

Porter had a preference for daring young officers, and he soon became acquainted with Charlie Ellet. At first, he did not know what to think of the brazen young colonel. But when the big Confederate steamer *City of Vicksburg* slipped into the moorage once occupied by the C.S.S. *Arkansas*, Charlie Ellet volunteered to run down in the ram *Queen of the West* and put her out of business. Porter thought the effort too risky, but Ellet persisted. On February 1, 1863, Porter finally approved the mission, mainly because he hoped to get one or two vessels below Vicksburg to stop the flow of supplies by river to the city's defenders.

Queen now carried a pair of small Parrotts

mounted on the deck. Porter suggested they be loaded with turpentine balls and shot into the enemy steamer to set her on fire. He told Ellet to make the attack at night, as it was more important to get *Queen* below Vicksburg than to lose her under the city's batteries.

Ellet banked *Queen* with cotton bales to make her shot-proof and early in the morning started down the river. For added protection, the steerage had been rearranged, but the pilot complained that he could not see his way. Ellet stopped the ram to make adjustments. Hours passed as the crew worked in the dark to return the wheel to the pilothouse. As *Queen* got underway, the first yellow streaks of dawn cracked the eastern sky. By the time she rounded De Soto Point, daylight flooded the valley.

Instead of postponing the attack, Ellet surged around the bend and bore toward his target. Vicksburg's batteries opened, but the ram moved so swiftly that only three shells nipped her. Coming fast abeam of *City of Vicksburg* , the helmsman came hard to port, swung across the river, struck an eddy, rammed the vessel at an angle, and glanced off her beam. Ellet, having loaded the starboard gun with turpentine balls, emptied it into the transport's upper deck and set the ship on fire. Shells from the

Above: Welles always accused David Porter (center) of being overly ambitious and difficult to control, but Porter got things done. Welles eventually promoted him to Rear Admiral and transferred him to the Atlantic.

Below: With cotton bales piled high to give protection to *Queen of the West*, 19-year-old Charles Rivers Ellet loaded his Parrott with turpentine balls, sped through heavy enemy fire, and mortally damaged *City of Vicksburg*.

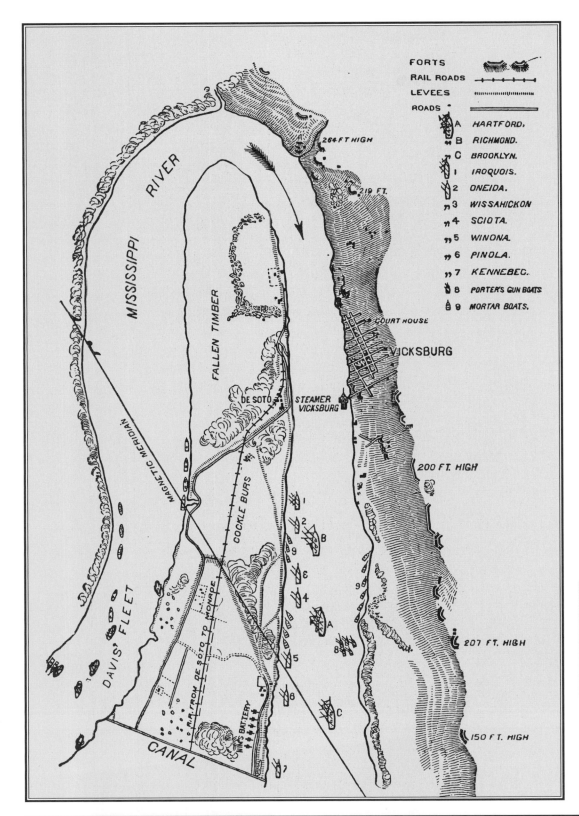

FORTS
RAIL ROADS
LEVEES
ROADS

A   HARTFORD.
B   RICHMOND.
C   BROOKLYN.
1   IROQUOIS.
2   ONEIDA.
3   WISSAHICKON
4   SCIOTA.
5   WINONA.
6   PINOLA.
7   KENNEBEC.
8   PORTER'S GUN BOATS
9   MORTAR BOATS.

Much to the chagrin of Farragut and Davis, the Confederate steamship *City of Vicksburg* slipped by the Union squadron with a cargo of supplies and docked at the town's wharf. No Union gunboat commander except for Charles Rivers Ellet volunteered to run Vicksburg's batteries and destroy the vessel. He was now a colonel and seemed willing to take on any mission in which there was a high probability of him being killed.

Below: The Ellets were always getting themselves in trouble with Admiral Porter. Alfred Ellet sent two rams past Vicksburg at daybreak, losing *Lancaster* to shell fire. *Switzerland* came through with heavy damage.

town's batteries plunged into *Queen's* cotton bales and soon set them ablaze. Fearing the loss of his boat, Ellet disengaged, and while men kicked the burning bales overboard, *Queen* beat a hasty retreat downriver – her woodwork battered and her mission ostensibly unfulfilled. Though *City of Vicksburg* quenched the flames, *Queen* had cracked her hull and she never sailed again.

Porter was annoyed by Ellet's daylight attack, but was pleased to learn that *Queen* had passed Vicksburg with only slight damage. So, on February 2, he ordered her down to the mouth of Red River with instructions to destroy trans-Mississippi traffic but not to lose his ship. Once again, Ellet did not wait until nightfall. He ran Warrenton's battery during the afternoon, sped down to Natchez at 20 knots, captured three prizes near the mouth of Red River, and herded them back upriver. His trophies, however, could not keep pace with *Queen*. With his bunkers low, Ellet removed the prisoners and set fire to the boats before reaching Grand Gulf.

Delighted with Ellet's successful outing, Porter floated down a barge filled with 20,000 bushels of coal and sent him back to Red River, this time with a 30-pounder Parrott and the tender *De Soto*. He warned Ellet to watch out for the C.S.S. *William H. Webb*, the only armed vessel cruising the Red. "If you get the first crack at her," Porter wrote, "you will sink her, and if she gets the first crack at you she will sink you." Before pushing off on February 10, Ellet received one final message from Porter: "Don't be surprised to see the *Indianola* below. Don't mistake her for a rebel; she looks something like the [river ironclad] *Chillicothe*."

Porter's long-sought objective to blockade the Mississippi between Port Hudson and Vicksburg was about to be realized. To ensure success he needed a gunboat working in tandem with the speedy *Queen*. *Indianola* joined Porter's squadron on February 7, three days before Ellet departed on his second raid, and the admiral's only mistake was not sending the vessels downriver together.

Built at Cincinnati for a cost of $200,000, *Indianola* was a grotesque rendition of a river ironclad embracing many new features, not all of them good. She carried four guns, two 11-inch Dahlgrens in the bow and two 9-inch Dahlgrens aft. Her deck was flat and barely

Right: Though most sailors liked their whiskers, they all carried a shaving kit with ditty bag and filled with grooming articles. Flaggs Shaving Soap made a little lather but was bought from a land-lubber.

above water. Her power plant was most unusual because she came equipped with twin propellers as well as two paddlewheels and an engine for each. She carried heavy armor on her bows but little aft. Her twenty-eight-year-old captain, Lieutenant Commander George W. Brown, sought an opportunity to distinguish himself in a war that promised quick promotion to the dauntless, so he spent a few days prepping the vessel before taking her past Vicksburg's batteries. He discovered the ironclad could generate only about six knots in still water, but this did not particularly trouble him. Nobody told Brown that *Indianola* represented the least suited vessel for the enterprise because she carried no guns in broadside. Porter, however, intended to find a way into the upper Yazoo so that Grant could flank Vicksburg, and he needed his other gunboats for the task.

In the meantime, Colonel Ellet went on a tear. Instead of patiently waiting for *Indianola* as directed, he raided down the Atchafalaya one day and up the Red the next. During *Queen's* escapades, First Master James D. Thompson received a disabling wound in the leg. Ellet retaliated and burned three plantations. When he learned that a steamer had passed up the Red with guns for *William H. Webb*, he began the pursuit. On the morning of February 14 he trapped *New Era*, loaded with passengers and corn, running downstream. He held the boat as a prize and continued the ascent of the Red.

From *New Era's* passengers, Ellet learned that three steamers had docked upstream at Gordon's Landing. He also learned that the landing was protected by Fort Taylor, a small earthwork still under development.

When Charles Rivers Ellet started down the Mississippi, he departed from a plantation located on the opposite side of the river between Vicksburg and Warrenton. His journey took him to Port Hudson, where Confederates had built another fort, and then up the Red River to Fort De Russy where, through a combination of taking unnecessary and desperate risks combined with bad luck, he lost the boat under his command.

Below: On most areas of the Mississippi River, the only way for sailors to get to shore was by boat. In this photo, two groups came ashore by dinghy, the other two groups by yawl.

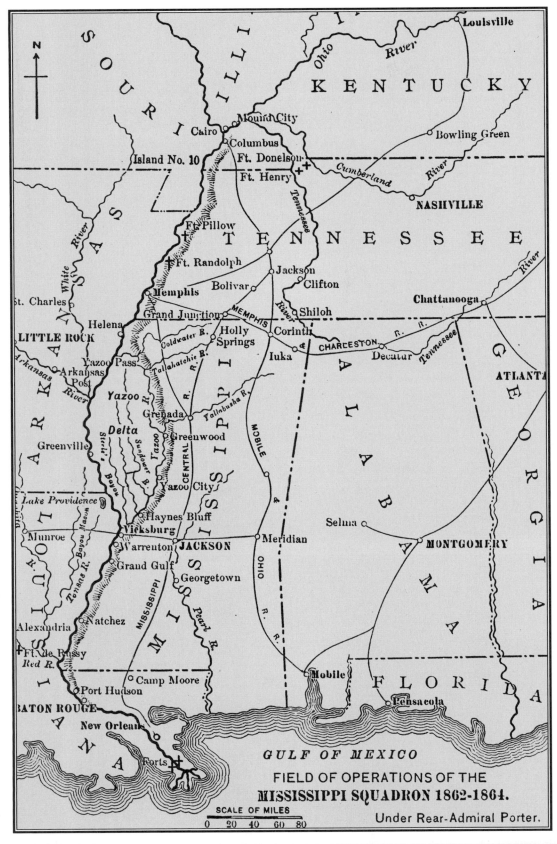

FIELD OF OPERATIONS OF THE
MISSISSIPPI SQUADRON 1862-1864.

SCALE OF MILES
0   20   40   60   80

Under Rear-Admiral Porter.

He assigned a prize crew to *New Era* and continued up the river.

Captain John Kelso commanded Fort Taylor. He had been forewarned of *Queen's* approach and prepared to meet her by bracketing all of his guns on a bend just below the fort. Ellet reached the bend at sunset, February 14, and as he inched *Queen* around the point he opened fire on three steamers attempting to flee from Gordon's Landing. Kelso replied with four 32-pounders, dropping the first shots a few yards off *Queen's* stern. Ellet shouted to the pilot, Thomas W. Garvey, to reverse the engines. Garvey panicked and grounded *Queen* on the exact point where Kelso had ranged in his artillery.

Shells crashed through *Queen's* deck, sliced through steam pipes, and enveloped the boat in clouds of scalding vapor. Men poured topside from the engine room and, before Ellet could control the situation, the crew deserted their guns. Men tossed bales of cotton overboard, jumped into the river, and began rafting down to the waiting *De Soto*. Ellet ordered the yawl lowered to remove the wounded, but the crew had gone off with it. Finding himself alone with the wounded, he dove into water, grabbed a floating bale of cotton, and drifted down to *De Soto*.

With First Master Thompson and other injured men still on board *Queen*, Ellet rounded up a group of men who volunteered to go back to the boat to save her. If that failed, they agreed to remove the wounded and set the boat on fire. As the rescue party climbed on board *Queen*, one of

Above: A six-man crew swabs an army field howitzer mounted on the deck of a gunboat, while an officer appears more interested in the camera. Because powder charges were loaded through the muzzle, swabbing was needed to quench residual

Above left: On February 13, 1863, U.S.S. *Indianola* ran the batteries at night in an effort to join *Queen of the West* off Red River. After pasing safely through heavy fire, her commander, George Brown, would find nothing but trouble ahead.

Left: Of all the mischief caused by the Ellets, nothing surpassed losing the *Queen of the West* to Confederates laying in wait at Fort De Russy, and the consequences that led to the loss of the U.S.S. *Indianola*.

Above: Most 100-pounder Parrotts were mounted on pivots, but this piece worked off a stationary mounting, making it far less effective. The barrel could be elevated or depressed, but not moved to lateral positions.

the volunteers peered into the darkness and spotted three boatloads of Confederate soldiers rowing toward the vessel. They could neither remove Thompson nor set the boat on fire with wounded men still on it. Those that could get away jumped into the yawl and fled, but they could not find *De Soto*. Small arms fire from shore, accompanied by the sound of many voices demanding her surrender, had driven the steamer ten miles downriver. Ellet waited for the yawl while contemplating his options – to escape or be captured.

In the dark and desperate dash downriver, *De Soto* lost both rudders. In unmanageable condition she drifted down to *New Era*. Ellet ordered *De Soto* destroyed and transferred his crew to *New Era*. In his eagerness to get away, he neglected to check *New Era's* supply of fuel and left a barge full of coal for the enemy. At 10:00 p.m., as the boat started down the river, a savage thunderstorm struck. Wind-driven rain blinded the steerage and, after the downpour stopped, fog smothered the valley. As the boat crept cautiously down the

river, a reporter who had shipped on *Queen*, wrote, "We know to a certainty that we shall be pursued. The gunboat *Webb* is lying at Alexandria, and we know that she will start in pursuit of us.... Our only hope is in reaching the Mississippi quickly."

During the bungled effort to capture more prizes, Ellet lost 62 men, and the remnants of his crew worked extra hard lightening the vessel as she bumped down the Red. The crew jettisoned the corn, forgetting that much of it could be used to stoke the firebox. Not until they reached the Mississippi on the morning of the 15th did Ellet learn that the vessel, having exhausted its fuel, would have to be taken ashore so men could cut wood. Pilot Garvey, who had run *Queen* aground off Fort Taylor, now ran *New Era* aground off Ellis Cliffs. Suspecting Garvey of treason, Ellet placed him under arrest. Were it not for the fog, Confederate batteries on Ellis Cliffs would have knocked *New Era* to pieces.

Ellet did not get *New Era* off the bar until late afternoon. Doing so damaged the boat's paddles, which had already been injured by storm debris awash in the river. He could not make much headway and stopped frequently to cut more cypress. On the morning of February 16, as *New Era* chugged toward Natchez, a lookout hollered, "There's a gunboat ahead of us." The crew believed that *Webb* had passed during the night and lay in wait for *New Era*, but above the thin veil of fog Ellet recognized the smokestacks of a Union ironclad. "It's the *Indianola*," someone shouted, and a cheer resonated across the valley. *New Era* tied up alongside *Indianola*, and for the first time in more than 48 hours,

Ellet's men enjoyed a hot meal and fresh clothes.

While carpenters repaired *New Era's* paddlewheels, Brown and Ellet sat together in the captain's cabin and discussed strategy. After coaling, Ellet would take the point and go downriver in search of the Confederates' *Webb*. Cloaked by fog, *Indianola* would follow, but only close enough to stay in contact with *New Era*. Should Ellet sight *Webb*, he would come about and lure the enemy under the guns of *Indianola*. The plan almost worked. Ellet spotted *Webb* off Ellis Cliffs and toggled the

Below: A selection of Confederate heavy artillery projectiles. Top left, a 5.3-inch Mullane shell for a rifled 18-pounder; top center, a 5.8-inch Selma shell for a rifled 24-pounder; top right, a 6.4-inch Brooke solid bolt for a 100-pounder. Bottom left, a 6.4-inch Read shell for a 100-pounder; bottom right, a 6.2-inch Read shell for a 100-pounder.

steam whistle to signal *Indianola*. Having no guns on *New Era*, the crew hooked a hose to the boilers and prepared for battle.

Lieutenant Colonel William S. Lovell, commanding *Webb*, had spoken with prisoners captured during the Fort Taylor fiasco and learned that Ellet expected to be met by an ironclad. *Webb*, a 656-ton wooden steam ram, was larger than *Indianola*, but she carried only one 32-pounder and a pair of brass 6-pounders. Lovell spotted *Indianola* lurking in the fog and beat a hasty retreat, taking with him the transports *Grand Duke*, *Grand Era*, and *Doubloon*, which had been

following with infantry. *Indianola* fired two 11-inch shells at the rapidly vanishing ram, but both dropped into the river. *Webb's* flight filled Brown with a sense of false confidence, leading him to believe that the ram would not fight.

Brown and Ellet moved down to the mouth of Red River and collaborated on another plan. Porter's instructions to *Indianola's* commander had been quite clear. He had told Brown to not separate from Ellet, and "whatever you undertake try and have no failure. When you have not the means of certain success, undertake nothing;

Below: When David Porter took command of the Mississippi squadron, he had his choice of *Benton* or *Black Hawk* as his flagship. He choose *Black Hawk*, the vessel being much more commodious and comfortable.

a failure is equal to defeat."

With *Queen* captured, Brown no longer had the "means of certain success." Nevertheless, Ellet made a case for going back up the Red to salvage *Queen*, along with his own reputation. Having learned that the ram was under repair, Brown agreed to the plan, mainly because Ellet assured him that *Indianola's* guns would be able to turn back any attack by *Webb* and the captured *Queen*. Taking advice from a young colonel could lead to grim consequences, especially since Ellet, after expressing his opinions, then departed with his rickety

riverboat *New Era* for Vicksburg.

Aboard *Indianola*, Brown wisely decided not to go up the Red, but he unwisely dallied around its mouth for five days. On February 21 he learned from an informant that *Queen* had been repaired, and with *Webb*, supported by several cottonclads, would start down the Red to attack him. Rather than making every effort to get out of harm's way, Brown steamed slowly up the Mississippi, stopping at plantations for cotton to barricade his decks. He also towed his two barges, thinking that if Porter sent another vessel downriver she might need

coal. *Indianola* had a head start, but by towing barges she made little more than two knots an hour.

Webb and *Queen* had the advantage of running with the current when descending the Red. Major Joseph L. Brent had replaced General Lovell, organizer of the River Defense Fleet, and on February 22 he shoved off from Gordon's Landing with *Queen*, *Webb*, *Grand Era*, and *Dr. Beatty*. *Indianola* had more than a 90-mile head start, but Brent made up half the distance quickly as he led the flotilla down the flooded Red. When the boats swung into the Mississippi, however, *Grand Era* and *Dr. Beatty*, heavily laden with bales of cotton for breastworks, slackened the pace.

Unless *Indianola* could find another two or three knots of speed, Brown would have to fight her guns. Though he had plenty of fuel to reach safety, he clung to the coal barges. He moved so slowly that sharpshooters along shore kept up a steady fire by doing no more than leisurely walking the bank. At noon Brown passed Grand Gulf, his engines laboring against the current.

Late afternoon, February 24, Brown spotted trails of smoke far downriver and suspected it came from the Confederate vessels. Night fell, and the lookout on deck reported lights three miles astern. Brown had just passed Palmyra Island, about 25 river miles below Vicksburg, and cleared for action. Assured by Ellet that the ironclad's 11-inch shell guns would make easy work of *Webb* and *Queen*, Brown came about and faced the Confederate flotilla. While waiting, he pulled in the two coal barges and lashed them to his beams. Feeling quite safe, he ordered the forward guns run out and steamed downriver to meet the Rebels.

Major Brent led the charge on *Queen*, with *Webb* following about 500 yards astern. Lashed together, *Dr. Beatty* and *Grand Era* trailed two miles to the rear. An overcast moon shed good light for ramming, but not so good for sighting-in the bulky Dahlgrens. *Indianola's* forward gun crews peered out the ports. Because of kerosene lanterns dimly glowing behind them, they could barely see the approaching enemy. But from the deck of *Queen*, Brent spotted the shadowy shape of *Indianola* moving slowly along the bank. Neither vessel fired, but as *Queen* closed to 150 yards Brent opened with both Parrotts and a 12-pounder howitzer. The shots whizzed away, lost in the darkness.

At almost point blank range, Brown's Dahlgren's opened with two 11-inch shells. Both shots missed. Seeing *Queen* sheer to bear down on his port wheelhouse, Brown backwatered and swung the ironclad sideways to let the barge absorb the impact. *Queen* crushed in the sides of the barge and became entangled, but *Indianola* had no broadside guns to rip her apart. While Brent worked with a crew to clear the wreckage, Rebel sharpshooters went to the bulwarks and blazed away at the ironclad.

Indianola's gunners reloaded just in time to see *Webb*, 70 yards off the bow, pressing forward under a full head of steam. The *Indianola's* 11-inchers roared and missed again. At thirty yards *Webb* replied with her

Below: A full year passed after the loss of *Queen of the West* **before Porter was able to bring his squadron up Red River and, in support of General Nathaniel Banks, capture Alexandria during another inept {poorly directed} army campaign.**

32-pounder, smothering the portholes of both vessels with smoke. Bows on, the two vessels crashed into each other. On both boats the collision knocked everyone off their feet. *Indianola* lost a few plates but crushed in eight feet of *Webb's* bow. Union gunners went back to their Dahlgrens and

quickly reloaded, but *Webb* slipped to starboard and in doing so swept away one of *Indianola's* barges. The impact jarred *Queen* loose and ripped off the other barge. After that, the engagement became general and often at close quarters.

Brent took *Queen* upriver and circled

for another run. With both barges gone, *Indianola's* exposed beams made tempting targets. Nobody in the ironclad's pilot-house could see a thing outside, so Brown went on deck to direct operations. Musket balls spattered off the casemate, and he could not tell whether they were fired from shore or from one of the steamers carrying infantry. He spotted *Queen* up-river, bearing towards him, and ordered the pilot to wheel about and take the blow on the bow. *Queen* struck *Indianola* on the forward quarter, glanced off, and in passing astern absorbed two ineffectual shells from the ironclad's 9-inch after guns. Knocked off his feet while standing on deck, Brown nearly tumbled into the river.

Webb stayed out of the action, enabling *Queen* to steam upriver for the kill. Bearing down on *Indianola* for the fifth time, Brent aimed the ram at the ironclad's starboard

wheelhouse, striking it head on. Planks cracked and plates dribbled off the casemate, but the impact heeled *Queen* over so sharply that Brent feared she would sink. When Charles Ellet had fitted his rams, he had made them superbly durable. *Queen* righted herself, and Brent ordered the crew to standby for another run.

Brown had seen enough. Whether he could get away or not, he decided to try. By doing so he slowly brought *Indianola* about, exposing the vessel's unarmored stern. He did not see *Webb* pressing up the river until one of the aft 9-inch Dahlgrens fired. The shot missed, but *Webb's* attack was right on target.

The impact sliced into *Indianola's* stern, cracking timbers and tearing away the starboard rudder. "Through and through," reported Brent, "crushing and dashing aside her iron plates, the sharp bow of the *Webb* penetrated as if it were going to pass entirely through the ship." Water poured through the fractures and flooded into the

hold, causing the vessel to list aft. *Queen* ranged above, and Brown knew that, if struck again, his ironclad would go to the bottom and take with her the crew. He tried to work the vessel to the Louisiana bank where he could blow her up, but *Webb* followed closely as *Indianola* hobbled toward shore.

Dr. Beatty came up, her decks swarming with infantry ready to board. Still too far from shore, Brown shouted, "I surrender!" The crews of *Webb* and *Beatty* attached hawsers to *Indianola* and tried to tow the prize downriver. The ironclad quickly filled, forcing the boats to pull her to a bar near Hurricane Island where she settled in 10 feet of water. Brent looked her over and knew she could be raised.

For 90 minutes Admiral Porter listened to the spasmodic firing of Brown's guns and considered it a bad omen. He suspected the ironclad had run into trouble. But during those minutes Brown fired only 11 shots from the 11-inch guns in the bow and six

from the 9-inch guns aft, and no more than three shells ever struck the enemy. Brown later reported only one killed, one wounded, and seven missing on *Indianola*. Brent got off even easier, losing two killed and one wounded on *Queen* and one wounded on *Webb*, but he collected 100 prisoners, including Brown, and a repairable ironclad with four big guns.

The loss of *Indianola* wrecked Porter's plans to control the river below Vicksburg. What made him even madder was Ellet's misadventures; his disregard of orders had led to the capture of two Union vessels. Both boats could now be used by the enemy, making Porter's chores even harder.

The intentions of the enemy became quite clear when on February 25 Brent brought *Queen of the West* up to Warrenton to obtain pumps. The following day he carried 100 workmen downriver. For protection, they mounted two 6-pounders on *Indianola's* deck and started work to raise her.

On March 2 Porter reported to Welles on

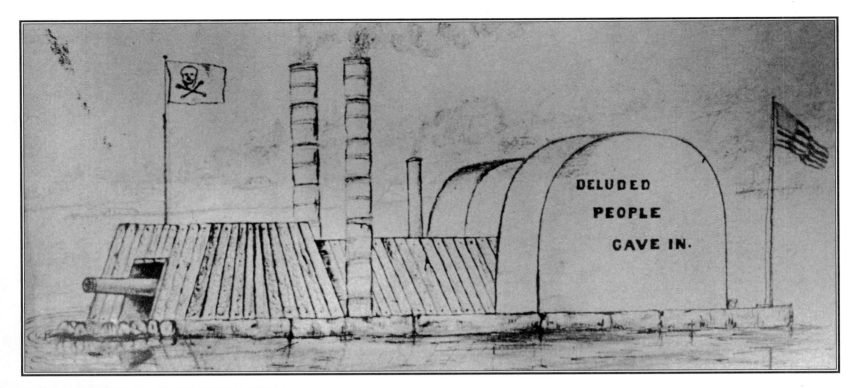

the loss of *Indianola*, writing, "The rams *Webb* and *Queen of the West* attacked her twenty-five miles from here, and rammed her until she surrendered. All of which can be traced to a noncompliance of my instructions.... If she is not sunk, she may be used against [Farragut's] fleet." Welles replied: "She is too formidable to be left at large, and must be destroyed."

Porter refused to risk another ironclad on a rescue mission, yet he shared Welles's view that *Indianola* must be rendered irreparable. Being an inveterate prankster, Porter believed the Confederates could be bluffed, so he conceived what he called "a cheap expedient." He put carpenters to work on an old flat-bottomed coal barge, fitting it with a raft of logs that increased its length to 300 feet. Behind low-slung bulwarks, the men built an enormous but flimsy casemate out of rough lumber and canvas and added a pair of giant hollow wheelhouses and a pilothouse. Into the casemate they cut five gaping portholes, behind which they rigged five huge wooden guns. For towering smokestacks, workmen nailed together dozens of pork barrels and set them on two pots filled with tar and oakum – flammable ingredients that when ignited discharged a thick black smoke similar to soft coal. To add the texture of credibility, an old yawl hung from broken davits on each beam. Having completed their construction work, the builders smeared the craft with tar and mud, and on the wheelhouse painted the inscription "DELUDED PEOPLE, CAVE IN."

Porter claimed the project cost $8.23 and 12 hours work. With the national emblem nailed to a pole aft and a black banner emblazoned with a skull and crossbones forward, tugs took her up to De Soto Point and in the early morning hours of February 26 set "Black Terror" adrift.

As the huge, unmanned dummy approached Vicksburg's upper water battery, signals flashed across the heights, guns roared, and projectiles splattered into the river. Drifting through the barrage undamaged, the creature bumped against the west bank below the city. Soldiers from

Above: Porter's so-called $8.23 dummy ironclad, built from an old coal barge and fitted with Quaker guns, so terrified Confederates attempting to raise the U.S.S. *Indianola* that they blew her up and abandoned her.

Left: After word reached Rebel publishers of the destruction of *Indianola*, they condemned Confederate General John Pemberton for the action and asked, "Why build costly ironclads when $8.23 will do?"

General Sherman's command pushed it back into the current and pointed its nose downriver. They followed the craft for a few miles and, when another eddy carried it ashore, they gave it another push. A four-knot current picked up "Black Terror," and the troops reported last seeing it moving at good speed right down the center of the river.

From Major General Carter L. Stevenson's command center at Vicksburg, Major Brent received word that a powerful ironclad was pressing down the river towards Warrenton. Brent took *Queen* upriver and caught a quick glimpse of "Black Terror" heading straight for his boats. Without losing a moment of valuable time, he returned to Warrenton and ordered *Dr. Beatty* and *Grand Era* to cut loose and run. In the panic to get underway, *Queen* rammed *Grand Era*, stove in her after port quarter, and all but disabled her. From his headquarters in Jackson, Mississippi, General John C. Pemberton wired Stevenson at Vicksburg, "You must, if possible, blow up the *Indianola*."

Brent stopped briefly at Hurricane Island and removed half of the salvage crew from the ironclad. The others nervously volunteered to remain behind, serve the guns, and refloat her. As night fell on February 26, men with overly exercised imaginations sighted a phantom squadron of Union vessels approaching from above. Whatever they saw created an instant panic. They spiked *Indianola's* guns, tossed the fieldpieces into the river, lit a fuse to the magazine, and pushed off in boats for shore. As they reached the woods, *Indianola* exploded with a deafening roar. Off Young's Point, Admiral Porter heard the detonation and guessed its source.

A week later a detachment of wandering Confederates found "Black Terror" stuck on a mud bank. The *Vicksburg Whig* newspaper confirmed *Indianola's* fate, writing, "The Yankee barge sent down the river last week was reported to be an ironclad gunboat. The authorities, thinking that this monster would retake the *Indianola*, immediately issued an order to blow her up…. Who is to blame for this folly? […] It would seem that we had no use for gunboats on the Mississippi, as a coal barge is magnified into a monster, and our authorities immediately order a boat – that would have been worth a small army to us – to be blown up." A few days later the *Richmond Examiner* picked up the story and suggested that if Porter could build a few more monitors of logs and canvas, the Union Navy could do without ironclads and win the war with dummies.

The Confederates, after losing *Indianola*, still had *Queen of the West* and *Webb*, but neither boat ever again become a factor in the war on the Mississippi. Porter never undid the damage caused by Ellet, but for $8.23 and a few hours of work, he gave a new meaning to the definition of warfare.

Right: The sailor carried all his tools of war in leather casings – (top) revolver holster, boarding ax, rifle cartridge box, (bottom) pistol cartridge box, percussion cap boxes, and carbine cartridge box.

CHAPTER EIGHT

CHARLESTON-IRONCLADS AND IRON COFFINS

By the summer of 1863, the Confederate ironclad program began to stagnate, not because the ships were not needed, but because those which had been put into service proved to be poor performers. Those built near southern ports along the Atlantic seaboard were meant to go to sea, destroy Union blockading vessels, and reopen the ports to foreign commerce. Most ironclads carried so much weight they could barely stem the tide, and in moderate weather seas washed over the decks, poured through portholes, and inundated the vessels with tons of water. So frustrated did some officers become with the clumsy ironclads that they looked for other ways to break the blockade.

Since the early days of the war, innovators and investors worked on designs that would create a small submersible boat that could steal out of the harbor at night, approach blockading vessels without being seen, and by using a torpedo device, blow a hole in the hull of an enemy warship. Experiments failed first at New Orleans and then at Mobile, until finally all the collective technology came together at Charleston, South Carolina. Without failures and experimental disasters, there would never have been a submarine during the Civil War. But the Confederates gave a new weapon to the world's navies – one that others perfected – and in the process created a little history for themselves.

On September 24, 1862, General Pierre G. T. Beauregard took command of the Department of South Carolina and Georgia and made Charleston his headquarters. He had been there before, where on the morning of April 12, 1861, artillery under his command fired on Fort Sumter and started the war. Charlestonians liked the swarthy Creole from Louisiana, but Beauregard preferred a field command. After being blamed by President Davis for losing the battle of Shiloh in April 1862, Beauregard sought to redeem himself through his new command.

Of all the Confederate seaports along the Atlantic coast, Charleston, though heavily blockaded, remained commercially active. Blockade runners preferred it to Wilmington, North Carolina, and Savannah, Georgia, but which of the three ports they used most often was determined by their point of departure – Bermuda, Nassau, or Havana.

The city of Charleston lay about five miles inside the mouth of its harbor. The main shipping channel carried about 18 feet of water and flowed into the Atlantic off Sullivan's Island, where Fort Moultrie, Battery Beauregard, and Battery Bee guarded the northern entry into the harbor. Two miles across from Sullivan's Island lay Morris Island with Battery Gregg at Cumming's Point and, farther down the island, Battery Wagner and Fort Shaw. Between the two islands lay Fort Sumter. Inside the harbor were another four batteries, and any Union vessel attempting to enter Charleston's harbor came under an instant cross fire from no fewer than four directions.

Jefferson Davis and his cabinet considered Beauregard quarrelsome and unmanageable, so it came as no surprise to them when the general attempted to take control of the naval forces in his department. Navy

A class of Southern submarines known as "Davids" were constantly being tested and on occasion drowning their crews. Here, *David No. 4* had just been brought up from the bottom and set aside for disposition.

Above: A recently captured blockade runner, the famous *R. E. Lee,* had made many runs into Charleston. The Union refitted the steamer at Norfolk, Virginia, and added her to the North Atlantic Blockading Squadron.

Below: The U.S.S. *Santiago de Cuba,* a former packet ship once running between New York and Havana, was purchased by the Union and armed with ten guns as a blockading vessel to chase runners creeping in southern ports.

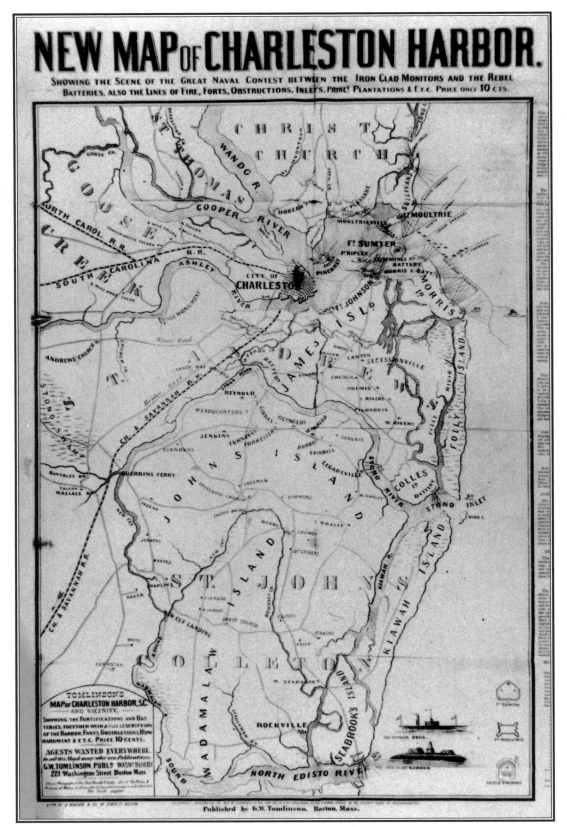

Charleston harbor and much of the surrounding area, as depicted by a contemporary artist, contained batteries bearing on the ocean and on surrounding inlets, such as Stone and Edisto to the south. Once inside the harbor, a hostile vessel entered an area of crossfire capable of blowing a wooden vessel to pieces. Shore batteries had been strategically located as much to protect incoming blockade runners as to ward off enemy attacks.

Secretary Mallory disliked Beauregard and exercised measures to thwart the general's efforts. Charlestonians liked Beauregard much better than they liked Mallory, which made the secretary's job no easier. Yet Beauregard and Mallory had much in common. They both understood the importance of sea power without fully agreeing on how to use it, and they both sought vessels strong enough to disrupt the blockade.

Commodore Duncan M. Ingraham had been in Charleston for nearly a year, and during that time he had assembled a small squadron of wooden gunboats and started construction of two ironclads. A 60 year old native of the city, he had served in the Navy for 50 years. Though no one questioned his personal courage in battle, many of his younger officers described him as "too deliberate," and "overly cautious; a perfect old woman." Such remarks had more to do with the commodore's diminutive appearance and cultured manners than with his competence.

Blockade runners continued to slip in and out of the harbor, some bringing munitions and supplies, others bringing luxury items in exchange for gold and silver. Flag Officer Samuel F. Du Pont, a tall, dignified, and wealthy Union naval officer, commanded the South Atlantic Blockading Squadron that lay off the harbor. His officers tried to nab the fleet-footed runners but, to the flag officer's utter frustration, they could not put an end to the traffic. Du Pont's so-called siege of Charleston never worked, and as months passed he received

Below: The Confederate rams *Palmetto State* and *Chicora*, both sluggish ironclads, make a rare appearance outside Charleston's harbor and for three hours raise havoc among the Union blockaders.

Right: The *Hornet* made many fast passages through the blockade until finally being caught attempting to creep into Wilmington. The Union Navy bought her and commissioned her *Lady Sterling* just as war ended.

Above: Supply vessels and small gunboats crowd the river near a Confederate encampment across from Charleston, where regiments train in the fine art of defending the city against Union attack.

increasing pressure from Navy Secretary Welles to take his squadron into the harbor and capture the city. Rather than complain to Welles, he shared his concerns with Assistant Secretary Fox, writing, "the industry of these Rebels in their harbor defenses is beyond all praise. It has been ceaseless day and night."

After Du Pont's attack failed to materialize, Beauregard continued to apply his engineering skills to improve the harbor's defenses. When Northern newspapers reported that several monitors were on their way to reinforce Du Pont, Beauregard hurried work obstructing the harbor to keep the monitors out. He knew heavy ironclads would be useless in chasing blockade runners and were being sent for one reason – to invade the harbor.

Meanwhile, Commodore Ingraham

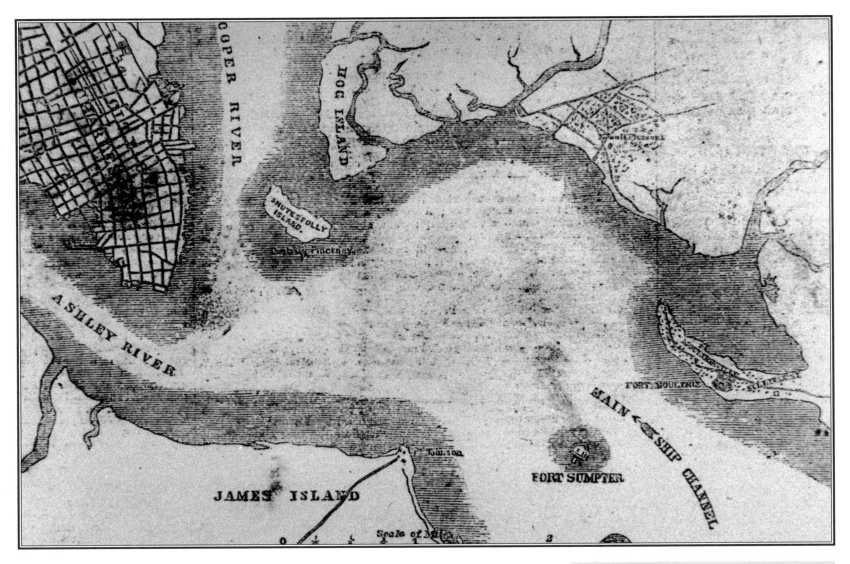

rushed work on his two ironclads – *Chicora* and *Palmetto State*. By November both vessels were ready for service but without crews. Ingraham appealed to Beauregard, who put an honest effort into recruiting seamen from within his ranks but could not produce enough volunteers. In late November a draft arrived from the Yazoo River. It included veterans from the C.S.S. *Arkansas* who filled the vacancies on both ironclads. Compared with other gunboats in the home-based Confederate Navy, Ingraham's squadron contained some of the best officers and seamen in the service. The vessels, however, were not so good.

Financed through fund-raising efforts by the ladies of Charleston, *Chicora* and *Palmetto State* were both 150 feet long, 35 feet in beam, and 12 feet in depth of hold. Like all Confederate ironclads, each featured a sloped casemate armored with 500 tons of iron that rode on a deck having 12 inches of freeboard. Their engines had been salvaged from small steamers and could not develop more than five miles and hour in still water. When acting as a picket boat between Forts Sumter and Moultrie, *Chicora* once dropped anchor because she could not stem the ebb tide. Comparatively weaker in firepower than other Confederate ironclads, *Chicora* carried two 9-inch shell guns and four rifled 32-pounders. *Palmetto State* mounted only four guns – a rifled 7-inch cannon forward, a rifled 60-pounder aft, and one 8-inch shell gun in each broadside.

Never satisfied with the progress of the Navy, and especially not pleased with the performance of the two ironclads,

Beauregard looked vigilantly for other alternatives. One of his engineers, Captain Francis D. Lee, showed him plans for a torpedo ram. Having tinkered with underwater explosives, Lee believed a partially submerged vessel, having no more than a smokestack, pilothouse, and a little armor showing above water, could be designed to carry a torpedo on a spar, drive it into the belly of a warship, and blow the vessel up. No one listened to Lee's proposal until Beauregard came to Charleston.

Bypassing the government in Richmond, the general went directly to the governor of South Carolina for money to fund the project. He convinced the state that an ordinary gunboat would have little effect on the Union's new monitors. "We must attack them underwater where they are the most vulnerable," said Beauregard, and, "if we wish to destroy them… the torpedo ram is the only probable way of accomplishing that… end." The governor thought so, too, and transferred funds from the state gunboat appropriation for the project.

When Ingraham learned that Beauregard had inched his way onto Navy turf, he complained to Mallory. The secretary tried to revert the project to the Navy, not because he believed in submarines but because he believed in ironclads and did not want resources for building them lost to silly ideas. Two more ironclads had already been started, *Charleston* and *Columbia*, but Beauregard had seen enough of Mallory's "hen houses" to know they were no good. The War Department agreed and gave Beauregard permission to build boats to

Fort Sumter sat in the center of Charleston's outer harbor with the main shipping channel running between it and Fort Moultrie. The Charleston bar crossed the channel to the east, about two miles beyond Fort Sumter. Additional batteries rimmed Sullivan's Island, James Island, Morris Island, and Mount Pleasant, with another heavy battery emplaced at Castle Pinckney near the mouth of the Cooper River.

Right: Captured in open water between Havana, the blockade runner *Columbia* made a nice prize. Like all runners, she was adjudicated in a prize court before taken to the Brooklyn Navy Yard for refitting as a gunboat.

Below: The crew of U.S.S. *Passaic*, a single-turreted monitor stationed off Charleston, turn out on a balmy Sunday morning for Sunday services near the ducts used to circulate air below decks.

carry spar torpedoes. Doing so merely fueled more resentment between Mallory, Ingraham, and the general. Mallory attempted to frustrhinery and iron, and Ingraham did the same. The general countered by exerting pressure on Ingraham to attack the blockading squadron before the monitors arrived.

On January 6, 1863, Welles ordered five monitors to join the Union's South Atlantic Blockading Squadron. The original *Monitor* was among them, but she foundered in a storm off Cape Hatteras and never completed the voyage. Du Pont, who always seemed to have an excuse for not forcing an entrance to Charleston harbor, sent two of the monitors, *Montauk* and *Passaic*, to Savannah. This left Du Pont with *New*

Ironsides, an enormous armor-belted ironclad, at Port Royal for repairs and Welles with the problem of finding other monitors to send to the squadron off Charleston. So on January 28, when the weather began to clear, there were still no Union monitors off Charleston.

Ingraham did not want to take his ironclads beyond the bar, but Beauregard insisted. The general had talked with the commanders of English and French vessels in port who agreed that, if Ingraham could chase away the Union squadron for 20 hours, they would sail out and proclaim the blockade lifted. Referring to Ingraham's patent excuse that the ironclads lacked sufficient motive power, one of his officers wrote, "How the Devil is he going to find out unless he tries?"

On January 30, Beauregard's horse artillery set a trap along the Stono River and forced the surrender of the U.S.S. gunboat *Isaac Smith*, reducing by one the number of Union vessels off Charleston. Late in the afternoon the U.S.S. *Commodore McDonough* ran up to Stono Inlet to investigate the firing, temporarily removing herself from blockading chores. By early evening, an unusual period of winter calms had flattened the seas. With Beauregard stealing his thunder, Ingraham decided to get underway with his ironclads to see what they could do.

At 10:00 p.m. Ingraham came aboard *Palmetto State* and an hour later stood for the bar. Fifty-year-old John Randolph Tucker, a member of an early and distinguished

Above: An artist provides a sketch of the deck under a monitor's turret and gives an impression of a high-ceilinged, commodious compartment filled with mechanical apparatus, all of which is exaggerated.

Right: After Charleston fell in February, 1865, a few blockading vessels, such as the USS *Catskill*, moved into the harbor. Lt. Comdr. Edward Barrett is seated in the turret, directly over a 15-inch Dahlgren.

Virginia family, followed with *Chicora*. The ironclads moved so slowly that they did not clear the ar – having barely a foot to spare – until half past four in the morning.

Powhatan and *Canandaiqua*, two of the Union's largest vessels, had gone to Port Royal for coal, leaving off Charleston a thin cordon of smaller gunboats. With *Isaac Smith* captured and *Commodore McDonough* down at Stono Inlet, *Keystone State*, *Flag*, *Mercedita*, *Memphis*, *Augusta*, *Quaker City*, and *Housatonic* tried to cover some 20 miles of shore.

The moon had set, and a light mist settled over the dim shapes of Union vessels off the bar. Ingraham spotted *Mercedita* dead ahead and ordered *Palmetto State's* captain, John Rutledge, to ram her. Mercedita carried nine guns, one being a 100-pounder rifled

Above: The gundecks of old ships-of-line, such as the U.S.S. *New Hampshire*, often seemed cluttered with ropes, tackle, stays, and ratlines, and on some occasions, with sailors having nothing to do but have a photo taken.

Parrott, but her commander, Henry S. Stellwagen, had just gone to bed after an exhausting chase of a steamer. Not yet asleep, he heard the voice of Lieutenant Trevett Abbot, who was topside, shout, "She has black smoke! Watch, man the guns, spring the rattle, call all hands to quarters!" Stellwagen reached for his pea jacket just as Acting Master Thomas J. Dwyer came to the cabin door and said, "Sir, a steamboat is close aboard."

Stellwagen sprinted to the deck, climbed the poop ladder, and observed what appeared to be a tug chugging slowly toward his ship. "Train your guns right on him," he said to Abbot, "and be ready to fire as soon as I order!" He then hailed, "Steamer ahoy! What steamer is that? Drop your anchor or you will be into us!" He hailed again, but all he heard in reply was, "Halloo," followed by a few indistinct words. Seconds later came a more distinct reply, "This is the Confederate States steam ram -----!"

Stellwagen hollered, "Fire! Fire!" but by then his guns could not be depressed enough to hit the ironclad. *Palmetto State* fired a shell from the 7-inch bow gun and seconds later crashed into the *Mercedita's* starboard quarter, stoving in several rows of planking. The shell ripped through the hull diagonally, passed through both boilers, and exploded against the other side of the ship, blowing in it a hole five feet in diameter. *Mercedita* filled with scalding steam, water poured through the hull, and from below

reports filtered topside that men had been killed and the vessel was sinking.

Palmetto State swung abeam, touching *Mercedita*, and a voice from below hollered, "Surrender, or I'll sink you!" After a pause, Ingraham called out again, "Do you surrender?"

Stellwagen replied, "I can make no resistance. My boiler is destroyed."

It was not the answer Ingraham wanted, so he asked again, "Then do you surrender?"

Stellwagen replied, "Yes."

Abbot rowed over to *Palmetto State* to

Above: Standing watch on a sailing ship is usually not done on the gundeck, but this sailor looks quite smart standing with a telescope in front of the cutlass rack and the arms chest.

arrange for the surrender of his vessel, *Mercedita*. Ingraham had no idea where to put prisoners or what to do with a sinking gunboat. The longer he procrastinated, the more impatient Abbot became. With daylight approaching, one of Ingraham's officers said, "Commodore, you must think quick for we must get along!" The reminder served its purpose. Ingraham paroled the prisoners on their pledge of honor that "neither… the officers and crew of the *Mercedita* will again take up arms against the Confederate States during the war, unless you are legally and regularly exchanged as prisoner of war." Abbot gave his pledge and returned to the sinking ship. In parting, he assured Ingraham that because of shallow water, the vessel "will not go lower than the upper deck," thereby implying that the Confederates could get her off whenever they wished.

Thinking the matter settled, Ingraham went in search of *Chicora*, which earlier had fired a few shots into *Mercedita* and steamed on by. Other blockaders heard the reports but thought nothing of it, such noise being almost a nightly occurrence.

After passing *Mercedita*, 30 minutes elapsed before Commander Tucker brought *Chicora* in sight of the 11-gun sidewheel steamer U.S.S. *Keystone State*, commanded by William E. Le Roy. Being a nervous chap, Le Roy came topside at the first sound of gunfire. He beat to quarters and ordered the cables slipped. Through the mist, lookouts spotted a steamer approaching, and when no one answered the challenge *Keystone State* opened fire. *Chicora* replied, one shell

tearing through the enemy's berth deck, killing and wounding several men, and setting fire to the wood work. When Ingraham came up, he found *Chicora* blasting away at the enemy but not using her ram. Tucker had spoken with the chief engineer and the pilot, and both warned that *Chicora* did not have the motive power to extract her prow once it became embedded in the much larger *Keystone State*. Second Assistant Engineer James H. Tomb, who had served on *McRae* during the battle of New Orleans, disagreed and said so, but Tucker preferred using conservative tactics and contentedly stood off and traded shots. Ingraham, seeing *Keystone State* on fire, also stood off and opened with *Palmetto State's* guns.

Having the advantage of speed, Le Roy worked *Keystone State* up to 12 knots, moved off, and extinguished the fire. It was now daylight, and he could see his attackers – two small ironclads pursuing slowly in the distance. Enraged by the attack, he came about to ram *Chicora*. When bearing down on her, a shot from *Chicora* hulled *Keystone State's* portside, swept through the ship, and damaged both steam drums. Scalding vapors enveloped the vessel, driving those who survived topside. During the confusion and disorder, *Chicora* continued to hammer the distressed ship as fast as her men could reload and fire.

During the battle, a fight of a different sort occurred on the deck of *Keystone State*. The executive officer, Lieutenant Thomas H. Eastman, noticed that the ship's flag had been lowered. On *Chicora*, Tucker also observed the flag down, so he suspended

Above: Capt. Stephen C. Rowan commanded the U.S.S. *New Ironsides* off Charleston harbor and led the attack on the forts. He constantly fretted about the vessel, and in 1864 was relieved and placed in waiting orders.

Below: Many of the early monitors, such as the U.S.S. *Weehawken*, were not seaworthy. During a storm off Charleston Harbor, *Weehawken* took water through the vents and turret and on December 7, 1863, sank.

firing and lowered a boat to accept the ship's surrender. Meanwhile, Eastman turned to the officers on *Keystone's* deck and snorted, "Who hauled down the flag?" Le Roy replied, "I ordered it down. We are disabled and at the mercy of the Ram who can rake and sink us. It is a useless sacrifice of life to resist further." Eastman hurled his sword to the deck and said, "God D--n it. I will have nothing to do with it." Shocked by the reply, Le Roy asked, "What would you do? Will you take responsibility?" Eastman replied, "Yes, sir, I'll take responsibility," and picking up his sword hollered to the officer on the poop deck, "Hoist up the flag. Resume firing."

By a stroke of good luck, *Keystone's* starboard wheel continued to operate on the engine's vacuum, and she moved off faster than *Chicora* could keep stride with her. Aboard *Chicora*, Tucker still would not fire because her quarry's flag was down and, by the time he saw it back at the masthead, the distance between the two vessels had hopelessly widened. What Tucker did not see was the U.S.S. *Memphis*, which had entered the scene under a screen of smoke, passed a hawser to *Keystone State*, and towed her to Port Royal, leaving Tucker angrily complaining that "her commander, by this faithless act plac[ed] himself beyond the pale of civilized and honorable warfare."

At daylight, four other blockaders blundered into the fight. Seeing that they were up against a pair of ironclads, they stayed safely out of range – all but *Quaker City*,

which absorbed a shell in her engine room.

With the blockaders scattering, *Chicora* and *Palmetto State* returned to the bar and waited for the next tide to carry them into the harbor. They expected to be pounced upon by the Union squadron, but not a vessel could be seen on the horizon. At 4:00 p.m. they steamed inside, greeted by salutes from the forts and the cheers of thousands. Beauregard wired Richmond, "I am going to proclaim the blockade of Charleston lifted," and the following day Ingraham signed it. If so, the Union would have to go through lengthy diplomatic formalities before it could re-established a formal blockade. Every foreign consul in the city received a copy of Beauregard's declaration, but engineer Tomb of *Chicora* lamented, "They say we have raised the blockade, but we all felt we would rather have raised hell and sunk the ships."

On the following evening the Union blockaders returned, and all of Beauregard's blusterings came to nothing. The battle over whether the blockade had been lifted raged on for another 15 years, but by then the fight had diminished to merely words.

Chicora and *Palmetto State* never again made much of a difference in the defense of Charleston. On March 28 Confederate Secretary Mallory relieved Ingraham and transferred command of the squadron to Tucker. *Chicora's* former commander faced new problems, because on April 6, 1863, Du Pont crossed the bar in his flagship, *New Ironsides*, and with a squadron of seven

Above: The Confederates went through a cycle of submarine yearning, contriving large submersible vessels with iron prows (as imagined in these contemporary drawings) that they had neither the technology, facilities, nor the funds to build.

Above: The Confederates called them torpedoes, but what they planted in Charleston's harbor and inlets were a wide variety of mines, some submersible, and others that floated, that exploded on contact.

Above right: The unreliable keg-type mine floated just above the surface. The U.S.S. *Pawnee* had the misfortune of wandering into a pair of kegs cabled together and the crew barely had enough time to abandon ship.

monitors and the tower ironclad *Keokuk,* launched the long expected attack on Charleston harbor. Du Pont's first objective was to reduce Fort Sumter by bombardment. Tucker held the Rebel ironclads in readiness to make a desperate and final assault should the monitors succeed in passing the forts. Beauregard saved him the trouble. Shore batteries opened with a withering cross fire and two hours later drove Du Pont's monitors back to sea.

New Ironsides, more than any other vessel in Du Pont's command, worried Beauregard. At 230 feet and 3,486 tons, she was the largest and most heavily armed man-of-war in the Union arsenal. She carried seven 11-inch Dahlgren smoothbores in each broadside, two 100-pounder rifled Parrotts forward, and a pair of 50-pounder rifled Parrotts aft. Armored with $4^1/2$ inches of iron backed by 27 inches of oak, she was virtually invulnerable to any projectile the enemy could throw at her.

Ironsides' commander, fifty-four-year-old

Stephen Rowan, anchored her in the shipping channel directly off Morris Island. Rowan had participated in amphibious assaults at Hatteras Inlet, Roanoke Island, and New Berne, and these impressive victories led to his promotion to captain and commodore. Not all of Rowan's peers considered him the best officer to command *Ironsides*, the kingpin of the blockading squadron. But, between the months of July and September 1863, Rowan brought her under the guns of Beauregard's batteries 14 times, during which she fended off 164 projectiles.

Beauregard grew weary of watching *New Ironsides*, which drew his attention daily, but he noticed that each evening she returned to the same anchorage. One foggy night after she departed on patrol, a boat from shore pushed out to sea and planted a mine directly under the vessel's anchorage. To explode the so-called "torpedo" required a set of wires running underwater to galvanic batteries on shore. For several days, while Rowan slumbered in his cabin, a

detail attempted to explode the device, but it failed.

During the winter of 1863, Beauregard had raised funds to build a semi-submersible vessel that could carry a torpedo fitted to the end of a spar, one when driven into the hull of a ship would detonate on impact. Such an apparatus was installed on the bow of *Palmetto State*, but because the ironclad never went anywhere, the explosive rig remained at the testing stage.

Besides Beauregard, two other men took special interest in the program, Captain Lee of the army and Lieutenant William T. Glassel, an officer on *Chicora*. While Lee worked on a partially submersible vessel to carry the charge, Glassel went to Ingraham and offered to lead 40 small boats equipped with spar torpedoes out to sea to blow up the blockaders. Ingraham refused, giving as a silly reason that Glassel, as a lieutenant, was not entitled to command more than one boat. So Glassel formed a crew of six volunteers, loaded them into one of Lee's

specially fitted boats, and led them outside the harbor to blow up the 2,400 ton sidewheel steamer *Powhatan*.

At 10:00 p.m. the tide ebbed, the moon set, and the sea became smooth. The men rowed quietly, coming within 600 feet of *Powhatan* before a sentinel on watch hailed, "What ship is that?" Glassel answered evasively, drawing closer, until an officer on *Powhatan* threatened to fire upon the boat unless Glassel stopped and identified himself. At that point, one of the oarsmen began to back and stopped the boat, causing it to drift by the side-wheeler. Glassel cut the torpedo adrift and made for shore. The failure discouraged the Confederate Navy from pursuing the torpedo boat concept, but not Beauregard.

The arrival of the Union's *New Ironsides* rekindled interest in Lee's torpedo ram, still lying unfinished on her stocks. This time a board of naval engineers looked her over and urged Tucker to finish her. On August 1 she quietly slipped into the water. James

Carlin, a volunteer pilot who knew every inch of Charleston's harbor, took the torpedo boat on a short shakedown cruise and reported her ready for service, having exceeded expectations "both in speed and seaworthiness."

On the moonless night of August 20, Carlin cast off and steamed toward Fort Sumter. The ram plowed through the harbor with only her stack, pilothouse, and a few inches of decking showing above the water line. With her furnaces stoked with anthracite, only the thinnest ribbon of smoke marked her position. Stopping at Fort Sumter, Carlin took on board a guard of 10 soldiers armed with rifles. A half-hour later he pushed off again, riding gentle swells raised by a light southwesterly breeze. At 11:30 he passed through the line of obstructions blocking the channel and steered for *New Ironsides*, anchored off Morris Island among five other ironclads. At 400 yards, Carlin lowered the torpedo-armed spar and commenced his attack, keeping the

target slightly to port. From a distance of 50 yards, Ensign Benjamin H. Porter, *Ironsides'* officer of the deck, spied the strange vessel and gave the hail: "Ship ahoy!"

Carlin expected the ram to strike at a slight angle but saw that she was beginning to take too much of an angle. To the hail, Carlin merely replied, "Hello!" while at the same time stopping the engine and sending word to the helm to come "hard-a starboard." The helmsman misunderstood the order and failed to respond. The tide took hold of the ram and carried her alongside *Ironsides.*

Ensign Porter leaned over the side and hollered, "What ship is that?"

Carlin replied, "The steamer Live Yankee."

Growing more suspicious by the minute, Porter asked, "Where from?"

Carlin now regretted having shut down the engine. He replied, "Port Royal," and ducked below to execute a quick escape, only to learn that the engine had jammed.

Porter had seen enough and beat to quarters. Rockets streaked from *Ironsides'* deck to warn the squadron, and marines formed along the deck with muskets trained on the torpedo boat. Porter demanded her surrender, and Carlin, to gain time, replied, "Aye, Aye, Sir, I'll come on board." As the ram drifted away, small cannon opened on the boat, but she was too low in the water to be seen clearly, and the shots skittered away in the darkness.

After Carlin got her engine running, he considered attacking some other vessel, but having lost the element of surprise he wisely decided to return to Charleston. Once safely in port, Carlin wrote Beauregard condemning the semi-submersible and her engine as too defective for further service. Although the general held hope that her defects could be corrected, the ram passed, without a name, into obscurity.

Beauregard soon found another option

equally as devious as the unnamed ram – a little contraption called *David.* Built by a group of Charlestonians calling themselves the Southern Torpedo Company, the diminutive semi-submersible vessel was no more than a 50-foot iron shell built around a powerful engine and designed in such a way as to admit water into ballast tanks until her sloped deck became awash. She carried a 100-pound torpedo on a hollow folding shaft connected to her bow. Glassel volunteered to command the vessel and for a crew collected three equally courageous daredevils – James H. Tomb, who had served on *Chicora,* and two men from *Palmetto State,* pilot Walker Cannon and fireman James Sullivan. Before Beauregard could direct her activities, *David* was absorbed by the Navy, but the objective remained the same – to sink *New Ironsides.*

On the night of October 5, Glassel took her down the harbor on the ebb tide and into

Left: Unlike a submarine, the torpedo boat pictured here was equipped with a small steam engine and was meant to remain just above the surface, using as its sole weapon a spar torpedo fastened to the bow.

the Atlantic. At her customary anchorage off Morris Island, *New Ironsides* came into view. Glassel paused, waiting for nine o'clock when the tide would change and the Union ironclads would pipe down for the night. *David's* crew, armed only with double-barreled shotguns and .36 caliber revolvers, lowered the spar torpedo and throttled the engine to full power. The little vessel shot across the water, unseen but for an eerie phosphorescence churned up by the wake.

New Ironsides' officer of the deck Ensign Charles W. Howard, warned by Rowan to watch for boarding parties, came to the gangway and hollered at the disturbance in the water, "Boat ahoy! Boat ahoy!" Glassel replied with his shotgun, felling Howard with a spray of buckshot. Seconds later the torpedo struck with a deafening roar, jolting the iron ship with enough force to bring down her rigging, knock guns off their positions, and send shot and shell rolling

across the decks. *Ironsides* heeled over, and when she rebounded cast a wave over *David* that came through the hatch and doused the fire that fed the boiler. When it became evident that *David* might sink, the four-man crew stripped off their coats and dove overboard.

Glassel swam away and Tomb struck out for Morris Island. Cannon could not swim, so he clung to *David*, while Sullivan stroked to *Ironsides* and grabbed onto her anchor chains. When Tomb looked back and saw *David* still afloat, he returned to the vessel, pulled Cannon on board, restarted the engines, and steamed back to Fort Sumter. A Union picket boat rescued Glassel and took him to the U.S.S. *Ottawa*, where an old friend from the Navy gave him a parole. In the morning, men on *Ironsides* found Sullivan on the anchor chain. They dragged him on board and unceremoniously tossed him into a cell.

Glassel believed the torpedo failed to damage *Ironsides* by striking her too close to the water line. Officers on the Union ironclad shared his opinion, but as coal was removed from her bunkers a closer inspection disclosed signs of serious damage. Towboats hauled her to Port Royal, and from there to Philadelphia for repairs. Her damage remained a secret until after the war, mainly to keep from giving the Confederates any encouragement for developing this new abominable mode of warfare.

Rear Admiral John A. Dahlgren replaced Du Pont and took measures to prevent further attacks from Confederate submersibles. On occasion, sentinels continued to report nighttime sightings, either real or imagined, of strange vessels mingling about the Union squadron. There is no further record of *David's* activities, nor further damage reports to Union vessels from this cause, and months passed before another creature

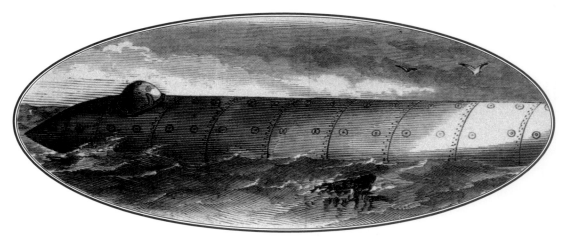

Right: The Confederacy did not have an exclusive corner on submarine design. De Villerou created a concept for an unknown customer, but on May 16, 1862, the government seized it at Philadelphia.

Below: A submarine designed to sink the U.S.S. *Minnesota* never got beyond the trial stage. One cranker could not get the craft in motion. Four crankers did a little better. The torpedo dragged by cable often overran the boat.

caused consternation among the Union blockaders.

While the Southern Torpedo Company gave birth to the semi-submersible *David*, a New Orleans consortium backed by sugar broker Horace L. Hunley and three local financiers began work on a true submarine. Twenty feet long, four feet deep, and six feet wide, she looked like a big fish with a single hatch amidships. She had no pilothouse and no engine, just a few glass-covered portholes forward and a pair of diving vanes operated from within. Two men inside used cranks connected to a shaft to turn the propeller. The owners named the vessel *Pioneer*, put her through several tests, and on March 31, 1862, received a letter of marque certifying her as a privateer. Hunley and his friends had big ideas, but Farragut captured New Orleans, and the owners scuttled their boat.

Hunley and the builders fled to Mobile with their blueprints and raised money for another boat, this one larger and with many refinements. They added more room for crankers, improved the lighting by adding more glass and, to monitor the amount of oxygen when submerged, they introduced a small candle. Instead of using a spar torpedo fitted on the bow, they attached to the stern a long rope carrying a floating torpedo. Their concept was to dive under the target, pulling the device into the side of a ship, and at the time of detonation, to resurface on the opposite side of the victim and get away fast. After several trials at Mobile, a tug took *Pioneer II* down the bay to attack the Union squadron off Fort Morgan. Choppy seas poured into the hatchways, and before the vessel got halfway to her destination, she sank.

Hunley went right back to work building

Top: The early torpedoes, known by most sailors as "infernal machines," were operated from shore using a galvanic battery wired to the device and tripped by an operator when a vessel passed over the charge.

Right: Horace L. Hunley and his partners designed at New Orleans the first operating submarine. Hunley eventually sent his creation to Charleston and met his death inside when she sank.

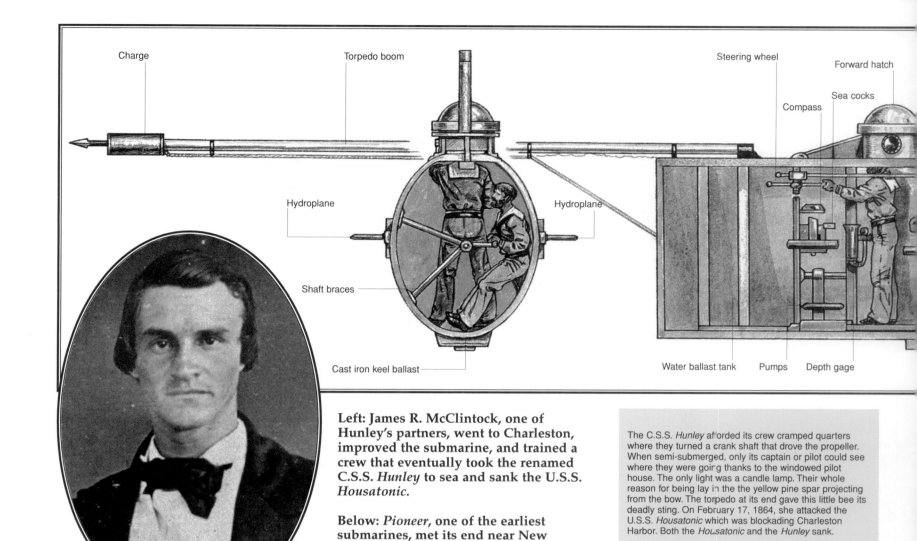

Charge

Torpedo boom

Steering wheel

Forward hatch

Sea cocks

Compass

Hydroplane

Hydroplane

Shaft braces

Cast iron keel ballast

Water ballast tank   Pumps   Depth gage

Left: James R. McClintock, one of Hunley's partners, went to Charleston, improved the submarine, and trained a crew that eventually took the renamed C.S.S. _Hunley_ to sea and sank the U.S.S. _Housatonic_.

Below: _Pioneer_, one of the earliest submarines, met its end near New Orleans after the city was captured. Dredged from the mud years later, it sat at Bayou St. Johns at the State Home for Confederate Soldiers.

The C.S.S. _Hunley_ afforded its crew cramped quarters where they turned a crank shaft that drove the propeller. When semi-submerged, only its captain or pilot could see where they were going thanks to the windowed pilot house. The only light was a candle lamp. Their whole reason for being lay in the the yellow pine spar projecting from the bow. The torpedo at its end gave this little bee its deadly sting. On February 17, 1864, she attacked the U.S.S. _Housatonic_ which was blockading Charleston Harbor. Both the _Housatonic_ and the _Hunley_ sank.

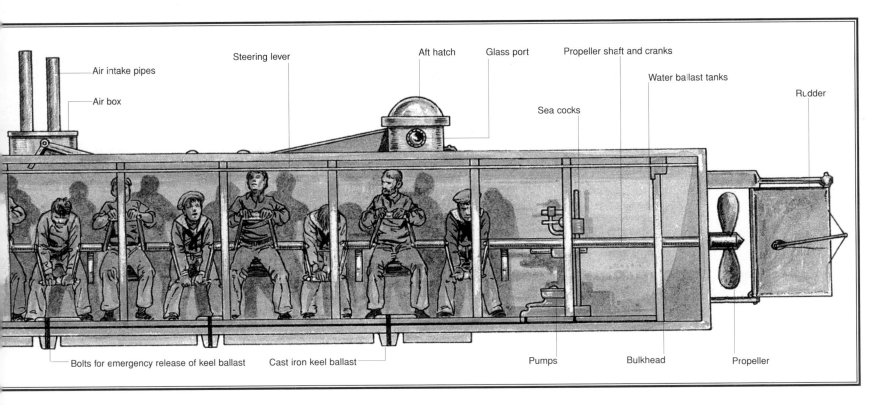

Air intake pipes · Air box · Steering lever · Aft hatch · Glass port · Propeller shaft and cranks · Water ballast tanks · Rudder · Sea cocks · Bolts for emergency release of keel ballast · Cast iron keel ballast · Pumps · Bulkhead · Propeller

another vessel, this one from a 25-foot ship's boiler that measured four feet in diameter. He had it cut in two, the ends lengthened and tapered, and the inner shell expanded to accommodate eight crankers and two hatches cut about 14 feet apart. Hunley added devices to accelerate submerging and rising by fitting seacocks and pumps to water ballast tanks fore and aft and iron castings to the keel that could be jettisoned to lighten the vessel by pulling a lever. Coamings were added to give the pilot better vision and a petty officer provided to operate the seacock and pump. Hunley also added an air tube, which could be turned on and off with a key inside, but he had not solved the problem of supplying oxygen to the craft once she dove.

With every detail checked to the designer's satisfaction, *Pioneer III* slid beneath the surface towing a 90 pound torpedo, passed under an old barge, and blew it up. The explosion unseated everyone in the submarine and caused the boat to roll, but she came to the surface in triumphant success.

Hunley soon discovered that a floating torpedo could be carried along by the wind faster than the crankers could keep ahead of it, so he wisely adopted the system of a spar torpedo used in Charleston.

He also learned that John Frazer & Company of Charleston had offered $100,000 to anyone who sank New Ironsides and a somewhat lesser amount for sinking one of the other monitors. Finding Mallory's attitude toward submarines circumspect, Hunley wrote Beauregard and offered to send his boat to Charleston. The general responded with the necessary flatcars, and in August 1863, Hunley's creation rode the rails to South Carolina.

At Charleston, Lieutenant John Payne rounded up eight volunteers and spent the next few days familiarizing the men with the boat. After a few practice dives, Payne declared the submarine ready for duty. A tug took her to Fort Johnson on the south side of the bay, and at midnight the crankers

headed for sea. She had barely cleared the wharf when wake from a passing steamer broke over her and spilled through the open hatches. Payne escaped through the hatchway, but eight seamen went to the bottom with the boat. The Confederate Navy raised the boat, cleaned it out, and buried the victims with full honors.

Undaunted, Payne tried again, this time from Fort Sumter. The new crew pushed off from the wharf and moments later the boat went inexplicably to the bottom. Payne and two others fought their way back to the surface. A few days later mourners listened to "Dixie" played during burial services for seven more seamen.

Beauregard had seen enough. The Navy had not handled the boat properly, so he invited Hunley to come to Charleston and bring with him men of experience. Lieutenant George E. Dixon of the 21st Alabama Infantry took command of the vessel, and with William A. Alexander of the same regiment ran a new crew through a series of successful exercises. Hunley agreed to personally take the vessel on a trial dive under the Confederate receiving ship *Indian Chief*. Three hundred feet from the target, he closed the hatches, marked his compass, and then made the fatal error of opening the forward cock too quickly. The boat plunged nose first into the mud, sticking fast as water seeped into the cabin. Men frantically worked the hand pumps, but Hunley had forgotten to shut off the valve to the ballast tank. In 30 minutes everybody, including Hunley, died of suffocation.

After a fourth unsuccessful test, bringing the death toll to 30, Beauregard said, "Enough! Let her lie in the mud. She will kill no more!" But Dixon and Alexander wanted to raise the vessel and nine days later brought her back to the surface. They cleaned her out, made repairs, and after setting up a submarine school on the north side of the harbor, passed the winter training volunteers. To honor her designer, they renamed the submarine C.S.S. *H. L. Hunley* and put what Charlestonians

called the "peripatetic coffin" on display for all to see.

Dixon and Alexander made amazing progress. Four times a week *Hunley* could been seen cranking about the harbor, traveling as many as 15 miles a day. As the crews became more proficient, the instructors began making endurance dives. The vessel would stay submerged until one of its members said, "Up!" Observers on shore would clock the dive. On one occasion they watched for two hours, and when the boat did not return to the surface, they reported another disaster to Beauregard. But, below the surface, the crew gasped for bits of air in an enclosure that had become unbearably wet and stuffy. Thirty minutes later they surfaced and, after filling their lungs with fresh air, cranked over to the dock. A lone guard, startled by the unexpected resurrection of the recently departed submarine, whooped with joy.

In February, Alexander received orders to return to Mobile, and Dixon lost a valuable resource. Nonetheless, he proceeded with his plans.

At 7:00 p.m. on February 17, 1864, the bay calmed to a sheet of glass, Dixon pushed off from the dock and headed for sea. He had set his sights on a 1,240-ton screw corvette carrying 13 guns, and told his men, "Tonight, we sink the *Housatonic!*" The vessel lay in the main channel off Beach Island, a few miles south of the entrance to Charleston harbor. Not far off twinkled lights from other Union blockaders anchored another mile or two away. Soldiers at Battery Marshall watched *Hunley* go, a thin sliver nearly awash, and soon she passed into the night.

All was quiet on *Housatonic*, where Lieutenant Francis W. Higginson stood watch. Captain Charles W. Pickering had settled in his cabin. Acting Master John K. Crosby, officer of the deck, was making the rounds when at 8:45 he noticed a ripple on the surface about 100 yards away. It had, he said, "the appearance of a plank moving in the water." Having been warned about

torpedo boats, Crosby gave the alarm. Higginson took a look and beat to quarters, later reporting, "It came directly toward the ship, the time from which it was first seen till it was close alongside being about two minutes." Sailors scurried to slip the cable, the ship's engines began to back, and men on the after pivot gun tried to bear on the creature slithering through the water. As Crosby recalled, the torpedo struck the ship forward of the mizzenmast, on the starboard side in a line with the magazine.

A deafening explosion jolted *Housatonic* partly out of the water, heeling her over on her side. Guns, shot, and fixtures flew in every direction. Men on deck slammed into the bulkheads and toppled overboard. Seawater filled the hold, and as the ship righted herself she heeled to port and, almost in the blink of an eye, sank stern first. Before help arrived, *Housatonic* settled on the bottom.

To the bottom with her went *Hunley.* A few years later a diver located the submarine lying in the sand near *Housatonic.* Alexander reviewed the findings and concluded that *Housatonic* had backed down upon *Hunley* just as Dixon dove and attacked. When the spar torpedo exploded, *Hunley* became trapped under the larger vessel and was carried to the bottom. More than likely the enormous concussion, which was said to rattle windows in Charleston, knocked all of the men in *Hunley* senseless, and what happened afterwards one can only guess.

During the brief career of the C.S.S. *Hunley,* she took at least 40 lives to prove the merits of submarine warfare. Admiral Dahlgren, who once condemned the Confederacy "for using an engine of war not recognized by civilized nations," now recanted, admitting to Assistant Secretary Fox, "The secrecy, rapidity of movement, control of direction and precise explosion indicate… the introduction of the Torpedo element as a means of certain warfare – It can be ignored no longer."

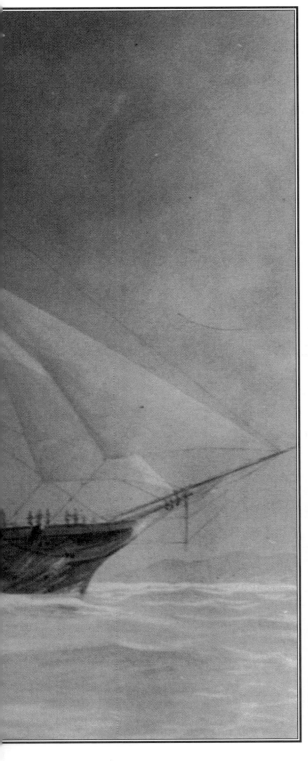

Above: The 1,240-ton U.S.S. *Housatonic* was by no means a small steamer, but on the night of February 17, 1864, she just happened to be singled out by the roving C.S.S. *Hunley* and became the only victim of a Rebel submarine.

Right: What appears to be an unnamed submarine turned up in a Union navy yard between two monitors. She appears much larger than a Hunley or a David, and was probably captured in a Rebel port and hauled away.

CHAPTER NINE

THE ALBEMARLE AFFAIR

The Confederacy lost control of the North Carolina Sounds early in the war, and now, in the winter of 1864, its government wanted them back. As was customary, the Army of the Potomac and the Army of Northern Virginia had gone into winter quarters. No serious fighting was expected along the Rapidan or Rappahannock Rivers until the many muddy country roads dried. While the two armies waited for the drying sunshine of springtime, General Robert E. Lee detached a force to recapture several small ports bordering Albemarle and Pamlico Sounds. To secure the flanks of his liberating brigades against renewed Union naval and amphibious attacks, he asked for ironclads. By 1864, small ironclads could be framed and fitted beside any strip of water having enough depth to float them. Most of the rivers 30 miles inland remained especially deep until after the late winter and early spring runoff. During the latter months of 1863, Mallory started five ironclads at different sites, at least two of which were intended to support the Rebel army's effort to recapture control of the Sounds. Like all of Mallory's best intentions, he tried to do too much with too little, and the end result always fell short of fulfilling his own expectations. One of his ironclads, however, arrived in time to participate in the Confederate attack on Plymouth, Virginia, and created a fascinating history of its own.

In early 1862, Union Brigadier General Ambrose Burnside captured Roanoke Island, North Carolina, and soon thereafter gained complete control of Albemarle Sound, Pamlico Sound, and the surrounding coastal towns, one of which was Plymouth. To recover the sounds, Confederate Secretary of the Navy Mallory needed to drive away the Union Navy, take possession of Roanoke Island, and provide protective cover for three Confederate infantry brigades under the command of Brigadier General Robert F. Hoke. To spearhead the drive to break the blockade and recover lost territory, the South needed an ironclad. Having no facilities for such a project, they built the vessel in a cornfield owned by Peter E. Smith at Edward's Ferry, 40 river miles up the Roanoke River.

To supervise the work, Mallory dispatched Chief Naval Constructor John L. Porter, the same man who had transformed *Merrimac* into the ironclad *Virginia*. When Porter arrived at Edward's Ferry, he brought a set of plans for an armored ram shaped like *Virginia* but much smaller, being only 152 feet in length, 34 feet in beam, and having a 9-foot draft. For cannon, he gave her only two 100-pound Brooke rifles on pivots forward and aft. But at Edward's Ferry, Porter found no equipment to build the boat, only a crew of willing men supplied with hammers and saws. Porter eventually sequestered a derrick and a few power tools, but by January 15, 1864, his dour personality and constant complaining over the lack of resources compelled Mallory to replace him with Commander James W. Cooke.

Cooke came from Beaufort, North Carolina, and knew the sounds as well as anyone in the Confederate Navy. After 33 years of service in the United States Navy, he resigned as a lieutenant on May 1, 1861, and a month later joined the Confederate Navy. During the battle at Roanoke Island in 1862, he fought ferociously, taking a musket ball in his arm and a bayonet wound in his leg. He refused to surrender until subdued. A fellow officer described Cooke as being *so*

The U.S.S. *Miami*'s pivot gun crew goes through a training exercise. They would have been under the watchful eye of an officer (out of picture). Ten men jack the piece into position, fix it in place, load the charge, aim, and fire the piece.

Above: During quieter moments, the officers of the U.S.S. *Miami* pose with their hunting dogs on the hurricane deck. They would soon find themselves engaged in one of the toughest naval battles of the Civil War.

tenacious in battle that he would "fight a powder magazine with a coal of fire." This was exactly the type of man Mallory needed to finish work on the ironclad named after the sound she was built to liberate – *Albemarle*.

When Cooke arrived at Edward's Ferry, he found *Albemarle* launched. Porter had installed two 100-horsepower engines, each powering a separate screw. He had built the casemate, but her four inches of plating had been diverted to another ironclad building on the Neuse River. Cooke soon understood why Porter became so quarrelsome but, instead of grumbling, he sent a detail of scavengers into the countryside and soon expropriated enough scrap iron to forge the needed plates.

Rumors of an ironclad building up the Roanoke dribbled into the office of Union Secretary of the Navy Gideon Welles with enough persistence that he began to believe the rumor. Lieutenant Commander Charles W. Flusser, in command of the Union naval force in Albemarle Sound, voiced no reason for concern. During the fall of 1863 Commander Henry K. Davenport, senior Union officer in the sounds, began sending Flusser old hulks to be sunk in the river above Plymouth. He believed that no matter how powerful the ironclad, she would be of no service to the Confederacy if barricaded

in the river. Flusser found the hulks so shallow in depth that he doubted whether they would do any good. Privately, he believed "it scarcely worthwhile to block up the river," but he did so anyway.

Flusser failed to credit *Albemarle* as a serious threat, mainly because Confederate informants told him that she would never venture down to Plymouth without support of land troops. Those informants were telling him the truth. Confederate strategists expected to deploy her as the linchpin for reoccupying Plymouth and a large portion of coastal North Carolina. The plans had been laid. All that remained was for Cooke to finish work on *Albemarle* and bring the ironclad down the Roanoke.

Flusser commanded a squadron of four light wooden gunboats. His flagship, the double-ended eight-gun sidewheeler *Miami*, had already seen an abundance of action, having been part of Commander Porter's mortar squadron during the bombardment of Fort Jackson. The seven-gun *Southfield*, next in power and of the same class, was commanded by Lieutenant Charles A. French, a volunteer officer and not a member of the regular Navy. Two other small side-wheelers, *Ceres* and *Whitehead*, carried four or five small cannons – Parrott rifles and field howitzers. What Flusser expected to do with four flimsy gunboats

Union forces controlled both Pamlico and Albemarle Sounds, and the Confederacy wanted them back. To support an expedition by land, Mallory began building ironclads up the Neuse and Roanoke Rivers. The operation had to be closely coordinated because land forces had been borrowed from General Robert E. Lee, who wanted them back before the spring campaign began, and time was running short.

Below: Simple side view and plan of the Confederate ram, *Albemarle*. As built, the vessel had a draft of nine feet, was 152 feet long and 34 feet in beam, and was powered by two 200 horsepower engines.

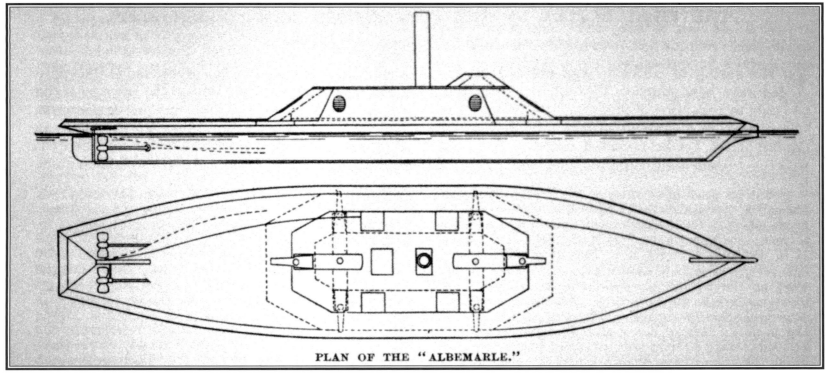

PLAN OF THE "ALBEMARLE."

against an ironclad – should she make an appearance – is questionable, but he got through each day believing that such an eventuality would never occur.

Flusser used the bar at the mouth of the Roanoke as his ace in the hole. Since he could not get *Miami*, with a draft of eight feet six inches over it, he concluded that an ironclad, which he assumed to be of deeper draft, could never get beyond it. He then learned that *Albemarle*, after receiving her plating, had a much shallower draft than he anticipated. "...she may pass over our obstructions," he warned Rear Admiral Stephen P. Lee, commanding the North Atlantic Blockading Squadron, and recommended that a force of five hundred cavalry be dispatched to destroy the ram before she started down to Plymouth. When Flusser heard nothing back from the admiral, he appealed to Major General Benjamin F. Butler, the district commander for the Army. Butler, whose contribution to the war effort came mainly in the form of incompetence, replied, "I do not believe in the ram," intimating that such mundane matters should be looked after by the Navy.

Flusser now began to worry, and for good reason. On April 10 he received word that Cooke had floated the ram down to deeper water off Hamilton and that General Hoke, "accompanied by a land force of eleven thousand men," intended to assault the Union garrison at Plymouth. Flusser's information contained a few cloudy details but was otherwise accurate. On that day, Hoke received orders from Richmond directing him to attack Plymouth, Washington, and New Bern. Brigadier General Henry W. Wessels, commanding the Union troops at Plymouth, also learned of the planned assault and on April 13 frantically applied to Butler for 5,000 additional troops.

Albemarle still needed several days of work before she could operate under her own power. To expedite the process, Hoke

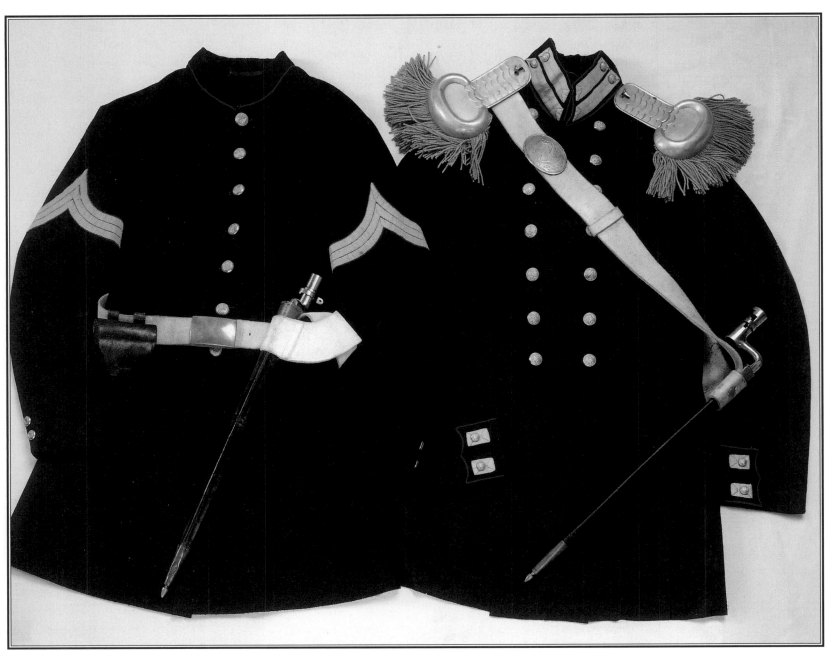

Left: Captain James W. Cooke, commanding the C.S.S. *Albemarle*, had seen a lot of action during the Civil War, and on May 4, 1864, he was about to see a lot more as he prepared to support an attack on Plymouth, Virginia.

Above: Every vessel carried a few Marines. A sergeant's field frock coat is to the left. To the right is a full dress, double-breasted coat on which yellow dress shoulder scales were required at all times.

Right: A Marine shield on full dress headgear had a french horn with an "M" inside the twist, distinguishes the wearer as a Marine. A kepi (right) was the standard field cap for Marines.

Left: The *Albemarle* ready for action. Smaller than the C.S.S. *Virginia* at 152ft long and 34ft in beam, with a 9ft draft, the Rebel ram was underestimated by Union forces, and it took an act of daring to destroy her.

supplied a dozen mechanics. Cooke suggested the work would take 15 days. Hoke replied that he needed the ram ready for service in seven. Cooke did not want to throw a cog into the Confederacy's war machine and made every effort to comply.

On April 17 Cooke picked up two officers and twenty men and prepared to descend the river in the morning. At dawn

Albemarle started down the Roanoke, towing on a barge a heavy forge needed to finish work on the casemate. He exercised the men at the guns, hollering, "In vent and sponge! Load with cartridge! Load with shells – prime!" On deck, ten smaller forges continued to hammer out rivets. On the casemate, men worked off scaffolds fastening the last iron plates. After getting underway, *Albemarle's* engines failed, and mechanics spent six hours repairing a coupling on the mainshaft.

Late in the afternoon of the 17th, Acting Ensign George W. Barrett took the U.S.S. *Whitehead* a few miles above Plymouth to make certain the sunken hulks obstructing the river had not been removed. At 5:30 p.m. Barrett heard firing near Plymouth and went back downriver to investigate. He met Ceres and learned that Confederate field artillery placed along shore had opened on her, killing two and wounding seven. Ceres brought a message from Flusser warning that a Rebel army was on the road and five miles from Plymouth. Barrett knew better. The Rebels were already there.

Three miles above Plymouth, Cooke spotted obstructions in the river and came to anchor. A detail found the waterway blocked by sunken vessels and seeded with mines. Gilbert Elliott, the builder of the ram, had helped bring her downriver and volunteered to scout the obstructions. Taking a pilot and two men in a boat, he located a passageway through the obstructions having a 10-foot clearance. Elliott marked the spot and returned back to the ram. Cooke aroused the crew, and at 4:00 a.m. on April 19, *Albemarle* passed down to Plymouth. A Union battery at Warren's Neck opened on the ram as she passed. Elliott thought "the noise made by the shot and shell as they struck the boat sounded no louder than pebbles thrown against an empty barrel."

During the 18th, Hoke had brought his Rebel force to Plymouth and spent the day skirmishing. He waited for *Albemarle*, mainly because the Union's *Miami* and *Southfield* had come up to shell his position. Two Union transports worked through the day evacuating women and children. Confederate fieldpieces disabled one of them, the transport *Bombshell*, and drove away the other. Not until the morning of

19th did he learn that Cooke had come down during the night.

With *Albemarle* came the merchant steamer *Cotton Planter*, carrying a detachment of sharpshooters. U.S.S. *Whitehead*, on picket duty, spotted the lights of both vessels above the obstructions on the night of the 18th. Barrett fired a rocket to warn Flusser that enemy vessels had come in sight. Flusser read the signal and returned to his cabin, writing Davenport, "The ram will be down tonight or tomorrow... if she doesn't stay under cover of their battery established above Fort Gray... we shall whip her." He dispatched the message by steamer and moved with *Miami* and *Southfield* about a mile below Plymouth. Using chains and long spars, Flusser put both crews to work lashing the vessels loosely together. He planned to snare the ironclad in the chains, wedging her between *Miami* and *Southfield*, after which marines from both ships would board her with ladders, climb the casemate, and drop explosives down her smokestack.

About 4:00 a.m. officers aboard *Ceres* spotted *Albemarle* running down the river and she steamed back to warn Flusser. Instead of coming directly into open water, Cooke frustrated Flusser's plan of entrapment by keeping the ram close to the riverbank. As *Albemarle* drew abreast of the Union gunboats, Cooke called for full throttle and sheered to port. Using the current for extra speed, he swung into the center of the river and bore obliquely on *Miami*. Flusser shouted orders to attack. Both vessels slipped their cables and opened on the ram. Shots bounded harmlessly away, leaving small dents in the ram's armor.

Miami and *Southfield*, chained together, bore down on *Albemarle*. Instead of maneuvering to avoid the Union vessels, Cooke let them come. With the ram but a few yards away, Flusser ran to the 9-inch

Left: An officer of the deck assumed a special responsibility during his watch. Wherever he went, his telescope followed, and if danger threatened, every minute counted when preparing for a fight.

Below left: Glancing off Miami, the ram Albemarle plowed clean through Southfield's forward storeroom and into her fireroom. The chains between Miami and Southfield were cut, and the latter sank.

Above: After Union forces recaptured Plymouth, the mighty *Albemarle* was refloated, patched, and towed to Norfolk where Union engineers could inspect the creature that had been built in a cornfield.

Below: Confederate prisoners from both services crowded into old Fort Warren at Boston, Massachusetts. They lived quite well, compared with Union prisoners living and dying in the hellhole at Andersonville.

Dahlgren in the bow. As he reached the gun, *Albemarle* struck *Miami* on the port forward quarter, slicing through two planks near the water line and ripping open a hole ten feet long. Glancing off *Miami*, the ram plowed into Southfield at an angle, smashing clean through her forward storeroom and into her fireroom.

Flusser, standing by the 9-inch Dahlgren, ordered the gun loaded with shells. One shell struck *Albemarle's* casemate and shattered. Pieces hurtled back upon the gun

crew, piercing Flusser's face, skull, and chest. He slumped to the deck, one fragment having "cut his heart out." With Flusser killed and *Southfield* sinking, *Miami*'s boarding party lost spirit and hunkered down behind the bulwarks. Sharpshooters on *Albemarle* kept up a steady fire, picking off any bluecoat foolish enough to expose himself.

Southfield filled rapidly and began to sink. The impact had severed the forward chain lashings between the two Union vessels, and those aft were quickly cut. Of 117 men on *Southfield*, some leapt into boats and headed for safety. Others dove into the river and swam for shore. Those who could jumped on board *Miami*, which had gone out of control and was paddling toward the bank. Lieutenant French made the leap, took command of *Miami*, and got the engines reversed before she grounded. He had seen enough of *Albemarle* and hurried *Miami* back down the river, followed by two small Union steamers that had stood off during the fight.

Albemarle had bitten so deeply into *Southfield* that Cooke could not extricate her prow. Chain-plates on the ram's forward deck caught on the frame of the gunboat. As the bow of the ram angled downwards, water rushed through the forward port, threatening to sink the victor along with the victim. *Albemarle*'s engines backed frantically and slowly the prow pulled free.

Minutes after the ram came level with the surface, *Southfield* sank and settled, leaving her pilothouse and smokestacks protruding above the river. With his ram undamaged by the fight, Cooke picked up a number of *Southfield*'s survivors and steamed back upriver to confer with General Hoke.

On the morning of April 20, Cooke began shelling Fort Williams, the Union citadel at Plymouth. Designed to defend against a land attack, the fort was most vulnerable from the river approaches. Cooke lobbed shells into the earthwork throughout the day, and on April 11 General Wessels surrendered 2,834 bluecoats, thirty guns, tons of supplies, and the town of Plymouth unconditionally to Hoke. Referring to *Albemarle*, Wessels complained to General Butler, "This terrible fire had to be endured without reply, as no man could live at the guns...."

Much of the credit for the quick capture of Plymouth went to Cooke, and cautious Confederates wanted to keep *Albemarle* there to protect the area from another enemy invasion. Navy Secretary Mallory felt differently. He envisioned using the ram to repatriate every town fringing the sounds, beginning with the removal of the Union naval base at Roanoke Island. Jefferson Davis preferred bringing the ram around to Pamlico Sound to aid Hoke in capturing New Bern, a town equally as important as Plymouth and located 60 miles

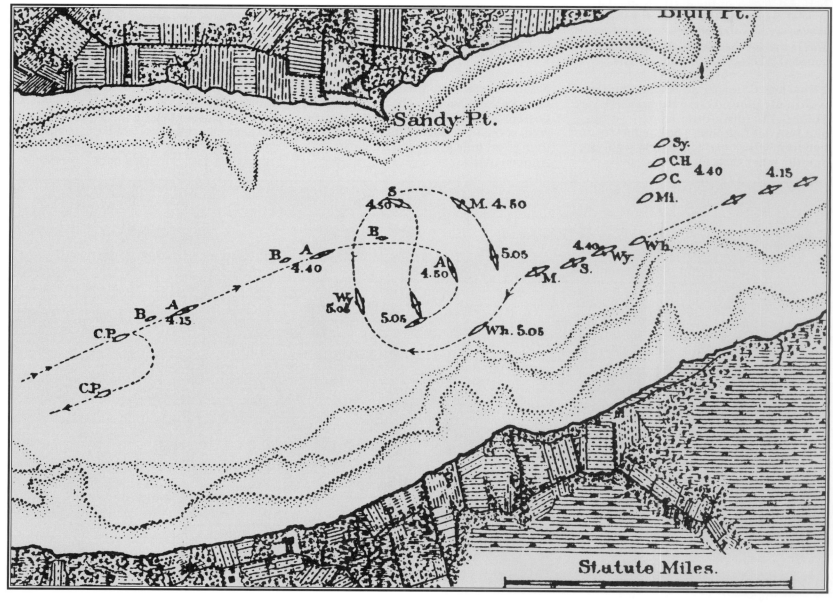

Left:Young Acting Paymaster Henry M. Meade of the U.S.S. *Mattabesett* probably never expected to find himself running powder to the deck when his rickety sidewheeler went into action against *Albemarle*.

Above: U.S.S. *Sassacus*, commanded by Roe, rams *Albemarle* on her after shield, heeling the Rebel ram over and sending a wave of water through her after port.

On May 5, 1864, when the *Albemarle* met the Union squadron in the mouth of the Roanoke River, a furious fight took place between Lt. Comdr. Francis A. Roe's seven gunboats and Capt. Cooke's ironclad and two small gunboats, both of which stood off. Cooke retired with little damage. *Albemarle* had little room to maneuver because of the shallows, while the flimsier Union vessels drew far less water.

away on the Neuse River. Another ram was already under construction up the Neuse, but Davis did not want to wait. General Robert E. Lee wanted Hoke's brigade returned to the Army of Northern Virginia, but Davis believed that, by using *Albemarle*, Hoke could retake New Bern and still return to Lee in time for the spring campaign.

In General Butler's department, dispatches flew back and forth. Major General John Peck, commanding Union forces in North Carolina, warned that "unless we are immediately reinforced, both by the army and the navy, North Carolina is inevitably lost." Butler brushed off the warning by blaming the navy for deserting the garrison at Plymouth. Among the officers in the department, "ram fever" reached new heights. Only General Butler

began each day in stubborn denial.

On April 23 Union Navy Secretary Welles sent Captain Melancton Smith to Roanoke Island and placed him in overall command of the sounds. Ironclads were not a new phenomenon to Smith. He had been on the Mississippi with Farragut, fought *Manassas* during the New Orleans expedition, and lost his ship under the guns of Port Hudson. With him came a ponderous amount of advice on methods for destroying an ironclad, little of which was practical. The Navy also placed at his disposal three sidewheel double-enders, *Mattabesett*, *Sassacus*, and *Wyalusing*. The ships were so nearly alike that one could barely be distinguished from the other. They each carried two 100-pounder rifled Parrots, four 9-inch Dahlgrens, and several smaller cannon.

Welles also filled the vacancy created by Flusser's death with another veteran of the New Orleans campaign, Lieutenant Commander Francis A. Roe, formerly an officer on *Richmond*. Smith assigned Roe to Albemarle Sound with instructions to patrol the mouth of Roanoke River and watch for the ram. Roe took command of *Sassacus* while another officer from the New Orleans campaign, Lieutenant Commander Walter W. Queen, took charge of *Wyalusing*.

On May 5, with orders to support Hoke's attack on New Bern, Cooke started down the river with *Albemarle*. With him came two steamers carrying troops, the captured and repaired *Bombshell* and *Cotton Planter*. *Miami* had just started into the river with two small gunboats, *Commodore Hull* and *Ceres*, and an army transport, *Trumpeter*, to lay torpedoes. When Hull, steaming in advance, reported

Above: After Flusser's death during the earlier action with the *Albemarle*, Lt. Comdr. Francis A. Roe took command of the Union squadron and fought the ironclad to a tactical draw, forcing her to retire.

Above: When the U.S.S. *Sassacus* **rammed the** *Albemarle,* **she ripped a huge hole in her own bow, and though she gave the enemy ironclad a severe jolt and knocked people to the deck, she almost sunk herself.**

the ram coming down, Roe sent *Trumpeter* back to Roanoke Island to inform Smith. He then backed slowly down the river, keeping the enemy in sight.

When Smith spotted *Trumpeter* beating toward the island, he knew the reason. He had already designed a plan of action and from the deck of *Mattabesett* signaled *Sassacus, Wyalusing,* and *Whitehead* to follow. He intended to use all seven vessels. The large double-enders were to pass as close as possible to the ironclad *Albemarle* without endangering their paddlewheels, concentrate their attack on her stern, and foul her propellers with fish netting. *Miami,* fitted with a torpedo on the end of a spar, would come abeam and drive the explosive into the ram's side. If the ironclad should succeed in embedding her prow in any Union vessel, the others were to immediately attack, board her, and throw

grenades down her smokestack.

Smith led the attack in *Mattabesett,* and at 4:40 p.m. *Albemarle* opened with the 100-pounder in the bow. The first shell exploded near *Mattabesett's* forward gun, wounding six men and smashing the ship's launch. A second shot ripped through the rigging. Five minutes into the engagement *Mattabesett, Wyalusing,* and *Sassacus* turned their guns on *Bombshell* and knocked her to pieces. *Cotton Planter* escaped up the river, leaving *Albemarle* alone to deal with the Union squadron.

At 4:50 *Mattabesett* opened at 150 yards and fired a broadside into the after-section of the ram, knocking 23 inches off the underside of the barrel of the stern gun. Despite its damaged condition, the crew continued to fire the gun. Smith passed around the stern of the ram and circled for another broadside.

Left: Confederate gunners, barely balancing on the *Albemarle*'s pitching deck, fire a 6.4-inch gun through an embrasure in the ram's casemate. A Union shell sliced 20 inches from the barrel of another cannon, but the Rebels kept right on firing the damaged gun as they withdrew.

Sassacus, which had drawn off a quarter-mile to engage *Bombshell*, used the distance to build a head of steam. Roe, commanding the vessel, ordered the throttle opened full and "laid the ship fair for the broadside of the ram to run her down." When Roe started his run, *Albemarle* was fully engaged with *Wyalusing* and *Whitehead*. The ram's gun crew aft saw her coming and, moments after impact, sent a shell into *Sassacus* that entered her starboard and spilled out the port side. *Sassacus* struck *Albemarle* on her after shield, heeling the ram over and sending a wave of water through the after port. A member of *Albemarle's* crew recalled, "The shock was not great... [but] there was a good deal of confusion.... Most of the men left their station and ran around. Captain Cooke was standing in the hatch and was knocked down. He looked kinder sacred like."

Roe believed he had injured the ram and at first thought she was going down. "I kept the engine going," he recalled, "pushing, as I hoped, deeper and deeper into her, and also hoping it might be possible for some one of the other boats to get up on the opposite side of me and perhaps enable us to sink her." When no help came, Roe kept *Sassacus* beating against the ram for 10 minutes while the crew hurled grenades down her deck hatch and tried in vain to lob one or two down her smokestack. The stern of *Albemarle* began to swing around, bringing her port broadside to bear on *Sassacus*. The ram's 100-pounder sent a shell through the starboard side of *Sassacus* that passed through the berth deck, smashed the starboard boiler, and lodged aft in the wardroom.

Steam engulfed *Sassacus*, scalding dozens of men who would later die. Roe tossed the signal books overboard, knowing that once he pulled free of the ram his ship would sink. But the engine continued to run, and Roe threw the helm hard aport. As the vessel came about, her wheel passed over *Albemarle's* stern, damaging the braces on the ram's hull and destroying a launch she had been towing. As *Sassacus* eased off, men went back to the guns, fired at point-blank range, and damaged one of the enemy's gun ports.

For three hours and fifty minutes *Albemarle* held off the Union squadron. At times the battle became so hectic that several of Smith's gunboats could not fire for fear of striking one of their own. Lieutenant French made one pass at the ram with *Miami's* spar torpedo, but Cooke saw the ship coming and backed just in time. French could no longer control *Miami's* wheel, so he decided not to make another attempt. During the first torpedo run, the vessel had been severely injured by friendly fire. French wisely pulled away from the firing of *Mattabesett* and *Wyalusing* before they could sink his ship.

Wyalusing had been struck so many times that at one point Lieutenant Queen thought she would sink. He signaled a tender for assistance, but after a closer examination discovered that she was leaking no more than usual.

With *Sassacus* disabled and *Wyalusing* standing off, Smith continued to fire

Left: Toward the end of the war, the Union began fitting some of their vessels with spar torpedoes. The monitor U.S.S. *Casco* carries one on her bow, using it as a better weapon for destroying enemy vessels than ramming.

Below: A selection of Union and Confederate grenades. Top left , Federal Ketcham 5-pound and 1-pound percussion grenades, with wooden tail and paper wings to assist stabilization of the projectile in flight, and (next to these) a Confederate spherical 1-pound hand grenade. Below left and bottom, Confederate Rains hand grenades, similar to the Ketcham but with a modified plunger head; the bottom one has kite-like tail for stability. Top right, a Ketcham 3-pound hand grenade lays over printed instructions for charging and use. Below these are (left to right) Confederate speherical hand grenade, an Adams hand grenade, and Haynes Exelsior patent (1862) hand grenade which came in two halves – an outer casing surrounded an inner sphere containing the charge; detonation was by percussion caps on the sphere hitting the outer casing.

Mattabesett's broadsides. No projectile seemed to have any effect on the ram, but a 100-pounder from *Albemarle* entered the portside abaft *Mattabesett's* wheel, ripped through the bowels of the vessel, and settled in the small-arms locker. By then, all seven Union vessels bore the scars of battle. *Sassacus* sustained the most damage, being totally disabled. French discovered water seeping into *Miami's* hold at the rate of five inches an hour from holes punched in her hull, some having come from chunks of shell ricocheting back from the ram's armored casemate.

At 7:30 p.m., as darkness approached, *Albemarle* started back up the river, her steering mechanism injured, one gun disabled, and her port shutters damaged. Her smokestack had been badly riddled, making it necessary for Cooke to rob the larder for combustibles. The only way *Albemarle* could generate enough steam to

stem the current was to burn all the ship's bacon, fat, and butter. Smith followed in *Mattabesett,* keeping at a safe distance and content to see the ram retire. During the three and one-half hour engagement, his four gunboats had shot 456 projectiles at the ram without subduing her.

In the end, *Albemarle* won the battle, but Smith won the day. In her weakened condition, the ram never kept her appointment at New Bern. As a consequence, the Confederate attack failed.

Commander Roe of *Sassacus* summarized the day's action against the ram by simply admitting, "She is too strong for us." Captain Smith sent Admiral Lee a fragment from one of *Albemarle's* 100-pound projectiles, stating that "the various reports heretofore made of the invulnerability of the ram have not been exaggerated." When *Albemarle* came to rest at the Plymouth wharf, repairs could be readily made. She

still represented a formidable force in the sounds. Something had to be done to eliminate the threat. But what?

Having missed the action at New Bern, Cooke repaired the ram and kept her posted at Plymouth, mainly because she had no other place to go. Her presence kept a strong Union squadron constantly on patrol. On occasion she would steam down to the mouth of the Roanoke dragging for torpedoes, but mainly she languished up the river, doing nothing. For several weeks Cooke kept the ram well hidden, and prowling Unionists could not find her.

Welles did not want to send wooden ships against her, and every proposal to destroy the ram carried overtones of a suicide mission. Yet, when five men on *Wyalusing* came forward with a plan, Queen approved it.

At 2:00 p.m. on May 25, the volunteers pushed off in a dinghy and ascended a

Left: A selection of Confederate naval arms and accoutrements. The flag is a typical Second National Bunting Flag as displayed by warships and other vessels of the South. Laying across this are a British Pattern 1859 cutlass-type design of bayonet with protective scabbard, for use in conjunction with British Wilson breechloading naval rifle below, complete with ramrod in stowed position; short-barreled type of pistol used for firing warning flares or colors of the day; canvas sea bag; naval cutlass complete with canvas waist belt and protective scabbard; Thomas, Griswold and Company design of naval cutlass (far right) with belt, the buckle of which displays an embossed "CS" motif; and (bottom right) firing mechanism for ship-borne cannon armament embarked on Cofederate ships of the line.

Below: Most Confederate torpedoes dredged up from the waterways were already ruined by the infiltration of water. Torpedoes that did not detonate in the water were hauled ashore, taken apart, and defused.

branch of the Roanoke. Landing along shore across from Plymouth, over an island swamp they carried two 100-pound torpedoes in stretchers. Coxswain John W. Lloyd and Coal-heaver Charles W. Baldwin slipped into the water at 11:00 p.m. and, dragging a line to haul across the torpedoes, swam to the opposite shore. The two men came ashore a few hundred feet above the ram, pulled the torpedoes across the river, and bridled them together in such a way that Baldwin could place one along each side of the ram's bow. As Baldwin swam toward the ram, Lloyd remained on shore paying out the guide rope and letting the current carry the explosives downstream. Fireman Allen Crawford waited on the

opposite shore for a signal from Baldwin to explode the devices.

Baldwin came within a few yards of the ram before being sighted by a sentry. Seconds later, Confederates with muskets tumbled out through the hatch and spattered the river with small arms fire. Baldwin ducked beneath the surface and swam downriver. Lloyd cut the torpedoes loose and vanished in the brush. Crawford ran for the dinghy and hastily departed with the two oarsmen. On the morning of the 27th, after a mission consuming 38 hours, the trio returned to *Wyalusing*. They reported Baldwin and Lloyd missing, but the pair showed up two days later, totally exhausted. For their efforts, both men

received the Medal of Honor, but the deadly *Albemarle* remained intact and unmolested.

The weeks of constant strain wore on both sides. Cooke, *Albemarle's* commander, fell ill from nervous exhaustion, so Mallory dispatched Lieutenant Commander Alexander F. Warley to relieve him. It seemed like old enemies from the *Mississippi* were being joined together for one last fight. Warley had commanded the ram *Manassas* during Farragut's fight off Fort Jackson and St. Philip. He had rammed the U.S.S. *Mississippi*, on which Roe had been an officer, and Roe had been among the detail that boarded *Manassas* and set her on fire. It now seemed evident they would face each other again, but not if Lieutenant William B.

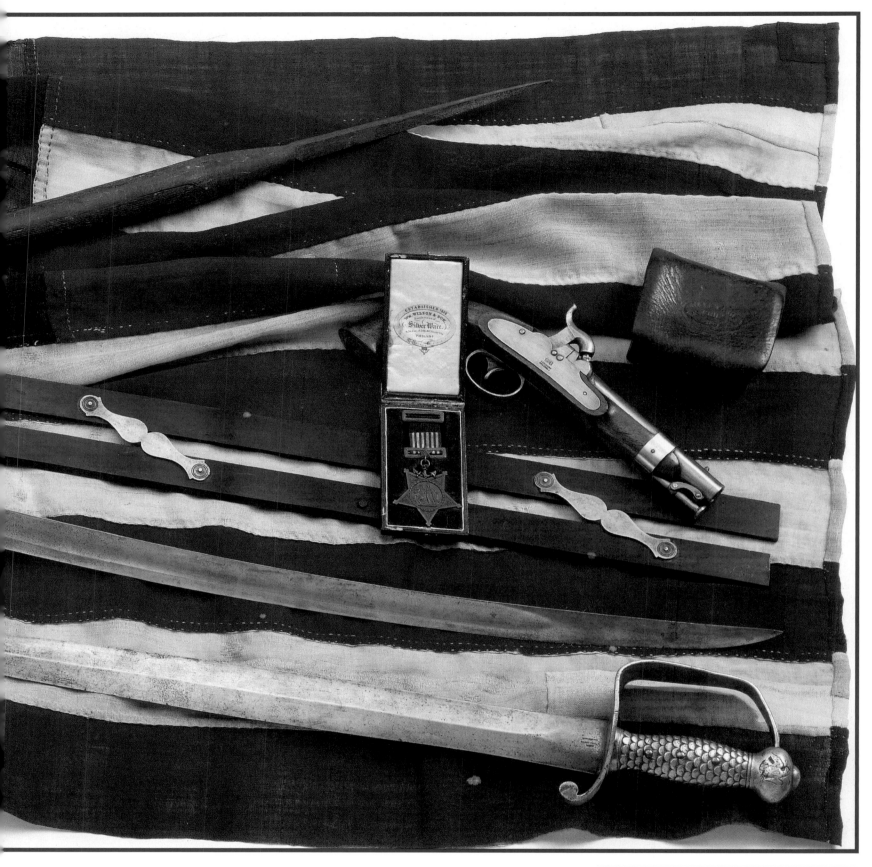

Above: A selection of Union naval arms and accoutrements. The flag is a typical National Bunting Flag as displayed by Union warships during the war. Laying across this are a type of pike used to facilitate boarding of Confederate warships during close-order engagements; a stand of grape shot (bottom left); a Dahigren-manufactured Bowie-type bayonet with scabbard; two officers' cutlasses, the top one being of Model 1860 design, the bottom one being of Model 1841 design. Above these are a parallel ruler used in navigation; a presentation case with 1862 design Navy Medal of Honor; U.S. Navy Model 1842 muzzle-loading percussion pistol with ramrod; and leather box containing primer.

Cushing had his way.

During the summer of 1864, numerous schemes had been proposed for destroying Albemarle, and none since May had been implemented. In July, as Admiral Lee leisurely paged through official correspondence, he came across a report describing one of Cushing's extraordinary escapades along the Cape Fear River. The twenty-one year-old daredevil seemed to enjoy any assignment involving great risks and had demonstrated an aptitude for pulling them off successfully.

After making a few inquiries into Cushing's record, Lee turned to an aide and said, "Get Lieutenant Cushing! Bring him to me as quickly as you can!" What Lee did not

know was that Cushing and Flusser were the closest of friends. When the lieutenant learned that Miami's battle with Albemarle had taken Flusser's life, he said, "I shall not rest until I have avenged his death." By coincidence, Admiral Lee gave him that opportunity.

Cushing enjoyed making surprise raids using small boats, and to attack Albemarle he chose a pair of 30-foot steam launches under construction at Brooklyn. He armed each vessel with a 12-pound howitzer in the bow and attached a complicated device for holding a torpedo fastened to a 14-foot boom. To explode the device required a careful manipulation of a lanyard connected to a trigger line. After testing the apparatus in the Hudson River, Cushing finally mastered the sequence and believed he could explode the torpedo blindfolded.

On September 22 he started south, but only one launch reached Hampton Roads. The other boat suffered engine trouble, and though Cushing searched for her, she was never found. So with a single launch, he pushed off for Roanoke Island, arriving there on October 23.

Much to the lieutenant's surprise, Admiral Lee showed him a newspaper article explaining how Cushing intended to destroy *Albemarle*. Though the newsclip described the plan inaccurately, the warning could not have gone unnoticed by the Confederates.

After explaining the mission to 14 volunteers, Cushing spent the next two days drilling the men while acquainting himself with the lower section of the Roanoke River. Satisfied that he could find the ram in the dark, he pushed off on the night of October 26. The launch chugged toward the mouth of the river, the Union flag at her masthead. The boat grounded on a bar, and Cushing did not get her afloat until 2:00 a.m. He did not want to waste the night and started upstream, only to be hailed by a Union picket boat. Learning from the sentinel that the launch's steam engine could be heard from several hundred yards away, Cushing returned to the squadron to have the steam system muffled.

During the 27th, three escaped slaves warned that the Confederates had posted pickets on the partially submerged *Southfield* and established a signal system with sentinels on *Albemarle*. When he shoved off that night, Cushing towed a cutter containing 12 men. He intended to cast it off when approaching *Southfield*, thereby enabling the men in the cutter to sneak up to the sunken vessel and capture the lookouts. But during the night rain fell, muffling

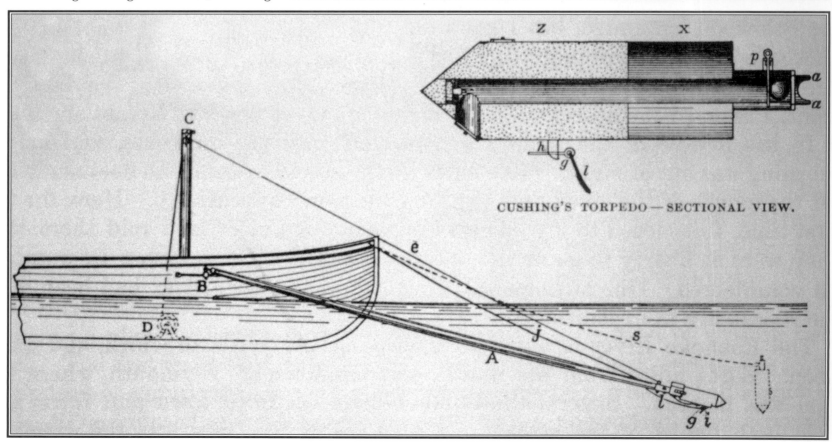

CUSHING'S TORPEDO — SECTIONAL VIEW.

engine noise, and Cushing's launch slipped by the Union picket boat unnoticed, which meant that there was a good chance that the enemy, too, would not hear his launch coming. Keeping the launch near shore, he passed *Southfield* unseen and continued upstream, still towing the cutter. With 12 extra men, his plan of action began to change. Instead of blowing up the ram, why not capture it?

The dark form of *Albemarle* loomed ahead, and Cushing steered along the far bank. Passing upstream of the ram, he headed for a wharf to discuss his change of plans with the men in the cutter. A dog barked along shore, waking a sentry who challenged the launch. With the opportunity to board *Albemarle* lost, Cushing quickly cut loose the cutter and sent it downstream to capture the pickets on *Southfield*. Then, with a full head of steam, he swung the launch across the river and steered directly for the ram.

Men emerged from the *Albemarle's* casemate, and musket fire began spattering the water around the charging launch. As Cushing squinted into the darkness ahead, he gingerly fingered the ropes controlling the spar. Grayclads ignited bonfires along shore, and in the eerie light cast by the flames Cushing observed a circle of logs surrounding *Albemarle*, the best defense against a torpedo attack. He sheered off, taking the launch back to the far side of the river. With every ounce of steam the boilers could generate, Cushing brought the launch about and ran at full speed for the log pen. Moments before impact, he fired the 12-pounder, sending a double charge of canister across the deck of *Albemarle*. With a

grinding lurch, the bow of the launch hurdled the pen and hung suspended over the obstruction.

Bullets zipped through the air, tearing into the launch, but Cushing concentrated only on the ram. He lowered the spar and swung it under the bow of the ram. Ten feet away he heard a shutter of a gunport open and the sound of a 100-pounder running out. He had but seconds before it fired. With practiced deftness, he jogged the trigger. The ball dropped on the pin and the device detonated with a mighty roar, lifting the ram partly out of the water. At almost the same instant the Brooke rifle erupted. The gun, having been lifted slightly by the exploding torpedo, spewed a hundred pounds of canister over the heads of the men in the launch. With a gaping hole in her side, *Albemarle* settled on the bottom of the Roanoke River. The top of her casemate remained above water to mark her grave.

Overwhelmed by Confederates on shore, most of the men in the launch surrendered. Two jumped into the river and drowned. Cushing somehow survived musket fire, the river, a day in the swamp, and made it back to the safety of the squadron.

Admiral David Farragut, who had come home from the Gulf on furlough, declared that "young Cushing was the hero of the war." Congress rewarded Cushing with advancement to lieutenant commander. A few months later he distinguished himself again during the Union assault on Fort Fisher, and spent the next year, deservedly so, as a national celebrity.

With *Albemarle* destroyed, Captain Smith moved his squadron into the Roanoke River on October 31 and forced the surrender of the Confederate garrison at Plymouth. The loss induced the Confederates to destroy two unfinished rams building on other rivers feeding into the sounds. The South's aspirations to recover control of coastal North Carolina had died with the explosion of a single torpedo carried by a launch driven by a navy lieutenant and 12 volunteers.

Ironically, the first so-called torpedoes of the war were developed by the Confederacy. Cushing never liked them. After blowing up *Albemarle* he admitted that the device had so many defects, "he would not again attempt its use." For those who cared, once was enough.

Above: Lieutenant William B. Cushing had already earned the reputation as a daredevil before he suggested to Admiral Lee a method for destroying the *Albemarle*. Lee agreed, only because Cushing would lead it.

Below: A selection of Confederate naval buttons, including officers' uniform buttons imported from Britain, with (far right) an enlisted man's hard rubber coat button.

Bottom: a selection of Union naval buttons, including five brass officers' buttons, and a (larger) Goodyear naval button.

Left: Farragut declared Cushing the "hero of the war" when he heard the young lieutenant had blown up the troublesome *Albemarle*, which lifted partly out of the water with the explosion and settled on the bottom of the Roanoke River.

Left: Contemporary drawing showing side elevation of Cushing's launch with 14-foot boom to which was attached a "torpedo" with which he planned to blow up the Albemarle. The "torpedo" would be exploded by manipulation of a lanyard connected to a trigger line.

CHAPTER TEN

THE BATTLE IN THE CHANNEL

Every ship-to-ship naval battle during the Civil War took place on inland or coastal waters – except one, and that fight took place in the English Channel. It marked the last great tournament between two ships of wood and sail.

There would never be another to match it.

From the heights overlooking the Channel near Cherbourg, France, thousands of Europeans and a few Americans would follow the action through binoculars. Others would hear the thunder of heavy guns as they tried to focus on a fight seven miles away. Dozens standing in yachts and launches would enjoy a ringside seat near the outer fringes of the action. Oddsmakers enjoyed an active business among the betting public. Artists brought sketchbooks or planted their easels on the heights to capture for posterity a once-in-a-lifetime event.

No one who watched the fight would ever forget it.

The Confederate vessel had been a ship of prey. For two years she had prowled the seas destroying American commerce. The Union vessel had been the hunter, always searching but never finding the fast and elusive commerce raiders built in British shipyards for the Confederacy. In June, 1864, the hunt ended, and two vessels, evenly matched, went to sea, one of them for the last time.

When learning of the battle some weeks later, Admiral David Farragut, who had the most distinguished record of any officer in the Union Navy, lamented, "I would sooner have fought that fight than any ever fought on the ocean." Hundreds of brother officers shared the same sentiment.

During the Civil War, few Confederate sailors plied their trade as tenaciously or as effectively as Raphael Semmes, who for three years roamed the seas in search of American merchantmen. The South never mobilized more than eight commerce destroyers, and Semmes commanded two of them.

Semmes affected people strongly. Those he met instantly either liked or disliked him. Of medium height, thin, and small-boned, Semmes had piercing eyes, a quick intellect, and a strong personality, with a habit of direct speech. He minced no words and kept his counsel to himself. In foreign ports he could be delightfully sociable or, on matters of international law, legalistically brutal. In the quiet of his cabin, he enjoyed his books and his privacy. His other distinguishing feature – tightly pointed waxed mustaches –

gave vent to a sailor's search for amusement in the forecastle. They called him "Old Beeswax," but not to his face.

Born in Maryland on September 27, 1809, Semmes joined the navy at the age of 17, learned his craft at sea, and passed his examination in 1832, ranking as a passed midshipman. Between tours of duty, while other naval officers found work on packet ships, Semmes studied law at his brother's office in Cumberland, Maryland. In 1834 he became a member of the bar, and in 1837 a lieutenant in the navy. Having established himself in two professions, he married and eventually moved to Mobile, Alabama, where he occupied his time doing both.

Rear Admiral David Dixon Porter of the United States Navy knew Semmes well, having served with him on *Porpoise* in 1846. He remembered the man who would

At Capetown, South Africa, Capt. Raphael Semmes of the C.S.S. *Alabama* stands behind his favorite gun, the 110-pounder Armstrong. Behind him against the wheel is Lt. John M. Kell, the executive officer.

Above: Two Confederate commerce destroyers came from British shipyards, the first being the C.S.S. *Florida*. Pictured in chase of the magnificent clipper ship, *Jacob Bell*, *Florida* caught her and burned her.

Below: Semmes was called a pirate by Secretary Welles, who threatened to hang him when caught. About the only semblance given Semmes by this cartoonist was the captain's handlebar moustache.

become his foe during the Civil War as one having no particular taste for the navy but having a fondness for literature and international law. Porter might also have added that Semmes had many interests, including the science of the seas and the geography of the world. Porter found Semmes "indolent and fond of his comfort" – a man of little energy. Intellectual conversation, however, stimulated Semmes. Evidently, time spent with Porter did not.

When war erupted in 1861, Commander Semmes had reached the age of 52. He resigned from the Old Navy, where he had spent the past several years idling away in the U.S. Lighthouse Service. Confederate Secretary of the Navy Mallory put him quickly to work in New Orleans converting the packet steamer *Havana* into an armed commerce raider, the five gun, 520-ton C.S.S. *Sumter*. Porter's impression of Semmes lost credibility when the clumsy little *Sumter* outsailed the faster U.S.S. *Brooklyn* and escaped into the Gulf. Porter later hunted for Semmes as far south as Brazil and never found him. In the meantime, *Sumter* captured 18 American merchant vessels before limping into Gibraltar with rotten boilers and a leaking hull.

During Semmes's seven months at sea, Commander James D. Bulloch went to Liverpool, England, as Mallory's secret purchasing agent. Mallory had visions of building a great Confederate fleet by using England's shipyards. Applying many ruses to outwit British authorities, Bulloch hired agents and through them built two of the Confederacy's greatest commerce raiders – *Florida* and *Alabama*. While Lieutenant John Newland Maffitt commanded *Florida*, Bulloch aspired to command *Alabama*. But

because the United States Navy had bottled-up the leaky *Sumter* in Gibraltar's harbor, Semmes became available, and the command of *Alabama* went to him.

No other warship in the Confederate Navy could match the size, beauty, and overall performance of the steam propeller sloop *Alabama*. Built to the highest standards of the Royal Navy, her bark-rig made her fast under sail and fast under steam. She could stay at sea for months, having a desalination system that worked off her steaming system, and provisions other than coal she could get from her prizes.

To overhaul the fast clipper ships, Bulloch had designed her for speed and, in case she ran into trouble, he had also given her a potent battery – eight English Blakely cannons, a 7-inch 100-pounder rifle in pivot, one 8-inch solid shot 68-pounder aft, and six 32-pounders, three in each broadside. Bulloch had pierced the ship for 12 guns, leaving two empty ports on each side which could be filled by moving two 32-pounders from one side of the ship to the other if needed in battle.

Bulloch slipped *Alabama* away from England a few hours before the British government sought to seize her. He sent her to a lonely island in the Azores to be fitted with guns and to await the arrival of Semmes and his officers. Bulloch also recruited a crew in Liverpool, luring seamen by offering them lots of prize money. *Alabama* would have the unique distinction of fighting a war with officers from America's South and sailors from England.

British merchant shippers wanted *Alabama* to succeed in her quest for prizes equally as much as did Semmes and his officers – but for different reasons. For the past 10 years the American merchant fleet

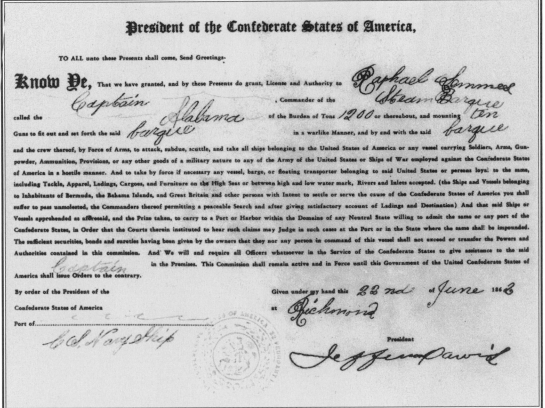

Above: Every officer commanding a ship of war goes to sea with a certificate of authority. In Semmes's case it was granted by Jefferson Davis, the president of the Confederacy. The document served as a passport in foreign countries.

Above left: Commander. James D. Bulloch went to England as a special agent to buy or build commerce destroyers for the Confederacy. He did so by building the finest two vessels in the entire Confederate navy.

Left: Great Britain was not supposed to take sides during the Civil War, but English blockade runners could be found along every wharf loading with supplies, guns, ammunition, and dry goods for the South.

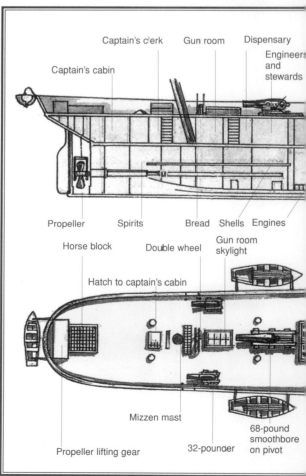

Captain's clerk   Gun room   Dispensary

Captain's cabin

Engineers and stewards

Propeller   Spirits   Bread   Shells   Engines

Horse block   Double wheel   Gun room skylight

Hatch to captain's cabin

Mizzen mast

Propeller lifting gear   32-pounder   68-pound smoothbore on pivot

had snatched a huge amount of carrying trade away from the British. English shippers could not compete with the new, efficient American sailing vessels. With men like Semmes and commerce raiders like *Florida* and *Alabama*, British merchants took heart. They now had the means to destroy their competition without lifting a finger and, when Bulloch built the two cruisers, many in England looked the other way.

Most of the officers on *Alabama* came from *Sumter*. Having been trained by Semmes, they had come to know his skills and developed enormous confidence in his decisions, all of which would have to be imparted to a crew of 120 Englishmen and 20 junior officers.

Semmes placed complete confidence in his executive officer, Lieutenant John Macintosh Kell, of Georgia, a 20-year veteran from the Old Navy. Thirty-nine years of age and six feet two, Kell was a powerhouse of strength. His fiery, reddish-brown beard and fierce blue eyes stood out in sharp contrast to his fair and even-tempered management of the crew. The men liked him more than they did Semmes.

Second Lieutenant Richard F. Armstrong, a slim six-foot, blue-eyed, 20-year-old, outranked everyone on board but Semmes and Kell. After graduating from the U.S. Naval Academy and receiving his commission, Armstrong resigned and returned to his home in Georgia. He joined Semmes on *Sumter* and took command of a gun division. On *Alabama* he would command the 100-pounder Blakely rifled pivot gun – the most important gun on the ship – and two 32-pounders in broadside.

Third Lieutenant Joseph D. Wilson, a former cadet at the Naval Academy, had resigned at the outbreak of war and finished his training under Semmes on *Sumter*. Wilson commanded *Alabama's* after gun division, the next in order of importance. Fiery and impulsive by nature, he loved a fight. Before the war ended, he would have one.

Fourth Lieutenant Arthur Sinclair had already been in one fight, having served on

Far left: Two of Semmes's junior officers, Lt. Arthur Sinclair (left) and Lt. Robert F. Armstrong pose on *Alabama*'s deck. Sinclair looks like he is dressed to go into Capetown for a little recreation.

Above and left:The C.S.S. *Alabama* began life as "Hull No. 290" in Liverpool, England. Quickly named *Enrica* for her launch on May 15, 1862, she was officially turned over to her Confederate masters out in the Atlantic, near the Azores, on August 24. She was commissioned as a cruiser, armed, and and renamed *Alabama*. The ship was a barque-rigged steamer, 220 feet long and 31 feet 8 inches in beam. She displaced 1,050 tons, and was powered by a single-shaft engine that could propel her at up to 13 knots. In addition to running the ship, her crew of 145 officers and men also had to man six 32-pound smoothbores in broadside, a massive 68-pounder smoothbore pivot gun aft, and a powerful 6.4-inch Blakely muzzle-loading rifle as bow pivot.

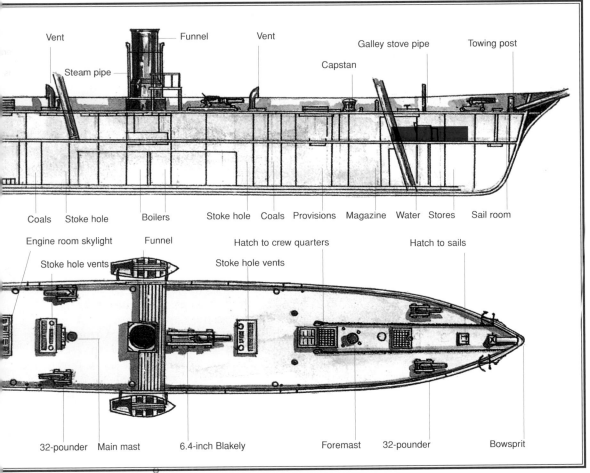

Vent — Funnel — Vent — Galley stove pipe — Towing post

Steam pipe — Capstan

Coals — Stoke hole — Boilers — Stoke hole — Coals — Provisions — Magazine — Water — Stores — Sail room

Engine room skylight — Funnel — Hatch to crew quarters — Hatch to sails

Stoke hole vents — Stoke hole vents

32-pounder — Main mast — 6.4-inch Blakely — Foremast — 32-pounder — Bowsprit

Above: Officers of the U.S.S. *Kearsarge* gather for a photo after the deck had been cleared following the fight with *Alabama*. Captain John Winslow is third from the left with a thumb tucked into his jacket.

Top: The U.S.S. *Kearsarge* had been built to chase Confederate cruisers and assigned to Europe to search and destroy all that could be found. Until the first week of June, 1864, *Kearsarge* had been a bad luck ship.

the C.S.S. *Virginia* during her two-day rampage in Hampton Roads. A Virginian by birth, Sinclair followed in the footsteps of his father and grandfather, each having held high rank in the Old Navy. Next to Semmes, young Sinclair was probably the most insightful and gifted officer on *Alabama*. In years after he wrote a marvelous book of his life on the ship, surpassing in many respects the lengthy apologia penned by Semmes in his "Memoirs."

On September 5, 1862, Semmes captured his first prize, a whaling ship off the Azores, and before the year ended he had burned or bonded 25 more. By then, the Union had a dozen warships scouting from the coast of Nova Scotia to Brazil looking for *Alabama*. Semmes, however, had slipped into the Gulf

of Mexico looking for Union transports. He lured the 5-gun U.S.S. *Hatteras* off blockade duty at Galveston, Texas, and sank her after a 13-minute engagement. Using shells, Armstrong's 100-pounder blew five-foot holes in the sides of *Hatteras*.

Semmes then went on a cruise that took *Alabama* around the Cape of Good Hope and east to Singapore. Merchant ships from the United States no longer dotted the seas. Those not destroyed had holed up in ports, waiting for the war to end. Shippers changed their registers, seeking protection under foreign flags. Some firms sold their ships, unable to pay wartime insurance rates or unwilling to risk their assets against the probability of loss by capture.

After 22 months of hard sailing, *Alabama*

began to show signs of wear. The copper sheathing on her hull began to peel, her boilers and engines needed repair, and age and exposure to the climates of the seas had sapped strength from her powder. Even Semmes, who had withstood the strain of endless days at sea, sought refuge in a friendly European port where he, along with his ship, could rehabilitate. By burning almost all of the 66 American vessels he had captured, Semmes had created a diplomatic crisis in Great Britain and, to a lesser degree, in France. By mid-1864, many of the nations of Europe had deserted the Southern cause, but Semmes chose a port in France. On June 11, after disguising the ship as a merchantman, he slipped into Cherbourg and dropped anchor.

On June 12, Semmes visited the port admiral and requested the use of the government's dry dock to repair his ship. The admiral temporized, stating that only the emperor, Napoleon III, could make that decision but he was away on vacation and was not expected to return for several days.

Semmes returned to the comfort of his cabin to await developments, but they were not of the kind he expected.

News of *Alabama's* presence at Cherbourg spread rapidly. At Flushing in the Netherlands, Captain John Acrum Winslow, commanding the U.S.S. *Kearsarge,* learned that the most wanted ship in the Confederate Navy lay less than a day's sail away. He had spent most of his career chasing Rebel raiders and had never caught one. Now was his chance.

Welles had sent Union warships all over the world in search of Confederate cruisers. He had spent millions on the effort. Shipping firms constantly hounded him for results. Nothing frustrated him more than failing to put a stop to commerce raiding. The U.S.S. *Kearsarge* had once kept the C.S.S. *Florida* penned-up at Brest, on the west coast of France, but only for a while, and later had missed a chance to capture the C.S.S. *Georgia.* After two years of patrolling the English Channel, the Bay of Biscay, and the Mediterranean, *Kearsarge's* record

Below: *Kearsarge* **did not carry many guns, but her two 11-inch Dahlgrens on pivots gave her great flexibility. Acting Master James R. Wheeler (left) and Engineer Sidney L. Smith (right) flank the Dahlgren's trunnion.**

remained so remarkably unproductive that some of her men called her an unlucky ship.

Winslow had not always commanded *Kearsarge*. When she was launched from the Portsmouth Navy Yard and commissioned on January 24, 1862, the 1,031-ton sloop of war left New Hampshire for foreign service under the command of Captain Charles W. Pickering. Pickering took her into the Mediterranean and blockaded *Sumter* at Gibraltar, but Semmes never expected to get the defective cruiser back to sea and left her there for Pickering to waste time watching. Late in 1862 Welles detached Pickering and sent Winslow to Europe to take command of *Kearsarge*. Winslow found her in dry dock at Cadiz, Spain, where she remained out of service for three and a half months.

Winslow did not like his new command. Being third rate men-of-war, ships like *Kearsarge* usually drew as a skipper either a commander or lieutenant commander – not a captain. Winslow felt he deserved a squadron or, at minimum, one of the new double-turreted monitors. He had complained so loudly in Washington about being passed over for command of a squadron that Welles sent him to Europe to

rid himself of the nuisance.

Winslow also suffered from chronic malaria, an ailment that invaded his system during his early years in the navy. He joined his new command ill, his condition complicated by an infected eye, and spent his first days bedridden. Winslow expected no rewards. Only a deep sense of duty gave him the strength to carry on.

A native of Wilmington, North Carolina, Winslow grew up in the navy, one of his closest friends being Raphael Semmes. During the Mexican War they served together on the U.S.S. *Cumberland*. During that war, each had the good fortune of commanding a ship. Winslow lost his on a reef off Tampico; Semmes lost his to a sudden norther that capsized his vessel and nearly took his life. Misfortune brought their roles as "captains" to an abrupt end. Both were reassigned to the U.S.S. *Raritan*, where once again they shared the same stateroom and joked about their bad luck. Eighteen years later they were captains again – this time pitted against each other.

For more than a year Winslow had cruised his station watching for *Alabama*. He chased every rumor emanating from a

network of Union agents placed among the ports of Europe, but he always came up empty-handed. When word came on June 13 that *Alabama* had entered Cherbourg, he assembled his crew on deck and said, "Men, I congratulate you in saying that the *Alabama* has arrived at Cherbourg, and the *Kearsarge*, having a good name in France and England, is to have her cruising ground off that port."

Confederate cruisers rarely fought, nor did Mallory's orders to Semmes's encourage it. Winslow expected to conduct another lengthy blockade. Semmes' genius for escape gave Winslow much to worry about. The latter's entire career had been a series of small personal embarrassments. He did not need another. Much to his surprise, his old friend supplied the solution.

When *Kearsarge* appeared off the eastern breakwater to Cherbourg's harbor on June 14, Semmes reflected on his alternatives. He found the French unfriendly and doubted whether they would put *Alabama* in dry dock as he first had hoped. At home, the South was losing the war, and in diplomatic circles France and England no longer espoused the Confederate cause. *Alabama's* officers and men were exhausted, and the

Far left: The Union sailor's work uniform, especially during the balmy days of summer, consisted of light cotton work trousers, a wool undershirt, and a wool cap. Most light woolens breathed well during the summer.

Left: Instead of foot lockers, sailors stored their clothing is sea bags, which hung next to their hammocks below deck. During hours of idlements, sailors found ways to adorn their bags with embroidered designs.

ship's powder showed signs of decay. Even if he escaped from *Kearsarge*, where and how far could he go before the ship suffered irreparable damage? American merchant ships had all but disappeared from the seas, so why continue cruising for prizes that could no longer be found? And how many days would pass before more Union ships came off Cherbourg to keep *Alabama* in her pen, even should she try to escape? From Semmes's perspective, his only alternative was to fight. *Alabama* had been a lucky ship, but would that be enough when pitted against the bigger *Kearsarge*?

Kearsarge had been built to fight; *Alabama* had been built to raid, her advantage being speed. But, with copper sheathing curling on her hull, she had lost that advantage. *Kearsarge* carried seven guns to *Alabama's* eight, but two on the Union vessel were 11-inch Dahlgren smoothbores – not very effective at a distance but deadly up close. The only rifle on *Kearsarge* was a 28-pounder, the other four being 32-pounders. *Alabama* had the advantage in long guns, a 100-pounder and a 68-pounder, both rifled Blakelys. Yet in weight *Kearsarge* could throw 430 pounds of projectiles to *Alabama's*

360 pounds. On paper the vessels were closely matched, but *Kearsarge* had another advantage. She had recently been overhauled. While Semmes had always tried to save his powder, Winslow regularly exercised his guns, sharpening his men for battle.

When *Alabama* had captured the ship *Rockingham* on April 23, Semmes had given the gun crews a small amount of target practice before burning the prize. When he announced that he had decided to challenge *Kearsarge*, Kell privately reminded him that every third shell fired at Rockingham had failed to explode. But Semmes had no trouble whipping up enthusiasm to fight *Kearsarge*. The gun crews, being mostly Englishmen, were anxious to match their skill against the Yankees.

Semmes signified his determination to fight on June 15 when he sent his treasury ashore – five bags of gold sovereigns worth $25,000. He deposited them with the Confederate agent at Cherbourg, along with the paymaster's records of crewmen's accounts and ransom bonds for vessels he had captured and released. From every prize Semmes had collected a trophy – the

ship's chronometer – and for safe keeping he transferred the timepieces into the care of the captain of the British yacht *Hornet*.

For three days Semmes prepared his ship for battle. His strategy was simple. He would stay at long range, using his rifled Blakelys to disable *Kearsarge*. Then, having silenced the enemy's guns, he would come alongside, sweep her decks with the 32-pounders, and assault the vessel with a strong boarding party. To accomplish this end, men practiced during the day with pikes and cutlasses and at night honed them to a razor-sharpness. Gunner Thomas C. Cuddy overhauled the guns and drilled the crews. Boatswain Benjamin P. Mecaskey detailed men to take down the light spars, stopper the standing rigging, and dispose of the top hamper. On Saturday, June 18, Kell reported the ship ready for battle. Semmes advised the port admiral that he intended to go out and fight *Kearsarge* on Sunday morning – his lucky day.

Semmes harbored no misgivings about the risks involved. On Saturday night he penned an entry in his journal, writing, "My crew seem to be in the right spirit, a quiet spirit of determination pervading both officers and men. The combat will no doubt be contested and obstinate, but the two ships are so equally matched that I do not feel at liberty to decline it. God defend the right, and have mercy on the souls of those who fall, as many of us must."

As each day passed, Winslow watched for *Alabama*. He had come ashore in a boat on June 14, only to be tantalized by a challenge from Semmes carried by the local Confederate agent. Welles did not approve of officers accepting challenges, so Winslow said nothing and hurried back to his vessel to prepare for a fight. He expected to see his old friend come out of the harbor on June 15 or 16, but Semmes needed time to get his ship in fighting trim and failed to appear. When nothing happened, Winslow began to despair, but he used the extra time to put his gun crews through rigorous drill. Those not serving the guns distributed tourniquets and bandages along the gundeck and made preparations for receiving the wounded.

News of the forthcoming battle spread through France and across the English Channel. Not since the War of 1812 had one ship from the United States challenged another in an old-fashioned sea battle. Hordes of people from Great Britain, France, Belgium, and the Netherlands flocked to Cherbourg to witness the fight. The yacht *Deerhound*, owned by wealthy Englishman John Lancaster, slipped into the harbor on the night of June 17 to pick up the owner, who had been on vacation in France with his family. Confederate naval personnel landlocked in Europe came to Cherbourg to join *Alabama*. Prisoners released by Semmes when reaching France volunteered to join *Kearsarge*. French authorities intervened. The two belligerents must fight it out with no increase in manpower, firepower, or armament, but nobody told the Lancasters and the owners of dozens of other vessels in the harbor that they could not go out in the morning to watch the battle.

On Sunday, June 19, 1864, daylight burst upon Cherbourg, bringing a soft balmy breeze blowing off the Channel. Sunlight drenched the heights on Querqueville Point at West Pass, where at an early hour 15,000 spectators dressed in their finest clothes had massed to watch the fight. Artists set up

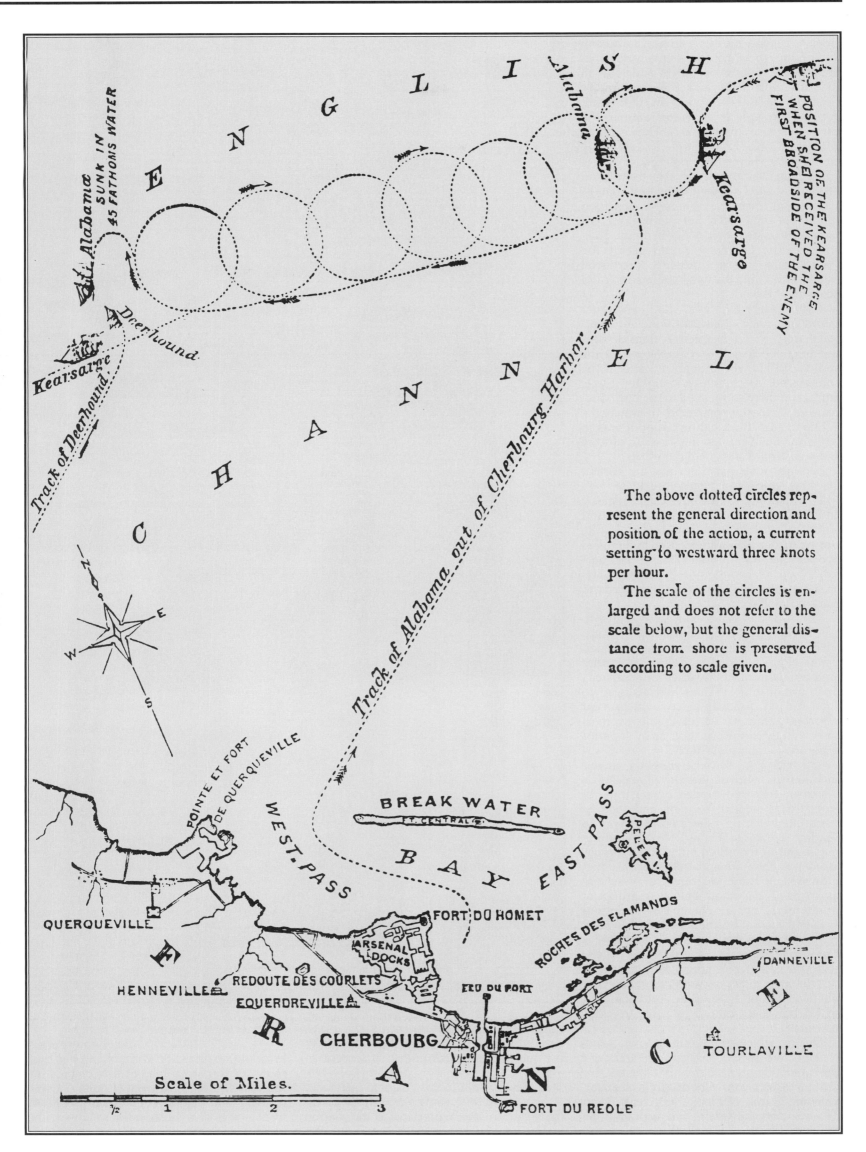

The above dotted circles represent the general direction and position of the action, a current setting to westward three knots per hour.

The scale of the circles is enlarged and does not refer to the scale below, but the general distance from shore is preserved according to scale given.

easels to capture the scene on canvas, among them Edouard Manet. Residents hung from upper story windows, others squatted on rooftops, and here and there miniature Confederate flags flapped in the wind, dappling a splash of color among the gawking swarm of onlookers. They came to witness a once-in-a-lifetime event. They would not go home disappointed.

Captain Penhoat of the French ironclad *Couronne* waited nearby for the first signs of activity on *Alabama*. When he observed sparks spewing from her smokestack, he came alongside, informing Semmes that, when ready, *Couronne* would escort the Confederate vessel outside territorial waters. After that, the two combatants could do as they wished.

John Lancaster, who had anchored *Deerhound* near *Alabama*, watched with equal interest. He wanted a ringside seat and intended to follow *Alabama* out of the harbor, but his wife thought it better if the family went to church. A daughter, niece, nurse, and three sons called for a vote. Nine-year-old Catherine preferred to watch the fight and cast the deciding ballot. It was to Catherine that Semmes and 41 of his officers and men would soon owe their lives.

Semmes took his time, making certain the crew enjoyed a hearty breakfast. Kell and Armstrong walked the deck, making doubly certain that guns, shot, shell, and powder were in position to do battle. During earlier preparations, Kell had moved two of the 32-pounders from the port battery and placed them in the empty ports on the starboard side, giving him seven to guns to face the enemy.

Winslow had made similar changes to his battery, equalizing the number of guns, but as an extra defensive measure he draped chains along his hull to deflect projectiles fired by *Alabama*. Kell warned of *Kearsarge's* chain armor, but Semmes had resolved to fight and no disadvantage would prevent him from doing so. At sea, battles were as often won by fortuitous shots as by superior arms, and Semmes felt lucky.

At 9:45 a.m. *Alabama* weighed anchor and fell in with *Couronne*. Lancaster's *Deerhound* followed, trailed by a parade of boats flying colorful banners and looking much like weekend sailors on their way to Sunday regatta. During the 45-minute respite out to the seven mile limit, Semmes called the crew aft and delivered his first address since commissioning the vessel. He spoke as if he stood before a group of Southerners, not Englishmen, reminding them that the achievements of *Alabama* must not be tarnished by defeat. "The thing is impossible!" he said. "The flag that floats over you is that of a young Republic, who bids defiance to her enemies, whenever and wherever found. Show the world that you know how to uphold it! Go to your quarters!"

During the same interval of time, Winslow conducted services on *Kearsarge*. The quartermaster only half listened. He kept a glass on Cherbourg's harbor, watching a trail of smoke as *Alabama* and *Couronne* came into view. "She's coming!" he hollered. Winslow closed the service and

came to the rail. He borrowed the glass, nodded affirmatively, and handed it back to the quartermaster. Turning to his executive officer, Lieutenant Commander James S. Thornton, he said calmly, "Beat to quarters." Winslow did not want *Alabama*, if badly damaged, to seek refuge inside the marine league, so he steamed farther into the

Channel before coming about to fight.

At first, *Alabama's* crew interpreted Winslow's tactics as a withdrawal, but they soon saw *Kearsarge* helm over to engage. As the vessels closed to within a mile, *Alabama* opened with her pivot guns, but the shots went wild. Two broadsides followed, the projectiles soaring over the masts of

Kearsarge. Winslow wheeled hard and came at full speed, giving the impression that he intended to ram, but at 900 yards he sheered off and fired a full broadside. The shots fell short, bringing a cheer from the Confederates. *Alabama* replied with another broadside, sending shells screaming harmlessly through *Kearsarge's* rigging.

The pace of firing from *Alabama* reached frenzied proportions, the gun crews loading, firing, swabbing, and re-loading at one-minute intervals. *Kearsarge* replied more deliberately, her gun crews cycling their fire every two to three minutes and taking care to make every shot count. Each ship concentrated their heaviest fire on the stern

Above: On even small steamers like the 1,031-ton *Kearsarge*, it takes a lot of men just to run the engineering department, including five officers, being the chief engineer and four assistants.

of the other, hoping to disable the engines or the steerage.

When Winslow discovered that *Kearsarge* could outmaneuver her enemy, he attempted to cross the Confederate's unprotected stern and rake her with 11-inch shells. Surprised by *Kearsarge's* speed, Semmes barely escaped having his decks swept by the Dahlgrens. Instead of standing off and using his rifled Blakelys, Semmes jockeyed for position, exchanging broadsides at distances ranging between 800 and 1,300 yards. The two warships attempted to batter each other into submission while making seven complete clockwise circles. Semmes found he could neither pull out of range of *Kearsarge's* heavy shell guns nor get close enough to board her. What he needed was that lucky shot.

Fifteen minutes into the fight, Semmes got his lucky shot. He stood on the horseblock shouting at his gun crews to aim lower and to make every shot count. A shell from the 100-pounder passed through *Kearsarge's* hull, and Semmes watched, suspecting it had struck the enemy's vital sternpost. For anxious seconds he waited for the shell to explode, but it never did. Perhaps at that moment he recalled Kell's warning – that when practicing on the prize *Rockingham*, two out of every three shells had failed to detonate.

Winslow felt the ship shudder when the 100-pounder struck the sternpost. At the

wheel, Quartermaster William Poole also knew something had happened. The shell had bound the rudder so tightly that it took three men to turn the wheel. Several days after the battle a detail cut the shell from the sternpost and sent it to Washington. Later, Semmes learned the shell had actually lodged in the sternpost. When reflecting on the battle, he wrote, "If the cap had performed its duty and exploded the shell, I

Bottom: Union naval flag, like that which would been flown from U.S.S. *Kearsarge*.

Below: Confederate States Navy Ensign of the Second Pattern. This actual flag was captured on the C.S.S. *Florida* after that ship was seized under cover of night in the neutral harbor of Bahia, Brazil, in October 1864.

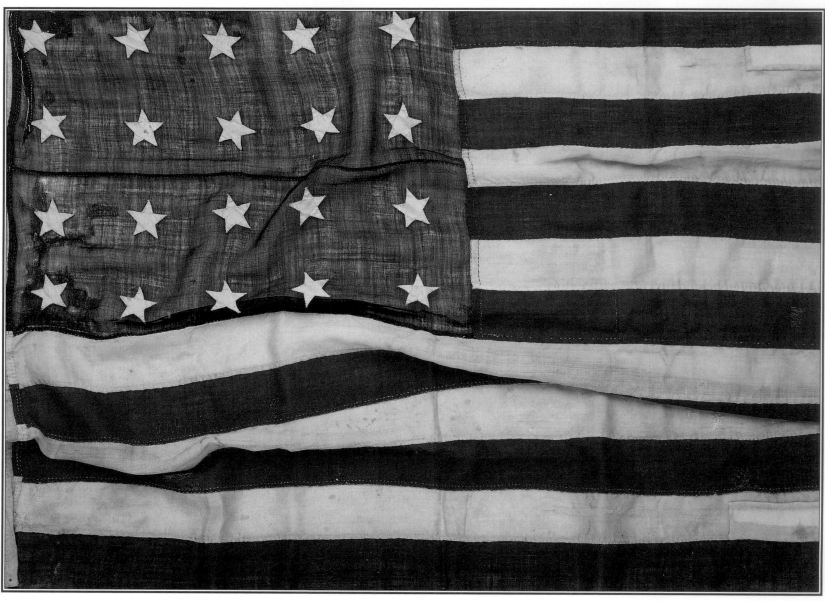

Left: Union naval artillery-related implements. The wooden tompion at the left with the brass star ring pull was used to plug the muzzle of a 9-inch gun when not in use. The leather pass box with strap was used to carry the projectile to the gun.

should have been called upon to save Captain Winslow's crew from drowning, instead of his being called upon to save mine. On so slight an incident – the defect of a percussion cap – did the battle hinge. The enemy were very proud of this shell. It was the only trophy they ever got of the *Alabama*."

Twenty minutes into the engagement, *Alabama's* guns began to find their mark. A Blakely shell ripped through *Kearsarge's* bulwarks and exploded on the quarterdeck, wounding three men serving the 11-inch gun aft. Two more shells plowed through open gun ports but failed to explode. A third shell exploded in the hammock nettings, setting them on fire. A shot from a 32-pounder struck the forward 11-inch Dahlgren, almost toppling both gun and carriage, but, like the shell embedded in the ship's sternpost, it failed to explode. But for decaying shells, Semmes's gun crews fired many lucky shots, and had the powder and caps been fresh, Winslow may have lost two of his 11-inch shell guns, and in all probability, his ship.

What puzzled Semmes was the number

of shots he observed striking *Kearsarge's* hull which, instead of penetrating, fell into the water. From the horseblock he shouted, "Mr. Kell, our shells strike the enemy's side, doing little damage.... Try solid shot." Kell alternated with shot and shell, pummeling the enemy's hull, but the unseen chain armor absorbed the impact and rejected the projectiles. Such was not the case on *Alabama*.

Winslow's superbly trained gun crews took their time loading, finding the range, and firing. They wasted barely a shot. Eleven-inch shells shot from Dahlgrens crashed through *Alabama's* beam, hurling huge splinters topside and below deck. Shells exploded, ripping enormous holes in her side, blowing out her bulwarks, disabling her rudder, and rendering her steerage unmanageable. Above the roar of guns and the explosion of shells came the screams of the wounded. As the crew ran out the after pivot gun, an 11-inch shell plowed through the port and exploded, killing or wounding 19 men and covering the gundeck with a mass of human fragments. One man was miraculously spared, Michael Mars, who grabbed a

shovel, scooped up the heap of human remains, and hurled them overboard.

A shot from *Kearsarge* carried away *Alabama's* gaff, and with it her colors. Union sailors gave a cheer, but Kell raised a new ensign on the mizzenmast. He might well have left it lowered, but Semmes intended to fight his ship to the end. *Kearsarge's* Dahlgrens roared again, tearing through the decks, slaughtering more men. A third shell struck the carriage of the aft pivot gun but failed to explode. It spun around on the deck until a seaman picked it up and threw it overboard. Another shell plunged through the hull at the waterline and smashed into the engine room. Seawater poured into the hold.

Though knocked to pieces, and with fires raging in the engine room, *Alabama* fought on. Armstrong leveled the 100-pounder on *Kearsarge's* midsection and fired a shell in desperation. Semmes watched as the projectile plunged through the Union ship's engine room skylight. Once again he waited for the detonation, knowing that when it came it would destroy the enemy's boilers. But this shell, too, failed to explode. By then

Left: As *Alabama* sinks in the English Channel, rescue parties begin circulating through choppy waters in search of men drifting about, clutching onto grates and slivers, or anything that floats.

Below: As *Alabama*'s flag comes down, cheering breaks out around the pivot gun on *Kearsarge*, but a few more rounds came from the Union vessel before Winslow was satisfied that Semmes had actually surrendered.

Right: Executive officer John McIntosh Kell came from Georgia and had great confidence in Semmes. Kell, more so than Semmes, ran the *Alabama* and ran it well. His flowing red beard set him off as a man who meant business.

Semmes must have realized this was not his lucky day. Conscious that victory had deserted him, he still fought on, hoping in vain for some miracle to save the day.

Kearsarge continued to gut *Alabama* with 11-inch shells. Fires raged below, water poured into the hull, and the Confederate raider began to list. A fragment of shell gashed Semmes's right arm, cutting a vein. Blood gushed to the deck. As the quartermaster wrapped the wound and fitted the captain with a sling, Semmes looked down the deck at the men fighting the guns. They seemed to be steady, but there were barely any starboard guns left to do battle. If he could not fight, perhaps there was still a chance to escape. As the two vessels completed their seventh circle, Semmes turned to his executive officer and said, "Mr. Kell, as soon as our head points to the French coast... shift your guns to port and make all sail for the coast."

Winslow observed *Alabama*'s change of direction and moved into position to rake. For several minutes, he held his fire. *Alabama* had begun to wallow from water in her bilge, and she could make little headway. Her guns had fallen silent, so Winslow, either out of pity or old feelings of brotherhood, followed with guns ready.

When Kell sent seaman John Roberts aloft to loose a jib on *Alabama*, *Kearsarge* opened with a single gun. A shell fragment sliced through Roberts's groin, "slitting it open like a fresh-sliced melon." Lieutenant Arthur Sinclair remembered it as "the most remarkable case of desperate wounding and after-tenacity of life" he had ever witnessed. "In this pitiful state, Roberts clung to the jib boom and worked his way along a foot-rope

to the topgallant deck, climbed to the spar deck, and hesitated. Shrieking and beating his head with his arms, he died where he stood, his entrails spewing out in a red mass."

Kearsarge circled and moved into position between *Alabama* and the coast, blocking any further attempt by the Confederates to escape. Semmes, however, would not surrender. When Chief Engineer Miles J. Freeman came topside to report the engine room flooding, Semmes sent him back with an order to raise more steam. Kell followed Freeman to assess the situation and was shocked at the damage found below. Partitions had been smashed, water poured into the engine room from holes in the hull, and when Kell looked in on the surgeon, a shell struck the operating table and swept the patient out from under the doctor's bloody hands.

Kell returned to deck and informed Semmes that the vessel could remain afloat for no more than 10 minutes. "Then, sir," said Semmes, "cease firing, shorten sail, and haul down the colors. It will never do in the nineteenth century for us to go down and the decks covered with our gallant wounded." Kell executed the order and struck the colors. Winslow observed the ensign lowered but fired five more shots. He later explained to Secretary Welles his reason for doing so, stating that Semmes could not be trusted and he suspected another ruse. Kell ordered the men back to *Alabama*'s guns, but after finding the situation hopeless he went aft and raised a white flag.

Now convinced the ship would sink, Semmes ordered the dinghy lowered and

dispatched Masters Mate George T. Fullam to *Kearsarge* to get help in removing the wounded. Kell loaded as many of the wounded as possible on the least damaged quarterboat and sent it along with Fullam. The wounded made it safely to *Kearsarge*, but from Semmes's perspective Winslow showed no urgency in lowering boats to rescue the men still on board *Alabama*.

Having lost much blood, Semmes became wobbly and clutched the rail for support. Turning sadly to Kell, he gave the order to abandon ship and for all the men to save themselves. Overboard went spars, grating, an oar, a splinter – anything that would float – and then went the men

tumbling feet first into the cold English Channel. Paddling with all their strength, they made haste to escape the sucking vortex that would come when the ship went down. *Kearsarge* still stood off, seeming to drift farther away.

Semmes and Kell were among the last to leave. As they prepared to jump into the water, Semmes remembered his diary and the ship's papers in his cabin. Michael Mars volunteered to get them and returned with the two bundles wrapped in oilskin and tied between slats. Mars and Quartermaster Freemantle each took half. As a token of disgust toward Winslow's tardiness in saving Alabama's crew, Semmes and Kell

removed their swords and threw them overboard.

Feet first from the taffrail they jumped. Semmes wore a life preserver, but with his injured arm he could not swim and soon became exhausted. Kell grabbed a grating and pushed it over to Semmes, then together they kicked and struggled to get away from the ship. Holding the captain fast to the grating, Kell looked about for a lifeboat, but none came.

Alabama sank stern first in 40 fathoms of water. From a hundred yards away, Lieutenant Sinclair watched, later writing, "She shot up out of the water bow first, and descended on the same line, carrying away

Left Acting Master Eben M. Stoddard (left) went to some effort to have a shell and a charge of grape brought to deck for this victory photo. Chief Engineer William H. Cushman (right) left his chores below to sit by the Dahlgren.

Below: When Semmes was convinced that *Alabama* was about to sink, he dispatched Masters Mate George T. Fullam to *Kearsarge* to seek help in removing the wounded, loading as many of the wounded as possible aboard a quarterboat and sending it to the Union victor.

with her plunge two of her masts, and making a whirlpool of considerable size and strength." For *Alabama*, it had not been a lucky day, but for Semmes, a small amount of luck remained.

During the 1 hour 27 minute battle, the English yacht *Deerhound* stood off, her crew and passengers witnessing the most exciting spectacle of their lives. At 12:30 p.m. John Lancaster noticed that *Kearsarge* had made no effort to rescue the Confederates struggling in the Channel. He steamed over to the Union vessel to ask why and learned the reason. *Alabama's* shells had so riddled the warship's lifeboats that Winslow could not float them without first making repairs.

From the taffrail, Winslow pointed to the heads bobbing in the water and shouted down to Lancaster, "For God's sake, do what you can to save them!"

Minutes later *Deerhound* began picking up survivors, among them "Old Beeswax," who was recognized by his mustaches, and Kell, by his wet, red beard. When the crew lifted Semmes on board, they found him half-conscious and still bleeding from his wound. They wrapped him in a sheet and laid him in the stern. A boat from *Kearsarge* passed and the officer in charge asked if anyone had seen Semmes. Kell replied, "Captain Semmes is drowned." The boat passed on, resuming its search for survivors.

Deerhound's two boats picked up 12 officers and 30 men. *Kearsarge* recovered five officers and 65 men, including the wounded delivered by Fullam. Because Winslow had difficulty getting his boats repaired and in the water, he ordered Fullam to stay with the dinghy and save whomever he could. Fullam gathered a few survivors but, instead of returning with them to *Kearsarge*, he took them to Deerhound. A boat from *Kearsarge* rescued Lieutenant Sinclair and a sailor, both of whom had slipped overboard and swum to *Deerhound* when no one was watching. Two French pilot boats came upon the scene and rescued 15 more; one carried half the men to

Kearsarge but the other boat took her half to Cherbourg.

With *Deerhound* crammed with survivors, Lancaster asked Semmes, "Where shall I land you?" The captain replied, "I am under English colors; the sooner you land me on English soil, the better." Lancaster agreed, came about, and headed for Southampton. Winslow's officers, watching *Deerhound* steam away, now speculated that Semmes must be on board. They urged that a shell be fired to halt the vessel's escape, but Winslow temporized, replying that "the yacht was simply coming around." After admitting his error, he still refused to fire on the yacht. He had sunk *Alabama*. That was enough for one day. Besides, Semmes had drowned, or so he had been told.

The tally of the 87-minute carnage heavily favored the *Kearsarge*. *Alabama* had fired 370 projectiles, dismounted a gun carriage, torn up some of *Kearsarge's* rigging and woodwork, and wounded three men, one of whom died later. Dozens of shots had hit the Union ship's hull, only to be deflected by her chain armor. In contrast, *Kearsarge* had fired only 173 times, but her shells had killed nine on *Alabama*, wounded 21, and caused another 12 to be lost by drowning. Of the 21 men killed or lost, most had been Englishmen.

Though Winslow received criticism for letting so many prisoners escape and for paroling those he captured, he nonetheless became a national hero. Welles sent his congratulations, Lincoln petitioned Congress for a vote of thanks, and Winslow became a commodore.

When Semmes landed safely in England with 41 officers and men on board *Deerhound*, relations between Great Britain and the United States festered anew. Semmes recovered during the harmless diplomatic squabbles and, with Kell, enjoyed the hospitality of his many British admirers.

Semmes returned to the Confederacy in January, 1865. Mallory made him a rear admiral and on February 10 placed him in command of the James River Squadron. Semmes never experienced another opportunity to fight. When the Confederate government abandoned Richmond during the last days of the war, Semmes blew up his squadron and, with his naval brigade, followed General Lee's retreating army. At Danville, Virginia, President Davis made him a brigadier general. Semmes became the only officer during the Civil War to hold both an admiral's commission and a general's commission simultaneously.

During *Alabama's* rampage on the high seas, she destroyed $4,613,914 in American shipping and bonded vessels worth $562,250. Her raiding, more than any other vessel built in Great Britain for the Confederacy, gave rise to a postwar suit wherein the United States sought reparations from the British crown. The new battle, known appropriately as the "Alabama Claims," continued until 1872. At an arbitration held in Geneva, the judges awarded the United States $15,500,000 in gold. By then, the Federal government could no longer find all the claimants and pocketed a share of the money.

The victory at the arbitration table represented a small sum compared with what the Union lost. Great Britain, by building commerce raiders for the Confederacy, regained her dominance of the seas at the expense of the American carrying trade. Diplomats in the United States accused the British of hatching a strategy to aid and abet the Confederate Navy at the outbreak of war. *Alabama* did little to win the war for the Confederacy, but she played a major role in winning Britain's economic battle for the commerce and control of the seas.

The battle in the English Channel marked the end of another era – stand-up fights between wooden ships of sail. The fight between *Alabama* and *Kearsarge* gives a special distinction to the officers and men who came together on June 19, 1864, to give the world one last great show. There would never be another quite like it.

Left: Lieutenant Arthur Sinclair kept an extensive record of his adventures on board the *Alabama*. After the war, he wrote one of the finest accounts of the men of the cruiser and their experiences as men of prey.

Below: A selection of powerful Union shells. Top left, 7-inch Schenkl for 7-inch rifle. Note that papier mache sabot is still in place over projections cast onto base of shell to fit the 7-inch rifling. Below left, a stand of 6.4-inch grape shot for a 100-pounder rifle. Top right, background, 5-inch Whitworth shell for an 80-pounder. Right center, 5.1-inch Stafford shell for a 50-pounder Dahlgren gun. Below right, 5.8-inch shell. Note the cast-on projections designed to fit the rifling of the gun's barrel.

CHAPTER ELEVEN

DAMNING THE TORPEDOES

By August, 1864, the only Confederate vessel worthy of the name battleship lay in Mobile Bay, not because she looked the part of a battleship but because she could be fought like one. Arrayed against her were the finest Union vessels in the Gulf Blockading Squadron and four new heavily armed monitors. Once again, Confederate Secretary of the Navy Mallory had tried to build five ironclads, this time to defend the city of Mobile against attack from the Gulf of Mexico. Once again, his larger strategy had been to send the ironclad squadron into the Gulf of Mexico to dismantle the Union blockade. And once again, only one of the five vessels ever became a useful and formidable ironclad ram.

The last great naval battle of the Civil War matched Admiral Farragut's squadron of 14 wooden warships and four monitors against Admiral Buchanan's three gunboats and the best ironclad ram built in the Confederacy. Mobile Bay, however, also contained two forts at the main entrance to the bay and an underwater minefield fringing the main shipping channel that posed a threat of catastrophic proportions. Even if Farragut could get his squadron past the forts and into the bay, he had no guarantee that he could remain there. Buchanan had great confidence in his powerful ironclad. Though slow and cumbersome, he did not believe she could be destroyed.

But even before Farragut could engage her he had to find a way to get his squadron inside the bay, and doing so was replete with many problems.

On July 20, 1864, Rear Admiral David Glasgow Farragut lay off the entrance to Mobile Bay, Alabama, in the Gulf of Mexico, in his flagship *Hartford*. He thumbed through a stack of old newspapers delivered by a dispatch boat from Washington. His work in the Mississippi River had ended. The only unfinished business for his squadron dated back to January, 1862, when his original orders from Secretary Welles stated several objectives – among them being the capture of Mobile. Farragut had spent most of his time in the river, fighting forts and rams with ships that belonged on the sea. He never relished the work, nor did the prospect of entering Mobile Bay, passing more forts, and fighting more ironclads, fill him with any special enthusiasm.

But his eye caught an article in one of the newspapers that detailed the fight in the English Channel between the C.S.S. *Alabama* and the U.S.S. *Kearsarge*. Farragut had been in the navy for 54 years, and since the battle between the frigate U.S.S. *Essex* and the British H.M.S. *Phoebe* and *Cherub* on March 28, 1814, he had never engaged another ship in a fight at sea. "The victory of the *Kearsarge* over the *Alabama* raised me up," he wrote his son. "I would sooner have fought that fight than any ever fought on the ocean."

To fight at sea had been Farragut's lifetime dream. As the years of the Civil War passed, he saw the dream slipping away and the days of the sailing navy coming to a close. He despised ironclads and never wanted to command one. Men of his age were becoming obsolete as rapidly as the vessels they commanded. Now, in the closing months of the war, he had but one final act to perform – to capture Mobile Bay – thereby sealing off the last of the great Confederate ports in the Gulf of Mexico.

Gideon Welles had asked him to wait for

Union vessels communicated with each other at night with lights. During the day, they used signal flags; some were raised on one of the masts, but to communicate back and forth, they were waved by signalmen.

On the morning of August 5, 1864, Farragut started his squadron through the Main Shipping Channel and into Mobile Bay. His fleet would be wedged between the powerful batteries in Fort Morgan on his starboard and the obstructions and minefield on his port. Once clear of those impediments, his vessels then faced the Confederate squadron and the only vessel that gave him grave concern, the formidable *Tennessee*.

example for them to follow. The war had made him meanspirited, so much so that he held no compunctions about dying in one last fight. According to the officers closest to him, Old Buck savored the opportunity to battle Farragut, admiral to admiral.

While *Hartford* languished at anchor off Mobile Bay, Farragut watched for Buchanan to come out with his ironclads to attack the flotilla of wooden Union warships standing off Fort Morgan. But Buchanan never ventured out of the Bay, and Farragut could not be certain of the cause. Buchanan knew the reasons. The engines of *Tuscaloosa* and *Huntsville* could not generate enough speed to move the vessels about, so they became worthless stationary floating batteries anchored up the Bay near the city of Mobile. *Nashville* had been armed with six guns, but she lay naked without her covering of armor and still required months of work. This left Buchanan with *Tennessee* and three gunboats – *Selma, Morgan,* and *Gaines* – all with batteries ranging from four to eight guns. Had Farragut been able to get an accurate picture of Buchanan's difficulties, he may have launched his attack without waiting for the monitors.

The C.S.S. *Tennessee* represented the finest and most dangerous ironclad built in the South, but like all her predecessors she was underpowered and could barely make six knots in still water. At 209 feet in length and 48 feet in beam, she was second in size only to the converted *Merrimac*. Her armored casemate, 79 feet long, 29 feet wide, and 8 feet high, made her so heavy that she drew 14 feet of water. She was the only ironclad to carry six inches of plating on her forward casemate and five inches on her sides and aftershield. The plating ran two feet below her water line and formed a knuckle strong enough to fracture the bow of any vessel attempting to butt her. She also carried two inches of plating on her deck, but the designers did not seem to know what to do with her steerage chains and merely set them in two channels running down her afterdeck.

Tennessee did not carry a big battery, but all her guns were rifled, new, and carried a punch. The two 7-inch Brookes in pivot fore and aft came from Commander Catesby ap R. Jones's foundry operation in Selma, Alabama. Jones had been Buchanan's executive officer at Hampton Roads. Now he was "Old Buck's" gunmaker. In broadside *Tennessee* mounted four 6.4-inch rifled cannon, two on each beam, which when coupled with the two pivot guns enabled

reinforcements. Inside the Bay lay the C.S.S. *Tennessee*, the deadliest ironclad in the Confederate arsenal. Welles feared that Farragut's wooden warships would be chewed to pieces by the ram, so he promised to send the admiral four monitors. As each day passed, Farragut fended off the idea of fighting iron with wood, his better judgment interceding to quell his impatience, for to fight without monitors would be foolishly rash.

Farragut had more to worry about than *Tennessee*. Admiral Franklin Buchanan, who on March 8, 1862, had commanded the C.S.S. *Virginia* and nearly destroyed the Union squadron in Hampton Roads, now commanded the Confederate squadron on Mobile Bay. Like Farragut, Buchanan was an old but energetic and determined fighter. Soon after he recovered from his injury at Hampton Roads, Mallory sent him to

Mobile to finish work on four ironclads. Buchanan found *Huntsville* and *Tuscaloosa* launched on the Tombigbee River, and *Tennessee* sitting upriver on the Alabama. With the rivers falling during the spring of 1863, he ordered the unfinished vessels down to Mobile. To complicate matters for Farragut, a fourth ironclad, *Nashville,* had been started at Montgomery, 150 miles up the Alabama River – which was precisely the reason why Welles did not want Farragut to enter Mobile Bay without four monitors.

Farragut knew Buchanan well, the two having served together during their early twenties. There was no question in Farragut's mind but that "Old Buck" would give him a heap of trouble. Buchanan had always been a man of action – seldom cautious, always hasty – and when he picked a fight, he held nothing back. He demanded the same from his men and set an

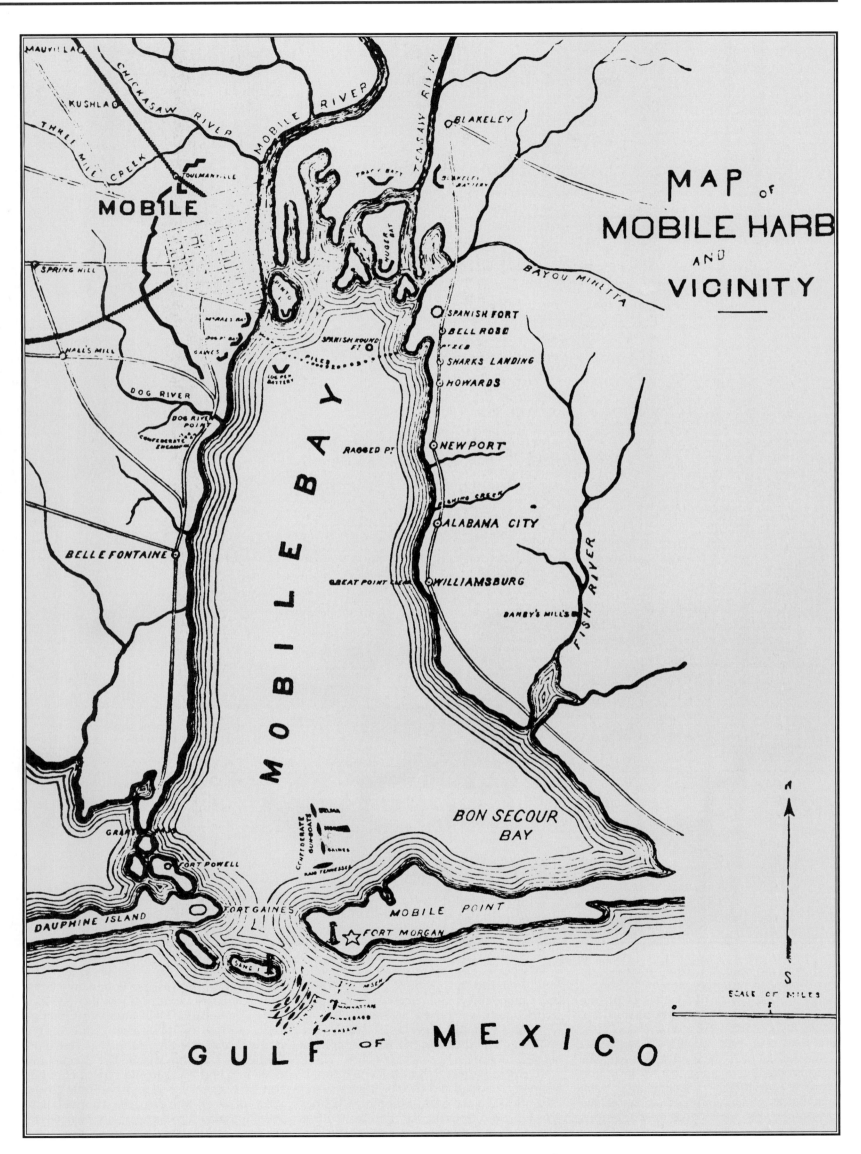

MAP OF
MOBILE HARB
AND
VICINITY

Buchanan to present four muzzles in broadside. Each gunport contained a sliding shutter covered with five inches of plating and connected to a system of pulleys and tackles that enabled the gun crew to open and close the port quickly. Though the vessel did not have the motive power or the maneuverability to make her 24-inch iron prow particularly menacing, she nonetheless came equipped with all the technology to make her a dangerous antagonist.

No vessel cost more or took longer to build than did the *Tennessee*. For $595,800, the Confederacy had created their finest ironclad ram, but she still had many defects.

When Farragut developed tactics for entering Mobile Bay, he had more to consider than Buchanan's monolith. There were two entrances to the Bay, one through Mississippi Sound and Grant's Pass, and the other through the Main Shipping Channel which flowed from the Bay into the Gulf of Mexico. Fort Powell stood squarely in the

middle of Grant's Pass, but because of the shallowness of Mississippi Sound only light-draft gunboats could pass into the bay. Two forts guarded the Main Shipping Channel, Fort Morgan on the eastern side of the channel and, three miles to the west, Fort Gaines on Dauphin Island. The channel ran close into Fort Morgan and carried about 22 feet of water. Less than a half-mile to the west of Fort Morgan, the channel rose quickly into shoal water, so any vessel passing into the Bay had to go under the

Left: Farragut aligned his columns so that
the monitors would come close under
Fort Morgan and engage the water
batteries while the wooden vessels fired
their broadsides into the upper parapets.

Farragut expected his four monitors to pass the forts
undamaged, and he placed them on his starboard so they
could pound Fort Morgan with their Dahlgrens. In the port
column, he faced the broadsides of his strongest vessels
toward the fort but, fearing one or more ships could be
disabled during the passage, he lashed a gunboat to their
sides, in this way ensuring that a crippled ship would still
have mobility.

guns of Fort Morgan for about 30 minutes while receiving a small amount of cross fire from the rifled pieces mounted in Fort Gaines.

Fort Powell at Grant's Pass was the least of Farragut's worries. The earthwork mounted four rifled 32-pounders and two larger cannon, an 8-inch and a 10-inch columbiad. Lieutenant Colonel James M. Williams of the 21st Alabama Infantry commanded the fort, but the sandy works were weak and watery and always under repair.

The guns of Fort Gaines bore mainly on the channel, but over the years the main channel had moved to the east and away from Gaines, making it difficult for the batteries to operate against vessels coming into the Bay. Colonel Charles D. Anderson of the 21st Alabama commanded the fort. Having been a regular army man in the 4th U.S. Artillery, his experience should have served him well in commanding the fort's 864 officers and men, but his leadership in battle had never been tested. The fort,

having been solidly constructed of brick, mounted 27 guns. Aside from three 10-inch columbiads and four rifled 32-pounders, all were smoothbores – good at short range but not much use otherwise.

Brigadier General Richard D. Page commanded the defenses of Mobile Bay and made his headquarters at Fort Morgan. In appearance, he closely resembled his first cousin, General Robert E. Lee. As a prewar commander in the United States Navy, he lived in Norfolk and had been a neighbor on

Above: Blockade duty meant days of boredom, a good time for photographs for *Hartford* officers. Surgeon Philip Lansdale wore his straw hat, Asst. Eng. William H. Whiting drew on his pipe, while others showed mixed interest in the sitting.

Above right: The boring days of blockade duty off Mobile Bay led to regular Sunday morning inspections. A gun crew from the U.S.S. *Metacomet* stood their turn before one of the ships 100-pounder rifled Parrotts.

Right: A Confederate floating "torpedo," a device now known as a sea mine. These weapons usually consisted of a metal cylinder with a powder charge and buoyancy chamber. The charge could be detonated by means of a spring mechanism connected to a trigger wire floating on the surface, although more sophisticated designs were set off with electric or chemical detonators.

friendly terms with Farragut. He rose to the rank of captain in the Confederate navy before trading occupations for a brigadier general's star. His associates called him "Ramrod Page" because he got things done, and when he arrived at Mobile Bay he concentrated on strengthening Fort Morgan.

By the summer of 1864, Fort Morgan mounted seven 10-inch, three 8-inch, and 22 32-pounder smoothbores, and two 6.5-inch and four 5.8-inch rifled cannon, all in casemates or en barbette. A number of guns located behind the brick embrasures had been mounted on a semi-circular track so that they could be moved from one place to another along the upper parapets. Page placed another 29 guns in external batteries, the most formidable being a water battery armed with 10-inch columbiads, one 8-inch rifle cannon, and two rifled 32-pounders. An informant had told Farragut that he had been through Fort Morgan and counted "from 120 to 125 guns," five or six being 11-inchers. Had the admiral known that General Page could bring no more than 70 guns to bear on the channel, he might have slept easier.

Page and his predecessor had mined the entrance to Mobile Bay and driven piles to obstruct the flats off Fort Gaines. Where torpedoes had been planted, small buoys marked their location. The devices ranged in style, the earlier torpedoes being operated from shore using galvanic batteries. Farragut had recently observed

Rebels seeding the channel with new devices designed to detonate on impact. To steer clear of the minefield, a ship must run close under the guns of Fort Morgan. Page believed that any ship eluding the minefield and passing into the Bay would be hammered so severely by Fort Morgan's guns that Buchanan would be able to mop up the few survivors. Until now, Farragut had dismissed torpedoes as a dangerous threat, but after a recent reconnaissance he ordered heavy iron cutters installed on the bows of some of his ships.

Farragut knew little of how the minefield had been arranged, only that the devices had been anchored below the surface of the water. When the tide rose, the mines went deeper, but Farragut did not know how deep, and when the tide fell, the mines rose closer to the surface. Hence, the best time to attack would be during high tide.

One hundred eighty torpedoes had been laid in over a period of several months. The easternmost edge of the minefield lay 226 yards off Fort Morgan's water battery and stretched westerly to the piles off Fort Gaines. Farragut wanted to move his squadron into the bay in two columns, and doing so would not leave much room for maneuvering. But he would not be going into the Bay until his monitors arrived, and the longer the torpedoes remained submerged, the sooner they deteriorated.

Without the monitors, Farragut's squadron contained many of the same

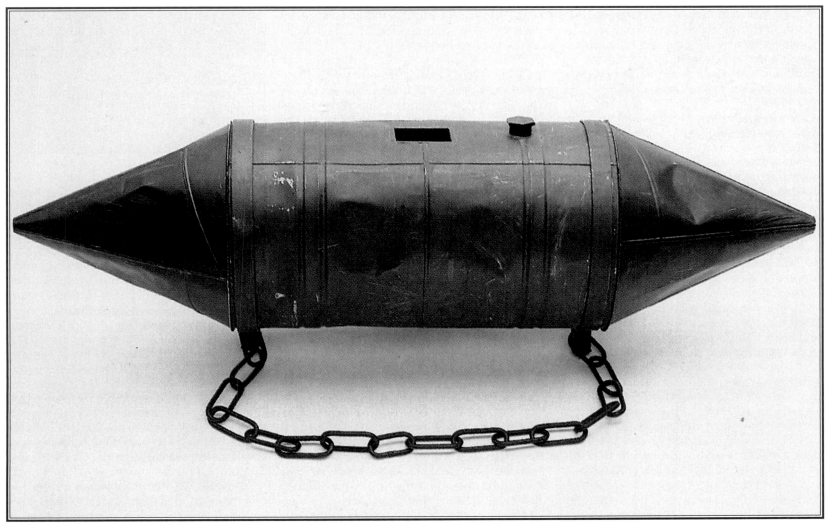

Farragut held several meetings on board his flagship to detail the best approach into Mobile Bay. This sketch, believed to have beeen made by him on board *Hartford*, was an attempt to illustrate the direction of fire from Fort Morgan. The edge of the Main Shipping Channel actually ran a few yards off Fort Morgan, not in the center of the outlet, which was three miles wide. The sketch also omits Fort Gaines, directly opposite Morgan.

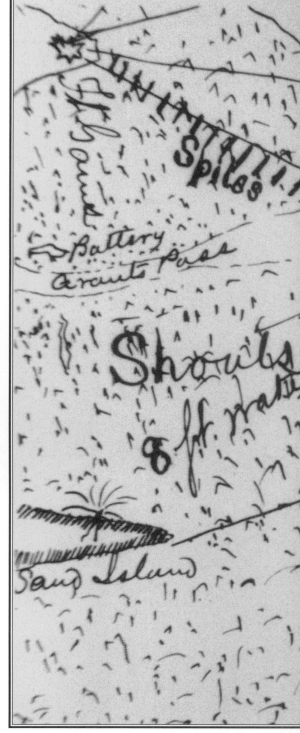

vessels that had been with him since the capture of New Orleans. *Hartford, Brooklyn,* and *Richmond* had always been part of the backbone of his squadron. *Kenebec, Itasca,* and *Oneida* had gone with him up the Mississippi. Off Mobile Bay, two more large sloops of war fashioned after *Hartford* – *Lackawanna* and *Monongahela* – joined the squadron, along with the gunboats *Octorara, Metacomet, Port Royal, Seminole, Galena,* and *Ossipee.*

As the first week of July passed, Farragut paced the deck, waiting for his monitors. The delay became a subject of personal embarrassment because arrangements had been made with the Army for a joint operation. Brigadier General Gordon Granger stood by with 2,400 troops to land on Dauphin Island and assault Fort Gaines the morning of the attack. Granger – a short and fiery West Pointer – was not well liked by his troops but had earned a solid reputation as a fighter. The balding, black-bearded Union general had little in common with the congenial admiral, but Farragut liked the pugnacious nature of his partner and knew he could depend upon the general in the days ahead.

On July 8, the long wait began to end. Admiral Porter released two new river ironclads, *Chickasaw* and *Winnebago,* and sent them down the Mississippi with the warning that the vessels had been built for service on the river and, because of their low decks, would probably founder in the Gulf. Two days later the monitor *Manhattan* arrived at Pensacola, followed by a message that she had caught on fire.. Farragut dispatched Fleet Captain Percival Drayton

to investigate and from him learned that the fire had occurred in the engineer's storeroom and no serious damage had been done. From the fourth monitor, *Tecumseh,* no word had come. Farragut feared she had been lost at sea, so in late July he decided to attack without her.

Farragut was not the only admiral feeling pressure to act. Since May 22, 1864, Jefferson Davis, anticipating an attack on the city of Mobile, had been pressing Buchanan to move the C.S.S. *Tennessee* down to Fort Morgan and "strike the enemy before he establishes himself in the Bay with his land forces." Buchanan grumbled to a friend, "Everybody has taken it into their heads that one ship can whip a dozen and if the trial is not made, we who are in her are damned for life, consequently the trial must be made. So goes the world."

Buchanan had just gotten the ram over the Dog River bar and into the Bay. He reluctantly decided to attack, knowing that to succeed it must come as a surprise and be done before the blockaders spotted the ram in the Bay. Using the cover of darkness, he steamed for the channel and, while pausing for better weather, went aground. Having been sighted by Farragut's picket boats, Buchanan changed his mind, and after high tide refloated the ram, he came to anchor off Fort Morgan.

On July 28 *Tennessee* came out from behind Fort Morgan and paraded inside the Bay, exercising her guns. Farragut had decided to attack as soon as the river ironclads arrived, but Buchanan's demonstration of power convinced him that "Buck" intended to fight and it would be

best to wait for the arrival of *Tecumseh.* Toward evening Farragut received word that she had just steamed into Pensacola. *Tecumseh* needed work on her engines, so Farragut used the extra time to prepare for the attack.

Manhattan, commanded by Comdr. James W. A. Nicholson, and *Tecumseh,* commanded by Comdr. Tunis A. M. Craven, were sister ships, each single-turreted monitors carrying two huge 15-inch Dahlgren smoothbores. Being 190 feet long and 38 feet in beam, they were about 19 feet shorter and 10 feet narrower than the C.S.S. *Tennessee* and not as heavily armored. Each vessel had cost the government $650,000 and represented some of the latest technology in monitor design. Unlike the original *Monitor,* they could develop a speed of eight miles an hour and steam through a storm with less fear of foundering.

On July 31 the river monitors arrived after coming through a day of turbulent weather. *Winnebago,* commanded by Comdr.

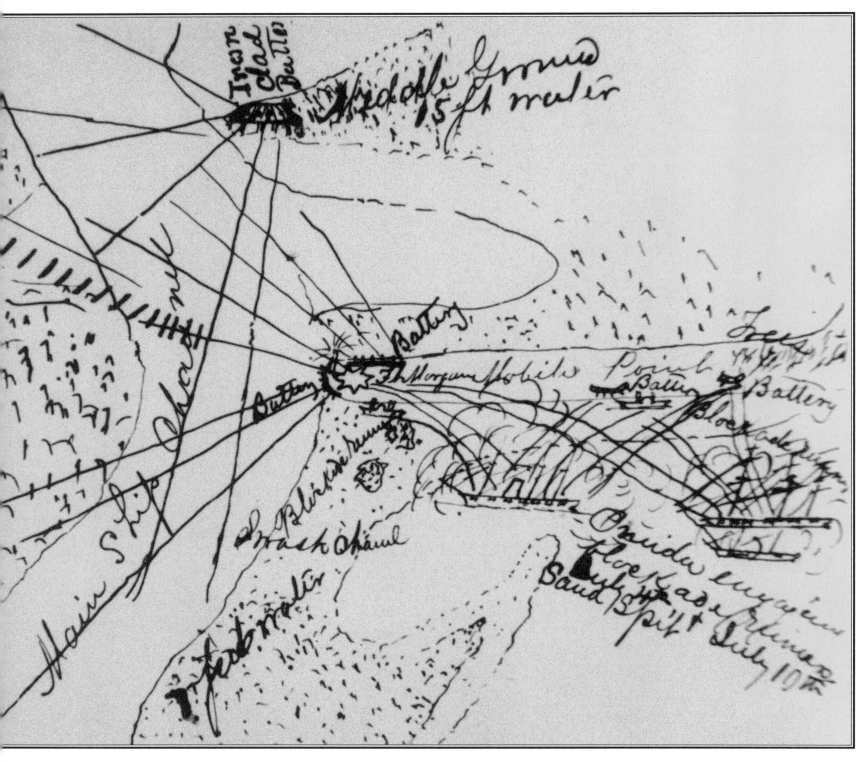

Thomas H. Stevens, and *Chickasaw*, com-manded by Lt. Comdr. George H. Perkins, were both 970-ton double-turreted monitors armed with two 11-inch Dahlgrens in each turret. The vessels were about 257 feet long with beams of 57 feet. Both vessels were well balanced and, contrary to Admiral Porter's admonishment, quite steady in rough water. With all four monitors present for duty, Farragut had marshaled a formidable squadron for assaulting Mobile Bay, but he still had to get past Fort Morgan and evade the minefield before engaging Buchanan's force.

Farragut and Granger planned the attack for the morning of August 3, but once again *Tecumseh* forced a postponement because of engine trouble. The delay gave the admiral another day to go over his plans with his officers. Leaving nothing to chance, he instructed his carpenter to shape miniature ships from wooden blocks so he could lay them out on a large table covered over with an enlarged map of Mobile Bay. At the

conclusion of the conference, each officer con-firmed that they understood their orders.

Because of the nearness of the Main Shipping Channel to Fort Morgan and the closeness of the minefield directly opposite the fort, Farragut took a chance by arranging his squadron in two columns. He placed the four monitors on the right flank where their heavy guns could engage the fort and the water battery. Because Commander Craven held the position of senior officer, Farragut put *Tecumseh* in the van, followed by *Manhattan*, *Winnebago*, and *Chickasaw*. The left column contained the wooden ships, and to the portside of every large vessel he ordered a gunboat lashed. The sloops of war – *Brooklyn*, *Hartford*, *Richmond*, *Lackawanna*, and *Monongahela* – would engage Fort Morgan and, should any of them become disabled, the gunboats lashed abeam would lug them into the Bay, helped along by the morning flood tide.

Every officer in the squadron urged Farragut not to put *Hartford* at the head of

the column because only *Brooklyn* had been fitted with a pair of snippers on her bow to cut the cables holding torpedoes. They argued that *Brooklyn*'s commander, Captain James Alden, had worked with the Coast Survey and had charted Mobile Bay in 1856, and therefore knew the location of its bars better than anyone in the squadron. After much debate the admiral agreed to let *Brooklyn* lead the wooden vessels so long as *Hartford* went next.

In addition to the main attack, Farragut sent five gunboats under Lt. Comdr. James C. P. de Krafft over to Dauphin Island to support the landing of General Granger's infantry. Thinking that Farragut intended to initiate his attack on the morning of August 3, Granger landed without opposition and proceeded across the island to invest Fort Gaines. Discovering that the Union squad-ron had not yet moved, he put the infantry to work digging entrenchments and mounting batteries.

On the afternoon of August 4, Farragut

scheduled his attack for 5:45 in the morning. At sundown rain began to fall, and the admiral went to bed distressed over the prospects of another delay. He felt poorly and could not sleep. At midnight the breeze shifted around to the southwest, which is exactly what Farragut wanted because the wind would blow smoke from the cannon into the eyes of Fort Morgan's gunners. At 3:00 a.m. he sent word to his steward, John H. Brooks, to go topside and check the weather. Brooks returned, reporting the skies clear, the night calm, but the air hot and heavy with humidity. Now fully awake and full of fight, the admiral began to dress, and to his steward said, "We will go in, this morning."

When the orders reached the deck of *Manhattan*, a member of the watch observed a comet streaking across the heavens to the northeast and predicted certain victory. Others saw it, too, and word of the celestial display spread through the squadron. The timely omen provided a calming effect, offsetting the sailors' dread of fighting on a Friday.

August 5 dawned clear and cloudless, the southwest breeze having moved a point or two to the west. Boatswains' pipes shrilled down the line of ships, followed by the call "All hands!"

At 4:00 a.m. the wooden warships began forming in line. The smaller gunboats eased under the port side of their designated partner and lashed together. The four monitors steamed into position on the right flank. At 5:00 a.m. Farragut sent the gunboats *Sebago, Pembina, Genesee,* and *Bienville* east of Mobile Point to enfilade Fort Morgan from the rear. Then, at 5:30 a.m., while sipping coffee with his fleet captain, Farragut casually remarked, "Well, Drayton, we might as well get underway." Drayton went topside and hoisted the signal. The entire fleet, standing by, instantly replied and began easing into position.

As the wooden vessels formed off Sand Island, gun crews stripped to the waist and grimly assembled at their posts. Because the monitors moved so slowly, they cut across the head of the line, advancing first to engage Fort Morgan. At 6:00 a.m. both columns crossed the bar. Twenty minutes later *Tecumseh* fired a 15-inch shell at Fort Morgan's water battery. It fell short. As if on cue, daylight suddenly flooded the Bay. The squadron unfurled its banners – Farragut's blue admiral's pennant making a fine target as it streamed from *Hartford's* mizzenmast. *Tecumseh* fired again, the second shell bursting high above the fort. At 6:50 the fort opened on *Brooklyn*, still a half mile off. The first shot plunged into the water. Alden replied with the 100-pounder Parrott mounted in *Brooklyn's* bow. Then all hell broke loose.

Farragut signaled the wooden ships for closer order. Each pair of vessels on the left moved to within a ship's length of the other.

Above: A detail of *Hartford*'s afterguard gather on the afterdeck for a rare photo of the men who seldom ever got the opportunity to be recognized for their presence and work guarding the vessel day and night.

Right: The U.S.S. *Manhattan*, the first monitor to join Farragut's squadron, had a difficult voyage and required a tow. After reaching Pensacola, a fire broke out in her supply room, adding to Farragut's daily anxieties.

On *Brooklyn*, shot and shell began to rip through her tops, sending splinters and rigging whipping across the deck. At 7:11 shots began to fall around *Hartford*, one clipping the foremast, but Farragut could not bring the ship's broadsides to bear without sheering into the minefield. For 20 minutes he could reply with only one gun, the 100-pounder mounted in the bow. He had depended upon the monitors to silence the enemy's batteries, but for some reason *Tecumseh* and *Manhattan* had neither closed on the fort nor reached an effective range for their 15-inch shells to crush the parapets.

At 7:20 *Brooklyn* came abreast Fort Morgan and fired a broadside. *Hartford* followed, a hundred yards back, and, sheering slightly to port, sent a dozen 9-inch shells set with 10-second fuses into the upper palisades. Ahead, a mile above the fort, lay Buchanan's three gunboats, spread across the Middle Ground with broadsides waiting to rake the Union squadron. *Tennessee*, laying in wait under Fort Morgan, pushed into the channel and presented her broadside. All four Confederate vessels opened, hurling a hail of projectiles across the decks of *Brooklyn* and *Hartford*. The U.S.S. *Octorara*, lashed to *Brooklyn*, absorbed three shots in her wheelhouse, four in her tops, causing Alden to cut her loose. As other wooden vessels closed on the fort, gunners cut their fuses to five-second shells and two-second shrapnel. By the time *Brooklyn* and *Hartford* entered the narrow gap opposite the fort, Confederates in the water battery and the upper enclosures had been driven into their bombproofs.

Farragut, however, could see nothing. Smoke poured over the channel, obscuring not only the fort but also the monitors formed to starboard. To get a better view the admiral climbed the port main rigging, ascending the ratline step by step "until he found himself partly above the futtock bands and holding onto the futtock shrouds." One of *Hartford's* pilots, Martin Freeman, had preceded him and stopped just beneath the top. When he observed Farragut hanging precariously on the lines below him, Freeman offered his foot and suggested that the admiral hold it to steady himself. Captain Drayton had been preoccupied by *Brooklyn's* erratic steering and did not see Farragut scramble up the mast. When he spied the admiral swaying aloft, he sent Quartermaster John H. Knowles up the ratlines with a lead-line, instructing him to loop it around Farragut to keep him from falling. When Knowles began lashing the admiral to the after shroud, Farragut said, "Never mind, I am alright," but, said the quartermaster, "I went ahead and obeyed [Drayton's] orders, for I feared [the admiral] would fall overboard if anything should carry away or he should be struck."

Farragut enjoyed a panoramic but hazardous view of the battle, and each broadside sent him careening about in the tops with one hand on the rigging and a marine glass in the other. Having Freeman nearby with a speaking tube provided an unexpected benefit. He could communicate with Drayton on the poop deck and with Lieutenant Commander James E. Jouett, who stood atop the wheelhouse of the U.S.S. *Metacomet*, the gunboat lashed alongside. He also had a clear view of *Brooklyn*, which appeared to be slowing and inexplicably veering to port.

At 7:25 Alden signaled, "The monitors are right ahead. We can not go on without passing them. What shall we do?" Craven, having become lost in the smoke, had led *Tecumseh* and the slow-moving monitors into the path of *Brooklyn* and, instead of going straight ahead, had sidled to port. Farragut lost time getting a signalman to read the message, who then wigwagged the admiral's reply, "Go ahead!"

Five minutes later *Tecumseh*, after crossing the path of *Brooklyn*, passed too far to port, entered the minefield, struck a torpedo, and sank in two minutes. Craven appeared to be overanxious to engage *Tennessee* and had the misfortune of striking one of the few surviving live torpedoes. Farragut had specifically warned all his commanders to pass inside the buoys marking the minefield, and though the space was narrow he emphasized that if every ship stayed in formation there would be no accidents.

Alden not only witnessed *Tecumseh* sink, but the monitor's unexpected appearance caused him to con *Brooklyn* toward the very edge of the minefield. By staying on his present course, Alden had visions of following *Tecumseh* to the bottom. He then observed *Tennessee* dead ahead and "making for us." Panic gripped Alden. Disregarding Farragut's order to push on into the Bay,

Above: Fleet Captain Percival Drayton was also the admiral's warden. Farragut practised poor eating habits, and Drayton constantly scolded him, demanding that he eat less rich food and get more exercise.

Right: Nobody could keep Farragut out of the shrouds during a battle. Had he not been there on the morning of August 5, he may not have "damned the torpedoes" and ordered full steam ahead.

Alden stopped his engines. When the tide began drifting *Brooklyn* into the minefield, he threw the engines into reverse and began to back into *Hartford*, signaling, "Our best monitor has been sunk."

Farragut could not see any reason for *Brooklyn* to back. Fearing the column would stack-up under the guns of Fort Morgan, he signaled Alden, "Tell the monitors to go ahead and then take your place." Off course, paralyzed by the sight of buoys directly under his beam, warned by the pilot of shoal water ahead, and distressed by the approach of *Tennessee,* Alden froze.

Farragut could not get *Brooklyn* out of the way, but in his elevated perch he had put himself in the right place to make the most crucial decision of the morning attack. He could see the field of battle better than any officer in the squadron, but he had no trusted subordinate with whom he could confer. With broadsides roaring below and the lead vessel backing into the column, Farragut hollered up to Freeman, asking if there was sufficient water for the flagship to swing clear and pass off *Brooklyn's* port side. Freeman affirmed there was. Farragut

replied, "Then I will take the lead," and he sent orders through the speaking tube to go ahead at full speed.

To lead meant going through the minefield, the very thing he meant to avoid. As the flagship came abeam *Brooklyn*, Drayton trumpeted, "What's the trouble?" Alden replied, "Torpedoes!" Farragut heard the answer and shouted, "Damn the torpedoes! Full speed ahead, Drayton! Hard a starboard! Ring four bells!" Then he shouted down to Jouett, ordering *Metacomet* to back, thereby swinging Hartford's bow straight into the minefield.

Satisfied that the trailing *Richmond* had followed his lead, Farragut shouted down to *Metacomet*, "Jouett, full speed!" Chief Engineer Thom Williamson became confused by all the orders being passed down from aloft, so he shouted up to the admiral, "Shall I ring four bells, sir?" Farragut scowled down from the shrouds, hollering, "Four bells – eight bells – sixteen bells – damn it, I don't care how many bells you ring." Williamson reacted with alacrity, and the flagship surged past the drifting *Brooklyn* and led the squadron into the minefield.

The sinking of *Tecumseh* by a torpedo would have been enough to discourage any senior officer from entering the minefield, but not Farragut. Refugees had informed the admiral that most of the devices had been spoiled by seawater, but *Tecumseh's* descent to the bottom gave Farragut every reason to pause. It was his decision to make, and he gambled his squadron to fit his fighting instincts. Had the situation been reversed, the only other officer in the navies of the Civil War who might have done the same was Franklin Buchanan, who waited off the minefield in the C.S.S. *Tennessee* to fight Farragut to the end.

By swinging into the minefield, Farragut also ran the risk of grounding the heavy sloops on shoals bordering the channel. Between deck-jarring broadsides, leadsmen took soundings as *Hartford* steamed ahead. With all the commotion on deck, few of the men heard the scraping of torpedoes against the hull and the snapping of primers as the flagship passed through the minefield.

As *Hartford* crossed into the bay, the C.S.S. *Selma* opened with a broadside, raking the flagship fore and aft and doing

Above: The monitor U.S.S. *Tecumseh* arrived off Mobile Bay a day before the attack. She led the ironclads into the bay, got off course, veered into the minefield, struck one of the few active mines, and sank.

Right: Seven gunboats lashed themselves to the larger wooden vessels. The gunboat U.S.S. *Galena* (seen here) tied herself to the U.S.S. *Oneida*, which brought up the rear of the column containing the wooden vessels.

Below: Of seven large wooden warships, Comdr. James H. Strong commanded one of them, the U.S.S. *Monongahela*. She was one of the newest wooden screw steamers in the Union Navy's arsenal, and Strong fought her well.

more damage than all the projectiles fired from Fort Morgan. On *Tennessee*, Buchanan had lined-up to ram *Brooklyn*, but when he spied Farragut's flagship passing into the Bay, he helmed over a few points to starboard to bear upon *Hartford*. Buchanan told his pilot that if he could get the ship's prow into the Union flagship, then he would not care if *Tennessee* went down with her.

Farragut observed the ram bearing off the starboard quarter and easily outmaneuvered her. Buchanan opened the forward port and fired two 7-inch shells at point blank range, but neither of them did any damage. In passing, *Hartford* delivered a broadside that caromed off *Tennessee*'s shield and bounded harmlessly away. Farragut later declared that after firing the first broadside, he "took no further notice of her than to return her fire."

Having come into the Middle Ground, being the deeper section of the bay, *Hartford* opened on all three Confederate gunboats, crippling *Gaines* and driving her under the protective guns of Fort Morgan. A few minutes later the C.S.S. *Morgan* disengaged and, after grounding temporarily on shoals off Navy Point, also ran in under the fort.

At 8:02 Farragut cut *Metacomet* loose and sent her after *Selma*. Earlier in the action, *Selma* had fired a shell into *Metacomet*'s storeroom and started a fire, killing one man and wounding another. Jouett sought revenge and ordered the engine room to pour on the steam. Lieutenant Peter U. Murphey, commanding *Selma*, quickly surmised that he could not match *Metacomet*'s speed and tried to escape. Jouett pressed forward and at close range fired a pair of 9-inch shells that ripped through *Selma*, wounded Murphey, killed the first lieutenant, and disabled two of the vessel's four guns. While Jouett reloaded with grape, Murphey fired one last volley and surrendered before *Metacomet* could reply. Unlike the commanders of the other Confederate gunboats, Murphey fought well and quit only after his deck had been

reduced to "a perfect slaughter pen."

Buchanan, after missing his chance to ram *Hartford*, helmed *Tennessee* over to engage the drifting *Brooklyn*. He aimed for her bow, but at the last minute sheered over and fired a broadside. Alden replied with no effect. Buchanan came about and made a pass at *Brooklyn*'s stern. *Tennessee*'s attack snapped Alden out of his fog. He shed his worries about the minefield, steamed through it to the Middle Ground, and at 8:05 came alongside *Hartford*.

Richmond, commanded by Captain Thornton Jenkins, had closed up on *Hartford* after *Brooklyn* stopped. When Jenkins saw *Tennessee* bearing down on *Brooklyn*, he opened on the ram. Thinking *Tennessee* might strike *Brooklyn* on the starboard side, Jenkins moved into position to run over the ram and sink her before she could extract her prow. But Alden steamed away, leaving *Richmond* to deal with the ram. Jenkins loaded with solid shot, drove home his heaviest powder charge, and at ranges varying from 50 to 200 yards fired three full broadsides from his 9-inch Dahlgrens. The projectiles flitted away, leaving a few scratches in the ironclad's armor.

Lackawanna, following behind *Richmond*, clanged another broadside off *Tennessee*'s shield before passing the ram. Next in line came *Monongahela*. Commander James H. Strong made the mistake of passing off *Tennessee*'s port, thereby exposing *Kenebec*, lashed alongside, to the ram's broadside. *Tennessee* nipped the bow off *Kenebec* and sent a shell through her berth deck, wounding five men. *Ossipee* passed off the ram's starboard side, and Buchanan greeted her with a broadside, but *Ossipee* could not return the fire without hitting *Kenebec*.

Oneida, bringing up the rear, did not have the advantage of hiding in the smoke and received heavy fire from Fort Morgan. A 7-inch shell passed through her chain armor, penetrated the starboard boiler, and exploded. A second shot struck near the water line, burst in the cabin, and cut both

wheel ropes. *Galena* took over the work of bringing *Oneida* into the bay, but *Tennessee* ranged off the latter's beam and shattered her with more broadsides. With eight killed and 30 wounded, *Oneida* limped into the Middle Ground.

The only wooden vessel lost was the ordnance supply ship *Philippi*, whose skipper ignored orders, followed the squadron up the channel, and for his impertinence received a disabling shot from the fort. He ran the ship ashore, deserted the vessel, forgot his signal book, and left tons of ammunition for the enemy. Farragut vowed to court martial *Philippi*'s commander and eventually did.

At 8:35, a little more than two hours after the action first opened, *Hartford* anchored in the Middle Ground, four miles northwest of Fort Morgan. Every vessel in the squadron joined the flagship but *Tecumseh*, and Farragut, for the first time, learned what became of the monitors in the smoke-shrouded battle.

Commander Craven, in his eagerness to engage *Tennessee*, had failed to hold formation, given the fatal order to steer westward, crossed the path of *Brooklyn*, and had led the monitors into the minefield. At first, observers on *Brooklyn* thought *Tecumseh* had sunk *Tennessee*, leading to five minutes of loud cheering before Alden discovered the truth. *Tennessee*'s 7-inch rifle in the bow had fired a bolt at the monitor minutes before she sank, and her gunners incorrectly prided themselves on discharging the fatal shot. Twenty-one men escaped through *Tecumseh*'s hatch before she sank, carrying the other 93 sailors to the bottom, including her captain. One survivor claimed that, when Craven observed the monitor heading for the minefield, he had said, "I cannot turn my ship," suggesting there had been problem with the steerage. *Tecumseh* had sunk a hundred yards from *Tennessee*, and at the time, *Manhattan* had closed to within a hundred yards of the sinking monitor.

When Commander Nicholson had sighted the minefield, he steered *Manhattan* away from it. In his battle report he oddly omitted any mention of *Tecumseh* while claiming to maintain a steady fire on *Tennessee*. If so, his 15-inch Dahlgrens had done no more damage to the ram than that of a peashooter. *Winnebago* and *Chickasaw* had stayed on their assigned course and engaged the water battery. Neither monitor

Left: All kinds of weird vessels were conjured up by overly imaginative contemporary artists. This monster never existed, though the artist attempted to add authenticity by drawing Fort Morgan and the wrecked U.S.S. *Philippi* on the horizon.

Below: President Lincoln forever respected the men of his navy, from admiral to jack tar, and was ever happy to lend his support for their care after service. This letter wishes success to a fair in 1864 which raised $200,000 to build a sailors' home.

had made contact with *Tennessee* because Buchanan had gone in chase of *Hartford* and engaged the column of wooden vessels. All three monitors had then filed into the Middle Ground to await further orders.

Farragut signaled the squadron for damage reports and soon learned that, with the exception of *Tecumseh* and the injured *Oneida*, his ships remained in good fighting trim. He believed he had damaged Fort Morgan, although according to General Page most of the firing passed over the fort, killing only one man and wounding three, and not a single Confederate gun had been dismounted or a carriage disturbed.

The admiral's most serious concern lay off the fort. *Tennessee* remained as invincible as ever, her steam up and spewing an angry, black smoke. She had been through a cordon of fire and truly seemed impervious to the combined firepower of the Union fleet. For Farragut, the real test lay before him, and the question he persistently asked himself would finally be answered – could vessels of wood stand against those made of iron? Soon he would know.

Executive Mansion,
Washington, Nov. 9. . 1864.

The Managing Committee of the
Sailor's Fair:
Boston, Mass.
Allow me to wish you a great success. With the old fame of the Navy, made brighter in the present war, you can not fail. I name none, lest I wrong others by omission. To all, from Rear Admiral, to honest Jack I tender the Nation's admiration and gratitude

A. Lincoln

CHAPTER TWELVE

THE BATTLE ON MOBILE BAY

No two admirals came through the Civil War with more fighting spirit and a tenacious determination to win at all costs than Farragut and Buchanan, two old friends from the prewar navy. For Buchanan, it seemed most fitting for him to command the last worthy Confederate ironclad, as he had commanded the first, the C.S.S. *Virginia* (*Merrimac*). It also seemed fitting for Farragut, who won the first great naval battle of the Civil War, to be the admiral in command of the last.

During the second phase of the morning battle, Buchanan nurtured one objective, to destroy *Hartford*, Farragut's flagship, and then casually go about the work of destroying the other ships in the Union fleet. Farragut's one objective was to destroy *Tennessee*, Buchanan's flagship. He had already lost one monitor crossing the minefield, and if necessary he would lose them all. And when his monitors were gone he would sacrifice, if necessary, every other vessel under his command to defeat the *Tennessee*. Neither Farragut nor Buchanan were men who could face defeat gracefully, no matter how honorably they fought.

The morning battle for the possession of Mobile Bay would attract much attention from abroad. Any lingering doubts among the admirals of the world regarding the viability of wooden warships against iron were answered during a furious fight that lasted but one hour.

Coming up to 9:00 in the morning, August 5, 1864, Admiral Franklin Buchanan stood on his Confederate ironclad *Tennesse* and stared over at Admiral David Farragut's Union squadron anchored in the Middle Ground, four miles northwest of Fort Morgan, protecting Mobile Bay. Aboard his flagship *Hartford*, Farragut stared back. For thirty-five minutes, Farragut and Buchanan surveyed each other's ships while pausing for crackers and coffee.

On the Union vessels, details washed the decks, cleared away the wreckage, and carried the dead to the port side to await a sailor's burial. Farragut remained on the poop, scanning *Tennessee*. He turned to Drayton and said, "As soon as the people have had their breakfasts I am going after her."

While Farragut discussed methods for attacking *Tennessee*, Buchanan stomped about the deck of the ram and waited impatiently for his men to refresh themselves. The temperature in the engine room had topped 145 degrees, making it

impossible for anyone to remain below. Aside from heat prostration, not a man had been injured in the two-hour fight earlier that morning. With ports flung open to air out the vessel, Buchanan inspected the ram inside and out. Except for holes in her smokestack that would reduce her speed, Buchanan found her fit for battle and, in his opinion, impregnable.

He overheard one of the crew suggest that, with Farragut in the Bay, *Tennessee* and her crew were by default made prisoners of the Union Navy. Buchanan whirled about and faced the speaker, angrily retorting, "No, I will be killed or taken prisoner, and now [that] I am in the humor I will have at it at once." He turned to the ram's captain, Commander James D. Johnston, and said sharply, "Follow them up, Johnston; we can't let them off in that way." The *Tennessee*, rather than dwell under the protective batteries of Fort Morgan, ventured forth to engage the entire Union flotilla.

A lookout on *Hartford* reported the movement of *Tennessee* to Captain Drayton, who believed that Buchanan intended to

Rear Admiral Farragut and Maj. Gen. Gordon Granger meet on U.S.S. *Hartford* to discuss amphibious operations against Fort Gaines, a bastion of Dauphin Island, across the channel from Fort Morgan.

Below: Sailmakers carried ditty bags filled with the tools of their trade, such as a palm, needle case, beeswax, wooden fids, and seam rubbers. The braided rope whip, though outlawed, still saw occasional use.

Right: *Hartford* made a mighty rush at the C.S.S. *Tennessee*, gave the ram a good butt, and only caused damage to herself. Others Union vessels also tried, only to learn that butts could not disable the *Tennessee*.

pass into the Gulf and attack the gunboats left outside the Bay. Farragut peered through his glass, watching every movement of the ram. He observed her turn towards the Middle Ground and shouted, "No! Buck's coming here. Get underway at once; we must be ready for him." Drayton believed that Farragut, whose eyes were bad, was experiencing a delusion. He did not react with speed until the boatswain, hearing Farragut's comments, piped to quarters. Men scurried to their guns and shouted, "The ram is coming!"

Buchanan had given Farragut no time to organize either an attack or a defense. All Farragut could do under the circumstances was to signal for *Manhattan* to run down the ram. Most of the squadron could not read the signals being used. Fleet Surgeon James C. Palmer was about to push off from *Hartford* in a dispatch boat to visit the squadron's wounded when Farragut stopped him and said, "Go to the monitors and tell them to attack the *Tennessee*." A few minutes later Lt. Comdr. Perkins steamed by on the top of *Chickasaw's* turret and waved at Farragut, who thought it a bit peculiar for the ship's commanding officer to go into battle in his shirt sleeves and wearing a straw hat.

Tennessee, being the only Confederate vessel in the impending contest, gave Buchanan a rare advantage. Any ship he

fired upon would be an enemy, and with so many targets clustered in close range he could fire in almost any direction and hit one. Convinced that Union shell guns could not injure the ram, and hopeful of catching Farragut unprepared, Buchanan actually believed that he could whip the Union squadron.

Hundreds of Confederate soldiers watched from the parapets of Fort Morgan as *Tennessee* steamed into battle. They knew the stakes – the preservation of Mobile and the lives of many, because if Farragut won the fight, the next Union assault would be waged on the forts.

With *Tennessee's* speed reduced by half, Buchanan chugged slowly toward the Middle Ground. He focused on one target, Farragut's flagship, believing that by sinking *Hartford* the squadron would become demoralized and without a leader. Union vessels began converging on the ram from all sides, but Buchanan ignored them, never wavering from his solitary objective.

Commander James H. Strong surmised Buchanan's intentions and, having raised a full head of steam, drove the 1,378-ton *Monongahela* into the forward deck of the ram. Buchanan did not see her coming until the last moment, and just before the collision he steered the ram hard aport. The oblique impact spun the ram around and knocked everybody inside to the floor. For a

moment, *Tennessee* sagged in the water, her deck submerged, but she bounded back to the surface unharmed. The butt snapped off *Monongahela's* prow and carried away her cutwater. Two shots from *Tennessee* plunged through her bow. One exploded, wounding three men. *Monongahela* stood off 10 yards and pounded *Tennessee* ineffectually with her 150-pounder and her 11-inch Dahlgrens. Buchanan replied with two 6.4-inch shells and the 7-inch pivot gun, the shot from the latter plowing through the port side and out the starboard, leaving *Monongahela's* hull with a hole large enough to see through.

Captain John B. Marchand waited for *Tennessee* to pass under the guns of *Monongahela* before lining up the 1,533-ton *Lackawanna* for a run at the ram's beam. At full speed, the big sloop struck the ram dead center, directly opposite a gunport. *Tennessee* listed slightly, but *Lackawanna* suffered all the damage. Her stem buckled, planks splintered five feet below the water line, and water began pouring into her hold. As the two vessels turned head and stern abeam each other, *Tennessee's* ports opened and two 6.4-inch projectiles ripped through *Lackawanna's* hull. Marchand could bring only one 9-inch gun to bear. At a distance of 12 feet, the shot struck one of the ram's shutters dead center, buckled it, and scattered fragments of iron inside the casemate. With water spilling into

Above: Farragut consistently put himself in harm's way, but he believed that a commander, in order to direct the battle, must see the field, and to see it meant climbing the ratlines to get above the smoke.

Lackawanna's hold, Marchand wanted to make one more attack before standing off for repairs, so he ordered the helm to bring her about.

As *Lackawanna* cleared into the Bay, *Hartford* made her move. Farragut wanted to strike *Tennessee* on her beam and, to make certain the flagship did not bungle the attempt, he climbed into the port mizzen

rigging to direct operations. Lieutenant John C. Watson noticed Farragut going up the ropes, grabbed the tails of his coat, and unsuccessfully tried to stop him. Knowing that Farragut would probably be jolted off his perch when *Hartford* collided with the ram, Watson grabbed a rope and followed the admiral into the tops. Farragut took the rope, wrapped it around his body, and

collision, but the impact bent the anchor's flukes flush with the shaft. Had the vessels met head-on, they would probably have sunk each other, a risk Farragut had been prepared to take, but not Buchanan. When Drayton saw *Tennessee* sidle to port, he shook his lorgnette at the ram and shouted, "The cowardly rascal; he's afraid of a wooden ship."

For several minutes both vessels lay locked together, port to port. Farragut rocked several feet above the ram when the guns of both ships, which almost touched each other, burst into action. *Hartford's* Dahlgrens made little dimples on the ram's casemate. Buchanan returned fire with shells that ripped through *Hartford's* berth deck, killing five and wounding eight men, but they failed to explode. So close were the vessels that powder from *Hartford's* guns blackened the ram's casemate.

Drayton caught sight of Buchanan standing near an open port. Having no weapon nearby, he ripped off his binoculars and threw them at the Confederate admiral, hollering, "You infernal traitor!" The port closed and *Tennessee* passed aft. From the shrouds Farragut yelled down to Drayton to come about for another run at the ram.

Having all but stopped after the collision, *Hartford* began a wide circle to build momentum. *Lackawanna,* bearing down on *Tennessee* for a second time, crossed *Hartford's* path and crashed into the flagship near the mizzenmast where Farragut had been perched. The admiral had just returned to the deck and got knocked off his feet. The collision cut into two of *Hartford's* ports, dismounted one of her Dahlgrens, and opened a hole two feet above the waterline.

When men on deck looked aloft for Farragut and found him missing, they first thought he had toppled into the water. Up went the cry, "Save the Admiral! Save the Admiral!" Others, not knowing the cause of the yelling, thought the flagship was sinking and shouted, "Get the Admiral out of the ship!" Farragut did not understand all the hullabaloo and climbed up the starboard mizzen rigging to assess the damage to the hull. Finding the hole well above the waterline, he hollered down to Drayton to keep after the ram and to hit her again.

The collision had not been caused by *Lackawanna* but by *Hartford;* in battle, nobody owned a right of way. Angered by the accident, Farragut turned to signal officer Lieutenant John C. Kinney and said, "Can you say 'For God's sake' by signal?" Kinney replied, "Yes, sir."

"Then," said Farragut, "say to the *Lackawanna,* 'For God's sake get out of our way and anchor!'" Kinney began wigwagging the message, and in his zeal to please the admiral, struck him on the head with the signal staff and nearly knocked him to the deck. The signalman on *Lackawanna* read only the first five words before a large flag on the masthead flapped in his face and obscured the last five words. *Lackawanna's* signalman interpreted the five words to mean that he should get down from aloft and take shelter below, which he promptly did, and never conveyed any part of the message to Captain Marchand.

secured it to the shrouds. Watson stayed with him, drawing a revolver to shoot anybody on the ram who drew a bead on the admiral.

Having never taken his eye off *Hartford,* Buchanan saw her coming and helmed over to meet her head-on. Drayton had no time to change the Union flagship's course. With both vessels running at full speed, the 1,273- ton ram faced a 2,900-ton sloop of war bows-on, iron against oak, with Farragut lashed to the shrouds. Had Buchanan not sheered to starboard a few seconds before impact, the collision might have snapped *Hartford's* masts and brought the tops crashing to the deck, admiral and all. *Hartford's* uncatted port anchor caught on the ram's gunwale and buffered the

While *Hartford* untangled herself from *Lackawanna,* Perkins brought *Chickasaw* off the stern quarter of *Tennessee* and began battering the ram with steel and iron shot. *Tennessee's* surgeon, Daniel B. Conrad, remembered that moment as a time when projectiles striking the casemate created "one continuous roar," making it almost impossible to "hear voices when spoken close to the ear," the concussion being so great that men bled from their noses. Maintaining a distance of from 10 to 50 yards, Perkins dogged the ram, hammering her afterport with 11-inch shot. *Winnebago* took position off the ram's other stern quarter, but both of her turrets had jammed, and she could fire on target only by manipulating her steerage.

Chickasaw's accurate and persistent fire on *Tennessee's* aftershield collapsed the ram's shutter, leaving Buchanan without the use of his after gun. Perkins fired 52 projectiles, knocking to pieces *Tennessee's* smokestack, ripping away her partially exposed steerage chains, and shot by shot slowly disabled her.

Farragut had put his faith in *Manhattan's* 15-inch Dahlgrens, but Commander Nicholson never fired more than six shots. Every time he fired, smoke engulfed the turret and blinded the gun crew. One of the guns jammed early in the action, and after that, Nicholson failed to close on the ram, blaming it on faulty steerage. He would later attempt to take credit for disabling *Tennessee,* but only one of *Manhattan's* shots caused the ram any injury.

From inside *Tennessee's* casemate, Lieutenant Arthur D. Wharton observed that one lone shot, for he had peered out a port and observed "a hideous-looking monster... creeping up our port side, whose slowly revolving turret revealed the cavernous depth of a mammoth gun. A moment later, a thundering report shook us all, while a blast of dense sulphurous smoke covered our portholes, and 440 pounds of iron, impelled by 60 pounds of powder, admitted daylight through our side where, before it struck us, there had been two feet of solid wood, covered with five inches of solid iron. This," said Wharton, "was the only 15-inch shot which hit us fairly. It did not come through; the inside netting caught the splinters, and there were no casualties from it. I was glad to find myself alive after that shot."

Buchanan knew that for his ship to survive he must somehow repel *Chickasaw.* He sent four men with sledgehammers to the port shutter aft to knock away the bolt that had jammed it shut. Two men held the bolt while the others pounded it with sledges. A shot from *Chickasaw* struck the casemate near the workers, and the men whose backs were braced against the shield "split to pieces." Surgeon Conrad rushed to their aid, but was interrupted by a man dropping down from the gun deck who shouted, "Doctor, the admiral is wounded!" "Well, bring him below," Conrad replied. "I can't do it," said the messenger, "I haven't time. I am carrying orders for Captain Johnston."

Conrad climbed to the gun deck and asked, "Where is the admiral?" Nobody knew. They were all too busy at the guns. So Conrad sifted through the smoke until he found an "old white-haired man... curled up under the sharp angle of the roof." Buchanan seemed oblivious to the extent of his injury, but Conrad noticed one of the admiral's legs "crushed up under his body." A heavy object had fractured the large bone of Buchanan's leg, comminuting it, and the ragged ends of the severed bone protruded through the skin and muscles.

Nobody could hear the surgeon's call for help, so Conrad lifted the admiral gently and carried him down the ladder, but as he did so he could feel the damaged leg "slapping against me as I moved slowly along." While Conrad set the leg in a crude splint, the captain came below. "Well, Johnston," said the admiral, "they have got me again. You'll have to look out for her now; it is your fight." Johnston replied solemnly, "I'll do the best I know how."

Five minutes before being disabled,

Buchanan had issued orders to take the ram back to Fort Morgan. When Johnston started for the pilothouse, his objective was not to fight the ship so much as to save her. Because *Chickasaw* had shot away the steerage chains, men on the ram tried to maneuver the vessel with relieving tackles, but another shot from *Chickasaw* ripped the tackles away and separated the tiller from the rudderhead.

As Johnston approached the pilothouse, *Monongahela* struck the ram on the port quarter and sent the captain tumbling to the floor. By then, all the shutters on the gun ports had been jammed, and the ram's stack hung over the casemate, supported by only a remnant of bent metal.

For 15 minutes *Tennessee* limped toward Fort Morgan, having neither steerage nor sufficient power to stem the tide. Her guns fell silent, the men on deck lamenting opportunities lost to sink Farragut's wooden ships because of defective fuses. Johnston soon realized that he could neither fight the ship nor navigate her and reported the sad news to the admiral. "Well, Johnston," said Buchanan, "fight her to the last! Then to save these brave men, when there is no longer any hope, surrender."

Johnston returned to the pilothouse to make a final assessment. Shot continued to batter the casemate. Off to port he spied *Ossipee* steaming toward him on a ramming run. To starboard he saw *Lackawanna* and *Hartford*, now untangled, both bearing on

the ram's starboard quarter. Having no mobility, he could not avoid being struck. Johnston ordered the engines stopped and crawled outside to lower the ensign, but the firing did not stop, nor did the rapidly approaching *Ossipee*. "I then decided," Johnston declared, "although with almost a bursting heart, to hoist the white flag, and returning again onto the shield, placed it in the same spot."

The moment Commander Le Roy observed the white flag, he ordered *Ossipee's* engines stopped, but the ship's momentum carried her into the ram, knocking men to the floor and giving Buchanan another shot of pain. Le Roy came abeam the ram and shouted, "Do you surrender?" Johnston replied, "Yes," adding, "Admiral Buchanan is wounded." Le Roy replied, "This is the United States steamer *Ossipee*. I accept your surrender for Admiral Farragut."

The fight that began at 6:20 a.m., with the briefest pause at 8:35, ended three hours and forty minutes later – exactly at 10:00 a.m. Farragut believed that *Tennessee* had not fired another shot after being rammed by *Hartford*, but he was wrong. It was not the ramming that disabled *Tennessee* but the 11-inch guns of George Perkins's *Chickasaw*, one of the two river monitors from which Farragut had expected the least. The admiral later learned that more men had been killed and wounded by firing from the ram than all those lost during the passage of Fort Morgan.

When Conrad stepped on board *Hartford* to explain the seriousness of Buchanan's wound, he could not believe the immense amount of wreckage on the flagship's deck. "The scene was one of carnage and devastation," he recalled, "with a long line of grim corpses dressed in blue lying side by side." Conrad found Farragut on the poop and asked permission to personally attend to Buchanan. The admiral replied, "Of course," and offered to provide whatever help the surgeon required.

After Conrad returned to *Tennessee*, Farragut dispatched Fleet Surgeon Palmer to the ram to offer aid. Palmer, after almost falling in the water while trying to get aboard the ram, found Buchanan lying near a pile of debris. Palmer extended Farragut's offer "to take him aboard *Hartford*, or send him to any other ship he might prefer." Buchanan did not want any help from Farragut and said so. When Palmer returned to *Hartford* with Buchanan's rejection, Farragut felt hurt, but he told Palmer to transfer "Old Buck" to *Metacomet* and to look after him whether he liked it or not. Men died from lesser injuries than the one

Below: U.S.S. *Richmond* **works its broadsides against the casemate of** *Tennessee*, **only to discover that shot and shell merely carom off the plated behemoth, with some even rebounding back toward the very guns that had fired them.**

Above: Farragut expected little from the U.S.S. *Chickasaw*, a double-turreted river monitor, but her commander, George Perkins, got on the rear of *Tennessee* and forced her surrender.

Right: The U.S.S. *Chickasaw* ranges off the beam of *Tennessee* as *Hartford* approaches to offer aid. The ram's smokestack and steerage had been shot away, and she lay all but dead in the water.

The two phases of the Battle of Mobile Bay show the arrangement of the Union and Confederate squadrons as Farragut entered the bay, and the subsequent fight with *Tennessee* in the Middle Ground. The insert shows the numerous efforts made by Farragut's wooden vessels to disable *Tennessee* by ramming. The efforts failed, proving for all time to come that the wooden navies of the world had rendered themselves obsolete.

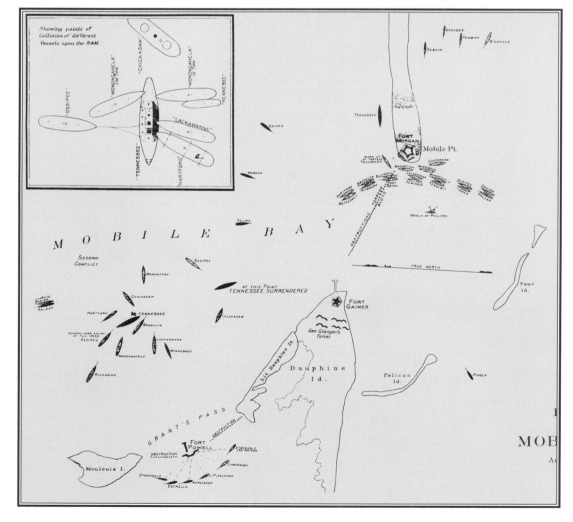

suffered by Buchanan, but Palmer treated the wounded admiral faithfully and eventually saved his leg as well as his life.

Like every battle that ends in victory, there are always those who want the credit. Nicholson tried to steal it from Perkins by claiming that *Manhattan* had ripped apart the ram's decking and carried away the steering gear. Farragut did not know who to credit because he had lost partial sight of the battle after *Lackawanna* collided with the flagship. When Lieutenant Commander Jouett took *Metacomet* to Pensacola with the wounded, the pilot of *Tennessee* asked him, "Who commanded that Monitor that got under the ram's stern?" Jouett replied, "Perkins." "Damn him," said the pilot, "He stuck to us like a leech; we could not get away from him; it was he who cut the steerage gear, jammed the stern port shutters, and wounded Admiral Buchanan." Referring again to *Chickasaw*, the ram's pilot added that Perkins fired "the two eleven-inch guns in her forward turret like pocket pistols, so that she soon had the plates flying in the air."

It is difficult to determine what the outcome of the battle would have been if Farragut had not had *Chickasaw*. Of his best two monitors, *Tecumseh* had sunk and *Manhattan* had developed steerage problems. The twin turrets on *Winnebago* had jammed, making her no more effective than a gunboat firing fixed cannon.

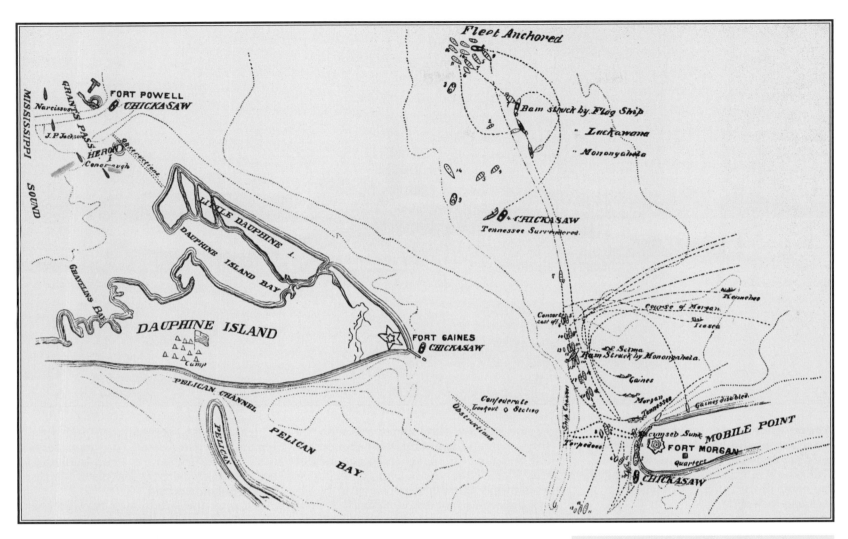

Although design technology certainly improved during four years of war, at least two of the monitors in Mobile Bay had come into the action with serious defects.

During the morning battle, Farragut lost 327 men – 52 killed, 170 wounded, and 93 by drowning when *Tecumseh* sank. Four were taken prisoner after they swam to Fort Morgan, and the balance came from those missing from the storeship *Philippi*. *Hartford's* casualties – 25 killed and 28 wounded – mainly occurred during her battle with the ram. Conversely, most of the flagship's damage was caused by her collision with *Lackawanna*. *Brooklyn* lost 11

killed and 43 wounded from Captain Alden's poor management of the ship when off Fort Morgan. The three surviving monitors came through the fight with no damage and no battle casualties.

All of Farragut's wooden vessels wore chain armor on the starboard beam. The flagship collected 20 hits, five of them passing through the hull. Were it not for the chains, three more shots would have penetrated her hull, and one hitting at the waterline could have sunk her. *Brooklyn* reported 30 hits, 13 entering her hull with two penetrating just above the waterline.

Captain Jenkins of *Richmond* inspected

Below: After the battle for the bay ended, all the forts fell except Morgan. Farragut's squadron, which now included the *Tennessee*, opened on the Fort Morgan in support of Gen. Granger's amphibious landing.

Above: After Farragut captured the C.S.S. *Tennessee*, he did not change her name, only her ownership. Having two *Tennessee*'s in his command, he changed the name of the other, a sidewheel steamer, to *Mobile*.

Below: During the late August bombardment of Fort Morgan, the captured *Tennessee* hurled huge shells at the bastion, punching enormous holes in the lighthouse and demolishing the eastern face of the fortress.

the ram after she surrendered and reported "fifty indentations and marks of shot on her hull, deck, and casemate," and many smaller ones all over the vessel. Nine of the deep dents in her aftershield appeared to be 11-inch projectiles shot from *Chickasaw* at close range. *Tennessee's* hull showed no visible damage from being rammed, which again suggests that, without *Chickasaw*, Farragut could have battered his wooden warships to pieces without doing the enemy any physical harm. And Farragut could have been counted upon to do exactly that.

Below: With the sea battle ended, Farragut's fleet anchored in Mobile Bay and his sailors joined the Army forces to capture the three forts, Powell, Gaines, and Morgan, seen here with much damage after she fell on August 23.

Jenkins also reported that, with minor repairs, *Tennessee* could "do good service now." All she needed was a new smokestack, her shutters repaired, a few plates replaced, and ventilation added.

During the afternoon, Farragut sent *Chickasaw* across the Bay to shell Fort Powell at Grant's Pass. Lietenant Commander de Krafft fired on the fort from Mississippi Sound. Caught in a cross fire, Colonel Williams spiked his guns and abandoned the fort that night.

With Fort Powell out of the way, Farragut turned his attention to Fort Gaines. General Granger had moved 1,200 Union troops up Dauphin Island on August 3 and opened on the fort the moment Farragut started into the Bay. After dealing with Buchanan, Farragut sent his light draft vessels down to Fort Gaines to support Granger. On August

Left: When the Civil War ended, most of Gideon Welles's thousand-ship navy ended with it. Among the casualties was Farragut's famous flagship, but several artifacts from *Hartford* were saved, such as the pictured carving.

Below: After the capture of Mobile Bay, an appreciative public rushed to honor him. Among others, the City of New York provided him with both an elegant home and a beautifully carved presentation sword.

7 Colonel Anderson dispatched a message under a flag of truce to Farragut and surrendered the following day.

The only remaining bastion of Confederate resistance in the lower reaches of Mobile Bay was Fort Morgan, commanded by General Page. Farragut could now supply his squadron through Mississippi Sound, thereby lessening the urgency to force the fort's surrender. On August 9 the Union squadron landed Granger's infantry in the rear of the fort. The U.S.S. *Port Royal* towed the repaired *Tennessee* to a position off the fort where her guns, now served by men of the United States Navy, could bear on the water battery. On August 22 Granger opened on the rear of the fort and set the citadel on fire. At 6:30 the following morning General Page surrendered. Thus ended the battle of Mobile Bay.

On September 3 President Lincoln tendered national thanks to Admiral Farragut and General Granger for one of the nation's better examples of combined operations. In a separate announcement, he added General Sherman's capture of Atlanta to the Mobile Bay victory and ordered a three-day, hundred-gun salute at every navy yard and arsenal in the Union.

For Davy Farragut, the war had ended. He returned to New York as the most distinguished admiral of the Civil War. Two years later, Congress decided the time had come to recognize the contribution of the navy by raising one of its members to full admiral. On July 25, 1866, David Glasgow Farragut became that man. On Sunday, August 14, 1870, the first admiral died, leaving a void for another to fill. In one of the great coincidences of the war the highest office in the navy went to David Dixon Porter, the man who had become Farragut's foster brother and served under him during the early campaigns on the lower Mississippi River.

The battle of Mobile Bay settled a question in Farragut's mind that had already been settled in the minds of others, such as Mallory and Welles – the question of wood versus iron. Without *Chickasaw*, Farragut would have battered his ships against *Tennessee* until they sank or withdrew. Nine months later the war ended, and with it went the old men-of-war made of wood. The Civil War in America not only brought to a close the Southern rebellion, it also dropped the curtain on the wooden navies of the world.

Right: No officer came out of the Civil War with more distinction that David G. Farragut. It took Congress a while to give him the recognition he deserved, and when they finally did, they made him the first admiral.

BIBLIOGRAPHY

Alden, Carroll S., *George Hamilton Perkins, U.S.N.: His Life and Letters*

Ballard, G. A., "British Battleships of the 1870s: the Warrior and Black Prince," *Mariner's Mirror*

Barnes, J. S., *Submarine Warfare*

Baxter, James P,. *The Introduction of the Ironclad Warship*

Belknap, George E., *Letters of Capt. Geo. Hamilton Perkins, U.S.N.*

Boatner, Mark M., III., *The Civil War Dictionary*

Boynton, Charles B., *The History of the Navy During the Rebellion*, 2 Vols

Bradlee, Francis B., *A Forgotten Chapter of Our Naval History: A Sketch of the Career of Duncan N. Ingraham*

Brooke, John M., "The Virginia or Merrimac: Her Real Projector," *Southern Historical Society Papers, XIX*

Bulloch, James D., *The Secret Service of the Confederate States in Europe*, 2 Vols

Butler, Benjamin F., *Private and Official Correspondence of General Benjamin F. Butler during the Period of the Civil War*, 5 Vols

Butler, Edward D., "Personal experiences in the navy, 1862-65," *Papers read before the Maine Commandery of the Loyal Legion of the United States*, Vol. 2

Church, William C., *The Life of John Ericsson*, 2 Vols

Civil War Naval Chronology, 1861-1865, 6 Vols

Clark, Charles E., *My Fifty Years in the Navy*

Coffin, Charles C., *My Days and Nights on the Battlefield*

_____. *Drum-Beat of the Nation*

Crandall, Warren D., and Newell, Isaac D., *History of the Ram Fleet and the Mississippi Marine Brigade*

Daly, Robert W. (ed.), *Aboard the USS Monitor, 1862: The Letters of Acting Paymaster William Frederick Keeler*

Davis, Charles Henry, *Life of Charles Henry Davis, Rear Admiral, 1807-1877*

Davis, William C., *Duel Between the First Ironclads*

Dew, Charles B. *Ironmaker of the Confederacy: Joseph R. Anderson and the Tredegar Iron Works*

Dewey, George., *Autobiography of George Dewey, Admiral of the Navy*

Drayton, Percival, *Naval Letters from Captain Percival Drayton, 1861-1865*

Dufour, Charles L., *The Night the War Was Lost*

Duncan, Ruth H., *The Captain and Submarine CSS H. L. Hunley*

Durkin, Joseph T., *Stephen R. Mallory, Confederate Navy Chief*

Ellicott, John M., *The Life of John Acrum Winslow, Rear Admiral, United States Navy*

Farragut, Loyal, *Life and Letters of Admiral D. G. Farragut*

Faust, Patricia L. (ed.), *Historical Times Illustrated Encyclopedia of the Civil War*

Franklin, S. R., *Memories of a Rear-Admiral*

Gift, George W., "The Story of the Arkansas," *Southern Historical Society Papers*

Glassel, W. T., "Reminiscences of Torpedo Service in Charleston Harbor," *Southern Historical Society Papers*

Gosnell, H. Allen, *Gunboats on the Western Waters: The Story of River Gunboats in the Civil War*

Hackett, Frank W., *Deck and Field*

Hearn, Chester G., *The Capture of New Orleans, 1862*

_____. *Admiral David Dixon Porter, The Civil War Years*

_____. *Admiral David Glasgow Farragut, The Civil War Years*

_____. *Ellet's Brigade: The Strangest Outfit of All*

_____. "The Brief But Illustrious Career of the Ram Albemarle," *Blue and Gray Magazine*

Holden, Edgar, "The Sassacus and the Albemarle," *Magazine of History*

Johnson, Robert U., and Buell, Clarence C. (eds.), *Battles and Leaders of the Civil War* Vols. 1, 2, 3, & 4

Jones, Catesby ap R., "Services of the 'Virginia' (Merrimac)," *Southern Historical Society Papers*

Jones, Samuel, *The Siege of Charleston and Operations off the South Atlantic Coast*

Jones, Virgil Carrington, *The Civil War at Sea*, 3 Vols

Kell, John McIntosh, *Recollections of a Naval Life*

Lewis, Charles L., *Admiral Franklin Buchanan. Fearless Man of Action*

_____. *David Glasgow Farragut*, 2 Vols

Long, John S., "The Gosport Affair," *Journal of Southern History*

McClure, Alexander K., *The Annals of the War, Written by Leading Participants North and South*

McKay, Richard, *South Street, A Maritime History of New York*

Mahan, Alfred T., *The Gulf and Inland Waters*

Marvel, William, *The Alabama and the Kearsarge: The Sailor's Civil War*

Merrill, James M., *Battle Flags South: The Story of the Civil War Navies on Western Waters*

_____. *The Rebel Shore: The Story of Union Sea Power in the Civil War*

Miers, Earl Schenck (ed.), *Lincoln Day by Day, A Chronology, 1809-1865*

Military Essays and Recollections, *Papers Read Before the Commandery of the State of Illinois*, Vol. 1

Milligan, John D., *Gunboats down the Mississippi*

Morgan, James Morris, *Recollections of a Rebel Reefer Naval Actions and History 1799-1898*

Niven, John, *Gideon Welles, Lincoln's Secretary of the Navy*

Official Records of the Union and Confederate Armies in the War of the Rebellion, 128 Vols

Official Records of the Union and Confederate Navies in the War of the Rebellion, 30 Vols

O'Neil, Charles, "Engagement Between the 'Cumberland' and the 'Merrimack,'" *United States Naval Institute Proceedings*

Parker, Foxhall A., *The Battle of Mobile Bay*

Parker, William H., *Recollections of a Naval Officer, 1841-1865*

Perkins, Susan G. (ed.), *Letters of Capt. Geo. Hamilton Perkins*

Perry, Milton F., *Infernal Machines: The Story of Confederate and Submarine Warfare*

Personal Recollections of the War of the Rebellion: *Papers Read Before the New York Commandery*, Vol. 2

Porter, David Dixon, *The Naval History of the Civil War*

Ramsay, H. Aston, Worden, J. L. , and Greene, S. D., *The Monitor and the Merrimac*

Reed, Rowena, *Combined Operations in the Civil War*

Rochelle, James H., *Life of Rear Admiral John Randolph Tucker*

Roman, Alfred, *The Military Operations of General Beauregard in the War Between the States, 1861 to 1865*, 2 Vols

Roske, Ralph J., and Van Doren, Charles, *Lincoln's Commando: The Biography of Commander W. B. Cushing, U.S.N.*

Scharf, J. Thomas, *History of the Confederate Navy*

Selfridge, Thomas O., *Memoirs of Thomas O. Selfridge, Jr., Rear Admiral, U.S.N.*

Semmes, Raphael, *Memoirs of Service Afloat during the War between the States*

Sinclair, Arthur, *Two Years on the Alabama*

Still, William N., Jr, *Iron Afloat: The Story of the Confederate Ironclads*

Stimers, Alban C., "An Engineer Aboard the Monitor," John D. Milligan (ed.) *Civil War Times Illustrated*

Summersell, Charles G. (ed.), *C.S.S. Alabama: Builder, Captain, and Plans*

_____. *The Journal of George Townley Fullam, Boarding Officer of the Confederate Sea Raider Alabama*

Thompson, Robert M., and Wainwright, Richard (eds.), *Confidential Correspondence of Gustavus Vasa Fox, Assistant Secretary of the Navy, 1861-1865*, 2 Vols

Walke, Henry, *Naval Scenes and Reminiscences of the Civil War in the United States*

War Papers; Read Before the Commandery of the State of Michigan, Vol. 2

Welles, Gideon, *Diary of Gideon Welles*, 3 Vols

West, Richard S., Jr., *Mr. Lincoln's Navy*

_____. *Gideon Welles: Lincoln's Navy Department*

Williams, Frances L., *Matthew Fontaine Maury, Scientist of the Sea*

Williams, Harry T., *Beauregard: Napoleon in Gray*

Winters, John D., *The Civil War in Louisiana*

Wise, John S., *End of an Era*

INDEX

MANAGING THE TRAINING PROCESS
Second edition

Managing the training process

Putting the principles into practice

Second edition

Mike Wills

Gower

First edition published 1993 by McGraw-Hill International (UK) Limited

This edition published by
Gower Publishing Limited
Gower House
Croft Road
Aldershot
Hampshire GU11 3HR
England

Gower
Old Post Road
Brookfield
Vermont 05036
USA

British Library Cataloguing in Publication Data
Wills, Mike, 1946–
 Managing the training process: putting the principles into
 practice. – 2nd ed.
 1. Employees – Training of
 I. Title
 658.3'124'04

 ISBN 0 566 08017 6

Library of Congress Cataloging-in-Publication Data
Wills, Mike, 1946–
 Managing the training process: putting the principles into
 practice / Mike Wills – 2nd ed.
  p. cm.
 Includes bibliographical references and index.
 ISBN 0–566–08017–6 (hardcover)
 HF5549. 5. T7W4934   1998   98–9618
 658.3' 124–dc21   CIP

Typeset in Great Britain by Saxon Graphics Ltd, Derby and printed in Great Britain by MPG Books Ltd, Bodmin.

Contents

List of figures

List of tables

Acknowledgements

The trouble with acknowledgements is that it is nearly impossible to list everybody who has influenced the writing of a book. Even if I were to try, I am sure I would miss out some of my most important influences.

So, rather than attempt the impossible, I would like to dedicate this book to all the people I have ever taught, and to all my colleagues who have influenced me by way of suggestions, discussion, argument or demonstration of good training practice. Thank you all.

MW

Introduction

'Training and education are now being given the prominence and priority that they deserve throughout business and industry.'

Such an optimistic statement might perhaps be a headline from a future newspaper, but when I wrote the introduction to the first edition of *Managing the Training Process* I had the impression that many companies were putting, and keeping, training on the agenda.

Today, even more companies are taking training seriously, although I am also detecting the beginnings of a polarization between companies who take a long-term view and those who concentrate on the short term. Companies taking the long-term view are investing heavily in training and other parts of their businesses. Unfortunately, the companies that take the short-term view are cutting back furiously – perhaps even to the point of organizational anorexia.

Far-sighted companies are not investing in training because of altruism but because of a deeply held value that successful companies are the ones who take the training of their people very seriously. Of course, this is not a simple cause-and-effect relationship. If good training guaranteed spectacular results we could simply sink vast amounts of money into training and immediately have highly profitable companies. It sounds too easy and it is too easy.

The relationship between training and business results is a very complex one. This is because results are affected by many differing and varying influences. Economic influences are some of the most prevalent. Identifying training's contribution to the business would involve filtering out the effects of all these other influences.

Although it is doubtful whether this calculation could ever be done with any sort of accuracy, it is something training managers often find themselves having to attempt – simply because they are asked to justify their current training curriculum.

Another approach is to assess the business needs regularly. The skills required are then identified and a training plan is developed to eliminate the skills deficiencies. In this way training becomes an essential and integral part of the business strategy and plans.

Even though training makes an essential contribution to the business, it should be remembered that training does not provide a complete solution for the development of a company's employees. I estimate that attending training courses probably accounts for about 10 per cent of people's development, with experience accounting for the remaining 90 per cent. Sometimes people are surprised at how low this estimate is – especially coming from someone in the training and development profession! However, I would maintain that this is a vital 10 per cent. Unless people have the skills, knowledge and theoretical framework to make sense of what is going on around them, how can they make the right decisions and take the right actions?

'Total quality management' is an example of a business strategy that cannot succeed without a huge investment in training. The quality principles were first put forward by Deming and Juran, taken up with shattering success by the Japanese, and are now being used by increasing numbers of Western companies.

Quality is defined as meeting customer requirements. This can only be achieved by every single person in the organization taking individual responsibility for the quality of their work. People cannot take responsibility for their own quality if they are not able to use the new quality processes and technologies. A once-off injection of training is not enough because quality means continually improving business processes. Improved processes require new skills and knowledge.

Additionally, skills can quickly go out of date because customer requirements are becoming more stringent by the day. Competition is growing fiercer and the pace of change is ever accelerating. If this isn't bad enough, the older style of organization is just not responsive enough to cope with today's changing environment because no one dares to make a move until decisions have been made and received from the people at the top of the hierarchy.

Organizations are also becoming flatter, with technology helping people to take on more work and greater spans of control. This kind of structure can be very cost effective. However, the flatter organization can only be effective, flexible and responsive if the workforce is highly motivated, trained and educated.

Another effect of flatter organizations is that responsibility for training is fragmented throughout the organization. Different processes and standards start to emerge and there is a consequent fall in quality coupled with a waste of meagre training resources. Often, exactly the same training need is met by different courses in different parts of the company. For example, one large multinational company once had 37 different courses on 'presentation skills' throughout the world. Apart from wasting resources, this approach leads to confusion and poor communication because people from different parts of the company end up using different processes and terminology.

The instinctive reaction to this situation is to centralize the training operation, but this approach can create an inflexible and unresponsive bureaucracy.

The training process described in this book arose out of a real need to standardize the quality of training delivery in a large multinational organization without the necessity for a centralized bureaucracy. In fact, writing this book helped me to refine the process further.

The first draft was a training process with elements that all our training and human resource managers recognized. Although all of the steps were familiar, very few of us had seen the entire process put together on one sheet. The power of this was that we could quickly and easily see where our current processes fell short of this benchmark.

Having a benchmark process only solved part of the problem; the process still had to be locked into the organization's business cycle and responsibilities for each step of the process had to be assigned. The development of the process and the writing of this book then proceeded together – the one feeding off the other.

The way that this book has been structured means that it can be used as:

- A checklist for training professionals.
- A guide for people, such as directors, human resource

managers and line managers, who need to understand how the training process is managed.

- A detailed explanation for those such as training managers, trainers and training administrators whose job it is to make the process work.

The purpose of this book is to provide a guide to managing the training process, one which meets the needs of today's organizations. The emphasis throughout the book is one of practicality. This does not mean to say that the theoretical basis of training, which has been covered in detail by other books, has been ignored. Rather, this book concentrates on what you have to do when you are identifying the need, bringing on new trainers, sourcing new courses and deciding how you are going to integrate the many demands that are cascaded down from corporate, head office or the board.

Of course there are no easy answers to all of this, but this book offers some practical approaches you can take to help you through the training jungle.

The structure of the book is driven by a series of flow charts. Chapter 1 describes the top-level process. The subsequent chapters take one or more steps from the top-level process and describe them in more detail. Each of these steps has its own process and flow chart.

The second edition of the book has given me the opportunity to develop some of the themes identified in the first edition and to include some of the latest developments in the ever-changing world of training and development.

I have done this by dividing the book into two parts. Part I retains the original flow chart structure to describe the basics of the training process – basics which remain constant and form the foundation of new developments.

Part II is a collection of short papers or briefings which are designed to keep you up to date on the latest developments in training and development. Brevity is achieved by reference back to Part I for detailed explanations of the basics.

Future editions of *Managing the Training Process* will include further revisions of Part I and enlarged or changed contributions to Part II. It is my intention to publish draft versions of the new briefings on the Internet to judge reaction and obtain feedback before including the most popular briefings in a later edition of the book. You will find them, plus other training topics, on my home page, which can be found on:

http://ourworld.compuserve.com/homepages/mikewills

Also look out for details of a proposed electronic version of *Managing the Training Process*. If you would like me to send you details when these publications become available, or if you have any comments on this book or other training-related topics, please e-mail me on:

mikewills@compuserve.com

Mike Wills

Part One

The Training Process

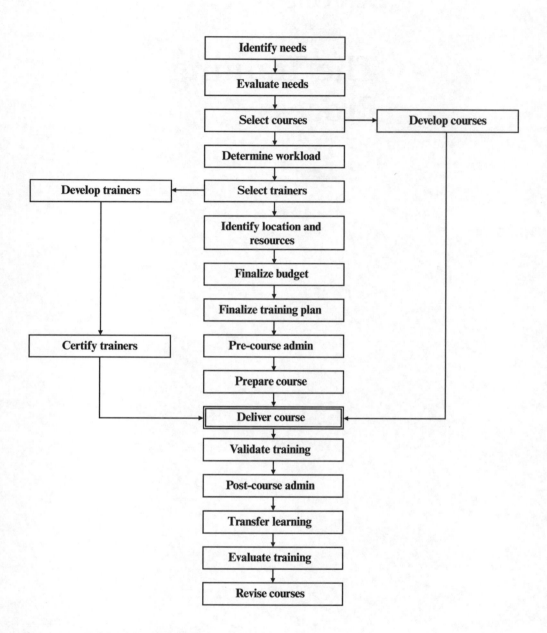

Figure 1.1 *Top-level flow chart of the training process*

1 The process of training

When people talk about the training process they usually mean the day-to-day activities that make up the annual training cycle. Concentrating on the process is the best place to start if you want a quick and significant improvement in training efficiency. Indeed, the greater part of this book is devoted to describing this basic training process.

There are, however, several dangers in considering the training process in isolation. The most obvious is that the training provided will have little or no relevance either to business requirements or to the development needs of the people. Another danger is that maintaining the process can become an end in itself. Then training becomes inflexible and insensitive to change.

It is very easy to say that effective training has to be aligned with a company's business directions and values; that the training department has to provide courses which support the company's goals; and that anyone who is involved in managing the training process has to have a clear idea of where the business is going.

All this assumes that those involved in running the business have a clear idea of where they are going. Unfortunately, this is not always the case and proactive training managers will often find themselves involved with senior management in getting the basics right. If this foundation is not firm, no training process can successfully support the business objectives.

As well as giving an overview of the training process, this chapter also describes how successful companies define their businesses and how they clarify their attitudes towards training.

Getting the basics right

Not every company uses the same method to ensure that the business is built on firm foundations, but the following is a summary of current thinking on the subject. Much of this thinking comes from Japan. If you are interested in understanding the Japanese approach in more detail, Masaaki Imai's book *Kaizen: The Key to Japan's Competitive Success* gives a detailed account.

Alignment

The key to getting the basics right is making sure that everybody has the same understanding of the current situation and that everyone is pulling in the same direction for the future.

The large arrow in Figure 1.2 represents the company's intended business direction. The small arrows are the directions of the individual departments. Each department is pursuing its own interests, and spends more time on in-fighting than on fighting the company's competitors.

Without the alignment shown in Figure 1.3 no company can make progress – and no training department could provide efficient and effective training. Training provided for one department would not be suitable for another, and little of the training would align with the company's business direction.

Philosophy

A philosophy is a statement of what the company stands for. It is a set of values and beliefs by which actions can be judged. A philosophy makes it clear which behaviours are

Figure 1.2   Misalignment of company organizations

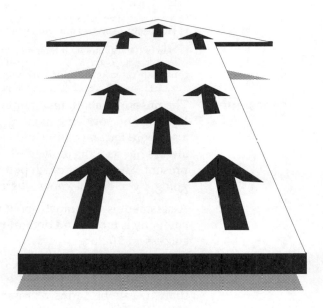

Figure 1.3   *Alignment of company organizations*

appropriate – and which are unacceptable. The following is an example of a typical philosophy. It is based on a large multinational's core values.

> We succeed through satisfied customers
> We value our employees
> We aspire to deliver quality and excellence in all that we do
> We require premium return on assets
> We use technology to deliver market leadership
> We are responsible members of society

Missions   A mission is a statement of what a company or organization is here to do today. It is the reason for the organization's existence. A mission should describe what is done for whom in such a way that it could not be confused with anybody else's mission. An example of a mission for a training department might be: 'To provide sales training for XYZ's UK-based sales staff'.

Communicating the mission to every employee ensures that everybody knows what business they are in. It also helps to highlight any duplication or gaps in a company's structure.

If you think a company's mission is so obvious that it hardly warrants the effort of defining it, be prepared to shock yourself. Try asking a selection of people what they think their department's mission is.

> A company had just embarked on the development of a new product.
> The design team was brought together to define their mission.
>
> Half of the team thought their mission was to look after the product
> from 'cradle to grave'. The other half of the team thought they were
> there to 'caretake' until the *real* design team was formed.

Assessment

The mission is about maintaining today's processes, but training and surviving in today's business environment are also about encompassing and loving change. Change always has its roots in the past and has to start in the present. There is not much point in deciding where you are going if you do not know where you are starting from.

Assessment is very much about understanding where the company is today, and determining the reasons for both success and failure.

Visions

A vision is a 'picture' of where the organization wants to be in the future. By describing the future in emotional rather than measurable terms, a vision can exert a strong pulling force which helps keep the organization aligned.

Examples of visions are: 'There will be a time when generations of people have lived, died and been born on Mars' and 'Every household will have their own wind-driven generator.'

Describing events in pictorial terms, and from a future viewpoint where success has already been achieved, greatly enhances the probability of a vision coming to fruition.

Like the philosophy, a vision provides a basis for deciding which actions should be taken.

Goals

Goals are quantitative figures, such as sales, profit and market share, that are established by top management. Goals put the flesh on the vision. Without goals the vision will remain only a dream.

Policies

A policy is a medium- to long-range course of action comprising a goal and a strategy (a 'what' and a 'how'). A strategy is the means of achieving the goal. Without the means a policy is only a slogan like 'Work Harder' or 'Think Smarter'. Imploring people to improve without providing the means cannot, and does not, work.

Be careful of how the word 'policy' is used, as it is often used interchangeably with 'philosophy' which has quite a different meaning.

Policy deployment

Policy deployment is the process of ensuring that the company's policies for quality, cost and delivery (QCD) are understood from the highest to the lowest levels in the company.

The way the system works in practice is that the policy is communicated across the organization as well as being cascaded down through the line managers.

Cross-functional communication of policies is very important because it binds the functions together in pursuit of the company goals. It helps functions co-operate instead of selfishly pursuing their own objectives at the expense of others. It is this subtle but important distinction that separates policy deployment from management by objectives (MBO).

As a policy cascades down, all line managers are expected to translate the 'what' in the light of their own responsibilities, and to identify 'how' they will achieve the goals. As a result of this, the 'how' at one level becomes the 'what' at the next level down.

Policy deployment is a cyclical process. Progress against the goals should be checked, the reasons for any deviations (both positive and negative) diagnosed and the policies modified in the light of the diagnosis.

Making change happen

Change is occurring far more rapidly than ever before. Companies have to adapt to change or become extinct. Resistance to change has to be overcome.

There are two basic approaches to bringing change about deliberately. The first is through innovation and the second is through continuous improvement. Western cultures concentrate on innovation but Eastern cultures put more importance on continuous improvement. In Japan the word for continuous improvement is *kaizen*.

Innovation causes leaps in efficiency and productivity, but competitors can copy the innovation and the competitive advantage is soon whittled away. Innovation is often dramatic and causes resistance to change.

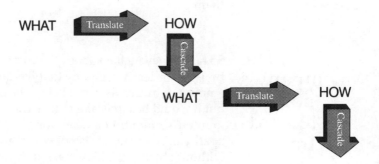

Figure 1.4 Policy deployment

Continuous improvement helps you keep ahead of the competition until your competitors introduce an unexpected innovation.

The most successful companies get the best of both worlds by both innovating and continuously improving.

The single most important factor in the successful management of change is the leadership shown by the people at the top of an organization. A company's employees rarely do what management exhorts them to do. Instead they follow the lead given by successful managers. If leaders do not model the new behaviours and attitudes, their followers cannot be expected to change.

Successful leaders provide vision and direction. They understand their people. They understand the factors that are working for them and those that are working against them.

Making change happen in an organization is like trying to light a bonfire. Although change cannot happen unless the 'logs' catch fire, you would not dream of lighting a fire by holding a match to the logs. You light the paper, add more fuel and fan the flames until the logs are consumed in the blaze.

Training plays a vital role in making change happen. Skills that once lasted for generations are now redundant. New skills have to be identified and trained.

Work processes In the end a company has to produce something, whether it be goods or services, that customers are willing to buy. No sales, no income, no company. Although much work has to be done to determine which products meet the customers' requirements, it is the work processes that ensure those requirements are met every time. So, an essential part of getting the basics right is to identify the critical work processes and constantly strive to improve them.

The company's attitude towards training So far we have talked about the company getting its own house in order. A company that has already gone to this amount of trouble is very likely to be committed to training, but it would be a mistake to take this commitment for granted. Commitment taken for granted often turns to apathy or resistance. It is not worth going any further without obtaining a high level of commitment to training. Senior management's actions and behaviours are crucial to the success of any venture.

Senior management commitment to training is not enough by itself. The training department has to get its own house in order and the organization has to be aware of the importance that is attached to training.

Getting the training function's house in order

The process for getting the basics right for any department is the same as for the whole company. This is no less true for the training function.

Training function alignment

As previously stated, training has to be aligned with the business direction of the company. If the company has got its basics sorted out, and communicated them effectively, the training function should be in no doubt as to which business directions and values should be supported.

In most companies, whether they be large or small, it is very rare for all training to be delivered by one department. This gives ample opportunity for fragmentation and misalignment of the training effort. As we have said before, it is not unknown for several different versions of the same course to exist within the same organization. One multinational corporation was said to have had 37 different 'presentation skills' courses!

Variability in the training process, as with other processes, increases the chances of poor-quality products. The answer to this is to ensure that all the key players within the training community agree on:

- the missions of the various training departments,
- a training philosophy,
- a training policy,
- training standards,
- definition of training,
- the training process,
- accountability and responsibilities.

The training forum

We tackled this problem in one organization by forming a training forum which comprised the following key players:

- total quality manager,
- human resource director,
- site human resource managers,
- group training manager,
- site training managers.

The forum first met to reach consensus on the basics. Once these had been established the forum then met twice a year to ensure continuing alignment on business direction and training needs.

Obviously the composition of a forum will depend on how the company is organized.

Training department's mission

Where there is more than one training organization within a company it becomes imperative that the 'coverage' provided by each training department is understood and well defined. This helps to avoid duplication and prevents training needs falling between the cracks. An example of a training department's mission could be:

> 'To provide sales and customer care training for all the sales representatives who work in the corporation's telecommunications division.'

Notice that this mission states what types of training are provided for which population of students. It can be inferred from the statement that this training department does not do technical training, but provides sales and customer training for telecommunications staff wherever they are located. If this is not true then the mission statement would have to be modified. For example, in a large multinational corporation the end of the statement might be modified to:

> '...who are based in France and work in the corporation's telecommunications division.'

Training philosophy

The training philosophy is a statement of a company or organization's attitude towards training. It has to define clearly the importance that is attached to training. It has to be communicated, with conviction, to every employee. If the philosophy is just a set of words without the backing of real and practical commitment, the authors of the policy will soon be 'found out' and the damage will, perhaps, be irreparable. The first paragraph of the following statement on training is a typical example of a training philosophy.

Group Education and Training Philosophy and Policies

1 We are committed to having a workforce prepared to meet current and future business objectives by providing our employees, at all levels, with appropriate education and training opportunities.

2 We are committed to defining clearly the minimum training requirements which are related to the job holder's role, responsibilities and needs, including total quality and customer satisfaction.

3 All new employees will be oriented in the philosophy, ethics, values, principles and business priorities of the company, including total quality management and induction into their own organization, within three months of their employment.

4 Our employees will only take up new job assignments when they have completed the minimum level of training specified for that job.
5 All newly hired or first-time people managers will successfully complete specified supervisory training within four months of appointment.
6 Our managers will successfully complete functional knowledge and skills training to properly coach, inspect and reinforce the work of their employees.

Training policy

In the same way that a business policy has a goal and the means to attain the goal, a training policy should also have targets and measures.

For example, having all employees oriented to the company's philosophy, ethics, values, principles and business priorities is a goal. Having new employees attend induction and quality training within three months of joining the company is the measure that will achieve the goal.

Following the principles of policy deployment, these measures now become the goals of the new employees' managers and of the training department. The managers will have to provide the means for releasing new employees for training within three months. The training department has to take measures to ensure the availability of training.

Training standards

The training policy will incorporate many of the training standards, such as:

- hours of functional training per employee,
- additional hours of training for managers,
- minimum level of training before starting a new job,
- the amount and timing of induction training.

There are many other standards that have to be agreed and met for the training process to run smoothly. The following are just a selection:

- trainer-to-student ratio,
- trainer training,
- trainer accreditation,
- face-to-face percentage,
- delivery-to-preparation ratio,
- cost per student-day,
- cost per trainer-day,
- classroom standards,
- administrative standards,
- course development standards.

These standards will be dealt with in detail in the rest of this book.

Definition of training

While it is essential to have a training philosophy, policy and standards, it is impossible to judge whether our training is in accordance with these if there is no clear definition of training.

For example, a company might have a target to give each of its employees five days of training every year. Depending on what is considered to be training, one company might say it is providing three days of training and another company might claim nine days – even though both companies' employees have received exactly the same amount of training and development!

An amazing number of activities might be considered as training. The following is just a selection:

- classroom (trainer led),
- distance learning,
- computer-based training,
- on-the-job training,
- external courses,
- large-scale workshops,
- attendance at seminars,
- attending exhibitions,
- attending conferences,
- attending communications meetings,
- evening classes,
- further education,
- assignments,
- participating in quality circles,
- reading articles and books.

Some of the above activities, such as classroom training and computer-based training, would always be considered as training. Activities such as exhibitions, conferences, assignments and reading would not usually be classified as training.

Clearly on-the-job training should be considered as training, but surely not all of the time spent under supervision should qualify for the employee's 'hours of training'. The conclusion we came to was that the time spent on producing usable output should not be included in the training time.

In Europe and the United States, participating in quality circles would probably not be considered to be training because the prime purpose of a quality circle is thought to be solving the company's problems. Any learning that comes about would be thought to be secondary. In fact, this is another indication of how Western culture misunderstood Japan's quality revolution, because one of Japan's main aims in starting quality circle activities was to enable the factory workers to study together and teach themselves quality control.

Without a definition of training, deciding whether an activity should be recognized as training becomes very subjective. The working definition of training that I use is:

> 'Training is the transfer of defined and measurable knowledge or skills.'

From this definition it can be seen that training activities should have objectives and a method for checking whether these objectives have been met.

Training, defined in this way, deals only with changes in behaviour and knowledge. Some definitions include changes of attitude as part of training. I have not included attitude change within the definition because, apart from being incredibly difficult to measure, it is the environment and culture of a business that primarily determine attitude. Training has an important part to play in this, and can help create the environment in which attitudes can change, but training alone will not change anybody's long-term attitude.

Many different attempts have been made to define what constitutes a training activity, and these all vary depending on the definition of training that is used. Having agreement on a definition of training is more important than which of the many good definitions you decide to use. This allows you to be aligned within your own company, and to make sensible comparisons with other companies.

If you have not already done so, this would probably be a good time to consider which activities in your company should be considered as training.

The French Ministry of Work, Employment and Professional Training considers that training activities are those activities which are paid for by employers and take place in accordance with a programme which:

- has pre-determined objectives,
- specifies the teaching methods,
- specifies the personnel to be used,
- has an implementation plan,
- assesses the results,
- is given in premises separate from the production area unless it includes practical training,
- can include correspondence courses, safety and security training and training outside of work hours.

The ministry specifies no set minimum duration for a training activity and any duration of course can be included in the minimum statutory time per worker (1.2 per cent) if the training agency agrees. However, in practice, the state does not often allow a training activity lasting less than a day to be included.

Training as part of the business

A useful approach for understanding the training process is to consider it as a system whose boundaries interact with the rest of the business (see Figure 1.5). Training needs are identified, training is provided to meet the needs, the output is compared to the requirements and any necessary changes are made to the system to obtain the desired output.

While this approach helps you understand how training processes operate, it does put training at the centre of the universe. The effect of this training-centred approach is that the business will see training either as a panacea for all problems or as having no direct relevance to the business. Neither of these impressions will help you manage the training process effectively.

A better approach is to extend the boundaries of the system so training is an integral part of the business (Figure 1.6).

The learning organization

Companies which have made this degree of progress have taken the first step towards being a 'learning organization'. There are many definitions of a learning organization but the one I like (based on Pedler, Burgoyne and Boydell) is:

The business

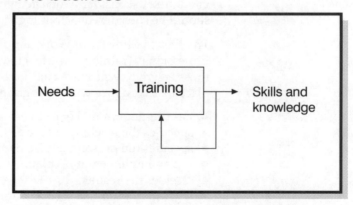

Figure 1.5   Training as a system whose boundaries interact with the business

'A learning organization is one which facilitates the learning of all its members and continuously transforms itself to achieve superior competitive performance.'

Figure 1.6 shows a system that is displaying 'single-loop learning'. The output of the system is compared to a set of standards and adjustments are made to counterbalance any deviations from the standards. More advanced learning organizations would have progressed to 'double-loop learning' where the standards themselves are challenged.

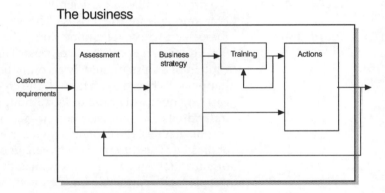

Figure 1.6 *Training as part of the business system*

The concept of the learning organization does not replace training. As you can see from Figure 1.7, training is a vital component of learning. It is important not to overlook this fact, as there have been examples of organizations which have been so intent on becoming learning organizations that they have, to their cost, overlooked the basics of training.

Figure 1.7 *Training as part of the learning organization*

The training process

Having established where training fits into the business, we can now take a look at the training process itself. The fundamental elements of any process are:

- accountability (ownership),
- identification of stakeholders,
- definition and documentation of the process,
- checkpoints,
- responsibility for the steps of the process,
- continuous improvement of the process.

Accountability and responsibility

No process will work efficiently unless somebody 'owns' or is accountable for the process. The accountable person is the person whose telephone rings when something goes wrong with any part of the process. This person is like the captain of a ship, ultimately accountable for everything that happens on board even though the crew are responsible for carrying out most of the tasks. Although the captain holds individual crew members accountable for their responsibilities, the captain's own accountability cannot be abdicated. The difference between an ordinary organization and a 'quality' organization is that in the latter people feel accountable for their own responsibilities.

The training manager is the 'owner' of the training process. This makes the training manager accountable for every step as well as the entire training process. Being accountable for every step is tough, because the responsibility for carrying out many of the individual steps lies with other people. It is the training manager who has to make sure nothing falls down the cracks between the steps of the process.

Identifying the stakeholders

A stakeholder is a person who has a vested interest in the outcome of the process. Stakeholders often have a positive or negative impact on the outcome of a process, even though they might not take a direct part in it. This is especially true if the process involves 'treading on their turf'.

This makes it vital for you to involve stakeholders during the early stages of process design. Managing directors, heads of departments, and human resource managers are all stakeholders in the training process.

Defining and documenting the training process

Definition of a process involves establishing the boundaries of the process. In theory, any process could be traced back to the 'big bang' or projected forward to 'the end of the universe'. In practice, this makes the process too large and cumbersome to handle, so you need to define the beginning and end points of your process. Although defining the boundaries is, to some extent, arbitrary, the following guidelines should help you decide:

- The beginning of your process is where you take over control from someone else.
- The end of your process is where you hand over control to another person.

The easiest way of documenting a process is to tape some sheets of flip-chart paper together and use 'Post-it' notes to represent the steps of the process. You already have the beginning and end points, so these can be stuck on to the sheets straight away. Stick additional steps on the sheets until you have a series of related steps that connect the end point to the beginning point.

Make sure you use a verb and a noun to describe each step in the process. This clarifies what is involved in each step and separates one step from another. 'Select course' is different to 'Develop course' which in turn is different to 'Deliver course'.

The flow chart shown at the beginning of this chapter (Figure 1.1) is an overview of the training process. Subsequent chapters in this book will expand on this 'level 1' process by describing a 'level 2' process for one or more of the steps. In the interests of clarity and simplicity, checkpoints, decision boxes and feedback loops have been left out at this stage.

A brief overview of the steps of the training process follows.

> **Identify needs**

The process starts off by identifying the business needs and turning these needs into training requirements.

> **Evaluate needs**

A check is made to ensure that the requested, or mandated, training is suitable for the people concerned. A check is also made to make sure that training can meet the identified need.

In the cases where training is not a suitable approach the need has to be analysed further so that alternatives to training can be suggested.

> **Select courses**

Given that the business need is one where training can make a contribution, the next step is to identify suitable courses. The choice will be between:

- using an existing company course,
- buying an external course,
- developing a new course.

Develop courses

If no suitable courses are available, new courses have to be developed and piloted.

Determine workload

At this stage you should be able to make your first estimate of the resources you will need to meet the training need.

Select trainers

Before a course can be delivered suitable trainers need to be identified. If you do not have sufficient trainers to meet the expected workload, you will need to start the process of recruiting new trainers. It often takes three months or more to recruit a new trainer so you will need to start this step as early as possible.

Develop trainers

It is likely that the trainers you select to run new courses will need further development of their own skills and knowledge. It is even more likely that trainers recruited from outside will require development.

If you are developing people to be trainers, you will need to put them through a programme of training and experiences before you allow them to train unassisted. Depending on the level and frequency of the courses, this could take from three months to a year.

Certify trainers

If a course is new to the trainers, they should undergo a programme of observation and practice to ensure that they reach the required standard before they are allowed to deliver the course by themselves.

Identify location and resources

Before advertising the dates of the proposed courses it is best to make sure that appropriate locations and resources are available.

Finalize budget

By this stage you should have enough information to know how much it is going to cost to meet the training need. Negotiations over the actual budget are started.

Finalize training plan

After budget negotiations are complete you will need to make adjustments to the training plan.

Often there will be more demand for a course than there are places available so it will be necessary to prioritize the candidates. Prioritizing should still be done even if sufficient places are available, because the people most in need of the course will still get trained if budgets are cut later in the year.

The training plan is built up throughout the early steps of the training process and it is at this stage that the finalized plan can be put together ready for presentation to senior management.

Pre-course admin

Once the training plan has been agreed the course administrator has to ensure that the identified people get to the right course, at the right time.

Prepare course

Before the courses can be delivered the trainers need to prepare themselves, the materials and the training rooms. The trainees also need to prepare themselves for the course.

Deliver course

Although course delivery is the culmination of all the efforts that have been put into the previous steps, it should be remembered that, as far as the rest of the organization is concerned, this is only the start of the change process.

Validate training

Validation is the process of ensuring that the course meets and continues to meet its stated objectives. Tests, observations and student feedback are all data which have to be analysed to determine whether the objectives are being met.

| Post-course admin |

As soon as the training has been completed attendance on the course should be noted on the students' training records.

| Transfer learning |

The students then have to use the knowledge and practise the skills to ensure that the learning is transferred into the business.

| Evaluate training |

As with any process, the training process should have a method of ensuring that it has had the desired effect.

| Revise courses |

The courses then need to be revised to incorporate the changes identified during evaluation.

Establishing checkpoints

You need to establish checkpoints to keep the process on track, under control and producing the required outputs. Checkpoints can occur at the beginning, during and at the end of the process. Checks at the beginning answer the question of whether the correct outputs will be produced. Checks during the process answer the question of whether the correct outputs are being produced. Checks at the end answer the question of whether the correct outputs have been produced. Deviations that you detect early on in the process are easier and cheaper to correct than those found at the end of the process.

The major checkpoints of the training process shown in Figure 1.1 are:

- needs analysis and evaluation,
- pilot courses (within course development),
- trainer certification,
- finalize budget,
- finalize training plan,
- course preparation,
- validate training,
- evaluation.

The most important checkpoint is evaluating the needs. If we identify the needs incorrectly, all else that follows is built on sand. Each process step has its own checkpoints and these will be discussed in the following chapters.

Responsibility for the steps of the process

The training manager should identify, by name, the people responsible for carrying out each task or step in the process. Attaching a person's name to a responsibility is a sure way of flushing out conflicting responsibilities, gaps and potential overloading.

If more than one person is involved in a process step, one of them should be given the prime responsibility so that nobody can ever say: 'I thought that was somebody else's responsibility to make sure that the task was completed.'

Table 1.1 shows how responsibilities could be allocated for the steps in the training process. This table gives job titles in the responsibility column. In practice you would also identify the people's names.

Additional responsibility matrices should be drawn up if there is more than one training organization in the company. The additional matrices should clearly show which courses or types of course are covered by the responsibilities.

Improving the training process

We should always be looking for ways of continually improving the training process. There are two main ways of improving a process:

- reducing errors,
- reducing cycle time (the time it takes to go from the beginning to the end of a process).

To do this you should have a close look at your process by documenting what actually happens at every step.

When you design a new process it is very likely that you will have designed an ideal one. It won't show gaps, duplication, dead ends, confusing responsibilities or activities that add no value to the end product.

You can now compare your actual process with the ideal and make sure that gaps are plugged, duplication and dead ends eliminated, and responsibilities clarified. Activities that add no value to the end product are:

- correcting errors,
- waiting time,
- storage,
- transport time.

By reducing these activities to a minimum you will reduce the cost of, and the time for, providing training.

Table 1.1   *Possible responsibilities for the steps in the training process*

Step	Responsibility
Identify needs	Training manager
Evaluate needs	Training administrator Training manager
Select courses	Training manager Training administrator
Develop courses	Course developers
Determine workload	Training manager
Select trainers	Training manager
Develop trainers	Training manager
Certify trainers	Course developers
Identify location and resources	Training manager Training administrator
Finalize budget	Training manager
Finalize training plan	Training manager Development committees
Pre-course admin	Training administrator
Prepare course	Trainers
Deliver course	Trainers
Validate training	Trainers
Post-course admin	Training administrator
Transfer learning	Participants, managers Trainers
Evaluate training	Trainers Training manager
Revise courses	Course developers Trainers

Training strategies

The training process is a cycle that you need to manage continuously. You respond to needs. You ensure that the training is aligned with the business. The cycle time is short term – usually no longer than a year. Managing the training process is essentially operational or tactical.

If we always manage training at this level we are in danger of being reactive rather than proactive: starting and stopping training programmes or perhaps even failing to deliver anything.

We need to have a clear idea of how we are going to deliver training over a longer period. Training needs analysis and training policies provide the 'what' and the 'how much'. A training strategy provides the long-term orientation.

To put a training strategy together you should have a 'vision' of what training in your organization should look like in, say, five years. You should then map out the years and the key milestones along the way. When you are putting a training strategy together you should ask yourself the following questions:

- How much training will you need to do each year?
- What type of courses will you need to provide?
- What types of people will you put on what type of course?
- What resources will you need in terms of space and trainers?
- Who will you use to do your training?
- Will you use full-time, part-time or consultant trainers?
- What delivery methods will you use?
- How will changes in technology affect delivery methods?
- What business, social and environmental changes are likely to take place?

Every time you cycle through the training process you should re-examine your training strategy to see if it still holds up in the light of new training requirements and corporate policies. This is an example of 'double-loop' learning. Try to make your strategy as robust as possible, and only change strategies when there are significant business, social and environmental changes. If your strategy is really robust you will find that you can respond to many changes by adjusting your tactics rather than throwing away your strategy.

It is difficult but essential to find the right balance between constantly chopping and changing strategies, and sticking with a useless and outmoded strategy.

Communicating the importance of training

Having a training philosophy and policy is the starting point for communicating the importance of training and it is very important that everybody is aware of them.

Posters, in-house magazines, staff briefings and memos are all methods of putting the message across. But no matter how much effort is put into communicating through the usual channels, there is still no getting away from the fact that the most powerful communication always occurs through the unwritten and unspoken channels:

- the amount of training that is done,
- the budget allocated to training,
- the status of training managers and staff,
- how often a training event has to be moved to another location to make room for another business activity,
- how often training is postponed or cancelled,
- the reasons managers give for pulling their people off courses,
- the standard of the training rooms,
- whether people are allowed to start a new job before they have been trained.

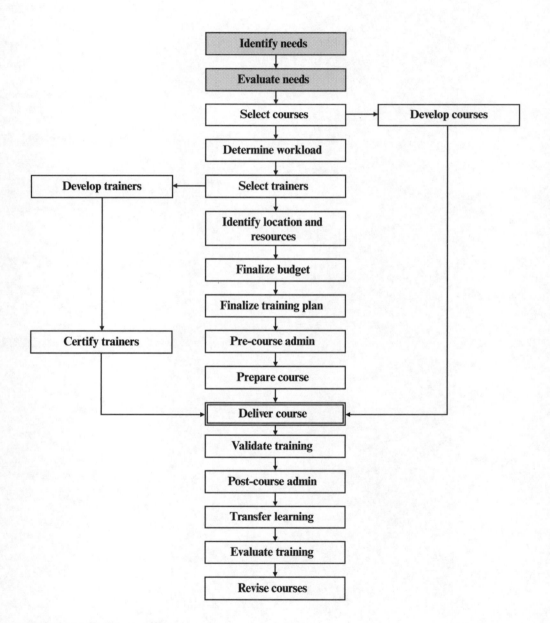

Figure 2.1   Training needs

2   Training needs

In this chapter we will be covering two steps of the training process (highlighted in Figure 2.1):

- identify needs,
- evaluate needs.

Identifying training needs is the starting point for managing the training process. Yet this is often one of the last steps to be considered seriously – probably because a proper needs analysis is both difficult and time consuming.

Initially, it might be quicker and easier to forget about analysing the needs and have your customers pick and choose from a catalogue, but this will ultimately lead to frustration and inefficiency.

Identifying training needs is not just a matter of finding the need and then simply satisfying it. There are often conflicting requirements from different interests within the company. The development needs of the individual have to be met while satisfying the skills requirements of the organization. These needs, once identified, have to be matched to appropriate training courses.

Sometimes there is a feeling that training will always be the solution for every identified development problem. However, there is no point in providing training if training is not an appropriate solution. When this is the case the training manager has to be brave enough to say that it is not appropriate – and creative enough to suggest alternative solutions.

Needs identification

Needs identification has to balance corporate demands, policies and strategies as well as individual and organizational requirements. Figure 2.2 outlines a process that balances these requirements. It shows that corporate policies and strategies should be the 'umbrella' under which individual and organizational training needs are identified. This helps to ensure alignment of training activities with the business direction.

> Collect corporate policies and strategies

Corporate policies and strategies form the boundaries within which all training and development activities should take place.

There are two ways in which corporate policies and strategies give rise to training needs. The first is directly through mandatory training. The other way is through indirect influence. When an organization puts its training plan together it should take account of both the business plan and individual development needs. This is where the process often breaks down and even the indirect influences start to disappear.

Policy deployment, which is a structured method of cascading corporate goals and strategies through the company, is a powerful method of ensuring that training needs are identified within the context of the company's business goals.

In Chapter 1 we discussed the importance of alignment and of getting the corporate basics right. If this has been done well, you will have no difficulty in collecting corporate policies and strategies. You will then be able to prepare a training plan that supports the direction of the business.

If your company is confused about its strategies, or does not communicate them effectively, you might as well miss this step out completely and be resigned to providing training that cannot completely support the business.

Figure 2.2   *Needs identification*

Start by reading your company's policies on training and development, reviewing the company's vision and understanding the current goals and objectives.

> Identify mandatory training

Company policy dictates which employee groups are required to undergo prescribed courses. Some courses, such as 'induction training' and 'total quality management', are an integral part of the company's culture so all new employees have to attend this training.

Company strategy may also require all personnel to go through specified forms of training in a relatively short period. Examples of this kind of training are:

- equal opportunities,
- empowerment,
- harassment,
- financial responsibility,
- new measurement systems (e.g. economic value added),
- new legal requirements.

Compulsory courses will usually be aligned with the company direction because they have been developed centrally for company-wide implementation.

> Identify business needs

Policy deployment and the training forum are two essential tools for identifying business needs. Policy deployment and the training forum's role in defining the basics of the training process are both covered in Chapter 1.

Policy deployment Policy deployment is the process by which a company's strategies are communicated to its organizations. An organization then determines what it needs to achieve by understanding its part in the company's strategy. The 'what' should be measurable and take the form of goals or objectives.

Once an organization has determined what it has to achieve, it then has to decide how these objectives will be met. Once the 'how' has been identified it is possible to determine the skills and knowledge the organization will require.

Training forum's role The training forum's role at this stage of the process is to:

- provide a 'forum' for identifying an organization's business needs,
- ensure that training plans are aligned with the company's direction,

- identify opportunities for sharing or exchanging resources.

The training forum comprises training managers and other interested parties who meet to discuss training plans. They also identify opportunities for sharing resources. A forum is particularly useful when there are several, dispersed training departments within a company.

The forum would normally need to meet twice a year: the first time to understand both corporate requirements and local issues; the second meeting to review draft training plans. Figure 2.3 shows typical timings for the two training forum meetings.

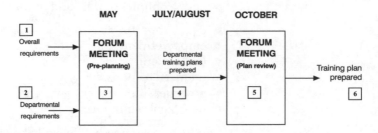

Figure 2.3   *Schedule for training forum meetings*

Timing of these forum meetings is critical and depends on which month is the start of the organization's financial year. The output of the second meeting needs to be available for inclusion in the annual business plan.

Individual development plans should be completed before the draft departmental training plans are put together. The training plans will be based on guesswork if the development plans are not available. If the development plans are available too early, the training plan could be out of time by up to six months. The following is a description of how the training forums work in practice.

1. Before the first meeting the group training manager has a meeting with the organization's general manager to understand the business direction and vision for the organization.

> Even a short statement from a general manager can have quite a profound effect on how the training plans are put together. For example, during preparation for the coming year's training plan at one company, the director said: 'If we sell a product in Europe, we will manufacture it in Europe.'
> The effect of this statement was to cause the training managers to reassess the skills that would be needed in their factories. A very different set of skills is needed to manufacture every machine that is sold rather than assemble small machines and pass the larger

machines through a warehouse. The director said he wanted everybody to make themselves thoroughly familiar with the organization's mission and objectives which could be found in the recently published 'Blue Book'.

He also highlighted the shift in technology that would be required. In the past the business had been built on optical and mechanical technology. Today's and tomorrow's emphasis would be on digital technology. Flexibility would be key: flexible people and flexible manufacturing processes. He also had a concern about the plethora of training courses being produced within the corporation and expressed a hope that they would be properly prioritized and integrated. Another concern was the transfer of learning into the workplace.

The group training manager also collects general training requirements and demands from:

- functional heads,
- human resource managers,
- corporate.

It is amazing how much information this type of digging around can unearth. In preparation for the coming year's training plan, the finance community forewarned us that functional managers were to be made more responsible for financial and other process controls. This would generate additional training for functional managers and buying staff.

2. Preparation notes for the pre-planning meeting are issued and the site training managers identify the following general training requirements and demands for their own areas:

- technical,
- induction and quality,
- business.

3. The training forum meets to understand overall requirements and issues, and to identify potential areas of co-operation. This is the pre-planning meeting. See Figure 2.4 on page 33 for the agenda of the meeting.

The first part of the meeting deals with general issues such as corporate business direction, human resources, quality issues and management training. This is to ensure that the site training managers understand the context within which they will be developing their final plans.

In preparation for the coming year's plan, the human resource director pointed out that the human resource challenges will have to be approached against a background of:

- resource constraints,
- flatter organizations,
- matrix management,
- new technical skills,
- population demographics,

- education levels,
- the European Union,
- workforce empowerment and flexibility,
- equal opportunities,
- the environment and recycling,
- the mix of permanent and contract staff,
- health, safety, security and export control.

The training plans will also have to take account of the 'total quality' initiatives – the main one being the company's application for the European Quality Award. Part of the application process will be 'self-certification' of the key business processes. It is anticipated that 'self-certification' will identify additional training needs.

During the second part of the meeting the site training managers present their draft plans. This gives an opportunity for resources to be shared and new ideas to be spread across the organization.

4. Preparation notes are issued and site training managers prepare the first drafts of their training plans, which include:

- the training needs that have been identified,
- what this would cost if the needs could be met fully,
- how many days of training per employee this would represent,
- how much of the above could realistically be provided during the coming training year,
- resources required,
- approximately when the training will be carried out,
- what this realistic estimate represents in terms of days per employee and total cost.

5. The forum meets again to review the site training plans. The meeting agenda is given in Figure 2.5. The site training managers present their draft training plans and an estimate is made of the amount of training that is planned to be delivered, as well as the cost and the resources required.

6. The site training managers finalize their training plans.

7. The group training manager prepares an overall training plan for the organization.

8. Training plans are submitted as part of the organization's business plan.

Identify individual needs

Identifying training needs via business requirements is a 'top-down' approach which satisfies the need for training to be in alignment with the business direction. If we were only to use this approach, the coverage would be too broad to pick up individual development requirements. We also

---

Pre-planning meeting agenda

Time   Topic

10.00   Review of purpose and agenda (10 min)

10.10   Business direction (20 min)

10.30   Total quality management (30 min)

11.00   Break (15 min)

11.15   Human resource management (30 min)

11.45   Management training and finance (30 min)

12.15   Lunch (45 min)

13.00   Site presentations (1 hr 30 min)

14.30   Break (15 min)

14.45   Next steps (30 min)

15.15   Next forum meeting (30 min)

15.45   Meeting review (15 min)

Figure 2.4   *Agenda for the pre-planning meeting*

need to consider 'bottom-up' training requests and to make sure that both sources of training requirements complement each other. Individual training requirements come either from direct requests or as a result of appraisal discussions.

Requests   If we were honest with ourselves, we would probably admit that the majority of training needs are identified through requests received from either the employee or the

Agenda

Time   Topic

10.00   Review of purpose and agenda (10 min)

10.10   Review action items (15 min)

10.25   Sites information sharing and processing
        (2 hr 55 min – including break)

13.20   Lunch (45 min)

14.05   Group (50 min)

14.55   Break (15 min)

15.10   Issues and opportunities identified
        (information processing 30 min)

15.40   Next steps and action items (15 min)

15.55   Meeting review (5 min)

16.00   End

Figure 2.5   Agenda for the plan review meeting

employee's manager. At their most basic these requests would be an informal approach to the training department with the prospective student or manager saying something like: 'Have you got a course on XYZ?'

The training administrator would then look through the training catalogues and say, 'Well, there doesn't seem to be an XYZ course, how about the PQR course in July?'

Appraisals Another route for identifying training needs is through the annual appraisal system. You know how it can go. The employee's salary is directly related to the outcome of the appraisal and the first hour and a half can be spent discussing what the person did, or did not do, seven months ago. With ten minutes left to go they happen upon a 'Training required' box at the bottom of the last page of the appraisal form.

'I've heard that the Welding for Pleasure course is pretty good,' suggests the appraisee.

'I think that Photographing Dustbins is a better course,' replies the manager.

'Well, perhaps I ought to do both courses.'

'That's a good idea,' agrees the manager, 'let's put them both down and then we can wrap this up and get some coffee.'

These sketches might seem a bit extreme but they illustrate the point that the training requests received by the training department often have more to do with perceived demand than actual need – although it has to be said it is much better to be demand led than place led.

Being place led is where the number of places on a training course has been previously fixed (usually by the size of the budget) and the training administrator has to search around to find people to fill the places.

Approaching needs analysis this way might, by chance, provide training which meets a need, but the odds of this aligning with the company's values and business directions are virtually non-existent.

The way to improve this situation is to take a developmental approach to training needs identification, and to have a broader view of where training needs originate.

A developmental approach to needs identification The whole idea behind a developmental approach to training needs identification is that a person's current skills level is established and compared with the skills or competencies required to do today's as well as tomorrow's job.

Some companies' training request forms have a section that asks what the development need is, and how the requested course would help the candidates do their jobs better. This gives the training administrator a much better chance of suggesting an appropriate course.

A good appraisal system can produce development-related training needs. However, the waters are muddied when the next promotion, or salary increase, is linked to the results of the appraisal.

It would be better if development could be entirely divorced from salary-related assessment. This, of course, would be difficult in companies that run performance-related salary schemes, but development planning and appraisal could still be two separate discussions. Even if no separation is possible, the appraisal can be improved by having the right balance of past performance and future development.

Too many appraisals spend too much time looking backwards and not enough time discussing future development. Although it is valuable to see what lessons can be learnt, the past cannot be changed. Only the future can be changed.

Average appraisers spend only 12 per cent of the appraisal talking about the future; expert appraisers concentrate on future behaviour for 40 per cent of the time.

A developmental approach to appraisal and training would have the discussion centred around the employee's current strengths and weaknesses and would put together a developmental plan to sustain the strengths and minimize the weaknesses. Notice that it is called a 'developmental plan' rather than a 'training plan'. This is quite deliberate, because there is sometimes an immediate assumption that training is the answer to all development needs and performance problems.

Occasionally there is a confusion between personal development and career development. Personal development is all about improving a person's skill and knowledge so that they can do today's job better. Career development is about preparing the person for the next career move.

It is very important to be clear about which type of development you are talking about when you are having discussions with your staff. Most people think that all development will give rise to better prospects and increased salaries. Given the flatter, leaner nature of our organizations, these kinds of expectations are less likely to be fulfilled, and will ultimately lead to anger and frustration – especially if people think that attendance on a training course will automatically give them their next promotion.

Career development depends on opportunity, capability and luck. Opportunity is simply the availability of job at the next stage of a person's career development. Capability is the person's skill and knowledge level. Luck is being in the right place at the right time.

A person's capability can be improved through development. There is even something that can be done about luck. Determine the 'right place' and the 'right time', and position yourself accordingly.

Luck can be created but, unfortunately, the one thing that is almost impossible to influence is opportunity. The number of opportunities that are available in an organization are probably more to do with the general state of the economy and where the company is in its life cycle than anything the organization or individual can do.

Even if the discussions are centred around career development, be very careful about giving the impression that attendance at a particular training course is an automatic ticket to promotion. Careless selection of courses can also lead to false expectations. For example, sending people who are not suited to being managers on a management training course would give them the wrong impression of their prospects and abilities.

Even worse is the avoidance behaviour of sending people on courses in the hope that the course will do the 'dirty work' of revealing their unsuitability for a particular kind of job.

Development is not something that can be done to someone. People have to take the responsibility for their own development. Having said that, the company should provide development opportunities and encourage development. Opportunities which are aligned with the business needs should be given priority, but bear in mind that any development of an individual is ultimately good for the business and should be encouraged. In reality, of course, resources are limited and priorities have to be decided.

So development is a shared responsibility between a person, the manager and the company. Ideally, the individual should take prime responsibility, the manager should have the secondary responsibility, and training and personnel should be third in line. It really does have to be a combined effort.

This is all very well, but is it reasonable to expect the individual and the manager to understand the details and ramifications of all the courses that are available? Providing a training catalogue can help, but even with the best catalogue the manager does not have the background knowledge that is required to make the optimum choices.

Expert systems

What managers and individuals really need is an expert training adviser sitting beside them as the choices are made. Obviously this would not be a cost-effective prospect, so it would be worth considering the use of artificial intelligence in the form of an expert system. An expert system is a computer program that can be given a set of rules which allow it to make the same decisions as an expert. Even at its simplest level an expert system could be of great assistance to a manager.

For example, you might provide both an 'Effective Meetings' course and a more advanced 'Meeting Facilitator's Workshop'. A person who has completed the 'Meeting Facilitator's Workshop' would not need to attend 'Effective Meetings' because its content is covered by the first day of the 'Meeting Facilitator's Workshop'.

Although the two courses are mutually exclusive it can be guaranteed that you will receive requests for people to attend both. It is no use complaining that the managers should have read the details in the training catalogue. Beating up already pressurized managers doesn't help anybody. An expert system could easily and unobtrusively avoid this problem. More advanced systems could take account of the person's job, training record and career path.

Development open days

Expert systems involve a certain amount of expense and, although they can provide instant advice, it will probably be a long time before they can be as effective as discussions with professional advisers.

A way of meeting this need, which also increases the profile of training and development, is to hold a development open day. The day could be in the form of an exhibition, with training and human resource professionals on hand to discuss development needs. Any member of staff would be able to attend the event, but it would primarily be designed for managers who want to understand what development opportunities are available for their people.

Frequency and timing of appraisals

Assuming that all the problems associated with running an appraisal session have been ironed out, there are still the questions of where the output from the appraisal fits into the overall planning cycle, and whether all the needs have been identified.

One of the problems of identifying needs through appraisal is that they are identified only once, or maybe twice, a year. New training needs can surface at any time of the year and, unless the training department can react quickly to train new skills requirements in well under a year, then a company's competitive advantage could be seriously eroded.

The timing of the appraisal is also important. Most companies start submitting their plans for the next financial year about three months before the end of the current financial year. If the appraisal occurs towards the end of the year, the needs analysis will not be done in time for the training plan to be included in the business plan. If the appraisal is done too early, over half of the training would need to have been completed before the business plan was approved.

Even if there were a perfect time to complete appraisals, the chances are that other important activities would need to be done at the same time.

Development plans
The answer to these difficulties is for each individual to have a development plan. A development plan is best produced as the output of a counselling session. Instead of being 'once-off' plans, they should be kept 'evergreen' – that is, they should be revised every time an existing development need has been met or a new one identified.

Notice that the development plan shown in Figure 2.6 includes activities other than training. This shows that the manager and employee who put this plan together have a good idea of what can, and cannot, be achieved by training.

Because these development plans are always up to date, the training needs analysis can be done at any time of the year. The training administrator can request copies of the current development plan when the needs analysis has to be done.

Identify departmental needs

So far we have seen how training departments can be aligned with each other and with the corporate business direction. We have also seen how individual development requirements can be identified. We now need to see how the detailed departmental training needs are identified.

The processes already described should ensure that the department's training demands are based on corporate or company business needs and requirements. The individual requirements give us a picture of the demand within a department but not necessarily the need.

Name *J Ford*   **DEVELOPMENT PLAN**   Date *15th March*

Strengths	Activities to maintain	Schedule/follow-up date
1. *Project Management*	1. *Run workshop on Project Management*	1. *22nd March, 25th March*
2. *Recognizing people*	2. *Provide information on creative use of recognition and reward*	2. *3rd April, 15th April*

Identified needs	Activities to develop	Schedule/follow-up date
1. *Problem solving*	1. *Use of problem-solving process at next staff meeting*	1. *3rd May, 17th May*
2. *Team building*	2. *Hold team-building session with direct reports*	2. *2nd April, 16th April*
3. *Meeting skills*	3. *Attend Meeting Management Workshop*	3. *17th March, 3rd April*

Figure 2.6 *An example of a development plan*

In fact, the process for identifying departmental needs is very similar to the process for identifying need at the corporate level. Each department should assess where it is. The department should have a vision, a mission and a strategy for realizing the vision.

> Identify skills and training required for each job

The department's mission, and the work processes the company uses, determine the jobs the department needs to produce its products and services. Each job has an associated set of skills. New jobs require new skills.

In its simplest form, identifying the training required for each job involves:

1. Identifying the skills required to do a job.
2. Comparing the required skills to the current skills level of the people who will be doing the job.

It is training's function to bridge the gap between current and required skills.

The skills and knowledge required for every job should be documented. You should also document the courses that a representative person will need to reach the required skills level. This makes it easier to select the correct courses. A representative person is the type of person you would normally employ to do the job.

The basis of identifying and documenting the required skills is the 'job description'. A job description should include the tasks that have to be performed and the outputs that have to be produced by the job holder. Outputs are products or services that are handed on to someone else. An output should have a standard or specification attached to it so that the quality of the output can be measured.

The next step is to prepare a 'person specification' from the job description. A person specification describes the ideal person to fill the job. It is a profile of the required personal skills and characteristics. These skills and characteristics are also known as competencies.

For job descriptions which cover a large number of employees it is worth producing a 'training specification matrix'. This matrix describes the training courses that correlate to the skills described in the person specification.

You shouldn't be surprised if all this sounds rather familiar. It is exactly the same as the recruitment process – the only difference being that we are developing existing people to fit the person specification rather than recruiting the 'ideal' person.

If you are recruiting to fill a vacancy, you may not be able to find anybody who fits the person description. You might also want to give people who do not yet meet the person specification a chance to work at a higher level. In such cases you will need to provide additional training to bring these people to the required level.

Identify affected individuals

Arising out of your analysis of corporate policies, mandatory training, business needs and job skill requirements, you will be able to identify which groups of employees will need what training. For example, all new managers will need training on the basics of management, and all electronics assembly people will need training on electrostatic protection.

Effective training processes need to be managed at the level of the individual, so the next step is to identify those individuals who are part of the group which needs the training. This task is made a great deal simpler by computerized personnel and training records. If each person's job is given a job code, the computer can print out a report on the people who have a particular type of job and have yet to receive the required training.

This task is made even easier if the personnel and training records are part of the same database. If you have separate records, you will need to update the training database every time someone joins, leaves or changes jobs.

> Enter potential needs on training records

A training record should not only list the courses a person has attended but also the training a person needs. It is easier to prepare a training plan if the record gives a range of dates for when the training is required. The potential need can be in the form of either a course or a skill.

It is important that the training record is a live reflection of current training requirements. It should be revised any time a new training requirement is identified. This can be after appraisal, when a training request form is received or after an individual has attended an assessment centre. This means that an up-to-date training plan can be pulled off the system at any time of the year.

> Produce training requirement reports

A training record shows the training that individuals have completed and the training that they need to do. The next step is to sift through all the training requirements so you can evaluate the needs and estimate the amount of training that needs to be done. This can be done manually, but it is much quicker if you have computerized training records.

A computer can produce training requirement reports that list:

- all the people who have requested a particular course,
- all the people who need a particular skill,
- the amount and type of training requested by a particular organization.

Needs evaluation

All training requests need to be validated to ensure the training is both appropriate and necessary. The amount of effort and time required to validate the training requirements depends on the quality of the input received. The best time to evaluate training needs is when the needs are being identified. This is why it is worth spending the time to run development open days and to train managers in development needs analysis. In an ideal situation the training administrator should only need to perform a quick check when the training department receives the training requests. These checks are shown in Figure 2.7.

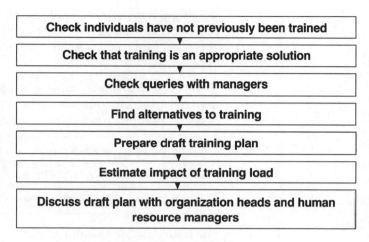

| Check individuals have not previously been trained |
| Check that training is an appropriate solution |
| Check queries with managers |
| Find alternatives to training |
| Prepare draft training plan |
| Estimate impact of training load |
| Discuss draft plan with organization heads and human resource managers |

Figure 2.7 *Process for evaluating training needs*

| Check individuals have not previously been trained |

It is amazing how many requests for training involve people who have already been trained. Sometimes this is because the person has forgotten the name of the course. On other occasions it is because a nomination has been put forward without consulting the person concerned. Whatever the reason, it is highly embarrassing when people turn up to courses they have already completed.

Usually this problem can be caught when the training request is entered on the training record. This is why it is absolutely essential to have accurate training records. If you forget to amend the training record when a person has completed a required training course, you could find that the person will be automatically renominated.

Even if the training records are not as accurate as they should be, many duplications can be identified by an experienced training administrator. As a further precaution, it is worth getting the trainers to review the training requirement reports.

| Check that training is an appropriate solution |

Sometimes a business problem cannot be solved by a training solution. Where this is the case, it is the responsibility of the training department to make this known. However, if a training analyst says that a business problem cannot be solved by training, and does not suggest any alternatives, the organization will soon get the impression that the training department is being inflexible and is not interested in the rest of the business.

If training is to be an integral part of a business's change process, it has the duty and responsibility to suggest alternative approaches when a training solution is not appropriate.

Many of the individual 'training' requests the training department receives are unsuitable for the person concerned or are inappropriate performance problem solutions.

> Some time ago I was observing a report-writing course. One of the students came up to me and said that he had been on report-writing courses five times before. Being surprised by this, I asked whether he really couldn't write reports. 'Oh, I can write reports all right,' he said, 'I just refuse to write them!'

The training administrator and trainers should look through the training requirement reports to see whether any of the requirements seem to be inappropriate or unsuitable. This again underlines the value of having experienced trainers and training administrators who have extensive local knowledge.

> Check queries with managers

When it is suspected that training is not an appropriate solution, you should check this out with the individual's manager. The following are examples of questions that you can ask the manager:

- Is there an important business or strategic need for this training?
- Does the individual already have the knowledge and skills?
- Is the individual willing to use the knowledge and skills?
- Has the individual received this training before?
- Does the individual have the ability to be trained?

To demonstrate how these questions are used for determining whether training is an appropriate solution, let's take the example of the student who refused to write reports even though he had been on a report-writing course five times before.

In answer to the first question, there is a business need for training in report writing. The second question asks whether the individual has the skill and knowledge. As he admitted he could write a report, the answer to this question is 'Yes'. The answer to the third question is 'No' – the individual is not willing to use his report-writing skills. The answers to these questions tell us that training would not be a suitable solution for this person.

Contrast this with a person who is unable to write reports. She needs to write reports as part of her job, so there is a business requirement for this skill. If we were to hold a gun to her head, she still would not be able to write a report, so we know she does not have the knowledge or skill. She has not been trained before, so it is not simply a matter of her forgetting how to write reports. We would then ask whether she has the ability to be trained. It is only after making all these checks that we would say that training is a suitable solution for this person.

> Find alternatives to training

If training is not an appropriate solution, other options need to be found.

If there is no important business or strategic need for training, we should not put people on courses just for the sake of it. 'No action required' is a perfectly acceptable alternative.

If a person already has the skills and knowledge, we have to look at what is preventing them from performing. The person might be willing, but inadequate resources or poor procedures are hindering their performance. In this case, we should recognize their willingness and help them remove their barriers. A counselling session might be required if a personal problem or unhelpful attitude is the source of the difficulty.

We may have to provide refresher training if the person has already been trained, but it is more likely that on-the-job coaching and practice will be required.

If a person does not have sufficient ability for training to be economic, we would have to consider redeploying them and finding someone else to do the job. We would certainly have to re-examine our recruitment procedures and selection standards.

In the case of the person who wouldn't write reports, he had the skills and knowledge but was unwilling to make use of them. If there were no obstacles, we would be led to the conclusion that we are dealing with an attitude problem.

So, instead of sending this person on yet another report-writing course, a better answer would be for him to be counselled by his manager. This is obviously not a training solution. If any training were to be required, it would be to send the manager on a counselling course.

Counselling   Counselling is a critical skill for managers and it is
especially important when training needs are being
identified. The steps in the counselling process are:

1. Set climate.
2. Set expectations.
3. Seek counsellee's views of strengths and weaknesses.
4. Agree a development plan.
5. Summarize.

Chapter 4 deals with the counselling process in more detail.
Although the process there describes a training manager
counselling a trainer, the techniques are just as applicable
to appraisal and development discussions.

> Prepare a draft training plan

When you have validated the training requirements you
are in a position to put a draft training plan together. This
should include estimates of:

- the number of trainer-days you think you will have to
  provide,
- the spread of the training load over the year,
- the cost of the training,
- the number of days of training per employee.

We cover how to put a detailed training plan together in
Chapter 6.

> Estimate impact of training load

Take the draft training plan and consider its impact from
two perspectives:

1. the impact on the training department,
2. the impact on the organization.

The impact on the training department is really a question
of whether it has the capability, space, budget and
resources to meet the demand. If it does not have the
capability to deliver the demand, now is the time to signal
that you may need more resources.

The impact on the organization is a little more subtle. Try
asking yourself the following questions to help you
understand the impact:

- What do the estimated hours of training per person
  mean in terms of people being away from the
  workplace?

- What are the expected short-term penalties, in increased production times and costs, compared with the long-term benefits?
- How many people can you afford to have absent from one department at the same time?
- What other claims are there on the budget you need to deliver the training plan?

> Discuss draft plan with organization heads and human resource managers

Considering the impact of the training puts you in a good position for discussing the draft plan with senior management, departmental managers and human resource managers. The purpose of this step is to get 'buy-in' from the stakeholders before you go public with the final plan. It is far better to deal with 'fatal flaws' and objections at this stage than later on in the training cycle.

You can discuss what the demand and training load mean to avoid 'nasty surprises' later in the year. You can get agreement to the proposed budget. You can discuss issues. You can discuss whether all the requested training is appropriate.

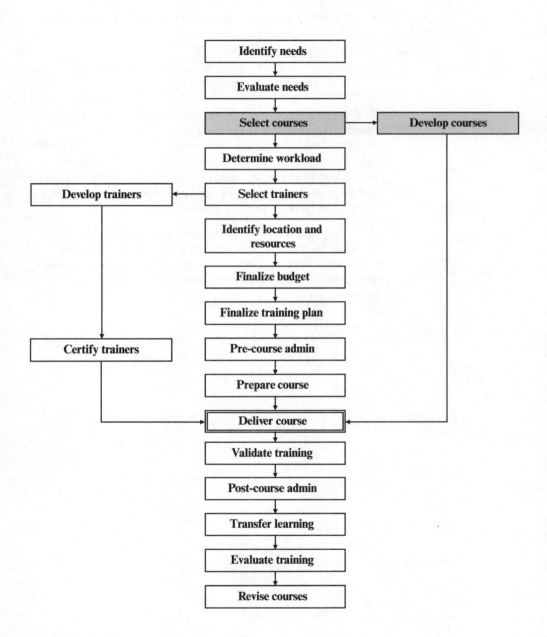

Figure 3.1 *Training courses*

3   Training courses

In this chapter we will be covering two more steps of the training process:

- select courses,
- develop courses.

Having established that training is appropriate for the identified development needs, the next step is to find courses that meet the needs. We have to make choices about whether we buy or develop our courses. Developing a course from scratch can be both expensive and time consuming. Even purchasing a course that exactly matches all the requirements is not as easy as it sounds.

Course selection

When it comes to selecting courses you have the following options:

- using an existing course,
- modifying an existing course,
- buying or licensing an external course,
- developing your own course,
- using an 'in-house' course,
- using a public course.

Whichever of these options you choose, you need to consider the availability of existing material and the urgency of and demand for the course. Figure 3.2 is an algorithm that will help you make this decision.

> Consider using company course

First, check whether a suitable course already exists within your own training department. If you're fortunate, and you have a good system for storing your materials, you will be able to find a course on the shelf that exactly fits the bill. If you are managing a new training department, the chances of your finding a suitable course on the shelf are considerably reduced.

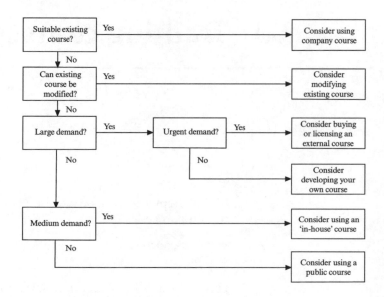

Figure 3.2 *An algorithm for selecting courses*

If you work for a small company, your search may have to end there. However, don't give up too quickly if your first searches draw a blank. You'll be surprised how many courses are developed and run over the years. Tracking these courses down can be a bit like finding a needle in a haystack.

First try the personnel department – personnel often get called on to run training courses. Also try asking supervisors and section managers – sometimes managers independently arrange training courses for their own people.

Did your company disband its training department some years ago? This can be a cyclical process. In good times training departments expand, and in difficult times training is often one of the first activities to be hit. If you are fortunate, the trainers may still be in the company but working in other departments. In these circumstances you will have to use all your powers of tact, persuasion and diplomacy. Nurture these ex-trainers. Their cupboards, shelves and filing cabinets are often gold-mines of training material.

If you work in a large or multinational company, you will have a much larger search area with which to contend. Spend some time on the telephone to the other training departments within your company. Ask for copies of their training catalogues. Follow up items that you read in the house magazines. Check out rumours you hear on the grapevine. It can take some time and persistence to get to the right person and the right training course, but it can be very rewarding.

Another approach is to form links with training managers in other companies in your area. This is always a good idea because it is very useful to exchange notes and compare methods of working. You may also find that it will be mutually beneficial to exchange training material – provided that no proprietary information is involved.

Despite all your efforts you may still not be able to find an existing course that will meet your needs. Even more frustrating will be the times when you are faced with the classic response of: 'I only threw that out last week – I didn't think that it would ever be needed again!'

| Consider modifying an existing course |

Having exhausted all the possibilities for finding a suitable existing course, the next step is to see whether any other course could be modified to meet the need.

How easy this is depends on how the course was originally developed. Some courses are so tightly structured that it is impossible to remove parts of the course without destroying the structure of the whole, or losing the meaning of the individual parts. Any change in one part of this type of course will have a ripple effect through the entire course. You will find yourself entering into a major rewrite.

If the course has a modular structure, the tasks of modification and adaptation become much easier. Parts can be added, removed and rearranged until you have the course you require.

When you come to develop your own courses you should consider using modular structures which are easy to adapt for future requirements. In some areas of training, such as management training, the content will remain constant over many years. Yes, the emphasis may change and some topics may be added or subtracted, but the basics will still be the same. Good management is still good management whatever you like to call it. Good managers have been exhibiting the same skills over the centuries.

An introduction to management will nearly always have modules on:

- communication,
- motivation,

- leadership,
- the role of the manager,
- coaching and counselling,
- decision making,
- planning and organizing,
- meetings,
- delegating,
- interviewing.

You also might want to throw in modules on time and stress management. To do all these topics justice would probably take about 60 hours.

A menu of these modules, showing what is involved for each subject, will help you or your client prioritize and make decisions about the content. See Figure 3.3 for an excerpt from a typical menu.

There is a great deal of argument among trainers about the use of 'training menus' or 'training catalogues'. Many trainers feel uneasy about giving clients a menu because they feel the customers will just choose what they 'fancy'. You can avoid this danger by being present to provide advice when the customer is making a selection.

One of the main advantages of a menu is that you can quickly draw up a specification for a course which is based on your interpretation of the customer's requirements. Any misunderstanding is soon flushed out by presenting the specification to the customer.

Consider buying or licensing an external course

If you have a large and urgent demand, you will need to buy or license an external course.

Buying suitable courses

Even if you have a large budget, which few of us do, finding a suitable course can still be very difficult. Looking through magazines and putting yourself on mailing lists can be helpful, but be warned that you will have to spend some time wading through all the mail you will receive. You will also need a very good filing system to recover the relevant brochure when you need it. A small database on a computer will help you retrieve the information, although you will have to be very disciplined about inputting the data as you receive it.

Some courses come as a complete package with transparencies, lesson plans, student materials and a video. Look very carefully at packages that come with a video as standard. Sometimes I feel that a video has been included

```
BASICS OF MANAGEMENT

A. Role of the manager (3 hr)

        1. Challenges of management (0.4 hr)
        a) Video: 'Role of the Supervisor'                      0.2 hr
        b) Discussion: Challenges facing participants           0.2 hr

        2. Functions of management (2.6 hr)
        a) Exercise: 'Operation Land Deal'                      1.3 hr
        b) Case Study: 'Computer Systems Inc'                   1.3 hr

B. Decision making and problem solving (4.5 hr)

        1. Decision making (2.5 hr)
        a) Lecturette: What is decision making?                 0.3 hr
        b) Lecturette: Decisions & problem solving              0.2 hr
        c) Lecturette: The steps of decision making            0.5 hr
        d) Example: 'Replacement Windows' case study           0.5 hr
        e) Exercise: 'The New Cars' case study                 1.0 hr

        2. Problem solving (2.0 hr)
        a) Discussion: Review of problem solving               0.3 hr
        b) Exercise: 'Carry the Torch' case study              1.7 hr

C. Communication (2 hr)

        1. Communication principles
        a) Lecturette: Communications model                    0.4 hr

        2. Communication barriers
        a) Exercise: 'Silencers Ltd'                           0.4 hr
        b) Exercise: 'Chinese Whispers'                        0.4 hr

        3. Communication helps
        a) Exercise: Feedback                                  0.5 hr
        b) Lecturette: Effective communication                 0.3 hr

D. Understanding finance (2.5 hr)

        1. Budgetary control (2.5 hr)
        a) Lecturette: Budgeting process                       0.3 hr
        b) Lecturette: Cash forecasting                        0.3 hr
        c) Lecturette: The profit and loss account             0.6 hr
        d) Lecturette: The balance sheet                       0.3 hr
        e) Exercise: 'XYZ plc' budgetary planning              1.0 hr
```

Figure 3.3   *Excerpt from a training menu*

because it is the 'thing to do' rather than being an essential part of the training.

Also look out for whether you have been given the copyright to make photocopies of the student materials. Otherwise, you might find yourself with the unexpected cost of purchasing more student materials every time you run the course. Some of these materials are very well produced and you may want to use them instead of photocopies. This is fine if you do this knowingly when you buy the package.

You also might like to look at the support you get with these packages. For example, there may be no 'trainer training'. This is all right if you have very experienced trainers, who have an in-depth understanding of the subject. Otherwise you might find that you are leaving your trainers very exposed – especially with the 'livelier' classes.

Licensing courses   There is another approach you can take if you do not have enough time to develop your own course. You can have your own trainers licensed to run a commercial course. You will have to pay to have your own trainers trained. Additionally, you may have to pay a fee to give you the rights to run the course, plus a licence fee every time the course is run. Licensing has a large initial cost, but the more people you put through the course the more cost effective it becomes. Another reason for needing a reasonable demand to make this approach viable is that it can take up to four courses to bring a trainer up to speed. (See the section on trainer certification in Chapter 4.)

Licensing is not commonly advertised, but you may notice one or two advertisements in the training magazines. Even though a training company may not advertise the licensing option, a surprising number will be willing to negotiate the licensing of their courses if you are likely to put some more business their way.

> Consider developing your own course

Even assuming that you have all the expertise and time, it is only economic to develop your own course if you have a large demand. You can either use the expertise of your own trainers or you can hire consultants to develop the course for you. This will prove more expensive than using your own staff to develop the course, so only follow this approach if the course is specific to your company, and there is a large and urgent demand for the course.

Developing your own courses is covered later in this chapter.

> Consider using an 'in-house' course

An 'in-house' course is one where a training company runs one of their courses on your premises. This keeps your travel costs low and training providers usually charge less. An 'in-house' course is a good solution when there is medium demand for a course that is not in your own repertoire.

Using consultants continually over a long period is considerably more expensive than having your own staff.

If you have to use consultants over a long period, it is worthwhile negotiating the fees. Most consultants do not expect to have paid work every day of the year. They factor the time they spend selling into their daily fees. This means they might be willing to give you a discount in return for a guaranteed medium- to long-term commission.

You are more likely to get a discount from one-person bands and small groups of consultants. Surprisingly, the big institutions stick to their standard rates even in times of recession. Don't let this put you off. Make sure that you negotiate with the head of the institution. If you still meet resistance over discounts, try talking in terms of free places.

Some companies charge by the trainer-day and this can be very expensive when a course needs two trainers. If the course requires a lead trainer and a co-trainer, you can save some money by offering to supply your own trainer as the co-trainer. This is particularly appropriate when the co-trainer's role is to observe and give feedback.

> Consider using a public course

Where there is a small or individual demand, the most cost-effective approach is to send people on an externally run public course. Judging the quality of external courses is difficult without going on all the courses yourself – which is perhaps not the best use of your time. This is especially true if you are only going to send one or two people on each course.

The reputation of the company running the course and the experiences of other training managers can help here. Don't be afraid of asking for the names of companies that have used the course. When you telephone these companies you nearly always get an honest appraisal of the course.

Talk to the providers of the training and to the potential delegates. This also will help you form an opinion of the course's suitability. Some training companies hold open days where they present extracts from their courses. This will help you gain a feeling for the style, content and professionalism.

Developing your own courses

In many ways developing your own courses can be very satisfying, even though it can be expensive and time consuming.

Course development is an extremely large subject. It is very important that you understand what it involves because it is a vital and intrinsic part of the training process. Being such a large subject, the development process really requires its own dedicated book. However, the following description should give you a very good idea of what it is all about.

The process I use has evolved over the years. Like all the processes described in this book, developing your own training courses is much messier than the neat, linear diagram shown in Figure 3.4. Real life is usually a great deal more circular and iterative.

You don't have to follow this process slavishly. By all means explore some other methods of course development and – if you do get lost – you can use this process as a guide for getting you back on track. The process given here will help you produce excellent training materials but it is no substitute for your own creativity. You could follow the process to the letter and still produce a deadly dull course.

> Define subject

The training needs analysis should have clearly defined the subject matter of the course. Do make sure that the training you think you have been asked to develop is what is really required.

Lack of clarity is one of the most common pitfalls. For example, you might have been requested to develop a course on planning and control. This seems simple – but is it 'project management' or 'personal organization' that is required? 'Project management' would cover subjects like critical path analysis and Gantt charts, whereas 'personal organization' would include topics such as time management and coping with paperwork.

Another example of this is the common request for 'finance for non-financial managers'. Typically this course would cover balance sheets, profit and loss statements, and the common financial ratios. However, in large companies most managers would never have to deal with these. Although these subjects might be interesting, they would only be useful if the managers were to leave the company and set up their own businesses. What is really required is an explanation of how their departments' budgets are formed and controlled.

> Describe aims

The aims of a course should be closely related to the business requirements that first generated the need for a new course. It is here you describe what you want the people to know, or do, when they have left the course. You will also want to describe the effect the training will have on the business results or the business environment.

If you have carried out a good needs analysis, you will already know what you are trying to change or improve. If

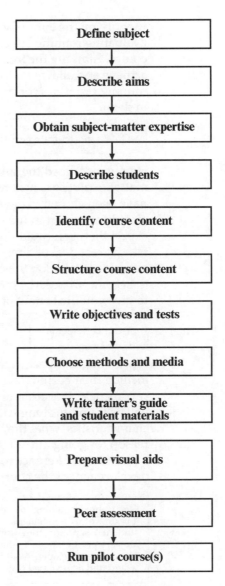

Figure 3.4   Process for developing training courses

so, this step of the process should be comparatively easy. Also think of this step as a checkpoint. After you have written down what you believe to be the aims of the course, you should go back to your clients and check whether you have interpreted their requirements correctly.

Do not fall into the trap of thinking that training is the complete solution. A course is usually only a solution to part of a much larger problem. Therefore, you should be very careful that the aims of the course describe which part of the problem the course will solve.

Identifying the aims of your training is essential for evaluating training effectiveness as well as developing the course. Aims are the indicators of what you are trying to achieve and allow you to 'complete the loop' as far as the training process is concerned. Chapter 12 covers evaluation in detail.

> Obtain subject-matter expertise

Having described the subject and aims, a source of subject-matter expertise is next required. In many cases you will have been chosen to develop a course because you are already an expert in the relevant subject. If you are not an expert then you could do the research required but this can take a great deal of time – often more time than you have available to develop the course. If there is not enough time to become an expert, you will need to call on other people to give you the benefit of their knowledge.

> Describe students

As you might expect, a description of the students should include their current level of skill and knowledge. More surprisingly, it also should describe the types of people you will be training, along with their attitudes, physical characteristics, what they enjoy and what they dislike. The reason for going into all this detail is that it can make a tremendous difference to how you approach the development of the course.

> One technical training course required service engineers to read vast amounts of written material. If the course's authors had written a student description, they would have realized that service engineers are very practical people who spend little of their leisure time reading. The course developers would also have realized that the engineers would find a text-based course boring and frustrating.

Physical characteristics should include hearing ability, sight and strength. All these will influence the training methods, practical exercises, and the colour and size of the visual aids.

> I was once running a train-the-trainer course in Singapore and one of the trainees was having difficulty in choosing a suitable training project. As he was an engineer I suggested he teach the resistor colour code. (The resistor colour code is a numbering system where numbers are represented by coloured rings.)
> When I was coaching him on 'Describe the students' I emphasized how important it is to describe the physical characteristics of the students – including colour blindness.
> I then heard laughter and chattering in Chinese from the rest of the class. When I asked what was causing the laughter, I was told that the

> student himself was colour blind. I had made the incorrect assumption that engineers would not be colour blind – there is nothing like being hoisted by your own petard.

If the students come to training with a negative attitude about the course, you know you will have to allow extra time to diffuse these feelings. Learning cannot occur while grievances are being aired.

Above all, build up a mental picture of your students which will allow you to develop the course specifically for them. Novelists often use this technique: when they are writing a novel they imagine that they are telling the story to a typical reader who is sitting in front of them.

Identify course content

The content bridges the gap between the students' current level and the level they should have after the learning experience. The use of the term 'learning experience' rather than 'course' is deliberate. Only part of the required behavioural change can develop during the short duration of a course. It is unrealistic to expect a course to do any more than develop an awareness of the required changes. A course also provides supervised practice of the new skills.

In very simple terms, you should take the desired knowledge and skills (as described by the course aims) and subtract the students' current knowledge and skills (as given in the student description).

A useful technique for doing this is called 'mind mapping'. Mind mapping is a creative technique that is described in Tony Buzan's book *Use Your Head*. 'Mind maps' are also known as 'spidergrams' or 'bubble diagrams'.

To apply this technique you first draw a bubble shape in the middle of a sheet of paper. You then write the subject of the course in this shape. The main categories of topics that make up the course are written in 'bubbles' that are attached to branches radiating from the central bubble shape. You can then have the detailed topics radiating from the main category bubbles (see Figure 3.5).

Structure course content

This is where you determine the structure and timing of the course. It helps if you have an overall framework to work within. A good framework for the structure of a course comes from the 'Army School of Training':

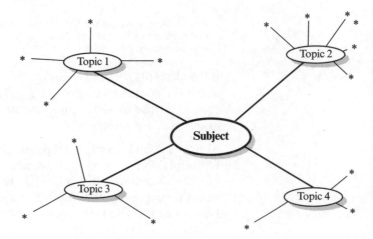

* = detailed topics

Figure 3.5 *Using a mind map to determine course content*

- Tell 'em what you're goin' to tell 'em.
- Tell 'em.
- Tell 'em what you told 'em.

Or put another way:

- overview,
- body and
- summary.

The main course modules are to be found in the body of the course. The body needs to be sequenced so that there is a logical flow from one topic to another. A logical flow goes from:

- the simple to the complex,
- the general to the specific and
- the known to the unknown.

Although the detailed topics shown on the mind map form the content of the course, the larger bubbles will not necessarily be the course modules. You created the mind map while you were coming to understand the relationships between the detailed topics. This means that the structure that develops may not be the most efficient one for learning the subject. Some people can write down the correct order straight away, but I find it easier to use 'Post-it' notes.

Start by writing one of the course components (it doesn't matter which one) on a 'Post-it'. Then stick this on a sheet of flip-chart paper and ask the following questions to help decide which components should come before or after:

- What has to be taught before this component can be taught?
- What can be taught now that this component has been taught?
- What can be taught at the same time?

The answers to these questions will suggest which components should be stuck on to the chart next. Keep asking these questions as each new 'Post-it' is added. Draw lines to connect the components and a network will be built up showing a logical sequence for the course.

There are two basic methods for determining the length of the course. The first is to estimate the duration of each component and simply add them up. The second is to start with a fixed time and see what you can fit in.

Obviously the second method is the less satisfactory, but there is always something that can usefully be taught – no matter how little time you have. It's just a matter of you, and the person who requested the course, being aware of the resulting limitations and consequences.

The effectiveness of a limited amount of training depends very much on the students' current state of knowledge. If there is no existing knowledge, any amount of training will make an improvement. Where knowledge is very limited, simply communicating 'three things you need to know to get you through the day' can have a large and significant effect.

When there is a limited amount of time, or when you have to shorten a course to reduce costs, there are only two viable ways of doing this. The first is to look at the training methodology to see if there are more efficient ways of meeting the same objectives. For example, you might use the same exercise to give practice for both coaching and counselling rather than having two separate exercises.

The other method is to take content out of the course. In this case the decisions you have to make are all about what you put in and what you leave out.

We shouldn't make the mistake of thinking that we can shorten a course by simply running faster or exerting very high pressure on the students. The effectiveness of the course will suffer. A training menu described earlier in this chapter is one method of helping the client prioritize what should be done in the available time.

> One of my clients once asked for all the content shown in the training menu to be taught in four days. A quick addition of the times soon revealed that it would take more than 60 hours to complete the training. Further discussions about the client's requirements and priorities resulted in 50 hours of training, spread over five days. To keep disruption to a minimum the course was split into two parts. The first part was to run for two working days and the second, three-day module was to run three weeks later from Thursday to Saturday.

When you have to make complex decisions it is better to analyse the content of the course very carefully against certain criteria. Agree the criteria with your client, because you will be using them for including or rejecting course content. The actual criteria you use depend very much on your client's requirements, so it is very important that these criteria are determined very early on in the process. An example of how you can use criteria to determine the content of a course is given in Appendix 6.

The output of structuring the course content should be a course agenda or programme. If the course is short and uncomplicated the agenda will be like a meeting agenda (see Figure 3.6). You would use the type of course programme shown in Figure 3.7 when the course is longer and more complex.

| Write objectives and tests |

An objective is a statement of what the students should be able to do once they have completed a section of the course. It is an indicator of what learning has taken place. Notice that I said indicator rather than measure. Learning is what goes on inside a student's head and therefore cannot be directly measured. So while it is perfectly possible to have an objective of 'understanding interpersonal skills', this is not very useful for measuring the effectiveness of the training. The students could be asked whether they understand interpersonal skills, or the trainer could gain a 'feeling' for how much has been understood by general questioning or observing body language.

Another approach is to use indirect indicators such as something the students should be able to do if learning has taken place. The skill in this approach is deciding what these indicators should be.

For example, a student who really understands interpersonal skills should be able to recognize and use all the different categories of verbal behaviour. Although a trainer can hear the trainees using the verbal behaviours, checking whether somebody has recognized something is a

```
AGENDA

Introduction                                          9:00
– Introductions
– Expectations
– Agenda

Why total quality management?                         9:20
– The need
– Initial steps
– Quality gurus
– Birth of a strategy
– Key elements of the strategy

What is quality?                                      9:40
– Definition
– Standard
– System
– Measurement

Quality is free?                                     11:00
– Cost of quality
– Conformance
– Non-conformance
– Lost opportunities

Who's the customer?                                  11:20
– Suppliers
– Internal customers
– External customers

Tools of the trade                                   12:00
– Problem-solving process
– Quality improvement process
– Process capability
– Fishbone diagram
– Pareto analysis
– Forcefield analysis
– Interactive skills

Where do we go from here?                            16:00

Review                                               16:30
```

Figure 3.6   *Course agenda*

little more difficult. One way round this would be to show a videotape of a number of different behaviours and have the student state the name of each behaviour.

The next question is how many of the responses would have to be correct to satisfy the trainer that the student had really understood interpersonal skills. Would it be 5 per cent, 20 per cent, 80 per cent or 100 per cent?

Taking all this into account, the objectives for 'understanding' interpersonal skills would look like this:

- Given a videotape showing 20 examples of verbal behaviour, the student will be able to name correctly at least 18 of the behaviours.

	DAY 1	DAY 2		DAY 3	DAY 4	DAY 5
8.00	Introduction	Motivation		Financial		Project
9.00	Role of the	and		planning		management
10.00	manager	leadership			Staff	(2)
11.00					selection	
Lunch				Effective		
13.00	Communication			meetings		
14.00		Managing				Stress
15.00	Decision	time		Coaching	Project	management
16.00	making			and	management	
17.00		Wrap-up		counselling	(1)	Wrap-up
Evening	*Desert Survival exercise*			*The Numbers Game*	Plan project	

Figure 3.7　*An example of a course programme*

- Given a list of 11 verbal behaviours, the student should be able to give correct examples for a minimum of 10 of those behaviours.

A good objective has three components:

1. Behaviour – what the student will be expected to do.
2. Conditions – the conditions under which the behaviour has to occur.
3. Standard – the acceptable level of performance.

In the interpersonal skills example the behaviours are:

- naming behaviours,
- giving examples of behaviours.

The conditions are:

- 'Given a videotape showing 20 examples of verbal behaviour...'
- 'Given a list of 11 verbal behaviours...'

and the standards are:

- '...at least 18 out of 20 behaviours correctly named.'
- '...a minimum of 10 correct examples of behaviours.'

Writing objectives is hard work, but if they are done to the above standard writing the tests becomes very easy. As a good objective gives the standards and conditions under which the behaviour should occur, it also gives the conditions and standards for the test.

A test does not have to be an 'examination'. The minimum condition is that the trainer should be able to observe the desired behaviour so the standards can be checked to see whether the training has been effective.

Objectives are an essential tool for course developers, course presenters and students. Course developers use objectives to determine the content of the course; course presenters use them to measure what has been learnt; and students use objectives as an overview of what they are going to learn. Be careful of giving students the same detail on the objectives that you would use for presenting or developing a course. Although detailed objectives are required for presenters and developers, students would be confused if they were presented with the following objective at the beginning of the course:

> 'By the end of the module you will be able to identify the central processing unit, the random access memory, the read-only memory, the visual display unit and the input/output interfaces.'

After all, if they already knew what these terms meant they would not have to attend the course.

A better objective to give a student at the start of a course would be:

> 'By the end of the module you will be able to identify all the main components of a microcomputer.'

Some objectives describe behaviours or conditions that can only exist in the classroom, such as 'will have participated in three simulations'.

It is much better to have objectives that describe behaviour and conditions that can be measured both inside and outside the classroom. This allows you to monitor learning inside the classroom and monitor the transfer of learning to the business.

Written question-and-answer tests should only be used when it is not possible to use a practical example of a task that has to be done in the workplace.

As a final check, make sure that every objective has a corresponding test and that every test item is related to an objective.

> Choose methods and media

There are many different points of view about what are the 'best' training methods. The following is a summary of the most frequent arguments:

- Should courses be 'trainer led' or 'self-directed'?
- Should students be told the facts or be encouraged to go on a 'voyage of discovery'?

- Should you use a case study or should you use a real-life example?
- Should you start with a 'big-picture' overview and then work down to the details, or should you start with the basic 'building blocks' and develop the learning upwards from there?

Some trainers insist that trainees be given freedom of choice. One method of doing this is to have a course map that has alternative routes through the course (see Figure 3.8).

The students are allowed to take any of the routes through the course as long as they have completed the prerequisites. The prerequisite modules are the ones that are above, and on the same path as, the module the student wants to take.

But does this approach mean that the trainees have a real choice? Do they have enough information to come to sensible conclusions? It could be argued that if the students did have enough information to make rational rather than random choices, they wouldn't need to take the course in any case!

Proponents of any training method can be very persuasive with the arguments they bring forward to support their favourite approach. Training managers, personnel managers and directors should be very careful of being seduced into spending huge amounts of money on new training technologies that are the 'only way to train'.

There are two other warnings when it comes to training technology. The first is that the vision of what people want from the technology is often years in advance of what the technology is able to deliver today. The second, counterbalancing warning is not to look at technology with

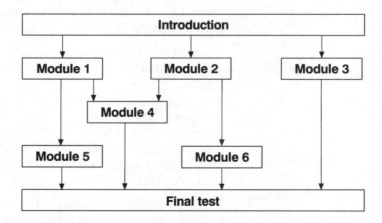

Figure 3.8 *An example of a course map*

a jaundiced eye, even though the last 20 demonstrations you attended were little more than gimmicks. One day you will miss that significant innovation you really need.

The truth is that there never will be one 'best' method or one 'best' medium for training people. Every student is different and every person learns in a different way. Some people have to know the detail first. Others couldn't possibly understand the detail until they have a mental framework to pin it on. Some people like facts and figures, others like a more inspirational approach to training.

There are many personality theories and questionnaires that claim to classify people into different types. Many of these are based on the work of Jung, who identified four basic classifications:

- thinker,
- feeler,
- sensor,
- intuitor.

Each approach has its own names for the four types, but usually the types fall into the following categories:

- logical people,
- people people,
- task-oriented people,
- intuitive/entrepreneurial people.

Given an understanding of how people are different, we can make better choices of which methods and media to use on our courses. Table 3.1 indicates how different types of people learn. It also shows the types of learning activities to which they respond.

Table 3.1   Learning methods and media for different types of people

	Suitable methods and media
Logical people	Lecture, reading, case studies, underlying theory, debate, programmed instruction
People people	Case studies, discussion, role play, games coaching, simulation
Task-oriented people	Practice, experimenting, simulation, demonstration, coaching, self-directed learning
Intuitive/ entrepreneurial people	Video, multimedia, discovery, OHPs, experimenting, simulation

This again emphasizes the importance of having a good description of the students who will be attending your course.

If you have a homogeneous group of students, you will have a good idea of which types of methods and media you should be using. If you have a varied group of people to teach, the chances are that there will be a fairly even spread of the four different types. In this case it would probably be advisable to have a wide range of differing methods and media so that you can reach as many different types of people as possible.

However, considering the learning preferences of the group is not all the story. Consideration should also be given to which methods and media are the most suitable for each part of the course. The best courses have a wide range of media and learning experiences.

Table 3.2 shows the range of media that are available, along with their advantages and disadvantages.

> Write trainer's guide and student materials

In one of his *Lettres Provinciales*, Blaise Pascal wrote: 'I have written a long letter because I did not have time to write it shorter.' In the same way, it is much easier and quicker to write a long course than a short one. It takes time to analyse what is essential and what could be left out. The virtue of writing at length is that you will probably include everything you need. The problem is that you will never know what you could have left out. Writing the materials as lean as possible has the advantage of producing succinct training and it will become obvious if anything has been left out.

Make sure that the manuscripts are given a really good proofread. Although it seems unfair, you have to come to terms with the fact that some students judge the overall quality of the materials on their first impressions. Spelling and grammatical errors interfere with their learning. If the materials have been written on a word processor, you will be able to put them through a spellchecker.

Some words of caution here. Only the very sophisticated spellcheckers, those which dabble in artificial intelligence, can do anything more than to tell you whether a particular word exists. Generally, spellcheckers don't take any account of the grammar, context or meaning of the words. So, a sentence such as: 'Thee employees took there complained too their manger' would hardly cause a spellchecker to stutter.

Table 3.2 *Advantages and disadvantages of different media*

Step	Advantages	Disadvantages
Presenter	Relatively quick and inexpensive, flexible response	Quality depends on the individual presenter
Flip chart	Inexpensive, flexible	Good handwriting required
Whiteboard	Clean, easy to alter	Difficult to clean if wrong pens used
Blackboard	Easy to alter	Dusty, reminiscent of school
Overhead transparencies	Easy and economic to produce, equipment widely available	Tendency to be over-used
35 mm slides	High quality, standard format, equipment widely available	Equipment unreliable, slides prone to jamming
35 mm slide/tape	Moderately easy and economic to produce	Unreliable synchronization of audiotape to slide projector
Videos	Wide range of videos available, reliable	Expensive, difficult to make, varying standards around the world
16 mm film	Good quality	Expensive and difficult to produce, unreliable, equipment obsolescent
Text	Fairly easy and economic to produce and revise	Not suitable for all students
Audiocassette	Fairly easy and economic to produce, equipment widely available, easily used outside classroom	Limited by lack of visual content
Text/tape	Economic and easy to produce, good combination of sound and visuals	Student has to keep pace with audiotape
Computer-based training	Paced to student, wide range of programs available	Expensive and time consuming to produce. Becoming very accessible as more homes and offices have access to multimedia computers
Interactive video	Paced to student, high-quality graphics	Expensive and time consuming to produce, very expensive equipment

There are also some grammar checkers on the market. The following shows what one of these made of the above example:

ARCHAIC: Thee
SHOULD 'too their' BE 'two' OR 'to their'?

The grammar checker caught some of the problems, but it didn't catch 'complained' instead of 'complaints' or 'manger' instead of 'manager'.

Also be very careful that you do not 'teach' the spellchecker to be a bad speller. When the spellchecker does not recognize a word it gives you the choice of skipping the word, correcting the word or adding the word to its dictionary. When you are working through a long document pressing the 'add' button almost becomes a reflex reaction and, before you know it, another misspelt word is added to the computer's dictionary. Another way of adding errors to a spellchecker's dictionary is when you are convinced a misspelt word is correct. After all, you have been spelling the word this way for nearly all your life! For some unknown reason it is nearly always much easier to add than to remove a word from electronic dictionaries.

Although there is no substitute for a thorough proofread, a spellchecker is a very useful tool. It can spot many errors that we overlook. A computer, unlike the human brain, does not 'see' what it thinks should be there.

Trainer's guide   A good trainer's guide includes:

1. Course objectives.
2. Course programme.
3. Course prerequisites.
4. Course pre-work.
5. Number of training and break-out rooms required.
6. List of student materials.
7. List of equipment required.
8. List of audiovisual materials (transparencies, posters, prepared flip charts, audiotapes and videotapes).
9. Room layout.
10. Preparation notes for each session.
11. Lesson plans for each session.
12. Masters for the overhead transparencies.

Items 1 to 7, taken together, form the course specification which provides essential information for the course administrator. The order shown above reflects the structure of a trainer's guide – not necessarily the order you would write it in.

If you have been following the process for developing training materials, you will find that you have already prepared some of the components of the trainer's guide. You would have already written the objectives (1) and you would also have determined the course programme (2).

The course prerequisites (3) are determined by comparing the course content with the student description. A prerequisite is a level of competence that a student should have before attending a course. It could be attendance at another course, a certain level of education or a particular skill.

You would normally identify the other components of the trainer's guide as you write the lesson plan. In fact, it is a good idea to have sheets of paper headed 'Student materials', 'Videotapes' etc. so that you can note the requirements as you identify them.

Lesson plans Writing a course is writing the lesson plan. It is a 'script' that not only provides you with your 'lines' but also describes detailed timings, structure and activities.

There are many formats that you can use for a lesson plan. My preference is for a three-column format. The first column is for timings and type of activity, such as State, Ask, Stress, Action and Exercise. The middle column is reserved for the actual statements, questions and directions, and the third column lists the media. Figure 3.9 shows an example of this type of lesson plan. Notice that the timings are clock times. You have more than enough to do when you are running a course without adding up the times of the individual modules to see whether you are running to time.

> Prepare visual aids

Preparing the visual aids is something that can be done at any time during the development of the student materials and lesson plan. My preference is to do it as I am writing the lesson plan. As you develop the course, you should be

NEW COURSE		First module
08:30	**FIRST MODULE** (1 hr 20 min)	
	Introduction	
State:	Welcome to the new course.	OHP 1
Ask:	How many people have been on a similar course to this?	
Action:	Count the number of people and write this on a flip chart.	FLIP CHART
Stress:	That this course builds on similar courses.	
Show:	'Attending Courses'.	VIDEO

Figure 3.9 *Example of a lesson plan format*

constantly thinking whether a learning point could be better illustrated with a visual aid.

During this step of the process you should review the visual aids you have prepared so far, and create any additional visual aids that are required.

The most popular form of visual aid is the overhead projector transparency (OHP). Keep the OHP uncluttered and simple. Resist the temptation to put too much on it. A copy of an existing document rarely makes a good overhead. The following guidelines will help you produce OHPs:

- Don't make the lettering too small
  Rule of thumb: 18 point (approximately equivalent to 6 mm for capital letters) is about as small as you want to go; 44 point (15 mm) is good for titles and 28 point (10 mm) is good for the main text.
- Don't put too much on one OHP
  Rule of thumb: Six words per line and six lines per slide is a good guideline.
- Restrict the number of fonts that you use
  Rule of thumb: Restricting yourself to two proportionally spaced fonts plus careful use of bold and italics will cover most of your needs. Underlining is rarely necessary and OHPs usually look better without it. A good combination is a sans serif font (e.g. Arial, Univers) for the titles and a serif font (e.g. Times New Roman, Century Schoolbook) for the text.
- Restrict the number of colours that you use
  Rule of thumb: Two colours will cover most of your needs.

If you follow these guidelines you shouldn't go far wrong, but don't feel that you have to follow them slavishly. There will be times when you will have to bend these rules to get the effect that you want. The final test is what it looks like on the screen.

Computer programs such as Microsoft PowerPoint and Lotus Freelance will help you create professional transparencies quickly. You can also use PowerPoint and Freelance to produce the student notes. The 'Slide Sorter' views of these programs can be of great assistance in getting the structure of the course right. You can use the mouse to drag the slides to different positions (see Figure 3.10).

> Peer assessment

Before you unleash your course on a group of unsuspecting students, it is a very good idea to have your colleagues

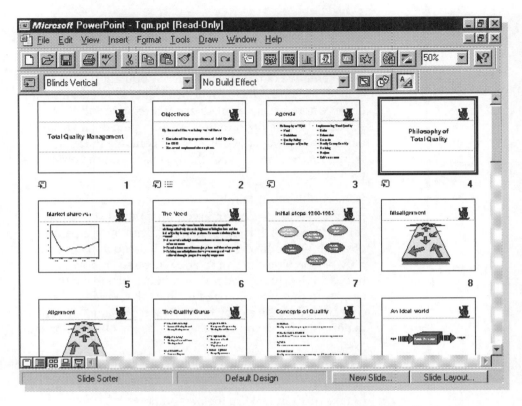

Figure 3.10 *Using a graphics program 'Slide Sorter' to structure a course*

review the materials. It is an even better idea to teach the course to your peers.

After all this time you will be too close to the course to notice even the more obvious mistakes. An experienced colleague will be able to spot the fatal flaws, annoying inconsistencies and irritating errors.

> Run pilot course(s)

Pilot courses are the 'test flights' for your newly developed course. With a brand new course you will normally need to run two pilot courses. The first, sometimes called a developmental test, is run to get all the bugs and gremlins out of the course. It is not essential to have representative students on the developmental course, but it is risky to have stakeholders present. A stakeholder is a person who has a vested interest in the course and could damage its reputation.

The reason for this is that the errors and the pauses will only serve to distort an observer's perception of the course.

Reports of the 'disaster' will still be heard long after the course has established itself as a great success.

The second pilot course should have students who are representative of the target student population. This second course is a good time to invite some stakeholders along to observe and give some feedback. The course will be sufficiently developed to prevent annoying errors from getting in the way, but not so set in concrete that you would not be able to make changes based on the observers' feedback.

If the course is self-taught, you can take on the role of passive observer – only intervening if things start to go seriously wrong. It is much more difficult to be a passive observer when the course is trainer led and you are the only person who can run it. You will be too involved to notice all the subtle, and not so subtle, reactions to the course. In this case you need to enlist the services of a colleague. Provide a copy of the lesson plan and student materials and ask your colleague to do the observations for you.

If the course is large, and you are leading a team of training developers, you can either do all the observations yourself or take turns in making the observations.

When you are running a pilot course you must be extremely careful to avoid rationalizing away any negative reactions the students might have. It is all too easy to think that a problem was a chance occurrence. You might be persuaded that 'real' students wouldn't have the same difficulty. Always assume that minor difficulties, encountered on the pilot course, will become major problems if they are left uncorrected for the final version of the course.

Be a fly on the wall. Record any difficulty, hesitancy or problem. Avoid coming up with solutions or rewriting the material at this stage because you might miss some of the other problems. Try not to interfere with the training.

Immediately after the training get the students to fill in a written feedback form. Then have general discussions about what went well and what could have gone better. Again, don't try to solve any of the problems at this stage. Don't try to explain why you wrote in a particular way. Above all, don't argue if you think their comments are wrong. Just record, without editing, all their comments on a flip chart. Some students will make suggestions for changing the course. These should also be recorded. This does not commit you to making those changes if, after reflection, you do not agree with them.

Always try to understand why the student wanted to have that change. Even if the suggested change is not a good idea, there is nearly always an underlying problem that needs to be addressed. Other students might just feel uncomfortable about something or feel that something is 'not quite right'. By all means ask some questions to help you understand what the problem might be, but don't pressurize them to come up with explanations or solutions. After all, solving training problems is your job, not theirs.

When you have finished collecting information from the students, have a meeting with the trainers to get their feedback. Now you can work with the trainers to develop proposals on how the course should be changed, amended or revised.

Appendix 5 gives an example of how this process was used to develop a real course.

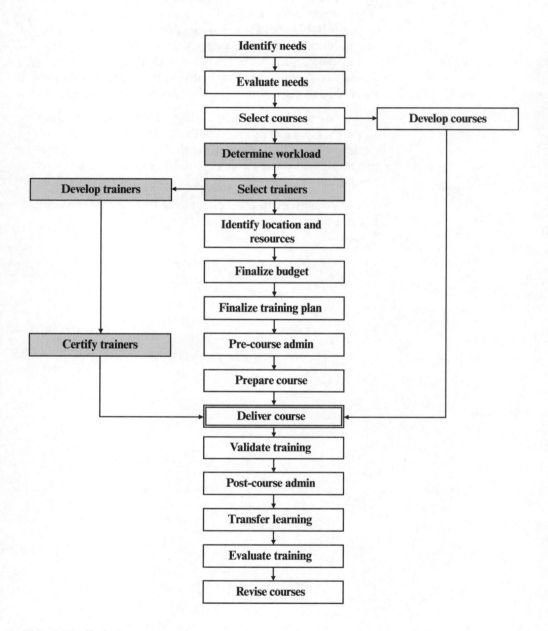

Figure 4.1   *Trainers*

4 Trainers

In this chapter we will be covering four more steps of the training process:

- determine workload,
- select trainers,
- develop trainers,
- certify trainers.

The first step is to determine the workload. If you have sufficient staff or contractors to meet the training needs, you can then select the most appropriate trainer(s) to run each of the identified courses. You also need to consider whether these trainers will need any further development.

If you cannot cover the load with your existing resources, you will need to recruit additional trainers or find more contractors. This will involve you in writing job descriptions and vacancy notices as well as interviewing prospective trainers. If you are unable to find experienced trainers you will need to consider which people would make good trainers and what training these new trainers should receive.

Even if you recruit experienced trainers, they may not have had experience of the type of training you will be asking them to provide. They will also need to undertake a programme of development. To do this you need to understand what skills and knowledge your trainers should have for these courses.

Once the trainers have the basic skills and competencies needed to run the courses, you still have to plan how they will learn to train the new courses that you will be running. This is the process of certification.

Determining the workload

When you decide how many trainers will be required, you have to make an estimate of the workload each trainer can handle. The factors you have to take into account are:

- the number of courses,
- the duration of the courses,
- face-to-face ratio (the amount of time a trainer spends in front of a class),
- the number of trainers needed to run each course,
- how much time is spent in preparing courses,
- how much time is spent in developing courses,
- how much time is spent in other activities such as planning, supervising and evaluating,
- the learning curve of new trainers.

Number and duration of courses

The number of courses you need to run depends on:

- the number of people you need to train,
- the number of people you can train per course.

The number of people you need to train comes from the needs analysis. The course specification will tell you the maximum number of people each course can accommodate, but don't base your estimates on this figure. It is unlikely you will be able to run with the maximum number on every course. The availability of people as well as sickness and cancellations will erode this figure. Always try to book the maximum number of people on to the course and you will probably find that you will be running the course with the optimum number of students.

Rule of thumb: Assume you will put people through the course at the rate of two-thirds of the maximum number.

If you find you can train people at a faster rate than this, nobody will complain if you finish a training programme ahead of time.

The course specification will give you the duration of the course.

Face-to-face ratio

The amount of time a trainer can spend in front of a class depends on many factors, such as the difficulty of the course and the number of different courses that the trainer has to train.

It is possible for trainers to spend 100 per cent of their time in the classroom if they have full administrative support and the courses always fill a complete week (it is difficult to schedule courses without any gaps between them).

Eventually fatigue will set in, with a corresponding decline in standards. If you have to support a massive training effort, and your trainers are committed to the programme, it is possible to sustain a face-to-face ratio of 80 per cent.

More realistically, you would expect trainers to spend some of their time on preparation, administration, revision of existing materials and development of new materials. The proportion of time spent on these activities will vary depending where the trainers are in their career development. We will consider what these proportions might be when we look at developing trainers.

Rule of thumb: You would normally expect trainers to have a face-to-face ratio of 50 per cent.

This is supported by data from several benchmarking exercises that I carried out with other companies.

Number of trainers per course

The number of trainers you need to run a course depends on the complexity of the course and the number of students on the course. These are the factors you take into account when you plan the number of trainers required for a new course. The course specification should tell you how many trainers you need for existing courses.

The complexity of a course is driven by:

- the course logistics (the amount of preparation and 'scene shifting' that has to be done before each session);
- the amount of observation, facilitation and coaching required;
- the amount of data processing that is required (e.g. running computer simulations or producing graphs and ratios from observation data).

It seems sensible to say that the more students you have, the more trainers you will need; and the more students each trainer has to deal with, the less effective the training becomes.

This would seem to be borne out by the argument about the size of classes in our schools. The problem of having a simple measure of effectiveness makes it difficult to put this hypothesis to the test. However, we had the opportunity to test it out when we introduced Trainee Centred Learning (TCL).

The idea behind Trainee Centred Learning is the same as that for self-paced learning:

- Students learn better at a pace which matches their own abilities.
- They do not move on to the next stage of learning until they have demonstrated competence at the previous stage.
- All the students have their own learning station and a set of training materials.
- Trainers are on hand to answer questions, demonstrate techniques and check that the course objectives are being met.

Managing the training process

Using this approach it is intended that everybody leaves the course having reached a common standard, even though people may have taken different times to reach that standard.

Individually the time taken to go through the course depends on the person's own learning pace and starting ability, but the average duration can be used as a measure of training effectiveness.

When the course durations were correlated to the 'student-to-trainer' ratio we found, as expected, that the course duration increased as the ratio went up from 6:1 to 10:1. Imagine our surprise when the course duration also increased as the ratio fell below 6:1 (see Figure 4.2). While it is easy to explain the increase in duration with greater numbers of students in terms of longer waiting times, it is much harder to explain why the length of the course should increase when there are more trainers on hand.

We came to the conclusion that there must be an optimum level of trainer intervention. Too little contact from the trainer and the student starts to flounder. Too much contact and the trainer starts to interrupt the learning process, or worse still takes over the learning tasks from the student!

Another interesting result that came out of this exercise was that a ratio of 20:2 is not the same as a ratio of 10:1. What this means is that two trainers spread over 20 students is not as effective as making each trainer primarily responsible for a sub-group of ten students. With this approach the trainer only has to remember and monitor the progress of ten trainees in detail, rather than remembering the details of all 20 students.

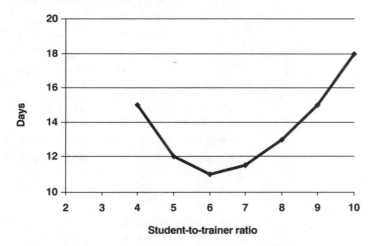

Figure 4.2 *The effect of student-to-trainer ratio on course effectiveness*

So we concluded that the best student-to-trainer ratio for this type of training was in the region of 6:1. Of course this optimum is different for different types of training; in some cases such as tutoring or coaching 1:1 will be the optimum ratio. You should always consider the effect that this ratio will have on your training and not always assume 'the more, the better'.

Each course should have a course specification which specifies the number of trainers, observers and so on who are needed to run the course. The 'student-to-trainer' ratio should be expressed as two ranges: an optimum range, and a minimum to maximum range.

For example, an optimum range might be from 10:1 to 16:1. This means that the course works best when there are between 10 and 16 students for every trainer. The 'minimum to maximum' range for the same course might be from 8:1 to 18:1. This means that the course is either unworkable outside this range, or its effectiveness is seriously eroded above 18:1, or it is uneconomic to run the course with fewer than eight students.

Rule of thumb: Generally speaking, courses will work well up to the following student-to-trainer ratios:

Simple courses: 18:1
Complex courses: 12:1
Individual feedback: 6:1

Preparation time   The amount of time it takes to prepare for a course depends on the complexity of the course and the trainer's familiarity with the course. If a trainer is unfamiliar with the material, it can take as much as a day of preparation for every hour of presentation time.

A great deal of time and effort may be required to calculate the preparation times for courses of different complexity. Often the results are no more accurate than taking a 'broad-brush' approach. A useful guide for determining preparation time is given below.

Rule of thumb: On average, it takes one day of preparation for every three days of training.

This means that trainers would normally spend a maximum of 75 per cent of their time in front of the class. This figure also takes interruptions into account (it is impossible to do a day's preparation without other business issues intervening).

Course development time   The time required to develop a new course is about as long as the proverbial piece of string. It depends on:

- the complexity of the course;
- how much material has to be produced;
- the standard of the materials;
- what is already available.

What is clear is that most people have no idea how long it takes to develop a course; and when they find out they are very shocked.

Rule of thumb: Table 4.1 gives estimated development times for different types of course.

If you need to make a significant revision to an existing, complex, five-day course, then you would need to plan 85 person-days to do the job. At first sight 85 days is a very long time, so let's see where the time goes.

The first thing to note is that the figure is a planning assumption – it assumes that very few days will pass without interruption and it is unlikely that development will take place in one, uninterrupted block. The figure also assumes that the trainers are producing their own materials. Using a secretarial service will reduce the time by about 25 per cent, but it will also increase the costs.

A significant revision is one where every page of the lesson plan and the student materials needs to be changed and substantially retyped. A five-day course could have 400 page-equivalents of lesson plans, student materials, handouts, posters and slides. This means that the trainer will have to research, revise and restructure the course at the rate of five pages per day.

The same considerations apply when you are writing a new course, but you also have to add in a substantial amount of time for researching, learning and condensing the subject matter.

Table 4.1 *Development times for different courses*

Type of course	Development time
Computer-based training	100:1
Complex/technical courses	40:1
Extensive restructuring/revision of an existing course	17:1
Moderate restructuring/revision of an existing course	11:1
Constructing a modular course from existing modules	6:1

Time spent on other activities

In addition to standing up in front of a class, trainers also need to spend time on planning, supervising and benchmarking. The proportion of time spent on these activities varies depending on the individual. Generally, these activities will increase as a trainer progresses from instructor to training manager. We look at these issues in greater detail in the section on developing trainers.

Rule of thumb: The proportions of time spent on activities, other than preparing and training courses, are as follows:

Instructors: 30 per cent
Trainers: 40 per cent

Learning curve time

A trainer who is 'learning the ropes' will be less productive than an experienced trainer. You also have to allow time for experienced trainers to learn new courses. You can calculate the length of time based on the experience of the trainer and the number of new courses that have to be taught. The section on trainer development looks at this in more detail.

Rule of thumb: A new trainer will take about three months to become partially productive, and a year to become fully productive.

Rule of thumb: It will take an experienced trainer two courses to become familiar with a short, simple course, and four courses for a long, complex course.

Selecting trainers

In this step you are selecting trainers to match the type and number of courses you need to run.

Using existing trainers

There are only two factors to consider:

- experience;
- availability.

Does the trainer have, or can the trainer acquire, the experience to run the course? Will the trainer be available to run the course when the client needs it?

When I discuss training needs with my clients I ask them whether it is possible for them to give me a 'window', or range of dates, for when they want a specified number of people trained. Matching trainers to a range of dates is much easier than matching them to fixed dates.

Full-time trainers or consultants?

Whether you use full-time trainers or external consultants depends on the criteria (such as cost and flexibility) you use for making your decision.

Rule of thumb: If the decision is on the basis of cost, consultants start to become more expensive than full-time employees when you employ the same consultants for more than 50 per cent of their time.

Some training organizations prefer to use only external consultants for training. They like the flexibility and the cross-fertilization from other companies. External consultants also specialize, which means that they are able to be experts in their field. Full-time trainers can only specialize if there is enough demand for their speciality to keep them fully utilized. Otherwise, the trainers will have to spread themselves thinly over a larger number of subject areas.

If you choose external consultants at random you will have the problem of ensuring consistency and quality. The answer is to have a core of consultants, or associates, to whom you have given your organization's seal of approval. External trainers and courses should be certified in the same way you certify your own trainers and courses.

Using external consultants for delivery is expensive but the cost is generally well understood. However, the cost of using external consultants for development of materials can give you a shock.

If you assume that an average development time for a five-day course is 10 days of development for every day of training, and take a consultant day rate of £500, the cost for developing this course would be £25 000. It would be far more cost effective to buy an off-the-shelf course or to use one of your full-time employees to develop the course.

The problem arises when the consultant's day rate is applied to the development of the course. As far as you are concerned you are not interested in how much time the consultant spends developing the course as long as it is ready by the time you need it. What is important is how much you think the finished product is worth to you.

If your application is a very specialized one, you may be prepared to pay a lot of money to have the course developed. If the course has wide applicability, you may feel you should not pay anything for the development – because the consultant can defray the development costs over a number of different customers. The situation is similar to buying a new car. If you were the first customer for a new model you would not expect to pay millions of pounds to cover the manufacturer's research and development costs. It is important to remember that the negotiating issue is not time but price.

External consultants will obviously not want to make a loss over the deal so, before taking on the contract, they will carefully consider:

- whether they have existing materials which can be modified rather than developing the course from scratch;
- whether they could charge less because of the prospect of having two months of continuous work (day rates are calculated on the basis of not being able to get work every day, a certain amount of personal preparation that is required before every course, and a certain amount of product development);
- how much they would expect to earn in a year, and what proportion of that expectation would be met by a fixed-price contract;
- whether there are any costs or time associated with being away from base which would not be incurred during the development of the course;
- as it is not possible to work continually on course development (it is often more productive to give it a rest and work on something else for a while), whether there are any other money-making activities that could be worked on in parallel;
- what additional work this project could lead to;
- whether there is a guaranteed minimum number of courses the consultant will be asked to run;
- whether the client will be tied to the consultant for running future courses;
- whether the consultant will be able to run the course for other clients and thus be able to defray the development costs over a larger number of courses.

Recruiting trainers

If you cannot cover the workload with your existing trainers or consultants you will need to recruit additional trainers.

Ideally you would want somebody who is currently very successful at doing the same kind of job. This unfortunately poses the questions: 'Where do "new starters" get their experience?' and 'If someone is already doing this job, why would they want to come and work for our company?'

Internal or external recruitment?

First see if there are experienced trainers in other parts of the company. Resist the temptation of always bringing in 'new blood' from outside. New ideas and different experiences will add richness to a training department, but don't underestimate the importance of company knowledge and experience. Avoid the 'grass is greener' trap.

Internal candidates bring with them a record of achievements, failures, strengths and weaknesses. Unless you probe very thoroughly external candidates will only tell you their strengths and achievements. The first time you get to find out about external candidates' failures and weaknesses may be after you have employed them!

If you have time you can develop somebody who does not have training experience but has the desire and potential to be a trainer. Recruiting internally for someone who has no experience is a risk. Recruiting inexperienced people externally is an even greater risk. But how do you tell whether somebody has the potential and the desire?

Training is an activity you have really got to want to do, so it is very likely that people with the desire to train will approach you. If a person has always wanted to do something, it is also very likely that they have always done it. This would not necessarily be formal training, but they would have a history of successful presentations, or of coaching their colleagues.

As with all things it is a matter of getting the balance right. You need both experience and 'new blood'.

Rule of thumb: If you need a team of six trainers, you would probably want four existing trainers with company experience, one externally recruited trainer and one 'apprentice' trainer.

As far as I am concerned there is no difference between recruiting a permanent member of staff and finding a new consultant, except that you probably would not want to use an inexperienced consultant. The criteria for deciding whether you would recruit a new employee or find a new consultant are exactly the same as we discussed in the section on selecting trainers.

The recruitment process

Recruitment is the process of finding and attracting a person who matches the requirements of the job.

Recruiting trainers is much the same as recruiting for any other profession. Employers have to identify potential candidates and satisfy themselves as to which candidate is best able, and most willing, to do the job. Many interviewers concentrate on ability to the exclusion of willingness.

This matching process cannot start unless we understand what the job involves, and the type of person best suited to the job.

Job descriptions

The job description tells you what the job entails. It is the basis on which you can decide the kind of person you need for the job.

The way to do this is to identify which tasks have to be completed to meet the requirements of the job. 'Developing a lesson plan' and 'Analysing training needs' are examples of tasks. Note that both a verb and a noun are required to define the task.

Person specifications

The person specification describes the ideal person to fill the job. It is a profile of the personal skills and characteristics you will look for in the recruitment and selection process. The best way of writing a person specification is to take the job description and analyse the knowledge, skills and behaviours that are needed to perform the tasks.

The interview

The selection method in which most companies put their trust is the interview. The purpose of selection interviewing is 'to determine whether an applicant fulfils the requirements of the job'. A good interviewer does this by investigating past experience for evidence of the candidate's strengths, weaknesses and attitudes.

Don't be misled by your perceptions, but don't ignore them either – they often serve as warning bells, indicating areas where you will need to dig up some more facts.

Being an interviewer is like being a detective. While intuition is useful, the final conclusion must be firmly based on facts and data.

Most jobs are filled through interviews, but the widespread reliance on this method is often based on assumptions which do not bear close examination. It cannot be automatically assumed that all experienced managers are good judges of an applicant's character and skills who are able to sum up an individual in an interview that often lasts for no more than an hour.

Even when the job lends itself to practical selection tests, or when companies are able to use extensive psychometric testing, the interview almost invariably forms the final selection process.

Given these limitations, it is important that the interview is used effectively, and that those likely to be involved in interviewing are given training.

In any interview, the interviewer's task is to determine whether the candidate is both willing and able to do the job. As we have already said, sometimes we concentrate on one of these to the exclusion of the other.

Checking a trainer's ability

Checking a candidate's ability is easier for training than for many other professions. It is relatively easy to simulate a training environment where you can observe a trainer's performance. A training session is the culmination of all the work and preparation the trainer has done. Most of the candidate's strengths and weaknesses will become apparent in a 45-minute session. The more accurately you can simulate the training environment, the better data you will get. Many companies ask the candidates to make a presentation when they come for a second interview.

Unfortunately, the trainer will often try to do something 'special'. This, combined with performing in front of an interview panel, can give a distorted and misleading impression of the trainer's true abilities. Try to provide a natural environment for the presentation. Presenting to a single interviewer is very different to making a presentation to a large group.

Ideally, it would be better to observe trainers in their 'natural' environment such as a course they had already planned to run. Of course, this is very difficult if the person is currently working for another company. It is unlikely that a trainer's present employers would allow you to 'poach' on their own premises unless it was part of an 'outplacement' programme.

During the interview you will have established which courses the trainer is already able to train. If there is a good match between the candidate and the job, it is more than likely that one of these courses will meet one of your training requirements. In this case you could invite the trainer to run a training session for a group of your own students.

If the prospective trainers are consultants who want to take up full-time employment, it is relatively easy to get permission to observe them. You could even offer a fixed-term contract and observe the trainer in the environment in which they would be working.

The observation form shown in Figure 4.4 (page 98) can be used as a checklist of points to look out for. Don't just observe the trainer, also look at the students to gauge their reaction.

Another good indicator of a trainer's abilities are the lesson plans they have prepared. Ask prospective trainers to bring examples of lesson plans they have developed and use them as a basis for discussion. Examples of handouts and other student materials also give a lot of information about a trainer's ability.

One of the best predictors of future performance is past and present performance. During the interview get the candidate to talk about how they have handled past situations. It is not a good idea to ask them how they would handle a hypothetical situation, because they will either be stuck for words or they will describe how they feel the situation should be handled – not how they would actually perform.

Don't reject people just because they have been made redundant – many excellent, dedicated people only come on to the job market in times of redundancy. The fact that a person is redundant is not as important as the reason for the redundancy.

In any case, you should always take up references and talk to people the candidates have worked for and to the students they have trained.

Experience may be related to age, but this can be a trap. Someone may claim to have fifteen years' experience, but this may turn out to be one year's experience fifteen times over. Some companies have age blocks which are difficult to justify. An age block is even more difficult to justify for trainers, because many trainers continue to work as consultants long after they have taken 'early retirement'.

You can easily check whether the person's education and training meet the requirements of the job, but be careful not to use education and qualifications as predictors for all job requirements.

Physical qualities such as stamina are important for a trainer. Good hearing, vision (including colour vision where necessary) and clarity of voice are essential for communicating with students. Boxes of training materials are surprisingly heavy, so a trainer needs to be physically fit. Don't make assumptions on the basis of physical stature or disability. Small people can have immense strength, and the physically disabled learn to be enormously resourceful. The only way you can be sure the person is physically able to do the job is to observe them prepare and run a training session.

Appearance can be a trap for the unwary. It is unreliable to assess a person on the basis of appearance, but it is important that a trainer's mode of dress does not distract or intimidate the students.

Intelligence is difficult to assess without testing. Obviously trainers have to be intelligent enough to understand the concepts they are teaching, and not to look foolish in front of the class. A secondary indicator of intelligence is knowledge and it is relatively easy to check this out during an interview.

Maturity and emotional stability are essential to gain respect and credibility. Again, achievement in the past can help. Pure gut feelings will probably mislead.

Checking a trainer's willingness

A trainer's attitude to work answers the important question of whether the candidate will do the job as well as being able to do it. Probe the candidates' reasons for applying for the job as well as their aims, intentions and ambitions.

Make sure they understand what the job means in terms of carrying boxes, unsocial hours, travelling and nights away from home. Watch for any hesitancy in their reactions as you describe the job. Don't fudge the issue of describing the demands of the job for fear of discouraging a 'good candidate'. It is far better for applicants to be put off at this stage rather than after they have been employed.

Training is the kind of job that can be hell if you don't thoroughly enjoy it and get some kind of buzz out of teaching people. In some ways this characteristic of training makes it easier for an interviewer to judge a candidate's willingness. If enthusiasm for training and the subject matter does not shine through at the interview, it is unlikely that the applicant will be able to survive as a trainer.

Selection and the law

Every interviewer should be aware of how the law applies to recruitment. The following are not law in every country, but you will find that they encapsulate the policies and values of most multinational companies.

- It is unlawful, unless the job is covered by an exception, to discriminate on the grounds of a candidate's belonging to a particular category (i.e. gender, marital status, race, religion etc.).
- It is advisable to keep records of interviews, showing why applicants were rejected, for at least six months.
- Questions at interviews should relate to the requirements of the job. Questions about marriage plans or family intentions should not be asked, as they could be construed as showing a bias against women. Information for personnel records can be collected after a job offer has been made.
- Each individual job applicant should be assessed according to their personal capacity to meet the requirements of a given job. Applications from men and women, married and single, of whatever race or

religion should be treated in the same way. Where it is necessary to assess whether personal circumstances will affect the performance of the job (e.g. unsocial hours) this should be discussed objectively without detailed questions based on assumptions about marital status, children and domestic obligations. Interview questions should probe the experience and skills necessary to carry out the job.

- Employers should give careful consideration to the selection criteria that they use (including age bars, mobility and hours of work) and whether this would discriminate disproportionately against a particular category. Criteria which cannot be shown objectively to be necessary should be withdrawn.
- Selection criteria (job description and person specification) should be determined before the recruitment process starts.
- There are very few exceptions where it is legal to select a person of a particular category while excluding people of other categories (e.g. gender or race). These are called genuine occupational qualifications (GOQs). Basically these are authenticity, privacy, decency, and laws regulating the employment of women. Be very cautious about using a GOQ as a reason for not employing a person. You need to be very sure of your ground, and you will need to have demonstrated that you were unable to make suitable alternative arrangements for the person concerned.

You should not assume that:

- women are less ambitious or committed than men;
- women put their family commitments before their careers;
- men put their careers before their families;
- women work for 'pin money';
- a man will not work for a woman;
- women with children cannot work long or unsociable hours or attend residential training courses;
- women are not prepared to relocate to follow their careers;
- women are unsuited to certain kinds of work (e.g. scientific, technical, heavy manual or senior management).

Allowing your treatment of employees to be influenced by any of these assumptions may result in unlawful discrimination.

Developing trainers

Developing your trainers is a very important part of managing the training process. There are three areas of development:

- developing the skills required to run courses, identify needs and develop new courses (trainer training);
- continuous development (assessing trainer performance);
- finding career paths either within or through the training department (career development).

Training trainers   The exact process for training new trainers depends on the trainer's experience and the type of training to be done. The process given in Figure 4.3 is for a management trainer. It certifies trainers at two levels: instructor and training officer. An instructor is a person who has the professional skills to deliver courses. Training officers also carry out needs analyses and develop courses.

Induction into training department

This step is used to introduce both new and experienced trainers to the department. It assumes that the person has

Figure 4.3   Train-the-trainer process

attended the company's induction course and it includes:

- the mission of the training department (see Chapter 1 for an explanation of what a mission is);
- where the training department fits into the organization;
- roles and responsibilities of the training department's personnel;
- meeting members of the training department, clients and suppliers;
- location of offices, training rooms, storage areas, photocopying and other facilities;
- current issues;
- future direction of the department.

> Use of technical equipment

There are very few courses that are run without any technical equipment. An overhead projector seems to be the absolute minimum – even though it is perfectly possible to run a course without one. In addition a trainer can be expected to deal with audiocassette recorders, video recorders, video cameras, camcorders, computers, multimedia, interactive video, satellite links, 35 mm slide projectors and 16 mm film projectors.

Film and 35 mm slide projectors are becoming less common, which is just as well as they are notoriously unreliable. I would always try to avoid these 'technology traps' by having the films transferred on to video.

Although all trainers cannot be expected to be technical experts and to fix every fault, they should at least have a minimum level of expertise. This will keep delays due to embarrassing equipment failures down to a minimum.

Table 4.2 shows the minimum technical knowledge that a trainer should have for each type of equipment.

> Interpersonal skills observers course

The ability to observe and give feedback on students' interpersonal behaviour is an important tool for management trainers but, while this would be a useful course for many trainers, it would not be essential training for all trainers. Technical trainers, for example, could miss out this step.

> Techniques of instruction course

Many organizations provide techniques of instruction courses and choosing one is the same process as for

Table 4.2 *Minimum knowledge of technical equipment*

Equipment	Minimum technical knowledge
Overhead projector	Changing the lamp Cleaning the optics Adjusting colour fringes Keystone effect (how to adjust for)
Audiocassette recorders	Head cleaning Azimuth adjustment
Video recorders	Formats and standards (VHS, Super-VHS, 8 mm, Hi8, Betamax, Betacomm, U-matic, PAL, NTSC, SECAM) Colour, hue, brightness, sharpness, contrast, tracking and skew adjustments Cuing Head cleaning Leads and connectors Counter/time relationship
Video cameras Camcorders	Manual/auto iris, focusing, panning, tilting, zooming, tracking Sound and lighting Leads and connectors
Computers Interactive video	Operating systems Booting up Random access memory Copying and deleting files Disk formats (5¼", 3½", single-sided, single-density, double-density, hard disk, CD-ROM) Word processing Databases Graphics Desktop publishing
35 mm projectors	Loading Lamp changing Optics cleaning
Film projectors	Film threading Lamp changing Leaders and lead-in Sound leads and connectors Splicing broken film Rewinding

choosing any other course (see Chapter 3, Training Courses). I would recommend selecting a supplier who issues a recognized certificate or award as this sets the standard. A professional qualification is good for trainers' morale and the credibility of the training department.

> Trainer goes through at least one course certification process

The course certification process is the means by which an instructor or trainer becomes proficient to train a course without assistance. This process is described later in this chapter.

> Training manager certifies instructor

At this point the training manager reviews the new instructor's progress. This should be no more than a formality if the process described here has been followed up to this point. If your trainers are following the path of vocational qualifications, you may want to delegate this step to an external assessor.

> Train-the-trainer course

Once an instructor has become proficient in delivering courses, a development discussion may reveal a desire on their part to become a training officer. The first step is to attend a train-the-trainer course, followed by gaining a recognized qualification or award.

> Training officer develops new course

New training officers will now demonstrate what they have learnt on the train-the-trainer course by developing a new course. This should be done under supervision and using the process described in Chapter 3.

> Training manager certifies training officer

The training manager reviews the training officer's progress and provides formal certification. Again, you may want to delegate this to an external assessor.

Assessing trainer performance

Assessing trainer performance is a very important skill. Good assessment ensures that suitable trainers are employed as well as maintaining and improving the quality of existing trainers. To be effective, an assessment must:

- provide the training manager with relevant data which enable appropriate development activities to be recommended;
- provide an opportunity for trainers to explore their performance strengths and weaknesses;
- motivate trainers to investigate new developments in instructional techniques.

How often should trainers be assessed?

There are no 'hard and fast' rules on how often a trainer should be assessed but intervals of three to six months usually give the maximum benefit. New trainers should be observed more often than experienced trainers. The final decision on how often assessment should be conducted also depends on the workload of the trainer and the availability of the observer.

How long should assessment take?

The time an assessment takes also depends on many factors, but it is unlikely that sufficient data would be collected in under 45 minutes of observation. It is also unlikely that any meaningful feedback could take place in under 20 minutes.

How objective is assessment?

Although observation is more reliable than selection interviewing it is not entirely objective. If all students were influenced by trainer performance in the same way, to the same degree and at the same time, then it might be possible to have objective assessments.

But it isn't that simple. Every trainee is an individual and each will respond differently to the trainer. An action which may have the desired effect on one trainee may not have the same effect on another. What makes objectivity even more difficult is that it sometimes takes many hours to see the effects of that action. Sometimes it is impossible to assess the effects of a trainer's actions.

Similarly, observers' evaluations are influenced by their own subjective reactions. Sometimes observers confuse style with substance and will give a low rating simply because the trainer has a different style and feels more comfortable with different jokes and anecdotes. While assessment should be designed to be as objective as possible, it is important to understand the influence of subjective factors.

Even though assessment may be influenced by subjective factors, it is still vital for maintaining and improving the standard of training. Training managers must have a basis for evaluating what their trainers do and how well they do it. All trainers are entitled to an evaluation of their performance, and most trainers will actively request it.

Trainers will also have their own opinions of how well or how poorly they are performing their tasks. These opinions are extremely important to the trainer – and to the training manager. Yet the fullest benefit cannot be obtained from both the trainer's and the training manager's opinion unless comparison and discussion take place.

This means that training managers must base their opinions on what they actually see. They must observe trainers in the classroom and then set up a meeting where both the manager and the trainer can share their opinions and agree on appropriate follow-up activities.

What is assessed? Trainers are sometimes regarded primarily as subject-matter experts. Whatever other qualities they bring to the classroom they are, by definition, subject-matter experts. Trainers tell, show, test and then decide when a topic has been adequately covered.

There is, however, much more to training than the mechanics of presenting information. Trainers work with individuals. They must be able to deal with student motivation. They should try to remove the obstacles that prevent learning.

Trainers also need to pay attention to the fact that they are role models for the trainees. Their enthusiasm for a subject or their adherence to policies affect student behaviour. Although being a role model will not necessarily cause students to follow suit, its absence will almost certainly be copied by students – 'If the trainer doesn't care, why should I?'

How should assessment be handled? Although there are many different views on how an assessment should be done, all workable systems have four elements in common:

- preparation;
- observation;
- feedback;
- follow-up.

As each of these elements involves both the trainer and the observer, planning the availability of suitable observers is essential.

Preparation (45 minutes) Before any assessment takes place, training managers should discuss the process with the trainers. When everybody involved understands what is involved, individual observations can be scheduled. At least one week's notice should be given.

Managing the training process

Observation   The observer should be seated as unobtrusively as possible.
(45 minutes)   The best position is off to one side and behind the students.
                       Try not to sit in the middle at the back of the classroom as
                       trainers will feel that they are being stared at all of the time.
                       The trainer should not be interrupted at any stage of the
                       observation period.

                       During the observation the training manager should record
                       the observations. If a new trainer is being observed an
                       observation checklist (see Figure 4.4) should be completed.
                       If an experienced trainer is being certified on a new course,
                       notes can be made on a copy of the lesson plan.

Feedback   Feedback should be given immediately, or as soon as
(20 minutes)   possible after the evaluation. Only the trainer and the
                       observer should be present. It is recommended that a
                       counselling approach be taken. Counselling, in this

Trainer:	Date:
Session:	Observer:

(1) = Not acceptable   (2) = Poor   (3) = OK   (4) = Master performer

Behaviours	**Assessment and comments**
<u>Preparation</u> — Rehearsed lesson — Administration — Classroom layout — Materials and equipment prepared — Arranged to be free from interruptions	(1) (2) (3) (4) (5)
<u>Presentation</u> — Introduced subject — Communicated objectives — Communicated agenda — Followed logical sequence — Summarized — Checked students' understanding — Kept to time — Kept to subject	(1) (2) (3) (4) (5)
<u>Manner</u> — Showed commitment — Showed enthusiasm — Created interest — Sensitive to group — Credible — Knowledgeable	(1) (2) (3) (4) (5)
<u>Technique</u> — Voice — Questioning — Pace — Movement — Eye contact — Mannerisms — Use of audiovisual aids	(1) (2) (3) (4) (5)

Figure 4.4 *Observation checklist*

situation, is an attempt by the observer to help the trainer explore strengths and weaknesses so that the strengths are reinforced and suitable actions are taken to improve performance. Figure 4.5 gives the elements of counselling.

The observer should start off by *setting the climate*. This is to make sure that the trainer is relaxed. If the observer knows the trainer well, setting the climate will only take a few minutes. Always be sincere. Do not delay getting down to business any longer than necessary or tension will be needlessly increased.

The observer must take the time to *set expectations*. This means that the trainer understands the purpose and process of the session.

The next step is to *seek trainer's views of strengths and weaknesses*. Here the observer invites the trainer to express opinions on the trainer's own performance strengths and weaknesses. Questioning techniques should be used appropriately to ensure that the trainer fully explores all of the observed strengths and weaknesses. Where opinions differ, evidence should be provided by the observer.

It is much better if trainers are able to identify their own strengths and weaknesses. They are more likely to want to do something about improving their performance. However, they can be unaware of some of their performance strengths and weaknesses, so the observer should not be afraid of prompting and giving direct feedback. There are guidelines for giving constructive feedback in Figure 4.6.

Towards the end of the feedback session the observer should help the trainer *develop an action plan*. List the strengths and weaknesses on a development plan (see

1. Set climate

2. Set expectations

3. Seek trainer's views of strengths and weaknesses

4. Develop an action plan

Figure 4.5   *Elements of counselling*

1.   IT IS NOT JUDGEMENTAL

         Making judgemental statements such as 'You really are a bad listener' is not very useful and they
         can cause the receiver to react defensively.

2.   IT IS SPECIFIC
         A far better approach is to describe a specific incident, e.g. 'At the end of the lesson you interrupted
         Hazel before she could finish explaining her problem.'

3.   ITS PURPOSE IS TO HELP THE RECEIVER
         Sometimes we give feedback to make ourselves feel better. It helps us to get things off our chests.
         This might be good for the giver but it does nothing for the receiver. Ensure that the only reason for
         giving feedback is to help the receiver improve performance.

4.   IT IS ABOUT BEHAVIOUR THAT CAN BE CHANGED
         Frustration is only increased when a person is reminded of some shortcoming that cannot be
         controlled.

5.   IT IS CLEAR
         One way of making sure that the feedback is clear is to have the receiver paraphrase the feedback.

6.   IT IS TIMELY
         Generally, feedback is most effective immediately after the behaviour. The exception to this is when
         the receivers are not ready to hear the feedback, such as when they are feeling depressed or are 'on a
         high'.

Figure 4.6   *Guidelines for giving constructive feedback*

Figure 2.6 in Chapter 2) and then invite the trainer to suggest appropriate activities that will maintain the strengths and minimize the weaknesses. Figure 4.7 gives guidelines for improving performance.

Follow-up
(unspecified time)

After the session the observer should assess how well the feedback session went and what would be done differently during another feedback session.

The trainer's performance should be monitored and, if necessary, additional observations and feedback sessions planned.

Career
development

There are two ways in which training can be part of a person's career development:

● training as a profession;
● training as part of a development plan.

Training as a
profession

Many trainers consider themselves to be career trainers. They would like to develop their careers within the training profession. Although they enjoy training, they don't want to spend the rest of their working lives doing wall-to-wall training. It is important to have a career path within the training department if these trainers are not to lose their motivation.

- Do not try to change too much at once. It is better to improve one or two aspects of performance than to make no progress on twenty.

- Always agree a completion date for each of the activities.

- It is easier, and probably healthier, to do more of a new behaviour than suppress an existing behaviour. For example, if the trainer talks for too long it is better and more helpful for them to use more visual aids and ask more questions than to simply suggest that they talk less.

- Always summarize what is going to be done, by whom and by when.

Figure 4.7 *Guidelines for improving performance*

Figure 4.8 shows part of a career path within a management training department. The right-hand side shows the skills and education that are needed to perform at each level. The left-hand side of the diagram shows the activities that each job involves.

Notice that even the most senior trainers are still expected to do the basic activities. What does change is the proportion of time spent on these activities at each level. Figure 4.9 shows how this varies for the management training jobs.

If you do this kind of analysis for your own training jobs, your compensation and benefits manager will be able to assess the jobs and fit them into your company's existing grading structure.

Somebody with no training experience could 'learn the trade' by starting as a training administrator, progressing to a training assistant and then on to a management skills trainer. If they had managerial experience, they could also progress to higher levels.

If trainers have insufficient experience, skills or knowledge to progress from one level to the next, actions would be identified for their personal development plans. This might include leaving the training department for a year or two to gain managerial experience.

Training as part of a development plan
The career path shown in Figure 4.8 is essentially a longitudinal progression with each step serving as an entry point. Training can also be used for the development of

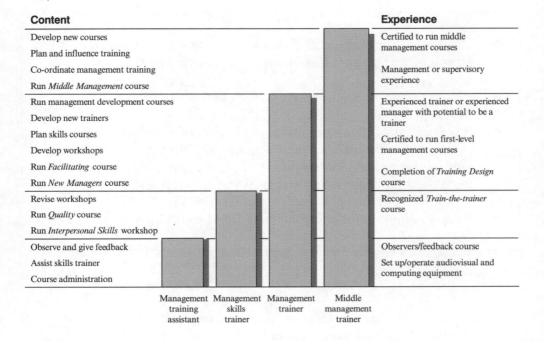

Content		Experience
Develop new courses		Certified to run middle management courses
Plan and influence training		
Co-ordinate management training		Management or supervisory experience
Run *Middle Management* course		
Run management development courses		Experienced trainer or experienced manager with potential to be a trainer
Develop new trainers		
Plan skills courses		Certified to run first-level management courses
Develop workshops		
Run *Facilitating* course		Completion of *Training Design* course
Run *New Managers* course		
Revise workshops		Recognized *Train-the-trainer* course
Run *Quality* course		
Run *Interpersonal Skills* workshop		
Observe and give feedback		Observers/feedback course
Assist skills trainer		Set up/operate audiovisual and computing equipment
Course administration		

Management training assistant　　Management skills trainer　　Management trainer　　Middle management trainer

Figure 4.8　*Part of a career path in a management training department*

people from other parts of the company. There is nothing like teaching for learning and forming contacts!

A secondment to the training department is particularly useful for managers and 'high fliers'. It also broadens the experience of people whose career paths have been within one department.

The benefit works both ways because secondment brings new ideas into training and helps keep training in touch with reality.

Certifying trainers

Certification or accreditation is the process of ensuring that a trainer is ready to train a new course. The exact process that is used to accredit or certify trainers depends on the complexity of the course and the trainers' experience. The trainers' experience also affects the time it takes to go through the certification process:

- Are the trainers experienced trainers?
- Have they trained this type of course before?
- Do they already understand the underlying concepts?
- Have they practised the skills in the workplace?

Figure 4.10 shows a process that is used for a complex five-day course.

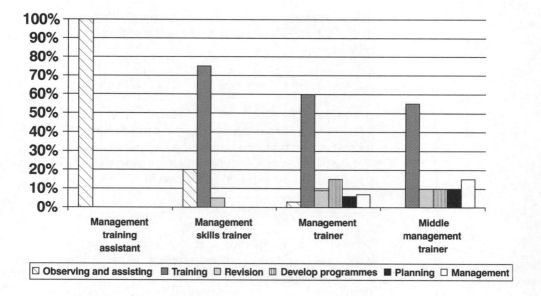

Figure 4.9 *Activity profiles for different levels of trainer*

Trainer attends course

The first step is to have the trainer take the course as a student. This is very important for two reasons. The first reason is the obvious one: to have any credibility trainers need to possess the knowledge and skills that they will be teaching. The second reason, although not so obvious, is just as important. Trainers who take a course under the same conditions and pressures as the students will be better

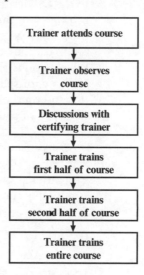

Figure 4.10 *Certification process for a complex five-day course*

able to appreciate their students' learning difficulties. This makes for greater empathy and a better student–trainer relationship.

> Trainer observes course

After taking the course as a student the trainer is then given a lesson plan so that the next course can be observed and followed. The trainer is encouraged to make copious notes during this observation and to start considering which parts of the course should be tackled first.

> Discussions with certifying trainer

Soon after the completion of this observation the trainer has a discussion with the certifying trainer. The certifying trainer should ideally be the course originator or a trainer who has extensive knowledge and experience of the course. The discussion should include any questions the trainer has and the final decision as to which modules should be practised first.

> Trainer trains first half of course

On the third course the trainer co-trains with the experienced trainer. Usually half of the course is trained, but it may be advisable to train only a third of a very complex course.

The experienced trainer should observe and give feedback to the trainer throughout the course. For maximum effect it is important that this feedback is given as soon as practically possible. Trainers vary in the formality of the feedback they require. For some a few words at the end of the session is all that is required; others may want a full-blown counselling session at the end of the day. It will all depend on their experience, confidence and ability to teach this type of course.

> Trainer trains second half of course

The other sessions should be practised on the fourth course. Again, this should be done under observation and with feedback.

> Trainer trains entire course

With the feedback that has been received so far, the trainer should be able to teach the fifth course alone. So you can see that for a complex course, which is run only once a quarter, it can take over a year for a trainer to be brought up to speed.

At the other end of the scale it should be possible for a trainer to take a simple one-day course as a student and then, given a comprehensive lesson plan, be able to teach the next course alone.

Although it is possible for an experienced trainer to train straight from a lesson plan without having seen the course before, you should really try to avoid this as even the best lesson plans cannot capture all the details that are required to make the course a success.

Certifying the certifiers

Of course, all this begs the question of who certifies the certifiers. Ideally accreditation should be done by the people who originally developed the course. However, this is not always possible because of time, distance and cost. These problems are further compounded in large multinational organizations because of language and cultural difficulties. Foreign subsidiaries of these multinational corporations do not always appreciate having to pay for the cost of flying somebody in from abroad every time they need to have a new trainer accredited. In any case, not all trainers have sufficient expertise in the corporation's primary language that would enable them to train and be observed in that language. In fact, it could be argued that a trainer's certification would not really be valid unless their performance is observed under the conditions in which it would be taught.

The answer to this is to have some trainers developed to the point at which they would be able to certify their own trainers in their areas. Where language is an issue the local certifiers would have to be bilingual and would probably have to run a course at the corporation's own training centre. A certain amount of trust would have to be in place for this scheme to work, but the advantage is that the quality of the training is maintained at a level which meets the corporation's standards while at the same time giving flexibility to the local organizations.

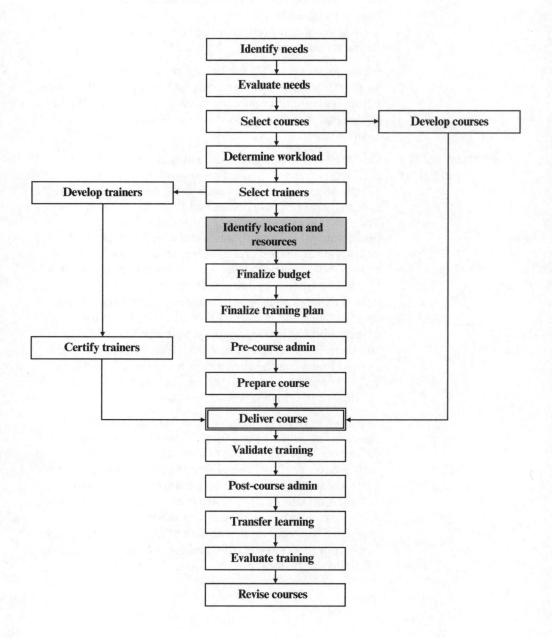

Figure 5.1 *Training locations and resources*

5 Training locations and resources

This chapter covers another step in the training process:

- identify location and resources.

By this stage you will have selected the courses and trainers. The next decision you have to make is where you are going to run the courses, what the best learning situation will be, and where you are going to obtain the equipment and materials.

If you run residential courses the accommodation costs can be the single biggest item in your training budget. Running courses on your own premises will allow you to keep travel and accommodation costs low.

Identifying training locations and resources

Figure 5.2 illustrates the process I will be describing for identifying training locations and resources.

> Obtain course specification

The course specification details the facilities, materials and equipment that are needed to run the course. This information is essential for deciding the type of learning environment required for the course. It allows you to check whether a location meets your specification. The specification is also an excellent method for communicating your exact requirements to a training centre.

> Determine type of learning environment

The factors that affect your choice of learning environment are the cost, the facilities you need, the type of instruction and whether the students need to be separated from home and work pressures.

Don't assume that all training has to take place in the classroom. 'Open learning' and 'distance learning' widen

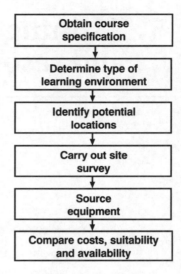

Figure 5.2 *Process for identifying training locations and resources*

the choice of learning environments. (See Chapter 9, Delivering the Course, for a discussion of open and distance learning.) Choices of learning environment can cover:

- at home,
- the workplace,
- open learning centres,
- meeting rooms,
- dedicated training rooms,
- hotels,
- sports centres and social clubs,
- residential training centres.

Home Home learning is suitable for programmed instruction, it is inexpensive and many people would welcome the opportunity to learn at home.

The disadvantages are:

- possible distraction by home pressures,
- isolation from tutors,
- lack of specialized equipment.

When we think of home learning we often think it is limited to text-based training. Home learning can be more creative if ways are found to overcome the disadvantages of isolation and lack of access to equipment.

Isolation can be overcome by using the telephone or computer links. Messages can be sent between tutor and students by e-mail. Access to learning materials all over the world can be obtained via the Internet. Videos can be broadcast from existing television stations, either during the day for large audiences or as a scrambled signal during the night for small specialist audiences. The night-time programmes can be automatically recorded by anyone who has a suitable decoder.

The Open University sends laboratory kits to its science and technology students by road. It is also possible for service engineers to learn how to repair small photocopiers on their kitchen tables!

In the workplace People do most of their learning outside the classroom, but much of it is random and unstructured. To make the most of experiential learning the student needs to have an experienced coach and a planned series of structured experiences.

Open learning centres Open learning centres are purpose-built rooms fitted with all the equipment and materials needed for private study. They provide flexibility in terms of time and students can learn at their own pace. Open learning centres are particularly useful in manufacturing areas because breaks in production are difficult to predict.

Meeting rooms Purpose-built meeting rooms are suitable for short training courses, but they are usually too small and the wrong shape for larger classes.

Dedicated training rooms Dedicated training rooms may well be ideal if you were involved in the design and paid attention to the following:

- size and shape of training room,
- capacity of training room,
- heating and ventilation,
- lighting,
- light switches,
- acoustics,
- equipment.

Further details of these aspects are given in the section on carrying out a site survey.

Distraction by work-related problems is the main disadvantage of an on-site training room. Some companies have dedicated training rooms at their head offices which means that most people have to travel to their courses. This helps to minimize disruptions. They also block-book bedrooms at a local hotel. This is cheaper than running courses at a commercial residential training centre, and avoids the problems and cost of running your own residential centre.

Hotels Many hotels are properly equipped to function as conference centres, but too many others see conferences and training courses only as a means of filling empty rooms. They often have to hire-in all the training equipment. Function rooms double as meeting rooms, and bedrooms have the beds removed to provide syndicate rooms. I have even seen instances of syndicate rooms not being ready until 11 o'clock because the hotel had rented them to guests the night before!

Sports centres and social clubs Much of what has been said about hotels also applies to sports centres and social clubs, except that the standard is even more variable. Don't automatically disregard these venues, however, because some of them provide excellent service and facilities at competitive prices. Always make sure that you carry out a thorough site survey nevertheless.

Residential training centres Residential training centres are in the business of providing excellent training facilities in suitable surroundings. They are also very expensive. You would only use a residential training centre for longer, more complex courses.

Identify potential locations

Once you have decided on the type of training location, the next step is to identify a number of potential alternative locations. You may already have a number in mind from past experience, but if you are new to the job or have just relocated to a new area you will need to look further afield. Training magazines and *Yellow Pages* are useful sources of advertising.

Many of the country's largest companies run their own training centres and, although they do not always advertise, they are often willing to hire rooms to other companies to improve their own utilization rates.

Finally, don't forget to ask your own colleagues – they may have attended training centres with other companies.

Carry out site survey

If you have never used a particular training centre before, it is imperative that you carry out a site survey to make sure the training location is suitable for your needs. It is worth taking a couple of hours really getting the feel of the place. The centre's management will be only too pleased to show you around – after all, it could lead to a great deal of business.

Talk to the staff, trainers and students. Explore the buildings and the grounds. Use a checklist like the one shown in Figure 5.3.

Date:		Location:

Checkpoint	Comments
Location	
Parking	
Reception	
Contacts	
Delivery arrangements	
Staff	
Access to training room	
Size/shape of training room	
Capacity of training room	
Heating and ventilation	
Lighting	
Power sockets	
Light switches	
Acoustics	
Equipment	
Wall space and fixings	
Syndicate rooms	
Toilets	
Access for preparation	
Food	
Meal and break arrangements	
Bedrooms	
Leisure facilities	
Security	
Emergency procedures	

Figure 5.3   *Checklist for doing a site survey*

Location   Most training centres are situated in remote areas. This is
not usually a problem for residential courses but you will
need to check whether:

- the centre is accessible by public transport with, perhaps,
  just a short taxi journey at the end (you would normally
  expect very remote training centres to provide a minibus
  service to and from the nearest train station, bus
  terminus or airport),
- there is a reasonable connection to the motorway
  (expressway) network,
- foreign students have enough time to get to the airport
  after the course has finished,
- students who arrive by car have no more than a five-
  hour drive.

If the course is not residential, the training centre needs to be far more accessible.

Parking It is another of those universal laws that the number of cars expands to fill the available parking space. When you arrive to carry out the site survey you will soon see how easy it is to park your car. When you leave, check to see if anybody is blocked in and whether cars are parked on the road outside.

Reception The first impression you get of a training centre is of the reception area. It is at the reception where frustrations and inefficiencies surface. The receptionist should be expecting you and you should not have to wait too long to be seen. This will give you an indication of how well the place is being run. For a better indication you should try to be in the reception area when students are booking in and booking out.

Contacts It is best to get the names of the staff you will need to contact if you decide to use the training centre. As well as making your life easier, it will also give you an indication of whether people have specific roles and responsibilities.

Delivery arrangements If you need to have materials delivered to the training centre, check out the process for receiving the deliveries and getting them to the classroom. Again, get the name of a contact for this purpose.

Staff The relationship you have with the training centre's staff can make all the difference between a smoothly run course and a course that is a series of irritations. Make sure you talk to the staff to get a feeling for their attitude towards you and the training centre.

Access to training room If your trainers intend to bring their own materials, see how close they can park their cars to the classroom, how many steps have to be climbed and check the width of the passageways. Also see what help is available – either in the form of trolleys or willing hands.

Size and shape of training room Generally speaking, training rooms tend to be rectangular and too narrow. This is especially true if you have a preference for a horseshoe layout of tables and chairs.

With a class of fifteen then you would probably have five people down each of the sides and five people along the back.

Rule of thumb: Allow 80 cm of desk space per person.

Allowing 80 cm per person you would need a horseshoe of tables five metres long and four metres across. The width of the room would need to be increased to about seven metres to allow space for the chairs and a passageway down the sides. To allow room at the front for the trainer and equipment, plus space for movement round the back, would require a room that is eight metres long.

Obviously you can use a narrower room if you have a longer horseshoe (with three or four people along the back) and less room for movement along the sides. This squeezes everyone in, but the people along the sides will have difficulty in seeing all the audiovisual equipment. This can be overcome, but you will probably find that you will have to indulge in a bit of 'scene shifting' by moving the television monitor and flip-chart stands. Building training rooms back-to-back permits a small room for audiovisual equipment to be built between them.

Rule of thumb: An ideal shape for a training room is a square. Try to keep the ratio of length to width at less than 4:3.

This might give the impression that the larger the training room, the better. However, there is a limit to the size of the room and this is determined by whether the students can read the visual aids. A person with good eyesight can usually read a flip chart up to nine metres away.

Rule of thumb: Try to limit the distance between the flip-chart stand and the furthest student to eight metres.

Capacity of training room

Taking all the above into account, you should be able to see whether the room is large enough for your course. The horseshoe layout takes more room than theatre style or a traditional classroom layout.

The training centre brochure should give an indication of the capacity of the room in these configurations. These estimates are usually on the optimistic side.

Heating and ventilation

Check that the training room has adequate heating and ventilation. Students who are too hot, too cold or too stuffy do not learn as well as those who are comfortable – but not too comfortable! In fact, students seem to be unable to concentrate if the temperature is more than 5°C above or below their comfort zone. For optimum learning it is probably better to have a slightly cool rather than a slightly warm temperature. Don't underestimate the value of having an air-conditioned training room – even in temperate countries.

Rule of thumb: Try setting the thermostat to 18°C.

Lighting

Many rooms have far too low a level of lighting. This is especially true if you use hotel function rooms. Here the lighting has been designed to provide a certain ambience.

It is also possible to have too much light. This makes it difficult to view videos and overhead transparencies. Check the efficiency and ease of use of blinds and curtains.

Some training rooms have no natural light and air. When the question is asked why the training room does not have any windows, the rationale is nearly always that a view would be distracting. Perhaps the students might occasionally look out of the window, but if they are constantly looking out of the window then I would question the effectiveness of the course and the trainer. On balance, the motivational benefits to be gained from having a pleasant environment and undisturbed body clocks far outweigh any potential distraction.

Power sockets Check the positioning of the power sockets and that the room has sufficient sockets for the equipment. It is surprising how many you need: one for the OHP, two for the video, three for the computer set-up...

Rule of thumb: Have a minimum of four power sockets available at the front of the room.

Light switches Make sure that the light switches are conveniently placed. You don't want to rush from one side of the room to the other every time you start or stop a videotape. Dimmer switches are useful for getting the optimum light level and for getting people's eyes used to the light after showing a videotape.

Acoustics Acoustics are not usually a problem unless you are using a very large room. Make sure you test the acoustics when people are in the room, as an empty room sounds very different.

Check the sound insulation from the outside and from neighbouring classrooms. A raucous class or a lawn mower can be very distracting.

Equipment You would normally expect a training or conference centre to supply flip-chart stands, an overhead projector and a screen. Some centres have their own video equipment, others have to hire it in. Check the positioning, ease of use and the operation of the equipment.

Wall space and fixings Many courses need to have posters and flip-chart sheets fixed to the walls, so it is surprising how little attention is given to the space and fixings required. Many training centres, especially the converted manor houses, abhor the use of Blu-tack or masking tape but don't provide sufficient alternatives such as pin-boards or rails.

Syndicate rooms Check that the syndicate rooms are conveniently situated and are large enough to accommodate the number of people in each sub-group plus any observers. Look out for other areas that can be used for paired, or triad, activities.

Toilets Check the number, position and cleanliness of the toilets.

Access for preparation Depending on the complexity of the course, you may spend anything from 30 minutes to three hours preparing the training room. Ideally, you would like to do this the night or the Friday before the course. You will need to check whether the training rooms are used during the evenings or over the weekends. Even if the rooms are not being used, you will need to check whether you can gain access at the time you need to prepare.

Food There can be considerable variation in menus from one training centre to another. Some provide meals to gourmet standards! You will need to decide whether the standard of the food and service is compatible with the type of course you are running. When you are doing a site survey you would normally expect to be provided with a meal so that you can judge the standard for yourself.

Meal and break arrangements Check the times and the flexibility of the meal and coffee arrangements. Also check to see how long it takes to serve a complete meal, as this can be critical if you are running evening sessions.

Bedrooms With the increase in the standard of living and holidays abroad most people expect a high standard of accommodation. Most training centres now provide:

- desk, chair and reading light,
- bed,
- wardrobe (but never enough coat hangers!),
- separate bath/shower/toilet/wash basin,
- television,
- clock/radio/alarm,
- coffee/tea-making facilities.

Look at the variation in standard and size between bedrooms. People do compare notes and it is inconsistency of standards rather than the absolute standard that causes people to complain.

Leisure facilities If the course is more than a couple of days long, the training centre should provide sport and leisure facilities. This is especially important if the centre is in a remote area.

Security Check that the training and accommodation blocks are secure and that the car park is supervised. Is it possible to open the windows in the bedrooms without providing access for an intruder? If the accommodation is separate from the training block, are the paths well lit and supervised?

Emergency procedures

Ask what the procedures are in the case of a fire or bomb alert. Gathering locations should be identified and, in the case of a bomb alert, these should be over 800 metres away and out of direct sight of the training centre.

> Source equipment

If you are running courses in a commercial training centre, all you need to do is to hand over a precise specification of your requirements and the equipment will be provided as and when you need it. If you do a lot of training on your own premises it is worthwhile buying the equipment you need. This is especially true of overhead projectors and video players which are also needed for meetings.

Unless you make frequent use of the more expensive and specialist equipment such as computers and projection televisions, you will find it more economic to hire rather than buy.

> Compare costs, suitability and availability

The results of the site survey will allow you to compare the suitability of alternative training venues. Comparing costs will prove to be a little more difficult. Most residential training centres will give you a day rate and a 24-hour rate, but these rates are not always directly comparable.

It is very important that you understand what the rate includes. Some rates include everything, others provide a minimum and make additional charges for anything else. The golden rule is to ask for a written summary of what is included in the price. The following is a list of items which may, or may not, be included in a 24-hour rate:

- main classroom,
- syndicate rooms,
- pencils,
- paper,
- flip-chart stands,
- flip-chart pads,
- flip-chart pens,
- food,
- coffee,
- audiovisual equipment,
- computers,
- special table arrangements in restaurant,
- making use of empty rooms for short exercises.

The costs of telephone calls (often priced at hotel levels), photocopying and faxes (sending and receiving) vary widely from centre to centre.

The other method of comparing prices is to have training centres quote against a pre-determined specification. The following is the specification that I use when I am getting quotes for non-residential training:

- 1 main classroom for 12 people with OHP, screen, flip-chart stand, flip-chart pad and flip-chart pens.
- 1 VHS player and monitor.
- 1 syndicate room with flip-chart stand, pad and pens.
- Coffee/tea and biscuits in morning.
- Cooked lunch (two courses).
- Tea/coffee in afternoon.

Running your own training centre

As the amount of training you do increases, one question that will come up is whether it is worthwhile to have your own training centre. Your own training centre can vary from a dedicated room to a separate building or a residential centre.

The disadvantage of having your own residential centre is that you have to worry about making sure it is full. If you cannot fill the centre yourself you will have to hire it out to external customers – and then you might find yourself in the hotel business rather than the training business.

Many companies do not want to be in the hotel business, and they do not like to have their cash tied up in a training centre, so they get a specialist company to buy and run the establishment for them. These companies make an annual charge for running the centre. If this charge is independent of the number of students, you will again be faced with the problem of filling the place. Unless you have nearly 100 per cent utilization rates this option will be just as expensive as hiring a commercial training centre only when you need it.

Designing a new training centre is a skilled activity. Architects are not trainers and do not always come up with the most practical layout. If you follow the advice given in this book you should be able to work with the architect and design the rooms you need.

Another possibility is to go to one of the suppliers of audiovisual equipment who will design the training rooms and will also provide a project manager to oversee the installation. Of course, there will always be a suspicion that the design will be more biased to the sale of equipment rather than what is exactly required. The most common problem people have when training rooms are designed for them is over-specification.

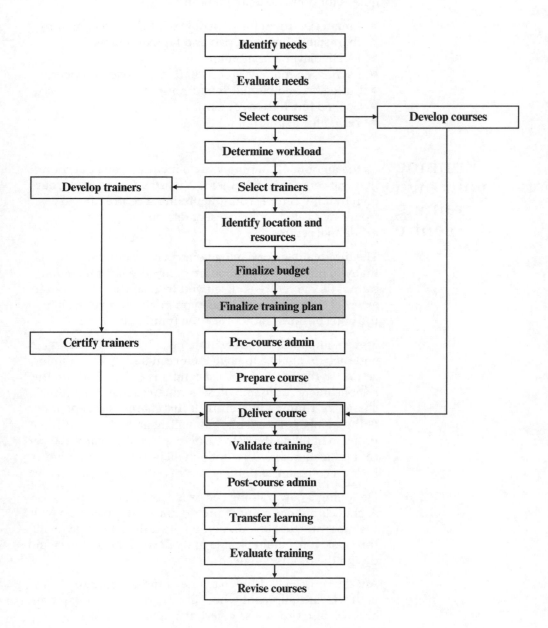

Figure 6.1 *Training plans and budgets*

6 Training plans and budgets

This chapter covers the content of a training plan and the preparation of a training budget, both of which are required to complete the next two steps of the training process:

- finalize training budget,
- finalize training plan.

In previous steps of the process we have covered the need, identified the courses to meet the need and estimated the resource required to deliver the workload. Now we have to prepare a budget, match the desired level of training to the available resource and prepare the final training plan.

Finalize training budget

One of the questions that has to be answered when a training plan is being put together is: 'How much will the training cost?' It is interesting to note that we are nearly always asked how much training will cost rather than what is the size of our training investment. A better question might be: 'How much would it cost us if we don't do this training?'

Whatever question is asked, and no matter what we call it, working out the figures may not be quite as simple as it first appears. This is because of the difficulty of deciding what should be included in the costs. For example, should you include the trainers' salaries, the students' salaries and the loss of production during training? You may end up doing a very detailed cost analysis or you may decide only to count what is normally deducted from your budget.

You may also have to decide whether your training department should be run as a profit centre. A profit centre means that you will sell your courses and training expertise in order to defray the expense of running your own training operation. This will involve you in preparing estimates and working agreements.

119

Whatever you include or exclude from your budget, the golden rule is to be consistent and to make your assumptions very clear. With all these parameters sorted out you will then be in a position to prepare a training budget.

The size of the budget is one of the main limiting factors when it comes to determining how much of the training demand will be delivered. There are many ways of preparing a budget and the way you choose will depend on your company's accounting systems. What you include or exclude from the budget depends on these practices. The steps for finalizing the budget are shown in Figure 6.2.

> Determine whether to be a profit centre

This step will not be necessary for many training organizations – you are there to provide training only for your own organization or company. However, in a large company you could be asked to run your training organization as a profit centre. In this case you will need to consider this step very carefully and include an estimate of your income in the budget.

Being a profit centre can mean many different things so you will need to clarify the rules of the game. For example, it may simply mean you have to contribute to the budget by selling any excess training capacity. At the other end of the scale the intention might be for the training department to have a 'zero-based' budget. This means that it has to justify and completely maintain its existence by selling all its 'products' to other departments and perhaps to customers outside the company as well.

You will also need to understand the reasons for making the training department a profit centre. It might be to put a value on the training so that managers can make a business

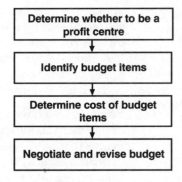

Figure 6.2   Process for finalizing the training budget

decision as to which training they buy. It might be to keep internal training competitive with external suppliers, or maybe a profit centre was the only way to justify the cost of a brand new, purpose-built training centre.

Strictly speaking, it might be impossible to have a true profit centre without making the training department a separate company. The reason for this is that it is extremely unlikely that any company would let the training department make its own decisions with regard to staffing levels, salaries, benefits and capital investments. Even if the training organization were given this free hand, you could imagine the amount of aggravation that would occur if you were busy recruiting trainers while the rest of the company was making people redundant.

The decision to form a separate company would be a very brave one but it also has its advantages. One curious example of this is a measure called the 'direct to indirect ratio'. This ratio, of how many direct staff you have compared to the number of indirect staff, is one of the more popular measures of a company's efficiency. By direct staff we mean the people who touch the product or its design. That is, they are directly involved with the design, manufacture or sale of a product. People who provide a service to an external, paying customer would also be considered to be direct staff.

Indirect staff are the people, such as managers and administrators, who support the direct staff. It is said that in the UK it takes one manager to supervise ten production workers, whereas in Japan it takes only one manager to ensure that 200 workers go home on time. So you can see that in the interests of efficiency, pressure will always be on to reduce the numbers of indirect staff.

All the staff in a training department would, without a moment's hesitation, be classified as indirect staff. Yet if that department were made a separate company, the trainers would then be classified as direct staff even if they were doing exactly the same work for the same people.

There is another important consideration that must be taken into account before launching yourself into a profit centre mode of operation. This is the question of who the customer is.

In a large company the training department was probably formed to meet the training needs of one organization. This organization would probably expect to have first call on the services of its own trainers – not an unreasonable request, you might think. Now the paradox of the situation is that the more successful you are as a profit centre, the less likely you are to be able to meet the needs of your own organization, because you will be too busy training other departments' staff. (You might even be asked which department you are working for.) This need not be a problem if your organization's needs analysis and planning have been done really well. In this case you will know how much spare capacity you have and you will be able to start taking bookings from other departments.

If you have spare capacity you might be asked why the training department needs to be as large as it is. On the other hand, if you do not have the capability to provide additional training you cannot expect your potential customers to wait a year to get their training. They will simply go elsewhere. That lost business will be very hard to regain.

The real problem arises when circumstances change, such as an urgent need to train every manager on financial control. You are asked to provide additional training for your own organization at the same time as you have contracted to train other departments. Obviously the first thing you will do will be to try to re-negotiate the contracts with your paying customers. You might be lucky and find that their circumstances have changed as well. If this doesn't work then you are faced with the question of who your customer is. Is it your own organization? After all, supporting them is the very reason for your training department's existence. Or is it the paying customers? If you cancel the contracts you will not get any business from them again. Your reputation will be destroyed and it is unlikely that anyone else would use such an unreliable supplier. Perhaps the only way around this, if you are really serious about running the training department as a profit centre, is to take a loss on these contracts and bring in consultant trainers to take on some of the workload.

> Identify budget items

The following is a list of items that can find their way into a training budget:

- cost of external courses,
- purchase and hire of equipment, books and videos,
- production of training materials,
- training staff wages/salaries,
- training staff overheads,
- hire of training venues,

- student accommodation costs,
- student travel costs,
- student wages/salaries/overheads.

Rule of thumb: Include everything that will be charged to the training department's budget during the financial year.

The aim of the exercise is to determine whether the cost of the training plan exceeds, falls below or meets your allocated budget. Most budgets also show the expected spend by month so that you will be able to monitor the budget during the year.

If you are selling training to other departments you will also need to show the expected income for each month.

Be sure to find out what your company's financial year is. Some start in April, some start in November, while others are the same as the calendar year. Confusion can arise over financial years, especially if your suppliers or customers have a different financial year to your own, so be very careful about what should be in this year's budget and what should be in the following year.

> Determine cost of budget items

The cost of some of the budget items is fairly easy to determine. Others, like the cost of a trainer or the cost of a day of training, can become quite involved.

How much does a trainer cost? The cost of employing anybody is not just the cost of their wages. There are other employment costs and overheads that have to be taken into account. Table 6.1 gives a fictitious example of the real cost of employing a trainer whose current salary is £22 000. I have assumed that the job involves a great deal of travel so that a car will have to be provided.

After taking away holidays a trainer is available for work for about 220 days a year. This means that this trainer costs

Table 6.1 *Example annual employment cost of a trainer*

Item	Cost (£)
Trainer's salary	22 000
National Insurance	1 600
Benefits	340
Car	5 500
Accommodation and facilities	2 700
Computer and information systems	1 000
Total	33 140

about £150 a day to employ. If the trainer is working at a face-to-face ratio of 50 per cent, the trainer will cost about £300 per training day.

How much does a training course cost?

This is a reasonably easy question to answer for a commercial course. It is simply the advertised price plus anything else such as travel, accommodation and wages that would normally be charged to the training budget.

To answer the same question for an internal course is more difficult. It all depends on:

- the type of training,
- the number of delegates per course,
- whether you train off-site or on your own premises,
- whether you use your own or external trainers,
- whether the course is residential or non-residential.

Not that you should let the difficulty daunt you. Your training plan should give you a good idea of the type and number of courses you need.

While I cannot give you any definitive answers to how much a training course costs, I can give you some examples of cost estimates for a number of different training courses. At least that will give you an approximate idea of how much training courses cost and it will certainly allow you to calculate your own costs.

In the following examples I have made the following assumptions:

- Neither the trainees' wages nor any costs due to lost production have been included.
- When training on your own premises I have not shown a direct cost for the training rooms but have assumed that this is covered by the general overhead which has been included in the cost of the trainer. (This would only reflect part of the cost of the training rooms because every employee's overhead contributes to this cost.)
- When using your own trainers the costs shown are the trainers' wages plus the general overhead plus an allowance to cover the trainers' salaries when they are not training. The same figure is used when the trainers work off-site because the overheads still have to be paid.
- Tax is not included.
- Travelling expenses are not included.

The cheapest classroom training that you can do is to use your own trainer on your own premises. Table 6.2 (Decision Making) is a one-day, on-site workshop and is non-residential. The calculation has been made on the basis of

Table 6.2 *Example of the cost of a Decision Making course*

Decision Making Course

Type of training	Non-residential
Duration (days)	1
Number of students	10
Number of trainers	1
Type of trainer	Own
Location	Off-site
Additional rooms	1
Trainer cost/day	£300
Materials/student	£15
Main room hire/day	£0
Seminar room hire	£0
Accommodation/student	£5
Equipment hire/day	£0
Simulation costs	£0
TOTAL COST	£505
COST/STUDENT	£51
COST/STUDENT/DAY	£51

ten students. This is a fairly typical number for skills
courses that are run to meet individual development needs.

- I have used the figure of £300 per day for the trainer cost.
  This was the figure that we estimated in the section on
  'How much does a trainer cost?'
- The sum of £15 for 'Materials/student' is to cover things
  like copies of the training materials, binders, pens,
  pencils and flip-chart pads.
- No charges are shown for room hire as the cost of the
  room is covered by the general overhead.
- The £5 shown under 'Accommodation/student' only
  needs to cover coffee for breaks and sandwiches for lunch.
- Because it is a very straightforward course no equipment
  needs to be hired, and no expensive simulations are
  required. The cost per student turns out to be just over
  £50, but naturally this would change if the number of
  students is different.

This example, and the others that follow, were worked out
using a spreadsheet on a small computer. The advantage of
doing this is that once you have set up the parameters you
can quickly work out the costs for a wide range of different
courses.

A spreadsheet is also useful because you can 'experiment'
with different numbers of trainers and students (but

keeping the student-to-trainer ratio the same) to see which combination would be the most cost effective. The formulae used for this spreadsheet are given in Appendix 1.

Table 6.3 is very similar to the previous example with the exception that a consultant trainer was used to run the course.

Costs for consultant trainers can vary wildly depending on the type of training and whether the trainers are part of a large consultancy organization or just running their own show. These fees can range from £300 to over £1000 a day! The fee of £500 shown in this example is below the commercial average of £700 a day for management training, but you can still get some really excellent training for around £350.

With this, as in all things, a higher price does not necessarily mean better training. You have to make your own decisions on what you can afford, the type of training, the fees that the type of training normally commands and your own assessment of the consultant.

The quality training shown in Table 6.4 was part of the company's introduction of total quality management. The decision was taken to use the company's own trainers where possible, and it was also decided to use an off-site training facility to avoid monopolizing the company's

Table 6.3   *Example of costs for an Assertiveness at Work course*

Assertiveness at Work Course

Type of training	Non-residential
Duration (days)	1
Number of students	10
Number of trainers	1
Type of trainer	Consultant
Location	On-site
Additional rooms	1
Trainer cost/day	£500
Materials/student	£15
Main room hire/day	£0
Seminar room hire	£0
Accommodation/student	£5
Equipment hire/day	£0
Simulation costs	£0
TOTAL COST	£705
COST/STUDENT	£71
COST/STUDENT/DAY	£71

Table 6.4 *Example of costs for a Quality course*

Quality Training Course

Type of training	Non-residential
Duration (days)	3
Number of students	12
Number of trainers	1
Type of trainer	Own
Location	Off-site
Additional rooms	1
Trainer cost/day	£300
Materials/student	£40
Main room hire/day	£0
Seminar room hire	£50
Accommodation/student	£49
Equipment hire/day	£50
Simulation costs	£0
TOTAL COST	£3 591
COST/STUDENT	£299
COST/STUDENT/DAY	£100

meeting rooms for the two years it would take to train every employee.

- The training centre did not make a direct charge for the main training room but included it in the day charge of £49 per delegate.
- The trainer was counted as a delegate for the purposes of meals etc.

Table 6.5 is a five-day residential course for first-time managers.

- The course runs with 15 to 20 students.
- Two trainers are needed to run the course.
- Four seminar rooms were required because of the number of sub-group exercises.
- The accommodation charge of £120 per student included the main lecture room and audiovisual equipment.
- A computer was hired for £50 per day to analyse the observation data collected during the day.

The final example, Table 6.6, is for a middle managers' course which involves a computer simulation and extensive behavioural observations of the participants. The simulation was specially commissioned by the American parent company to ensure that, as well as giving middle managers practice in running a large organization in

Table 6.5　*Example of costs for a Basics of Management course*

Basics of Management Course

Type of training	Residential
Duration (days)	5
Number of students	20
Number of trainers	2
Type of trainer	Own
Location	Off-site
Additional rooms	4
Trainer cost/day	£300
Materials/student	£50
Main room hire/day	£0
Seminar room hire	£50
Accommodation/student	£120
Equipment hire/day	£50
Simulation costs	£0
TOTAL COST	£18 450
COST/STUDENT	£923
COST/STUDENT/DAY	£185

coalition with other middle managers, the corporation's vision and values were clearly communicated to the participants.

- The simulation costs include licence fees for the simulation, air fares and accommodation costs for the computer simulation consultant.
- The three trainers are the company's own middle management trainer and two facilitators who observe the teams and give feedback throughout the course.
- The equipment costs include the hire of five computers that are needed to run the simulation.

So, the cost of one day's training can vary from £50 to over £300 even when you are arranging the courses yourself. Although this sounds like a great deal of money, it is still cheaper than sending everybody to public courses.

If you only have one or two people to train on a particular topic, then sending people on public courses would be more cost effective. Again, the cost of a day's training varies tremendously.

For example, sending someone to a course, similar to the Decision Making workshop in Table 6.2, at a local management training centre would probably cost something in the region of £150. A one-day non-residential

Table 6.6   *Example of costs for a middle manager's training course*

Middle Manager's Course

Type of training	Residential
Duration (days)	5
Number of students	20
Number of trainers	3
Type of trainer	Own
Location	Off-site
Additional rooms	4
Trainer cost/day	£300
Materials/student	£50
Main room hire/day	£0
Seminar room hire	£50
Accommodation/student	£120
Equipment hire/day	£250
Simulation costs	£9 000
TOTAL COST	£30 550
COST/STUDENT	£1 528
COST/STUDENT/DAY	£306

course with one of the large London-based training organizations would work out at about £250 a day. Residential courses would add at least another £50 to the daily costs.

If a famous business 'guru' has come to town, you could easily sit in a room with a thousand other people and be entertained for the day for the princely sum of £300. Whether these seminars could be considered to be training as defined in this book is debatable. In any case, you might well consider whether you would get a better deal by buying the book or the video!

Rule of thumb: If you want to get a 'wet-finger' estimate of the size of your training budget, work on an average of £150 per student-day of training. This includes the trainer's employment costs but excludes the trainee's employment costs.

> Negotiate and revise budget

You now know how much it will cost to deliver the training demand. I am willing to bet that this figure is larger than your allocated budget. In this case you will need to negotiate a larger budget or agree what training should be left out. Understanding what a reasonable training budget is can help enormously during these negotiations.

How big should a training budget be?

The size of the training budget is one of those perennial questions which will always be difficult to answer. A way of approaching this is to use 'benchmarking'. Benchmarking is a process by which you compare yourself to the best of your competitors with the aim of exceeding or surpassing their performance in all aspects. So, if a company in your sector is doing better than you are, it would be reasonable to assume that its level of training contributed to its business success. Therefore it would be valid to compare its training investment to your own.

Getting to the figures can be difficult. This is not because of any reluctance to disclose the figures (many training managers are only too willing to share ideas and information) but because of a lack of systems to retrieve the information. It will also take time to arrange and make these visits.

You may also find that the figures have been calculated on a different basis to your own. Differences occur over the inclusion or exclusion of items such as employment costs, overheads and loss of production. You will find that most training managers exclude as many items from the cost of training as they can get away with. The most common difference is the inclusion or exclusion of trainees' wages. This is not an insuperable problem because it is possible to make an estimate.

Rule of thumb: Inclusion of wages doubles the cost of training.

To give you an idea of a 'benchmark' for training budgets, successful multinational corporations recommend that each employee should receive five days of training per year. Managers should receive a further five days of management training.

Another guideline given by these companies is that the training budget, exclusive of wages and other employment costs, should be about 2 per cent of the total labour cost.

Most companies fall far short of these recommendations. Typical figures range from half-a-day to three days' training for each employee per year, with annual expenditure on training per employee varying from 0.4 per cent of total labour costs to 1.0 per cent. These figures are averages and the actual figures vary according to region, industry and size of company. Textile, footwear, clothing, construction and distribution industries are to be found at the lower end, and banking, finance, insurance and high-technology industries are to be found at the higher end of the range.

Training costs as low as 20p (excluding wages) a year per employee can be found in textile, footwear and clothing firms with fewer than 50 employees. Other typical spending levels are £4.80 a year in the food, drink and tobacco industry, £3.66 in the timber and wooden furniture sector and £31 in electrical and electronic engineering.

There is a direct relationship between the numbers of employees and level of training expenditure. Large employers have a consistently better record of training and have shown the greatest improvement over time.

The conclusion from this is that a training budget (excluding wages) of 1 per cent of labour costs is a reasonable figure, but this would need to be increased to nearer 2 per cent for 'benchmark' performance.

Finalize training plan

The kinds of information that you need on a training plan are:

- Who is to be trained?
- Why are they to be trained?
- When are they to be trained?
- What course has been identified to meet the training requirement?
- What is/are the occupation(s) of the people who need to be trained?
- How long is the course?
- How much will the training cost?

An example of a training plan is given in Figure 6.3.

Figure 6.4 shows the overall process for finalizing the training plan.

Assess capability to deliver

In some ways this step is just a summary of what you have done before. From 'Determining the workload' you will know how many courses you will need to run, and you will have had the opportunity to 'lobby' for additional resources. You will also know what training locations are available and when they are available. From this information you can tell how much of the training demand you can deliver with your existing resources.

WHEN	COURSE	WHO	NUM	WHY	HOW	WHERE	TRAINER/S	COST
13 December – 15 December	Total Quality	Managers, supervisors, engineers, clerical staff	9	Company-wide programme to support introduction of total quality	Classroom	Studley	PH	465
8 December	Equal Development Opportunities	2nd/3rd level managers, supervisors	11	Awareness training to comply with company policy	Classroom	Marlow	IPD	1036
10 January – 12 January	Total Quality	Line operators	15	Company-wide programme to support introduction of total quality	Classroom	Studley	PH	465
12 January	Noise seminar	Designers and engineers	17	Future skills requirement	Classroom	Engineering Centre of Learning	JD	N/A
17 January	Understanding Personnel	L Fage	1	New appointment	Open learning	Open Learning Centre	RBP	50

Figure 6.3 *An example training plan format*

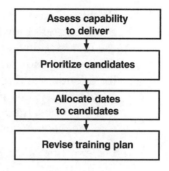

Figure 6.4 *Process for finalizing the training plan*

Prioritize candidates

As a result of capability or budget restrictions you may find that you are unable to meet the training demand. In this case, before you can finalize the training plan you need to prioritize the list of candidates. Another reason for prioritizing candidates is to determine who should attend the early courses on the basis of the urgency and importance of the training. Prioritizing also minimizes the damage that would be done by a budget cut towards the end of the financial year.

These priorities could be decided by the training department, but I feel that the organization should be responsible for its own priorities. One mechanism for doing this is the human resource development committee (HRDC).

Human resource development committees

An HRDC is a committee of peer managers who meet to make, review, validate or approve decisions which are related to the organization or development of people in their own areas.

The training department brings a list of people who have been nominated for the courses which are within the committee's responsibility. As the training department has already validated the demand there should not be many people on the list who obviously should not receive the training. The committee makes a final check on the validity of the list and then concentrates on prioritizing people for the limited number of training places.

Allocate dates to candidates

The timing of a course depends on when skills are required and the availability of training rooms, trainers and trainees.

Public holidays are another complication. Some are easy to avoid because they have a fixed date or because they are the first Monday after a fixed date. Other public holidays are just too 'moveable'. There has been a recent tendency for calendars and diaries not to show public holidays and, if they do, they only give the dates for the current year. This is not very useful if you are trying to put a training plan together six months in advance.

Easter is one of the trickiest holidays. It can catch out even the most wary. Originally Easter was associated by the early Church with the Jewish Passover, but the exact date has been a matter of controversy for centuries. In AD 325 a method of determining the date was agreed at the Council of Nicaea. This definition, which is still used today, is (wait for it):

'The first Sunday after the first full moon after or on the vernal equinox.'

This means that Easter can fall on any Sunday between 22 March and 25 April. No wonder moves are being made to have Easter on a fixed date. In fact, on 15 June 1928, a Bill was passed by the House of Commons which would 'fix' Easter to be the Sunday after the second Saturday in April. This would have the effect of restricting Easter to between 9 April and 15 April. However, this Bill can only take effect after it has been agreed by the World Council of Churches. Assuming that this agreement may be some time in coming, Appendix 2 gives the expected dates for Easter Sunday well into the twenty-first century.

If you train abroad or if you have students coming from abroad, then things are further complicated because of all the different holidays observed in various countries. Don't be too surprised if there are only three weeks in the year when you can avoid a public holiday. To reduce these complications for planning purposes I usually only recognize the public holidays of the country hosting the training course. This may mean that people miss their public holidays when they are travelling, but this is usually far more acceptable than training when the rest of the country is having a day off.

> Revise training plan

Now that the budget has been agreed and the priorities have been decided, the final touches can be made to the plan in readiness to take its part in the company's business plan. The next phase of the training process is to implement the plan.

Respon-sibilities

It is very important that one person has overall responsibility for the training plan. This does not mean to say that all the training has to be delivered or arranged by this person. It means that somebody should be responsible for the quality, timely delivery and cost of the training.

Will your plan be successful?

To a large extent the question of whether your training plan is successful will depend on how over- or under-optimistic you have been about your training department's capability for delivering the plan. Over-optimism leads to rushed preparation, fire-fighting and a general reduction in the quality of the training. Under-optimism means that your trainers will be under-utilized and the cost effectiveness of the training will be diminished. If the under-utilization is extreme, low motivation and lethargy will set in. This also will lead to a reduction in quality.

In most planning there is usually a tendency to err on the side of over-optimism. This syndrome is sometimes known as 'planning for success'. What it really means is that absolutely everything in the plan will go right, there will be no setbacks and it is assumed that all tasks will be completed in the shortest possible time. This, of course, is a recipe for failure. So, rather than 'planning for success', I prefer to 'plan to succeed'. This means that you take a realistic view of your department's capability, have contingency plans and put the emphasis on preventing things from going wrong.

Having a realistic view of the capability of your training process will depend on your experience, but you should also collect data from previous years. This will give you the most accurate estimate of the department's capability. If you are new to managing the training department then the guidelines given in this chapter on student-to-trainer ratios and trainer workload will give you a pretty good starting point.

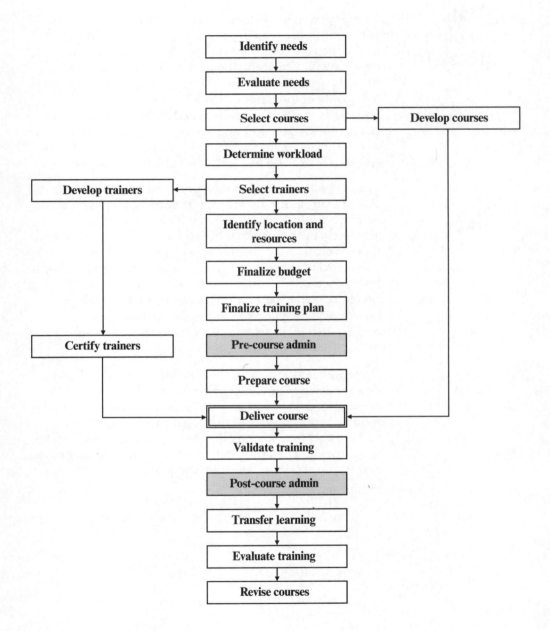

Figure 7.1　*Training administration*

7 Training administration

Training administration – the 'glue' of the training process – is covered by two steps of the training process:

- pre-course administration,
- post-course administration.

Although training and development needs are becoming more complex, you still have to get the right people to the right courses at the right time. This, as anyone who is involved in training administration will know, is much easier said than done. Just filling the course places and keeping the drop-out rates low are major challenges in themselves – let alone meeting the development needs of the individual and the business requirements of the organization.

In addition to all the work that was done in completing the training needs analysis and training plan, there are still myriad details to be seen to:

- booking the trainers,
- booking the rooms,
- booking courses,
- booking accommodation,
- ordering materials, food and coffee,
- notifying delegates of their course places,
- keeping cancelled places to a minimum,
- ensuring delegates are fully prepared,
- getting them to the right course, on the right day and at the right time,
- keeping training records up to date,
- paying the bills.

Pre-course administration

Figure 7.2 shows the pre-course administration process.

> Book location, accommodation, food, refreshments, equipment and trainers

Once you have finalized the training plan you need to book specific dates at your selected training locations. You need

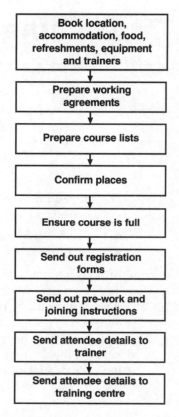

Figure 7.2   *Pre-course administration process*

to do this as early as you can. On-site meeting rooms need to be booked between two and three months ahead. Residential training centres often have their most popular dates booked a year ahead.

When you make the booking, make sure that you have your preferred dates, plus several alternative dates, to hand. You should previously have made sure that the trainers are available on these dates. Confirm the booking in writing and be very specific about your requirements (you should already have the requirements listed on your course specification). Finally, confirm the dates with your trainers.

> Prepare working agreements

If you decide to set up as a profit centre it will be necessary to increase the administrative part of the process to keep track of what is being re-charged to other departments.

- The trainers (or sales staff) let the training administrator know of any future re-chargeable work.

```
┌─────────────────────────────────────────────────────────┐
│                  WORKING AGREEMENT                        │
│                                                           │
│         Supplier                     Customer             │
│      doing the work              paying for the work      │
│   ┌──────────────────────┐    ┌──────────────────────┐    │
│   │ Division: Manufacturing│   │ Division: Manufacturing│  │
│   │ Department: Training   │   │ Department: Training   │  │
│   └──────────────────────┘    └──────────────────────┘    │
│                                                           │
│   Description of work being undertaken                    │
│   ┌──────────────────────────────────────────────────┐   │
│   │ Course: Coaching          Dates: 15–19 June        │  │
│   │ Number of trainers: 2     Sets of materials: 24    │  │
│   └──────────────────────────────────────────────────┘   │
│                                                           │
│   Re-charge                                               │
│   ┌──────────────────────────────────────────────────┐   │
│   │ Amount: £1760.00                                   │  │
│   │ Cost centre: 631270       Payment: Within 30 days  │  │
│   └──────────────────────────────────────────────────┘   │
│                                                           │
│   Supplier approval              Customer approval        │
│   ┌──────────────────────┐    ┌──────────────────────┐    │
│   │ Name:                │    │ Name:                │    │
│   │ Signature:           │    │ Signature:           │    │
│   │ Date:                │    │ Date:                │    │
│   └──────────────────────┘    └──────────────────────┘    │
└─────────────────────────────────────────────────────────┘
```

Figure 7.3   *An example of a working agreement*

- The training administrator draws up a numbered working agreement (see Figure 7.3).
- Signatures to authorize the payment are obtained. A copy of the working agreement is given to the customer and the original is kept on file.

A working agreement is simply a contract between yourself and your paying customer. It should cover what work is going to be done, when it will be done, how much it is going to cost, when the charge is going to be made and who will be paying for the work.

┌─────────────────────────┐
│ Prepare course lists   │
└─────────────────────────┘

The heart of an administration system is the course list. On receipt of the course dates and numbers, the administrator prepares a set of blank course lists. There should be a list for every course. When it is complete it should show:

- the title, date and location of the course,
- the maximum number of places,
- the names and locations of the delegates,
- unfilled places,
- reserve and 'wait-listed' delegates.

Reserves are people who:

- did not get a place on the prioritized list,
- are on a later course but are on standby for an earlier one.

If there are no 'wait-listed' people you can nominate students who are on later courses to be reserves. This also makes it easier for a student to change from one course to another.

There should be only one list for each course and only one person responsible for its maintenance. The list can be a sheet of paper in a book or it can be part of a computerized administration system. Although only one person should own the list, its information should be available to anyone who has a need to know.

I believe in 'charts on walls' or, in this case, 'lists on walls'. Managers of the training process need to know the status of course bookings at any time. They need to do this quickly and without disturbing the course administrator. A wall display showing all the course bookings allows them to do this. The display could be hand-written charts, a computer printout or a whiteboard.

A method that we have found very useful is the 'T-card system'. It is made up from a set of metal frames that have slots cut into them. 'T-shaped' cards fit into the slots. The 'ears' of the 'T' prevent the cards falling through the slots. The trunk of the 'T' is hidden when the card is in the frame. Each card has a space for the name and location of one

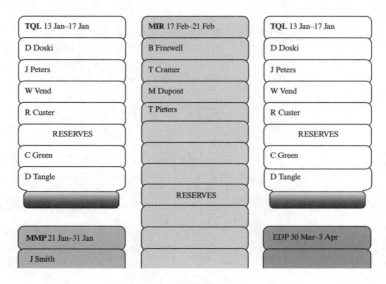

Figure 7.4   *'T-Card system' for displaying course places*

student. Other less frequently used information is shown on the hidden part of the card. Different colours represent the different courses. Details of the system are shown in Figure 7.4.

When the blank course lists have been drawn up the training administrator has to assign candidates to each course. This is most easily done from a priority list or on a first come, first served basis.

The system is more complicated than this in larger companies because the individual organizations will want to decide who goes on which course. In this case the training administrator allocates blocks of places to each organization.

The administrator determines the size of the block from the demand forecast. Figure 7.5 shows how the blocks would be reserved using the 'T-card system'. The allocations for the different organizations or locations are identified by an abbreviation, e.g. LON.

Getting the names right A customer's perception of quality depends on the care the supplier takes to get the details right. The details that matter are those which many suppliers would consider to be trivial.

Misspelling a student's name is a good example of this. Although it might be as trivial as spelling a name with 'tt' instead of 't', the student will form an immediate and unshakeable perception of the course's quality.

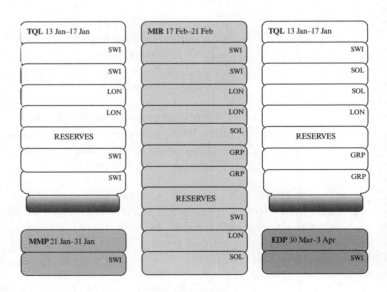

Figure 7.5 *Allocating training places to other parts of the organization*

Getting the names right is not simple. Often we rely on the original training request for the correct spelling of the names. This is the first mistake. Training requests can pass through many hands before they reach the training department. It is also surprising how many managers do not know the correct spelling of their people's names.

A good source of information is the internal telephone directory. Although not infallible, people do complain if their names are not correct in the directory. Often these directories will only have the initials of the forenames and this will make it difficult to discriminate between similarly spelt surnames. It is also difficult if the course is to be run on a first name basis.

Personnel, pensions and payroll records are the most accurate sources. As these records deal with formal names, they are less useful when people prefer to use their middle names or nicknames.

The only foolproof way of getting a name right is to ask the people themselves. This need not be arduous if the administration process makes use of a registration form.

> Confirm places

The next step is to inform the candidates, and their managers, of the course dates. Also inform the local training representatives.

Inform candidates of their places as early as possible so that they can book the dates in their diaries. The reserves should also block out the dates in their diaries.

> Ensure course is full

The training administrator should keep a constant eye on how the course places are being taken up. If anybody drops out, the administrator informs one of the reserves that a place is now available.

Keeping cancellations to a minimum

The main cause of cancelled places is 'pressure of work'. A cancellation fee can help keep cancellations to a minimum. Some people think this is punitive, but this is not the idea behind the fee.

One of the reasons for charging a cancellation fee is that an unfilled place is a wasted opportunity. It reduces the amount of training that can be done because an empty place costs nearly as much as a filled place. At least a cancellation fee will pay for an additional place on another course.

Sometimes you have to cancel a course because there have been too many cancellations. Always consider a cancelled course as a failure because it is a total loss of learning and resource. It might be worth re-charging the entire cost of the cancelled course to the organizations that pulled their people off the course.

Another reason for introducing a cancellation fee is to allow managers to make a business decision on whether they should withdraw their people from a course. For example, a manager might withdraw someone to write an important report. If there is no consequence, many managers would put the report before the course. However, if the cost of cancelling a place is £1500 then managers can make a business decision. Is getting the report written in the next five days worth an expenditure of £1500? If it is, then the right business decision is to withdraw the person from the course.

Having a good reserve system and letting people know the dates well ahead of the course may also help avoid cancellations.

Then there is the question of double booking. The airlines favour this to make sure that there are no empty seats. I am against this practice because we should never promise a customer something we cannot deliver. When I am told that the seat that I have booked and paid for has been taken by somebody else, I am a very unhappy customer. I am not the slightest bit interested in the airline's problems or its utilization rates.

Double booking sets an expectation that cancellations will occur and that we condone cancellations. We should set the expectation that the only reason for a cancellation is a personal emergency.

Always try to book the maximum number of students allowed by the course specification. If there are last-minute cancellations, you should still have the minimum number of students required to run the course successfully.

All the above suggestions for keeping cancellations to a minimum are no substitute for people, and their managers, really wanting the training to happen. People and organizations do what they believe to be important. This underlines the importance of getting the basics right and delivering the training that meets both the individual's and organization's requirements.

> Send out registration forms

The registration form reminds students of their attendance. It also flushes out the people who are unable to attend. Send out the registration forms six weeks before the course is due to start. If you send the forms much earlier there is a chance that the course will be forgotten. Sending the forms much later will not leave enough time to find a replacement if somebody drops out. An example of a registration form is given in Figure 7.6.

The form should have the name of the course as well as its start and end dates. It is always a good idea to put both the date and the day. This helps to identify mistakes and avoid misunderstandings.

Clearly show charges and cancellation fees on the registration form. This will keep future arguments to a

---

COURSE REGISTRATION FORM

PLEASE COMPLETE IN **BLOCK CAPITALS** AND RETURN TO:
The Training Administrator, Group Personnel

COURSE TITLE:

COURSE DATES:

COURSE FEE:

COURSE LOCATION:

NAME:
(As you would like it to appear on a certificate, e.g. Bertram J Bloggs)

NAME:
(As you would like to be called during the course, e.g. Bert Bloggs)

STAFF NUMBER:

JOB TITLE:

GRADE:

ORGANIZATION:

DEPARTMENT:

LOCATION:

ELECTRONIC MAIL ADDRESS:

INTERNAL TELEPHONE NUMBER:

MANAGER'S NAME:

MANAGER'S LOCATION ADDRESS:

MANAGER'S ELECTRONIC MAIL ADDRESS:

MANAGER'S INTERNAL TELEPHONE NUMBER:

COST CENTRE:
(For course cancellation charge – does not apply in a personal emergency)

MANAGER'S SIGNATURE: _____

Figure 7.6   An example of a course registration form

minimum. Also identify the person, or organization, responsible for paying the fee. A budget or cost centre number does this unambiguously.

Advising students of the course venue at this stage allows them to plan their travel arrangements.

It is a good idea to ask for the students' full names as well as the names they would like to use during the course. It is surprising how different these can be. Don't forget to amend the course list if you discover any spelling differences here.

If certificates are awarded it is also a good idea to check how candidates would like their names spelt on the certificates.

It is better not to use the term 'Christian name' as this may cause irritation, if not offence, in multicultural societies. A better term would be 'first name' or 'given name'.

A staff number uniquely identifies a person's personnel or training record. This is the only way to ensure that the right person is coming on the course. Having the staff number also makes it easier to update the training records. It also makes it more likely that changes to the training record will be made after the course.

The job title, grade and organization provide a final opportunity to make a check on the course's suitability for the delegate. This information also allows the trainer to make better decisions about sub-group composition. Many courses work better with diverse sub-groups, other courses require homogeneous sub-groups. Chapter 8 deals with the composition of sub-groups in more detail.

The registration form should also ask whether the delegate has any special dietary, access or other requirements.

Send out pre-work and joining instructions

Send out the pre-work and joining instructions no later than two weeks before the course. Increase this time if the students have to gather information, if there is a lot of reading or if there is a holiday period before the course.

Keep pre-work to a minimum. Never issue pre-work that is not a prerequisite for the course. Similarly, do not go over the pre-work in class. This irritates the students and it also discourages them from completing the evening work.

Joining instructions should cover the following at a minimum:

Internal Memo

From: **A Traynor**   Location: **Newark**   Division: **Human Resources**
                           Extension: **2542**

To: **Attendees**   Location: Date: **25 May**

Facilitation Workshop

Date: Wednesday 16 June–Thursday 17 June
Location: Conference Room 1, Newark
Start: 8.30 am
Finish: 6.00 pm (both days)
Trainer: Andy Traynor

I am writing to confirm your place on the above workshop and to provide you with information on the following:

• The purpose, desired outcomes and agenda of the workshop

• Your pre-workshop assignment

Please find enclosed the above attachments and a copy of *Facilitating for Gold.*

Notes on the pre-work:

• Please read *Facilitating for Gold*

• Summarize the main learning points from the first three chapters

My experience of this workshop is that completion of the pre-work is essential.

The time we have available for useful practical work is limited, so we will need to make the best use of our time between 8.30 and 6.00.

A thorough understanding of the contents of *Facilitating for Gold* will enable us to make best use of this time. I estimate that the pre-work will take you at least three hours.

I look forward to seeing you on 16 June. Please contact me if you have any questions or concerns.

Regards

Andy Traynor

Figure 7.7   An example of a joining instruction letter

- the course title,
- the start and finish dates of the course (use the day as well as the date),
- the location,
- starting and finishing times,
- directions to the venue,
- accommodation arrangements,
- dress code,
- what they have to pay for (e.g. drinks in the bar).

An example of a joining instructions letter is given in Figure 7.7.

Delegates also find it useful to have a booklet which gives additional details about the training centre. These details include:

- meal arrangements,

- message arrangements,
- sport and recreational facilities,
- smoking policy,
- emergency and security procedures,
- local shops and banks.

Electronic mail, if it can handle graphics, is a convenient way of sending out pre-work and joining instructions. Sending large volumes of pre-work electronically gives some electronic mail systems a headache, so check with your system expert before you do so.

> Send attendee details to trainer

During the week before the course starts, the administrator should send the trainer the names of the attendees. This can be either a list or copies of the registration forms. The advantage of using the registration form is that the information is supplied by the trainee and so is less likely to be wrong. It also has information which will help the trainer decide on seating plans and sub-group arrangements.

> Send attendee details to training centre

The week before the course, the administrator should send the hotel or training centre details of the attendees. This list includes the delegates' names, the nights they need accommodation, special requirements and whether they will be needing a meal the night before the course.

Post-course administration

Figure 7.8 shows the details of the post-course administration process.

> Trainer confirms students' attendance

After the course the trainer should give a list of the attendees to the training administrator. Copies of the course critique should also be sent to the administrator.

> Amend training records

Keeping the records accurate and up to date should be the responsibility of one named person. In our organization the responsibility for the records lies with the training administrator. Training administrators can only keep control if they are the only people given authority to access and amend the training records. Even training managers should merely be allowed to read the records!

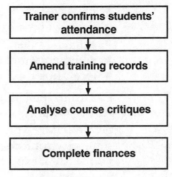

Figure 7.8   Post-course administration process

The training records should be amended as soon as the training administrator receives the confirmed list of attendees from the trainer.

When a person goes on an external course extra precautions should be taken to ensure that the training is recorded. The way to do this is to give the students a critique form to take with them. At the end of the course the student returns the completed form to the administrator. If the students do not return the form, the administrator contacts them to check whether they attended the course. Using a critique form in this way helps to control the quality of external courses.

The risk of incomplete records increases when training has been organized from within another department. It is a good idea to have all training requests pass through the training department and for the training department to hold the budget for all training.

The intention is not to control what functional training should be given to an individual. There is no way that anyone in the training department could have enough knowledge of all the professions to make any kind of sensible judgement. That decision is best left to the individual's manager. What the training department can do is to check whether good value for money is being obtained, co-ordinate separate demands for the same kind of training and ensure that the amount of training received is not being under-reported.

> Analyse course critiques

The course critiques are analysed for trends in the students' perception of the course. Details on how to do this are given in Chapter 10, Validation. Keep the analysis and the critique forms on file for at least three years.

> Complete finances

After the course the administrator should pay the invoices that relate to the course. Re-charges should also be made for unfunded places, cancellations and work that has been completed for other organizations.

Controlling the budget

The amount you have spent needs to be checked at regular intervals so that you can detect deviations from your plan before they become an irrecoverable problem. How often the checks need to be carried out depends on the rate at which you are spending the money. It is unlikely to be more than monthly or less than quarterly. You will also need to check the accuracy of the invoices you receive.

If you find you are overspending you will obviously need to determine what the causes were so that the problems can be avoided in the future. However, do not spend a lot of time beating yourself up. Those problems are in the past and you can do nothing more to prevent them. The problems that you can do something about are in the future and that is where you need to concentrate your efforts. Come up with solutions which will allow you to meet your targets with the budget you have left.

You need especially to look out for the problem of invoices received after the financial year has finished. You need to be able to carry forward an amount of money into the next year to cover these charges, otherwise you will find either that there will be no money to pay for them or that you will have less money to fund the training plan.

Computers and admin- istration

One of the things you will notice as you get more involved in training administration is that the same information keeps on cropping up in different circumstances. This means that the administrator spends a great deal of time typing, and perhaps correcting, the same information. It is precisely these circumstances which lend themselves to the use of computers.

Take the simple example of a student's name. This information appears in all of the following documents:

- course demand lists,
- course place notifications,
- course lists,
- registration forms,
- joining instructions,
- name cards,
- attendance sheets,

- drinks lists,
- sub-group composition,
- observation sheets,
- course certificates.

Not only does the student's name have to be typed or written on every one of these documents, the chances of getting the name wrong are considerably increased.

If the students' names and other information are kept on a computer database, standard letters and documents are produced quickly and accurately.

There are several training administration training programs on the market, but you may find that some of these programs have been developed for a particular industry sector. This makes it even more important that you have a demonstration to make sure that the program is suitable for your needs.

Facilities of a computerized administration system

To help you assess a particular system, the following is a list of facilities that you would expect a computerized administration system to provide:

Programme planning

- Proposed course schedule
- Trainer allocations
- Locations
- Budget allocation
- Schedule revisions

Course booking

- Course place status
- Vacancy details
- Reserves
- Block bookings (without specified student names if required)
- Unconfirmed bookings
- Waiting lists
- Notification letters
- Joining instructions
- Pre-work enclosure list
- Invoicing
- Cancellation fees

Accommodation

- Room allocation
- Daily register of residents' details
- Registration
- Invoicing
- Visitors' accommodation

Course documentation

- Certificates
- Name cards

- Lapel badges
- Delegate lists
- Seating plan
- Groupings
- Drinks lists
- Contact lists

Charging
- Internal re-charges
- Variable invoicing
- Separation of delegate-incurred expenses

Statistics
- Profit/loss statements
- Number of delegates
- Number of delegates per course
- Drop-out rate
- Resource utilization
- Hours of training per employee
- Cost of training per employee
- Cost per course place

Training records
- Employee training record
- Record of bookings, transfers, cancellations and fees
- Enquiry and report facilities
- Training records update

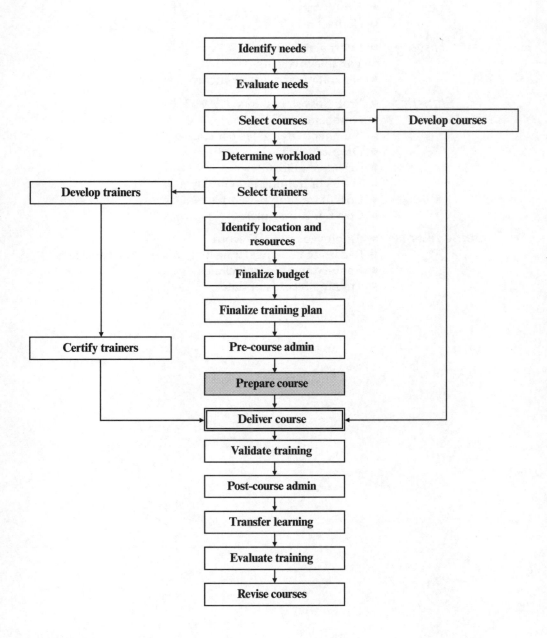

Figure 8.1   *Course preparation*

8 Course preparation

The more effort put into the preparation of a course, the more trouble free that course will be. Always plan to prevent (or at least have a contingency for) what you know could go wrong. As Murphy's law says: what can go wrong will go wrong, and at the worst possible time.

When you are dealing with these known emergencies you will be leaving no time for the hundreds of other gremlins that you didn't know about. Murphy's lesser-known second law – 'Murphy's law of time estimation' – also applies when you are preparing for a course. This law runs as follows: 'To determine the true time that a task will take, you should first make an estimate of the time. Double it and then move it up into the next time unit.'

For example, if you estimate that it will take five minutes to alter a document on your word processor, it will actually take 10 hours. If you estimate that you can write a one-day workshop in three days, it will probably take you six weeks to complete.

There is an inverse relationship between the amount of effort you put into preparation and the perceived difficulty of your job. The harder you work, the easier it seems. It is unfortunate that your strengths will always seem easy, simply because of smooth and professional execution. So don't be surprised when you are asked: 'When are you going to go back to doing a "real" job?'

Figure 8.2 shows that there are two parallel streams of preparation activity. Not only do trainers have to prepare, but students also have to prepare themselves for the course. For this reason this chapter has been divided into two parts: student preparation and trainer preparation.

Student preparation

> Students do pre-work

If you were to take a survey of how many students do their pre-work before arriving at the training centre, you would

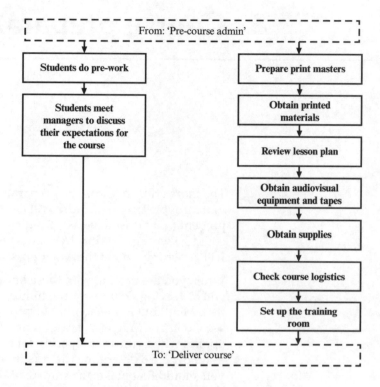

Figure 8.2 *Course preparation activity*

find the proportion to be less than 60 per cent. Of these, more than half would have left the pre-work to the last one or two days before the course.

Given these depressing statistics, it has to be asked why we bother with sending out pre-work. The usual reason for doing pre-work is to shorten the time it takes to do the course. This, by itself, is not a good reason.

However, there are activities which do not make the best use of course time. Examples of these activities are:

- background reading,
- collecting data,
- filling in questionnaires.

As students also vary widely in the time they take to complete these activities, it makes sense to set such tasks as pre-work.

The guidelines given in Figure 8.3 will help to ensure that the pre-work is done in good time.

- Always make sure that the pre-work is essential to the running of the course.

- Give an accurate estimate of how long the pre-work will take.

- Prioritize the pre-work tasks.

- Let the students know why the pre-work is necessary.

- Let them know how the pre-work is to be used.

- Let them know when the pre-work will be used.

Figure 8.3   *Guidelines for setting pre-work*

Students meet managers to discuss expectations for the course

An important part of ensuring that training is effective is to make sure that the participants know why they are on the course, and how they are going to use the training after the course.

You would be right in thinking that this is a bit late in the day for the participants to find out why they are going on a course, but if you need convincing that this step is necessary, try asking your next group of students why they think they are on the course.

A certain proportion will know the developmental reasons for their attendance, but a significant minority will, after a few seconds of stunned silence, come up with some serious and some not so serious responses such as:

- 'I don't know.'
- 'I was told to come.'
- 'I came for the free lunch.'
- 'John couldn't attend, so I'm here as a substitute.'

The right time for people to know why they are on the course is at the time they are nominated. This is part of needs analysis, which is dealt with in detail in Chapter 2.

Once the participants have a clear idea of why they are attending the course they can discuss what their managers will expect them to do differently as a result of the course.

If the course is skills based it is a good idea for the participants and their managers to select tasks that can be practised during, and used for application after, the course.

For example, depending on the course, you could select:

- tasks that need to be delegated,
- projects that need to be managed,
- reports that need to be written,
- problems that need to be solved.

Not only does this concentrate the mind but it also provides a final check as to whether a person needs to come on the course. It is very difficult for people to justify their need for a project management course when they are unable to find any projects they need to manage.

Trainer preparation

> Prepare print masters

Some years ago the idea of the paperless office was much discussed. While there is a great deal of merit in having visions of the future, it will be a long time before people will feel comfortable without a piece of paper in their hands.

Undoubtedly computer technology has made tremendous strides already and will continue to do so. However, a computer's window on the world is still very small (about 200 words compared with an open book's 800). A computer prefers to act like a scroll rather than a book, and when it can be coaxed to turn pages it does so very slowly. It just cannot compete with leafing through a book. Surprisingly, even when supercomputers were used to simulate the speed and capacity of a book, people still found fewer errors in a proofreading experiment.

Computers do not like being folded up like a piece of paper and they always need more batteries and power than a book. Where computers do score is in their ability to search for a given word, present information in different ways (depending on the learning need) and link with other sources of information.

So, it looks as if printed documents (also known as hard copy) will be with us for some time to come. More and more materials will be prepared electronically but they will not be committed to paper until much later in the process. One of the main advantages of having electronic masters is the ease of revision and modification. There is no theoretical reason for the masters to be held in any form other than electronically.

However, electronic storage of information is always susceptible to being lost or corrupted. Surprisingly, a flimsy sheet of paper can take much more damage than an electronic file before it is impossible to retrieve the information. This is why computer users are always being urged to make 'backups' (additional copies) of their work. Although this has the effect of doubling the cost of storing information, it is still far cheaper than losing all your work.

I would still recommend keeping a paper version of your materials – if the worst comes to the worst you can always have the paper document scanned electronically.

In the future you could imagine a small terminal in the training room that prints the material as the students arrive and produces the handouts only when they are needed. In this way there should be no wastage whatsoever.

Currently most people make copies of paper masters that have been produced electronically. With this approach you can still produce the materials even if the whole of the computer system has 'gone down' because you can find a photocopier in nearly every office.

Another disadvantage of using electronic masters is that they may be compatible with only one word-processing program. However, most systems can read simple files on disks that are compatible with the MS-DOS format.

For this reason, it is advisable to keep a copy of your text files in the simplest format possible (usually called an ASCII file) or to make sure that you know how to convert your text to an ASCII file. Appendix 3 gives some tips on how to do this.

Although this seriously restricts what can be done (the document will be unformatted and you will not be able to have combined text and graphics), it does mean that you can access your text from almost any word-processor program. Convertibility between programs and even platforms (Windows and Macintosh, for example) is also becoming more common in the latest systems.

The other possibility is to keep an HTML (HyperText Mark-up Language) version of your documents which can then be read and printed from any computer with browser software. HTML can handle graphics and a wide range of formatting including tables.

Obtain printed materials

Be sure you have enough copies of the training materials ordered, printed or photocopied in time for the course. Ideally you would want the printed materials to arrive at the training venue on the day you set up the training room.

This ideal is risky unless your suppliers are of the highest quality. You will probably arrange for the materials to arrive a couple of days before the course as a contingency measure. What you don't want to do is have your office or storage area cluttered up with training materials months before you need them.

How many copies should you make?

In an ideal world you would have exactly the same number of copies as you have students. Yes, I know that, in spite of all the administrative systems we have put in place, it is still almost impossible to ensure full attendance. I also know that on occasions more students than you expect turn up. Sometimes the materials have defects and you need spare copies to replace them.

Assume that you order two extra sets of materials when you run a workshop for ten people. This may not seem a lot, but you are increasing the cost of the training materials by 20 per cent. This is a significant chunk out of your training budget. You may argue that having additional materials does not really matter as you can always use them on the next course. But when will the next course be? Where will you store the extra materials from this workshop and the materials from the other courses that you run? What happens if you revise the course? Will you have the time to 'rework' all the binders you have in the stores? Can you be certain that all your materials will have the same revision level? Can you ensure that the materials will not get dirty or be damaged while they are being stored? In fact, you might be better off throwing the spare materials away.

This might seem to fly in the face of today's emphasis on conservation and recycling, but it need not. First, concentrate on ensuring that the right number of people turn up to the course. Then have a really close look at the materials. Check to see whether they have been printed simplex or duplex (single sided or double sided). If the materials can be printed double sided, there will be a 40 to 50 per cent saving on paper usage and cost.

See if the materials can be printed on recycled paper. Rather than throwing excess materials in the bin, remove the sheets from their binders and arrange for a recycling company to come and collect the waste paper. Return the binders to your printer or copy centre or hold on to them yourself if you must. At least you can re-use them quickly because they will hold the materials for any of your courses.

If you have the impression by now that I am not in favour

of storing anything, you would be pretty close to the truth. This might seem counter-intuitive, because trainers find a certain amount of comfort in having large stacks of materials. They also have difficulty in throwing anything away – you never know when you might need it.

The trouble with storage is that you can never have enough of it. The quantity of materials you have to store will always increase to exceed the amount of storage space you have available. Good systems have to be in place to help you find the items you require and there is always a danger of damage to the materials while they are in storage.

Storage is very expensive. Ask your financial director how much a square metre of floor space costs your company. This money is locked up and doesn't earn a penny. The stored materials do not add any value to the business until they are removed from the store and are either used or sold.

Just-in-time materials

This concept of stock-less operation is called 'just in time' (JIT). It is one of the many ideas that have come over from Japan. The idea is that you train your suppliers to deliver the materials you need at the exact time you need to use them. So, in a supermarket, a new delivery of toothpaste would arrive just as the last tube was being taken from the shelf. Not only do your suppliers have to be well disciplined but you also have to be able to use the materials immediately. If you don't you will be buried under a mountain of stock.

This mode of operation seems to be a little strange to some British suppliers...

> Komatsu, the Japanese manufacturer of bulldozers, took over a factory that used to be owned by the Caterpillar company in the north of England. In keeping with European Union regulations, the Japanese needed to use a proportion of locally manufactured parts in their bulldozers. One such part was the fuel tank. Komatsu asked one supplier when it could supply the tanks.
> 'Next week,' came the reply.
> 'No, you don't understand,' said the Japanese, 'Which day? Which hour?'

This does not mean that this kind of approach cannot be transferred to a Western culture. Neither does it mean that everyone has to do exercises and sing the company song before starting work in the morning. There are many Marks & Spencer stores in England that now have first-floor sales areas where their stockrooms used to be.

Applying the 'just-in-time' approach to training means that you have the materials copied just before you run the training courses. In this way you will only have to find storage space for about four boxes at a time. The clever bit about this is that it is your printer who has to find storage space for the paper and binder stocks.

Even if you copy the materials yourself, it is still better to print off what you need when you need it, because there is less money tied up in the raw materials than there would be in the final product.

There is always the temptation to order a whole year's worth of materials because you can get a better discount from the printer. Think very carefully before you do this. Are your training materials so good and your company so stable that the materials will need no revision during the coming year? It can be very expensive throwing away or 'reworking' half a year's stock.

Also compare the savings that you make with the discount with what you would have to pay for extra storage. Estimate the cost of stocktaking and damaged materials. Ask what else you do with the money that you have 'invested' in the stock.

Storing the masters
All this assumes that you have a superb system for storing, revising and retrieving the masters for your course materials. One of the first decisions you are going to have to make is where the masters are going to be stored. The major options are: with the trainers, with the training administrator or at the printers. The final choice of location depends on the security of the masters and the stability of the course. If a course is stable and run many times a year, it can be very convenient to store the masters at the printers and just make a phone call when you need some more copies printed.

Electronic storage of masters is becoming more practical. When copies of the materials are required the 'digital masters' are retrieved and the materials are printed off. It is also possible to create a document on a personal computer and send it electronically to a printer for printing and finishing.

Take the security of your paper and electronic print masters very seriously. Masters should be kept in file boxes, and the file boxes should be in a locked cupboard or stored on shelves in a secure room.

With paper masters, every handout or sub-section of a student binder should be in its own plastic document wallet. The wallet should have a label that identifies the master and gives instructions to the printer on how the masters should be copied and bound (see Figure 8.4).

```
Module 7  Visions
• Single-sided
• 4-hole punched
• White, recycled, A4
```

Figure 8.4 *Example of labelling a print master*

This should be sufficient for relatively simple jobs. For more complex materials you should also provide a printer's dummy. A printer's dummy is an example of the finished materials so the printers can see exactly how they should produce the materials.

When you have the handouts printed, ask the printer to put them straight into the file you will be using during the course. It will not take the printer much longer, but it will save you a great deal of time and bother.

Handouts v binder material When I see a course that has a large number of handouts, I start to suspect that the course is becoming out of date (it is easier to produce another handout than to revise and reprint the student binder). This suspicion becomes stronger if the trainer does not make full use of the materials that are in the binder.

Review lesson plan

Make sure that you have enough time to prepare yourself for teaching the course. If you are unfamiliar with a course this can take as much as a day of preparation for each hour of trainer presentation. For a familiar five-day course you may need no more than a hour to skim through the lesson plan.

No matter how familiar you are with the course, don't be tempted to miss out this step entirely. Familiarizing yourself with the course provides reminders of all the things you need to do before and during the course. Over-confidence leads to disaster.

Obtain audiovisual equipment and tapes

The course specification should have a complete list of all the audiovisual equipment required for the course, such as:

- overhead projectors,
- flip-chart stands,
- cassette recorders,
- video recorders and cameras,
- computers and printers.

The technical specifications need to be very precise when you order or hire video equipment and computers. There are many different standards and, if the equipment supplied is not compatible with your tapes or software, you will not be able to use it.

The most common standards are VHS for video and IBM-PC for personal computers. I say standards, but even these popular 'standards' come with several different variations.

Overhead projectors　Most training locations supply an overhead projector as standard. There is not a lot to choose between the different makes of overhead projector, although there are a couple of features you should look out for. The first is an internal spare bulb that can be changed quickly and easily by turning a handle. The second is the ability to 'tune' the optics so that blue and orange colour fringes can be eliminated.

Flip-chart stands　Check to make sure that your transparency frames do not foul the column that supports the optics head.

Flip-chart stands seem to be innocuous pieces of equipment, but like deckchairs they can be a trap for the unwary. Here are some pointers to look out for:

Height　Check that the stand can be adjusted for both your shortest and tallest trainer.

Weight　If you have to transport your own flip-chart stands check the weight and bulk of the unextended stand.

Rigidity　Check that the stand does not move around or bend when you write on it.

Method for holding the paper　Look at the method for retaining the paper. This can be a spring-loaded jaw or a pair of pegs. Check that the pegs align with the holes in your flip-chart paper. (Why on earth isn't there a standard for this?) Many of these stands have screw-on clamps which make it difficult to tear off sheets cleanly.

The jaw method of retaining the paper has the advantage of not needing a particular spacing for the holes but it does not retain the pad so well. Some methods use a retaining bar and I have seen it take two people to insert the pad – one to hold the bar out of the way and the other to push the pad into the jaws!

Check to see whether the stand will retain single sheets, either by themselves or in addition to the pad. This feature is essential if you have sub-groups reporting back to the main classroom.

Video recorders

VHS is the most popular format for video recorders but unfortunately it comes in three different standards: PAL, NTSC and SECAM depending on which country you happen to be in. (See the glossary at the end of the book for an explanation of these abbreviations.) Most European countries use PAL. France and the former Soviet Union use SECAM and the USA uses NTSC.

Unless you can buy or hire a multistandard video recorder which will play PAL, SECAM and NTSC, you will need to make sure that all your tapes are in the same format as the machine you are using. You can check this by looking at the label on the cassette or its case. If this doesn't give you a clue, try playing the tape on your machine. A different standard usually runs the soundtrack at a different speed and produces horizontal lines on the screen.

If your tapes are in a different standard you will need to get them converted by one of the specialist video houses. A word of warning – if your tapes are commercially produced, you will be breaching the owner's copyright if you have the tape converted. So when you buy a commercial tape make sure that it is in the standard you will be using.

The introduction of camcorders, i.e. portable video cameras with a built-in video recorder, has led to two new formats (plus variations): VHS-C and 8 mm. This isn't a problem if you are using video feedback that will be played back during the course, but it will cause problems if you want to give the students their tapes to take away with them. The VHS-C cassette has to be either copied on to a standard tape or clipped into a special carrier before it can be viewed on a domestic video recorder. 8 mm has to be copied on to a standard tape.

A more recent introduction is Super VHS. This has a cassette the same size as an ordinary VHS cassette. It achieves higher definition and picture quality. An ordinary VHS cassette can be played on a Super VHS machine, but a Super VHS cassette cannot be played on a standard VHS machine.

Modern video recorders are very reliable and the most common problems are dirty recording heads and damaged connecting leads. The main symptom of a dirty recording head is a snowy type of interference. This problem can easily be solved using a head-cleaning videocassette. Scotch makes a version that has a pre-recorded video message and audio tone. The cassette is played until the tone is clear and the message is legible.

Audiocassette recorders

Until the introduction of digital tapes, audiocassettes followed a universal standard. There is not a great deal to choose between the different makes of recorder. It is convenient if the recorders have an internal microphone. A battery indicator light gives an early warning of flat batteries and helps you prevent spoilt recordings.

The most common problems you are likely to get with an audiocassette recorder are:

- flat batteries,
- dirty recording head,
- dirty pinch roller and capstan.

If you have poor sound quality always check the batteries first, and then use a head-cleaning cassette. If the problem persists refer to the user manual and clean the capstan and pinch roller. The capstan is a metal spindle that turns to drive the tape. The pinch roller is a rubber wheel that holds the tape against the capstan.

Computers and printers

The situation with computers is very similar to the video situation – different standards with many variations. Always check that your computer matches the system requirements that are printed on the software packaging or in the software manual. Appendix 4 explains computer specifications in more detail.

Obtain supplies

Supplies are consumables that you need for every course – and they have a habit of running out just when you need them. The trainers' checklists in Appendix 7 suggest a selection of supplies that you will need during a course. It is a good idea to use the checklists before each course to ensure that you have a sufficient stock of supplies.

Fixings

It is almost certain that every course you run will involve displaying charts or posters on a wall. If you are working in a purpose-built training room, there should be rails or pin-boards on the wall for displaying posters and charts. It is an unwritten law of the universe that you will always need more display area than is provided.

Masking tape is the best all-round method for sticking charts to walls. If you are careful, it should not pull off paint and wallpaper when it is removed.

Blu-tack is less satisfactory as it can be difficult to remove without leaving a mark. A tip for removing Blu-tack is to roll up another piece into a small ball, and then roll it over the wall so that it picks up the pieces like a snowball. Doing it this way decreases the likelihood of removing any paint.

Flip-chart pads

The holes in the flip-chart pads should align with the pegs on your flip-chart stand. Some pads are stapled together which makes it difficult to tear off single sheets. One way to overcome this problem is to buy pads with perforations, but this leaves the holes behind which makes it difficult to put the sheets back on the stand. Another way around this problem is to buy pads which are held together by an adhesive rather like a note pad.

A square grid printed faintly on the sheets helps you draw diagrams and keeps your writing on the level. Considering the amount of flip-chart paper that is thrown away at the end of a course, it is a good idea to buy pads made of recycled paper.

Flip-chart pens

Flip-chart pens or markers come in several different types: spirit based, water based and dry wipe. Black and blue are the best colours for reading from the back of the room, while red and orange are the worst. The pens' tips should have a minimum width of 5 mm.

Whiteboards should only be written on with dry-wipe pens. Too many whiteboards have been spoilt by writing on them with permanent pens. If this should happen to you, all is not lost because there are several methods that you can use for removing the marks.

First there are proprietary sprays. If you do not have any of these around when you need them, you can try Snopake or White-out thinners. An effective but lengthy method is to scribble over the permanent marks with a dry-wipe pen. Then use a dry cloth to remove both marks together. As this method is also quite tiring it teaches you not to use the wrong pens on the board. You could also try using a plastic eraser to remove the marks.

The manufacturers of some water-based pens say that these pens can be used on whiteboards. This is true but the marks have to be removed with a damp cloth. This can turn out to be a somewhat messy operation.

Some trainers take the preventive route by banning all pens except dry-wipe pens. The only problem with this is that dry-wipe pens are not very suitable for flip-chart work. The lines they draw are not broad enough to be read from the back of the class and the colours are not strong enough.

I prefer to use water-based pens for flip-chart work. If you do accidentally use them on a whiteboard, it is not too much hassle to remove the marks using a damp cloth. Another advantage of using water-based pens is that you do not spend all day breathing in fumes.

Throw flip-chart pens away as soon as they dry out. Repeatedly picking up the same exhausted pen is a frequent source of frustration. No amount of shaking or standing the pens on their heads will get more than a few extra minutes of life out of them. It is advisable to bring your own flip-chart pens with you as it is amazing the number of training locations that provide exhausted or unsuitable pens.

Overhead projector pens

There are two types of overhead projector pens: permanent and water soluble. Pens with a medium tip are generally the most useful thickness but you might find you will also need a set of fine pens. Red, blue, green and black stand out well on the slides.

Use permanent pens if you don't want them to rub off. Water-soluble pens are useful if you want to make corrections as you go along, or if you want to re-use the slide, but cleaning the slide can be a bit messy. Another option is to place a blank transparency on top and write on that with a permanent pen. I prefer to use this method even when I am using water-soluble pens because it is easier to throw the top sheet away than clean up the prepared transparency.

Whatever you do don't get the two types of pen mixed up. Buy pens that allow you to see easily which is which. For example, Staedtler makes permanent pens with a black barrel and water-soluble pens with a grey barrel. Permanent pens do not always write very well on some types of transparency material. If you have a problem, try a water-based pen instead.

Check course logistics

Some courses are more complex than others when it comes to preparation. Scanning through the lesson plan will remind you of what you have to do.

Course specifications

When you provide many different courses it is always difficult to remember exactly what has to be prepared. The kind of details you need to remember are:

- How many syndicate rooms does this course need?
- For what time should we order the coffee?
- What are the start and end times?
- What videos do we need to bring along?

This problem is compounded when you are training away from your home base. You may have to rely on somebody else to prepare the classroom and to make all the necessary arrangements.

As suggested above, you could scan through the lesson plan to answer these questions, but you need to attend to the logistics long before you start in-depth preparation of your sessions. The answer to this problem is to have a specification for every course you run. A course specification only needs to be two or three pages long at the most. Figure 8.5 gives an example.

**Project Management
Course Specification**

Venue
On-site

Duration
2 days

Times
8.30 am–4.30 pm

Rooms
1 training room
1 breakout room

Dress
Normal business

Breaks*
Coffee and biscuits 8.15 am,
10.00 am and 2.45 pm

Lunch
12.30

Audiovisual equipment
OHP + screen*
VHS player* + monitor* + leads*
2 flip-chart stands* (one in each room)
Fresh flip-chart pads*
Fresh flip-chart pens*

No. of attendees
6–12 (min–max) †
8–10 optimum

Date
Wednesday and Thursday
14 and 15 October

Trainer
Andy Traynor

Pre-work (at least 1 week in advance)
Discussion with manager
Selection of suitable project
Completion of 'terms of reference'

Student materials
1 per student

Slides
1 set

Handouts
1 set

Charts
1 set

Video and audio tapes
'Managing Projects' (VHS format)

Computer equipment
PC with Microsoft Project Version 4

Course description
Project Management is a two-day workshop. The first day concentrates on skill building (including critical path analysis and Gantt charting) and covers:

- What is a project?
- Video
- What is project management?
- Stages of a project
- An example project
- Team leading
- A case study

* To be arranged by local administrator

† Course cannot run below minimum number

Figure 8.5 An example of a course specification

I usually send my customers a copy of the course specification as soon as the course dates have been confirmed. You will notice that I give a detailed specification for computer and video equipment. This is to avoid the embarrassment of not being able to play the tape, or run the software, on your customer's equipment.

I also make it clear what equipment I will be bringing and what equipment needs to be supplied by the customer.

Fred's list The course specification is sufficient for short, straightforward courses. Courses that have complex logistics need the equivalent of a course specification, or a checklist, for every module. This checklist details the items that you need to prepare or obtain for the module.

We call the complete set of checklists 'Fred's list' in honour of a colleague of ours whose lists helped us through the logistics of a particularly tricky course.

You will still need a course specification for the course's general requirements. 'Fred's lists' are for trainers' eyes only – they are far too detailed to be of use to the customer.

Seating plans When students ask me how I choose the seating plan, they are disappointed to learn the simplicity of the criteria. (They suspect that I use some complex psychological method.)

There are two basic approaches for seating people on a course. The first is to have them sitting next to somebody they know, the second is to have them sitting next to somebody they don't know.

One of the advantages of a residential course is the opportunity to meet people with different backgrounds. To foster this, I often arrange the seating so the students sit next to someone they don't know.

If the course intends to do team building I would have the participants sitting in their natural work groups. This situation is one of the few times that I would have managers and their people in the same group. Having a manager and one of that manager's people on the same course can make it difficult for both parties to act naturally.

Before you can make any decisions on the seating plan you have to have some data on the students. The registration forms have information which indicates whether the participants know each other. Look to see whether they work in the same location, are part of the same organization or work for the same manager. Although this approach is no substitute for local knowledge, it does have a high success rate. In the absence of these data, a random seating plan is as good as any other. Having the students sit in sub-group order helps the logistics (and the trainer's memory) considerably.

If you know the students well enough, you may be able to avoid potentially explosive seating combinations. In practice, predicting the interactions of 20 people is just too difficult to get right. Having too many criteria makes it impossible to find a suitable seating plan.

Sub-group assignments The guideline of keeping the criteria simple also applies to sub-group assignments.

The composition of the sub-groups should match the objectives of the course. Diverse groups allow people to learn about other departments. Homogeneous groups permit delegates to share knowledge and experience.

Be careful if you use criteria of race, age, gender, religion or nationality for creating diverse sub-groups. You must have a good training reason for using these criteria. 'Let's split the girls up' is not a good reason. Giving people practice in managing diversity is a better reason. The safest selection criteria are experience, location and the delegate's job.

Mixing the sub-groups A good way to have a nervous breakdown is to change the sub-group composition for each exercise. For an even better nervous breakdown, try arranging the groups so that every student has worked with every other student by the end of the course.

After a few hours of brain bashing, you will come to the conclusion that only certain combinations of course and group size provide a complete solution.

Set up the training room

Setting up a training room, checking the equipment, putting up posters and laying out materials for 20 people can take up to two hours. If the training room is free the day or evening before, I would recommend that you set up the room then – you still have all night to sort out any problems. There is nothing worse than trying to get the video recorder to work as the students are walking in. Even better, get somebody you can trust to set up the room for you.

Of course, having somebody set up the training room for you does not work this well every time. It takes several years to build up this kind of relationship with a supplier and you would not normally want to cut things this fine – even with your most trusted supplier. However, this

One of the training venues I had been using for many years understood my requirements so well that they would lay out the training room exactly as I would have done it myself.

This arrangement worked well for both parties. I did not have to book the room for the night before to lay out the materials, and the squash club could run profit-making functions into the early hours of the morning. All I had to do was give the manager a copy of the course specification and a drawing of the room layout, and make sure that all the materials were on site.

To give you an idea of how well this worked, I was once delayed by a traffic jam and arrived at the training venue just as a team-building event was due to start. Everybody had helped themselves to coffee, as indicated by a notice on the flip-chart stand, and I was able to walk in, switch on the overhead projector and say, 'Good morning and welcome to ...'

episode does underline the importance of having the training room set up as early as possible.

Room layout Check that the tables and chairs are positioned so that everybody will get a clear view of you, the video monitor and the overhead projection screen. Walk round the room and look at the layout from every student's viewpoint.

If you want to encourage discussion between the participants, avoid having students sitting with their backs to each other.

Arranging the tables in a 'U' shape is a good layout, but don't get stuck with only one kind of layout. Try out some more interesting variations. You could use groups of tables, or you could have gaps to allow for freedom of movement in the room.

Audiovisual equipment Checking the audiovisual equipment should be one of the first things you do when you are setting up a classroom. This will give you the maximum time to have the equipment replaced, or repaired, in the event of a major malfunction.

Check the sound level of the video, but bear in mind that the soundtrack will appear louder in an empty room than in a room full of sound-absorbing students.

After you have checked the sound and picture, wind the tape back to the beginning. Cue the tape by playing it up to where you want it to start. You may have to experiment with the exact stopping point as some recorders do not restart at the same place as they were stopped. This should help you avoid showing a blank screen and the copyright notice. The few seconds that it takes for the video recorder to get itself started will give you time to turn out the lights.

People do not have a great tolerance for video recorders
that do not show a picture as soon as you press the play
button. It must be due to a basic mistrust of technology.

> This basic mistrust of technology was once demonstrated to me when
> I lent a videotape to a group of senior managers. The video was in two
> parts, separated by a period when the screen faded to blue.
> When the first part had finished the managers assumed that the video
> recorder had gone wrong so they switched it off. Later I timed the
> interval between the two sections of the tape. It was six seconds!

If you are using audiocassette recorders, make a test
recording on every recorder to make sure that the batteries
aren't flat and that the recorders are recording properly.

Switch on the overhead projector and, using one of your
own slides, check that the projector is in focus and the
optics are clean.

I usually remove the clamp from the flip-chart stand and
remove the staples and cover sheets from the flip-chart pads
to make it easier to tear off sheets. I also attach short lengths
of masking tape lightly to the back of the stand so that I have
tape readily available when I want to stick sheets on the wall.

Student materials Lay the students' binders, pens, pencils and erasers on the
tables. Use this opportunity to do a final quality check on
the materials.

Locate the handouts in an easily accessible place. If you are
training in your permanent location, consider investing in a
wheeled set of hanging files. If portability is your first
consideration then a card 'concertina' expanding file will be
more convenient.

Name plates Name plates are essential for the first few hours of the
course so that you are able to learn the students' names.
There are several types of name plates. The simplest is a
sheet of A4 card folded along its length.

Other types use individual plastic letters. The letters have
small pegs on the back so that you can press them into the
holes on the name plate. Not only do these seem to take for
ever to prepare, but they are also an irresistible temptation
for the members of 'Anagrams Anonymous'. You will be
amazed at their creativity. You will never catch them in the
act because they strike when you least expect it.

A popular type of name plate has a shiny, white surface
which can be written on with dry-wipe pens. These are
quick to prepare but the name can only be written on one
side and the lettering is easily smudged.

One of the best name plates that I have seen was made in-house by one of the large conference centres. The base was a piece of wooden moulding that had a groove cut into its length. A name card was held by a piece of perspex (Plexiglas) that had been bent in half along its length. The perspex fitted into the groove on the wooden moulding.

You can get the students to fill in their own names as part of the warm-up. This helps if you are not confident of who is going to turn up. It also helps if you are not sure whether the names are spelt correctly.

My preference is to have the names already filled in on the name plate. This allows you to decide where the students will sit and it also makes the students feel expected when they walk in.

Consider having the names printed or written on both sides of the name plate. If you can withstand the jokes about students not knowing their own names, you will be able to see who the students are from any part of the room. This also helps participants find their places when they first walk into the training room.

> There was one incident that convinced me that the names should be on both sides of the name plate. This was a course when some of the students knew everybody's names except those of the people they were sitting next to.

Prepare syndicate rooms

Visit each syndicate room to make sure that the correct wall charts have been put up. Check the lighting. See if there is enough flip-chart paper. Test the felt-tip markers to make sure they have not dried out.

Check that there are sufficient supplies of other consumables such as masking tape, 'Post-its' and drawing pins.

Trainer materials

Finally, set out the trainer's guide and transparencies at the front of the room. Check that all the supplies you need are close to hand. Make sure that you have the latest version of the student materials in front of you. In this way you will not have the embarrassment of referring to the wrong page or to an exercise that was removed three courses ago.

Final check

When you think you have finished setting up the room, take a few moments to look round the room and check that everything is in place. Make sure that you know:

- where the keys are kept,
- where the light switches are,
- how to control the heating,

- how to open and close the windows and the window blinds.

Then turn off all the equipment at the wall, turn off the lights and lock up the room.

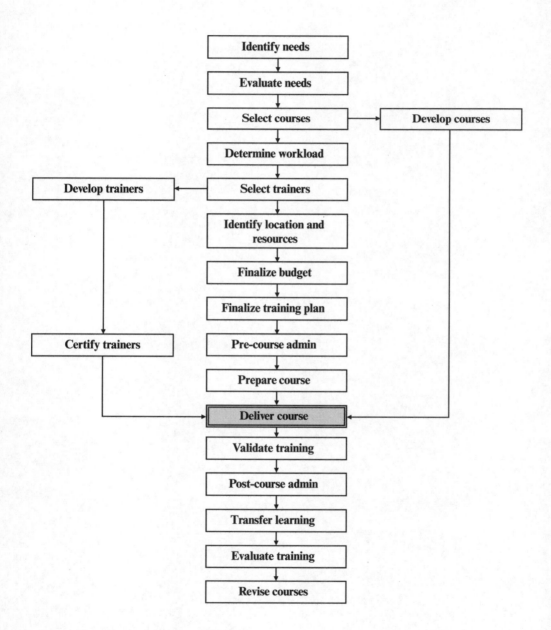

Figure 9.1   *Delivering the course*

9 Delivering the course

This chapter deals with the pivotal step of the training process:

- course delivery.

Because the thrust of this book is about managing the training process, rather than learning to be a trainer, the emphasis in this chapter is on the principles associated with the steps of the delivery process plus consideration of the following three topics:

- open and distance learning,
- training in other languages and cultures,
- the use of computers in the classroom.

Course delivery process

The process for delivering a course is shown in Figure 9.2.

Pre-course check

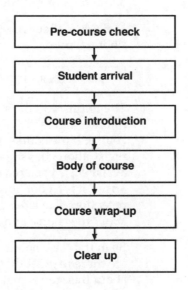

Figure 9.2 *Course delivery process*

Although you should already have prepared for the course, it is worth taking a few minutes to check that the following are still in order:

- lights,
- materials,
- overhead projector,
- video equipment.

The telephone　You will already have asked reception not to put calls through to the training room. As an extra precaution I would also recommend diverting calls or disconnecting the telephone from the socket – it's amazing how persuasive some people can be in trying to contact their staff.

If you forget to disconnect the telephone and it rings while you are in the middle of a session, keep talking while you walk over and disconnect it. Ignore the gasps of amazement – some people are psychologically unable to resist the call of a ringing telephone.

Spike Milligan once drew a cartoon of a person who was tied, head to toe, to a post. The only part of this person's anatomy you could see was an arm sticking out between the coils of rope.
A ringing telephone was placed on a pedestal that was just out of reach of the arm. The cartoon was titled: 'Chinese telephone torture'.

Don't worry about the call being urgent – they seldom are and most things can wait for 45 minutes. If it were a matter of life or death you can be sure somebody will ring the alarm bells or run round to the classroom.

Make sure that everyone has turned off their mobile phones and pagers.

Student arrival

The impression the students get within the first few minutes can make all the difference to the success of the course. If the course is residential it is essential that registration goes smoothly and the rooms are clean and available. If you are not able to meet the students as they arrive, it is a good idea to leave a welcoming letter at reception. The letter can also include additional details about the course and its location.

Be in the classroom before the first student arrives so you are there to greet them. The important thing to remember about this step is that you want the students to feel comfortable about the training.

Coffee　　One way to help students feel comfortable when they arrive is to have coffee and other beverages available. This gives people a chance to relax and get to know each other.

Dress code　　The participants' joining instructions will have advised them of the type of clothes that are expected to be worn on the course. The recommended level of clothing is part of the course design and depends on where the course is being run and its training philosophy.

Some training courses are designed to have a more informal atmosphere so students are asked to dress casually. No matter what is put in the joining instructions, it is another one of those unwritten laws of the universe that at least one of the students will turn up wearing a business suit and will continue to wear a suit for the rest of the week. There is no problem with this as long as the person feels comfortable with what they are wearing.

Whatever the dress code, the cardinal rule is that trainers should not be dressed very differently from the students. If a trainer adopts a dress style which is the same as the most casually dressed student the more smartly dressed may start to feel uncomfortable, and vice versa. The best approach is for trainers to try to adopt a level of dress that is at about the middle of the students' range.

As the students arrive you will get a feeling for the level of dress. If the level of dress is biased towards one end of the dress code, you can subtly amend your own clothes. This can be as simple as removing a jacket.

Late arrivals　　Always insist that training courses start on time. I know there is a temptation to wait for late arrivals, but there is no way of knowing how long they are going to be or whether they are going to turn up at all. Waiting punishes the people who have been punctual and destroys the momentum that is required at the start of a course. Five minutes lost at the start of a course often translates into an hour's loss by the end.

When the latecomers arrive do not make any fuss and do not stop the course to bring them up to speed. Making a fuss just disrupts the course and could lead to strained relationships. Stopping to summarize communicates that it is all right to be late because the trainer will always bring you up to date.

Course introduction

The course introduction is for:

- you to get to know the students,
- the students to get to know you,
- the students to get to know each other,
- communication of the course aims and structure,
- validating student expectations,
- understanding the reasons for their being on the course,
- communicating course logistics.

If there are two trainers consider having both take part in the introduction as the co-trainer is often disadvantaged by having to sit at the back of the room.

Student introductions The standard course introduction is to go round the room and have the students give a brief autobiography to include:

- name,
- job title,
- organization,
- how long they have been in the company,
- hobbies and interests.

This method is somewhat pedestrian and it often does not achieve what it sets out to achieve. People stop listening when they are thinking about what they are going to say. In a class of 20 this introduction can take up to an hour and each person is only directly involved for 5 per cent of the time. Here are some variations you might like to try:

Claim to fame Most people have met somebody famous or have done something excitingly different – and most people like talking about it. So instead of getting people to do the standard introduction you could get them to relate their claims to fame.

The best claims to fame don't always come out during the course introduction, so have another session later in the course if you want to hear the juicier stories.

Paired interviews Some people do not like talking about themselves in front of the class. In this type of introduction the students pair up with the person they know the least and interview each other. After about 15 minutes each person reports back with a brief biography of their partner.

A picture of my life Provide coloured pens and sheets of A3 drawing paper. Ask the students to draw a picture of who they are and what they do – both at work and at home. You will find that, despite initial reservations, people really get into this exercise and disclose more about themselves.

Catch ball Instead of going round the class in order, throw a ball (preferably a soft one) at one of the students who does the first introduction. This student then throws the ball to someone else. Challenge the class to complete the introductions without throwing the ball to the same person twice. It's probably a good idea to clear the coffee cups before starting this exercise.

Mugshot Ask the students to bring either a passport photograph or their identity badges to the course. Display the photographs on the wall along with an identifying letter (identity badges should have the names taped over). Supply each student with a list of identifying letters. The objective of the exercise is to write the names of the other students against their identifying letters on the list. This involves matching the people in the room with the photographs on the wall. When approached, people should only give their name. They should not say which photograph is theirs. The worse the photographs, the better this exercise works.

Course logistics

At the beginning of the course only communicate the most vital course logistics – very little is remembered of an information dump. Obviously emergency procedures have to be given at the beginning, but coffee, lunch and dinner arrangements etc. can be communicated as they are needed.

Training course or assessment centre?

It is important to communicate whether a report will be sent back to participants' managers.

Unfortunately, some managers expect training courses to assess how good their people are at doing their current job. Apart from the fact that this would be an abdication of one of the manager's prime responsibilities, training courses are not adept at and, for that matter, not designed for carrying out this task. The environment on a training course is very different to the work environment. If it were exactly the same, there would be no difference between formal training and on-the-job training. This difference in environment means that observed behaviour on a training course would not necessarily be a good predictor of behaviour back at work. The ability of a trainer to assess accurately 20 individuals on a week's course would also have to be questioned. It can take up to two days just to learn all the names!

If you assume that each student participates equally and that the exercises where behaviour could be assessed make up 60 per cent of the course, you would only have a maximum of one hour's data on each person – not a very efficient assessment process.

If the students work in sub-groups, it is the other members of the sub-group who are in the best position to make an assessment of a particular individual. I am not suggesting that students should 'spy' on their fellow students, but feedback from other class members can, if handled sensitively, be very powerful.

At this point it is worth pointing out the difference between training courses and assessment centres. Training courses are for increasing knowledge and the development of new skills. Assessment centres are designed to measure or assess existing skills.

In the development of new skills it is essential for a person to be able to reveal their current deficiencies and then to experiment and make mistakes without being punished. It follows that confidentiality is an essential part of a training course. If a person feels that everything they do is being reported back to the organization or their manager, they will be very reluctant to participate openly and the training will not be as effective.

With assessment centres the question of confidentiality does not arise because everybody knows and accepts that a report will be made.

It might be argued that it is essential for a person's manager to know whether that person has reached the desired standard in the skills that they were expected to learn. This is a reasonable request and complying with it need not be inconsistent with the principles outlined above.

With self-paced training a person could in theory remain on the course, receiving additional coaching until the desired level of expertise is attained. Thus completion of the course itself would be the indicator of meeting the required standards.

Of course, it would not be good business practice to allow everybody to stay on a course for an indefinite period, so most courses would have an upper limit on their duration. Above this limit it would be uneconomic to continue the training to completion. It would also probably indicate that the student concerned would be very unlikely to make the grade under any circumstances.

You should consider any failure to complete a course as an error in the process and a waste of your limited training resources. The cause of this kind of error is usually in the selection of the student for the course or the selection of the course for the student.

With trainer-paced courses the completion of the course does not give an indication of the standard reached. So how can the organization be assured that individuals have attained the necessary standards without reducing the effectiveness of the training? The answer is to make a distinction between the parts of the course where learning is taking place and the parts of the course which are assessed.

You would have to make this distinction very clear at the beginning of the course and assure the students that no reports are being made during the teaching phase. Under no circumstances should you imply that there is confidentiality where in fact there is none. Not only would this breach professional etiquette but it would quickly lose you all trust and ruin your reputation.

Expectations and reasons for being on the course

Take some time to understand what people are expecting from the course and why they are attending it. You will find that the course will meet most of their expectations, but there will also be some expectations that the course was not designed to meet. Be open about the extent to which the course will meet your students' expectations.

Understanding the reasons for the students being on the course will help you deal with any emotional issues that might arise during the course.

Course aims and structure

Describe the aims and structure of the course. Explain what will happen and when it will happen. Describe the linkages between the components. Take the opportunity to emphasize the parts of the course which best meet the students' expectations.

I like to have the course agenda displayed as a poster. (For a five-day course this could be as big as three sheets of flip-chart paper.) The students can then refer to this at any time to check where they are, and you can use it to reinforce the course structure as you move between components.

| Body of course |

I believe that there are four main phases in teaching:

- presentation,
- assimilation,
- practice,
- testing.

Presentation

In this context presentation has a broader meaning than is usually understood. It includes any method that presents the skills and facts to the students. So, in addition to the trainer standing up and making a presentation, it would include videos, demonstrations, text and self-discovery exercises.

We learn through all of our senses (the usual five plus sense of movement and rhythm) yet training makes limited use of only two – auditory and visual. Try introducing more colour into your presentations. Have exercises that involve movement and people doing things with their hands. Try presenting a lesson to the accompaniment of baroque music.

Assimilation   After presenting the facts or demonstrating the skills, the temptation is to go straight on to the next set of facts without allowing an opportunity for learning to take place. Even if the skills are practised and the knowledge tested, the assimilation phase is often left out. By assimilation we mean the process by which students are given 'space' to make sense of what they have just heard and seen. It also allows them to fit this new knowledge into their existing model of the world. If the training proceeds before they have had this opportunity, it will be building on a very shaky foundation.

This opportunity can be provided in several ways. You can give students a couple of minutes to reflect, you can get them to jot down a few notes or you can give them the opportunity to ask questions. If you presented the lesson accompanied by music, you could replay the music to help the assimilation.

Practice   The third phase is for the students to practise what they have been taught. Practice is an absolutely essential part of learning, so it is a pity that it is the first thing to go when the pressure is on to reduce the duration of a training course. The only circumstance under which you should permit the removal of practice from a course is when you can guarantee that supervised practice will occur immediately after the course has finished.

There is sometimes a debate on whether skills should be practised on case studies or on real examples. The argument against case studies is that it is difficult to transfer the skills being practised outside the classroom because case studies are too simple and unrealistic. The argument against using real projects is that they are too complex and students will spend far too much energy on the detail to the exclusion of learning the concepts. As with many 'either/or' arguments, the answer is not 'either/or' but 'both'.

The process I prefer for courses where the appropriate teaching style is more 'directed' rather than 'discovery' is as follows:

- First give an overview of the concept, principle or process.
- Then demonstrate using a simple example. Don't worry if the example seems trivial – this will allow some humour to creep in and will make demonstration of the skills all the more memorable. You could use a 'tea-making' example for teaching critical path analysis and have a heated discussion about whether the milk should be poured into the cup before or after the tea!
- After the simple example the students can then practise on a more complex case study.
- Finally students can be coached on an example from their own work area. If they have any difficulties they can always refer back to the example and the case study.

Testing   Finally you should check the extent to which the students have learnt the skills and knowledge desired. This could be a formal pencil-and-paper test but more effective, and incidentally less intimidating, is observing the student applying the learning to a project or their own work. This also increases the chances of the learning being transferred back into the business.

Another way of testing is for the trainer to ask questions in class. Even better, get the students to write the questions themselves.

Instead of using 'pose then pounce' or 'pounce then pose' techniques, try asking the question as you throw a ball to the student ('throw and pose' technique). Throwing the ball is not a gimmick: the idea is to distract the student's conscious attention so that the answer can surface from the subconscious. Suitable balls for this exercise are either sponge balls or balls that have been constructed from strands of rubber in the fashion of a pompom.

> I had some reservations about this 'catch ball' technique until I used it to help teach a dozen theories of motivation and leadership.
>
> The lesson included a videotape which described all 12 theories in 40 minutes, obviously too much to take in at one go. I had already split up the tape with discussions about the theories and I also had 'stills' from the video on display. Despite this it was still apparent that the students had little confidence that they could remember the theories. I decided it might be worthwhile using the 'catch ball' technique.
>
> After showing the video I called a coffee break to allow the students to relax and to give some time for assimilation. When they returned I named one of the theories and threw the ball to one of the students. Immediately the student explained what the theory meant. The ball was thrown from student to student, each student explaining one theory and naming another. To our amazement all the theories were accurately recalled.

Accelerated learning

Some of the techniques described above were first developed in 1956 at the University of Sofia by the Bulgarian psychologist Dr Georgi Lozanov. Colin Rose's book *Accelerated Learning* describes these techniques in more detail.

Level of intervention

One of the things that is most difficult to get right is the trainer's level of intervention in what students are doing. If students have problems with a task it is best if they can sort these problems out for themselves. If they can't sort out the problems for themselves, and the trainer does not intervene, they begin to flounder and lose confidence. If the trainer intervenes too early the students become frustrated and learn little. In extreme cases the trainer ends up doing the task for the student.

The best way to find the correct level of intervention is to identify the parts of the course where students are likely to have a problem, monitor them regularly and discreetly and err slightly towards intervening too late. (It is difficult to tell whether you intervened too early, because students might have got on to the right track if you had not intervened.)

The pudding shift

The pudding shift, otherwise known as the graveyard shift, is the session immediately following the lunch break. It is difficult to gain students' attention and concentration because they would rather be having a siesta. For this reason it is best to avoid presentations immediately after lunch and to have a participative exercise instead.

> Course wrap-up

During the course wrap-up you should:

- check whether the students' expectations have been met,
- have students complete a course feedback form,
- thank students for their participation and share your feelings about the course,
- if applicable, distribute certificates,
- stand near the door to say goodbye as students leave.

> At the end of every course, a colleague of mine used to say that this was the best course he had ever taught and that he loved all the students!
> The amazing thing about this was that he really believed it – and, more amazingly, so did the class!

> Clear up

The end of a course can be somewhat of an anticlimax, but you need to pack up the materials and take a few minutes to think about how the course went.

- Ask yourself how you feel. If you feel down, consider what you could do better next time. If you're on a high, the course might have gone exceedingly well, but check to make sure you were not playing games with the class. Feeling quietly pleased is a good position to be in.
- Look through the feedback forms. More on this in Chapter 10, Validation.
- Clear up the rubbish so the cleaners can distinguish between what should be thrown away and what should be kept.
- Pack up the materials that need to be sent back to the store.
- Send a copy of the feedback and attendance sheets to the appropriate administrator.

Open and distance learning

In Chapter 5 we discussed the 'Identify location and resources' step of the training process. An important part of this step is determining the type of learning environment. We usually think of the classroom when we talk about the learning environment. Although the classroom provides a controlled environment, it is usually more expensive and does not provide the flexibility of 'open learning' or 'distance learning'.

The terms 'open learning' and 'distance learning' are used interchangeably as this type of learning is usually 'open' to everyone (as with the Open University) and is carried out 'at a distance' from the creators of the material.

Learning can be at home, in the workplace or in specially adapted rooms known as 'learning centres'. These rooms are resource centres and usually come equipped with books, audiotapes, videotapes and computer programs – along with all the necessary equipment. The great advantage of open learning is that students can study at their own pace and at their own convenience.

The need, selection, development, administration and delivery of open learning courses should be given the same attention as any other type of course. If this is not done, the use of open learning will become haphazard and random and will fall into disrepute. The training process described in this book applies to open learning as much as it does to any other kind of learning. The principles of managing the training process remain the same.

Learning centres have variable success rates – some are over-booked while others are hardly utilized. Our research into learning centres has identified a number of factors which are critical to the success of the centre:

- Qualified tutors should be available all the time the centre is open.
- The centre should be open when it is needed, which means that it will probably have to be open both early morning and late evening.
- The centre should be located where it is easily accessible.
- The room should be purpose built.
- The organization's culture must be supportive of learning – people should not feel uncomfortable because they are perceived to be not working when they are in the centre.
- The programmes should be integrated with the organization's other learning activities.
- The materials and equipment must be up to date.

The need for a 'physical' learning centre will decrease as computers and access to the Internet become more widespread. This will enable time-of-need and point-of-need training.

Training in foreign languages and cultures

Unfortunately the British and Americans tend not to be fluent in any language other than their own. When compared to other nationalities such as the Scandinavians and the Dutch, we are truly put to shame. English is spoken widely, and few other countries speak Swedish or Dutch, which makes it easier for them and harder for us. However, this is not a good excuse for refusing to learn even a few words of someone else's language.

Whatever our level of linguistic expertise, most of us still have a problem when faced with a class of foreign students. Of course, the problem is minimized if all your students speak excellent English. In this case you should be able to train the course in the same way as you do for English students.

It is often assumed that the course should be presented in the students' own language and that all the materials should be translated if their command of English is less than perfect. Luckily, there are several levels of translation that can be applied and this can be critical when time or cost is at a premium. Table 9.1 shows the relationship between the level of translation and the standard of English.

When the language ability is very high, all the presentations, materials and exercises can be in English.

Where the command of the language is not perfect, but still very good, the presentation and materials can be in English

Table 9.1 *Relationship between language ability and the level of translation*

Ability	Exercises	Presentations	Materials
High	English	English	English
Good	Own language	English	English
Fair	Own language	Own language	English
Poor	Own language	Own language	Own language

but participants should be allowed to complete the exercises in their own language. It is still possible to use English trainers. If a translator is not available they will have to rely on their knowledge of the course, body language and tone of voice to understand what is going on. This is not as difficult as it might seem, because a trainer who has intimate knowledge of the exercises will soon be aware of any problems or difficulties. It is then just a matter of intervening and asking what is happening.

The next level is to have the course presented in the students' own language but still have the written materials in English. Videotapes would have to be over-dubbed. When producing videotapes that are to be used in other countries, make sure that the master has two soundtracks. The first track should have the music and sound effects, and the second track should have all the language-sensitive material. This makes dubbing in the foreign language very much easier.

As language ability decreases, more and more of the materials will need to be translated. However, not all of the written materials will need to be translated unless the language ability is very low. Articles and explanations of concepts would need to be translated but simple instructions may not have to be.

Some companies use a restricted vocabulary to write the service manuals for their engineers so that the time and cost of translation can be avoided. The author is asked to use only a vocabulary of about a thousand of the most commonly used words. The words in this vocabulary are carefully chosen and they are also defined to have only one meaning. If the user is taught the same vocabulary, the service manual can be understood by somebody with a minimal knowledge of the language.

The use of restricted vocabulary also makes computer-assisted translation easier. Computer translation has come a long way since the time when a computer translated 'The spirit is strong but the flesh is weak' into the Russian equivalent of 'The vodka is good but the meat is bad.'

However, the best use of computer-assisted translation is still as a translator's tool where the original and the computer's translation are shown side by side on the screen. The translator is then able to make adjustments for grammar, idiom and style.

Culture is a thin but very important veneer that you must be careful not to scratch. People from different cultures are basically the same and respond in the same way. However, make sure that you understand their basic customs and show an interest and willingness to learn the differences between your cultures.

> The meaning of Chinese words changes with the pitch of the voice. A word spoken at a low pitch has a completely different meaning to the same word spoken at a higher pitch.
>
> I was aware of this, but I was still caught out when I was teaching a class of Singaporeans.
>
> I was asking Tng a question but I didn't seem to be getting his attention. To make matters worse the whole class burst out laughing.
>
> When I asked what the problem was, they told me that I had been saying 'Tng' with a high instead of low pitch – I had been telling him to go home!

One of the most surprising things I have experienced is that there is often less difference between people of different nationalities who share the same profession than between people of the same nationality who work in different professions. The cultural differences between companies, between civilians and service people and between sales, marketing and manufacturing are fascinating and can easily catch out the unwary.

The use of computers in the classroom

A computer is a tool – no more, no less. Computers are excellent for running business simulations and can be used to present instructional material. There is some very effective computer-based training around.

When it comes to training, a computer is just one medium among many. Just like any other media, it is appropriate in some situations and less appropriate in others. The most effective training is usually a skilful blend of different media.

One of the most effective uses of computers is as part of a simulation. In this way it is possible to give students very fast feedback on their decisions and actions.

A computer is not only a useful tool for training but it can also bring large increases in the productivity of course administration. If you find yourself spending a great deal of time on a repetitive task, consider whether a computer could give you a productivity increase.

Interpersonal skills observations involve categorizing people's verbal behaviour. Every time a person speaks the observer records the interaction as one of 11 types of behaviour.

After the observation the observer has to perform a series of calculations which involve working out each type of behaviour as a percentage of the person's total number of behaviours. With a class of 20 this would typically require two hours to complete – even with the assistance of a calculator. Not only did this take up a lot of the trainer's time, but it also meant that the students would often not receive feedback until the following day.

This time was cut in half by using a computer with a spreadsheet program. After the observation, data were fed into the computer and the spreadsheet performed the calculations.

The time was cut even more dramatically by using a hand-held computer to record the observations directly. The hand-held computer was then connected to a printer and the students received a copy of their feedback within five minutes of the last observation being made!

The following is a checklist of activities where a computer may improve your productivity:

- preparing course materials,
- revising course materials,
- record keeping,
- presenting slides,
- making slides,
- course administration (delegate lists, sub-group composition, certificate lists, certificates),
- interactive skills observation and analysis,
- business simulations,
- analysis and presentation of course statistics,
- communication via electronic mail,
- access to centralized training records,
- computer-assisted learning,
- computer-assisted personality testing,
- computer-assisted career counselling.

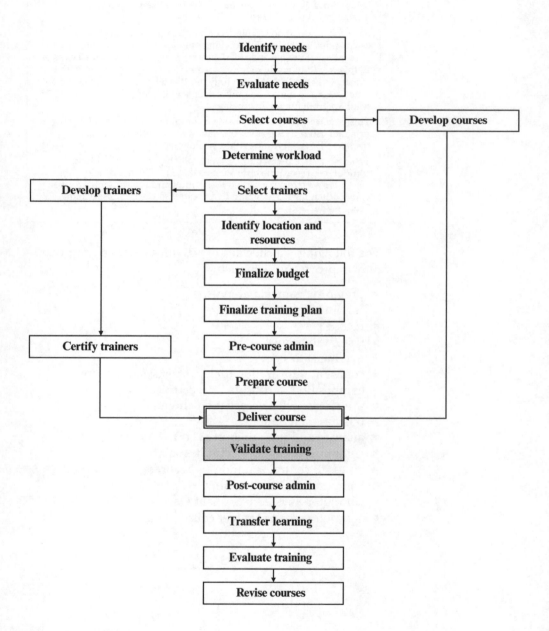

Figure 10.1 *Validation*

10 Validation

Validation ensures that the course meets, and continues to meet, the aims and objectives you set for it. Validation is an internal check on the course. The following is the definition of validation used in this book:

> 'A systematic analysis of data and judgemental information, collected during a training course, which is designed to ascertain whether the course achieved its specified aims and objectives.'

See Chapter 12 for a discussion of other definitions of validation and their origins.

Validation does not give you information on whether the students will use the skills and knowledge. It does not tell you whether those skills and knowledge contribute anything towards business effectiveness. Neither does it tell you whether the objectives were the right ones. I might have learned how to play Rachmaninov's Third Piano Concerto, but will this help me manage a group of sales people when I get back to work? It is evaluation, the subject of Chapter 12, that deals with these questions.

Validation is critical because learning cannot be transferred to the business unless the course has met its objectives. Good validation systems not only show us what needs to be changed, but they also prevent us from changing a course for change's sake. They give an early warning of a drift in the course's standards before disaster occurs.

Validation tells us whether the course has had the desired effect. There are two perspectives from which this can be done:

- validating against students' perceptions and comments,
- validating against the course objectives.

Validating against students' perceptions and comments

The first way of seeing whether the course meets its objectives is from the student's point of view. This is often done using end-of-course feedback sheets (sometimes called 'happiness sheets') comprising a questionnaire and a comments section. The questionnaire asks how much the students liked the course, whether they thought they met its objectives and what they thought of the trainer. It also gives them an opportunity to make open-ended comments.

Figure 10.2 is an example of a typical feedback sheet. Most courses have the students complete a feedback sheet at the end of the course.

The sheet could also have a space for the student's name. Some people feel that feedback should be anonymous so the students do not feel restricted in what they say. Unfortunately, anonymous sheets prevent you from

---

MANAGEMENT DEVELOPMENT PROGRAMME FEEDBACK

Directions: Please take a few minutes to respond to these statements about the course as a *whole* by placing a tick in the appropriate box to the right of the statement. Space has been provided for any comments you may wish to add.

1. Relevance of workshop to your present job

☐ ☐ ☐ ☐ ☐
Very low   Very high

Comments: _____

_____

_____

2. Confidence in your ability to use the skills

☐ ☐ ☐ ☐ ☐
Very low   Very high

Comments: _____

_____

_____

3. Usefulness of the pre-work

☐ ☐ ☐ ☐ ☐
Not useful   Very useful

Comments: _____

_____

_____

4. Overall satisfaction with the course

☐ ☐ ☐ ☐ ☐
Very low   Very high

Comments: _____

_____

_____

5. One change for improving the workshop _____

_____

_____

6. One thing that should be left as it is _____

_____

_____

THANK YOU FOR YOUR ASSISTANCE

Figure 10.2   An example of a course feedback sheet

following up comments to get further clarification or to clear up confusion.

Explain why it is useful to have the names on the feedback sheet, but let students know that their feedback can be anonymous if they prefer. If you have established trust and credibility during the course, the students should not feel that they need to withhold their names.

Feedback sheets give you data on how the students feel at the end of the course but they do not tell you much about how they felt along the way. This interim information is essential for continually improving the training process. Avoid giving the students a questionnaire to complete after every course module. You might get away with this on a pilot course, but under other circumstances students will rapidly become frustrated.

A technique we use is to provide the students with some cards. They write their comments on one of the cards whenever they feel they have some feedback to give us. A 'postbox' is provided at the back of the class. Once a day we review the comments, give responses to the feedback and, where necessary, clear up any misunderstandings.

Halo effect The danger with perceptions is that many different factors affect them. The halo effect occurs when a student judges a course in terms of a general feeling.

For example, some trainers are skilled performers: they have the class eating out of their hands and they get amazingly good feedback regardless of how good or indifferent the course. The students are judging the course in terms of how they feel about the trainer.

The halo effect also works in a negative direction. Students might give a course poor feedback because they had a bad experience on a previous course or because they have had problems with accommodation, or they might not feel too good because of a hangover.

Despite this weakness, student feedback is essential. Student perception is one of the main factors that determine a course's credibility and reputation. Students' perceptions and comments are also essential for identifying unexpected effects of the training.

Validating against course objectives

The second way of looking at validation is to see whether the students met the course objectives. Checking whether the students have met the objectives can be either very difficult or very easy – it all depends on the quality of the objectives.

If the objectives meet the guidelines given in Chapter 3 you will know what behaviours to test, the conditions under which to test them and the standards that should be reached.

Testing or measuring is implicit in validating a course against its objectives. A test does not have to be a 'pencil-and-paper' examination. It can just as easily be an observed exercise where the trainer records the results on a check chart.

Reacting to validation data

Be careful how you respond to validation data. It is all too easy either to over-react or to rationalize problems away. Over-reaction can make the course lurch from one extreme to the other.

For example, an exercise receives some negative feedback the first time you run a course, so you decide to remove the exercise. The next time you run the course you find that important objectives are not being met, so you reinstate the exercise. On the third course the exercise receives more negative feedback...

This is similar to the way some people adjust the thermostat on a radiator. The room is feeling a bit cold so they turn the control up to maximum. After a while they start feeling hot, so they turn the control down to minimum. When the temperature drops...

They end up spending all day adjusting the thermostat while the room temperature lurches from being too hot to being too cold and back again. What they should do is to let the system settle down and then only make minor adjustments when necessary. What is needed is a light touch on the steering wheel.

Although one piece of feedback may not mean anything by itself, you shouldn't fall into the trap of ignoring obvious problems. Too often we avoid taking action because we don't have a 'statistically significant' sample.

How many plane crashes does it take for us to think that something is wrong? How many times does a coin have to come up heads before we suspect that something is wrong with the coin?

Deciding when to react to feedback or a deviation is a difficult judgement to make. After the course has run several times you will begin to get a feeling for what is normal and what is a significant variation. The decision then depends on the intuition and experience of the individual trainer.

The problem is similar to deciding when to adjust a machine on a manufacturing line. Until the introduction of total quality management the decision was either left to the operator's experience, or nothing was done until the product drifted out of specification. The entire batch would then have to be inspected and as much as 20 per cent of production would have to be scrapped.

Statistical process control

Manufacturing's answer to the problem of when to react to deviations is statistical process control (SPC). The idea behind SPC is to collect data on a process and to determine statistically what is an abnormal variation. These data are displayed on a control chart. The chart has two lines drawn on it, an upper control limit (UCL) and a lower control limit (LCL).

The operator takes no corrective action as long as the data remain between the two control limits. If the data go outside the limits, the operator knows that the variation is significant and requires action before the process goes out of specification. This is similar to a driver turning the steering wheel before the car hits the kerb.

Figure 10.3 gives an example of a control chart for the manufacture of a 10 mm disc whose diameter should be a minimum of 9.90 mm and a maximum of 10.10 mm.

Applying SPC to training validation

When you are running the same course many times (such as when you are training every employee) it is possible to collect sufficient data to apply statistical process control to the validation results.

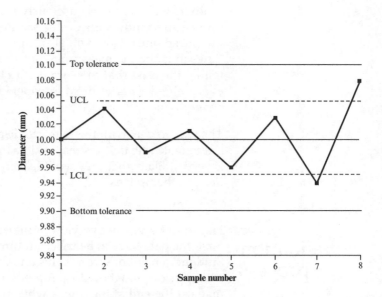

Figure 10.3 *An example of a control chart*

SPC allows you to detect changes in course performance that are due to significant causes. It allows you to check whether different trainers are training to the same standard. It shows you whether the course, in its present form, is capable of meeting the objectives. Most importantly, it gives you an indication of when you should not make changes to a course.

Measure-ments versus targets

The very act of measurement has the effect of distorting the data. If we are sensitive in how we carry out validation, the distortion should not make a significant difference to the results. Measurements are essential for maintaining the quality of our courses and we should do everything to reduce distortion to a minimum.

A single measurement is not a complete description of a course's quality. At best it is a prime indicator. The number of measurements required to define a course's quality completely would be so large as to make any validation system unwieldy. This need not be a problem as long as we take care in choosing the measurements we use as prime indicators of quality.

However, the moment a measure is turned into a target, the underlying weaknesses of using a few measures become apparent. (This is compounded when a trainer's pay increase is directly linked to measures such as student perception of 'trainer effectiveness'.)

Trainers will soon subconsciously realize which unmeasured indicators can be sacrificed to improve the measured ones. They will also learn which are the best times to make the measurements – such as just after telling the class that they are the best students they have ever trained, or after breaking open a bottle of champagne!

The way to deal with this is not to dispense with measures but to make the trainers responsible for their own quality. It is very unlikely that they would, even subconsciously, deceive themselves.

The validation process

Figure 10.4 gives an overview of the validation process. First, the data have to be collected throughout the course. Student perceptions, comments and test results are examples of validation data. A preliminary assessment is made at the end of the course while the course and any incidents are still fresh in the trainer's mind.

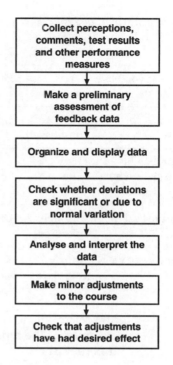

Collect perceptions, comments, test results and other performance measures

Make a preliminary assessment of feedback data

Organize and display data

Check whether deviations are significant or due to normal variation

Analyse and interpret the data

Make minor adjustments to the course

Check that adjustments have had desired effect

Figure 10.4 *The validation process*

Next the data have to be organized and displayed so that you can see whether the feedback is significant or just due to natural variation.

Then the data have to be analysed and interpreted so that you can determine the causes of the significant variations. Once you have understood the causes it is possible to make changes to the course. Always make the smallest adjustment consistent with solving the problem.

The next time you run the course you will need to go through the process of collecting and analysing the data again. This is to check that the changes have had the desired effect.

The remainder of this chapter looks at these steps of the validation process in detail.

> Collect perceptions, comments, test results and other performance measures

When collecting perceptions, it is common practice to use feedback forms with five-point response scales. The responses can be numbered or labelled. These responses have different labels depending on the type of questions asked.

Table 10.1 summarizes some of the more common labels

Table 10.1 *Relationship of different labels to a five-point response scale*

		1	2	3	4	5
A	What opinion do you have of the course?	Very poor	Poor	Fair	Good	Very good
B	How satisfied are you with the course?	Very unsatisfied	Unsatisfied	Fairly satisfied	Satisfied	Very satisfied
C	What is the probability of you using the skills when you go back to work?	Very low	Low	Medium	High	Very high
D	The course is the best that I have been on.	Strongly disagree	Disagree	Neutral	Agree	Strongly agree
E	The length of the course is...	Much too short	Too short	Just right	Too long	Much too long

and relates them to the five-point scale. It also gives examples of the types of questions that are used with the different labels.

Deciding whether '1' represents 'very poor' or 'very good' is an arbitrary decision. I use the convention of 'higher equals better'. The exception to this is the last scale in Table 10.1 where the best score is '3'. ('The length of the course is just right.') Be careful when you are using this type of scale as it can lead to confusion.

I also have the numbers run from '1' on the left-hand side to '5' on the right-hand side. This corresponds to the way Western cultures read across the page. It also makes it easier to use graphical display programs because this is the convention used for graphs.

Always stick to the same convention, no matter which one you decide to choose. And always give a warning when the scale changes.

People have varying views of what 'very poor', 'poor', 'fair', 'good' and 'very good' mean. You get better consistency when it is possible to frame the feedback questions in the form of opposites (see Figure 10.5).

This format produces a five-point continuum and the students put an 'X' in the column that best matches their perception.

The wording used in Figure 10.5 can have the effect of grouping the responses around the middle because of the 'all or nothing' nature of the extremes. One way round this

	1	2	3	4	5	
The trainer did not give satisfactory answers to any of my questions by the end of the course				X		The trainer gave satisfactory answers to all of my questions by the end of the course

Figure 10.5   Using opposites as feedback questions

is to use a seven-point scale so that there is more definition around the middle.

Another way to avoid the problem is to reword the questions. Don't make the wording too weak as this will introduce the problem of inconsistent definition. Figure 10.6 gives an example of weak wording. (Does 'most' mean 50 per cent, 60 per cent, 80 per cent?) Figure 10.7 gives a better example.

Make sure that the questions used are true opposites, otherwise this format becomes very confusing. Figure 10.8 gives an example of questions that are not true opposites.

Collecting comments   Although feedback on a five-point scale is easy to display and analyse, it is restrictive because you will only get feedback on what you asked for. Neither does an 'X' on a

	1	2	3	4	5	
The trainer gave unsatisfactory answers to most of my questions			X			The trainer gave satisfactory answers to most of my questions

Figure 10.6   Example of weak wording for feedback questions

	1	2	3	4	5	
I was very unsatisfied with the answers the trainer gave to my questions				X		I was very satisfied with the answers the trainer gave to my questions

Figure 10.7   Example of stronger wording for feedback questions

	1	2	3	4	5	
The trainer did not seem to care about whether I learnt		?		?		The trainer was very enthusiastic about the course

Figure 10.8   Example of questions that are not true opposites

one-to-five scale give many clues to the reasons for the response. To overcome this each question should have a comments space for the students to expand on their responses.

Also leave space at the end of the questionnaire for general comments that will give you feedback on aspects you never dreamt about when you were designing the questionnaire. Good questions for stimulating a response are:

- Is there anything that should be left out of the course?
- Is there anything that should be put into the course?
- What should be kept as it is?
- Is there anything that should be done differently?
- Any other comments?

Collecting test results

A test is a measure of whether the behavioural objectives of the course have been met. As tests should be based firmly on the objectives, your students should not be surprised by any of the test items.

The objectives should also give you the required standard, as in:

'Given a list of 20 countries you will be able to name the capital cities of at least 17 of those countries.'

Many objectives, like the one above, lend themselves to written tests. Others are best tested through observations of practical exercises. The observations can then be compared to a checklist or a profile of behaviours.

Good trainers constantly validate their training by asking questions as they go along. Although you can get a feeling for the level of knowledge by noting how many students want to answer, you can only be sure that one person knows the correct answer. One way round this is to ask multiple choice questions. Each student is given a device which allows them to display their response to the question. A Cosford responder (see Figure 10.9) is an example of such a device.

A Cosford responder is a cardboard, plastic or wooden tetrahedron which has a different colour on each of its faces. Each colour represents a different response to the question. In this way the trainer can easily see which students responded correctly.

Collecting other performance measures

Look out for other indicators which tell you how the course is progressing and whether you need to make any adjustments as you go along. Be as creative as you can. The following are some suggestions.

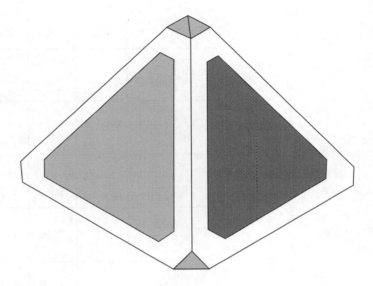

Figure 10.9 *A Cosford responder*

Room tidiness   A colleague of mine once said that the success of a course is inversely proportional to the tidiness of the room. At first I thought this was just a clever remark, but the more I think about it the more I am convinced that it has a relationship to the participants' energy level.

Smiley charts   A smiley chart (see Figure 10.10) is used to collect students' perceptions during a course. The chart is drawn on flip-chart paper and at the end of the day the students are asked how they feel. The trainer makes a mark or puts the student's initials in the appropriate square. These feelings are then explored by the trainer.

Stress level chart   A stress level chart (see Figure 10.11) works in a similar way to a smiley chart but it is based on the premise that everyone has an optimum stress level. If the stress level is too low, people become lethargic and are not motivated to learn. Too high a stress level interferes with learning. The stress level chart allows you to monitor the parts of the course that are too challenging and those parts that are too easy.

Working on   A measure of students' interest and motivation is whether groups continue working on projects after the 'official' end of the day. This does not mean that they have to 'burn the midnight oil' every night.

Talking on   On a residential course see whether your students make jokes or talk about the course content in the bar. This will give you a useful indication of interest and retention. An even better indicator is if they impose cash penalties on each other for talking about the course!

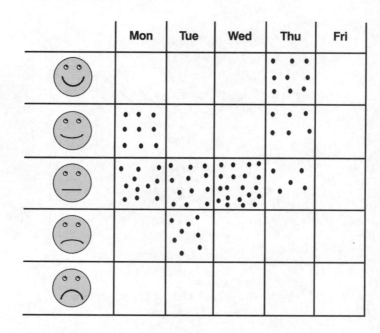

Figure 10.10   *Smiley chart*

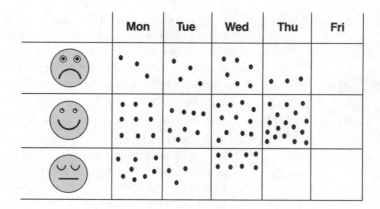

Figure 10.11   *Stress level chart*

Alertness   Note when the students start to drift off, are distracted or their eyelids start to droop.

Quiz challenge   Asking questions is a good method of measuring learning. A variation on this is to split the class into three or four groups and ask them to write questions for each other. The number and quality of the questions will give you an additional measure.

Make a preliminary assessment of the feedback data

At the end of the course you should collect all the evaluation sheets and test results. Immediately count the feedback sheets to make sure that you have received one from every person. Also check to see if there have been any omissions – sometimes people forget to complete part or some of the questions. It is much easier to collect the missing data now rather than after your students have returned to work.

Incidentally, you should initially suspect that omissions are caused by the feedback form rather than being a 'student problem'. For example, we should not blame the students for failing to complete the second side of a feedback sheet if we have not printed 'continued on other side...' on the first side of the sheet.

Scan through the sheets and look for obvious patterns and messages. Don't delay doing this – even if it means spoiling your evening or weekend! Timely feedback is the most effective feedback. Some comments are difficult to understand at the best of times. By the time you get back to the office, you will have even more difficulty understanding the comments.

Preliminary assessment of comments

Read the comments and try to recall any incidents that might have triggered the comment. Look for the same comment coming from different people. Make a mental note of those comments that will need further clarification, and those people to whom you will need to give additional explanation of the concepts.

Preliminary assessment of perceptions

Look at the scores that have been given for the feedback categories. You won't be able to make many conclusions without doing further analysis, but make a mental note of those scores which stand out as being very high or very low. Check to see if these scores have comments associated with them.

Preliminary assessment of test results

Look through the test results to see if the class was having the same type of difficulty throughout the course. (You should already have checked the individual test results immediately after each test to see what changes you needed to make during the course.) Detailed analysis of the test results can wait until you get back to the office.

Organize and display data

It is difficult to draw conclusions about data when the information is spread over a dozen or more evaluation sheets. The raw data need to be organized and, where possible, displayed graphically.

Organizing and displaying perceptions

The usual way of organizing this type of data is with a frequency chart. Figure 10.12 gives an example.

The process for constructing a frequency chart is as follows:

- Work through the evaluation forms and count the number of students who gave the course a relevance score of 1 (i.e. very low relevance).
- Enter this number (if any) in the '1' (Low) column on the relevance row.
- Count the number of relevance scores of 2, 3, 4 and 5.
- Enter these numbers in the '2', '3', '4' and '5' columns.
- Add up the number of responses to make sure you have not missed any out. This number is put in the 'Total' column.
- Calculate the average relevance score and put it in the 'Average' column. The calculation for the example given in Figure 10.12 is:

$(2 \times 2) + (9 \times 4) + (5 \times 5)$ divided by 16

- Follow a similar procedure for each of the response questions.

A computer with a spreadsheet program such as Lotus 1-2-3 allows you to make the calculations quickly and easily. Appendix 1 gives instructions for constructing this spreadsheet.

Although it is possible to draw conclusions directly from the frequency tables, it is much easier when the information is displayed graphically. The best tool for displaying distributed data is the histogram. A histogram is a set of vertical bars which represent the number of responses for each category of feedback. Figure 10.13 is a histogram for item (a), 'Relevance'.

Organizing and displaying comments

Qualitative data, like the feedback comments, are the most difficult to organize and display. The simplest way of

| | Low | | | High | | | |
Question	1	2	3	4	5	Tot	Ave
a. Relevance		2		9	5	16	4.1
b. Ability to apply			4	9	3	16	3.9
c. Probability of using		1	8	6	1	16	3.4
d. Overall satisfaction				10	6	16	4.4
e. Trainer effectiveness				6	10	16	4.6

Figure 10.12   Using a frequency chart to organize student feedback

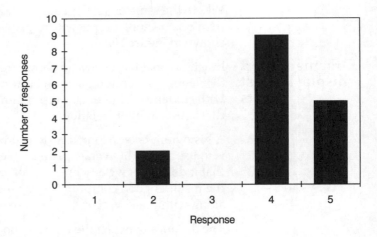

Figure 10.13   *Histogram of relevance scores*

organizing comments is to list them by question. Figure 10.14 gives an example of this. This is better than having the comments spread over all the evaluation sheets, but it is still difficult to detect patterns in the feedback.

Be careful when you group similar comments because there is a temptation to interpret the comments to fit into one of the existing groups. This has the effect of moving away from the original intent of the comments.

COMMENTS

1. **Relevance of workshop to your present job**
    — Very relevant, having recently acquired the responsibility for tracking projects.
    — Not for most day-to-day activities, but useful for two projects just starting.
    — Useful reminder, will be able to use positively in the future.

2. **Confidence in your ability to use the skills**
    — Only doubt is retaining correct skill level when I have a project to work on.
    — Useful revision of work previously covered at college.
    — I would now like to practise these skills.
    — My confidence will increase as I use these skills.

3. **Usefulness of pre-work**
    — Not completed as I have no project to work on.
    — Not relevant on this occasion.
    — Useful having a project in mind to increase relevance etc.
    — Would have helped if manager had given me proper terms of reference.
    — I received no pre-work.

4. **Overall satisfaction with the workshop**
    — Excellent workshop, especially with introduction of case study and monitoring.

Figure 10.14   *Organizing student feedback comments*

Where the same or similar comments are given by more than one person, it is possible to display this graphically as shown in Figure 10.15.

Organizing and displaying test results

Much of what has been said about organizing and displaying perception data can be applied to test results. As with students' comments, a histogram gives a good display that assists in interpretation.

A histogram takes a long time to produce so the temptation is to use a straight average. The problem with an average is that it does not give any information on the variability of the result. A good compromise is to display the average along with the lowest and highest scores (see Figure 10.16).

The distance between the highest and lowest scores gives an indication of variability and the position of the average indicates how the results are skewed. As the results are displayed in a compact format this method is ideal for showing trends over a number of courses (see Figure 10.17).

> Check whether deviations are significant or due to normal variation

It is essential that you make a judgement about whether deviations are significant and require action to be taken, or whether they are due to normal variation and can safely be ignored.

Checking comments for significant variation

When you read the comments there will be some feedback that 'rings true'. You know that it reflects a real problem and you won't need much more data before you do something about it. There will be other comments that are not so clear cut – others will be totally confusing. When you get confusing comments, go back to the students and ask for clarification. They might be surprised but you will be demonstrating that you take their comments seriously.

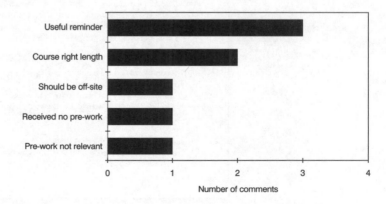

Figure 10.15   Displaying student comments graphically

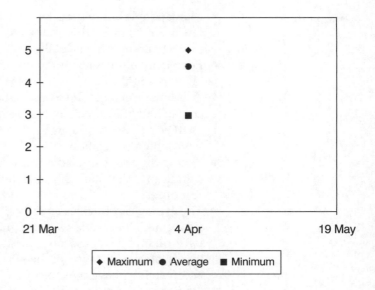

Figure 10.16 *An average displayed with maximum and minimum scores*

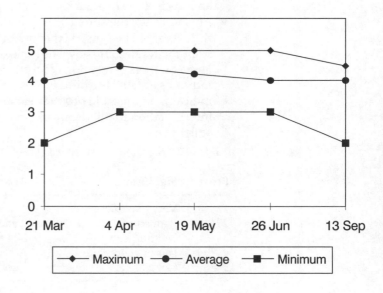

Figure 10.17 *Tracking the results over a period*

Checking perception scores for significant variation

You will need to run a course several times before you can definitely tell what are normal and abnormal responses for the perception scores. As it can take many months to gather statistically significant data, I use the following assumptions when I am making a preliminary assessment of significance. The assumptions are based on a five-point scale.

- Many people are reluctant to give a very high or a very low score. They do this on the basis that nothing is perfect and nothing is totally useless.
- People are more reluctant to give a '1' (very low) than a '5' (very high).
- '3' is a neutral score. It means that this aspect of the course had little effect on that person. Always consider a '3' to be a defect if you are aiming for your courses to have a high reputation.
- Taking the above into account, Table 10.2 indicates the significance that should be attached to individual responses.
- The average score gives an indication of how the course performed. It also allows you to track how course performance changes from course to course. Table 10.3 gives you an indication of the significance and acceptability of averaged scores.
- Do not use the average by itself: it smoothes out the scores and hides problems. It's like the person whose average temperature is just right – but his hair is on fire and his feet are in a bucket of ice!
- Always check the spread (range) of the scores as well as the average. The range is the lowest score subtracted from the highest. It shows how closely the students agree on their perceptions of the course. A small range indicates a stable learning process. A large range indicates an unstable process. Table 10.4 gives an interpretation for all the possible ranges on a five-point scale.

Table 10.2 *Significance and acceptability of individual scores*

Score	Significance	Acceptability
1	Very poor score	Totally unacceptable
2	Poor score	Unacceptable
3	Neutral score	Not acceptable
4	Fair or good score	Acceptable
5	Good or very good score	Very acceptable

Table 10.3 *Significance and acceptability of averaged scores*

Score	Significance	Acceptability
1.0–1.9	Very poor score	Totally unacceptable
2.0–2.4	Poor score	Unacceptable
2.5–3.4	Neutral score	Not acceptable
3.5–3.9	Fair score	Fairly acceptable
4.0–4.4	Good score	Acceptable
4.5–5.0	Very good score	Very acceptable

Table 10.4 *Interpretation of a score's range*

Range	Agreement	Training process stability
0	Extremely high	Extremely stable
1	High	Very stable
2	Good	Normally expected level
3	Low	Getting unstable
4	Very low	Unstable

Note: A course can be stable at the low end of the scale as well as at the high end. This is why the range should be taken into consideration along with the average.

- 'Overall satisfaction' and 'Trainer effectiveness' usually score higher than other questionnaire items.
- 'Relevance' and 'Probability of using' often score lower than the other items. 'Relevance' scores lower than other items because of poor needs analysis and student selection. 'Probability of using' often has a low score because we do not pay enough attention to learning transfer.

The above assumptions reflect what are generally regarded to be normal responses. We shouldn't be content with these. We should aim for zero defects (i.e. every student giving every feedback item a score of 4 or 5).

Checking test results for significant variation

Every test should have a standard attached to it. Any failure to meet that standard should be considered to be a defect. At this stage we are not assigning causes to the deviation. The cause might be that the student was not able to reach a sufficient standard or there might be a defect in the teaching of the course. We are simply noting that a significant deviation has occurred.

> Analyse and interpret data

Analysing and interpreting comments

It is always difficult to receive negative feedback about one of your courses – doubly so if you wrote the course. A course is part of you. Feedback can feel like personal criticism.

These feelings are natural but misguided. You should seek and welcome feedback. Students are your customers. Like other customers, they are reluctant to complain. Instead, they usually stop using your services and then loudly let their friends and neighbours know about it. You are the last person to find out, often too late to save your business from damage.

When people complain, it is for one of two reasons. The first is when their frustration with the product or service overcomes their reluctance to complain. The second is when they respect you enough to want to help. You should always pay attention when people take the trouble to give you feedback. Good feedback is very rare.

Reacting positively to a problem enhances your reputation. Customers are impressed by suppliers who correct mistakes quickly. Curiously, suppliers who never make a mistake are thought less of. Don't let this tempt you into making deliberate mistakes! There will be sufficient real mistakes to give you enough practice.

Always consider negative feedback as a symptom of a problem you need to solve. Remember, no matter how trivial you think a problem is, it is always significant to your customer.

Guard against rationalizing the feedback away. 'That person shouldn't have been on this course anyway' is a typical rationalization. Even if this were true, it's not the student's fault – it's a failure of our process. I find that the principle of 'guilty until proven innocent' helps me rationalize less.

When I receive a piece of criticism I make the assumption that something is wrong with the course or the way it was run. This doesn't mean that I will change the course every time I receive criticism. This would throw the course into confusion and cause even more problems. Instead, I keep the feedback in mind and collect more evidence until I can reach a clear verdict.

Criticism often comes in the form of a solution. An example of this is: 'I think you should scrap the session on company objectives.' Taking this at its face value will lead to a poor training decision. Removing the session from the course will stop the negative feedback but the course will fail to meet its design objectives.

There was obviously something wrong with the session on company objectives. You need to investigate further and find out what is causing the negative reaction. Could it be that students sit without a break for two hours listening to a presentation? Is the presenter unprepared? Perhaps the session makes no link between the company objectives and students' own objectives.

Analysing and interpreting perceptions

The shapes of the perception histograms are useful in analysing and interpreting student perceptions. The following is a discussion of what the different shapes indicate.

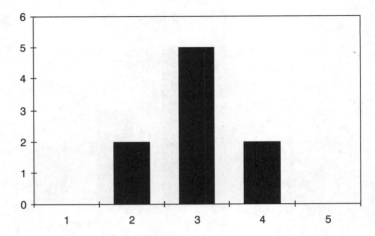

Figure 10.18 *Normal distribution*

The most common shape is the normal distribution, which is symmetrical and bell shaped (Figure 10.18). Most of the results are close to one value. Provided that the histogram does not have a large spread it indicates a consistency in student perceptions.

A negatively skewed distribution (Figure 10.19) shows that the feedback from the majority of students is positive. (I know this sounds contradictory but you'll have to argue that one with a statistician.) The trainer or training has had a significantly positive effect on the students.

A positively skewed distribution (Figure 10.20) shows that the feedback from the majority of students is negative. (Again, have a word with the statistician about the apparent inconsistency.) The trainer or training has had a detrimental effect on the students.

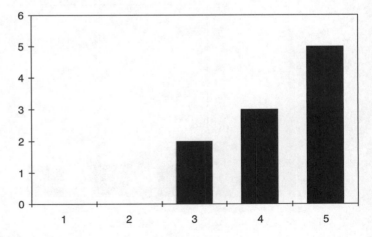

Figure 10.19 *Negatively skewed distribution*

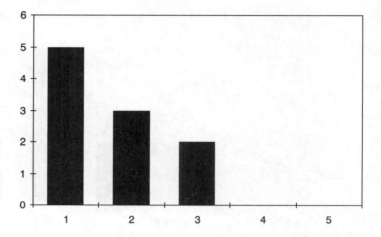

Figure 10.20   *Positively skewed distribution*

A negatively skewed distribution with a wide spread (Figure 10.21) is often seen as a reaction to a trainer who has charisma but whose style is not liked by some of the population. We find that videos starring business 'evangelists' often have this effect. The majority of the class is carried along with the energy of the presentation but some are 'turned off' by being shouted at.

An isolated peak distribution (Figure 10.22) indicates the inclusion of a small number of people from a separate population. For example, if this graph represented a relevance score it would indicate that the problem is more likely to lie with the process for selecting students than with the course itself.

The twin peak distribution occurs when the results of two

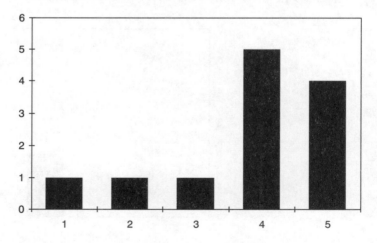

Figure 10.21   *Negative skew with wide distribution*

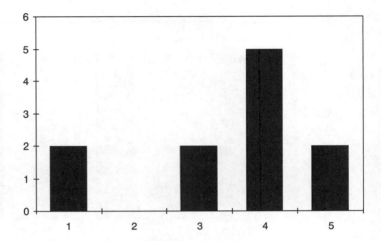

Figure 10.22   *Isolated peak distribution*

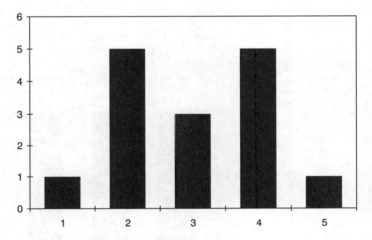

Figure 10.23   *Twin peak distribution*

distinctly different populations are mixed. For example, you might get this result when a course originally designed for sales people is given to a mixed sales and engineering class.

This interpretation can be checked out by stratifying the data. Stratifying the data involves displaying the data so that the two different populations can be easily identified. Figure 10.24 shows one way of doing this.

A flat distribution (Figure 10.25) usually results from a mixed reaction to the course. It can also mean that there are several different populations of students in the class. This is not a problem if you believe that the advantages of having a diverse group of students outweigh the disadvantages, and if the histogram does not have a wide spread.

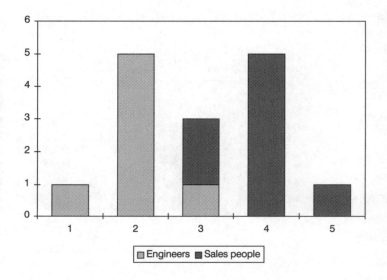

Figure 10.24　*Stratified twin peak distribution*

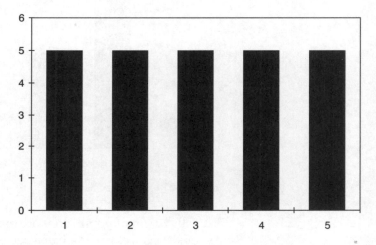

Figure 10.25　*A flat distribution*

Analysing and interpreting test results

A normal distribution means just what it says. It is the kind of distribution you would normally expect when things are left to themselves. If we get a normal distribution it may mean that our training has little effect on the students. Some examination results force the results into a normal distribution so that 50 per cent of the students pass, 25 per cent get credits and 25 per cent fail. As trainers we should be aiming for all our students to pass and to get the highest possible score. We want the distribution of our results to be skewed towards the top end (see Figure 10.26).

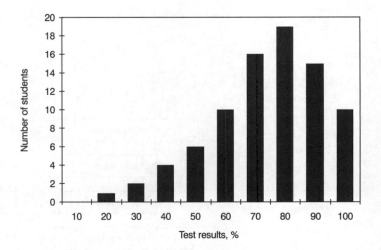

Figure 10.26 *An example of a positive effect on test results*

| Make minor adjustments to the course |

After you have assessed all the validation data you will be in a position to know what alterations to make the next time you run the course. Don't try to change too many things at once, otherwise you won't know what changes caused which results.

Corrections to printed materials

Many of the minor adjustments will involve making revisions to the printed materials. These could be typographical errors, changes to exercises or minor rewording of the text. You should correct these errors immediately or as soon as the course is finished.

If the materials are held electronically, make the corrections and then make sure that you replace the affected pages in the print masters. All this sounds obvious, but failure to make revisions while they are still fresh in your mind is one of the main reasons for the same mistakes turning up on every course.

| Check that adjustments have had the desired effect |

The next time you run the course you should collect exactly the same data as those which led you to make the change. This will give you confidence about whether the changes have had the desired effect. You should also check the other validation data to make sure that your changes have had no unexpected side effects – it has been said that the biggest causes of problems are solutions.

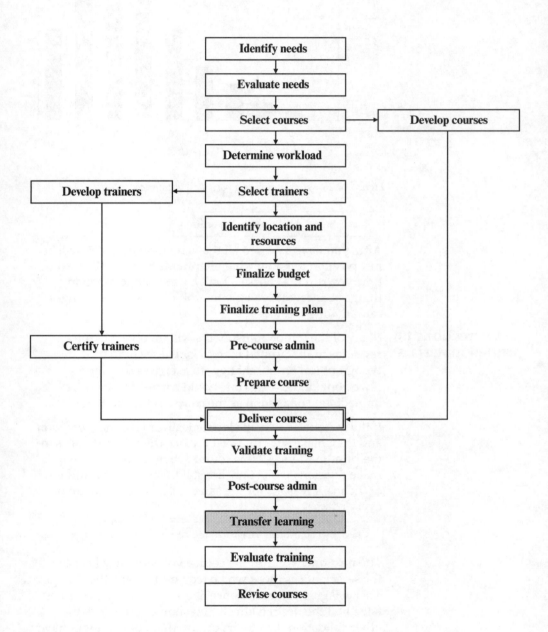

Figure 11.1 *Learning transfer*

11 Learning transfer

Training, no matter how good, is a waste of time if it does not help improve the business. Training will have no impact on the business unless the skills are used back at the workplace. Unused skills are soon forgotten: within six months it will be almost as if the training had never taken place.

As learning transfer is so important you would think that companies would put considerable effort into making it happen. Yet surprisingly few training organizations give learning transfer the priority it requires. Perhaps they think that learning transfer is a natural outcome of training and, as such, does not need nurturing.

Nothing could be further from the truth. New learning soon withers without constant attention. Unless considerable effort is put into learning transfer the effect on the business will be, at best, random and haphazard. Even companies that are aware of the importance of learning transfer find difficulty in making it happen.

In this chapter we will look at:

- the definition of learning transfer,
- what prevents learning transfer from taking place,
- what assists learning transfer,
- who is responsible for learning transfer,
- putting learning transfer into practice.

What is learning transfer?

The definition of learning transfer that I use is:

'The post-training application of the newly acquired knowledge and skills to improve the business.'

You may think this definition too lenient because the skills and knowledge could be used once and then promptly be forgotten. You might also argue that transfer is complete only when the students use the new skills and knowledge naturally, skilfully and automatically.

This stiffer definition should always be the ideal to aim for even though it is much more difficult to measure and attain.

What prevents transfer from taking place?

Given that learning is not efficiently transferred to the business, the next step is to understand the causes of the problem. Assuming that the students are not bothering to use the skills over-simplifies the problem. It just leaves us imploring them to use the skills. Unless we understand why the students are not using the skills, we will make very little progress towards solving the problem. Only understanding the root causes will allow us to remove the barriers.

The following is a selection of potential causes for poor learning transfer. You will need to check whether they apply in your situation and whether there are any additional causes.

Poor needs analysis

Curiously enough, the seeds of this problem are sown long before the training ever takes place. If there is to be any chance of the students using what they have learnt, there must be a need for the skills and knowledge.

This takes us right back to the beginning of the training process – needs identification and analysis. Far too many people are put on to the wrong course, for the wrong reason, at the wrong time. Typical of these misguided reasons are: 'It's a long time since that person's been on a course', 'It's the next course in the series' and 'We had a few spare places to fill.' If the training has little or no relevance, it should come as no great surprise if it is not used.

Skills not used immediately after the course

If the needs analysis has been done correctly, the next aspect to look at is the initial use of the learning after the course. There should be an opportunity to use the skills.

Ideally the students should use the skills and knowledge immediately after the course. However, significant transfer still occurs if the skills are used within three weeks. If this were to happen after every course, there would be a lasting impact on the business.

The work environment

There can be an aspect of the environment that 'punishes' people who use their new skills when they get back to work. This is known as the 'charm school effect'. It is particularly prevalent in management and behaviour training.

A person returns to the workplace, experiments with the skills and uses a new vocabulary. Other people in their work group, faced with strange and new behaviours, start to feel uncomfortable. Although they didn't like the old behaviours, at least they knew what to expect. This nervousness prompts them to make jokes like: 'Look who just got back from charm school!' In this way people are taught not to use their new knowledge.

Even if the returning trainee does not suffer verbal abuse, the work group's lack of training in the skills can still provide an impediment. Many skills need to have a critical mass of people using them before they can take root in an organization. If this critical mass is not reached, the skill becomes extinct. Once the critical mass has been exceeded, even those who were sceptical about the skills will be swept along with the rest.

The culture of the company often reinforces the behaviours we are trying to change. We take people out of this environment, train them to use new behaviours, and then put them back into the environment that caused the problems in the first place. We then wonder why the learning hasn't been transferred.

Little control over the transfer process Another reason for poor learning transfer is loss of control over the process. When the students are in the classroom they are a captive audience. You can monitor and give feedback, you can coach and counsel. But once the course is over that responsibility passes to the students' managers.

One way to gain more control over learning transfer is to spread the learning experiences. For example, in the BBC's 'Managing Change' course the delegates meet a few days before the course. They do the introductions and get to know each other. The course runs for five days. At the end of the course the students are given projects to do when they return to work. Three months later the delegates meet again to review how their projects are proceeding.

This approach goes a long way towards enhancing learning transfer. However, waiting three months to check a project is too long. It does not allow for the monitoring, feedback and coaching that are required in the early days of learning transfer. Another problem with projects is that the students see them as additional work and a burden that gets in the way of their priority tasks. Consequently, it is put off and the bulk of the project work is done in a rush, just before it is due to be checked.

Using a trainer to coach a student through the early stages of learning transfer is an effective but expensive method. It also has the disadvantage that it is usurping the manager's role. Managers can only fulfil their role if they have coaching skills and they become partners in the training process.

Skills not learnt on the course No transfer can occur unless the students develop the skills in the first place. Some training is of the 'hosepipe' variety.

The trainer sprays knowledge and experiences in the hope that all the students will grow.

Ideally, we should measure each student's performance, give feedback and coach until every student reaches the required standard. As we will never have the time or resources to do this, we need to understand what can be done with the resources we have.

Courses that intend to teach a specific skill, or set of skills, range from half a day to two days. Although the length of a course depends on the skill and knowledge complexity, the following guidelines will give you some idea of what can be done in a fixed time.

Half a day   You can teach some basic concepts, models and terminology. There will be little or no time for practice. Unless the students practise the skills very soon after the course, there is little chance that the learning will be transferred. However, half a day of theory in the classroom combined with coached practice in the workplace is a powerful combination.

One day   A full day's course allows time for some practice but not enough time for a significant amount of learning to take place. As there is only enough time for one practice session, the students end the course on a low note. The practice will give them feedback on what they cannot do. They will not have confidence that they can perform the skills correctly.

One and a half days   An extra half-day sees significant skill improvement so the chances of effective learning transfer are greatly enhanced. The intervening evening also helps because the students can reflect on what happened during the day. Learning still goes on even after the practice has stopped.

Two days   Two days of training also allow the students to start a post-course project or to rehearse an application.

Complex skills need to be taught in stages. When there is time pressure on a course there is a temptation to move on before the basics are thoroughly understood. Students who are confused early on in a course get and remain hopelessly lost. They will neither hear nor understand anything that follows.

Longer courses have modules which cover different subject areas. Again, time pressure forces us to move on before the students have had time to breathe.

Assimilation time is important for both learning and its transfer. The students need to check whether they have understood the information and how it fits into what they already know. They need to consider how they would use the learning back at work. Figure 11.2 gives an example of an assimilation aid.

Time also has to be given for the trainer to summarize what has gone before and to introduce what is coming next. There also needs to be constant reinforcement of where the modules fit into the overall scheme of the course.

Difference between work and classroom environments

Another reason for poor learning transfer is the difference, and sudden transition, between the classroom and work environment. The classroom can be compared to a gymnasium: its purpose is to develop skills. Work is like a sporting event – skills have to be used in a complex environment to produce results.

An athlete works out in the gym, practises on the field and then enters a competition. No athlete would go straight from the gym to the Olympics. Yet this is what we do with our students. We give them the skills, send them back to work and expect them to perform like champions.

We need to manage the transition from the classroom to the workplace. We need to create a transition environment that is more challenging than the classroom and safer than the workplace.

The transition between the two environments is not helped by the common perception that training is not work and work is not training. Training and learning need to be seen as a continuous process, an unending journey. The type of

---

Learning Assimilation Aid

1. What do you consider to be the main learning points of the module?

2. How do you currently behave when you find yourself in the situation described in the module?

3. Given what you have learnt from the module, as well as what you have learnt about yourself, what will you do differently in the future?

Figure 11.2 An example of an assimilation aid

organization where the distinction between learning and work becomes blurred is a learning organization.

> The European design managers of a large multinational organization were to be trained in counselling.
>
> The training started with a four-hour introduction to counselling and its techniques. Soon after the course each manager had a meeting with a facilitator to prepare for a real counselling session.
>
> Facilitators observed the managers carrying out their first counselling session. The facilitators explained to the counsellees that they were solely to observe the managers.
>
> After the session the facilitators gave the managers feedback and, where necessary, further coaching in counselling techniques.
>
> One of the benefits of this training was that more appraisals were completed on time than ever before.

Trying to do too much

A journey of a thousand miles starts with a single step. It should not start with a giant leap. Trying to cover too much ground too soon risks injury and exhaustion.

The same is true for learning transfer. Too many people return to their workplace and try to change the world overnight. Not only does this contribute to the 'charm school effect' but it is also a recipe for failure.

The first application of the skills and knowledge should be chosen very carefully. People need to succeed and to see the value of what they are doing.

> Major-General Jeremy Moore, commander of the British land forces during the Falklands War, was asked what should be the first objective for a newly arriving battalion of paratroopers. 'A battle you are going to win,' he replied.

What assists learning transfer?

The lessons to be learnt from what hinders learning transfer help us understand what assists the transfer of learning. These are:

- Training people from the same work group together aids learning transfer.
- Post-course project work assists learning transfer, but it is only effective if it is suitably supported and controlled.
- Some skills can only be transferred successfully if there is a cultural change in the company.
- Involve the managers before, after and, in some cases, during the training.
- Ensure that managers have the necessary coaching skills to assist learning transfer.
- Ensure that competence is demonstrated at one level of difficulty or complexity before proceeding to the next.

- Ensure that there is enough time to practise the skills on the course.
- Have at least two practice sessions. Complex skills require up to five practice sessions over a week's course.
- Allow time for assimilation between different subjects.
- Advise the students to be selective about what they apply the training to when they get back to work. Advise them against trying to do too much too soon.
- Manage the transition from the classroom to the workplace.
- Reduce the perception that training is not work and work is not training.

Vocational qualifications

Vocational qualifications can be used to assist in both learning transfer and the evaluation of the course. Vocational qualifications measure a person's effectiveness in the workplace rather than in the artificial environment of the classroom. A person is not awarded the qualification for passing a course. A course provides the background skills and knowledge that allow someone to demonstrate competence in the workplace.

If you design a course so that it is consistent with vocational qualifications you have an automatic link with the workplace. The skills are practised, managers function as mentors and competence is assessed.

Accrediting learning

Accreditation of your courses by an academic establishment rewards the effort put into learning and gives students a recognizable, transferable qualification. Students have to satisfy the requirements of the qualification and usually have to complete a project, thesis or dissertation which further facilitates learning transfer.

The Rover Body and Pressings Business, based at Swindon in the UK, is a good example of an organization using this type of accreditation. Students studying their 'Total Quality Leadership' programme have obtained qualifications at certificate, diploma and master's degree levels.

It is essential that a good relationship exists between your company and the accrediting body so that accreditation supports the course objectives rather than the other way round.

Who is responsible for learning transfer?

The people who are responsible for learning transfer are, in order of importance:

- the student,
- the manager,
- the trainer.

It is often thought that learning transfer is most affected by what the trainer and student do during the course but, in reality, what is done by the student and manager before and after the course have a far greater effect.

Putting learning transfer into practice

As you can see, transferring the training into the business can be both difficult and complex. Figure 11.3 shows a process for putting learning transfer into practice.

> Train managers, coaches and assessors

The essence of learning transfer is support for the student before, during and after the training course. You would normally expect the trainer to provide support during the course. Support before and after the course is often a chance occurrence.

A process has to be installed and a support network has to be established and trained. Coaching and counselling are essential skills for managers and coaches. If you are linking your training with vocational qualifications, you will also need to have assessors trained and accredited.

> Student/trainer selects skills and knowledge for initial application

Time is given during the course for the student to decide which skills and knowledge they should use during the initial application of the training.

> Student identifies initial application opportunities

Students should have a clear idea of the situations where they can use the skills and knowledge. The initial application will not happen unless they have a vivid mental picture of the situation. They should be able to imagine what it will look like and how it will feel.

For this reason a student should not leave the course without being sure of when the application will happen and who will be involved. Do not accept a fictitious or generalized situation.

> Student discusses practice opportunities with manager

For learning transfer to be successful the manager must support the skills and knowledge application. This step of the process happens more than once. Potential application opportunities should be identified before the course as part of the student's preparation.

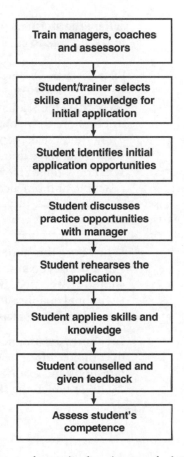

Figure 11.3 *A process for putting learning transfer into practice*

The discussion that occurs after the course is to let the manager know what is going on and to enlist their help and support.

Student rehearses the application

Rehearsing the application in a simulated but safe environment is a powerful way to make a bridge between the classroom and the workplace. It allows the new skills and knowledge to be tried out, mistakes to be made and feedback to be given.

Student applies skills and knowledge

By this time students should be fully prepared for their first application of their training. Where possible a coach should observe this initial application. The coach can be the person's manager or someone from a specially trained network of coaches. An alternative is the 'buddy system' where the students pair up and provide support, coaching and feedback to each other.

| Student counselled and given feedback |

As soon as the students have completed their first application, they should review their own performance. They should ask themselves what they did well and what they could have done better. Give them feedback to cover what they might have missed. Then provide any additional coaching and practice that they might require.

| Assess student's competence |

When both the student and coach feel that the correct standard has been reached, the student's competence should be assessed. If you have been following the vocational qualifications path the job will done by an internal or external assessor.

An alternative method is to give the student a project book to complete after the course. The project book would have questions and exercises that allow the trainer to assess the extent to which the skills were applied after the course.

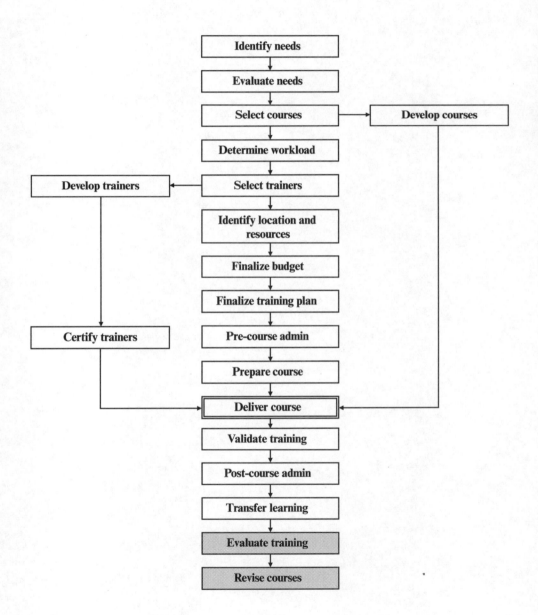

Figure 12.1 *Evaluation and revision*

12 Evaluation

This chapter covers the two final steps of the training process:

- evaluation,
- revision.

Chapter 11 described a process for facilitating the transfer of learning from the classroom to the business. Evaluation checks whether transfer has occurred and makes sure that the training has had the desired effect.

Validation (Chapter 10) is an internal check, it assesses whether the students have reached the required standard before they leave the course. Evaluation is about determining the effect of the course after the students return to the workplace.

A course might have the objective of being able to ice a cake. Validation would show that the students were able to ice a cake before they left the course, but you would have no idea of whether they would continue to ice cakes to the same standard or whether icing cakes is a skill that enhances the business.

In addition to covering the evaluation of training programmes we will also consider how to evaluate our training process. One outcome of evaluation is the identification of changes and additions to the training courses and process.

Evaluation versus validation

In my research for this book I came across many different definitions for both evaluation and validation. None of these definitions seemed to be satisfactory for the practical purpose of managing the training process.

The *Glossary of Training Terms* (Department of Employment, 1971) defines evaluation as:

'The assessment of the total value of a training system, training course or programme in social as well as

229

financial terms. Evaluation differs from validation in that it attempts to measure the overall cost-benefit of the course or programme and not just the achievement of laid down objectives. The term is also used in the general judgemental sense of the continual monitoring of a programme or of the training function as a whole.'

The two problems with this definition are to do with 'the total value in social terms' and 'overall cost-benefit'.

From a practical point of view I have absolutely no idea of how to measure the total value of a course in social terms. Even if I did, I have a feeling it could be a lifetime's work.

It is also not always possible to translate all the benefits of a training programme into financial terms. Even benefits which lend themselves to mathematical analysis involve complex calculations and the validity of the conclusions is nearly always suspect. Every outcome has more than one cause, so it is very difficult to apportion financial benefit to one activity rather than another. I have a suspicion that if you were to add up all the cost benefits claimed for training and other activities in a company, the total would exceed the annual revenue!

The *Glossary of Training Terms* defines two types of validation: internal and external. Internal validation is defined as:

'A series of tests and assessments designed to ascertain whether a training programme has achieved the behavioural objectives specified.'

The definition of external validation is given as:

'A series of tests and assessments designed to ascertain whether the behavioural objectives of an internally valid training programme were realistically based on an accurate initial identification of training needs in relation to the criteria of effectiveness adopted by the organisation.'

Many writers reject these definitions as being too narrow. Validation also needs to reflect the perceptions of the participants and consider other, perhaps unintended, effects of the training. From a practical perspective, I have great difficulty in drawing the line between where external validation ends and evaluation begins.

Peter Bramley, in *Evaluation of Training* (BACIE, 1986), suggests that it is better to take evaluation as a general term to cover the whole area rather than splitting it into three parts. He offers Goldstein (1980, p 237) as a broad definition:

> 'Evaluation is the systematic collection of descriptive and judgemental information necessary to make effective training decisions related to the selection, adoption, value and modification of various instructional activities.'

This approach certainly simplifies the business of defining evaluation. However, in my view there is a world of difference between checking whether a course does what you expect it to do on the day and the long-term effects of training on the individual, the department and the organization.

For the practical purposes of managing the training process, I have arrived at the definition of validation already given in Chapter 10:

> 'A systematic analysis of data and judgemental information, collected during a training course, which is designed to ascertain whether the course achieved its specified aims and objectives.'

This definition corresponds most closely to the definition of internal validation given in the *Glossary of Training Terms* but it also covers participants' perceptions of the course. Validation is primarily at the individual level – individual performance and reaction to the course. My working definition of evaluation is:

> 'A series of tests, assessments and investigations designed to ascertain whether training has had the desired effect at individual, departmental and organizational levels.'

Each of these three levels of evaluation can be further divided into quantitative and qualitative measures. See Table 12.1 for the types of quantitative and qualitative questions that can be asked at each of the three levels.

Figure 12.2 is a simplified diagram showing the relationship of evaluation to the rest of the training process. It shows evaluation taking a 'helicopter view' of the process. An evaluation strategy needs to take account of:

- the original aims of the course as identified in the needs analysis,
- the behavioural objectives as identified during course development,
- the validation data collected during and at the end of the course,
- assessment data taken during and after learning transfer.

Table 12.1 *Quantitative and qualitative measures for each evaluation level*

Level	Quantitative	Qualitative
Individual	Do the individuals still have the knowledge they gained on the course? Are they still able to perform the skills?	Do the individuals still believe the training to have been worthwhile?
Departmental	Have the desired improvements or changes occurred at the departmental level?	Does training have a good reputation in the participants' departments?
Organizational	Has the organizational aim been achieved? (e.g. profitability, productivity, flexibility, morale, commitment, achievement of business plan)	What is the organization's attitude towards training?

Our definition of evaluation covers the effect of training as a whole and includes two broad areas:

- evaluation of training programmes,
- evaluation of the training process.

Evaluating training programmes

Evaluation, according to the definition given in this book, is carried out after the end of the course. The question is how long after the course this should be.

When should training be evaluated?

Evaluation would not be done after every course. With a new course you would want to make a check three to six months after the first course. When a course is established there is little need to do evaluation. Validation is normally sufficient to let you know that the course has not wandered off track and is still delivering to the required standard.

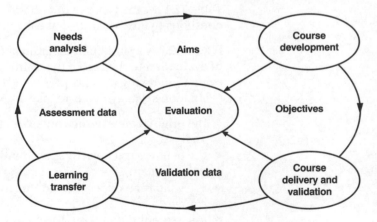

Figure 12.2 *Evaluation and its relationship to the training process*

Another time evaluation is required is when there has been a significant change in the organization or when the course is due to be revised or replaced by a new course.

Ideally, evaluation of training should also occur annually when the organization is assessing the success of its business plan.

How should training be evaluated? The way evaluation usually works is that the person doing the assessment goes into the workplace, sees the problems and successes that the organization, departments and individuals are having, questions whether training has helped them and then determines what additional training is required.

This type of evaluation is usually qualitative and also involves sending out questionnaires. The questionnaires and their analysis follow a similar format to that used for validation (see Chapter 10).

I prefer interviews to questionnaires. With questionnaires people can only answer the questions they have been asked. Questionnaires assume that the originator already has a good idea of what the problems with the course might be.

However, the problem with free-form interviews is that they do not have a structure. This raises questions about the validity of the data because different people are answering different questions. It certainly makes analysis of the data very difficult.

Structured interviews give the best of both worlds. In essence, they are interviews based on a questionnaire that includes all the basic questions that need to be covered. A sensitive interviewer will also be able to pick up and probe for any other feedback on the course.

A half-way house between free-form and structured interviews is to start the interview with a series of open questions such as: 'Tell me about any problems you have in doing your current job.'

Evaluation is not only done with the students. Their managers should also be asked if the course met the objectives from their point of view. With large-scale programmes feedback should also be sought from organizational and departmental heads. This ensures that the training is evaluated at all three levels. Different techniques are used depending on the level of evaluation and whether a quantitative or qualitative investigation is being carried out. Table 12.2 shows some of the techniques that can be used.

Table 12.2 *Techniques for use at different levels of evaluation*

Level	Quantitative techniques	Qualitative techniques
Individual	Tests Observations Vocational assessment	Interviews Questionnaires
Departmental	Production indices Quality indices Staff turnover	Interviews Questionnaires Attitude surveys
Organizational	Assessment and diagnosis of business results Financial results	Interviews Questionnaires Customer satisfaction

A process for evaluating training

The intuitive way of evaluating training programmes is to start at the first level of evaluation (individual level) and then proceed to the other two levels (departmental and organizational). This is the way in which most evaluation is carried out, except that few investigations get beyond the first level.

If you start evaluating at the lowest level, the process becomes training centred rather than business centred. It is difficult to assess whether the course's objectives are the right ones because you are actively looking for examples of the course objectives being met in the workplace.

Starting at Level 1 also makes it difficult to prove that training is an essential contributor to the business, because this narrow focus does not allow you to identify and isolate the other contributory factors.

Starting at Level 3, the organizational level, is more difficult but it is the only way to prove whether training has contributed to the business. Figure 12.3 shows a process that, when used with this 'top-down' approach, is an effective method for evaluating training.

> Review aims

In Chapter 1 we talked about the importance of training being aligned with the business. All training should support the maintenance or improvement of the business. When we evaluate at the organizational level (Level 3) we need to look at the original business aims that the training was meant to support.

> Have aims been met?

Evaluating whether business aims have been met is not something that can, or should, be done by the training

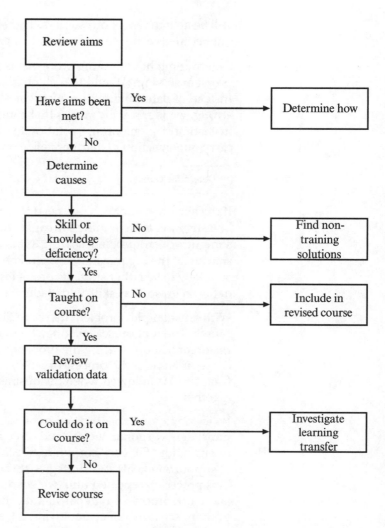

Figure 12.3 *A process for evaluating training's contribution to the business*

department alone. Well-run businesses assess the success of their strategies regularly – certainly at least once a year.

The assessment should be carried out by representatives of the company's main functions. Traditionally, the training function is not involved in these assessments. If we are serious about training being an integral part of the business, however, this is a critical omission.

> Determine how

If the answer to 'Have aims been met?' is 'Yes', we should understand how we met our aims. A good result without understanding is just luck. There is no guarantee that we will be able to repeat our success. This step is often missed out because we are so pleased and amazed by our success.

Determining how the aims were met is really a type of problem solving. (Would that all problems were like this!) Instead of determining the causes for something going wrong, we identify the factors that contribute to success; instead of implementing a solution to correct a problem, we carry out an action plan to capitalize on our success.

Determine causes

If the aims were not met, we need to carry out an investigation to determine the causes of this. This is straightforward problem solving. Notice, we are still starting at the organizational level. The causes at this level are likely to be either strategic problems or widespread deficiencies such as skill, knowledge or motivation.

With any complex problem there are likely to be several causes. The root causes will often be found further down the organization. Tracing the problems down to their root causes is easier if the process of policy deployment (see Chapter 1) is followed when the business plan is put together.

Policy deployment is the process of cascading and translating corporate visions and directions throughout the organization. For each corporate direction, there is a series of supporting goals and strategies at the next level down. This process is repeated until we get down to objectives and work processes at departmental and individual levels. You can see how policy deployment lends itself to our model of evaluation.

If an important corporate aim has not been met, we can see which of the supporting goals are contributing to the problem. We can look at the supporting goals that we have not achieved and see which work processes are not meeting expectations.

Provided that the training plan was put together as part of the original policy deployment, this process gives us a method of evaluating training's contribution to the business. It also allows us to evaluate the training process as well as the individual courses.

Skill or knowledge deficiency?

Skill and knowledge deficiencies can be in terms of quantity as well as quality. If qualified individuals are not meeting the course objectives, the course needs to be revised. If we have not trained the numbers of people we said we would train, the training process needs to be investigated.

Skill and knowledge deficiencies should be investigated at all three levels of evaluation. Deficiencies in the number of people trained are first investigated at the organizational level. We then need to determine the extent of the deficiency across all relevant departments. Finally, we should identify the individuals who have not been trained and ensure that they are included in the next revision of the training plan. Deficiencies in the quality of skills and knowledge are handled in a similar manner.

> Find non-training solutions

If the causes of a problem cannot be attributed to a skill or knowledge deficiency, we have to look elsewhere for solutions. Chapter 2 describes a process for finding alternatives to training. This process was designed for use during needs analysis but it can also be used at all levels of evaluation.

> Taught on course?

If one of the contributing factors to a business problem is a skill or knowledge deficiency, the next step is to check whether it was included in the course. This can be done by reviewing the course objectives.

> Include in revised course

If the deficient skills and knowledge were not taught in the original course, we need to make sure that they are included when we revise the course.

> Review validation data

The next step is to review the validation data collected at the end of each course. These data should already have been analysed and displayed graphically as described in Chapter 10. It is during evaluation that you realize the benefits of having a good filing and retrieval system for your validation data.

> Could do it on course?

The purpose of reviewing the validation data is to see whether the students were able to demonstrate the skills and knowledge while they were on the course.

> Investigate learning transfer

If the students were performing to the required level on the course, their performance must have deteriorated after the training. The next step is to look at the output of learning transfer.

Chapter 1 (The process of training) recommended that every job should have a description of the competencies needed to perform the job. It also recommended that everyone should have their competence assessed before being allowed to do the job by themselves.

Chapter 11 (Learning transfer) showed how vocational qualifications could be used to carry out this assessment. Without job certification evaluation becomes a time-consuming and costly additional exercise.

If you do not have access to assessment data, you will need to re-test a selection of students to see whether they are still able to meet the course objectives in the workplace. This underlines the importance of having objectives that are meaningful in both the classroom and the workplace. For example, an objective that states:

> 'By the end of the course you will have participated in three simulations'

is not useful because it cannot be measured in the workplace. It is more a description of the training content rather than an objective.

If your objectives are meaningful, you can use exactly the same approach as described in Chapter 10 (Validation). In this case the only difference between validation and evaluation is *when* you carry out the investigation.

If your investigation or assessment data show that there has not been a successful transfer of learning, you will need to find the causes of this and modify the learning transfer process. Chapter 11 (Learning transfer) considers the most common causes of poor learning transfer.

The assessment data may show that learning was transferred successfully but that it waned after a period of use in the business. In this case it is unlikely that you will need to modify the original course. The usual response in these cases is a demand for refresher training.

Be cautious about making an immediate response to demands for refresher training. First look for environmental or cultural reasons for the decline in skills. If an environmental or cultural cause is prevalent, no amount of refresher training will overcome these factors.

If refresher training is appropriate, don't put people through the same course again. You will only be 'telling them what you told them' and it is unlikely that you will get better learning transfer. As a colleague of mine says: 'If you always do what you always did, you'll always get what you always got!'

The answer is to run a different course which covers the same skill and knowledge from a different angle or at a different level. Another approach is to run a simulation which requires skilful application of the skills and knowledge.

> Revise course

If the students were not able to do what was required on the course, the course will need revising. However, it should be said that if you reach this step as part of evaluation, you should look at the other parts of the training process.

Poor performance on the course should be picked up during validation. If the needs analysis and course development were done properly, you should need to make only minor adjustments between courses.

As an example of how this process works in practice, consider a company whose customer satisfaction ratings are disappointingly low.

The managing director calls a meeting to assess and diagnose the problem. The data suggest that there is a widespread lack of skill in dealing with customers. Customer satisfaction training had not been given to any of the people who have direct contact with the customer.

This evaluation at the organizational level led to customer satisfaction training being included in training of sales people, customer representatives, service engineers, telephone operators and receptionists.

Further investigation of the data showed that manufacturing defects, administration errors and service engineer response time all contributed to customer dissatisfaction.

Investigations continued by looking at each of these departments in detail. For example, in the manufacturing area most of the defects were attributed to materials problems. Only a few defects were attributable to workmanship. These workmanship defects were eliminated by minor modifications to the training.

Measuring training effectiveness

One of the best ways of evaluating your training is to benchmark yourself against companies who have a known high reputation for their training. To do this you will have to decide which are the important indicators you wish to measure yourself against.

Training measures can be divided into four categories:

- financial,
- utilization,
- time,
- process.

The first three categories are quantitative. They are relatively easy to measure but can be perceived as bureaucratic. Quantitative measures have to be used with caution – one of the most popular time measures is the number of hours of training received by each employee per year. Many companies have a blanket target of 40 hours. Although this is useful as a guide, it is possible to imagine a situation where a highly skilled workforce would need only two hours of training per year. Training should always be related to the need.

Financial measures

The two types of financial measures are costs and earnings.

Costs

The following are some examples of training cost measures:

- total annual budget for providing training,
- training investment per employee per year,
- training investment per manager per year,
- cost of providing a day's non-residential training,
- cost of providing a day's residential training,
- cost of employing a trainer per day,
- cost of hiring a consultant per day,
- annual training budget expressed as a percentage of the company's total employment costs,
- annual training budget expressed as a percentage of the company's revenue.

The annual cost of providing training can include or exclude the students' wages while they are being trained, depending on the convention used in the benchmark company.

Earnings

If you are running your training organization as a budget centre, you will also be interested in measurements that allow you to compare your earnings with those of similar organizations. The following is a selection of measurements you can use:

- earnings per trainer per year,

- earnings per trainer per day,
- earnings as a percentage of the training budget,
- earnings per day of developed course,
- earnings per square metre of training space.

Utilization measures

The main two areas of utilization are trainer utilization and facility utilization.

Trainer utilization

- Face-to-face ratio – the percentage of time a trainer spends in front of the class.
- Delivery to preparation ratio – how much time is spent delivering a course compared to the time spent preparing for it. Often expressed as a percentage.

Facility utilization

Facility utilization is simply the percentage of time that the training rooms are in use. If you have an open learning centre, you will need to express the utilization as the percentage of time that the learning stations are in use.

Time measures

Time measurements include:

- hours of training per employee per year,
- time between identification of training need and delivery of the training,
- number of hours to develop one hour of training,
- percentage of training completed within agreed time limits (the target should always be 100 per cent).

Process measures

Measuring training effectiveness promises to be a fruitful line of research from a process point of view. Process questions allow an assessment of training effectiveness to be made without getting bogged down in numbers.

One of the main questions would be whether the organization has a training process. Other possible questions are:

- Do all employees receive training for their job role?

- Is their competence certified on the job?

- Do you have people whose job roles specifically include:
  – training management?
  – training delivery?
  – training administration?

- Have training staff been accredited as:
  – professional trainers?
  – trainers of the subject matter?

- Are you using accredited training courses?

- Has a training needs analysis been completed?

- Where do the training needs come from:
  – individual requests?

   – manager requests?
   – corporate mandates?
   – job requirements?
   – organizational needs?
   – departmental needs?
   – individual development plans?

- Are training needs linked to the business plan?

- How do you validate these needs to ensure that training is an appropriate solution?

- How do you prioritize these needs?

- Do people have 'living' development plans?

- Do you have an overall training plan for your business?

- To what extent is the training plan achieved?

- How do you select new courses?

- How do you assure the quality of these courses?

- If you develop your own courses, what process do you use to develop them?

- How do you select trainers?

- How do you assure the quality of these trainers?

- Do you have a training budget?

- How often are courses cancelled because of other priorities?

- To what extent are people withdrawn from courses?

- Do you have a dedicated training room?

- If you use external training facilities, how do you ensure that they are of sufficient quality and suitable for your needs?

- Do your courses have behavioural objectives?

- Are these objectives tested?

- Do students complete an end-of-course questionnaire?

- Are these questionnaires kept on file?

- How are they analysed?

- Who receives the analysis?

- What other validation methods do you use?

- Is evaluation carried out after the course is completed?

- Does each employee have a training record?

- Does the record include:
  – required courses?
  – planned dates?
  – date courses completed?
  – test results?

Part Two

Extending the Process

13 Training quality

Training should be considered to be no different to any other business process – and as such it should be subject to the same rigorous quality controls as any other critical process. As more organizations outsource the delivery of their training, assuring training quality is assuming a higher profile and importance.

Many businesses talk about being 'world class' without really knowing what it means – apart from being the best in the world, which brings us back to where we started and does not really tell us how we are going to achieve it.

For me, being 'world class' is simply doing the basics, and doing them right. This might seem very easy – but how many organizations do you see getting the basics consistently right?

The elements of 'world-class training' are:

- a quality training process,
- certified courses,
- certified instructors.

This chapter describes an audit process that was designed to assure the quality of training suppliers by making sure that the basics were done consistently well. The audit is used to:

- clarify standards of training development, administration, delivery and evaluation,
- assess the standards currently provided by suppliers,
- facilitate supplier development,
- examine the relationship between the business and its suppliers,
- examine the training process in terms of determining training needs, learning transfer and evaluation.

The process described here can be used for internal as well as external suppliers.

Minimum standards of performance

The performance of training suppliers is assessed in six areas:

- business relationship,
- communication and administration,
- course development,
- course materials,
- course delivery,
- training evaluation.

The minimum standards shown here are only given as examples and should be modified to suit the circumstances in your own business.

Business relationship
Invoices

- The supplier should raise invoices two weeks before the start of the programme.
- The customer will settle payment within 30 days.

Cancellation and substitution

- The customer can replace any delegate with a substitute at any time without charge.
- Cancellation within four weeks of the start of the course incurs a 25 per cent charge.
- Cancellation within two weeks incurs a 50 per cent charge.
- Cancellation within one week incurs a 100 per cent charge.

Pricing

- Pricing and discount structures are subject to negotiation.
- The supplier will allow the customer to preview and evaluate training materials before purchase.

Expenses

- Additional expenses such as travel, subsistence and accommodation costs are to be agreed with the customer before the event.

Communication and administration
Enquiry handling by supplier

- The supplier's office should be staffed during normal working hours.
- Answering machines should be available at other times.
- Specialist enquiries should be answered by the appropriate consultant within 24 hours.

Course and service information

- Course and information brochures should be revised regularly and distributed to the business units.
- 'Training directory' entry should be revised annually.

Joining instructions

- These include details and map of the venue, the course timetable, the learning objectives and any pre-course reading.
- Joining instructions reach the delegate at least two weeks before the course starts.

Course development
Process

- New programmes should be developed using a recognized course development process.

- Programmes should have precise, behavioural learning objectives.
- Progress checks should be included in the course design to ensure that the learning objectives are being met.
- Existing programmes should be continuously developed in a manner which reflects the changing business need.
- Programmes should be tailored to the local need.

Case studies and
syndicate exercises

- Case studies and syndicate exercises should have clearly recognizable learning outcomes in line with the objectives of the programme.
- They should reflect current company policies and initiatives where relevant.

Course materials
Training manuals
and handouts

- A course manual is to be provided to the delegates for each programme.
- The style and format of the manual should be appropriate for the learning objectives.
- The content of the manual should faithfully reflect the content of the course.
- Delegates should be able to use the manual as a post-course reference document.
- The overall impression of the manual should be one of neatness and clarity.
- The manual should reflect current company policies and initiatives where relevant.

Overheads

- Overhead projection slides should be clear and legible, and avoid information overload.
- They should be appropriate to the size of room.
- Diagrams should be used wherever possible.

Training delivery

Ensure that each individual obtains the maximum possible learning from the programme by:

- motivating and coaching people in a way that facilitates learning,
- identifying and supporting those participants experiencing difficulty in learning,
- recognizing and adapting the course to the needs of the group,
- displaying a sympathetic and caring attitude.

Provide opportunities for participants to:

- learn from each other,
- demonstrate their learning,
- relate their learning to the workplace.

Training
evaluation

Suppliers will be expected to work with their clients to evaluate the contribution of the training to individual, organizational and business performance.

End-of-course
review

- A written end-of-course review form should be completed by each participant.
- The design of the form and the questions asked should be specific to the learning objectives.

Post-course transfer
of learning

- A continuous sampling process, including telephone surveys, questionnaires and interviews, should be introduced to assess the transfer of learning to the workplace.
- The size of the sample should reflect the amount of investment involved. For programmes in excess of four days or where there has been a significant financial investment, a sample size of 25 per cent would be appropriate. For the remaining programmes, a sample size of 10 per cent would be more realistic.

Training audit process

Although this audit process (see Figure 13.1) was designed to ensure the quality of training we receive from outsourced suppliers, it can easily be adapted to assess internal training suppliers.

As you get into the detail of the audit you will come to realize, as we did, that this audit is as much about assessing your own training process as about auditing your suppliers. The reason for this is that suppliers can only provide you with world-class training if your needs analysis and post-course follow-up are also world class.

In addition it is important to understand that the purpose of the audit is to develop your suppliers and your relationship with them. It isn't about finding reasons for dumping your current suppliers and finding new ones. Constantly changing suppliers can only lead to an unstable training process.

However, the process does allow for parting company with a supplier if the supplier, despite being given every chance and encouragement, still fails to meet your stringent standards.

Select course to be audited

The full audit is a long process so you will need to be selective about which courses you audit. The following are criteria which would increase a course's priority for audit:

- a new course,
- an important course that has not previously been audited,
- a course that is part of a company-wide initiative, e.g. 'Finance Training Framework',
- a course that has given cause for concern.

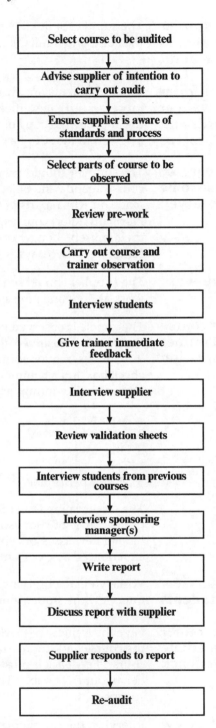

Figure 13.1   *Training audit process*

Advise supplier of intention to carry out audit The supplier should be advised of the intention to carry out the audit and a suitable date for the audit should be chosen.

Ensure supplier is aware of standards and process If the supplier is not aware of the audit standards and processes, arrange a meeting with the supplier to explain the approach. A copy of the process and standards should be given to the supplier.

Select parts of course to be observed The supplier should provide the assessor with a copy of the course agenda and objectives so that a decision can be made on which parts of the course should be observed. Normally, short courses (one to two days) are observed in their entirety. Longer courses would require a minimum sampling of two days.

Review pre-work The supplier should send the assessor a copy of the pre-work at the same time as it is sent to the students.

Carry out course and trainer observation The course is observed by keeping a log of comments and the trainer is observed against a number of attributes. The 'trainer observation form' (see Figure 13.2) has a 1–5 rating check box and a comments section for each of the attributes. The ratings are defined as follows:

1. Not acceptable
2. Poor
3. OK
4. Good
5. Master performer

The target rating is 4 or 5 for each of the criteria. The performance of your assessors should be moderated by having new assessors observing the same course as an experienced assessor until rating consistency is achieved.

Interview students While you are observing the course, take the opportunity to interview the students on their impressions of the course.

Give trainer immediate feedback Give the trainer feedback at appropriate points throughout the course and summarize the feedback at the end of the course. Feedback is most effective if it is as close to the behaviour as possible. The written report should contain no surprises.

Interview supplier Interview the supplier using a supplier questionnaire as a guide, similar to the one shown in Figure 13.3. The purpose of these questions is to determine the quality of the supplier's training process and to ascertain whether the supplier has met the standards for:

Trainer:	Date:
Session:	Observer:

(1) = Not acceptable   (2) = Poor   (3) = OK   (4) = Good   (5) = Master performer

Behaviours	**Assessment and comments**
<u>Preparation</u> — Rehearsed lesson — Administration — Classroom layout — Materials and equipment prepared — Arranged to be free from interruptions	(1) (2) (3) (4) (5)
<u>Presentation</u> — Introduced subject — Communicated objectives — Communicated agenda — Followed logical sequence — Summarized — Checked students' understanding — Kept to time — Kept to subject	(1) (2) (3) (4) (5)
<u>Manner</u> — Showed commitment — Showed enthusiasm — Created interest — Sensitive to group — Credible — Knowledgeable	(1) (2) (3) (4) (5)
<u>Technique</u> — Voice — Questioning — Pace — Movement — Eye contact — Mannerisms — Use of audiovisual aids	(1) (2) (3) (4) (5)

Figure 13.2   Trainer observation form

Supplier Questionnaire

Course:

Supplier:	Interviewer:
Interviewee:	Date:

1. How did you determine the objectives for this course?

2. How did you determine the length of the course?

3. How do you evaluate the effectiveness of this course?

4. Can you give me an example of how you have changed this course as a result of end-of-course feedback?

5. How do you evaluate the effectiveness of your training in terms of on-the-job performance?

6. Can you give me an example of how you have changed a training programme as the result of feedback on work-related performance?

7. How often do you run this course?

8. Who is your contact with the company and can you describe your working relationship with them?

9. How do you ensure that the course meets the specific needs of your students during the course?

10. How often do you revise the training materials?

11. What action do you take when a student fails to meet a course objective?

Figure 13.3   An excerpt from a supplier questionnaire

- business relationship,
- communication and administration,
- course development,
- training delivery,
- training evaluation.

Review validation sheets

Review validation sheets to see what additional insights can be derived from the students' perception of the course. A guide to interpreting validation sheets is given in Chapter 10, Validation.

Interview students from previous courses

The purpose of this step is to check the effect of the course three or more months after the student has left the course. Use a student follow-up questionnaire, similar to the one shown in Figure 13.4, as the basis of a structured interview. The questionnaire can also be sent out to graduates of the course to obtain a larger sample.

Student Follow-up Questionnaire

Course:	Date(s):
Venue:	Trainer(s):
Student:	Interviewer/date:

1. How good were the joining instructions?
   ☐ ☐ ☐ ☐ ☐
   Very poor   Very good

2. How good was the course pre-work?
   ☐ ☐ ☐ ☐ ☐
   Very poor   Very good

3. Did you discuss your personal development objectives with your manager prior to the course?
   ☐ ☐ ☐ ☐ ☐
   No   Yes

4. What was your overall impression of the course?
   ☐ ☐ ☐ ☐ ☐
   Very poor   Very good

5. How would you rate the effectiveness of the trainer(s) in the following categories:

   a. Subject-matter knowledge
   b. Presentation skills
   c. Enthusiasm for the subject
   d. Personal coaching
   e. Balance between lecture and practice
   ☐ ☐ ☐ ☐ ☐
   Very poor   Very good

6. How would you rate the quality of the course materials?
   ☐ ☐ ☐ ☐ ☐
   Very poor   Very good

7. How would you rate the relevance of the course to your work situation?
   ☐ ☐ ☐ ☐ ☐
   Very poor   Very good

8. How would you rate the duration of the course?
   ☐ ☐ ☐ ☐ ☐
   Too long   Too short

9. Did the course cater for your own preferred learning style?
   ☐ ☐ ☐ ☐ ☐
   No   Yes

Figure 13.4   *An excerpt from a student follow-up questionnaire*

Interview sponsoring manager(s)   The students' attendance on a course will have been sponsored by their immediate managers. Interview a sample of managers to see whether they have observed an improvement in performance as a result of course attendance. Also interview the organization's training manager to gain additional data on the effectiveness of the course.

Write report   Structure the report around the supplier standards and provide copies of questionnaires and observation forms.

Discuss report with supplier   Always meet the supplier to discuss the report and to communicate your recommendations. Sending the report without a meeting or an explanation is not as effective and it misses an opportunity to strengthen the customer–supplier relationship.

Supplier responds to report

Ask the supplier to make a written response to the report which will include their reaction to the observations and their plans for improving their performance.

Re-audit

If the initial audit was satisfactory, it may not be necessary to carry out a complete re-audit, but it will be necessary to assure yourself that your recommendations and the supplier's action plans have been carried out.

The audit will have to be repeated in its entirety if the initial audit was unsatisfactory. The supplier will be given every chance and assistance to reach the required standards, but you will have to look for alternative sources of supply if the second audit is unsatisfactory.

14 Training networks

Many large companies are concerned that they are 're-inventing the wheel' all over their organizations, with the consequent duplication of effort and loss of efficiency. A common solution to this problem is the formation of networks which allow learning to be shared across the business. This chapter looks at the purpose of networks, the characteristics of successful networks, and how to make the most of technology including e-mail and the Internet.

Networks come in two forms:

- physical networks – meetings of representatives from different parts of the organization,
- virtual networks – where members don't meet physically but use information technology to keep in touch.

Irrespective of whether they are virtual or physical, networks typically produce the outputs shown in Figure 14.1.

Physical networks

As most networks are physical networks, I am going to use a fictional example to illustrate the purpose of networks and why some networks function better than others. This example assumes a business with a fairly complex organizational structure:

- a large parent company,
- a central headquarters staff (including training and development staff),
- six or more relatively independent businesses (with their own headquarters),
- over 100 locations around the world.

The company established a training network whose main activity was a series of meetings which were held once a quarter at four different regional locations. Meetings were attended by training staff from sites within a 200 km radius but did not include representatives from the site's parent businesses.

The meetings were organized by headquarters' training staff who took the same agenda to each of the four regions.

Networking was limited to the parent company's home country and was thought of in terms of physical outputs such as network meetings and training directories rather than activities or results to be achieved. The network meetings, and hence the network, were calendar led rather than purpose driven. There were very few 'processing' and 'workshop' activities at the meetings.

After the initial novelty, attendance at the network meetings fell dramatically and only two or three stalwarts (plus a similar number of the central training staff) continued to attend each of the regional meetings.

The main sources of information sharing were a 'round table' session at the network meetings and the information contained in the training directory.

One of the root problems of this approach was that the network meetings were being run for their own sake. Although there was a purpose – to share learning – it was far too general to hold the network together and to provide a clear agenda for the meetings. The network only started to fulfil its initial promise when it was realized that its real purpose was to support a set of broader objectives:

- Training will be identified, delivered and evaluated to world-class standards by world-class processes.

- Maximum use will be made of the existing training resource.

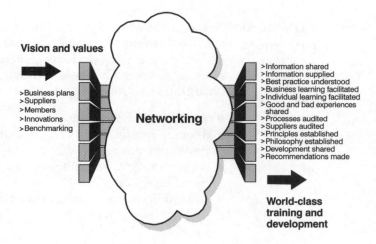

Figure 14.1   *Input–output diagram of a training network*

- Training will be a significant contributor to business success.
- Our employees will receive appropriate, timely training which will be admired and recognized throughout the world.
- Our businesses will have a shared training philosophy and principles.

Other problems that can be identified in the example are:

- Very little of the networking activity extended to the overseas parts of the business.
- The network meetings were held every three months irrespective of whether there was a real need.
- The majority of the meeting time was given over to 'information sharing'. This restricted the time that could be spent on 'information-processing' items such as discussion and problem solving. This was further compounded by trying to cover too much in the time allowed.
- Some of the network's members had influence on training and development at their own site but were not able to influence their parent business directly.
- The network's structure did not have representation from the people who ran the main businesses.

Factors which contribute to a successful training network

Taking the lessons of this example into account, we can summarize the factors that contribute to the success of a training network.

Definite purpose

The network should have a definite purpose, preferably in support of a broader set of objectives. All network activity should support the aim of providing your employees with world-class training and development. There should be no 'sacred cows'. Elements of the training network should be continued only for as long as they are useful.

One of the main purposes of a training network is to ensure that training plans are aligned to the business strategies. Having the chief executive officer make a presentation to the training network early on in the business planning cycle is a powerful means of achieving this. (See Chapter 2, Training needs, for a detailed description of this process.)

Appropriate ownership

The network should be 'owned' and driven by someone who has access to, and influence with, the chief executive officer and personnel director.

The network owner should try to visit individual network members, at their own locations, at least once every two years. This helps to flush out issues which would not normally surface in network meetings.

Appropriate membership

It is essential that the right people (those who have the power to implement change in their own organizations) are members of the network. Don't ignore important levels within the structure of the company when selecting members for the network.

Appropriate structure

In a multinational company, the network should extend internationally – not just cover the organization's home country.

When the size and geographical spread of the network increase, having everybody attend the same network meetings starts to become unmanageable. One approach is to run duplicate 'regional' meetings around the country, but this involves the network owner in an unacceptable amount of wasted time and travel.

A better solution is to have self-directed 'daughter' networks (with representation on the main network). These can be formed on a business or regional basis. You can still have occasional conferences when you can get larger numbers of people together.

Remember, a network is far more than a series of meetings, so encourage members to interact outside the structure of the network meetings.

Effective sharing of resources

One of the main reasons for forming a network is to improve resource utilization. This can be achieved by:

- sharing development of new training programmes,
- negotiating discounts on a national and international basis,
- co-ordinating applications for national awards,
- co-ordinating responses to surveys,
- sharing materials, people and other resources.

Effective dissemination of learning

An essential function of the network is to disseminate learning to the different parts of the business. Rather than trying to capture all the learning itself – which would take an enormous resource – the network should concentrate on recording where the learning can be found, and on bringing together people with complementary needs. This can be done through a paper-based training network directory. The section on virtual networks describes an electronic training network directory.

The network can also co-ordinate benchmarking and conference attendance. A network member makes a benchmarking visit to an external company or attends a conference and reports back to the network and other parts of the business.

Effective meetings Don't just plan network meetings for every month or once a quarter. Time them to coincide with and support significant events such as the production of the business plan.

The majority of the time spent at network meetings should be used for discussion, decision making and problem solving. Don't waste time sharing information which could be communicated better by other means such as newsletters. (See the section on virtual networks for other methods of distributing information.)

It is better to have one or two 'information-processing' items covered thoroughly than to rush through a crowded agenda.

Attendees, location, timing and duration of network meetings should be determined by the purpose and content of the meeting.

Meetings can be made more interesting by having presentations from high-profile speakers and demonstrations by suppliers.

Virtual networks

Many of the problems associated with physical networks are caused by the separation of their members in time and distance. Fortunately, these are problems which can be overcome by the use of a virtual network.

A virtual network is one whose members do not meet physically. Of course, this does not mean that the members would *never* meet physically – successful networks use a combination of physical and virtual networking.

As virtual networking has been made a great deal easier with the introduction of e-mail and the Internet, you could overlook the fact that virtual networks have been with us for many centuries, with members keeping in touch via letters, newsletters, magazines and books.

The following are a number of additional methods which can be used to support a virtual network.

Voice mail Voice mail allows people to leave recorded messages when they telephone you. The messages are usually recorded digitally and can be accessed from any telephone that has tone dialling. Telephone answering machines were the original form of voice mail.

It is possible to leave a detailed message, so voice mail allows you to communicate with people who are rarely at their desk or who work in different time zones.

Dial-a-fax   Many commercial companies distribute information to their customers by fax. A refinement of this is where the customer requests and automatically receives the information by fax. This has obvious applications in a network where, instead of deluging your members with every single piece of information, reports and papers can be requested when needed.

Electronic mail   Electronic mail (or e-mail) is another system which allows you to communicate with people independently of time and geography. You will need a computer that can be linked to either a commercial service provider or your company's own e-mail system. The service provider will provide you with all the software you need.

Messages addressed to you are held at your service provider's computer until you make a connection. The messages can then be read immediately or transferred to your computer. If you are linked to your service provider via a telephone connection, it's cheaper to transfer the messages to your computer, break the connection and read the messages later.

When you send a message, you will need to know the e-mail address of the person you want to contact. E-mail addresses can look a bit strange. For example, mine is:

mikewills@compuserve.com

The characters to the left of the '@' sign identify the recipient of the message. These characters can be letters, numbers or a combination. You can also use some other characters, provided that their use has not been restricted.

The characters between the '@' and the '.' identify the service provider and the characters after the '.' identify the type of organization. For example, 'com' indicates commercial, 'co' is company, 'gov' is government, and 'ac' is academic. Many addresses also have a country identifier tagged on the end, as in '.uk'.

E-mail addresses have to be typed exactly as they are written. For example, in my address there should be no space between 'mike' and 'wills'.

The space is one of the restricted characters, so you will find that people either run the words together (as in 'mikewills') or replace the space with a dot or an underline character, as in 'mike.wills' or 'mike_wills'.

You type the message in exactly the same way as if you were using a simple word processor, and when you have finished you instruct the computer to send the message. It is sent to your provider's computer and is then transferred to the recipient's service provider. The transfer will not be instantaneous as there is unlikely to be a direct connection between the two service providers' computers. The message will have to travel round the world in a series of 'jumps' from one computer to another.

The same message can be sent or copied to several recipients at the same time, which makes e-mail an ideal medium for communicating with network members. You will also find that because there is a culture of informality surrounding the use of e-mail, many people will use e-mail in circumstances in which they would be reluctant to write a letter.

Electronic newsletters Newsletters are a traditional method of keeping network members in touch, but their use can be restricted because of printing and distribution costs (including addressing and filling envelopes). Other methods of distributing a newsletter while keeping your printing costs to a minimum are to use e-mail or a fax machine.

If you have a large network, standing by a fax machine for a couple of hours is not the best use of your time. Try to use a fax that can keep all the network members' fax numbers in its memory so you can get on with something else while it does the dialling. Using fax can be quite expensive, especially when you have overseas members, but it is still comparable to the cost of surface mail and is certainly much quicker.

The quality of a faxed newsletter can be improved if your computer has fax software. Compose the newsletter using a word processor and, instead of printing it out and feeding it into a fax machine, fax it directly from your computer. This is usually done by 'printing' the document to the fax software instead of the printer.

The cheapest way of distributing a newsletter is using e-mail – it costs the same and takes the same amount of time no matter how many copies you are sending out. You may be able to 'attach' the newsletter to a memo. The recipients can then save the newsletter to their hard disk and, provided that they have the same word-processing software, can either read it on screen or print it. The look of the received newsletter may vary if the recipients have different printers connected to their computers.

If you can't be certain about the software being used at the receiving end, it's probably safest to send the newsletter as plain text within the body of the memo – but this does mean there will be no graphics and you will have to use a very simple format. A guide on how to convert a word-processor file to a plain text (or ASCII) file is given in Appendix 3. Or, since most people who have e-mail also have an Internet browser, you can save the newsletter in HTML format that can be viewed using any browser software.

Electronic network directory

Many networks have directories which list the network's members and the expertise that they can share with other members of the network. Paper-based directories share the same problems as traditional newsletters in that they are expensive to print and distribute.

An electronic directory can be distributed either as an e-mail attachment or on a lightweight computer disk. It also provides links to other parts of the directory and allows you to search for the information you require. Figure 14.2 shows the first screen of an electronic network directory.

This directory was constructed by collecting the data in a database and then writing a program for viewing the data which could be used by people who had no previous experience of databases.

Internet home pages

An Internet home page is just like having a noticeboard that anyone in the network can access at any time they want. A well-designed home page will also have links to related information and other home pages, building a 'web' of useful information.

If you have e-mail it is likely that you already have the software (called a browser) for connecting to the Internet. You can pay to have a home page designed for you but it really isn't too difficult to do it yourself. A good book on the subject is *Teach Yourself html* (Bride, 1996).

You need to know the location of a home page (called a URL) before you can access it. The location of my home page (which you are welcome to access to see how a home page can be used to support a virtual network) is:

http://ourworld.compuserve.com/homepages/mikewills

URLs are constructed in a similar way to e-mail addresses, but may be much longer. However, some may be quite simple, such as http://www.bt.com for telephone company BT.

Networked computers

If the members of the training network are connected to the same computer network, you can make use of shared files for collaborating on projects and distributing information.

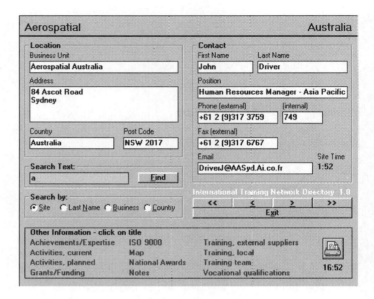

Figure 14.2 *An example of an electronic directory*

A private network may also have its own version of the Internet (called an intranet) where you can set up home pages that can only be accessed by people connected to your computer network.

Telephone and video conferencing

Instead of travelling to network meetings you could set up a telephone or video conference. Although these conferences can never be a complete substitute for a person-to-person meeting, they work remarkably well if there is a simple, prepared agenda and the participants know each other already.

A telephone conference for up to three people is relatively easy to set up using an ordinary telephone – contact your telephone company for details.

Once you get beyond three people it is best to use video conferencing so that you can keep track of who is talking. You will need to use a dedicated video link to get good quality and this can prove to be expensive – but not as expensive as flying everybody around the world.

Electronic conferences

Some Internet service providers have forums where people can 'talk' to each other electronically. It's rather like sending and receiving a series of e-mail messages where the response is almost immediate so long as members are on-line at the same time.

15 Using managers and others to deliver training

Along with other business functions, the training function is becoming leaner and flatter. Where once large, central training departments covered all aspects of the business, training is now being delivered by external suppliers, line managers and subject-matter experts in addition to in-house trainers.

Some organizations have the majority of their training delivered by external consultants. Although this is flexible, it can be a very expensive option. Many other companies are opting for the route of using line managers and subject-matter experts to deliver their training, not just because it is less expensive. Using your own people as instructors brings credibility to the subject matter and allows you to tailor the training to your exact needs.

Whatever method you choose for the primary delivery of your training, it is probably safest to keep your options open by not 'putting all your eggs in one basket'.

Using only in-house trainers can lead to over-resourcing and inflexibility. Depending on external consultants can drive up your costs enormously. Having only part-time instructors will eventually lead to lower quality standards.

The training professional's role

The trend towards using part-time instructors has implications for the role of the training professional. Rather than being responsible for the delivery of training, the role becomes more concerned with quality assurance and ensuring that the people who develop and deliver the training have the necessary skills.

You may decide to continue doing the training administration yourself or, depending on the organization, you may decide to devolve the administration as well.

Taking the empowered approach to training even further, you might even decide to set up 'faculties' which are aligned to specific 'disciplines' (such as engineering or sales) within the organization. The faculties would be responsible not only for developing, administering and delivering training in their areas, but also for research and capturing learning.

Assuring the quality of training

In Chapter 13, Training quality, I said that: 'Training should be considered to be no different to any other business process – and as such it should be subject to the same rigorous quality controls as any other critical process.'

This is just as true – perhaps even more so – when you are using managers and subject-matter experts to deliver your training. There is absolutely no reason why you should settle for standards which would be unacceptable if a full-time trainer or external consultant were delivering the material. Of course, you wouldn't necessarily expect them to be 'master performers', but you would expect them to be able to score '4' on a 1–5 scale.

The quality assurance process described in Chapter 13 can easily be adapted to audit internal rather than external suppliers. The only difference is that, as you will probably not be paying for the training, you won't need to examine the business relationship.

Developing part-time trainers

Chapter 4, Trainers, covers the development of full-time trainers. The process of developing part-time trainers is essentially the same but there are some additional factors which have to be taken into account.

The development needs to be more practical than theoretical and, because the instructor will not be training every day, the principles need to be simple and explicit.

When I was coaching a new part-time trainer, I remember giving advice similar to the following:

Training courses should have objectives and a method for checking that these objectives have been met. Putting it another way – if it doesn't have objectives and if it doesn't have a test, it isn't training!

Another consequence of this is that training does not have to take place in a training room but it does have to:

- be planned,
- be certified,
- be delivered by a certified instructor,
- be entered in the training records,
- have a record kept of the test results.

In other words – if it has objectives, and those objectives are tested, it *is* training!

Each objective should have an associated test item, and each test item should have an associated objective.

The course should also have been reviewed by colleagues of the author and at least one pilot course should have been run.

To begin with, part-time instructors will only need to understand the basic elements of a quality training process, which are:

- identifying the training need,
- developing the course,
- delivering the course,
- evaluating the training.

It is essential that trainers attend a recognized train-the-trainer course. For full-time trainers it is probably best that they attend train-the-trainer courses early on in their career so that they have the foundations of a strong theoretical framework that will allow them to make sense of the experiences they have during their development.

For part-time trainers, I have found it better to work very closely with them on a one-to-one basis during the development and presentation of their first course.

The section on 'Developing your own courses' in Chapter 3 will provide you with good reference material when you are coaching instructors on the development of their first course.

Similarly, the course delivery process described at the beginning of Chapter 9 will help trainers when they come

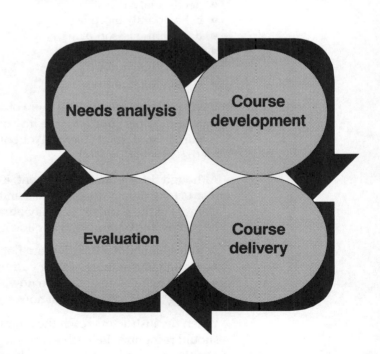

Figure 15.1　*The basic elements of a quality training process*

to prepare and present their first course. I would also provide them with a copy of the trainer observation form. Not only will this let them know how they are going to be assessed, but it is also a very useful summary of how to conduct yourself in the classroom.

When they present their first course, under your supervision, you should carry out a trainer observation as described in Chapter 4. This allows instructors to understand the need for the training and to concentrate on their development areas. It also allows you to have the train-the-trainer course tailored to the exact needs of your instructors based on objective observational data.

Based on previous experience, the content of a course for a part-time instructor is likely to include:

- presentation techniques,
- use of audiovisual equipment,
- learning principles,
- encouraging participation,
- questioning skills,
- facilitation skills,
- demonstrating,
- coaching,
- discussion leading,
- needs analysis,
- behavioural objectives,
- developing lesson plans,
- preparing visual aids,
- preparing handouts,
- evaluating training.

It will probably take several more observations after the train-the-trainer course for the instructor to reach the required standard of at least '4' out of '5' for all the criteria on the observation form.

Although the standard is stringent, it is possible for every instructor to attain the required standard because every element of the standard is behavioural and the criteria can be met by one or more of the following strategies:

- doing something that they are not currently doing,
- ceasing one or more of their current behaviours,
- doing more of what they do now,
- doing less of what they do now.

When the instructors reach the required standard, you should recognize their achievement, perhaps by issuing a certificate. Even better if the training can be accredited and put towards the award of a recognized qualification.

Don't forget to carry out observations after the trainer has been certified to ensure that the standards are being maintained.

The line manager's role

With the devolution of training development and delivery to the business, the line manager's role in identifying training needs and determining whether training is appropriate becomes even more critical.

When I was introducing this type of training approach into a US aerospace manufacturer, it rapidly became apparent that we would have to run a workshop to make line managers aware of what training can and cannot do, as well as underscoring the importance of the manager's role in the overall training process.

Although this workshop was run to support the strategy of training being delivered by non-trainers, it wouldn't be a bad idea to run a similar workshop for managers in any organization that values training and development.

An outline for such a workshop is given in Figures 15.2 to 15.5. Of course, you will need to extend and modify the outline to meet your local needs.

'Welcome to this presentation on the training process and your role in ensuring that we have world-class training in this organization.'

**Managers' overview
of the
training process**

[Review the session's objectives]

Objectives

By the end of this workshop you will be able to:

- Define training
- Identify the factors which contribute to world-class training
- Identify when training is appropriate
- Recognize the importance of course and instructor certification
- Describe a process for evaluating training

[Review the session's agenda]

Agenda

- Training quality
- Definition of training
- Getting the basics right
- Training process
- Identification of training and non-training solutions
- Alternatives to training
- Course and instructor certification
- Evaluating training

Figure 15.2   Managers' overview (page 1 of 4)

'Training should be considered no different to any other business process – and as such it should be subject to the same rigours as any other critical process.'

Training quality

Training is a critical process within the business. The quality requirement for training is no different from the quality requirement for all other critical processes.

'From this definition it can be seen that training activities should have objectives and a method for checking that these objectives have been met. Putting it another way – if it doesn't have objectives and if it doesn't have a test, it isn't training!'

'Another consequence of this is that training does not have to take place in a training room but it does have to:

• be planned;
• be certified;
• be delivered by a certified instructor;
• be entered in the training records;
• have a record kept of the test results.

'In other words – if it has objectives, and those objectives are tested, it *is* training!'

Definition of training

Training is the transfer of defined and measurable knowledge or skills.

'For me, being world class is simply doing the basics, and doing them right. This might seem very easy – but how many organizations do you see getting the basics consistently right?

'The elements of world-class training are a quality training process, certified courses and certified instructors.'

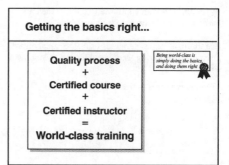

Getting the basics right...

Quality process
+
Certified course
+
Certified instructor
=
World-class training

Being world-class is simply doing the basics, and doing them right

Figure 15.3 *Managers' overview (page 2 of 4)*

'The basic elements of a quality training process are:

• identifying the training need;
• developing the course;
• delivering the course;
• evaluating the training.'

[Refer participants to Chapter 1, The process of training, for a more detailed description of the training process.]

Training process

'There is a tendency to assume that every business problem can be corrected by training. In reality training forms only 10 per cent of the solution – but this is a vital 10 per cent. If a person has not been trained properly, everything else that follows is built on sand.

'The questions shown in this slide will help you decide whether training is, or is not, an appropriate solution.'

[Go through the questions using the explanation and example given in the following sections in Chapter 2, Training needs:

• Check that training is an appropriate solution
• Check queries with managers]

Is training an appropriate solution?

• Is there an important business or strategic need for this training?
• Does the individual already have the knowledge and skills?
• Is the individual willing to use the knowledge and skills?
• Has the individual received this training before?
• Does the individual have the ability to be trained?

'If training is not an appropriate solution, then we have to find alternatives to training.'

[Go through these suggestions using the explanation given in the following section in Chapter 2, Training needs:

• Find alternatives to training]

Alternatives to training

• No action required.
• Remove barriers.
• Arrange coaching.
• Arrange practice.
• Arrange counselling.
• Re-design job/procedure.
• Look at recruitment standards.
• Move person into another job.

Figure 15.4 *Managers' overview (page 3 of 4)*

'A certified course will have objectives and tests. Each objective should have an associated test item and each test item should have an associated objective.

'The course should also have been reviewed by colleagues of the author, and at least one pilot course should have been run.'

[It should not be necessary to go into the details of how a course is developed at this stage, but if managers are interested you can refer them to Chapter 3, Training courses.]

'The training manager will work closely with the instructors during the preparation of their first courses.

'We will provide them with a train-the-trainer course which will be followed up by observation and feedback.

'Instructors will be certified when they score at least "4" out of "5" for every observation criterion.'

[See Chapter 4, Trainers, for a copy of the observation form and a detailed description of the instructor certification process.]

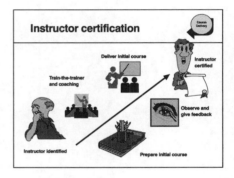

'Evaluation of training is essential for ensuring that the learning has been transferred into the business, and that we are providing the right kind of training to meet the business needs.'

[Go through the algorithm shown on this slide by referring to Chapter 12, Evaluation.]

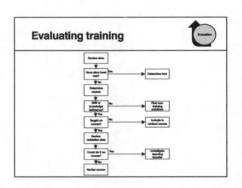

Figure 15.5   Managers' overview (page 4 of 4)

16 Competencies

Organizations are increasingly using competencies to help them identify and develop the characteristics in their staff that they need to be successful. Competencies provide a common language for describing performance. They help identify and prepare successors, allowing 'surprise fits' to be included while avoiding 'poor fits'; facilitate the selection process; and allow managers to have objective development discussions with individuals based on capabilities that the business needs.

There are many approaches to the use of competencies and this has resulted in much confusion. The purpose of this chapter is to provide an explanation of:

- what competencies are;
- their relationship to the training process;
- how they can be identified;
- how they are used.

What are competencies?

There are two types of competency (or competence):

- threshold (or essential) competence;
- distinguishing competency.

Threshold competences are characteristics that are causally related to effective or average performance. In terms of the training process, threshold competences are essentially the same as the skills and knowledge that are used in training needs analysis.

Distinguishing competencies are characteristics that are causally related to superior performance. In other words, they separate the superior performer from the average performer. (See Figure 16.1).

In a work context it is possible to evaluate an individual using a continuum of characteristics (see Figure 16.2). These range from results (what a person 'does') to innate characteristics (what a person 'is').

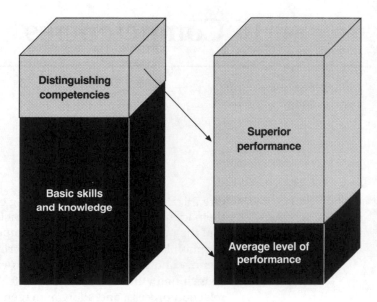

Figure 16.1 *Distinguishing competencies*

Knowledge and skills are relatively easy to develop (see Figure 16.3) but rarely differentiate outstanding performers from average performers. They are job dependent and usually indicate the minimum requirements (threshold competences) for doing a job adequately.

Although motives, traits, attitudes and values are hard to develop, it is often these which make the difference between average and superior performance. They are more generic, which means that they are less likely to be job dependent.

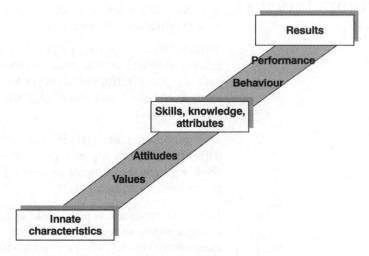

Figure 16.2 *Continuum of personal characteristics*

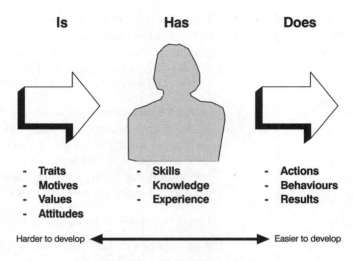

Is	Has	Does
- Traits	- Skills	- Actions
- Motives	- Knowledge	- Behaviours
- Values	- Experience	- Results
- Attitudes		

Harder to develop ←————————————→ Easier to develop

Figure 16.3   Ease/difficulty of developing personal characteristics

These ideas have profound implications for training because they imply that, although training courses may be excellent at developing threshold skills and *competent* performance, they may not be the best method for developing *superior* performance in an organization.

Using competencies

There are a large number of uses for competencies. Maximum benefit is gained by using competencies within key processes such as:

- selection,
- appraisal,
- personal development planning,
- training needs analysis,
- objective setting,
- training evaluation,
- succession planning.

Competencies are extremely powerful tools for shaping organizational culture. They help to change individuals' behaviour in directions required by the business by focusing their attention on 'what it takes to be successful' (e.g. 'has a broad business perspective'). Once businesses have identified and articulated the competencies they need, they can begin to focus employee development activities on acquiring them.

Identifying competencies

There are three main ways of deriving competencies:

- adopting an existing set,
- adapting an existing set,
- identifying a unique set of competencies.

Adopting an existing set

The advantage of this option is that it can be quick and easy to implement and, with careful selection, provides a high degree of actual as well as face validity. Some existing sets of generic competencies (such as McBer's) have an empirical basis and should be broadly applicable.

Using competencies that have been derived from an existing set saves time because you don't have to start with a blank sheet or an unprocessed list of characteristics, but you do need to make sure that they are appropriate for your application. An expert panel can be used to check whether the competencies are relevant to the needs of the business.

The disadvantages associated with this option are:

* It might be difficult to find a generic set of competencies that fit your business.
* Isolating the differentiating competencies might be more difficult.
* You might miss some of the unique aspects of the roles you are considering.

Adapting an existing set

Existing sets of competencies can be modified to reflect the needs, priorities and plans of the business – leading to an increased sense of ownership. An expert panel can be used to adapt the existing set, adding, deleting or modifying competencies where necessary.

Identifying a unique set of competencies

The advantage of this option is that the competencies will be developed by the people closest to the critical business issues and will therefore be driven by the specific business situation.

A potential disadvantage of this approach is that some of the processes used to identify competencies can be rigorous and time consuming. This is why many companies use external consultants to design and implement such processes. This approach should be considered when:

* businesses need to redefine job requirements to meet new demands and needs,
* when the jobs in question are 'key' roles,
* significant numbers of people are in these roles,
* a significant recruitment requirement exists for these roles.

The process outlined in Figure 16.4 is typically used to develop a set of tailor-made competencies.

Determine performance standards

As competencies are used to differentiate between average and superior performers, we need to know what constitutes superior performance. An effective way of doing

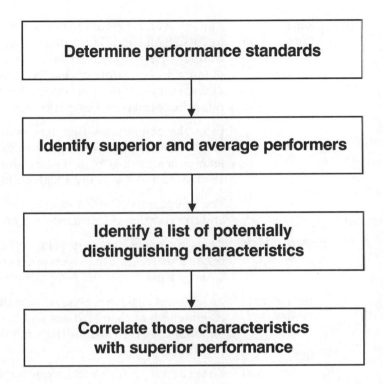

Figure 16.4 *Process for identifying competencies*

this is to have an expert panel determine the performance standards of the roles that are to be analysed.

Identify superior and average performers

The expert panel can now select a sample of superior and average performers. The sample should have at least 20 subjects: 12 superior and 8 average performers. If you are forced to use a smaller sample, make sure that you have twice as many superior performers as average performers because you will always learn most from your 'high fliers'.

Identify a list of potentially distinguishing characteristics

Use behaviour event interviews, job element analysis or a repertory grid (all described below) to identify potentially distinguishing characteristics.

Correlate those characteristics with superior performance

Distinguishing competencies are those that are shared by the superior performers but will not be in evidence for average performers. Use another sample to check whether the identified competencies can distinguish superior from average performers.

Tools for identifying competencies

The following is a description of the tools that are commonly used for identifying competencies.

Behavioural event interviews

The behavioural event interview is a technique developed by McClelland and Dailey that is used to identify competencies by getting detailed descriptions of a sample of individuals' performances. The sample includes both average and superior performers, but the interviewers are unaware of interviewees' performance records.

Examples of questions used in behavioural event interviews are: 'Describe a time when you had to work as part of a team to achieve a goal' or 'Tell me about a time in the last 18 months that was really a high point for you.'

The characteristics which emerge are coded, categorized and correlated to performance criteria.

Expert panels

An expert panel is a group of knowledgeable human resource specialists, managers and superior performers who are used to identify competencies.

Job element analysis

Job element analysis was developed by Boyatzis and uses a weighted list of characteristics that managers perceive as important in distinguishing superior from average performers.

Repertory grid

The repertory grid is a technique developed by Kelly that takes three individuals at a time from a sample that contains both average and superior performers. An expert panel is then asked in which way two of the individuals are similar to each other and different from the third. These similarities and differences form the basis of a set of competencies which are related to superior performance.

Assessing competencies

The two most common ways of assessing competencies are:

- assessment by the individual's manager,
- attendance at an assessment centre.

Assessment by the individual's manager

This usually takes the form of an appraisal or counselling session. It is at its most powerful when the manager and individual agree on the assessment.

Both the manager and the individual should make separate assessments of the individual's competency levels (usually on a 1–5 scale) before the session starts. The session can then concentrate on reconciling differences of opinion.

The process is made much easier if there is a description of the expected behaviour for each level of the competency.

An extension of this method is 360-degree appraisal, where the competencies are assessed by peers and subordinates as well as the individual's manager.

Attendance at an assessment centre

At an assessment centre individuals' levels of competency are measured by a series of tests and exercises. The scores and results of the exercises have to be converted to competency levels. Typical assessment tools are described below.

Tools for assessing competencies

The following is a description of tools commonly used for assessing competencies:

Personality questionnaires

Personality questionnaires usually take the form of self-reporting tests. A series of statements is rated or scored on the basis of how well they describe the person being tested. The results of the tests rate the individual against a number of factors on a 1–10 scale (stens).

The personality factors have to be correlated to the competencies you are measuring and the sten score has to be converted to the competency level.

Aptitude tests

There are a number of aptitude tests that cover areas of ability such as verbal and numerical reasoning. They are more objective than self-reporting personality questionnaires. The results are usually expressed in percentiles. A percentile score indicates a person's ranking in the group of people for whom the test was designed. For example, a person whose test results were in the 75th percentile in a test designed for senior managers would be ranked in the top 25 per cent of senior managers.

Aptitude tests have to be chosen to represent the competencies you are looking for and the percentile score has to be converted to the competency level.

In-tray exercise

This is a simulation exercise in which participants work through a typical basket of items. This includes 'big picture' items as well as looking at more detailed issues. Items include memos, data analysis and problems which require urgent attention. It is a timed exercise that most participants will not finish. They are expected to prioritize their responses and to complete a written review of how and why they made decisions about items in the exercise.

A scoring key has to be constructed that relates the in-tray items to the specific competencies. The person scoring the exercise looks at the decisions for evidence of the particular competency. The evidence is collated and each competency is given a rating.

Focused interviews

Focused interviews are used to assess competencies and involve using the same techniques as behavioural event interviewing. The purpose of the focused interviews is to elicit evidence of the required competencies. For example, a question that could be asked to elicit evidence of 'customer orientation' would be: 'Tell me about a time in the recent past when you personally have had to deal with a customer.'

Interviewers are provided with an interview guide for them to record and summarize the candidate's replies. Time is allocated at the end of each interview for completion, matching interview evidence with descriptions of the competency levels.

Although the questions target specific competencies, individuals would still be credited with other competencies if strong positive evidence of them emerged during the course of the interview.

Interviewers should compare notes at the end of each session to ensure consistency of their ratings.

Appendices

- Appendix 1 Spreadsheet examples
- Appendix 2 Public holidays
- Appendix 3 Hints for converting a word-processor file to ASCII format
- Appendix 4 Computer specifications
- Appendix 5 An example of course development
- Appendix 6 Using criteria to determine course content
- Appendix 7 Trainers' checklists

Appendix 1 Spreadsheet examples

The following examples of spreadsheets are provided so that you can use them as a basis for programming your own spreadsheets. The formulae are Lotus 1-2-3 compatible but you should have no difficulty in converting them for use on your own spreadsheet.

If you don't want to have the bother of typing in the formulae, please e-mail the author (mikewills@compuserve.com) for details of how you can obtain electronic versions of the spreadsheets.

Course cost calculations

This spreadsheet shows how Table 6.6 in Chapter 6 (Training plans and budgets) was put together.

- Set Default Currency to £
- Set width of column A to 20
- Set width of column B to 16
- Set range B11..B21 to Currency Format, 0 decimal places
- Type the following into the cells indicated:

A1: 'Middle Manager's Course

A3: 'Type of Training:
B3: "Residential

A4: 'Duration (days):
B4: 5

A5: 'Number of Students:
B5: 20

A6: 'Number of Trainers:
B6: 3

A7: 'Type of Trainer:
B7: "Own

A8: 'Location:
B8: "Off-site

A9: 'Additional rooms:
B9: 4

A11: 'Trainer cost/day:
B11: 300

A12: 'Materials/student:
B12: 50

A13: 'Main room hire/day:
B13: 0

A14: 'Seminar room hire:
B14: 50

A15: 'Accomm/student:
B15: 120

A16: 'Equip hire/day:
B16: 250

A17: 'Simulation costs:
B17: 9000

A19: 'TOTAL COST:
B19:
+(B11*B4*B6)+(B12*B5)+(B13*B4)+(B14*B4*B9)+(B15*(B5+B6)*B4)+(B16*B4)+B17

A20: 'COST/STUDENT:
B20: +(B19/B5)

A21: 'COST/STUDENT/DAY:
B21: +(B20/B4)

Spreadsheet for analysing student feedback

- Set the width of column A to 27
- Set the widths of columns B, C, D, E and F to 4
- Set the width of column G to 6
- Set the width of column H to 5
- Type the following into the cells indicated:

A1: \-
A2: 'Question
A3: \-

B1: \-
B2: "1
B3: \-

	A	B	C	D	E	F	G	H
1	----------							----------
2	*Question*		1	2	3	4	5	*Tot*	*Ave*
3	----------							----------
4	a. Relevance						0	ERR
5	b. Ability to apply						0	ERR
6	c. Probability of using						0	ERR
7	d. Overall satisfaction						0	ERR
8	e. Trainer effectiveness						0	ERR
9	----------							----------

Figure A1.1   *Spreadsheet for analysing student feedback before data entry*

C1: \-
C2: "2
C3: \-

D1: \-
D2: "3
D3: \-

E1: \-
E2: "4
E3: \-

F1: \-
F2: "5
F3: \-

G1: \-
G2: "Tot
G3: \-

H1: \-
H2: "Ave
H3: \-

A9: \-
A4: 'a. Relevance

B9: \-
A5: 'b. Ability to apply

C9: \-
A6: ' c. Probability of using

D9: \-
A7: 'd. Overall satisfaction

E9: \-
A8: 'e. Trainer effectiveness

F9: \-
G9: \-
H9: \-

G4: @SUM(B4..F4)
H4: (B4+(C4*2)+(D4*3)+(E4*4)+(F4*5))/G4
G5: @SUM(B5..F5)
H5: (B5+(C5*2)+(D5*3)+(E5*4)+(F5*5))/G5
G6: @SUM(B6..F6)
H6: (B6+(C6*2)+(D6*3)+(E6*4)+(F6*5))/G6
G7: @SUM(B7..F7)
H7: (B7+(C7*2)+(D7*3)+(E7*4)+(F7*5))/G7
G8: @SUM(B8..F8)
H8: (B8+(C8*2)+(D8*3)+(E8*4)+(F8*5))/G8

You can save time when entering the formulae by:

- Copying cell A1 to range (B1..H1)
- Copying cell A3 to range (B3..H3)
- Copying cell A9 to range (B9..H9)
- Copying cell G4 to range (G5..G8)
- Copying cell H4 to range (H5..H8)

Using the spreadsheet

This spreadsheet is used to analyse the end-of-course evaluation forms. The ERR which appears in the 'Ave' (Average) column stands for ERROR. The error is caused by the spreadsheet dividing something by zero. The ERRs will disappear as soon as data is entered on each line.

- Working through the evaluation forms, count the number of students who gave the course a relevance score of 1 (i.e. very low relevance).
- Enter this number in cell B4.
- Then count the number of relevance scores of 2, 3, 4 and 5.
- Enter these numbers in cells C4, D4, E4 and F4.

The 'Tot' column will show you the total number of responses that you received for course relevance. This number is used as a check on the counting. The average score is shown in the 'Ave' column.

Follow a similar procedure for each of the response questions.

Appendix 2
Public holidays

These dates are only given as a guide to help you identify when your training dates would coincide with a public holiday in the UK. The government has the final say on when public holidays occur each year. This is especially so when a public holiday falls on a Saturday or Sunday. Typically it would be held over until the following Monday.

Fixed holidays

New Year's Day

1 January (Scotland also has a holiday on 2 January).

Saint Patrick's Day

17 March (Northern Ireland only).

May Day

The first Monday after 1 May.

Spring Bank Holiday

The last Monday in May.

Orangeman's Day

12 July (Northern Ireland only).

Summer Bank Holiday

The first Monday in August (Scotland only).

Late Summer Bank Holiday

The last Monday in August (not Scotland).

Christmas Day

25 December. If Christmas Day falls on Sunday, an additional holiday is normally given on the Tuesday.

Boxing Day

26 December. If Christmas Day falls on a Saturday, Boxing Day is usually moved to the Monday and an additional holiday is given on the Tuesday.

Moveable holidays

Good Friday

The Friday before Easter Sunday. Falls between 20 March and 23 April. Not always taken by some British factories who will often take the following Tuesday instead.

Easter Sunday

The first Sunday after the first full moon on or after the vernal equinox. Falls between 22 March and 25 April. Table A2.1 is a list of dates for Easter Sunday that will take you well into the twenty-first century:

Table A2.1   Dates for Easter Sunday

Year	Date	Year	Date
1999	4 April	2009	12 April
2000	23 April	2010	4 April
2001	15 April	2011	24 April
2002	31 March	2012	8 April
2003	20 April	2013	31 March
2004	11 April	2014	20 April
2005	27 March	2015	5 April
2006	16 April	2016	27 March
2007	8 April	2017	16 April
2008	23 March	2018	1 April

Easter Monday   The day after Easter Sunday (UK but not Scotland).

Ascension Day   Celebrated in some continental countries. 40 days after Easter, counting Easter Sunday as the first day. Falls between 30 April and 3 May.

Whit Monday   Celebrated in some continental countries. The Monday following the seventh Sunday after Easter. Falls between 11 May and 14 June.

Appendix 3
Hints for converting a word-processor file to ASCII format

Hint 1: Check to see if your word processor has a facility to convert documents to standard ASCII text files. If it has such a facility, use it to create an ASCII text file. Many programs identify ASCII files as 'Text only' files. On a Macintosh system the term is also 'Text only'.

Hint 2: If this doesn't work, see if your word processor will allow you to create a print file on a floppy disk. Use this option to create a print file from your original document.

Hint 3: Many word processors and computers have a facility for creating and editing computer programs. If you use this facility to create your text files, you can usually use the normal word-processing mode to edit the files and add formatting commands.

Appendix 4
Computer specifications

When you buy software to use on a course or for training administration, it is important to make sure that it will work on the computers that you are using. If possible, try to see the software working on a computer system that is exactly the same as yours. Failing that, check that the system requirements shown on the software's packaging or in its manual conform to the specification in your computer's manual. Figure A4.1 shows an example of a typical set of system requirements.

System requirements

The things that you have to look out for are:

- the type of machine on which the software will run;
- the type of disk that the computer accepts;
- the amount of memory the program needs;
- the type of display it requires;
- the type of pointing device, if any, it requires;
- the operating system required.

Type of computer

There are many types of computer. Software written for one type of computer will not work on a different type of computer, although commercial programs are available in different formats.

The software shown in Figure A4.1 requires an IBM-compatible computer. Your computer's manual will tell you whether your machine is IBM compatible. The glossary at

---

System requirements

- IBM compatible PC

- 386SX or higher processor

- CD-ROM drive

- Audio board

- Headphone or speakers

- SVGA resolution monitor, 256 colors or higher

- 4MB RAM

- At least 3.5 MB of hard disk space

- Microsoft Windows version 3.1 or above

- MS-DOS operating system version 3.1 or later

- Microsoft mouse or compatible pointing device

Figure A4.1   Typical computer system requirements

the end of this book gives an explanation of many of the terms you will come across.

Disks When you buy a computer program it usually comes on flexible magnetic disks called 'floppy' disks or on plastic disks called CD-ROMs. It is essential that you buy the program on a disk that your computer will accept. A hard disk is a magnetic disk that is permanently installed inside the computer. If a program requires a hard disk (as most commercial programs now do), you will need to transfer the program from the floppy disks to the hard disk as part of the installation procedure. It is also possible to run some programs directly from a CD-ROM.

Memory This is known as RAM (random access memory) and is measured in kilobytes (Kb) or megabytes (Mb).1 Kb is approximately the memory it would take to store 1000 characters. Letters, digits and spaces are all characters. 1 Mb is 1000 Kb. As programs become more demanding, the amount of memory needed increases. Currently the minimum memory required for a machine running the Windows 95 operating system is 24 Mb.

Type of display A computer's display looks like a television screen and is called a VDU (visual display unit). Early computers were unable to display pictures (graphics) and were only able to display text. Today computers can display graphics in full colour and high definition. The development of graphics displays evolved over a number of years and consequently the number of different displays that a computer can have is quite bewildering.

Always check your computer manual to make sure that your 'graphics adaptor' is one of those supported by the software. The software shown in Figure A4.1 needs an SVGA display. See the glossary for an explanation of this abbreviation and other abbreviations you are likely to come across.

Pointing device Most programs require a pointing device to work properly. A pointing device allows you to access any part of a computer's screen faster than you can with the cursor (arrow) keys.

The most popular type of pointing device is called a mouse, so called because its plastic body approximates to the shape of a mouse and the lead looks like a tail.

Operating system When a computer is switched on it is like a new-born baby: all the wiring is in place and it can carry out basic functions but it needs to be 'educated' to carry out more complex functions. This 'education' is carried out by a program called an operating system.

Managing the training process

The most popular operating system for IBM compatibles is Microsoft Windows. It is essential that the software you are using has been written not only for the operating system but also for the correct version of the operating system, for example Windows 95 or the earlier Windows 3.1. The version is usually indicated by a decimal number, e.g. 2.0, 3.3, 6.0. A program that has been written for an early version will normally work on a later (higher-numbered) version, but it is unlikely that a program written for a later version will work on an earlier version.

Other operating systems include Macintosh and Unix.

Appendix 5
An example
of course
development

The following is an example of how a course was developed using the process described in Chapter 3. The chosen course is simple and straightforward but it illustrates all the relevant points.

Defining the subject

A company had embarked on training all its full-time employees on total quality management. As the culture and language of total quality started to embed themselves into the fabric of the company, it was realized that contract staff were becoming increasingly isolated from the rest of the company. They had no understanding of the language or processes of quality. It was not possible to justify giving them the six days of training that full-time employees receive. What was needed was a one-day overview that explained what total quality management was all about.

Describing the aims

The aim of running a one-day introduction to total quality management was to allow medium-term contractors to participate in 'quality circles'. They would not be expected to take a lead but they should not be confused when the company's permanent employees talked about total quality.

Obtaining subject-matter expertise

In this case the training analyst assigned to the development of this course had been training the full course for two years, so they already had subject-matter expertise. If the analyst had not had this previous experience, a considerable amount of time would have been required to bring them up to speed. Given the complexities of the subject, it could take about six months to gain sufficient subject-matter experience and knowledge. Without this experience the analyst would not be able to determine the critical content that should be included in the course.

Describing the students

The students were to be medium-term contractors. They would want to know what total quality is all about. Contractors may have concerns about being treated differently from full-time staff. They would also be concerned whether there would be another contract after the current one expires. Medium-term contractors may not have the same loyalty to the company as full-time staff but they have a professional approach and would be able to see how the concepts relate to their own businesses. In fact, it might be easier to communicate 'customer awareness' to these people than to permanent staff who rarely see an external customer.

Most of them would be designers with electrical/electronic, software or mechanical backgrounds. They would not appreciate a 'wordy' approach or put up with a significant amount of reading.

A significant minority would be translators with an arts background. Although English was not the mother tongue of many of the translators, the nature of their work obviously meant that they would not have any language difficulties. Reading would not present any problems.

All the contractors identified for the course were in good health with normal hearing and sight. Colour vision would normally be good for engineering people, but this would not usually be a requirement for translators.

Although some of the contractors may have done business studies at a university or college, the subject matter would be new to most of them.

Identifying the course content

In Chapter 3, I described how 'mind mapping' could be used to identify the content of a course. To apply this technique to the one-day 'Total Quality Management Overview', first draw a shape in the middle of a sheet of paper.

In this shape write 'TQM Overview', the subject of the course. Attached to branches radiating from this central shape are the main categories of topics that will make up the course. The categories come from thinking about the student description and the goals for this overview.

In this example the main categories were based on the questions the students would ask about total quality management and what the company would expect them to be able to do after they had completed the training. The

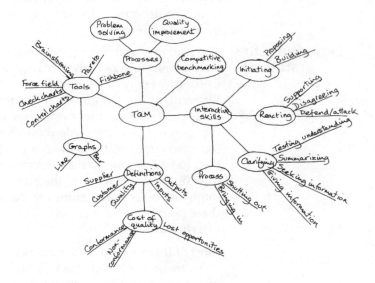

Figure A5.1　*A mind map for the TQM overview*

detailed topics radiate from the main category 'bubbles'. Although these detailed topics will form the content of the course, there are two other aspects that need to be considered before finalizing the content.

The first is to determine the level of the students' current knowledge. Teaching topics with which they are already familiar will be a waste of time. These familiar topics can be crossed out on the mind map. In the case of the 'Total Quality Management Overview' all of the topics will be new to the vast majority of the contractors, so no topics are omitted for this reason.

The other consideration is whether any of the topics are too advanced for the level of the course. In the example given in Figure A5.1, 'The use of control charts' was thought to be too advanced for a one-day overview.

Structuring the content

The modules chosen for this course were:

- Tools of the trade
- Why did we introduce total quality management?
- Quality is free?
- Who's the customer?
- What is quality?

The main course modules are to be found in the body of the course. The body needs to be sequenced so that there is a logical flow from one module to another. We used the 'Post-it' note method described in Chapter 3. The structure chosen for this course is given in the agenda shown in Figure A5.2.

Choosing the methods and media

Given the potentially wide range of students, we decided to base this introductory session on trainer presentations and student exercises. Short excerpts from existing videos would also be used.

We also had a tape/slide presentation put on to video. This was done to increase reliability and to keep the number of different media down to a minimum.

Writing the objectives and tests

After each module the students should be able to do something they could not do before. Objectives are best written by considering what this change of behaviour should be. For example, after completing the 'Tools of the trade' module the students should be able to 'Describe the basic tools of quality and their uses.'

You should keep the aims of the course in mind when you are writing the objectives. Although describing the tools and their uses would be a sufficient level for our target

```
┌─────────────────────────────────────────────────┐
│ AGENDA                                           │
│                                                  │
│ Introduction                              9:00   │
│ — Introductions                                  │
│ — Expectations                                   │
│ — Agenda                                         │
│                                                  │
│ Why total quality management?             9:20   │
│ — The need                                       │
│ — Initial steps                                  │
│ — Quality gurus                                  │
│ — Birth of a strategy                            │
│ — Key elements of the strategy                   │
│                                                  │
│ What is quality?                          9:40   │
│ — Definition                                     │
│ — Standard                                       │
│ — System                                         │
│ — Measurement                                    │
│                                                  │
│ Quality is free?                         11:00   │
│ — Cost of quality                                │
│ — Conformance                                    │
│ — Non-conformance                                │
│ — Lost opportunities                             │
│                                                  │
│ Who's the customer?                      11:20   │
│ — Suppliers                                      │
│ — Internal customers                             │
│ — External customers                             │
│                                                  │
│ Tools of the trade                       12:00   │
│ — Problem-solving process                        │
│ — Quality improvement process                    │
│ — Process capability                             │
│ — Fishbone diagram                               │
│ — Pareto analysis                                │
│ — Forcefield analysis                            │
│ — Interactive skills                             │
│                                                  │
│ Where do we go from here?                16:00   │
│                                                  │
│ Review                                   16:30   │
└─────────────────────────────────────────────────┘
```

Figure A5.2   *Structure for the TQM overview*

population, it would not be suitable for people who lead quality circles. They would need to demonstrate competence at using the tools. Figure A5.3 shows the objectives for the TQM overview.

Once the objectives have been written, tests become relatively easy to design. For example, the fourth objective is for the students to be able to identify customers and suppliers in a given situation. To test this we showed a video clip of a scene in the restaurant. There were four main characters:

- the paying customer;
- the waitress;

<u>OBJECTIVES</u>

After completing today's session you will be able to:

• State why the company introduced 'total quality management'

• Define quality

• Explain the basic concepts of quality

• Identify customers and suppliers in a given situation

• Describe seven basic tools of quality and their uses

Figure A5.3   *Objectives for TQM course*

- the cook;
- the owner.

Using the form shown in Figure A5.4, the students were asked which of the four characters was the customer and who was the supplier in the given situations. We developed the other tests in a similar manner.

Writing the trainer's guide and student materials
The trainer's guide and student materials were developed together. The student materials included a booklet which had a section for each of the modules. We also developed a set of cards that had objects, or pictures of larger products, glued to them. These cards were designed to help the students define quality. They would have to decide whether they considered the product to be a quality product. They would also have to give a reason for their decision.

Preparing the visual aids
Many of the visual aids were developed as the trainer's guide and the student materials were being written. We saved some development time by using artwork we had

OUTPUT	SUPPLIER	CUSTOMER
• Order taken		
• Order delivered		
• Dinner cooked		
• Dinner served		
• Money taken		

Figure A5.4   *Example of a test based on a course objective*

prepared for the student's guide as masters for overhead transparencies. The videotapes were already available as they had been developed for the full-length course.

Peer assessment The materials were given to a new trainer to review. It is a good idea to have one of your colleagues review the course at every stage of its development. The development of this course was also used to teach a new trainer the basics of course development.

Running the pilot course(s) We decided to use a group of 12 'target population' students for the pilot course. The maximum number of students for this course was 18 but we decided to restrict the numbers for the pilot course. I conducted the course and the new trainer made observations of the training process and the students' reactions. We asked the students to complete the feedback forms and then we had a debriefing session.

Appendix 6 Using criteria to determine course content

The following is a description of the process we used when we were asked to reduce a technical training course from 15 days to 5. At first sight this seems to be a particularly brutal reduction, but you should bear in mind that this condensed course was needed for a different population of students.

We would use this shortened course to train maintenance engineers. Maintenance engineers were recruited at a lower skill level than the service engineers for whom the original course had been designed. Their duties involved regular cleaning and maintenance of the machines as well as repairing some of the more frequently occurring faults. It was always expected that these maintenance engineers would not be able to repair every single fault they came across. From time to time, they would have to call in a service engineer for assistance.

So, giving maintenance engineers the same training as the service engineers, with all the associated travel and accommodation costs, was not a good investment. Service engineers would still need to have the full three weeks of training.

The criteria we chose for selecting the tasks were:

- frequency (how often would the task have to be done?);
- difficulty (how hard was it to do the task?);
- criticality (what is the impact of poor task performance?).

Frequency was the most important of the criteria because the strategy was to have the maintenance engineers performing the most commonly occurring tasks. The temptation might be to decide on the basis of frequency alone, but this approach would lead to difficulties. For example, if we decided to teach all tasks that occurred within a certain pre-determined period (say six months), we would find we would also be teaching tasks that are so easy that they need not be taught. Clearly, practising these tasks would be a waste of valuable teaching time.

Incorrect performance of other tasks, although infrequent, might lead to disastrous consequences. We would not want to take the risk of omitting them even though the task was performed infrequently.

The criteria of difficulty and criticality were introduced to overcome these problems.

Having determined the decision criteria, a method of rating the tasks against the criteria was required. We needed an objective method for determining how frequent, difficult or critical a task was. Tables A6.1, A6.2 and A6.3 show the ratings we used for our three criteria.

Table A6.1 *Frequency ratings*

Task interval (months)	Frequency rating
1–6	1
7–12	2
13–18	3

Table A6.2 *Difficulty ratings*

Difficulty rating	Definition
1	Without prior training, the maintenance engineer cannot or is not confident to perform the task without the assistance of a service engineer
2	Without prior training the maintenance engineer can perform the task correctly with the assistance of a service manual
3	Maintenance engineer can perform the task correctly without prior training, assistance of a service engineer or reference to a service manual

Table A6.3 *Criticality ratings*

Criticality rating	Definition
1	Incorrect completion of the task results in a safety hazard or catastrophic failure of the equipment
2	Incorrect completion of the task results in the equipment functioning at an unacceptable level
3	Incorrect completion of the task affects the look of the product only

Another method of assessing the difficulty is to compare the time a freshly trained novice and a master performer take to complete the same task. The greater the difference, the more difficult the task.

The next step is to find a method of making a decision based on combinations of these criteria. One method would simply be to add up the frequency, difficulty and criticality ratings for each task. If a task's total falls below a cut-off point, we would eliminate the task from the course. The problem with this approach is that it gives equal weighting to all the criteria.

To overcome this you can give more weighting to the more important criteria, producing different ratings. However, getting the relative ratings correct starts to become somewhat of a mathematical nightmare.

The approach we decided to take was to list every possible combination of the criteria (111, 112, 113...). For each combination we used our experience to decide whether a task with that combination of ratings would normally be included in a course.

So, a task with a 111 combination of ratings (task encountered at least once every six months, very difficult to perform and a safety hazard) would definitely be included in the course. A task with a rating combination of 132 would not be trained. (The '3' difficulty rating signifies that the task can be performed correctly without any training.)

The decision matrix (Table A6.4) gives the 'train' or 'no-train' decisions for all these combinations of frequency, difficulty and criticality. You should only use this matrix as a guide. Give the training analysts the authority to make different decisions on the basis of their judgement and experience – provided that the reasons for those decisions are recorded.

Very experienced training analysts would probably not need to use the matrix in the normal course of their work, but it is an extremely powerful tool for communicating the rationale of training decisions to your clients. The matrix is also very useful for providing 'instant experience' to less experienced training analysts.

Notice that some of the ratings in the difficulty and criticality columns have been highlighted. These are to remind the analyst to make some checks before finally making a 'no-train' decision.

When the warning occurs in the criticality column the analysts should satisfy themselves that labels on the equipment and the service manual cover any safety hazard.

When the warning occurs in the difficulty column the analyst should be satisfied that field support is available or that there is detailed support in the service manual.

Table A6.4   *'Train–don't train' matrix*

Frequency	Difficulty	Criticality	Decision
1	1	1	Train
1	1	2	Train
1	1	3	Train
1	2	1	Train
1	2	2	Train
1	2	3	Borderline
1	3	1	Don't train
1	3	2	Don't train
1	3	3	Don't train
2	1	1	Train
2	1	2	Train
2	1	3	Train
2	2	1	Don't train
2	2	2	Don't train
2	2	3	Don't train
2	3	1	Don't train
2	3	2	Don't train
2	3	3	Don't train
3	1	1	Don't train
3	1	2	Don't train
3	1	3	Don't train
3	2	1	Don't train
3	2	2	Don't train
3	2	3	Don't train
3	3	1	Don't train
3	3	2	Don't train
3	3	3	Don't train

Appendix 7
Trainers' checklists

Trainer's kit and supplies for the session

- Bulldog clips
- Paper clips
- Drawing pins
- Packing tape
- Masking tape (25 mm width)
- Adhesive tape (Sellotape, Scotch tape)
- Blu-tack
- Flip-chart marker pens (water based)
- Overhead projector pens (water soluble and permanent)
- Spare overhead projector bulb
- Lens cleaner
- Cloths
- Overhead transparencies (blank)
- Pencils
- Erasers
- Rulers
- Ring binders
- Folders
- Note pads
- Name cards
- Flip-chart pads
- Post-it notes
- Self-adhesive labels
- Calculators
- Pencil sharpener(s)
- 2-, 3-, 4-hole punch
- Correcting fluid (Snopake, White-out)
- Stapler
- Staples
- Staple remover
- Scissors
- Glue stick
- Hammer
- Extension lead (with two sockets)
- Batteries
- Screwdriver
- Penknife/scalpel
- Videotapes
- Audiocassettes
- Audio and video leads and adaptors

Training location survey

- Size, shape and capacity
- Location
- Heating, lighting and ventilation
- Power sockets, light switches
- Toilets
- Doors, windows, emergency exits
- Parking

- Access for preparation
- Contact established
- Acoustics
- Wall space for flip-chart pages
- Meal and break arrangements
- Bedrooms

Pre-course checklist
- Obtain printed materials
- Review lesson plan
- Obtain audiovisual equipment and tapes
- Obtain stationery and other supplies
- Check course logistics
- Check room layout
- Check waste bins, glasses, water etc.
- Lay out participant materials, pencils, pads, name cards
- Check visibility of screens, charts etc.
- Test felt-tip and dry-wipe pens
- Check lighting, ventilation and heating
- Display direction signs
- Disconnect telephone
- Check process for handling messages and phone calls

Post-course checklist
- Collect and analyse course feedback forms
- Clear up room
- Transport equipment back
- Pay bills
- Return keys etc.
- Complete training records

Bibliography

Argyris, C and Schon, D A (1978) *Organizational Learning*, Wokingham: Addison-Wesley

BACIE/ITD (1996) *The Training Directory*, London: Kogan Page

Barrington, Harry and Reid, Margaret (1997) *Training Interventions: Managing Employee Development*, London: Institute of Personnel and Development

Bartram, Sharon and Gibson, Brenda (1997) *Training Needs Analysis*, 2nd edn, Aldershot: Gower

Bentley, Trevor (1990) *The Business of Training*, Maidenhead: McGraw-Hill

Boam, Rosemary and Sparrow, Paul (1993) *Designing and Achieving Competency*, Maidenhead: McGraw-Hill

Boyatzis, Richard E (1982) *The Competent Manager*, Chichester: John Wiley

Boydell, T H and Leary, M (1996) *The Identification of Training Needs*, London: BACIE

Bramley, Peter (1996) *Evaluating Training Effectiveness*, Maidenhead: McGraw-Hill

Bride, Mac (1996) *Teach Yourself html*, London: Hodder & Stoughton

Buzan, Tony (1989) *Use Your Head*, 3rd edn, London: BBC Publications

Crosby, Philip B (1993) *Quality Is Free*, London: Signet

Department of Employment (1971) *Glossary of Training Terms*, London: HMSO

Goldstein, Irwin (1992) *Training in Organizations: Needs assessment, development and evaluation*, 3rd edn, New York: Brooks-Cole

Imai, Masaaki (1989) *Kaizen*, Maidenhead: McGraw-Hill

Kamp, Di (1996) *The Excellent Trainer*, 2nd edn, Aldershot: Gower

Kelly, George A (1980) *Theory of Personality: psychology of personal constructs*, New York: VVW Norton

Kenney, John and Reid, Margaret A (1986) *Training Interventions*, London: Institute of Personnel Management

Kolb, D A (1985) *Experiential Learning*, Hemel Hempstead: Prentice-Hall

Mitrani, A, Dalziel, M and Fitt, D (1992) *Competency Based Human Resource Management*, London: Kogan Page

Newby, A C (1994) *Training Evaluation Handbook*, Aldershot: Gower

Orridge, Martin (1996) *75 Ways to Liven Up Your Training*, Aldershot: Gower

Pedler, Mike (ed.) (1997) *Action Learning in Practice*, 3rd edn, Aldershot: Gower

Pedler, Mike *et al.* (1991) *Learning Company: A Strategy for Sustainable Development*, Maidenhead: McGraw-Hill

Peters, T and Waterman Jr, R H (1984) *In Search of Excellence*, New York: Harper & Row

Pickles, Tim (1995) *Toolkit for Trainers*, Aldershot: Gower

Prior, John (ed.) (1994) *Gower Handbook of Training and Development*, 2nd edn, Aldershot: Gower

Rackham, Neil *et al.* (1971) *Developing Interactive Skills*, Northampton: Wellens

Rae, Leslie (1991) *The Skills of Training*, 2nd edn, Aldershot: Gower

Rae, Leslie (1995) *The Techniques of Training*, Aldershot: Gower

Rae, Leslie (1997) *How to Measure Training Effectiveness*, 3rd edn, Aldershot: Gower

Rae, Leslie (1997) *Planning and Designing Training Programmes*, Aldershot: Gower

Rose, Colin (1985) *Accelerated Learning*, Aylesbury: Accelerated Learning Systems

Senge, Peter M (1990) *The Fifth Discipline: The Art and Practice of the Learning Organization*, New York: Doubleday/London: Century Business

Spencer Jr, L M, McClelland, D C and Spencer, S M (1992) *Competency Assessment Methods: History and State of the Art*, London: Hay/McBer Research Press

Stewart, A and Stewart, V (1981) *Business Applications of Repertory Grids*, Maidenhead: McGraw-Hill

Thurbin, Patrick J (1994) *Implementing The Learning Organisation*, London: Pitman Publishing

Glossary

8 mm A videocassette format used in camcorders. The tape is 8 mm wide.

A4 A standard paper size (210 mm × 297 mm).

Alignment The process of ensuring that all parts of a company are pulling in the same direction.

Artificial intelligence Apparent computer intelligence that allows a computer to solve problems.

ASCII American Standard Code for Information Interchange. A code which uses numbers to represent digits, upper- and lower-case letters, punctuation and additional characters such as RETURN.

Assessment The process of determining the company's or organization's current situation.

AT Advanced Technology. IBM PCs or compatibles which are more advanced than the standard PC or XT.

Attitude A predisposition to behave in one way rather than another.

Authoring tool Software used to create instructional material delivered on a computer system.

Azimuth adjustment The process of adjusting the angle of the recording/playback head of a tape recorder with respect to the tape.

Behavioural event interviews A technique developed by McClelland and Dailey, used to identify competencies by getting detailed descriptions of a sample of individuals' performances. The sample includes both average and superior performers but the interviewers are unaware of the interviewees' performance records. The characteristics that emerge are coded, categorized and correlated to performance criteria.

Browser A computer program used for searching for and reading information on the Internet.

Camcorder A portable video camera with a built-in video recorder.

CBT Computer-based training. Uses a computer to present and control the sequence of instructional information.

CD-ROM A disk for storing computer data. The information is recorded and read by a laser.

CGA Colour graphics adaptor. A standard for a computer's display which has a definition of 640 × 200 dots (pixels) in monochrome and 320 × 200 in four colours from a choice of 16.

Check chart A chart used for collecting and organizing data.

Competence The ability to perform a particular task to the required standard.

Competency A personal characteristic that differentiates the superior performer from the average performer.

Control chart A chart that displays statistical process control data.

Cycle time The time it takes to go from the beginning to the end of a process.

Database A large store of information.

Disk A magnetic disk that a computer uses for storing information. There are two types of disk: a hard disk which is rigid and a floppy disk which is flexible.

Displays Devices that allow users to see the computer's output on a monitor. PC displays have developed over the years to yield greater definition and more colours. Starting with the least sophisticated, the standards are: MDA, Hercules, CGA, MCGA, EGA, VGA, SVGA and EVGA.

Double-loop learning A process by which an organization not only checks itself against standards but also reviews and challenges those standards.

Duplex Printing on both sides of a sheet of paper.

DVI Digital video interactive. Technology that allows real-time compression and decompression of graphics and animated displays.

EGA Extended graphics adaptor. A standard for a computer's display which has a definition of 640 × 350 dots (pixels) in 16 colours from a choice of 64.

E-mail Electronic mail where messages are sent via computer networks.

EPSS Electronic performance support system. Software that helps users perform their jobs more effectively while they work.

EVGA Extended VGA (see *VGA*).

Expert panel A group of knowledgeable human resource specialists, managers and superior performers who are used to identify competencies.

Expert system A computer system that stores expert knowledge in the form of rules. It is a tool that can be used by non-experts to make decisions.

Face-to-face ratio The percentage of a trainer's available time that is spent teaching in front of a class.

Floppy disk See *Disk*.

Focused interviews Used to assess competencies with the same techniques as behavioural event interviewing.

Formatting (1) The process of defining what a document will look like. For example margins, top and bottom spaces, page length, tabs and font types.

Formatting (2) The process of preparing a disk so that it can be used by a computer.

Gantt charts Used to schedule project tasks. They take the form of a horizontal bar chart with time on the horizontal axis and the tasks on the vertical axis. The ends of the bars represent the start and finish times of the tasks. Invented by Henry Gantt.

Goals Quantitative figures that are established by top management.

GOQs Genuine occupational qualifications. Qualifications which make it legal to select a person of a particular category while excluding people of other categories (e.g. gender or race).

GUI Graphical user interface. A screen design employing graphics and colour in a consistent manner so that menus and other system features are easy for users to understand and use.

Hard disk See *Disk*.

Hardware Computer equipment such as computers, printers and plotters.

Hercules A graphics standard for a monochrome computer display giving a definition of 720 × 348 dots (pixels).

Histogram A graph in which frequency distribution is shown by means of vertical bars.

HRD Human resource development. Used to be known as personnel.

HRDC Human resource development committee. A committee of peer managers who meet to make, review or approve decisions related to the organization and development of people in their areas.

HRM Human resource management or human resource manager. Previously known as personnel or personnel manager.

HTML HyperText Mark-up Language.

Hypertext Electronic information that is linked so that users can easily move from one topic to another.

In-tray exercise A simulation exercise in which participants work through a typical basket of items. This includes 'big picture' items as well as looking at more detailed issues. Items include memos, data analysis and problems which require urgent attention. It is a timed exercise and participants are expected to prioritize their responses.

Internet A global network of interconnected computer networks.

IPD Institute of Personnel and Development.

IPM Institute of Personnel Management. Now combined with the ITD to form the IPD.

ITD Institute of Training and Development. Now combined with the IPM to form the IPD.

IVD Interactive video disk. Video images stored on an optical disk so that a companion computer can control their presentation, based on user responses.

Job element analysis Identified by Boyatzis as a weighted list of characteristics that managers perceive as important in distinguishing superior from average performers.

Kaizen Japanese for 'continuous improvement'.

Kilobyte (Kb) A measure of a computer's memory. One kilobyte of memory will store approximately 1000 characters, about two-and-a-half pages of A4.

Knowledge Usable information that an individual has in a particular area. Examples: understanding the art and science of management; understanding what motivates employees.

Learning organization According to Pedler *et al.*, an organization which facilitates the learning of all its members and continuously transforms itself to achieve superior competitive performance.

Management by objectives (MBO) An objective-setting process which increases commitment by involving employees in setting their own objectives. Championed by Peter Drucker.

MCGA Multicolour graphics array. A standard for a computer's display which has a definition of up to 640 × 200 dots (pixels) in monochrome and 320 × 200 in 256 colours from a choice of 262 144.

MCI Management Charter Initiative. A coherent framework for management education in the UK, based on a nationally agreed qualification structure.

MDA Monochrome display adaptor. The original standard for a computer's display. It can only display text in 25 lines of 80 characters.

Mission A statement of what the company or organization exists to do.

Motive Reasons (e.g. achievement, affiliation and power) that drive, direct and select an individual's behaviour.

Mouse A hand-operated device for selecting text and objects on a computer screen. Moving the mouse over a flat surface causes a corresponding movement in a pointer (usually an arrow shape) on the computer screen. Pressing a button on the mouse selects the text or object to which the arrow is pointing.

MS-DOS Microsoft Disk Operating System. The standard, single-user, base operating system for IBM and IBM-compatible computers on which Windows may be loaded.

NTSC National Television System Committee. A US television standard.

NVQs National Vocational Qualifications.

OCR Optical character recognition. The ability of a scanner to scan a paper document and read the text into a computer's memory.

On-line reference Reference information presented on a computer screen. Often employs hypertext technology.

Operating system A piece of software that carries out a computer's basic functions. A computer has to have an operating system installed before it can run other programs.

PAL Phase alternation by line. A television standard used mainly in Europe.

Panning The side-to-side rotation of a film or video camera.

PC Personal computer.

Philosophy A statement of a company's values and beliefs.

Pixels Picture elements – the individual dots of a computer screen's image.

Policy A medium- to long-term course of action comprising a goal and a strategy.

Policy deployment The process for ensuring that a company's policies are understood from the highest to the lowest levels in the company.

Printer's dummy An example of a finished document so a printer can see exactly how the materials should be produced.

QCD Quality, cost and delivery.

RAM Random access memory. A computer's internal memory, measured in megabytes.

Read-only access A restriction on a computerized record system that allows a person to read the records but does not allow them to amend, add or remove a record.

Repertory grid A technique developed by Kelly that takes three individuals at a time from a sample that contains both average and superior performers. An expert panel is then asked in which way two of the individuals are similar to each other and different from the third. These similarities and differences form the basis of a set of competencies that are related to superior performance.

Role play A simulation exercise in which participants 'act out' a typical situation.

Scientific management Sets out to increase productivity by developing performance standards on the basis of systematic observation and experimentation. Frederick Taylor was known as the father of scientific management.

SECAM Séquential à mémoire, a French television standard. Also used in the former Soviet Union.

Simplex Printing on only one side of a sheet of paper.

Single-loop learning A process by which an organization checks itself against standards but does not review and challenge those standards.

Skill An individual's demonstration by behaviour of proficiency or expertise – the ability to do something well. Examples are: interviewing effectively; selecting the best job applicant; assigning work clearly and effectively.

SME Subject-matter expert. People who support training development by providing expertise on specific topics to be covered in the training.

Software Programs used by computers. Software is to a computer what a compact disc is to a compact disc player.

SPC See *Statistical process control*.

Stakeholder A person who has a vested interest in the outcome of an event. Stakeholders usually have the power to influence positively or negatively the outcome even though they may not take any direct part in the event.

Standard deviation A measure of variability – the larger the standard deviation, the greater the variability of the sample. In normally distributed data, approximately 68 per cent of the data will fall between plus and minus 1 standard deviation.

Statistical process control A method used to determine whether variation in a process is normal or abnormal. A decision can then be made on whether to adjust the process.

Stens A means of giving a 1 to 10 score for normally distributed data. One sten is equivalent to one half of a standard deviation.

Strategy The means of achieving a goal.

SVGA Super VGA (see *VGA*).

Tilting The up-and-down rotation of a film or video camera.

Trackball A ball-shaped device on a computer keyboard which acts in a similar way to a mouse (see *Mouse*).

Tracking Physically moving a film or video camera either parallel or at right angles to the subject.

Trainee-centred learning A form of training where a student's progress (and hence pace) through a course depends on the student's readiness to move on to the next learning stage. Usually involves a form of programmed instruction. Also called self-paced learning.

Training philosophy A statement of a company's or organization's attitude towards training.

Trait A relatively enduring characteristic of an individual's behaviour. Examples: being a good listener; having a sense of urgency.

Triad A group of three students working together on an exercise.

U-matic A semi-professional video format. It used to be the standard for training videos but it is now being replaced by VHS.

UNIX A computer operating system that supports multitasking and is ideally suited to multiuser applications.

Value Something that is held to be important by the individual. Examples: education; honesty; openness.

VDU Visual display unit. The 'box' that houses a computer's screen.

VGA Video graphics array. A standard for a computer's display which has a definition of 640 × 480 dots (pixels) in 16 colours and 320 × 200 in 256 colours from a choice of 262 144. SVGA and EVGA are extensions of VGA with definitions of up to 1024 × 768 pixels.

VHS Video home standard. A domestic video standard, now increasingly being used as the standard format for training videos. See also *U-matic*.

VHS-C A videocassette standard that is used in camcorders. It can be clipped into a carrier which allows it to be viewed on a domestic video recorder.

Virtual network A network whose members do not meet physically.

Vision An inspiring 'picture' of where the company or organization wants to be in the future.

Voice mail A process by which recorded messages can be left and retrieved by telephone.

XT Extended technology. A more sophisticated version of the original IBM PC.

Zooming Adjusting the lens of a film or video camera so that the subject appears to get larger or smaller.

Index

The Business Approach to Training

Teresa Williams and Adrian Green

The role of the trainer is changing rapidly. Internal trainers are increasingly having to justify their proposed solutions in business terms, while external trainers can sell their services only by helping customers to fulfil their business objectives. In both cases, they need a knowledge of 'business speak' that will enable them to deal with other managers on an equal footing.

At the same time trainers are themselves having to operate in a businesslike way: to recover their costs, to market their services proactively, and so on. This book explains the main ideas governing finance, strategy and marketing. By relating concepts like business planning, cash flow, breakeven analysis, pay back, SWOT analysis and the marketing mix to the training process it removes some of the mystery that surrounds them. The authors use a variety of methods to reinforce the learning, including exercises and activities.

This is a book that bridges the gap between the practice of training and the realities of business. For the trainer determined to survive and flourish in today's demanding climate, it will be invaluable.

Gower

Dictionary of HRD

Angus Reynolds, Sally Sambrook and Jim Stewart

Providing succinct definitions of over 3,000 terms *Dictionary of HRD* is the most comprehensive work of its kind.

Based on Angus Reynolds' successful American dictionary, this new version by Sally Sambrook and Jim Stewart has been extensively reworked with a British and international readership in mind. The entries have been structured to meet the needs of the busy practitioner: definitions of theory are here, but the overall emphasis is on practice. Useful general business terms, which the professional would naturally encounter during the course of their work, are included too.

The *Dictionary* is organized as follows:

• Over 3,000 terms, arranged alphabetically. Definitions range from a succinct sentence, to a paragraph, depending on significance
• A list of '100 essential HRD terms'
• A list of acronyms and abbreviations
• A list of journals of interest to HRD specialists.

As well as being an invaluable source of reference and new ideas for training and HR professionals and academics, this will be welcomed by a much wider range of managers as an authoritative guide to HR issues, organizations and terminology.

Gower

Gower Handbook of Training and Development

Second Edition

Edited by John Prior, MBE

This *Gower Handbook*, published in association with the Institute of Training and Development, first appeared in 1991 and quickly established itself as a standard work. For this new edition the text has been completely revised to reflect recent developments and new chapters have been added on cultural diversity, learning styles and choosing resources. The *Handbook* now contains contributions from no fewer than forty-nine experienced professionals, each one an expert in his or her chosen subject.

For anyone involved in training and development, whether in business or the public sector, the *Handbook* represents an unrivalled resource.

Gower

A Handbook for Training Strategy

Martyn Sloman

The traditional approach to training in the organization is no longer effective. That is the central theme of Martyn Sloman's challenging book. A new model is required that will reflect the complexity of organizational life, changes in the HR function and the need to involve line management. This *Handbook* introduces such a model and describes the practical implications not only for human resource professionals and training managers but also for line managers.

Martyn Sloman writes as an experienced training manager and his book is concerned above all with implementation. Thus his text is supported by numerous questionnaires, survey instruments and specimen documents. It also contains the findings of an illuminating survey of best training practice carried out among UK National Training Award winners.

The book is destined to make a significant impact on the current debate about how to improve organizational performance. With its thought-provoking argument and practical guidance it will be welcomed by everyone with an interest in the business of training and development.

Gower

How to Set Up and Manage a Corporate Learning Centre

Samuel A Malone

The explosion in the type and availability of open, distance and flexible learning materials has created a revolution in the education and development of many employees. Through a corporate learning centre every employee can now have access to learning and development, when they want, where they want and how they want.

But setting up a cost-effective open learning centre in any organization and managing its continued development after the first flush of enthusiasm has worn off requires commitment from everyone, as well as careful research, planning and organization.

Sam Malone's book provides a concise and highly practical guide covering:

- the benefits, pitfalls and rationale behind corporate learning centres
- the mechanics of planning and setting up a new centre from scratch
- the launch and marketing of the new centre and its resources
- staffing, administration and support
- guidance on evaluating the usage of the centre and establishing the criteria for measuring success.

Also included is a 'learner's guide' to enable users to get the most out of their centre, and details of the experiences of Sun Life in setting up their learning centre.

Gower

The Techniques of Instruction

Roger James

What do effective instructors do that makes them effective? In this ground-breaking book, Dr James examines the whole process of instruction from the point of view of skill development to discover which are the best techniques and why. He shows:

- how to produce the best trainee performance possible in the shortest possible time
- how to structure practice sessions to maximize learning
- how to analyse the task involved so as to design the most appropriate exercise
- how to deal with the 'slow' trainee
- how to boost the trainee's confidence
- how to instruct 'at a distance'.

Although based on extensive research, the material in the book is presented in non-technical language and draws on a wide range of examples. The result is a comprehensive guide to the practice of instruction which will be of immense value to anyone involved in training, teaching or coaching.

Gower